How to access the supplemental online student resource

We are pleased to provide access to an online student resource that supplements your textbook, *Case Studies in Sport Law.* This resource offers an interactive learning experience that will enhance your understanding of how legal issues affect sport in today's society. We are certain you will enjoy this unique online learning experience.

Accessing the online student resource is easy! Follow these steps if you purchased a new book:

1. Visit **www.HumanKinetics.com/CaseStudiesInSportLaw**.

2. Click the <u>first edition</u> link next to the book cover.

3. Click the Sign In link on the left or top of the page. If you do not have an account with Human Kinetics, you will be prompted to create one.

4. If the online product you purchased does not appear in the Ancillary Items box on the left of the page, click the Enter Key Code option in that box. Enter the key code that is printed at the right, including all hyphens. Click the Submit button to unlock your online product.

5. After you have entered your key code the first time, you will never have to enter it again to access this product. Once unlocked, a link to your product will permanently appear in the menu on the left. For future visits, all you need to do is sign in to the textbook's website and follow the link that appears in the left menu!

→ Click the Need Help? button on the textbook's website if you need assistance along the way.

How to access the online student resource if you purchased a used book:

You may purchase access to the online student resource by visiting the text's website, **www.HumanKinetics.com/CaseStudiesInSportLaw**, or by calling the following:

800-747-4457 . . . . .U.S. customers
800-465-7301 . . . . .Canadian customers
+44 (0) 113 255 5665 . . . . European customers
08 8372 0999 . . . . Australian customers
0800 222 062 . . . . .New Zealand customers
217-351-5076 . . . . .International customers

For technical support, send an e-mail to:
support@hkusa.com . . . . U.S. and international customers
info@hkcanada.com . . . . Canadian customers
academic@hkeurope.com . . . . European customers
keycodesupport@hkaustralia.com . . . . . Australian and New Zealand customers

 HUMAN KINETICS
The Information Leader in Physical Activity & Health

02-2012

Product: Case Studies in Sport Law online student resource

Key code: PITTMAN-KNLFSW-OSG

This unique code allows you access to the online student resource.

Access is provided if you have purchased a new book. Once submitted, the code may not be entered for any other user.

HUMAN KINETICS ONLINE STUDENT RESOURCE

Case Studies in Sport Law

Andrew T. Pittman, PhD

Baylor University

John O. Spengler, JD, PhD

University of Florida

Sarah J. Young, PhD

Indiana University

Human Kinetics

Library of Congress Cataloging-in-Publication Data

Pittman, Andrew T., 1945-
  Case studies in sport law / Andrew T. Pittman, John O. Spengler, Sarah J. Young.
    p. cm.
  ISBN-13: 978-0-7360-6821-5 (soft cover)
  ISBN-10: 0-7360-6821-X (soft cover)
  1. School sports--Law and legislation--United States--Cases. 2. College sports--Law and legislation--United States--Cases. I. Spengler, John O. (John Otto), 1962- II. Young, Sarah J. III. Title.
  KF4166.A7P58 2008
  344.73'099--dc22

                                        2007042239

ISBN-10: 0-7360-6821-X
ISBN-13: 978-0-7360-6821-5

Acquisitions Editor: Myles Schrag
Managing Editor: Jillian Evans
Copyeditor: Sandra Merz Bott
Proofreader: Erin Cler
Graphic Designer: Robert Reuther
Graphic Artist: Patrick Sandberg
Cover Designer: Keith Blomberg
Photo Office Assistant: Jason Allen
Printer: Sheridan Books

Printed in the United States of America   10   9   8   7   6   5   4   3

The paper in this book is certified under a sustainable forestry program.

Human Kinetics
Web site: www.HumanKinetics.com

United States: Human Kinetics, P.O. Box 5076, Champaign, IL 61825-5076
800-747-4457
email: humank@hkusa.com

Canada: Human Kinetics, 475 Devonshire Road Unit 100, Windsor, ON N8Y 2L5
800-465-7301 (in Canada only)
email: info@hkcanada.com

Europe: Human Kinetics, 107 Bradford Road, Stanningley, Leeds LS28 6 AT, United Kingdom
+44 (0) 113 255 5665
email: hk@hkeurope.com

Australia: Human Kinetics, 57A Price Avenue, Lower Mitcham, South Australia 5062
08 8372 0999
e-mail: info@hkaustralia.com

New Zealand: Human Kinetics, P.O. Box 80, Torrens Park, South Australia 5062
0800 222 062
e-mail: info@hknewzealand.com

Contents

Preface

The study of sport and recreation law has gained both popularity and importance given the increasing amount of litigation in the sports realm and a growing interest among students in physical education, recreation, and sport management curricula. We now see more legal courses offered in undergraduate and graduate programs and more physical education, recreation, and sport management law textbooks entering the market. These textbooks serve an important purpose in presenting information on critical legal topics. We discovered an additional need, however, for a legal casebook designed to supplement these texts. A casebook allows students in these academic programs to generate thought on key topics relating to the information provided in the various sport law textbooks. This casebook is ideally suited to serving that purpose.

Recently several sport law casebooks designed for use in law school courses have been published. To the authors' knowledge, however, no one has attempted to publish a casebook designed for use in physical education, recreation, and sport management academic settings. One major advantage of this casebook is that only essential information is included. Each case was edited several times by the authors to eliminate information not pertinent to the disposition of the case.

This book is designed as a casebook and not as a narrative text. It is appropriate for use in either an undergraduate- or graduate-level course. Since this casebook contains cases found in a variety of legal content areas, it is suitable as a companion for any text. Some instructors use a topic approach when teaching sport law; others use a settings approach. The cases in this book allow the use of either approach. Periodic updates of this book will allow users to stay current as new precedent-setting cases are published.

The casebook is divided into nine major content areas: antitrust law (college and professional sport settings), constitutional law (college and high school settings), contract law, employment law, intellectual property law (copyright and trademark law), products liability law, statutory law, Title IX, and tort law (college, high school, professional, and recreational sport settings). At the beginning of each major content area is introductory information explaining that particular area. Following the introductory information is a number of edited cases pertinent to that area. Each area contains from 4 to 29 cases with a total of 90 cases in all. Through the use of the Delphi technique, a panel of experts identified the most important cases in their respective areas of law that illustrate primary legal concepts.

Review questions corresponding to each case are available in an online study guide for the purpose of evaluating students' knowledge of each case. An online instructor guide is also available to professors who adopt this text for their courses. It contains an answer key for the review questions and expanded versions of all 90 cases in the text. The expanded cases can be found in the student study guide as well. This book should become part of the professional library of all practitioners in college, high school, professional, and recreational sport settings.

Acknowledgments

I would like to thank J.O. Spengler and Sarah Young for allowing me to talk them into joining me on this project. Without their hard work, this casebook would not have been possible.

Thanks to J.O. for leading the effort in developing questions for the cases and providing input into other parts of the project and for also having a hand in convincing Human Kinetics that a book of this type was needed.

I also want to thank Sarah for taking the lead in conducting the Delphi portion of the study. Her persistence in keeping that part of the project moving kept this effort from dragging out. She also contributed in developing the questions for several sections of this casebook.

Last but not least are the staff at Human Kinetics, especially Myles Schrag. J.O., Sarah, and I know that you had to convince others at HK that this project was worthy of publication. It was a long, hard process, and we appreciate your efforts.

Andrew T. Pittman

I would like to thank my wife, Mariah, for her love and support throughout the making of this book. I also thank my parents for their endless encouragement and support. Well-deserved recognition goes to Andy and Sarah, whose diligence to the task was remarkable, and to all those who participated in the Delphi study.

John O. Spengler

First, I would like to thank Andy for asking me to be a part of this project and for his tireless effort in keeping the entire project moving forward. Andy has certainly been the glue that has held this project together, and for that I thank him.

Second, I would like to thank each of the members of the Delphi panel for their willingness to participate, review cases, and provide their feedback. I know they all had to get tired of seeing e-mail messages from me reminding them to reply by the deadlines! A heartfelt thanks and recognition go out to Ruth Alexander, Rob Ammon, Paul Anderson, Herb Appenzeller, Tom Appenzeller, Susan Brown-Foster, Linda Carpenter, Rod Caughron, Cathy Claussen, Dan Connaughton, Gil Fried, Merry Moiseichik, Anita Moorman, Tom Sawyer, Linda Schoonmaker, Todd Seidler, Bob Trichka, and John Wolohan. Without your help, the completed product would not be nearly as meaningful.

Sarah J. Young

Introduction

How This Text Was Developed

Reviewing the Sport Law Literature

In the mid-1980s when I first began teaching a sport law course, I encountered several problems that most faculty members face when developing a course from scratch. I had little idea of the major topics that should be covered and the important court cases in those areas. Furthermore, I had a difficult time figuring out what information a student should glean from each case.

I solved the first problem by convincing my dissertation committee at Texas A&M that I would do the profession a great service if they allowed me to design a sport law curriculum for my dissertation. Thank goodness they bought into the idea, and, after working on it for a couple of years, I was able to successfully complete it.

The second problem wasn't so easily solved. I found hundreds of court cases over the years and liked most of them. I was torn between using the tried but true cases and the current ones that may not have exhausted their appeals. Again, I went back to the same method I had used in determining the content areas—poll the experts. Unlike before, my problem wasn't solved. Little consensus existed as to which cases were most important, and I didn't know how to solve that problem. But I had collected some good information and, thank goodness, I kept it.

A short while later both of my remaining problems were solved. J.O. Spengler published a book of moot court scenarios he had developed based on published sport and recreation cases. His work on this project revealed his interest in developing creative learning tools for students. Even though I had a data bank of questions on approximately 500 cases, I realized that he could be of great help in developing questions for a casebook given his experience and expertise.

About that same time, Sarah Young was finishing her doctorate and used the Delphi technique to form a panel of experts as part of her study. I was fortunate to participate in that study. Suddenly I saw the solution to my problems. I would undertake the initial review of literature since I had accumulated information on thousands of court cases over the years. I reviewed 15 to 20 sport law texts and noted those cases that frequently appeared or were designated by the author as being a leading case. This initial list contained more than 120 cases. Sarah would direct the Delphi portion of the study, which would include putting the panel in place and analyzing their input.

Andy Pittman

Conducting the Delphi Study

When Andy proposed his idea to me of developing a casebook and asked for my involvement with the project, I jumped at the chance. As with Andy, one of the challenges I faced in teaching a legal aspects course was that I did not have easy access to recreation or sport case law. A supplemental text of classic cases illustrating the key concepts of each legal area with questions for each case was a tool that I could not only use myself but require my students to use as well.

My role in the project was to conduct a Delphi study as a method to gain consensus on the case law that best represented each legal area. The Delphi method uses a small group of experts through a series of three to five rounds of questionnaires designed to gain consensus on the topic under study. Our topic of study was to identify those cases that best represented various areas of law pertinent to sport management and recreation settings. There are several variations on how the Delphi can be administered, including the classical and modified methods. The classical Delphi asks the jurors to determine the items they will rate in subsequent rounds, whereas the modified Delphi asks the jurors to rate items prepared by the researcher. Since Andy had undertaken an extensive review of case law, the modified Delphi was selected as the best method for this project.

A panel of experts to participate in the Delphi was the next task that needed to be accomplished. In selecting a panel, one must consider individuals who have an interest in the topic area, who have pertinent knowledge and information to share, and who are motivated to involve themselves in a rather time-consuming process. Since the Delphi literature recommends a nomination process by peers and colleagues as a desirable method of selecting the panel, I contacted Tom Sawyer, the executive director of the Society of the Study of Legal Aspects in Sport and Physical Activity (SSLASPA; now Sport and Recreation Law Association, SRLA), to seek his recommendations for the panel of experts. Tom suggested contacting all professional members of SRLA, excluding student members, in an effort to seek nominations. In the fall of 2000, correspondence explaining the project and the Delphi were sent to 78 SRLA members requesting their nominations of individuals fitting the prescribed criteria for the panel of experts. As a result of this mailing, 161 nominations were received recognizing 52 individuals as experts in legal aspects of sport. Since some of the nominees had received more than one recommendation, I counted the number of times an individual was nominated and then listed them in order according to the number of nominations received. Letters of invitation were mailed to 25 people who had received a minimum of three nominations. From this mailing, 18 individuals consented to participate in the study.

Once the panel was established, Andy, J.O., and I concurred it would be too much of a burden to ask all panel members to give input on all the cases. Because of this, we asked the panel members to complete a self-assessment of their expertise in nine areas of law: antitrust, constitutional, contract, employment/labor, intellectual property, products liability, statutory, Title IX, and torts. Based on their assessments of expertise, individuals were assigned to no more than three legal areas. Thus, panel members would review the cases only in their assigned area of law.

Round 1 of the Delphi commenced in November 2000, with a total of 102 cases representing nine legal areas being sent to panel members via e-mail attachments. The e-mail method of correspondence was implemented in an effort to save both time and money. Panel members were asked to review case summaries of each case in their areas and rate the representativeness of each case for that area of law on a 5-point Likert scale (1 = poor case representativeness; 5 = best case representativeness). Panel members were also asked to list other cases of which they were aware that were representative of their legal area for inclusion in the second round of the study. Using this method, 63 new cases were recommended by the panel for round 2. Our panel of experts was so dedicated to this project that a 100% response rate was received in round 1!

Round 2 was distributed to panel members in January 2001 and indicated two tasks for the panel to accomplish. First, the results of round 1 with each case and its mean rating score were provided. Panel members were asked to indicate whether they agreed or disagreed with the group rating score for each case. If they did disagree, they were asked to write a score they thought was more appropriate for that case and briefly state their reason for doing so. The second task required panel members to review and rate the representativeness of new cases in their areas that had been suggested in round 1. As in round 1, a 100% response rate was received in round 2.

Since the goal of the Delphi was to identify those cases that were best representative of each legal area, a score of 3.51 on the 5-point Likert scale was chosen as the cutoff score for determining the cases that would be selected for the casebook. A cutoff score of 3.51 and higher represented the lower real limit of the "good case representativeness" category along with the "best case representativeness" category for rating cases. By the end of round 2, a general consensus had been achieved for 61 cases that received a consistent rating of 3.51 or higher on the 5-point scale over the first two rounds of the Delphi. While a portion of the Delphi was complete, round 3 was necessary in order to gain feedback on the new cases that had been rated in round 2. So, in March 2001, the final round of the Delphi was sent to the panel with instructions to review and rerate the group rating of each case in their areas. As a result of round 3, 48 additional cases had consistently been rated at 3.51 or higher. With the Delphi process completed, 109 cases had been selected as the best cases representing the nine legal areas for the casebook. Andy checked these cases to determine which ones were still good law. Any cases that had been overturned were eliminated. In one area—antitrust law in professional sports—the authors thought that 13 cases were a disproportionately large number of cases and subsequently eliminated those with scores of less than 4.00. One or two low-ranking cases in a couple of other areas were eliminated because they did not add additional understanding to their particular content area. Finally, one case was accepted for appeal and was therefore eliminated. As a result of all these changes, we ended up with a final total of 90 cases.

Sarah Young

Writing the Review Questions

These cases were then the focus for the next phase of the project, which was to edit and develop questions for each case (these questions can be found in the online student resource and the instructor guide). I would take my data bank of questions and oversee the development of questions for all the cases. The thought of developing questions for the important cases that Andy, Sarah, and I, along with our panel of experts, identified was exciting given my interest in sport and recre-

ation law as well as my desire to develop a way for professors in our field to challenge students and generate discussion on key legal issues. My excitement, however, was soon tempered by the tremendous amount of work involved in developing the questions. The challenge in writing the questions was to cover the central issues in the cases while avoiding duplication of issue questions and maintaining a degree of difficulty that was reasonable for undergraduate and graduate students in our field of study. Through many discussions, the three of us agreed that we would develop between 8 and 15 questions per case. This number would allow for a sufficient number of questions for generating discussions or creating a challenging assignment without extending beyond the central issues of the case. It was decided to make questions 1 through 4 standard to test the student's knowledge of the components of a case and challenge them to decipher the often difficult language of the law to determine the legal claims and who prevailed in a case. The remaining questions addressed the key issues that were presented in the cases. The questions were both fact and issue based and developed so that a student's knowledge of a particular case and the important issues to be derived from that case would be fully tested.

J.O. Spengler

This first effort was self-published in 2002, followed closely by a second edition later that same year. Because we now had a tangible product, we thought our idea was easier to sell to publishers as a text with merit and promise. Yet it took three years before we began serious negotiations with Myles Schrag at Human Kinetics. As a result, what you have in your hand represents input not only from the three coauthors and a panel of sport law experts but also from several people at Human Kinetics.

1

Antitrust Law

Antitrust law centers on the issue of competitive markets. Despite the fact that this is a complex area of law, the basic premise is easy to comprehend—markets should be competitive and free of restraints. To this end, state and federal laws have been enacted to protect markets from unlawful restraints on trade and from activities such as price fixing and the formation of monopolies (where there is only one provider of a product or service). Antitrust issues are more common than you might suspect and have been at the forefront of several highly publicized media events. Did you know that antitrust was at issue when

▷ Maurice Clarett decided to leave college early to enter the NFL;

▷ the NIT attempted to change the face of March Madness;

▷ teenage athletes sought to play in the National Basketball Development League (NBDL);

▷ the 1982 Heisman Trophy–winner Herschel Walker played for the United States Football League (USFL);

▷ the USFL sued the NFL and won, receiving $3 in damages; and

▷ Wrigley Field in Chicago was built?

The primary federal laws that govern antitrust issues are the Sherman Act, Clayton Act, Federal Trade Commission Act, and Robinson-Patman Act. The cases in this section address these laws. The Sherman Act, for example, makes it unlawful for organizations to form a conspiracy in restraint of trade. Sports league teams, however, have unique characteristics that have required the courts to take a close look at the application of this law to them. This interesting area of law is addressed in the cases of *AIAW v. NCAA, Federal Baseball Club v. National League of Professional*

Baseball Clubs, and *Flood v. Kuhn.* The cases that follow address antitrust issues involving such subjects as coach and player salaries (*Law v. NCAA* and *Brown v. Pro Football, Inc.*), the movement of professional teams to new cities (*LA Memorial Coliseum v. NFL*), draft and eligibility issues (*Banks v. NCAA* and *Smith v. Pro Football*), and broadcasting rights (*Chicago Professional Sports v. NBA* and *NCAA v. Board of Regents*). The cases are interesting and the questions are designed to strengthen your understanding of this complex but important body of law.

Association for Intercollegiate Athletics for Women v. National Collegiate Athletic Association

735 F.2d 577 (D.C. Cir. 1984)

This appeal arises from an antitrust action brought by the Association for Intercollegiate Athletics for Women (AIAW) against the National Collegiate Athletic Association (NCAA). AIAW alleged that NCAA unlawfully used its monopoly power in men's college sports to facilitate its entry into women's college sports and to force AIAW out of existence. On appeal, AIAW contests the district court's fact findings and legal analysis. Although we disagree in part with one portion of the district court's legal analysis, that court's disposition ultimately and properly turns on fact findings that are not clearly erroneous. We therefore affirm the district court's decision rejecting AIAW's claims.

From 1906 to 1980, NCAA sponsored programs only for men's intercollegiate athletics. In 1967, the Commission on Intercollegiate Athletics for Women (CIAW) was organized to provide a governing body for women's athletics. In 1971, CIAW was transformed into AIAW, an organization that throughout its existence governed only women's sports. By 1980-81, AIAW's membership had grown to 961 colleges and universities. AIAW's

standing as the major governing body in women's sports ended, however, in the fall of 1981.

In the 1981-82 sports season, NCAA introduced 29 women's championships in 12 sports. During the same season, AIAW suffered a significant drop in membership and participation in its events. AIAW's loss in membership dues totaled $124,000, which represented approximately 22% of the dues collected the previous year. Forty-nine percent of those institutions leaving AIAW elected to place their women's sports programs under NCAA's governance.

AIAW also suffered promotional losses. AIAW's diminished stature following NCAA's entry into women's sports also hindered AIAW's efforts to market its logo. AIAW had further difficulty securing national championship sites, holding volunteer staff, and realizing profits from its Division I championship events. Since AIAW's leadership expected these financial hardships only to worsen, it decided not to distribute membership renewal applications for the 1982-83 season. AIAW closed business on June 30, 1982.

FN1. Sections 1, 2, and 3 of the Sherman Act provide in pertinent part:

§ 1. Every contract, combination in the form of trust or otherwise, or conspiracy, in restraint of trade or commerce among the several States, or with foreign nations, is declared to be illegal.

§ 2. Every person who shall monopolize, or attempt to monopolize, or combine or conspire with any other person or persons, to monopolize any part of the trade or commerce among the several States, or with foreign nations, shall be deemed guilty of a felony. . . .

§ 3. Every contract, combination in form of trust or otherwise, or conspiracy, in restraint of trade or commerce in any Territory of the United States or of the District of Columbia, or in restraint of trade or commerce . . . between any such Territory or Territories and any State or States or the District of Columbia, or with foreign nations, or between the District of Columbia and any State or States or foreign nations, is declared illegal. 15 U.S.C. §§ 1, 2, 3 (1982).

On October 9, 1981, AIAW filed suit against NCAA in the United States District Court for the District of Columbia. AIAW alleged that NCAA violated §§ 1, 2, and 3 of the Sherman Act, 15 U.S.C. §§ 1, 2, 3 (1982), by using its monopoly power in men's college sports to facilitate its entry into women's college sports and to force AIAW out of existence. [FN1]

Specifically, AIAW asserted that NCAA's unlawful conduct consisted of predatory pricing, the use of financial incentives to link the sale of competitive services with the sale of monopoly services, and an illegal tying arrangement.

Before NCAA introduced women's events, NCAA members paid a single flat fee for the option of participating in all the events in their respective NCAA divisions. For the 1981-82 season, NCAA did not increase its flat rate, or charge a separate fee, for those members participating in the newly instituted women's events. NCAA continued this practice through June 1982 when AIAW closed business. AIAW asserts that the price for participating in a college sports program is the membership dues associated with that program. Since NCAA's price for participation in its women's program was effectively zero and thus well below the cost of the program, AIAW cites NCAA's dues policy as a classic example of predatory pricing.

Before 1981, NCAA guaranteed both transportation and per diem expenses to participants in all its championships. Also, after event administration expenses were deducted from revenues generated by a championship, remaining proceeds were distributed 50% to NCAA and 50% to institutions competing in the championship. When NCAA began to sponsor women's events, however, it changed this proceeds distribution formula. Although NCAA continued to guarantee reimbursement of transportation expenses, per diem expenses for championships were paid only from surplus revenue after event administration costs had been covered. Any revenues that remained after paying per diem expenses were used first to repay NCAA for the travel allowance, and only then were distributed to participating institutions. NCAA readily concedes that these changes reduced the likelihood of teams receiving either per diem reimbursements or championship proceeds.

AIAW argues that revisions in NCAA's distribution formula created financial incentives for schools whose men's teams already participated in NCAA events to enroll their women's teams in NCAA as well. The revisions, notes AIAW, decreased payments to current men's participants substantially below their former level. Because NCAA has monopoly power in men's sports, it allegedly did not fear losing participants in men's events due to the reduced proceeds allocated to those events. The only effect, AIAW argues, was to encourage coeducational institutions to enroll their women's programs in NCAA events to recoup lost proceeds shifted from men's to women's sports. AIAW contends that only by obtaining NCAA's relatively generous women's reimbursements could a coeducational institution avoid a net loss in subsidization for its entire athletic program. AIAW thus claims the revisions in NCAA's distribution formula produced irresistible inducements for coeducational schools to transfer their women's programs from AIAW to NCAA. These inducements allegedly constituted an unlawful linkage, tantamount to a coercive tie, of women's events to the monopolized men's events.

In the winter of 1981, NCAA negotiated the sale of television rights for its men's basketball championship with Columbia Broadcasting System (CBS) and National Broadcasting Company (NBC). In the course of negotiations, NCAA asked each network to clarify its position, *inter alia*, on a proposed rights fee for televising NCAA's women's basketball championship game. CBS originally offered $225,000 over three years for the women's basketball championship. NBC proposed $525,000 for the same television rights. NCAA, however, awarded CBS a contract covering both the men's and women's championships. NCAA's presentation indicates that its decision stemmed from CBS's offering some $3 million more than NBC for the men's championship, and from the efficiencies of selling both championships to the same network. AIAW contends, however, that NCAA tied the sale of television rights for its women's basketball championship to the rights for its men's counterpart. Because NCAA is a monopoly seller of television rights for men's college basketball championships, AIAW alleges NCAA was able to thrust its women's championship upon an unwilling purchaser. AIAW thus argues that CBS was forced to purchase the women's event, in which it had no interest, in order to obtain the men's event, which was of paramount importance.

NCAA argues that its nonprofit status and affiliation with higher education warrant special treatment under the antitrust laws. Its position rests primarily on a much-discussed footnote in *Goldfarb v. Virginia State Bar*, 421 U.S. 773, 788-89 n.17, 95 S.Ct. 2004, 2013-14 n. 17, 44 L.Ed.2d 572 (1975). There, the Supreme Court indicated that practices of professional organizations may not be interchangeable with those of commercial businesses for the purpose of antitrust analysis. NCAA contends that practices of nonprofit athletic associations are no more interchangeable with business activities than are practices of professions. NCAA therefore suggests that even where its conduct has significant anticompetitive consequences, that conduct may be justified by a motive to accomplish the legitimate nonprofit goals of the association.

We reject the district court's position that intent is a separate and essential prerequisite to civil antitrust liability of organizations such as NCAA. A party's intent is relevant only insofar as it helps predict the probable competitive impact of a disputed practice.

AIAW asserts that NCAA used its dues policy as a predatory pricing scheme and its proceeds distribution formula to create irresistible inducements to facilitate its entry into women's sports. AIAW claims that such conduct constituted alternatively an unlawful monopolization, an attempt to monopolize, or at least an unlawful use of monopoly power in one market to damage competition in another market.

To establish a monopolization claim, the plaintiff must demonstrate that the defendant in fact acquired monopoly power as a result of unlawful conduct. The district court determined that NCAA had acquired no monopoly power in women's sports by June 1982. To prevail in this court on its monopolization claim, AIAW must demonstrate that the district court's factual conclusion was clearly erroneous. The district court based its finding on a comparison of NCAA's and AIAW's respective standing in women's sports for 1981-82. In its final year of existence, AIAW enrolled more members and offered 12 more

women's championships in even more sports than NCAA. In every sport in which NCAA offered a women's championship, more NCAA members participated in the corresponding AIAW championship than in NCAA's championship. AIAW voluntarily ceased operations in June 1982, not because of current bankruptcy, but due to a business estimation of accelerating economic hardship in 1982-83. Because we do not find clearly erroneous the district court's conclusion that NCAA had not acquired a monopoly in women's sports by June 1982, we affirm its dismissal of AIAW's monopolization claim.

Attempted monopolization consists of a specific intent to acquire monopoly power by means of exclusionary conduct and a dangerous probability that such conduct, if unchecked, would produce the desired monopoly. Although AIAW proved that NCAA's eventual monopolization of women's sports was a likelihood, the district court found absent the requisite specific intent. AIAW asserts that the district court misconstrued the specific intent requirement by allowing altruistic motives to cleanse a purposeful attempt to monopolize. AIAW contends the district court held that NCAA intended to drive AIAW out of existence, but that such an intention was saved by NCAA's salutary motive to provide a singular governance and promotion system for women's sports. We agree that specific intent in attempted monopolization cases has little relation to the defendant's altruistic or malevolent motivations. Rather, specific intent in this context refers to a purpose to acquire monopoly power by driving one's rival from the market by exclusionary or predatory means. The law thus inquires not why, but whether, one intends to acquire unlawful monopoly power.

After considering the district court's full discussion of AIAW's attempted monopolization claim, we conclude that the court properly applied the law on specific intent. The district court cited and found persuasive considerable record evidence indicating that NCAA viewed the continued existence of AIAW as a healthy alternative to the NCAA and that NCAA's objective was not to take over women's athletics. The court then noted that NCAA's exhaustive and open debate on the appropriate objectives of its women's programs represented the antithesis of conspiratorial plotting to acquire surreptitious control of a market. Immediately thereafter, the court concluded that AIAW failed to prove the specific intent necessary to sustain its claim of attempted monopoly. The district court's frequent reference to NCAA's contemplated coexistence with AIAW reflects the court's recognition that the relevant inquiry was whether NCAA intended to destroy AIAW. Furthermore, the court's conclusion that NCAA's adopting a women's program did not represent an attempt to acquire surreptitious control of a market indicates that it resolved the relevant inquiry in the negative. We accordingly affirm the district court's finding of no attempted monopolization.

AIAW's third § 2 claim alleges that NCAA unlawfully distorted competition in women's sports, even though NCAA may not have sought or gained a monopoly in the market. NCAA allegedly caused this distortion by using its monopoly power in men's sports as a lever to facilitate its entry into women's sports.

Assuming *arguendo* that leveraging is a distinct § 2 offense, we note that a plaintiff still must prove the disputed use of monopoly power in fact caused economic injury and that such use was unlawful. AIAW argues that NCAA's dues policy and proceeds distribution formula were the unlawful means by which NCAA used its monopoly power in men's sports to injure AIAW's standing in women's sports. The district court, however, found that AIAW failed to establish the causal relationship between NCAA's disputed practices and AIAW's economic injury.

A review of the record does not reveal that the district court's conclusion was clearly erroneous. The court observed that two former AIAW presidents were unable to refer specifically to any institution that left AIAW in 1981-82 due to NCAA's economic incentives. Moreover, several witnesses indicated that their institutions participated in NCAA championships, not to receive the alleged irresistible economic inducements, but rather because NCAA offered a superior product. Thus, if AIAW's losses were NCAA's gains, the court properly concluded from substantial record evidence that the shift in membership and participation was not the product of anything but direct competition.

The court's conclusion is hardly remarkable given the nature of NCAA's dues and reimbursement policies. First, neither policy is exclusionary. The dues policy, which simply continued NCAA's past practice, did not make NCAA membership contingent on an institution's abstaining from AIAW's membership rolls or from participating in AIAW events. Additionally, the dues policy did not require NCAA members to enroll their women's programs in NCAA events or penalize them for not doing so. Similarly, the proceeds distribution formula did not condition reimbursement on exclusive NCAA membership or exclusive participation in NCAA events. Indeed, NCAA agreed to judge female participants' eligibility according to NCAA rules or the published rules of any recognized state, conference, regional or national organization of which an institution had been a member as of August 1, 1981. The disputed NCAA practices thus allowed coeducational institutions to maintain dual women's memberships and participate in both associations' events under either association's rules without suffering any penalty in membership dues or reimbursements.

Second, neither NCAA's dues nor its reimbursement policy sprung from a predatory intent that could indicate a potential anticompetitive effect. As discussed above, the district court rejected AIAW's argument, on the basis of insufficient persuasive evidence, that NCAA's purpose was to monopolize women's sports by unlawfully driving AIAW from the market. AIAW thus failed to prove that either policy represented anything other than NCAA members' rational judgment of how best and most equitably to promote men's and women's intercollegiate athletics.

Finally, both the dues policy and the reimbursement formula governed essentially noncommercial conduct. The dues policy regulated only the flow of funds from NCAA members to the association; it did not affect members' or the association's dealings with third-party commercial enterprises. Despite AIAW's effort to characterize NCAA's dues as a predatory pricing scheme, we believe the dues format is more accurately viewed as a mechanism by which members established the appropriate amount each must contribute to the organization. We conclude NCAA's dues policy was essentially an internal housekeeping matter that did not provide a means by which members or NCAA itself directly engaged in commerce. Similarly, we construe NCAA's reimbursement formula as a regulation governing the internal redistribution of NCAA's revenues among its members. Like the dues policy, the formula did not bear on members' or NCAA's interaction with third-party commercial enterprises.

That NCAA's disputed practices were not exclusionary, did not spring from a predatory intent, and regulated essentially noncommercial conduct further suggests that these practices would have a *de minimis* competitive impact. We, therefore, are especially reluctant to disturb the district court's factual assessment, based on substantial record evidence, to the same effect. We accordingly affirm the district court's holding that AIAW failed to establish that it suffered antitrust injury as a result of NCAA's dues policy or proceeds distribution formula.

AIAW contends that NCAA tied the purchase of television rights for its women's basketball championship game to the purchase of its men's counterpart. AIAW argues that such a tie is both a *per se* violation under § 1 and the unlawful means by which NCAA monopolized, attempted to monopolize, or gained a competitive advantage in women's sports in violation of § 2. The district court concluded, however, that NCAA in fact had not used this power to impose a tied sale on the television networks. AIAW again is faced with the heavy burden of demonstrating that the district court's factual conclusion was clearly erroneous.

AIAW focuses on three points in attacking the district court's finding of no coercive tie. First, AIAW notes that NCAA requested CBS and NBC to respond to 23 conditions in submitting their bids for the men's championship. One such condition requested the networks to assign a separate fee to NCAA's women's basketball championship game. Second, AIAW points out that both NBC and CBS felt obliged to submit such a bid. Finally, AIAW cites NCAA's awarding CBS its women's championship even though NBC's bid on the women's event was substantially higher. AIAW contends that these three facts, taken together, demonstrate conclusively that NCAA would sell its men's championship only to a network that agreed to purchase NCAA's women's championship. For the reasons presented below, we reject AIAW's argument.

In short, we find sufficient evidence to support the district court's conclusion that coverage of the women's championship game was not a *sine qua non* of a contract for the men's. Consequently, we reject AIAW's claim that NCAA's sale of television rights constitutes anticompetitive conduct violative either of § 1 or § 2 of the Sherman Act.

 For an extended version of the case and review questions to test your understanding of the material, please go to www.HumanKinetics.com/CaseStudiesInSportLaw.

Banks v. National Collegiate Athletic Association

977 F.2d 1081 (7th Cir. 1992)

Braxston Lee Banks appeals the district court's dismissal of his claim that the National Collegiate Athletic Association (NCAA) rules withdrawing athletes' eligibility to participate in collegiate sports in the event the athlete chooses to enter a professional draft or engages an agent to help him secure a position with a professional team are an illegal restraint on trade or commerce in violation of 15 U.S.C. § 1. We affirm the judgment of the district court holding that Banks failed to state a claim upon which relief can be granted.

Banks entered the University of Notre Dame on a full football scholarship in September 1986. As a freshman Banks started in four or five games and in fact played in all 11 contests. In the first game of his sophomore year, Banks injured his knee and, as a result of his injury, played in only seven games—he started in four of them. Again in his junior year, allegedly because of the knee injury, Banks played in only six games but again started in four. Banks chose to sit out his senior year (1989) because, as he stated, "of my desire to be sure that my knee was fully recovered before I played again."

Having completed three years of college eligibility, Banks was eligible to enter the National Football League (NFL) selection process or draft in the spring of 1990. Banks decided to enter the 1990 NFL draft after representatives of two scouting organizations employed by the NFL teams informed him that he would have been invited to the regular NFL scouting tryouts if he had completed his collegiate eligibility. After the news of Banks' entrance into the draft became public, representatives of virtually every NFL team visited Notre Dame and put him through athletic efficiency drills to test his skills. In addition, Banks participated in an NFL tryout in Indianapolis, Indiana for college players who had entered the draft before completing college eligibility. Banks apparently performed below par at the tryouts in Indianapolis, and as a result failed to be selected in the draft or as a free agent.

Under the NCAA rules, an athlete is eligible to play four seasons of an intercollegiate sport within five years of commencing his college education. As a result of sitting out his senior year of eligibility, Banks had one year of intercollegiate eligibility remaining when he graduated in August 1990. In spite of the fact that he was exposing himself to further injury, he decided that the only way for him to demonstrate his ability to compete on the professional level was to return to Notre Dame for graduate courses and reenter its intercollegiate football program during his final year of eligibility. Unfortunately for Banks, two NCAA eligibility rules stood in his way. Rule 12.2.4.2, the no-draft rule, provides that an individual loses amateur status in a particular sport when the individual asks to be placed on the draft list or supplemental draft list of a professional league in that sport. Rule 12.3.1, the no-agent rule, states: "An individual shall be ineligible for participation in an intercollegiate sport if he or she ever has agreed (orally or in writing) to be represented by an agent for the purpose of marketing his or her athletics ability or reputation in that sport." Since Banks participated in the draft tryouts and agreed to be represented by an agent subsequent to signing up for the draft, either of the two rules (NCAA Rule 12.2.4.2 or Rule 12.3.1) was sufficient to bar him from participating in his final year of eligibility at Notre Dame. The Notre Dame football coaches allegedly wanted

Banks to play in the 1990 season, but according to Banks, the school refused to request the NCAA to reinstate Banks' eligibility because no college had ever appealed to the NCAA to restore eligibility of a player who entered the NFL draft. The NCAA declined to consider Banks' personal request for reinstatement, as the bylaws provide only for member colleges to petition for restoration of an athlete's eligibility.

We will address the following issues in this appeal: (1) whether Banks has standing to act as a class representative for the purpose of seeking to enjoin the NCAA's enforcement of its no-draft and no-agent rules, (2) whether the district court erred in dismissing this antitrust claim under Rule 12(b)(6) for failure to state a claim upon which relief can be granted, and (3) whether the plaintiff stated a valid antitrust claim in his second cause of action.

Banks' primary contention on appeal is that because the record is not thoroughly developed, it was inappropriate for the district court to decide that the NCAA no-draft and no-agent rules were procompetitive in ruling on a Rule 12(b)(6) motion to dismiss. Banks asserts that without any evidence, the district court agreed with the NCAA that its no-draft and no-agent rules were reasonable and dismissed the complaint under Rule 12(b)(6) for failure to state a claim. We are unconvinced that the record in this case requires further development in order to determine whether the NCAA rules have a procompetitive effect, but it is immaterial to evaluating Banks' argument that the district court improperly decided that the rules were reasonable. The district court decided the case not on the basis of the relative anticompetitive effect of the rules versus the procompetitive impact, but on the ground of Banks' absolute failure to allege an anticompetitive effect. Mr. Banks does not suggest what anticompetitive effects result from either restraints in the football labor market or the group boycott, nor does he challenge the purported procompetitive impact of the NCAA no-draft rules. The court went on to hold that "[w]hile Mr. Banks claims that the NCAA rules in question accomplish a group boycott by way of restricting the football labor market, he ties those allegations to no competitive impact on any identifiable market. Mr. Banks has no antitrust injury that can be gleamed [sic] from the amended complaint." Since the district judge's decision was based on Banks' failure to allege an anticompetitive effect on an identifiable market, the argument that the court improperly determined that the rules were reasonable on a motion to dismiss is without merit.

The district court dismissed Banks' claim because he failed to allege that the NCAA rules had an anticompetitive impact on any identifiable market. Banks chose to appeal the judgment of the court rather than request leave to amend and reinstate his complaint. On appeal, Banks ignores the holding of the district court and asserts that the court found an anticompetitive impact on a relevant market.

The district court's conclusion that Banks has no antitrust injury was obviously based upon its holding that Banks failed to allege an anticompetitive impact on a relevant market. We confess that we are somewhat perplexed as to how Banks expects to get a reversal of the district court's judgment without assigning error to its holding.

We do not dispute the fact that the plaintiff could have alleged an anticompetitive impact. However, this court is not able to review what Banks could have alleged, but is called upon to review only what he actually alleged. Our review of Banks' argument shows that the plaintiff cited only examples of antitrust law violations (group boycotts, price fixing, control of output, refusal to deal) but failed to delineate much less explain which, if any, of these restraints of trade apply to the NCAA rules at issue.

This court has previously addressed the requirement of alleging anticompetitive effects on a market in order to make out a claim for a violation of the Sherman Act:

"The fundamental requirement at issue in this dispute is that of a sufficient allegation of anticompetitive effects that would result or have resulted from the defendants' actions; the absence of such allegations is ordinarily fatal to the existence of a cause of action. The purpose of the Sherman Act is to rectify the injury to consumers caused by diminished competition; it is for this reason that Congress provided a treble damage recovery for private parties willing to initiate an enforcement action. Thus, the plaintiff must allege not only an injury to himself, but an injury to the market as well. It is only when the plaintiff adequately states a *per se* violation of § 1 of the Sherman Act that an allegation of anticompetitive effects is not required." *Car Carriers, Inc. v. Ford Motor Company,* 745 F.2d 1101, 1107-08 (7th Cir. 1984)

Under the Supreme Court's ruling in *National Collegiate Athletic Association v. Board of Regents,* 468 U.S. 85, 104 S.Ct. 2948, 82 L.Ed.2d 70 (1984), allegations that the NCAA rules restrain trade or commerce may not be viewed as *per se* violations of the Sherman Act, but must be addressed under the rule of reason. Thus, in order for Banks' complaint to state a claim on which relief can be granted, it must allege anticompetitive effects on a discernible market.

Banks' complaint alleged that the NCAA no-draft and no-agent rules restrained trade or commerce in three ways:

(a) First, there is the restraint imposed by the NCAA on all of its member institutions that restricts them from offering a player such as Banks, who enters the draft and/or retains an agent, an opportunity to play college football again. The relevant market on which that restraint is imposed is all those players who wish to play football for major college football teams, a market which is dominated by the NCAA. (b) Second, the Rules operate as a restraint on all members of the NCAA requiring them to abide by the Rules, and not to change them or grant waivers from them. This restraint operates directly on member institutions such as Notre Dame and indirectly, although intentionally, on players such as Banks. The relevant market is all major college football institutions since all NCA [sic] member institutions are subject to similar restrictions, and hence players like Banks are foreclosed from choosing a major college football team based on the willingness of the institution to waive or change its rules, or consider doing so. (c) Third, the Rules also operate to restrain the ability of a player such as Banks from marketing his services to the NFL, by effectively giving him one and only one realistic chance to be drafted by the NFL. The relevant market being restrained is composed of players like Banks who are considering entering the NFL draft while they still have college football eligibility remaining.

These allegations identify two markets: (1) NCAA football players who enter the draft and/or employ an agent and (2) college institutions that are members of the NCAA. Another reading of the complaint might even have deduced a third market, the NFL player recruitment market. But regardless of how charitably the complaint is read, it has failed to define an anticompetitive effect of the alleged restraints on the markets.

As Banks states in paragraphs 5-7 of his amended complaint, the NCAA has adopted the no-draft, no-agent, and other substantive rules to which all NCAA member institutions have agreed, and do in fact, adhere. Contrary to Banks' erroneous allegations, an NCAA member institution may not waive or change the no-draft rule at its discretion for it is rather obvious that only the National Collegiate Athletic Association can waive or change one of its substantive rules. Any school that sought to waive or change the rules would forfeit its ability to participate in NCAA sanctioned events.

Second, as the district court held, the complaint has failed to allege an anticompetitive impact. The failure results from Banks' inability to explain how the no-draft rule restrains trade in the college football labor market. The NCAA rules seek to promote fair competition, encourage the educational pursuits of student athletes, and prevent commercialism. According to the constitution of the National Collegiate Athletic Association, the purposes of the NCAA Eligibility Rules are to maintain amateur intercollegiate athletics as an integral part of the educational program and the athlete as an integral part of the student body and by doing so, retain a clear line of demarcation between intercollegiate athletics and professional sports. The overriding purpose of the Eligibility Rules, thus, is not to provide the NCAA with commercial advantage, but rather the opposite extreme—to prevent commercializing influences from destroying the unique product of NCAA college football.

As the Supreme Court in *Board of Regents* stated: "most of the regulatory controls of the NCAA are a justifiable means of fostering competition among the amateur athletic teams and therefore are procompetitive because they enhance public interest in intercollegiate athletics." *Board of Regents*, 468 U.S. at 104, 104 S.Ct. at 2961. The Court further explained:

> "The NCAA seeks to market a particular brand of football—college football. The identification of this product with an academic tradition differentiates college football from and makes it more popular than professional sports to which it might otherwise be comparable, such as, for example, minor league baseball. In order to preserve the character and quality of the 'product,' athletes must not be paid, must be required to attend class, and the like. And the integrity of the product cannot be preserved except by mutual agreement; if an institution adopted such restrictions unilaterally [restrictions on eligibility rules], its effectiveness as a competitor on the playing field might soon be destroyed. Thus, the NCAA plays a vital role in enabling college football to

preserve its character, and as a result enables a product to be marketed which might otherwise be unavailable. In performing this role, its actions widen consumer choice—not only the choices available to sports fans but also those available to athletes—and hence can be viewed as procompetitive."

The no-draft rule has no more impact on the market for college football players than other NCAA eligibility requirements such as grades, semester hours carried, or requiring a high school diploma. They all constitute eligibility requirements essential to participation in NCAA-sponsored amateur athletic competition. Banks might just as well have alleged that only permitting a student five calendar years in which to participate in four seasons of intercollegiate athletics restrains trade. Banks' allegation that the no-draft rule restrains trade is absurd. None of the NCAA rules affecting college football eligibility restrain trade in the market for college players because the NCAA does not exist as a minor league training ground for future NFL players but rather to provide an opportunity for competition among amateur students pursuing a collegiate education. Because the no-draft rule represents a desirable and legitimate attempt to keep university athletics from becoming professionalized to the extent that profit-making objectives would overshadow educational objectives, the no-draft rule and other like NCAA regulations preserve the bright line of demarcation between college and play-for-pay football. We consider college football players as student athletes simultaneously pursuing academic degrees that will prepare them to enter the employment market in nonathletic occupations, and hold that the regulations of the NCAA are designed to preserve the honesty and integrity of intercollegiate athletics and foster fair competition among the participating amateur college students.

In order for the NCAA rules to be considered a restraint of trade in violation of section 1 of the Sherman Act, Banks must allege that the no-draft and no-agent rules, as the dissent explains, are terms of employment that diminish competition in the employment market (i.e., college football). Initially, we restate that the no-draft rule and similar NCAA rules serve to maintain the clear line of demarcation between college and professional football. In contrast to professional football, NCAA student athletes are required to attend class, maintain a minimum grade point average, and enroll and complete a required number of courses to obtain a degree. The no-draft rule is evidence of the academic priority of the NCAA because it forecloses a student athlete from hiring an agent or entering the NFL draft and after failing to meet the professional standards, returning to play college football to improve his football skills in hopes of entering an upcoming draft. In denying a college football player the right to play professional football (entering the NFL draft) and then return to college football, the no-draft rule merely serves as an NCAA eligibility requirement and precludes the existence of a college football labor market for athletes who are ineligible by NCAA standards.

Elimination of the no-draft and no-agent rules would fly in the face of the NCAA's amateurism requirements. Member schools might very well be exposed to agents offering the services of their football playing clients to the highest bidder. In representing their pro-athlete clients, the agents would in all probability attempt to bargain with the NCAA school and might very well expect the school to offer their client an attractive contract possibly involving automobiles, condominiums, and cash as compensation in contravention of the NCAA amateurism rules. Such arrangements might involve cash compensation payable only in the future after the player has completed his college eligibility and continues with an NFL club. The involvement of professional sports agents in NCAA football would turn amateur intercollegiate athletics into a sham because the focus of college football would shift from educating the student athlete to creating a minor-league farm system out of college football that would operate solely to improve players' skills for professional football in the NFL. We should not permit the entry of professional athletes and their agents into NCAA sports because the cold commercial nature of professional sports would not only destroy the amateur status of college athletics but more importantly would interfere with the athletes' proper focus on their educational pursuits and direct their attention to the quick buck in pro sports. The no-agent and no-draft rules are vital and must work in conjunction with other eligibility requirements

to preserve the amateur status of college athletics and prevent the sports agents from further intruding into the collegiate educational system.

Our review of Banks' amended complaint reveals that he has not alleged that college football players are regulated under terms of employment or that players are selling their services to their colleges. It is true that some colleges have been justifiably sanctioned by the NCAA for their violations of NCAA rules regarding cash compensation and free airline transportation between the athlete's school and home. The description of players selling their services to NCAA colleges stands in stark contrast to the academic and amateurism requirements of the vast majority of college athletic programs that, in compliance with the NCAA rules and regulations, are foreclosed from offering cash compensation or nonpermissible awards, extra benefits, or excessive or improper expenses not authorized by NCAA legislation. The fact that a minority of schools use athletes rather than encourage and foster their students' academic pursuits does not negate the fact that all NCAA member colleges encourage and require their student athletes to carry a minimum number of semester credits and maintain a minimum grade point average equivalent to the academic program the university's nonathletic students follow.

Specifically, the NCAA requires "to be eligible to represent an institution in inter-collegiate athletics competition, a student-athlete shall be enrolled in at least a minimum full-time program of studies, be in good academic standing and maintain satisfactory progress toward a baccalaureate or equivalent degree." *1992-93 NCAA Division I Operating Manual* § 14.01.1. The term "a full-time program of studies" in section 14.01.1 of the NCAA Bylaws is defined to mean: "the student-athlete shall be enrolled in not less than 12 semester or quarter hours, regardless of the institution's definition of a minimum full-time program of studies." The NCAA's definition of good academic standing in section 14.01.1 is "determined by the academic authorities [of the NCAA institution] who determine the meaning of such phrases for all students of the institution." Lastly, the

NCAA defines the "satisfactory completion" requirement in section 14.01.1 as "a student-athlete shall maintain satisfactory progress toward a baccalaureate or equivalent degree at that institution as determined by the regulations of that institution."

We acknowledge that some schools adhere more faithfully to the NCAA rules than others, but we need not reach the merits of whether the no-draft rule is a material term of employment as the dissent argues because Banks has failed to allege how the no-draft and no-agent rules are restraints of trade under section 1 of the Sherman Act. The most Banks alleges is that the relevant market is (1) NCAA football players who enter the draft (or employ an agent), or (2) NCAA member college institutions, and arguably a third market as the NFL player recruitment market. Beyond establishing these markets, Banks fails to illustrate how the NCAA no-draft and no-agent rules diminish competition in those markets. In evaluating the district court's Rule 12(b) (6) dismissal, we limit our review, as we must, to the well-pleaded allegations of the complaint.

Thus, any additional markets or anticompetitive effects upon them alleged outside the amended complaint are immaterial to our consideration of the district court's judgment. Although on review of a Rule 12(b) (6) dismissal we accept all allegations in the complaint as true, a complaint must contain either direct or inferential allegations respecting all the material elements necessary to sustain a recovery under some viable legal theory. The questions in regard to Banks' allegations of restraints on trade are whether the plaintiffs have successfully pleaded a contract, combination, or conspiracy in restraint of trade within the meaning of the Sherman Act. The pleader may not evade these requirements by merely alleging a bare legal conclusion; if the facts do not at least outline or adumbrate a violation of the Sherman Act, the plaintiffs will get nowhere merely by dressing them up in the language of antitrust.

We agree with the district court's finding that the plaintiff has failed to allege an anticompetitive effect on a relevant market; at best Banks has merely attempted to frame his complaint in antitrust language. While Banks alleges a restraint on the market of college football players, college institutions who are members of the NCAA, and perhaps an NFL player recruitment market, the complaint fails to explain how these alleged restraints diminish competition in or among the markets. In our review of Banks' arguments in his appellate briefs as well as our review of the oral argument, we have been unable to discern a cogent argument articulated even on appeal that the alleged restraints impose an anticompetitive effect on the alleged markets. The appellant merely claims that there is an anticompetitive effect, but he fails to explain what it is. While Banks might possibly have been able to allege an anticompetitive impact on a relevant market through a more carefully drafted complaint or an amendment to his complaint, he failed to do so. It is not for us, as appellate judges, to restructure his complaint for him.

We hold that Banks' failure to allege an anticompetitive impact on a discernible market justified the district court's dismissal for failure to a state claim on which relief can be granted. The appellant's argument that the district court erred in ruling that the NCAA rules were reasonable on a motion to dismiss is without merit, for the basis of the district court's holding was that Banks failed to allege an anticompetitive effect on a market. The judgment of the district court is AFFIRMED.

For an extended version of the case and review questions to test your understanding of the material, please go to www.HumanKinetics.com/CaseStudiesInSportLaw.

Brown v. Pro Football, Inc.

518 U.S. 231 (1996)

The question in this case arises at the intersection of the nation's labor and antitrust laws. A group of professional football players brought this antitrust suit against football club owners. The club owners had bargained with the players' union over a wage issue until they reached an impasse. The owners then had agreed among themselves (but not with the union) to implement the terms of their own last best bargaining offer. The question before us is whether federal labor laws shield such an agreement from antitrust attack. This court has previously found in the labor laws an implicit antitrust exemption that applies where needed to make the collective-bargaining process work. Like the court of appeals, we conclude that this need makes the exemption applicable in this case.

In 1987, a collective-bargaining agreement between the National Football League (NFL or League), a group of football clubs, and the NFL Players Association, a labor union, expired. In March 1989, during the negotiations, the NFL adopted Resolution G-2, a plan that would permit each club to establish a developmental squad of up to six rookie or first-year players who, as free agents, had failed to secure a position on a regular player roster. Squad members would play in practice games and sometimes in regular games as substitutes for injured players. Resolution G-2 provided that the club owners would pay all squad members the same weekly salary.

The next month, April, the NFL presented the developmental squad plan to the Players Association. The NFL proposed a squad player salary of $1,000 per week. The Players Association disagreed. It insisted that the club owners give developmental squad players benefits and protections similar to those provided regular players, and that they leave individual squad members free to negotiate their own salaries.

Two months later, in June, negotiations on the issue of developmental squad salaries reached an impasse. The NFL then unilaterally implemented the developmental squad program by distributing to the clubs a uniform contract

that embodied the terms of Resolution G-2 and the $1,000 proposed weekly salary. The League advised club owners that paying developmental squad players more or less than $1,000 per week would result in disciplinary action, including the loss of draft choices.

In May 1990, 235 developmental squad players brought this antitrust suit against the League and its member clubs. The players claimed that their employers' agreement to pay them a $1,000 weekly salary violated the Sherman Act. The federal district court denied the employers' claim of exemption from the antitrust laws; it permitted the case to reach the jury; and it subsequently entered judgment on a jury treble-damages award that exceeded $30 million. The NFL and its member clubs appealed.

The court of appeals reversed. The majority interpreted the labor laws as waiving antitrust liability for restraints on competition imposed through the collective-bargaining process, so long as such restraints operate primarily in a labor market characterized by collective bargaining. The court held, consequently, that the club owners were immune from antitrust liability. We granted *certiorari* to review that determination. Although we do not interpret the exemption as broadly as did the Appeals Court, we nonetheless find the exemption applicable, and we affirm that court's immunity conclusion.

The immunity before us rests upon what this court has called the nonstatutory labor exemption from the antitrust laws.

This implicit exemption reflects both history and logic. The implicit (nonstatutory) exemption interprets the labor statutes in accordance with this intent, adopted during the 1930s (prevent judicial use of antitrust law to resolve labor disputes), namely, as limiting an antitrust court's authority to determine, in the area of industrial conflict, what is or is not a reasonable practice. It thereby substitutes legislative and administrative labor-related determinations for judicial antitrust-related determinations as to the appropriate legal limits of industrial conflict.

As a matter of logic, it would be difficult, if not impossible, to require groups of employers and employees to bargain together, but at the same time to forbid them to make among themselves or with each other any of the competition-restricting agreements potentially necessary to make the process work or its results mutually acceptable. Thus, the implicit exemption recognizes that, to give effect to federal labor laws and policies and to allow meaningful collective bargaining to take place, some restraints on competition imposed through the bargaining process must be shielded from antitrust sanctions.

The petitioners and their supporters concede, as they must, the legal existence of the exemption we have described. They also concede that, where its application is necessary to make the statutorily authorized collective-bargaining process work as Congress intended, the exemption must apply both to employers and to employees. Nor does the dissent take issue with these basic principles. Consequently, the question before us is one of determining the exemption's scope: Does it apply to an agreement among several employers bargaining together to implement after impasse the terms of their last best good-faith wage offer? We assume that such conduct, as practiced in this case, is unobjectionable as a matter of labor law and policy. On that assumption, we conclude that the exemption applies.

Labor law itself regulates directly, and considerably, the kind of behavior here at issue—the postimpasse imposition of a proposed employment term concerning a mandatory subject of bargaining. Both the Board (the National Labor Relations Board) and the courts have held that, after impasse, labor law permits employers unilaterally to implement changes in preexisting conditions, but only insofar as the new terms meet carefully circumscribed conditions. The collective-bargaining proceeding itself must be free of any unfair labor practice, such as an employer's failure to have bargained in good faith. These regulations reflect the fact that impasse and an accompanying implementation of proposals constitute an integral part of the bargaining process.

Although the case law we have cited focuses on bargaining by a single employer, no one here has argued that labor law does, or should, treat multiemployer bargaining differently in this respect. Indeed, Board and court decisions suggest that the joint implementation of proposed terms after impasse is a familiar practice in the context of multiemployer bargaining.

Multiemployer bargaining itself is a well-established, important, pervasive method of collective bargaining, offering advantages to both management and labor. The upshot is that the practice at issue here plays a significant role in a collective-bargaining process that itself constitutes an important part of the nation's industrial relations system.

In these circumstances, to subject the practice to antitrust law is to require antitrust courts to answer a host of important practical questions about how collective bargaining over wages, hours, and working conditions is to proceed—the very result that the implicit labor exemption seeks to avoid. And it is to place in jeopardy some of the potentially beneficial labor-related effects that multiemployer bargaining can achieve. That is, because unlike labor law, which sometimes welcomes anticompetitive agreements conducive to industrial harmony, antitrust law forbids all agreements among competitors (such as competing employers) that unreasonably lessen competition among or between them in virtually any respect whatsoever. Antitrust law also sometimes permits judges or juries to premise antitrust liability on little more than uniform behavior among competitors, preceded by conversations implying that later uniformity might prove desirable.

If the antitrust laws apply, what are employers to do once impasse is reached? If all impose terms similar to their last joint offer, they invite an antitrust action premised on identical behavior along with prior or accompanying conversations as tending to show a common understanding or agreement. If any, or all, of them individually impose terms that differ significantly from that offer, they invite an unfair labor practice charge. Indeed, how can employers safely discuss their offers together even before a bargaining impasse occurs? A preimpasse discussion about, say, the practical advantages or disadvantages of a particular proposal invites a later antitrust claim that they agreed to limit the kinds of action each would later take should an impasse occur. The same is true of postimpasse discussions aimed at renewed negotiations with the union. Nor would adherence to the terms of an expired collective-bargaining agreement eliminate a potentially plausible antitrust claim charging that they had conspired or tacitly agreed to do so, particularly if maintaining the status quo were not in the immediate economic self-interest of some. All this is to say that to permit antitrust liability here threatens to introduce instability and uncertainty into the collective-bargaining process, for antitrust law often forbids or discourages the kinds of joint discussions and behavior that the collective-bargaining process invites or requires.

We recognize, as the government suggests, that, in principle, antitrust courts might themselves try to evaluate particular kinds of employer understandings, finding them reasonable (hence lawful) where justified by collective-bargaining necessity. But any such evaluation means a web of detailed rules spun by many different nonexpert antitrust judges and juries, not a set of labor rules enforced by a single expert administrative body, namely the Board. The labor laws give the Board, not antitrust courts, primary responsibility for policing the collective-bargaining process. And one of their objectives was to take from antitrust courts the authority to determine, through application of the antitrust laws, what is socially or economically desirable collective-bargaining policy.

Both petitioners and their supporters advance several suggestions for drawing the exemption boundary line short of this case. We shall explain why we find them unsatisfactory.

Petitioners claim that the implicit exemption applies only to labor-management agreements—a limitation that they deduce from case-law language and from a proposed principle—that the exemption must rest on labor-management consent. The language, however, reflects only the fact that the cases previously before the court involved collective-bargaining agreements; the language does not reflect the exemption's rationale.

Nor do we see how an exemption limited by petitioners' principle of labor-management consent could work. One cannot mean the principle literally—that the exemption applies only to understandings embodied in a collective-bargaining agreement—for the collective-bargaining process may take place before the

making of any agreement or after an agreement has expired. Yet a multiemployer bargaining process itself necessarily involves many procedural and substantive understandings among participating employers as well as with the union. Petitioners cannot rescue their principle by claiming that the exemption applies only insofar as both labor and management consent to those understandings. Often labor will not and should not consent to certain common bargaining positions that employers intend to maintain. Similarly, labor need not consent to certain tactics that this court has approved as part of the multiemployer bargaining process, such as unit-wide lockouts and the use of temporary replacements.

Petitioners cannot save their consent principle by weakening it, as by requiring union consent only to the multiemployer bargaining process itself. This general consent is automatically present whenever multiemployer bargaining takes place. As so weakened, the principle cannot help decide which related practices are, or are not, subject to antitrust immunity.

The government argues that the exemption should terminate at the point of impasse. After impasse, it says employers no longer have a duty under the labor laws to maintain the status quo and are free as a matter of labor law to negotiate individual arrangements on an interim basis with the union.

Employers, however, are not completely free at impasse to act independently. The multiemployer bargaining unit ordinarily remains intact; individual employers cannot withdraw. The duty to bargain survives; employers must stand ready to resume collective bargaining. And individual employers can negotiate individual interim agreements with the union only insofar as those agreements are consistent with the duty to abide by the results of group bargaining. Regardless, the absence of a legal duty to act jointly is not determinative.

More importantly, the simple impasse line would not solve the basic problem we have described above. Labor law permits employers, after impasse, to engage in considerable joint behavior, including joint lockouts and replacement hiring. Indeed, as a general matter, labor law often limits employers to four options at impasse: (1) maintain the status quo, (2) implement their last offer, (3) lock out their workers (and either shut down or hire temporary replacements), or (4) negotiate separate interim agreements with the union. What is to happen if the parties cannot reach an interim agreement? The other alternatives are limited. Uniform employer conduct is likely. Uniformity—at least when accompanied by discussion of the matter—invites antitrust attack. And such attack would ask antitrust courts to decide the lawfulness of activities intimately related to the bargaining process.

The problem is aggravated by the fact that impasse is often temporary; it may differ from bargaining only in degree; it may be manipulated by the parties for bargaining purposes; and it may occur several times during the course of a single labor dispute, since the bargaining process is not over when the first impasse is reached. How are employers to discuss future bargaining positions during a temporary impasse? Consider, too, the adverse consequences that flow from failing to guess how an antitrust court would later draw the impasse line. Employers who erroneously concluded that impasse had not been reached would risk antitrust liability were they collectively to maintain the status quo, while employers who erroneously concluded that impasse had occurred would risk unfair labor practice charges for prematurely suspending multiemployer negotiations.

Petitioners say that irrespective of how the labor exemption applies elsewhere to multiemployer collective bargaining, professional sports are special. We can understand how professional sports may be special in terms of, say, interest, excitement, or concern. But we do not understand how they are special in respect to labor law's antitrust exemption. We concede that the clubs that make up a professional sports league are not completely independent economic competitors, as they depend on a degree of cooperation for economic survival. In the present context, however, that circumstance makes the league more like a single bargaining employer, which analogy seems irrelevant to the legal issue before us.

We also concede that football players often have special individual talents, and, unlike many unionized workers, they often negotiate their pay individually with their employers. But this characteristic seems simply a feature, like so many others, which might give employees or employers more or less bargaining power, that might lead some or all of them to favor a particular kind of bargaining, or that might lead to certain demands at the bargaining table. We do not see how it could make a critical legal difference in determining the underlying framework in which bargaining is to take place. Indeed, it would be odd to fashion an antitrust exemption that gave additional advantages to professional football players by virtue of their superior bargaining power that transport workers, coal miners, or meat packers would not enjoy.

Ultimately, we cannot find a satisfactory basis for distinguishing football players from other organized workers. We therefore conclude that all must abide by the same legal rules.

For these reasons, we hold that the implicit (nonstatutory) antitrust exemption applies to the employer conduct at issue here. That conduct took place during and immediately after a collective-bargaining negotiation. It grew out of, and was directly related to, the lawful operation of the bargaining process. It involved a matter that the parties were required to negotiate collectively. And it concerned only the parties to the collective-bargaining relationship.

The judgment of the court of appeals is affirmed.

For an extended version of the case and review questions to test your understanding of the material, please go to www.HumanKinetics.com/CaseStudiesInSportLaw.

Chicago Professional Sports Limited Partnership v. National Basketball Association

95 F.3d 593 (7th Cir. 1996)

The Bulls want to broadcast more of their games over WGN television, a superstation carried on cable systems nationwide. Since 1991 the Bulls and WGN have been authorized by injunction to broadcast 25 or 30 games per year. We affirmed that injunction in 1992, and the district court proceeded to determine whether WGN could carry even more games—and whether the NBA could impose a tax on the games broadcast to a national audience. After holding a nine-week trial and receiving 512 stipulations of fact, the district court made a 30-game allowance permanent and held the NBA's fee excessive. Both sides appeal. The Bulls want to broadcast 41 games per year over WGN; the NBA contends that the antitrust laws allow it to fix a lower number (15 or 20) and to collect the tax it proposed.

Our 1992 opinion rejected the league's defense based on the Sports Broadcasting Act, 15 U.S.C. §§ 1291-95, but our rationale implied that the NBA could restructure its contracts to take advantage of that statute. In 1993 the league tried to do so, signing a contract that transfers all broadcast rights to the National Broadcasting Company. NBC shows only 26 games during the regular season, however, and the network contract allows the league and its teams to permit telecasts at other times. Every team received the right to broadcast all 82 of its regular-season games (41 over the air, 41 on cable), unless NBC telecasts a given contest. The NBA-NBC contract permits the league to exhibit 85 games per year on superstations. Seventy were licensed to the Turner stations (TBS and TNT), leaving 15 potentially available for WGN to license from the league. The Bulls sold 30 games directly to WGN, treating these as over-the-air broadcasts authorized by the NBC contract—not to mention the district court's injunction. The Bulls' only concession is that WGN does not broadcast a Bulls game at the same time as a basketball telecast on a Turner superstation.

Back in 1991 and 1992, the parties were debating whether the NBA's television arrangements satisfied § 1 of the Sports Broadcasting Act, 15 U.S.C. § 1291. We held not, because the Act addresses the effects of transfers by a league of clubs, and the NBA had prescribed rather than transferred broadcast rights. The 1993 contract was written with that distinction in mind. The league asserted title to the copyright interests arising from the games and transferred all broadcast rights to NBC; it received some back, subject to contractual restrictions. Section 1 has been satisfied. But the league did not pay enough attention to § 2, 15 U.S.C. § 1292, which reads:

> Section 1291 of this title shall not apply to any joint agreement described in the first sentence in such section which prohibits any person to whom such rights are sold or transferred from televising any games within any area, except within the home territory of a member club of the league on a day when such club is playing at home.

The NBA-NBC contract permits each club to license the broadcast of its games and then, through the restriction on superstation broadcasts, attempts to limit telecasts to the teams' home markets. Section 2 provides that this makes § 1 inapplicable, so the Sports Broadcasting Act leaves the antitrust laws in force.

Our prior opinion observed that the Sports Broadcasting Act, as a special-interest exception to the antitrust laws, receives a beady-eyed reading. The NBA could have availed itself of the Sports Broadcasting Act by taking over licensing and by selling broadcast rights in the Bulls' games to one of the many local stations in Chicago, rather than to WGN. The statute offered other options as well. Apparently the league did not want to use them, in part for tax reasons and in part because it sought to avoid responsibilities that come from being a licensor, rather than a regulator, of telecasts. Such business decisions are understandable and proper, but they have consequences under the Sports Broadcasting Act. By signing a contract with NBC that left the Bulls, rather than the league, with the authority to select the TV station that would broadcast the games, the NBA made its position under the Sports Broadcasting Act untenable. For as soon as the Bulls picked WGN, any effort to control cable system retransmission of the WGN signal tripped over § 2. The antitrust laws therefore apply, and we must decide what they have to say about the league's effort to curtail superstation transmissions.

Three issues were left unresolved in 1992. One was whether the Bulls and WGN, as producers, suffer antitrust injury. The NBA has not pursued this possibility, and as it is not jurisdictional (plaintiffs suffer injury in fact), we let the question pass. The other two issues are related. We concluded in 1992 that the district court properly condemned the NBA's superstation rule under the quick-look version of the rule of reason, because (a) the league did not argue that it should be treated as a single entity, and (b) the anti-free-riding justification for the superstation rule failed because a fee collected on nationally telecast games would compensate other teams (and the league as a whole) for the value of their contributions to the athletic contests being broadcast. Back in the district court, the NBA argued that it is entitled to be treated as a single firm and therefore should possess the same options as other licensors of entertainment products; outside of court, the league's Board of Governors adopted a rule requiring any club that licenses broadcast rights to superstations to pay a fee based on the amount the two Turner stations pay for games they license directly from the league.

The district court was unimpressed by the NBA's latest arguments. It held that a sports league should not be treated as a single firm unless the teams have a complete unity of interest—which they don't. The court also held the fee to be invalid. Our opinion compelled the judge to concede that a fee is proper in principle. But the judge thought the NBA's fee excessive. Instead of starting with the price per game it had negotiated with Turner (some $450,000), and reducing to account for WGN's smaller number of cable outlets, as it did, the judge concluded that the league should have started with the advertising revenues WGN generated from retransmission on cable (the outer market revenues). Then it should have cut this figure in half, the judge held, so that the Bulls could retain their share of these

revenues. The upshot: The judge cut the per-game fee from roughly $138,000 to $39,400.

The district court's opinion concerning the fee reads like the ruling of an agency exercising a power to regulate rates. Yet the antitrust laws do not deputize district judges as one-man regulatory agencies. The core question in antitrust is output. Unless a contract reduces output in some market, to the detriment of consumers, there is no antitrust problem. A high price is not itself a violation of the Sherman Act. WGN and the Bulls argue that the league's fee is excessive, unfair, and the like. But they do not say that it will reduce output. They plan to go on broadcasting 30 games, more if the court will let them, even if they must pay $138,000 per telecast. Although the fee exceeds WGN's outer-market revenues, the station evidently obtains other benefits—for example, (a) the presence of Bulls games may increase the number of cable systems that carry the station, augmenting its revenues 'round the clock; (b) WGN slots into Bulls games ads for its other programming; and (c) many viewers will keep WGN on after the game and watch whatever comes next. Lack of an effect on output means that the fee does not have antitrust significance. Once antitrust issues are put aside, how much the NBA charges for national telecasts is for the league to resolve under its internal governance procedures. It is no different in principle from the question how much if any of the live gate goes to the visiting team, who profits from the sale of cotton candy at the stadium, and how the clubs divide revenues from merchandise bearing their logos and trademarks. Courts must respect a league's disposition of these issues, just as they respect contracts and decisions by a corporation's board of directors.

According to the league, the analogy to a corporate board is apt in more ways than this. The NBA concedes that it comprises 30 juridical entities—29 teams plus the national organization, each a separate corporation or partnership. The teams are not the league's subsidiaries; they have separate ownership. Nonetheless, the NBA submits, it functions as a single entity, creating a single product (NBA Basketball) that competes with other basketball leagues (both college and professional), other sports, and other entertainments such as plays, movies, opera, TV shows, Disneyland, and Las Vegas. Separate ownership of the clubs promotes local boosterism, which increases interest; each ownership group also has a powerful incentive to field a better team, which makes the contests more exciting and thus more attractive. These functions of independent team ownership do not imply that the league is a cartel. The point is that antitrust law permits, indeed encourages, cooperation inside a business organization the better to facilitate competition between that organization and other producers. To say that participants in an organization may cooperate is to say that they may control what they make and how they sell it.

The district court conceded this possibility but concluded that all cooperation among separately incorporated firms is forbidden by § 1 of the Sherman Act, with certain exceptions. Even a single firm contains many competing interests. Conflicts are endemic in any multistage firm, but they do not imply that these large firms must justify all of their acts under the rule of reason.

We see no reason why a sports league cannot be treated as a single firm in this typology. It produces a single product; cooperation is essential (a league with one team would be like one hand clapping); and a league need not deprive the market of independent centers of decision making. The district court's legal standard was therefore incorrect, and a judgment resting on the application of that standard is flawed.

Whether the NBA itself is more like a single firm, which would be analyzed only under § 2 of the Sherman Act, or like a joint venture, which would be subject to the rule of reason under § 1, is a tough question. Unlike the colleges and universities that belong to the National Collegiate Athletic Association, which the Supreme Court treated as a joint venture in NCAA, the NBA has no existence independent of sports. It makes professional basketball; only it can make NBA Basketball games; and unlike the NCAA the NBA also makes teams.

After this case was last here the NBA created new teams in Toronto and Vancouver, stocked with players from the 27 existing teams plus an extra helping of draft choices. All of this makes the league look like a single firm. Yet the 29 clubs have the right to secede and rearrange into two or three leagues. Professional sports leagues have been assembled from clubs that formerly belonged to other leagues; the National Football League and the NBA fit that description, and the teams have not surrendered their power to rearrange things yet again. Moreover, the league looks more or less like a firm depending on which facet of the business one examines. From the perspective of fans and advertisers (who use sports telecasts to reach fans), NBA Basketball is one product from a single source even though the Chicago Bulls and Seattle Supersonics are highly distinguishable. But from the perspective of college basketball players who seek to sell their skills, the teams are distinct, and because the human capital of players is not readily transferable to other sports (as even Michael Jordan learned) the league looks more like a group of firms acting as a monopsony. That is why the Supreme Court found it hard to characterize the National Football League in *Brown v. Pro Football, Inc.*, 518 U.S. 231, ----, 116 S.Ct. 2116, 2126, 135 L.Ed.2d 521 (1996): "the clubs that make up a professional sports league are not completely independent economic competitors, as they depend on a degree of cooperation for economic survival. In the present context, however, that circumstance makes the league more like a single bargaining employer, which analogy seems irrelevant to the legal issue before us." To say that the League is more like a single bargaining employer than a multiemployer unit is not to say that it necessarily is one, for every purpose.

Most courts that have asked whether professional sports leagues should be treated like single firms or like joint ventures have preferred the joint venture characterization. These cases do not yield a clear principle about the proper characterization of sports leagues. Sports are sufficiently diverse that it is essential to investigate their organization, for we do not rule out the possibility that an organization such as the NBA is best understood as one firm when selling broadcast rights to a network in competition with a thousand other producers of entertainment, but is best understood as a joint venture when curtailing competition for players who have few other market opportunities.

However this inquiry may come out on remand, we are satisfied that the NBA is sufficiently integrated that its superstation rules may not be condemned without analysis under the full rule of reason. We affirmed the district court's original injunction after applying the quick-look version because the district court had characterized the NBA as something close to a cartel. After considering this argument, we conclude that when acting in the broadcast market the NBA is closer to a single firm than to a group of independent firms. This means that plaintiffs cannot prevail without establishing that the NBA possesses power in a relevant market, and that its exercise of this power has injured consumers. Even in the *NCAA* case, the first to use a bobtailed rule of reason, the court satisfied itself that the NCAA possesses market power. The district court had held that there is a market in college football telecasts on Saturday afternoon in the fall, a time when other entertainments do not flourish but college football dominates. Only after holding that this was not clearly erroneous did the court cast any burden of justification on the NCAA.

Substantial market power is an indispensable ingredient of every claim under the full rule of reason. During the lengthy trial of this case, the NBA argued that it lacks market power, whether the buyers are understood as the viewers of games (the way the district court characterized things in NCAA) or as advertisers, who use games to attract viewers. College football may predominate on Saturday afternoons in the fall, but there is no time slot when NBA basketball predominates. The NBA's season lasts from November through June; games are played seven days a week. This season overlaps all of the other professional and college sports, so even sports fanatics have many other options.

From advertisers' perspective—likely the right one, because advertisers are the ones who actually pay for telecasts—the market is even more competitive. Advertisers seek viewers of certain demographic characteristics, and homogeneity is highly valued. A homogeneous audience facilitates targeted ads: breakfast cereals and toys for cartoon shows, household appliances and detergents for daytime soap operas, and automobiles and beer for sports. If the NBA assembled for advertisers an audience that was uniquely homogeneous, or had especially high willingness-to-buy, then it might have market power even if it represented a small portion of air-time. The parties directed considerable attention to this question at trial, but the district judge declined to make any findings of fact on the subject, deeming market power irrelevant. As we see things, market power is irrelevant only if the NBA is treated as a single firm; and given the difficulty of that issue, it may be superior to approach this as a straight rule of reason case, which means starting with an inquiry into market power and, if there is power, proceeding to an evaluation of competitive effects.

Perhaps this can be accomplished using the materials in the current record. Although the judge who presided at the trial died earlier this year, the parties may be willing to agree that an assessment of credibility is unnecessary, so that a new judge could resolve the dispute after reviewing the transcript, exhibits, and stipulations, and entertaining argument. At all events, the judgment of the district court is vacated, and the case is remanded for proceedings consistent with this opinion. Pending further proceedings in the district court or agreement among the parties, the Bulls and WGN must respect the league's and the NBC contract's limitations on the maximum number of superstation telecasts.

 For an extended version of the case and review questions to test your understanding of the material, please go to www.HumanKinetics.com/CaseStudiesInSportLaw.

Federal Baseball Club of Baltimore, Inc. v. National League of Professional Baseball Clubs

259 U.S. 200 (1922)

This is a suit for threefold damages brought by the plaintiff in error under the Antitrust Acts of July 2, 1890, c. 647, § 7, 26 Stat. 209, 210 (Comp. St. § 8829), and of October 15, 1914, c. 323, § 4, 38 Stat. 730, 731 (Comp. St. § 8835d). The defendants are the National League of Professional Baseball Clubs and the American League of Professional Baseball Clubs, unincorporated associations, composed respectively of groups of eight incorporated baseball clubs, joined as defendants; the presidents of the two Leagues and a third person, constituting what is known as the National Commission, having considerable powers in carrying out an agreement between the two Leagues; and three other persons having powers in the Federal League of Professional Baseball Clubs, the relation of which to this case will be explained. It is alleged that these defendants conspired to monopolize the baseball business, the means adopted being set forth with a detail that, in the view that we take, it is unnecessary to repeat.

The plaintiff is a baseball club incorporated in Maryland, and with seven other corporations was a member of the Federal League of Professional Baseball Players, a corporation under the laws of Indiana, that attempted to compete with the combined defendants. It alleges that the defendants destroyed the Federal League by buying up some of the constituent clubs and in one way or another inducing all those clubs except the plaintiff to leave their League, and that the three persons connected with the Federal League and named as defendants, one of them being the president of the League, took part in the conspiracy. Great damage to the plaintiff is alleged. The plaintiff obtained a verdict for $80,000 in the Supreme Court and a judgment for treble the amount was entered, but the court of appeals, after an elaborate discussion, held that the defendants were not within the Sherman Act. The appellee, the plaintiff, elected to stand on the record in order to bring the case to this court at once, and thereupon judgment was ordered for the defendants. It is not argued that the plaintiff waived any rights by its course.

The decision of the court of appeals went to the root of the case and if correct makes it unnecessary to consider other serious difficulties in the way of the plaintiff's recovery. A summary statement of the nature of the business involved will be enough to present the point. The clubs composing the Leagues are in different cities and for the most part in different states. The end of the elaborate organizations and suborganizations that are described in the pleadings and evidence is that these clubs shall play against one another in public exhibitions for money, one or the other club crossing a state line in order to make the meeting possible. When as the result of these contests one club has won the pennant of its League and another club has won the pennant of the other League, there is a final competition for the world's championship between these two. Of course the scheme requires constantly repeated traveling on the part of the clubs, which is provided for, controlled, and disciplined by the organizations, and this it is said means commerce among the states. But we are of opinion that the court of appeals was right.

The business is giving exhibitions of baseball, which are purely state affairs. It is true that in order to attain for these exhibitions the great popularity that they have achieved, competitions must be arranged between clubs from different cities and states. But the fact that in order to give the exhibitions the Leagues must induce free persons to cross state lines and must arrange and pay for their doing so is not enough to change the character of the business. According to the distinction insisted on in *Hooper v. California*, 155 U.S. 648, 655 (1895), 15 Sup. Ct. 207, 39 L.Ed. 297, the transport is a mere incident, not the essential thing. That to which it is incident, the exhibition, although made for money would not be called trade of commerce in the commonly accepted use of those words. As it is put by defendant, personal effort, not related to production, is not a subject of commerce. That which in its consummation is not commerce does not become commerce among the states because the transportation that we have mentioned takes place. To repeat the illustrations given by the court below, a firm of lawyers sending out a member to argue a case, or the Chautauqua lecture bureau sending out lecturers, does not engage in such commerce because the lawyer or lecturer goes to another state.

If we are right, the plaintiff's business is to be described in the same way and the restrictions by contract that prevented the plaintiff from getting players to break their bargains and the other conduct charged against the defendants were not an interference with commerce among the states.

Judgment affirmed.

For an extended version of the case and review questions to test your understanding of the material, please go to www.HumanKinetics.com/CaseStudiesInSportLaw.

Flood v. Kuhn

407 U.S. 258 (1972)

For the third time in 50 years the Court is asked specifically to rule that professional baseball's reserve system is within the reach of the federal antitrust laws. "The reserve system, publicly introduced into baseball contracts in 1887, centers in the uniformity of player contracts; the confinement of the player to the club that has him under the contract; the assignability of the player's contract; and the ability of the club annually to renew the contract unilaterally, subject to a stated salary minimum. . . ."

At the age of 31, in October 1969, Flood was traded to the Philadelphia Phillies of the National League in a multiplayer transaction. He was not consulted about the trade. He was informed by telephone and received formal notice only after the deal had been consummated. In December he complained to the Commissioner of Baseball and asked that he be made a free agent and be placed at liberty to strike his own bargain with any other major league team. His request was denied. Flood then instituted this antitrust suit in January 1970 in federal court for the Southern District of New York. The defendants (although not all were named in each cause of action) were the Commissioner of Baseball, the presidents of the two major leagues, and the 24 major league clubs. In general, the complaint charged violations of the federal antitrust laws and civil rights statutes, violation of state statutes and the common law, and the imposition of a form of peonage and involuntary servitude contrary to the Thirteenth Amendment and 42 U.S.C. § 1994, 18 U.S.C. § 1581, and 29 U.S.C. §§ 102 and 103.

Petitioner sought declaratory and injunctive relief and treble damages.

Flood declined to play for Philadelphia in 1970, despite a $100,000 salary offer, and he sat out the year. After the season was concluded, Philadelphia sold its rights to Flood to the Washington Senators. Washington and the petitioner were able to come to terms for 1971 at a salary of $110,000. Flood started the season but, apparently because he was dissatisfied with his performance, he left the Washington club on April 27, early in the campaign. He has not played baseball since then.

Trial to the court took place in May and June 1970. An extensive record was developed. In an ensuing opinion, Judge Cooper first noted:

> Plaintiff's witnesses in the main concede that some form of reserve on players is a necessary element of the organization of baseball as a league sport, but contend that the present all-embracing system is needlessly restrictive and offer various alternatives which in their view might loosen the bonds without sacrifice to the game. . . . Clearly the preponderance of credible proof does not favor elimination of the reserve clause. With the sole exception of plaintiff himself, it shows that even plaintiff's witnesses do not contend that it is wholly undesirable; in fact they regard substantial portions meritorious. . . . 316 F.Supp., at 275-276.

He then held that *Federal Baseball Club v. National League,* 259 U.S. 200, 42 S.Ct. 465, 66 L.Ed. 898 (1922), and *Toolson v. New York Yankees, Inc.,* 346 U.S. 356, 74 S.Ct. 78, 98 L.Ed. 64 (1953), were controlling; that it was not necessary to reach the issue whether exemption from the antitrust laws would result because aspects of baseball now are a subject of collective bargaining; that the plaintiff's state-law claims, those based on common law as well as on statute, were to be denied because baseball was not "a matter which admits of diversity of treatment," 316 F.Supp., at 280; that the involuntary servitude claim failed because of the absence of "the essential element of this cause of action, a showing of compulsory service," and that judgment was to be entered for the defendants. On appeal, the Second Circuit felt "compelled to affirm." It regarded the issue of state law as one of first impression, but concluded that the Commerce Clause precluded its application.

We granted *certiorari* in order to look once again at this troublesome and unusual situation.

Federal Baseball Club v. National League, 259 U.S. 200, 42 S.Ct. 465, 66 L.Ed. 898 (1922), was a suit for treble damages instituted by a member of the Federal League (Baltimore) against the National and American Leagues and others. The plaintiff obtained a verdict in the trial court, but the court of appeals reversed. The main brief filed by the plaintiff with this court discloses that it was strenuously argued, among other things, that the business in which the defendants were engaged was interstate commerce; that the interstate relationship among the several clubs, located as they were in different states, was predominant; that organized baseball represented an investment of colossal wealth; that it was an engagement in moneymaking; that gate receipts were divided by agreement between the home club and the visiting club; and that the business of baseball was to be distinguished from the mere playing of the game as a sport for physical exercise and diversion.

Mr. Justice Holmes, in speaking succinctly for a unanimous court, said:

> The business is giving exhibitions of baseball, which are purely state affairs. . . . But the fact that in order to give the exhibitions the Leagues must induce free persons to cross state lines and must arrange and pay for their doing so is not enough to change the character of the business. . . . (T)he transport is a mere incident, not the essential thing. That to which it is incident, the exhibition, although made for money would not be called trade or commerce in the commonly accepted use of those words. As it

is put by the defendant, personal effort, not related to production, is not a subject of commerce. That which in its consummation is not commerce does not become commerce among the states because the transportation that we have mentioned takes place. To repeat the illustrations given by the Court below, a firm of lawyers sending out a member to argue a case, or the Chautauqua lecture bureau sending out lecturers, does not engage in such commerce because the lawyer or lecturer goes to another state.

> If we are right the plaintiff's business is to be described in the same way and the restrictions by contract that prevented the plaintiff from getting players to break their bargains and the other conduct charged against the defendants were not an interference with commerce among the States.

In the years that followed, baseball continued to be subject to intermittent antitrust attack. The courts, however, rejected these challenges on the authority of *Federal Baseball*. For the most part, however, the Holmes opinion was generally and necessarily accepted as controlling authority. And in the 1952 Report of the Subcommittee on Study of Monopoly Power of the House Committee on the Judiciary, H.R.Rep.No.2002, 82d Cong., 2d Sess., 229, it was said, in conclusion:

> On the other hand the overwhelming preponderance of the evidence established baseball's need for some sort of reserve clause. Baseball's history shows that chaotic conditions prevailed when there was no reserve clause. Experience points to no feasible substitute to protect the integrity of the game or to guarantee a comparatively even competitive struggle. The evidence adduced at the hearings would clearly not justify the enactment of legislation flatly condemning the reserve clause.

The court granted *certiorari* in three other cases and affirmed the judgments of the respective courts of appeals in those three cases. *Federal Baseball* was cited as holding "that the business of providing public baseball games for profit between clubs of professional baseball players was not within the scope of the federal antitrust laws," and "Congress has had the ruling under consideration but has not seen fit to bring such business under these laws by legislation having prospective effect. The business has thus been left for thirty years to develop, on the understanding that it was not subject to existing antitrust legislation. The present cases ask us to overrule the prior decision and, with retrospective effect, hold the legislation applicable. We think that if there are evils in this field which now warrant application to it of the antitrust laws it should be by legislation. Without re-examination of the underlying issues, the judgments below are affirmed on the authority of *Federal Baseball Club of Baltimore v. National League of Professional Baseball Clubs, supra,* so far as that decision determines that Congress had no intention of including the business of baseball within the scope of the federal antitrust laws." This quotation reveals four reasons for the court's affirmance of those cases: (a) Congressional awareness for three decades of the court's ruling in *Federal Baseball,* coupled with congressional inaction; (b) the fact that baseball was left alone to develop for that period upon the understanding that the reserve system was not subject to existing federal antitrust laws; (c) a reluctance to overrule *Federal Baseball* with consequent retroactive effect; and (d) a professed desire that any needed remedy be provided by legislation rather than by court decree. The emphasis in *Toolson* was on the determination, attributed even to *Federal Baseball,* that Congress had no intention to include baseball within the reach of the federal antitrust laws.

United States v. International Boxing Club, 348 U.S. 236, 75 S.Ct. 259, 99 L.Ed. 290 (1955), was a civil antitrust action against defendants engaged in the business of promoting professional championship boxing contests. Here again the district court had dismissed the complaint in reliance on *Federal Baseball* and *Toolson.* The Chief Justice observed that "if it were not for *Federal Baseball* and *Toolson,* we think that it would be too clear for dispute that the government's allegations bring the defendants within the scope of the Act." He pointed out that the defendants relied on the two baseball cases but also would have been content with a more restrictive interpretation of them than the Shubert defendants, for the boxing defendants argued that the cases immunized only businesses that involve exhibitions of an athletic nature. The Court accepted neither argument. It again noted that "Toolson neither overruled Federal Baseball nor necessarily reaffirmed all that was said in Federal Baseball." The Court noted the presence then in Congress of various bills forbidding the application of the antitrust laws to "organized

professional sports enterprises"; the holding of extensive hearings on some of these; subcommittee opposition; a postponement recommendation as to baseball; and the fact that "Congress thus left intact the then-existing coverage of the antitrust laws."

The parade marched on. *Radovich v. National Football League,* 352 U.S. 445, 77 S.Ct. 390, 1 L.Ed.2d 456 (1957), was a civil Clayton Act case testing the application of the antitrust laws to professional football. The district court dismissed. The Ninth Circuit affirmed in part on the basis of *Federal Baseball* and *Toolson.* The court did not hesitate to "confess that the strength of the pull" of the baseball cases and of International Boxing "is about equal," but then observed that "(f)ootball is a team sport" and boxing an individual one. This court reversed with an opinion by Mr. Justice Clark. He said that the court made its ruling in *Toolson* "because it was concluded that more harm would be done in overruling Federal Baseball than in upholding a ruling which at best was of dubious validity." He noted that Congress had not acted.

Finally, in *Haywood v. National Basketball Assn.,* 401 U.S. 1204, 91 S.Ct. 672, 28 L.Ed.2d 206 (1971), Mr. Justice Douglas, in his capacity as Circuit Justice, reinstated a district court's injunction *pendente lite* in favor of a professional basketball player and said, "Basketball . . . does not enjoy exemption from the antitrust laws."

Legislative proposals have been numerous and persistent. Since *Toolson* more than 50 bills have been introduced in Congress relative to the applicability or nonapplicability of the antitrust laws to baseball. A few of these passed one house or the other. Those that did would have expanded, not restricted, the reserve system's exemption to other professional league sports.

This emphasis and this concern are still with us. We continue to be loath, 50 years after *Federal Baseball* and almost two decades after *Toolson,* to overturn those cases judicially when Congress, by its positive inaction, has allowed those decisions to stand for so long and, far beyond mere inference and implication, has clearly evinced a desire not to disapprove them legislatively. Accordingly, we adhere once again to *Federal Baseball* and *Toolson* and to their application to professional baseball. We adhere also to *International Boxing* and *Radovich* and to their respective applications to professional boxing and professional football. If there is any inconsistency or illogic in all this, it is an inconsistency and illogic of long standing that is to be remedied by the Congress and not by this court. If we were to act otherwise, we would be withdrawing from the conclusion as to congressional intent made in *Toolson* and from the concerns as to retrospectivity therein expressed. Under these circumstances, there is merit in consistency even though some might claim that beneath that consistency is a layer of inconsistency.

The petitioner's argument as to the application of state antitrust laws deserves a word. Judge Cooper rejected the state law claims because state antitrust regulation would conflict with federal policy and because national "uniformity (is required) in any regulation of baseball and its reserved system." The court of appeals, in affirming, stated, "(A)s the burden on interstate commerce outweighs the states' interests in regulating baseball's reserve system, the Commerce Clause precludes the application here of state antitrust law." As applied to organized baseball, and in the light of this court's observations and holding in *Federal Baseball*, in *Toolson*, in *Shubert*, in *International Boxing*, and in *Radovich*, and despite baseball's allegedly inconsistent position taken

in the past with respect to the application of state law, these statements adequately dispose of the state law claims.

The conclusion we have reached makes it unnecessary for us to consider the respondents' additional argument that the reserve system is a mandatory subject of collective bargaining and that federal labor policy therefore exempts the reserve system from the operation of federal antitrust laws. We repeat for this case what was said in *Toolson*: "Without re-examination of the underlying issues, the (judgment) below (is) affirmed on the authority of *Federal Baseball Club of Baltimore v. National League of Professional Baseball Clubs, supra*, so far as that decision determines that Congress had no intention of including the business of baseball within the scope of the federal antitrust laws." And what the court said in *Federal Baseball* in 1922 and what it said in *Toolson* in 1953, we say again here in 1972: the remedy, if any is indicated, is for congressional, and not judicial, action. The judgment of the court of appeals is affirmed.

 For an extended version of the case and review questions to test your understanding of the material, please go to www.HumanKinetics.com/CaseStudiesInSportLaw.

Law v. NCAA

5 F.Supp.2d 921 (D. Kan. 1998)

This case is a consolidation of three class action price-fixing cases that came before the Court on Motions for Partial Summary Judgment. In all three cases, the National Collegiate Athletic Association [NCAA] seeks partial summary judgment with respect to groups of coaches for whom plaintiffs do not have and will not have evidence of impact because their final expert report contains no analysis or individualized finding of damage. It also seeks summary judgment as to (1) claims of any individual class member who failed to return a timely and accurate Restricted Earnings Coach Information Sheet; (2) claims of individuals who are not class members; (3) damages incurred

after May 25, 1995, when the NCAA rescinded the salary cap that violated § 1 of the Sherman Act, 15 U.S.C. § 1; (4) damages that represent a Consumer Price Index adjustment to plaintiffs' base damage calculation; and (5) plaintiffs' claim for injunctive relief.

On January 23, 1998, the Tenth Circuit affirmed this court's order, which permanently enjoined the NCAA from reenacting compensation limits such as those contained in the restricted earnings coach rule [the Rule] because, as a matter of law, the Rule violated § 1 of the Sherman Act, 15 U.S.C. § 1. In determining that the Rule constituted an unreasonable restraint of trade under § 1, the

Tenth Circuit inquired whether the challenged restraint had a substantially adverse effect on competition, and whether the procompetitive virtues of the alleged wrongful conduct justified the otherwise anticompetitive effects. The court of appeals answered the first question in the affirmative, holding that anticompetitive effect was established as a matter of law on the undisputed record. It noted that under a quick-look rule of reason analysis, anticompetitive effect is established, even without a determination of the relevant market, where the plaintiff shows that a horizontal agreement to fix prices exists, that the agreement is effective, and that the price set by such an agreement is more favorable to the defendant than otherwise would have resulted from the operation of market forces. It reasoned that the undisputed facts in this case supported a finding of anticompetitive effect. The NCAA adopted the Rule to reduce the high cost of part-time coaches' salaries, over $60,000 annually in some cases, by limiting compensation to entry-level coaches to $16,000 per year. The NCAA does not dispute that the cost-reduction has effectively reduced restricted-earnings coaches' salaries. Because the Rule was successful in artificially lowering the price of coaching services, no further evidence or analysis is required to find market power to set prices.

Having concluded that the Rule had a substantially adverse effect on competition, the Tenth Circuit inquired whether the procompetitive benefits of the restriction—retaining entry level jobs, reducing costs, and maintaining competitive equity—justified the anticompetitive effects. The court of appeals resolved this question in the negative, noting that the NCAA had failed to present evidence that the Rule would be effective over time in creating entry-level positions, reducing deficits, enhancing competition, leveling an uneven playing field, or reducing coaching inequities. It also noted that cost-cutting by itself is not a valid procompetitive justification. As a result, the Tenth Circuit concluded that the NCAA had not demonstrated a genuine issue of fact whether it had violated § 1 of the Sherman Act.

Proof that the NCAA committed an antitrust violation does not afford plaintiffs an automatic right to damages, however, under § 4 of the Clayton Act, 15 U.S.C. § 15; such proof establishes only

that injury may result and does not mean that any plaintiff has been actually injured within the meaning of § 4. In order to recover under § 4 of the Clayton Act, plaintiffs must establish that their injuries were caused by reason of defendant's anticompetitive activity. 15 U.S.C. § 15. The "by reason of" language is the starting point for analyzing causation and damages, the two aspects of plaintiffs' case that are at issue here.

The parties have sharply divergent views on two issues that pervade the motions for partial summary judgment: (1) whether the fact of antitrust injury has already been established as a matter of law, so that plaintiffs are relieved of any burden of further proof on that issue, or whether the matter remains to be determined at trial; and (2) whether plaintiffs are entitled to prove the fact of antitrust injury on a class-wide basis or whether they must do so on a coach-by-coach basis for more than 3,000 class members. Plaintiffs maintain that the fact of damage was conclusively resolved in the order that granted plaintiffs' motion for summary judgment on August 2, 1995, and the Tenth Circuit affirmance on January 23, 1998. Defendant disagrees, contending that the Tenth Circuit said nothing about whether any particular plaintiff sustained injury and did not mention § 4 of the Clayton Act. The NCAA further notes that a finding of anticompetitive effect under § 1 of the Sherman Act does not mean that every class member sustained antitrust injury and that in fact plaintiffs' expert, Dr. Robert D. Tollison, found that many coaches (some 60% of the class members) sustained no damages whatsoever.

The court agrees with the NCAA that the fact of antitrust injury remains an issue for trial. It disagrees with the NCAA's ancillary arguments that Dr. Tollison seeks to prove antitrust injury by estimating the amount of damages that plaintiffs incurred; that aside from Dr. Tollison's statistical analysis, plaintiffs have no evidence of antitrust injury; and that fact of injury cannot be established on a class-wide basis.

Causation evidence under § 4 must establish that the injuries that plaintiffs claim are attributable to the antitrust conspiracy, and not to other factors. The purpose of the antitrust injury requirement is to ensure that the harm claimed by plaintiff corresponds to the rationale for finding a violation of the antitrust laws in the first place. *Atlantic Richfield Co. v. USA Petroleum Co.*, 495 U.S. 328, 342, 110 S.Ct. 1884, 109 L.Ed.2d 333 (1990). The Supreme Court's observation in *Atlantic Richfield* underscores the salience of the fact of injury inquiry, as follows:

> Conduct in violation of the antitrust laws may have three effects, often interwoven: In some respects the conduct may reduce competition, in other respects it may increase competition, and in still other respects effects may be neutral as to competition. The antitrust injury requirement ensures that a plaintiff can recover only if the loss stems from a competition-reducing aspect or effect of the defendant's behavior.

In this regard, the Supreme Court reaffirmed *Brunswick Corp. v. Pueblo Bowl-O-Mat, Inc.*, 429 U.S. 477, 489, 97 S.Ct. 690, 50 L.Ed.2d 701 (1977), which held that plaintiffs seeking damages under § 4 of the Clayton Act must prove antitrust injury, which is to say injury of the type the antitrust laws were intended to prevent and that flows from that which makes defendants' acts unlawful.

In order to establish causation under § 4, plaintiffs must demonstrate that the anticompetitive activity was a material cause of their injury. They need not rule out all possible alternative sources of injury. If there is sufficient evidence in the record to support an inference of causation between the antitrust violation and the injury suffered, the ultimate conclusion as to what that evidence proves is for the jury. Once plaintiffs establish that defendant's anticompetitive activity was a material cause of some of their injury, however, the remainder of the damage inquiry is judged under the amount of damage standard.

While the evidence that links the alleged antitrust violation to plaintiffs' injuries must be more precise than the evidence establishing the amount of injury that they have suffered, plaintiffs' burden in proving fact of injury may be discharged by reasonable inferences from circumstantial evidence. Any evidence that is logically probative of a loss attributable to the violation will advance plaintiffs' case.

As a practical matter, in a class action context, proof of an effective conspiracy to fix prices will include facts that tend to establish—perhaps circumstantially—that each class member was injured. *Presidio Golf Club v. National Linen Supply Corp.*, 1976 WL 1359, *5 (N.D.Cal.1976). The district court in Presidio Golf noted that an inference of

antitrust injury is justified in certain circumstances, as follows:

> In the class action context the inference is predicated on the establishment of certain facts: (1) an antitrust violation, typically a conspiracy to fix prices or allocate markets; (2) an ability on the part of defendant-conspirators to effectuate the conspiracy; (3) generalized price increases or damages in the industry involved; and (4) purchase or, as here, rental by plaintiffs during the period of anticompetitive activity.

In such circumstances, unless it is clear that no plaintiff was injured, the fact that defendant may be able to defeat a showing of causation as to a few individual class members would not defeat the inference of antitrust injury; the exact amount of injury to each class member should be treated as an issue at the damage phase of the trial.

An antitrust plaintiff who is injured in his person or property by anticompetitive activity is entitled to recover damages. In economic terms, the amount of damages is the difference between what plaintiff could have made in a hypothetical free economic market and what plaintiff actually made in spite of defendant's anticompetitive activities.

Once an antitrust violation has been established, however, the burden of proving damages is to some extent lightened. Our willingness to accept a degree of uncertainty in fixing the amount of damages rests in part on the difficulty of ascertaining business damages, in that the vagaries of the marketplace usually deny us sure knowledge of what plaintiff's situation would have been in the absence of the defendant's antitrust violation. Our willingness also rests on the principle that it does not come with very good grace for the wrongdoer to insist on specific and certain proof of the injury that it has itself inflicted.

In *Zenith Radio Corp. v. Hazeltine Research, Inc.*, 395 U.S. 100, the Supreme Court accepted the proposition that damages could be awarded under relaxed rules, on the basis of plaintiff's damage estimate. In doing so, it repeated that in the absence of more precise proof, the fact finder may conclude as a matter of just and reasonable inference from the proof of defendants' wrongful acts and their tendency to injure plaintiffs' business, and from the evidence of the decline in prices, profits and values, not shown to be attributable to other causes, that defendants' wrongful acts had caused damage to the plaintiffs. In *Bigelow v. RKO Radio Pictures, Inc.*, the Supreme Court explained that any other rule would enable the wrongdoer to profit by his wrongdoing at the expense of his victim and that failure to apply it would mean that the more grievous the wrong done, the less likelihood there would be of a recovery. 327 U.S. at 264-65, 66 S.Ct. 574.

Therefore, to establish the amount of injury, plaintiffs need not establish their damages with mathematical precision. Plaintiffs need only provide such evidence that the jury is not left to speculation or guesswork in determining the amount of damages to award. Once the existence of injury is established by direct evidence or inference from the character of a sustained conspiracy, the proof necessary to set the amount of damages need not be exact.

It is hereby ordered that with one exception all defendant's motions for summary judgment be overruled.

 For an extended version of the case and review questions to test your understanding of the material, please go to www.HumanKinetics.com/CaseStudiesInSportLaw.

Los Angeles Memorial Coliseum Commission v. National Football League

726 F.2d 1381 (9th Cir. 1984)

These appeals involve the hotly contested move by the Oakland Raiders, Ltd. professional football team from Oakland, California, to Los Angeles, California. We review only the liability portion of the bifurcated trial; the damage phase was concluded in May 1983 and is on a separate appeal. After a thorough review of the record and the law, we affirm.

In 1978, the owner of the Los Angeles Rams, the late Carroll Rosenbloom, decided to locate his team in a new stadium, the "Big A," in Anaheim, California. Officials of the Coliseum then began the search for a new National Football League occupant.

The L.A. Coliseum ran into a major obstacle in its attempts to convince a team to move. That obstacle was Rule 4.3 of Article IV of the NFL Constitution. In 1978, Rule 4.3 required unanimous approval of all the 28 teams of the League whenever a team (or in the parlance of the League, a "franchise") seeks to relocate in the home territory of another team. Home territory is defined in Rule 4.1 as "the city in which [a] club is located and for which it holds a franchise and plays its home games, and includes the surrounding territory to the extent of 75 miles in every direction from the exterior corporate limits of such city. . . ." In this case, the L.A. Coliseum was still in the home territory of the Rams.

The Coliseum viewed Rule 4.3 as an unlawful restraint of trade in violation of section 1 of the Sherman Act, 15 U.S.C. § 1, and brought this action in September of 1978. The district court concluded, however, that no present justiciable controversy existed because no NFL team had committed to moving to Los Angeles. The NFL nevertheless saw the Coliseum's suit as a sufficient threat to warrant amending Rule 4.3. In late 1978, the Executive Committee of the NFL, which is composed of a voting member of each of the 28 teams, met and changed the rule to require only three-quarters approval by the members of the League for a move into another team's home territory.

Soon thereafter, Al Davis, managing general partner of the Oakland Raiders franchise, and the L.A. Coliseum officials, began to discuss the possibility of relocating the Raiders to Los Angeles in 1979. In January 1980, the L.A. Coliseum believed an agreement with Davis was imminent and reactivated its lawsuit against the NFL, seeking a preliminary injunction to enjoin the League from preventing the Raiders' move. The district court granted the injunction, but this court reversed, finding that an adequate probability of irreparable injury had not been shown.

On March 1, 1980, Al Davis and the Coliseum signed a "memorandum of agreement" outlining the terms of the Raiders' relocation in Los Angeles. In response, the League brought a contract action in state court, obtaining an injunction preventing the move. In the meantime, the City of Oakland brought its much-publicized eminent domain action against the Raiders in its effort to keep the team in its original home. The NFL contract action was stayed pending the outcome of this litigation, but the eminent domain action is still being prosecuted in the California courts.

After the NFL teams voted on March 10, 1980, 22-0 against the move, the Los Angeles Memorial Coliseum Commission renewed its action against the NFL and each member club. The Oakland-Alameda County Coliseum, Inc., was permitted to intervene. The Oakland Raiders cross-claimed against the NFL and is currently aligned as a party plaintiff. The action was first tried in 1981 but resulted in a hung jury and mistrial, and a second trial was conducted. The court was asked to determine if the NFL was a "single business entity" and as such incapable of combining or conspiring in restraint of trade. Referring to the reasoning in its opinion written for the first trial, the court concluded the League was not a "single entity."

On May 7, 1982, the jury returned a verdict in favor of the Los Angeles Memorial Coliseum Commission and the Oakland Raiders on the antitrust claim and for the Raiders on their claim of breach of the implied promise of good faith and fair dealing. The court then continued the case to September 20, 1982, to begin the damages trial. The damages trial was completed in May 1983 with the jury returning a verdict awarding the Raiders $11.55 million and the Los Angeles Coliseum $4.86 million. These awards were trebled by the district court pursuant to 15 U.S.C. § 15. The NFL and the other defendants have appealed.

The jury found that Rule 4.3 violates § 1 of the Sherman Act, 15 U.S.C. § 1. Section 1 literally prohibits every agreement, conspiracy, or other concerted activity in restraint of trade. Since Congress could not have intended that courts invalidate "every" such agreement, most restraints are analyzed under the so-called "rule of reason." The rule of reason requires the fact finder to decide whether under all the circumstances of the case

the agreement imposes an unreasonable restraint on competition. *Standard Oil*, however, reconciled the earlier categorical prohibition with its own rule of reason by declaring that some restraints remain inherently unreasonable. *Standard Oil of New Jersey v. United States*, 221 U.S. 1, 64-65(1911), 31 S.Ct. 502, 517 (1911).

The NFL contends the league structure is in essence a single entity, akin to a partnership or joint venture, precluding application of Sherman Act § 1, which prevents only contracts, combinations, or conspiracies in restraint of trade. The Los Angeles Coliseum and Raiders reject this position and assert the League is composed of 28 separate legal entities that act independently.

It is true, as the NFL contends, that the nature of an entity and its ability to combine or conspire in violation of § 1 is a fact question. It would be reversible error, then, to take the issue from the jury if reasonable minds could differ as to its resolution. Here, however, the material facts are undisputed. How the NFL is organized and the nature and extent of cooperation among the member clubs is a matter of record; the NFL Constitution and Bylaws contain the agreement. Based on the undisputed facts and the law on this subject, the district court correctly decided this issue.

The district court cited three reasons for rejecting the NFL's theory. Initially, the court recognized the logical extension of this argument was to make the League incapable of violating Sherman Act § 1 in every other subject restriction—yet courts have held the League violated § 1 in other areas. Second, other organizations have been found to violate § 1 though their product was "just as unitary . . . and requires the same kind of cooperation from the organization's members." Finally, the district court considered the argument to be based on the false premise that the individual NFL "clubs are not separate business entities whose products have an independent value." We agree with this reasoning.

NFL rules have been found to violate § 1 in other contexts. Most recently, the Second Circuit analyzed the NFL's rule preventing its member-owners from having ownership interests in other professional sports clubs. It recognized the cooperation necessary among league members, even characterizing the NFL as a joint venture, but nonetheless applied rule of reason analysis and found the cross-ownership rule violated § 1. As noted by the Second Circuit in *Soccer League* (*North American Soccer League v. National Football League*, 459 U.S. 1074, 74 L.Ed. 2d 639, 641, 103 S.Ct. 449 [1982]), a finding of single entity status would immunize the NFL from § 1 scrutiny: "To tolerate such a loophole would permit league members to escape antitrust responsibility for any restraint entered into by them that would benefit their league or enhance their ability to compete even though the benefit would be outweighed by its anticompetitive effects. Moreover, the restraint might be one adopted more for the protection of individual league members from competition than to help the league." *670 F.2d at 1257.*

Cases applying the single-entity or joint-venture theory in other business areas also contradict the NFL's argument. The facts make it clear the NFL does not fit within this exception. While the NFL clubs have certain common purposes, they do not operate as a single entity. NFL policies are not set by one individual or parent corporation, but by the separate teams acting jointly. It is true the NFL clubs must cooperate to a large extent in their endeavor in producing a "product"—the NFL season culminating in the Super Bowl. The necessity that otherwise independent businesses cooperate has not, however, sufficed to preclude scrutiny under § 1 of the Sherman Act.

The League itself is only in very limited respects an identity separate from the individual teams. It is an unincorporated, not-for-profit, "association." It has a New York office run by the Commissioner, Pete Rozelle, who makes day-to-day decisions regarding League operations. Its primary functions are in the areas of scheduling, resolving disputes among players and franchises, supervising officials, and discipline and public relations. The decision involved here on territorial divisions is made by the NFL Executive Committee, which is composed of a representative of each club. Even though the individual clubs often act for the common good of the NFL, we must not lose sight of the purpose of the NFL as stated in Article I of its constitution, which is to "promote and foster the primary business of League members." Although the business interests of League members will often coincide with those of the

NFL as an entity in itself, that commonality of interest exists in every cartel.

Our inquiry discloses an association of teams sufficiently independent and competitive with one another to warrant rule of reason scrutiny under § 1 of the Sherman Act. The NFL clubs are, in the words of the district court, "separate business entities whose products have an independent value." The member clubs are all independently owned. Most are corporations, some are partnerships, and apparently a few are sole proprietorships. Although a large portion of League revenue, approximately 90%, is divided equally among the teams, profits and losses are not shared, a feature common to partnerships or other "single entities." In fact, profits vary widely despite the sharing of revenue. The disparity in profits can be attributed to independent management policies regarding coaches, players, management personnel, ticket prices, concessions, luxury box seats, as well as franchise location, all of which contribute to fan support and other income sources.

In addition to being independent business entities, the NFL clubs do compete with one another off the field as well as on to acquire players, coaches, and management personnel. In certain areas of the country where two teams operate in close proximity, there is also competition for fan support, local television and local radio revenues, and media space. These attributes operate to make each team an entity in large part distinct from the NFL. It is true that cooperation is necessary to produce a football game. However, as the district court concluded, this does not mean, "that each club can produce football games only as an NFL member." This is especially evident in light of the emergence of the United States Football League.

For the foregoing reasons, we affirm the district court's rejection of the NFL's single entity defense. Of course, the singular nature of the NFL will need to be accounted for in discussing the reasonableness of the restriction on team movement, but it is not enough to preclude § 1 scrutiny. The NFL's related argument that Rule 4.3 is valid as a restraint ancillary to a joint-venture agreement will be discussed in the rule of reason analysis that follows. Contrary to the NFL's apparent belief, the ancillary restraint doctrine is not independent of the rule of reason.

As elaborated on by this circuit, "Rule of reason analysis calls for a 'thorough investigation of the industry at issue and a balancing of the arrangement's positive and negative effects on competition.'" This balancing process is not applied, however, until after the plaintiff has shown the challenged conduct restrains competition. To establish a cause of action, plaintiff must prove these elements: "(1) An agreement among two or more persons or distinct business entities; (2) Which is intended to harm or unreasonably restrain competition; (3) And which actually causes injury to competition."

Our rejection of the NFL's single entity defense implicitly recognized the existence of the first element—the 28 member clubs have entered an agreement in the form of the NFL Constitution and Bylaws. As will be developed in more detail, we have no doubt the plaintiffs also met their burden of proving the existence of the second element. Rule 4.3 is on its face an agreement to control, if not prevent, competition among the NFL teams through territorial divisions. The third element is more troublesome. It is in this context that we discuss the NFL's ancillary restraint argument. Also, a showing of injury to competition requires "[p]roof that the defendant's activities had an impact upon competition in a relevant market," proof that "is an absolutely essential element of a rule of reason case."

Other courts have applied rule of reason analysis to determine the legality of concerted action undertaken by the NFL and for the most part have found such action illegal. . . . The instant case is the first of this type in this circuit, however, and the first in which a member club has questioned the legality of NFL rules.

In a quite general sense, the case presents the competing considerations of whether a group of businessmen can enforce an agreement with one of their co-contractors to the detriment of that co-contractor's right to do business where he pleases. More specifically, this lawsuit requires us to engage in the difficult task of analyzing the negative and positive effects of a business practice in an industry that does not readily fit into the antitrust context. Section 1 of the Sherman Act was designed to prevent agreements among competitors that eliminate or reduce competition and thereby harm consumers. Yet, as we discussed

in the context of the single entity issue, the NFL teams are not true competitors, nor can they be.

The NFL's structure has both horizontal and vertical attributes. On the one hand, it can be viewed simply as an organization of 28 competitors, an example of a simple horizontal arrangement. On the other, and to the extent the NFL can be considered an entity separate from the team owners, a vertical relationship is disclosed. In this sense the owners are distributors of the NFL product, each with its own territorial division. In this context it is clear that the owners have a legitimate interest in protecting the integrity of the League itself. Collective action in areas such as League divisions, scheduling, and rules must be allowed, as should other activity that aids in producing the most marketable product attainable. Nevertheless, legitimate collective action should not be construed to allow the owners to extract excess profits. In such a situation the owners would be acting as a classic cartel. Agreements among competitors (i.e., cartels) to fix prices or divide market territories are presumed illegal under § 1 because they give competitors the ability to charge unreasonable and arbitrary prices instead of setting prices by virtue of free market forces.

On its face, Rule 4.3 divides markets among the 28 teams, a practice presumed illegal, but, as we have noted, the unique structure of the NFL precludes application of the *per se* rule. Instead, we must examine Rule 4.3 to determine whether it reasonably serves the legitimate collective concerns of the owners or instead permits them to reap excess profits at the expense of the consuming public.

The relevant market provides the basis on which to balance competitive harms and benefits of the restraint at issue. Such evidence is essential in a § 1 case.

In the antitrust context, the relevant market has two components: the product market and the geographic market. Product market definition involves the process of describing those groups of producers that, because of the similarity of their products, have the ability—actual or potential—to take significant amounts of business away from each other. A market definition must look at all relevant sources of supply, either actual rivals or eager potential entrants to the market. Two related tests are used in arriving at the product market: first, reasonable interchangeability for the same or similar uses; and second, cross-elasticity of demand, an economic term describing the responsiveness of sales of one product to price changes in another. Similar considerations determine the relevant geographic market, which describes the "economically significant" area of effective competition in which the relevant products are traded.

The claims of the Raiders and the L.A. Coliseum, respectively, present somewhat different market considerations. The Raiders attempted to prove the relevant market consists of NFL football (the product market) in the Southern California area (the geographic market). The NFL argues it competes with all forms of entertainment within the United States, not just Southern California. The L.A. Coliseum claims the relevant market is stadia offering their facilities to NFL teams (the product market) in the United States (the geographic market). The NFL agrees with this geographic market, but argues the product market involves cities competing for all forms of stadium entertainment, including NFL football teams.

That NFL football has limited substitutes from a consumer standpoint is seen from evidence that the Oakland Coliseum sold out for 10 consecutive years despite having some of the highest ticket prices in the League. A similar conclusion can be drawn from the extraordinary number of television viewers—over 100 million people—that watched the 1982 Super Bowl, the ultimate NFL product. NFL football's importance to the television networks is evidenced by the approximately $2 billion they agreed to pay the League for the right to televise the games from 1982-1986. This contract reflects the networks' anticipation that the high number of television viewers who had watched NFL football in the past would continue to do so in the future.

To some extent, the NFL itself narrowly defined the relevant market by emphasizing that NFL football is a unique product that can be produced only through the joint efforts of the 28 teams. Don Shula, coach of the Miami Dolphins, underscored this point when he stated that NFL football has a different set of fans than college football. The evidence from which the jury could have found a narrow pro football product market was balanced, however, with other evidence that tended to show the NFL competes in the first instance with other professional sports, especially those with seasons

that overlap with the NFL's. On a broader level, witnesses such as Pete Rozelle and Georgia Frontierre (owner of the L.A. Rams) testified that NFL football competes with other television offerings for network business, as well as other local entertainment for attendance at the games.

In terms of the relevant geographic market, witnesses testified, in particular Al Davis, that NFL teams compete with one another off the field for fan support in those areas where teams operate in close proximity such as New York City-New Jersey, Washington, D.C.-Baltimore, and formerly San Francisco-Oakland. Davis, of course, had firsthand knowledge of this when his team was located in Oakland. Also, the San Francisco Forty-Niners and the New York Giants were paid $18 million because of the potential for harm from competing with the Oakland Raiders and the New York Jets, respectively, once those teams joined the NFL as a result of the merger with the American Football League. Al Davis also testified at length regarding the potential for competition for fan support between the Raiders and the Los Angeles Rams once his team relocated in Los Angeles.

Testimony also adequately described the parameters of the stadia market. On one level, stadia do compete with one another for the tenancy of NFL teams. Such competition is shown by the Rams' move to Anaheim. Carroll Rosenbloom was offered what he considered to be a more lucrative situation at the Big A Stadium, so he left the L.A. Coliseum. In turn, the L.A. Coliseum sought to lure existing NFL teams to Los Angeles. Competition between the L.A. Coliseum and the Oakland Coliseum for the tenancy of the Raiders resulted.

It is true, as the NFL argues, that competition among stadia for the tenancy of professional football teams is presently limited. It is limited, however, because of the operation of Rule 4.3. Prior to this lawsuit, most teams were allowed to relocate only within their home territory. That is why Carroll Rosenbloom could move his team to Anaheim. This is not to say the potential for competition did not previously exist. There was evidence to the effect that the NFL in the past remained expressly noncommitted on the question of team movement. This was done to give owners a bargaining edge when they were renegotiating leases with their respective stadia. The owner could threaten a move if the lease terms were not made more favorable.

The NFL claims that it is places, not particular stadia, that compete for NFL teams. This is true to a point because the NFL grants franchises to locales (generally a city and a 75-mile radius extending from its boundary). It is the individual stadia, however, that are most directly impacted by the restrictions on team movement. A stadium is a distinct economic entity and a territory is not.

It is also undoubtedly true, as the NFL contends, that stadia attempt to contract with a variety of forms of entertainment for exhibition in their facilities. In the case of the L.A. Coliseum, this includes college football, concerts, motorcycle races, and the like. An NFL football team, however, is an especially desirable tenant. The L.A. Coliseum, for example, had received the highest rent from the Rams when they played there. We find that this evidence taken as a whole provided the jury with an adequate basis on which to judge the reasonableness of Rule 4.3 both as it affected competition among NFL teams and among stadia.

We conclude with one additional observation. In the context of this case in particular, we believe that market evidence, while important, should not become an end in itself. Here the exceptional nature of the industry makes precise market definition especially difficult. To a large extent the market is determined by how one defines the entity: Is the NFL a single entity or partnership that creates a product that competes with other entertainment products for the consumer (e.g., television and fans) dollar? Or is it 28 individual entities that compete with one another both on and off the field for the support of the consumers of the more narrow football product? Of course, the NFL has attributes of both examples and a variety of evidence was presented on both views. In fact, because of the exceptional structure of the League, it was not necessary for the jury to accept absolutely either the NFL's or the plaintiff's market definitions. Instead, the critical question is whether the jury could have determined that Rule 4.3 reasonably served the NFL's interest in producing and promoting its product (i.e., competing in the entertainment market) or whether Rule 4.3 harmed competition among the 28 teams to

such an extent that any benefits to the League as a whole were outweighed. As we find below, there was ample evidence for the jury to reach the latter conclusion.

The NFL has awarded franchises exclusive territories since the 1930s. In the early days of professional football, numerous franchises failed and many changed location in the hope of achieving economic success. League members saw exclusive territories as a means to aid stability, ensuring the owner who was attempting to establish an NFL team in a particular city that another would not move into the same area, potentially ruining them both. Rule 4.3 is the result of that concern. Prior to its amendment in 1978, it required unanimous League approval for a move into another team's home territory. That, of course, gave each owner an exclusive territory and he could vote against a move into his territory solely because he was afraid the competition might reduce his revenue. Notably, however, the League constitution required only three-quarters approval for all other moves. The 1978 amendment removed the double-standard, and currently three-quarters approval is required for all moves.

That the purpose of Rule 4.3 was to restrain competition among the 28 teams may seem obvious and it is not surprising the NFL admitted as much at trial. It instead argues that Rule 4.3 serves a variety of legitimate League needs, including ensuring franchise stability. We must keep in mind, however, that the Supreme Court has long rejected the notion that "ruinous competition" can be a defense to a restraint of trade. Conversely, anticompetitive purpose alone is not enough to condemn Rule 4.3. The rule must actually harm competition, and that harm must be evaluated in light of the procompetitive benefits the rule might foster.

The competitive harms of Rule 4.3 are plain. Exclusive territories insulate each team from competition within the NFL market, in essence allowing them to set monopoly prices to the detriment of the consuming public. The rule also effectively foreclosed free competition among stadia such as the Los Angeles Coliseum that wish to secure NFL tenants. The harm from Rule 4.3 is especially acute in this case because it prevents a move by a team into another existing team's market. If the transfer is upheld, direct competition between the

Rams and Raiders would presumably ensue to the benefit of all who consume the NFL product in the Los Angeles area.

The NFL argues, however, that territorial allocations are inherent in an agreement among joint venturers to produce a product. This inherent nature, the NFL asserts, flows from the need to protect each joint venturer in the "legitimate fruits of the contract, or to protect him from the dangers of an unjust use of those fruits by the other party." We agree that the nature of NFL football requires some territorial restrictions in order both to encourage participation in the venture and to secure each venturer the legitimate fruits of that participation.

Rule 4.3 aids the League, the NFL claims, in determining its overall geographical scope, regional balance, and coverage of major and minor markets. Exclusive territories aid new franchises in achieving financial stability, which protects the large initial investment an owner must make to start up a football team. Stability arguably helps ensure no one team has an undue advantage on the field. Territories foster fan loyalty, which in turn promotes traditional rivalries between teams, each contributing to attendance at games and television viewing. Joint marketing decisions are surely legitimate because of the importance of television. Title 15, U.S.C. § 1291 grants the NFL an exemption from antitrust liability, if any, that might arise out of its collective negotiation of television rights with the networks. To effectuate this right, the League must be allowed to have some control over the placement of teams to ensure NFL football is popular in a diverse group of markets.

Last, there is some legitimacy to the NFL's argument that it has an interest in preventing transfers from areas before local governments, which have made a substantial investment in stadia and other facilities, can recover their expenditures. In such a situation, local confidence in the NFL is eroded, possibly resulting in a decline in interest. All these factors considered, we nevertheless are not persuaded the jury should have concluded that Rule 4.3 is a reasonable restraint of trade. The same goals can be achieved in a variety of ways that are less harmful to competition.

As noted by Justice Rehnquist, a factor in determining the reasonableness of an ancillary restraint is the "possibility of less restrictive alternatives" that could serve the same purpose. . . . Here, the district court correctly instructed the jury to take into account the existence of less restrictive alternatives when determining the reasonableness of Rule 4.3's territorial restraint. Because there was substantial evidence going to the existence of such alternatives, we find that the jury could have reasonably concluded that the NFL should have designed its "ancillary restraint" in a manner that served its needs but did not so foreclose competition.

The NFL argues that the requirement of Rule 4.3 that three-quarters of the owners approve a franchise move is reasonable because it deters unwise team transfers. While the rule does indeed protect an owner's investment in a football franchise, no standards or durational limits are incorporated into the voting requirement to make sure that concern is satisfied. Nor are factors such as fan loyalty and team rivalries necessarily considered.

The NFL claims that its marketing and other objectives are indirectly accounted for in the voting process because the team owners vote to maximize their profits. Since the owners are guided by the desire to increase profits, they will necessarily make reasonable decisions, the NFL asserts, on such issues of whether the new location can support two teams, whether marketing needs will be adversely affected, etc. Under the present Rule 4.3, however, an owner need muster only seven friendly votes to prevent three-quarters approval for the sole reason of preventing another team from entering its market, regardless of whether the market could sustain two franchises. A basic premise of the Sherman Act is that regulation of private profit is best left to the marketplace rather than private agreement. The present case is in fact a good example of how the market itself will deter unwise moves, since a team will not lightly give up an established base of support to confront another team in its home market.

The NFL's professed interest in ensuring that cities and other local governments secure a return on their investment in stadia is undercut in two ways. First, the local governments ought to be able to protect their investment through the leases they negotiate with the teams for the use of their stadia. Second, the NFL's interest on this point may not be as important as it would have us believe because the League has in the past allowed teams to threaten a transfer to another location in order to give the team leverage in lease negotiations.

Finally, the NFL made no showing that the transfer of the Raiders to Los Angeles would have any harmful effect on the League. Los Angeles is a market large enough for the successful operation of two teams, there would be no scheduling difficulties, facilities at the L.A. Coliseum are more than adequate, and no loss of future television revenue was foreseen. Also, the NFL offered no evidence that its interest in maintaining regional balance would be adversely affected by a move of a northern California team to southern California.

It is true, as the NFL claims, that the antitrust laws are primarily concerned with the promotion of interbrand competition. To the extent the NFL is a product that competes with other forms of entertainment, including other sports, its rules governing territorial division can be said to promote interbrand competition. Under this analysis, the territorial allocations most directly suppress intrabrand, that is, NFL team versus NFL team, competition. A more direct impact on intrabrand competition does not mean, however, the restraint is reasonable. The finder of fact must still balance the gain to interbrand competition against the loss of intrabrand competition. Here, the jury could have found that the rules restricting team movement do not sufficiently promote interbrand competition to justify the negative impact on intrabrand competition.

To withstand antitrust scrutiny, restrictions on team movement should be more closely tailored to serve the needs inherent in producing the NFL "product" and competing with other forms of entertainment. An express recognition and consideration of those objective factors espoused by the NFL as important, such as population, economic projections, facilities, regional balance, etc., would be well advised. Fan loyalty and location continuity could also be considered. Al Davis in fact testified that in 1978 he proposed that the League adopt a set of objective guidelines to govern team relocation rather than continue to utilize a subjective voting procedure.

The NFL is a unique business organization to which it is difficult to apply antitrust rules that were developed in the context of arrangements between actual competitors. This does not mean that the trial court and jury were incapable of meeting the task, however. The lower court correctly applied and described the law. The reasonableness of a restraint is a "paradigm fact question," and our review of the record convinces us the jury had adequate evidence to answer that question.

We believe antitrust principles are sufficiently flexible to account for the NFL's structure. To the extent the NFL finds the law inadequate, it must look to Congress for relief. The judgment finding the NFL liable to the Los Angeles Coliseum and the Raiders, and enjoining the NFL from preventing the Raiders from relocating in Los Angeles is affirmed.

 For an extended version of the case and review questions to test your understanding of the material, please go to www.HumanKinetics.com/CaseStudiesInSportLaw.

National Collegiate Athletic Association v. Board of Regents of the University of Oklahoma

468 U.S. 85 (1984)

The University of Oklahoma and the University of Georgia contend that the National Collegiate Athletic Association has unreasonably restrained trade in the televising of college football games. After an extended trial, the district court found that the NCAA had violated § 1 of the Sherman Act and granted injunctive relief. The court of appeals agreed that the statute had been violated but modified the remedy in some respects. We granted *certiorari* and now affirm.

Since its inception in 1905, the NCAA has played an important role in the regulation of amateur collegiate sports. It has adopted and promulgated playing rules, standards of amateurism, standards for academic eligibility, regulations concerning recruitment of athletes, rules governing the size of athletic squads and coaching staffs, and conducted national tournaments in some sports. With the exception of football, the NCAA has not undertaken any regulation of the televising of athletic events.

The NCAA has approximately 850 voting members. The regular members are classified into separate divisions to reflect differences in size and scope of their athletic programs. Division I includes 276 colleges with major athletic programs; in this group only 187 play intercollegiate football. Divisions II and III include approximately 500 colleges with less extensive athletic programs. Division I has been subdivided into Divisions I-A and I-AA for football.

Some years ago, five major conferences together with major football-playing independent institutions organized the College Football Association (CFA). The original purpose of the CFA was to promote the interests of major football-playing schools within the NCAA structure. The Universities of Oklahoma and Georgia, respondents in this court, are members of the CFA.

On January 11, 1951, a three-person "Television Committee," appointed during the preceding year, delivered a report to the NCAA's annual convention in Dallas. Based on their report and additional input from the National Opinion Research Center (NORC), a television committee was appointed to develop an NCAA television plan for 1951.

The committee's 1951 plan provided that only one game a week could be telecast in each area, with a total blackout on three of the 10 Saturdays during the season. A team could appear on television only twice during a season. The plan received the virtually unanimous support of the NCAA membership.

During each of the succeeding five seasons, studies were made that tended to indicate that television had an adverse effect on attendance at college football games. During those years the NCAA continued to exercise complete control over the number of games that could be televised.

From 1952 through 1977, the NCAA television committee followed essentially the same procedure for developing its television plans. It would first circulate a questionnaire to the membership and then use the responses as a basis for formulating a plan for the ensuing season. Once approved, the plan formed the basis for NCAA's negotiations with the networks. Throughout this period the plans retained the essential purposes of the original plan. Until 1977 the contracts were all for either one- or two-year terms. In 1977, the

NCAA adopted principles of negotiation for the future and discontinued the practice of submitting each plan for membership approval. Then the NCAA also entered into its first four-year contract granting exclusive rights to the American Broadcasting Co. (ABC) for the 1978-1981 seasons. ABC had held the exclusive rights to network telecasts of NCAA football games since 1965.

The plan adopted in 1981 for the 1982-85 seasons is at issue in this case. This plan, like each of its predecessors, recites that it is intended to reduce, insofar as possible, the adverse effects of live television on football game attendance. It provides that all forms of television of the football games of NCAA member institutions during the plan control periods shall be in accordance with this plan. The plan recites that the television committee has awarded rights to negotiate and contract for the telecasting of college football games of members of the NCAA to two carrying networks. In addition to the principal award of rights to the carrying networks, the plan also describes rights for a supplementary series that had been awarded for the 1982 and 1983 seasons, as well as a procedure for permitting specific exception telecasts.

In separate agreements with each of the carrying networks, ABC and the Columbia Broadcasting System (CBS), the NCAA granted each the right to telecast the 14 live exposures described in the plan, in accordance with the ground rules set forth therein. Each of the networks agreed to pay a specified minimum aggregate compensation to the participating NCAA member institutions during the four-year period in an amount that totaled $131,750,000. In essence the agreement authorized each network to negotiate directly with member schools for the right to televise their games. The agreement itself does not describe the method of computing the compensation for each game, but the practice that has developed over the years and that the district court found would be followed under the current agreement involved the setting of a recommended fee by a representative of the NCAA for different types of telecasts, with national telecasts being the most valuable, regional telecasts being less valuable, and Division II or Division III games commanding a still lower price. The aggregate of all these payments presumably equals the total minimum aggregate compensation set forth in the basic agreement. Except for differences in payment between national and regional telecasts, and with respect to Division II and Division III games, the amount that any team receives does not change with the size of the viewing audience, the number of markets in which the game is telecast, or the particular characteristic of the game or the participating teams. Instead, the ground rules provide that the carrying networks make alternate selections of those games they wish to televise, and thereby obtain the exclusive right to submit a bid at an essentially fixed price to the institutions involved.

The plan also contains appearance requirements and appearance limitations that pertain to each of the two-year periods that the plan is in effect. The basic requirement imposed on each of the two networks is that it must schedule appearances for at least 82 different member institutions during each two-year period. Under the appearance limitations no member institution is eligible to appear on television more than a total of six times and more than four times nationally, with the appearances to be divided equally between the two carrying networks. The number of exposures specified in the contracts also sets an absolute maximum on the number of games that can be broadcast.

Thus, although the current plan is more elaborate than any of its predecessors, it retains the essential features of each of them. It limits the total amount of televised intercollegiate football and the number of games that any one team may televise. No member is permitted to make any sale of television rights except in accordance with the basic plan.

Beginning in 1979, CFA members began to advocate that colleges with major football programs should have a greater voice in the formulation of football television policy than they had in the NCAA. CFA therefore investigated the possibility of negotiating a television agreement of its own, developed an independent plan, and obtained a contract offer from the National Broadcasting Co. (NBC). This contract, which it signed in August 1981, would have allowed a more liberal number of appearances for each institution and would have increased the overall revenues realized by CFA members.

In response, the NCAA publicly announced that it would take disciplinary action against any CFA member that complied with the CFA-NBC contract. The NCAA made it clear that sanctions would not be limited to the football programs of CFA members, but would apply to other sports as well. On September 8, 1981, respondents commenced this action in the United States District Court for the Western District of Oklahoma and obtained a preliminary injunction preventing the NCAA from initiating disciplinary proceedings or otherwise interfering with CFA's efforts to perform its agreement with NBC.

There can be no doubt that the challenged practices of the NCAA constitute "a restraint of trade" in the sense that they limit members' freedom to negotiate and enter into their own television contracts. In that sense, however, every contract is a restraint of trade, and as we have repeatedly recognized, the Sherman Act was intended to prohibit only unreasonable restraints of trade. It is also undeniable that these practices share characteristics of restraints we have previously held unreasonable. The NCAA is an association of schools that compete against each other to attract television revenues, not to mention fans and athletes. As the district court found, the policies of the NCAA with respect to television rights are ultimately controlled by the vote of member institutions. By participating in an association that prevents member institutions from competing against each other on the basis of price or kind of television rights that can be offered to broadcasters, the NCAA member institutions have created a horizontal restraint—an agreement among competitors on the way in which they will compete with one another. A restraint of this type has often been held to be unreasonable as a matter of law. Because it places a ceiling on the number of games member institutions may televise, the horizontal agreement places an artificial limit on the quantity of televised football that is available to broadcasters and consumers. By restraining the quantity of television rights available for sale, the challenged practices create a limitation on output; our cases have held that such limitations are unreasonable restraints of trade. Moreover, the district court found that the minimum aggregate price in fact operates to preclude any price negotiation between broadcasters and institutions, thereby constituting horizontal price fixing, perhaps the paradigm of an unreasonable restraint of trade.

Horizontal price fixing and output limitation are ordinarily condemned as a matter of law under an "illegal *per se*" approach because the probability that these practices are anticompetitive is so high; a *per se* rule is applied "when the practice facially appears to be one that would always or almost always tend to restrict competition and decrease output." *Broadcast Music, Inc. v. Columbia Broadcasting Sys., Inc.*, 441 U.S. 1, 19-20 (1979). In such circumstances a restraint is presumed unreasonable without inquiry into the particular market context in which it is found. Nevertheless, we have decided that it would be inappropriate to apply a *per se* rule to this case. This decision is not based on a lack of judicial experience with this type of arrangement, on the fact that the NCAA is organized as a nonprofit entity, or on our respect for the NCAA's historic role in the preservation and encouragement of intercollegiate amateur athletics. Rather, what is critical is that this case involves an industry in which horizontal restraints on competition are essential if the product is to be available at all.

What the NCAA and its member institutions market in this case is competition itself—contests between competing institutions. Of course, this would be completely ineffective if there were no rules on which the competitors agreed to create and define the competition to be marketed. A myriad of rules affecting such matters as the size of the field, the number of players on a team, and the extent to which physical violence is to be encouraged or proscribed, all must be agreed upon, and all restrain the manner in which institutions compete. Moreover, the NCAA seeks to market a particular brand of football—college football. The identification of this product with an academic tradition differentiates college football from and makes it more popular than professional sports to which it might otherwise be comparable, such as, for example, minor league baseball. In order to preserve the character and quality of the product, athletes must not be paid, must be required to attend class, and the like. And the integrity of the product cannot be preserved except by mutual agreement; if an institution adopted such restrictions unilaterally, its effectiveness as a competitor on the playing field might soon be destroyed. Thus, the NCAA plays a vital role in enabling college football to preserve its character, and as a result enables a product to be marketed that might otherwise be unavailable. In performing this role, its actions widen consumer choice—not only the choices available to sports fans but also those available to athletes—and hence can be viewed as procompetitive.

Respondents concede that the great majority of the NCAA regulations enhance competition among member institutions. Thus, despite the fact that this case involves restraints on the ability of member institutions to compete in terms of price and output, a fair evaluation of their competitive character requires consideration of the NCAA's justifications for the restraints.

Our analysis of this case under the rule of reason, of course, does not change the ultimate focus of our inquiry. Both *per se* rules and the rule of reason are employed to form a judgment about the competitive significance of the restraint. A conclusion that a restraint of trade is unreasonable may be based either (1) on the nature or character of the contracts, or (2) on surrounding circumstances giving rise to the inference or presumption that they were intended to restrain trade and enhance prices. Under either branch of the test, the inquiry is confined to a consideration of impact on competitive conditions.

Per se rules are invoked when surrounding circumstances make the likelihood of anticompetitive conduct so great as to render unjustified further examination of the challenged conduct. But whether the ultimate finding is the product of a presumption or actual market analysis, the essential inquiry remains the same—whether or not the challenged restraint enhances competition. Under the Sherman Act the criterion to be used in judging the validity of a restraint on trade is its impact on competition.

Because it restrains price and output, the NCAA television plan has a significant potential for anticompetitive effects. The findings of the district court indicate that this potential has been realized. The district court found that if member institutions were free to sell television rights, many more games would be shown on television, and that the NCAA's output restriction has the effect of raising the price the networks pay for television rights. Moreover, the court found that by fixing a price for television rights to all games, the NCAA creates a price structure that is unresponsive to viewer demand and unrelated to the prices that would prevail in a competitive market. And, of course, since as a practical matter all member institutions need NCAA approval, members have no real choice but to adhere to the NCAA's television controls.

The anticompetitive consequences of this arrangement are apparent. Individual competitors lose their freedom to compete. Price is higher and output lower than they would otherwise be, and both are unresponsive to consumer preference. This latter point is perhaps the most significant, since Congress designed the Sherman Act as a consumer welfare prescription. A restraint that has the effect of reducing the importance of consumer preference in setting price and output is not consistent with this fundamental goal of antitrust law. Restrictions on price and output are the paradigmatic examples of restraints of trade that the Sherman Act was intended to prohibit. At the same time, the television plan eliminates competitors from the market, since only those broadcasters able to bid on television rights covering the entire NCAA can compete. Thus, as the district court found, many telecasts that would occur in a competitive market are foreclosed by the NCAA plan.

Petitioner argues, however, that its television plan can have no significant anticompetitive effect since the record indicates that it has no market power—no ability to alter the interaction of supply and demand in the market. We must reject this argument for two reasons, one legal, one factual.

As a matter of law, the absence of proof of market power does not justify a naked restriction on price or output. To the contrary, when there is an agreement not to compete in terms of price or output, no elaborate industry analysis is required to demonstrate the anticompetitive character of such an agreement. Petitioner does not quarrel with the district court's finding that price and output are not responsive to demand. Thus the plan is inconsistent with the Sherman Act's command that price and supply be responsive to consumer preference. We have never required proof of market power in such a case. This naked restraint on price and output requires some

competitive justification even in the absence of a detailed market analysis.

As a factual matter, it is evident that petitioner does possess market power. The district court employed the correct test for determining whether college football broadcasts constitute a separate market—whether there are other products that are reasonably substitutable for televised NCAA football games. Petitioner's argument that it cannot obtain supracompetitive prices from broadcasters since advertisers, and hence broadcasters, can switch from college football to other types of programming simply ignores the findings of the district court. It found that intercollegiate football telecasts generate an audience uniquely attractive to advertisers and that competitors are unable to offer programming that can attract a similar audience. These findings amply support its conclusion that the NCAA possesses market power. Indeed, the district court's subsidiary finding that advertisers will pay a premium price per viewer to reach audiences watching college football because of their demographic characteristics is vivid evidence of the uniqueness of this product. Thus, respondents have demonstrated that there is a separate market for telecasts of college football that rests on generic qualities differentiating viewers. It inexorably follows that if college football broadcasts be defined as a separate market—and we are convinced they are—then the NCAA's complete control over those broadcasts provides a solid basis for the district court's conclusion that the NCAA possesses market power with respect to those broadcasts. When a product is controlled by one interest, without substitutes available in the market, there is monopoly power.

Thus, the NCAA television plan on its face constitutes a restraint on the operation of a free market, and the findings of the district court establish that it has operated to raise prices and reduce output. Under the rule of reason, these hallmarks of anticompetitive behavior place on petitioner a heavy burden of establishing an affirmative defense that competitively justifies this apparent deviation from the operations of a free market. We turn now to the NCAA's proffered justifications.

Petitioner argues that its television plan constitutes a cooperative joint venture that assists in the marketing of broadcast rights and hence is procompetitive. While joint ventures have no immunity from the antitrust laws, a joint selling arrangement may make possible a new product by reaping otherwise unattainable efficiencies. The essential contribution made by the NCAA's arrangement is to define the number of games that may be televised, to establish the price for each exposure, and to define the basic terms of each contract between the network and a home team. The NCAA does not, however, act as a selling agent for any school or for any conference of schools. The selection of individual games and the negotiation of particular agreements are matters left to the networks and the individual schools. Thus, the effect of the network plan is not to eliminate individual sales of broadcasts, since these still occur, albeit subject to fixed prices and output limitations. Here the same rights are still sold on an individual basis, only in a noncompetitive market.

The district court did not find that the NCAA television plan produced any procompetitive efficiencies that enhanced the competitiveness of college football television rights; to the contrary, it concluded that NCAA football could be marketed just as effectively without the television plan. There is therefore no predicate in the findings for petitioner's efficiency justification. Indeed, petitioner's argument is refuted by the district court's finding concerning price and output. If the NCAA television plan produced procompetitive efficiencies, the plan would increase output and reduce the price of televised games. The district court's contrary findings accordingly undermine petitioner's position. In light of these findings, it cannot be said that the agreement on price is necessary to market the product at all. Here production has been limited, not enhanced. No individual school is free to televise its own games without restraint. The NCAA's efficiency justification is not supported by the record.

Neither is the NCAA television plan necessary to enable the NCAA to penetrate the market through an attractive package sale. Since broadcasting rights to college football constitute a unique product for which there is no ready substitute, there is no need for collective action in order to enable the product to compete against its nonexistent competitors. This is borne out by the district court's

finding that the NCAA television plan reduces the volume of television rights sold.

Throughout the history of its regulation of intercollegiate football telecasts, the NCAA has indicated its concern with protecting live attendance. This concern, it should be noted, is not with protecting live attendance at games that are shown on television; that type of interest is not at issue in this case. Rather, the concern is that fan interest in a televised game may adversely affect ticket sales for games that will not appear on television.

Although the NORC studies in the 1950s provided some support for the thesis that live attendance would suffer if unlimited television were permitted, the district court found that there was no evidence to support that theory in today's market. Moreover, as the district court found, the television plan has evolved in a manner inconsistent with its original design to protect gate attendance. Under the current plan, games are shown on television during all hours that college football games are played. The plan simply does not protect live attendance by ensuring that games will not be shown on television at the same time as live events.

There is, however, a more fundamental reason for rejecting this defense. The NCAA's argument that its television plan is necessary to protect live attendance is not based on a desire to maintain the integrity of college football as a distinct and attractive product, but rather on a fear that the product will not prove sufficiently attractive to draw live attendance when faced with competition from televised games. At bottom, the NCAA's position is that ticket sales for most college games are unable to compete in a free market. The television plan protects ticket sales by limiting output—just as any monopolist increases revenues by reducing output. By seeking to insulate live ticket sales from the full spectrum of competition because of its assumption that the product itself is insufficiently attractive to consumers, petitioner forwards a justification that is inconsistent with the basic policy of the Sherman Act. The rule of reason does not support a defense based on the assumption that competition itself is unreasonable.

Petitioner argues that the interest in maintaining a competitive balance among amateur athletic teams is legitimate and important and that it justifies the regulations challenged in this case. We agree with the first part of the argument but not the second.

Our decision not to apply a *per se* rule to this case rests in large part on our recognition that a certain degree of cooperation is necessary if the type of competition that petitioner and its member institutions seek to market is to be preserved. It is reasonable to assume that most of the regulatory controls of the NCAA are justifiable means of fostering competition among amateur athletic teams and therefore procompetitive because they enhance public interest in intercollegiate athletics. The specific restraints on football telecasts that are challenged in this case do not, however, fit into the same mold as do rules defining the conditions of the contest, the eligibility of participants, or the manner in which members of a joint enterprise shall share the responsibilities and the benefits of the total venture.

The NCAA does not claim that its television plan has equalized or is intended to equalize competition within any one league. The plan is nationwide in scope and there is no single league or tournament in which all college football teams compete. There is no evidence of any intent to equalize the strength of teams in Division I-A with those in Division II or Division III, and not even a colorable basis for giving colleges that have no football program at all a voice in the management of the revenues generated by the football programs at other schools. The interest in maintaining a competitive balance that is asserted by the NCAA as a justification for regulating all television of intercollegiate football is not related to any neutral standard or to any readily identifiable group of competitors.

The television plan is not even arguably tailored to serve such an interest. It does not regulate the amount of money that any college may spend on its football program, nor the way in which the colleges may use the revenues that are generated by their football programs, whether derived from the sale of television rights, the sale of tickets, or the sale of concessions or program advertising. The plan simply imposes a restriction on one source of revenue that is more important to some colleges than to others. There is no evidence that this restriction produces any greater measure of equality throughout the NCAA than would a restriction on alumni donations, tuition rates, or any other revenue-producing

activity. At the same time, as the district court found, the NCAA imposes a variety of other restrictions designed to preserve amateurism that are much better tailored to the goal of competitive balance than is the television plan, and that are clearly sufficient to preserve competitive balance to the extent it is within the NCAA's power to do so. And much more than speculation supported the district court's findings on this score. No other NCAA sport employs a similar plan, and in particular the court found that in the most closely analogous sport, college basketball, competitive balance has been maintained without resort to a restrictive television plan.

Perhaps the most important reason for rejecting the argument that the interest in competitive balance is served by the television plan is the district court's unambiguous and well-supported finding that many more games would be televised in a free market than under the NCAA plan. The hypothesis that legitimates the maintenance of competitive balance as a procompetitive justification under the rule of reason is that equal competition will maximize consumer demand for the product. The finding that consumption will materially increase if the controls are removed is a compelling demonstration that they do not in fact serve any such legitimate purpose.

The NCAA plays a critical role in the maintenance of a revered tradition of amateurism in college sports. There can be no question but that it needs ample latitude to play that role, or that the preservation of the student athlete in higher education adds richness and diversity to intercollegiate athletics and is entirely consistent with the goals of the Sherman Act. But consistent with the Sherman Act, the role of the NCAA must be to preserve a tradition that might otherwise die; rules that restrict output are hardly consistent with this role. Today we hold only that the record supports the district court's conclusion that by curtailing output and blunting the ability of member institutions to respond to consumer preference, the NCAA has restricted rather than enhanced the place of intercollegiate athletics in the nation's life.

Accordingly, the judgment of the court of appeals is affirmed.

 For an extended version of the case and review questions to test your understanding of the material, please go to www.HumanKinetics.com/CaseStudiesInSportLaw.

Smith v. Pro Football, Inc.

593 F.2d 1173 (D.C. Cir. 1978)

This private antitrust action challenges the legality of the National Football League (NFL) player selection system, commonly called the "draft." The plaintiff is James McCoy "Yazoo" Smith, a former professional football player who played one season for the Washington Redskins after being drafted by them in 1968. The defendants are Pro Football, Inc., which operates the Redskins, and the NFL. Smith contends that the draft as it existed in 1968 was an unreasonable restraint of trade in violation of §§ 1 and 3 of the Sherman Act, and that, but for the draft, he would have negotiated a far more lucrative contract when he signed as a player in that year. Smith alleges that he has been injured in his business or property in the amount of the difference between the compensation he actually received and the compensation he would have received had there existed a "free market" for his services.

Section 4 of the Clayton Act confers the right to sue for treble damages on "(a)ny person who shall be injured in his business or property by reason of anything forbidden in the antitrust laws. . . ." 15 U.S.C. § 15 (1976). After a trial to the court, District Judge Bryant held that the NFL draft as it existed in 1968 constituted a "group boycott" and was thus a *per se* violation of the Sherman Act. Alternatively, he held that the draft, tested under the rule of reason, was an unreasonable restraint because it was "significantly more restrictive than necessary" to accomplish whatever legitimate goals the NFL had. Judge Bryant awarded Smith treble damages totaling $276,000. The Redskins and the NFL have appealed the finding of antitrust liability; both sides have appealed the damage award.

The NFL draft, which has been in effect since 1935, is a procedure under which negotiating rights to graduating college football players are allocated each year among the NFL clubs in inverse order of the clubs' standing. Under the draft procedures generally followed, the team with the poorest playing-field record during the preceding season has the first opportunity, as among the NFL teams, to select a college player of its choice; the team with the next poorest record has the next choice, and so on until the team with the best record (the winner of the previous year's "Super Bowl") has picked last. At this point, the first "round" of the draft is completed. In 1968 there were 16 succeeding rounds in the yearly draft, the same order of selection being followed in each round. Teams had one choice per round unless they had traded their choice in that round to another team (a fairly common practice). When Smith was selected by the Redskins there were 26 teams choosing in the draft.

The NFL draft, like similar procedures in other professional sports, is designed to promote "competitive balance." By dispersing newly arriving player talent equally among all NFL teams, with preferences to the weaker clubs, the draft aims to produce teams that are as evenly matched on the playing field as possible. Evenly matched teams make for closer games, tighter pennant races, and better player morale, thus maximizing fan interest, broadcast revenues, and overall health of the sport. The draft is effectuated through the NFL's "no-tampering" rule. Under this rule as it existed in 1968, no team was permitted to negotiate prior to the draft with any player eligible to be drafted, and no team could negotiate with (or sign) any player selected by another team in the draft. The net result of these restrictions was that the right to negotiate with any given player was exclusively held by one team at any given time. If a college player could not reach a satisfactory agreement with the team holding the rights to his services, he could not play in the NFL.

Plaintiff Smith became subject to the draft when he graduated as an All-American football player from the University of Oregon in 1968. The Redskins, choosing twelfth, picked Smith as their first-round draft choice. After several months of negotiations, in which he was represented by an agent, Smith and the Redskins signed a one-year contract, a version of the Standard Player Contract that the NFL requires all players to sign. The contract awarded Smith a $23,000 "bonus" for signing, an additional $5,000 if he made the team, and a salary of $22,000, for a total first-year compensation of $50,000. Smith made the team and performed at a high level of play as a defensive back until he suffered a serious neck injury in the final game of the 1968 season. His doctors advised him not to continue his football career. After his injury the Redskins paid Smith an additional $19,800, representing the amount he would ordinarily have received had he played out the second ("option") year of his contract. Two years after his injury Smith filed suit in the district court. After finding that the draft violated the antitrust laws, Judge Bryant awarded Smith damages equal to the difference between his actual compensation and the compensation he could have received in a free market.

The legality of the NFL player draft under the antitrust laws is essentially a question of first impression. This case requires us to consider (1) whether the legality of the draft is governed by a *per se* rule or by the rule of reason; (2) whether the draft, if tested by the rule of reason, is a reasonable restraint; and (3) whether, if the draft violates the antitrust laws, the measure of damages adopted by the District Judge was proper. We discuss these issues in turn.

The traditional framework of analysis under § 1 of the Sherman Act is familiar and does not require extended discussion. Section 1 prohibits "(e)very contract, combination . . . or conspiracy, in restraint of trade or commerce." While this language is broad enough to render illegal nearly all commercial understandings, the Supreme Court established a judicial gloss on the statute that made the "rule of reason" the prevailing mode of analysis. Under this rule, the fact finder weighs all the circumstances of a case in deciding whether a restrictive practice should be prohibited as imposing an unreasonable restraint on competition. The inquiry mandated by the rule of reason, however, is often laborious, and as the courts gained experience with antitrust problems they identified certain types of agreements that were so consistently unreasonable that they could be deemed illegal *per se*, without elaborate inquiry into their purported justifications. Among the practices that have been deemed so pernicious as to be unreasonable *per se* are certain "group boycotts."

Plaintiff argues that the NFL draft constitutes a "group boycott" because the NFL clubs con-

certedly refuse to deal with any player before he has been drafted or after he has been drafted by another team, and that the draft is in consequence a *per se* violation of § 1. The district court accepted this argument. We reject it. We hold that the NFL player draft is not properly characterized as a "group boycott" at least not the type of boycott that traditionally has been held illegal *per se* and that the draft, regardless of how it is characterized, should more appropriately be tested under the rule of reason. The classic "group boycott" is a concerted attempt by a group of competitors at one level to protect themselves from competition from non-group members who seek to compete at that level. Typically, the boycotting group combines to deprive would-be competitors of a trade relationship that they need in order to enter (or survive in) the level wherein the group operates. The group may accomplish its exclusionary purpose by inducing suppliers not to sell to potential competitors, by inducing customers not to buy from them, or, in some cases, by refusing to deal with would-be competitors themselves. In each instance, however, the hallmark of the "group boycott" is the effort of competitors to "barricade themselves from competition at their own level." It is this purpose to exclude competition that has characterized the Supreme Court's decisions invoking the group boycott *per se* rule.

The NFL player draft differs from the classic group boycott in two significant respects. First, the NFL clubs that have "combined" to implement the draft are not competitors in any economic sense. The clubs operate basically as a joint venture in producing an entertainment product (e.g., football games and telecasts). No NFL club can produce this product without agreements and joint action with every other team. To this end, the League not only determines franchise locations, playing schedules, and broadcast terms, but also ensures that the clubs receive equal shares of telecast and ticket revenues. These economic joint venturers "compete" on the playing field, to be sure, but here as well cooperation is essential if the entertainment product is to attain a high quality: only if the teams are "competitively balanced" will spectator interest be maintained at a high pitch. No NFL team, in short, is interested in driving another team out of business, whether in the counting-house or on the football field, for if the League fails, no one team can survive.

Second, the draft differs from the classic group boycott in that the NFL clubs have not combined to exclude competitors or potential competitors from their level of the market. Smith was never seeking to "compete" with the NFL clubs, and their refusal to deal with him has resulted in no decrease in the competition for providing football entertainment to the public. The draft, indeed, is designed not to insulate the NFL from competition, but to improve the entertainment product by enhancing its teams' competitive equality.

In view of these differences, we conclude that the NFL player draft cannot properly be described as a group boycott at least not the type of group boycott that traditionally has elicited invocation of a *per se* rule. The "group boycott" designation, we believe, is properly restricted to concerted attempts by competitors to exclude horizontal competitors; it should not be applied, and has never been applied by the Supreme Court, to concerted refusals that are not designed to drive out competitors but to achieve some other goal. We are guided in reaching this conclusion by decisions in analogous areas of antitrust law. The courts have consistently refused to invoke the boycott *per se* rule where, given the peculiar characteristics of an industry, the need for cooperation among participants necessitated some type of concerted refusal to deal, or where the concerted activity manifested no purpose to exclude and in fact worked no exclusion of competitors. In view of the joint-venture characteristics of the professional football industry and the purpose of the concerted activity here, these decisions support our conclusion that the NFL player draft is not a group boycott that is illegal *per se*.

Whether the draft is a group boycott or not, we think it is clearly not the type of restraint to which a *per se* rule is meant to apply. A *per se* rule is a judicial shortcut; it represents the considered judgment of courts, after considerable experience with a particular type of restraint, that the rule of reason—the normal mode of analysis—can be dispensed with. A court will not indulge in this conclusive presumption lightly. Invocation of a *per se* rule always risks sweeping reasonable, procompetitive activity within a general condemnation, and a court will

run this risk only when it can say, on the strength of unambiguous experience, that the challenged action is a "naked restraint of trade with no purpose except stifling of competition."

The NFL player draft, we think, quite clearly fails to satisfy the demanding standards of prior Supreme Court decisions. Given that the draft's restrictive effect is temporally limited, we would hesitate to describe its impact on the market for players' services as pernicious. More importantly, we cannot say that the draft has no purpose except stifling of competition or that it is without any redeeming virtue. Some form of player selection system may serve to regulate and thereby promote competition in what would otherwise be a chaotic bidding market for the services of college players. The Redskins, moreover, presented considerable evidence at trial that the draft was designed to preserve, and that it made some contribution to preserving, playing-field equality among the NFL teams with various attendant benefits. The draft, finally, is widely used in our economy and has both judicial and scholarly support for its economic usefulness.

This is not to say, of course, that the draft in any one of its incarnations may not violate the antitrust laws. It is only to say that the courts have had too little experience with this type of restraint, and know too little of the "economic and business stuff" from which it issues, confidently to declare it illegal without undertaking the analysis enjoined by the rule of reason. Our conclusion that the legality of the NFL draft should not be governed by a *per se* rule parallels the conclusion of most courts and commentators that the legality of player restrictions in professional sports should be governed by the rule of reason. In the case most nearly on point, the Eighth Circuit recently declined, for reasons akin to ours, to apply a *per se* approach to the NFL's Rozelle rule. While we fully appreciate the administrative convenience of a *per se* rubric, ease of application alone cannot suffice to recommend it. In antitrust law, as elsewhere, we must heed Justice Cardozo's warning to beware "the tyranny of tags and tickets." When anticompetitive effects are shown to result from a particular player selection system "they can be adequately policed under the rule of reason."

Under the rule of reason, a restraint must be evaluated to determine whether it is significantly anticompetitive in purpose or effect. In making this evaluation, a court generally will be required to analyze "the facts peculiar to the business, the history of the restraint, and the reasons why it was imposed." If, on analysis, the restraint is found to have legitimate business purposes whose realization serves to promote competition, the "anticompetitive evils" of the challenged practice must be carefully balanced against its "procompetitive virtues" to ascertain whether the former outweigh the latter. A restraint is unreasonable if it has the "net effect" of substantially impeding competition.

After undertaking the analysis mandated by the rule of reason, the district court concluded that the NFL draft as it existed in 1968 had a severely anticompetitive impact on the market for players' services, and that it went beyond the level of restraint reasonably necessary to accomplish whatever legitimate business purposes might be asserted for it. We have no basis for disturbing the district court's findings of fact; and while our legal analysis differs slightly from that of the trial judge, having benefited from intervening guidance from the Supreme Court, we agree with the district court's conclusion that the NFL draft as it existed in 1968 constituted an unreasonable restraint of trade.

The draft that has been challenged here is undeniably anticompetitive both in its purpose and in its effect. The defendants have conceded that the draft "restricts competition among the NFL clubs for the services of graduating college players" and, indeed, that the draft "is designed to limit competition" and "to be a 'purposive' restraint" on the player-service market. The fact that the draft assertedly was designed to promote the teams' playing-field equality rather than to inflate their profit margins may prevent the draft's purpose from being described, in subjective terms, as nefarious. But this fact does not prevent its purpose from being described, in objective terms, as anticompetitive, for suppressing competition, is the telos, the very essence of the restraint.

The trial judge was likewise correct in finding that the draft was significantly anticompetitive

in its effect. The draft inescapably forces each seller of football services to deal with one, and only one buyer, robbing the seller, as in any monopsonistic market, of any real bargaining power. The draft, as the district court found, "leaves no room whatever for competition among the teams for the services of college players, and utterly strips them of any measure of control over the marketing of their talents." The predictable effect of the draft, as the evidence established and as the district court found, was to lower the salary levels of the best college players. There can be no doubt that the effect of the draft as it existed in 1968 was to "suppress or even destroy competition" in the market for players' services.

The justification asserted for the draft is that it has the legitimate business purpose of promoting "competitive balance" and playing-field equality among the teams, producing better entertainment for the public, higher salaries for the players, and increased financial security for the clubs. The NFL has endeavored to summarize this justification by saying that the draft ultimately has a "procompetitive" effect, yet this shorthand entails no small risk of confusion. The draft is "procompetitive," if at all, in a very different sense from that in which it is anticompetitive. The draft is anticompetitive in its effect on the market for players' services, because it virtually eliminates economic competition among buyers for the services of sellers. The draft is allegedly "procompetitive" in its effect on the playing field; but the NFL teams are not economic competitors on the playing field, and the draft, while it may heighten athletic competition and thus improve the entertainment product offered to the public, does not increase competition in the economic sense of encouraging others to enter the market and to offer the product at lower cost. Because the draft's "anticompetitive" and "procompetitive" effects are not comparable, it is impossible to "net them out" in the usual rule-of-reason balancing. The draft's "anticompetitive evils," in other words, cannot be balanced against its "procompetitive virtues," and the draft be upheld if the latter outweigh the former. In strict economic terms, the draft's demonstrated procompetitive effects are nil.

The defendants' justification for the draft reduces in fine to an assertion that competition in the market for entering players' services would not serve the best interests of the public, the clubs, or the players themselves. Confining our inquiry, as we must, to the draft's impact on competitive conditions, we conclude that the draft as it existed in 1968 was an unreasonable restraint of trade. The draft was concededly anticompetitive in purpose. It was severely anticompetitive in effect. It was not shown to have any significant offsetting procompetitive impact in the economic sense. Balancing the draft's anticompetitive evils against its procompetitive virtues, the outcome is plain. The NFL's defenses, premised on the assertion that competition for players' services would harm both the football industry and society, are unavailing; there is nothing of procompetitive virtue to balance, because "the Rule of Reason does not support a defense based on the assumption that competition itself is unreasonable."

We recognize that professional football "may differ significantly from other business services, and, accordingly (that), the nature of the competition" for player talent may vary from an absolute "free market" norm. Given the joint-venture status of the NFL clubs, we do not foreclose the possibility that some type of player selection system might be defended as serving "to regulate and promote . . . competition" in the market for players' services. But we are faced here with what amounts to a "total ban" on competition, and we agree with the district court that this level of restraint cannot be justified. The trial judge concluded, with pardonable exaggeration, that the draft system at issue was "absolutely the most restrictive one imaginable." Even though the draft was justified primarily by the need to disperse the best players, it applied to all graduating seniors, including average players who were, in a sense, fungible commodities. It permitted college players to negotiate with only one team. If a player could not contract with that team, he could not play at all.

Without imitating any view as to the legality of the following procedures, we note that there exist significantly less anticompetitive alternatives to the draft system that has been challenged here. The trial judge found the evidence supported the viability of a player selection system that would permit "more than one team to draft each player, while restricting the number of players any one team might sign." A less anticompetitive draft might permit a college player to negotiate with the team of his choice if the team that drafted him failed to make him an acceptable offer. The NFL could also conduct a second draft each year for players who were unable to reach agreement with the team that selected them the first time. Most obviously, perhaps, the district court found that the evidence supported the feasibility of a draft that would run for fewer rounds, applying only to the most talented players and enabling their "average" brethren to negotiate in a "free market." The least restrictive alternative of all, of course, would be for the NFL to eliminate the draft entirely and employ revenue-sharing to equalize the teams' financial resources, a method of preserving "competitive balance" nicely in harmony with the league's self-proclaimed "joint-venture" status.

We are not required in this case to design a draft that would pass muster under the antitrust laws. We would suggest, however, that no draft can be justified merely by showing that it is a relatively less anticompetitive means of attaining sundry benefits for the football industry and society. Rather, a player draft can survive scrutiny under the rule of reason only if it is demonstrated to have positive, economically procompetitive benefits that offset its anticompetitive effects, or, at the least, if it is demonstrated to accomplish legitimate business purposes and to have a net anticompetitive effect that is insubstantial. Because the NFL draft as it existed in 1968 had severe anticompetitive effects and no demonstrated procompetitive virtues, we hold that it unreasonably restrained trade in violation of § 1 of the Sherman Act. Affirmed in part, reversed in part, and remanded for proceedings consistent with this opinion.

 For an extended version of the case and review questions to test your understanding of the material, please go to www.HumanKinetics.com/CaseStudiesInSportLaw.

2

Constitutional Law

The Constitution of the United States is directly applicable to sports. Sports are an integral part of our free society, where athletes can learn, grow, and compete in a manner that is best suited to their lifestyle. The Preamble of the United States Constitution provides the citizens with a means to establish justice, insure domestic tranquility, promote general welfare, and secure the blessings of liberty. It is by understanding the words found in the Preamble that the purpose of sports in a democratic society can be comprehended.

There are four broad rights relevant to sports that all citizens enjoy. These include personal freedom, civil rights, due process, and privacy. The first broad right found in the Constitution is the right of personal freedom that includes freedom of movement, freedom of speech, freedom of association, and freedom of religious beliefs. Under the right to freedom of speech, citizens may disagree with decisions of others or the government, petition for change, or express displeasure. As illustrated in the case of *Tinker v. Des Moines Independent Community School District*, the right to protest does not always take the form of oral or written communication. Under the freedom of association, people are free to join teams as well as friendships and associations. Under the freedom of religion, one may practice his own set of religious beliefs by worshipping as he pleases, as illustrated in *Jager v. Douglas*. Some religious beliefs require dress standards that may contradict standards set forth by sport administrators as illustrated in the case of *Menora v. Illinois High School Association*.

The second broad right under the Constitution involves civil rights. Under this right, citizens are free from discrimination in sports in terms of race, color, creed, gender, religion, national origin, and age. Two examples of cases in this section are *Blair v. Washington State University* and *Doe v. Taylor Independent School District*.

A third broad right granted by the Constitution is the right of due process. Under this right, no one has the right to interfere in the lives of others without first proceeding in a legal and equitable manner. When athletes are denied their rights to life, liberty, and property, the Constitution guarantees them their rights cannot be denied without notice and a hearing (the opportunity to make their case). Cases in this section that address this right are *Denis J. O'Connell High School v. The Virginia High School League, Hall v. The University of Minnesota, NCAA v. Tarkanian, Palmer v. Merluzzi,* and *Spring Branch Independent School District v. Stamos.*

The fourth broad right under the Constitution and relevant to sports is the right to privacy. This right seeks to ensure that another cannot intrude on one's life by divulging private information in a public manner. Privacy rights prevent government interference in personal, intimate relationships, associations, and activities. Privacy issues often are raised in connection with drug testing. Cases in this section addressing this right are *Hill v. NCAA, Schaill v. Tippecanoe County School Corporation, University of Colorado v. Derdeyn,* and *Vernonia School District 47J v. Acton.*

Blair v. Washington State University

740 P.2d 1379 (Wash. 1987)

This is a sex discrimination action brought under the state Equal Rights Amendment, Const. Art. 31, § 1 (Amend. 61), and the Law Against Discrimination, RCW 49.60. Appellants are female athletes and coaches of female athletes at Washington State University. Respondents are Washington State University, its President, Executive Vice President, and Board of Regents.

The trial court concluded the university had discriminated against the plaintiffs on the basis of sex and awarded damages, injunctive relief, attorney fees, and costs. The plaintiffs now appeal, among other things, (1) the exclusion of football from the court's calculations for sports participation and scholarships, (2) the trial court's decision to allow each sport to benefit from the revenue it generates, and (3) the trial court ruling requiring them to file a claim under the Tort Claims Act, RCW 4.92.110, as a condition precedent to bringing this suit.

The comprehensive findings of fact of the trial court demonstrate that, despite marked improvements since the early 1970s, women's athletic programs have continued to receive inferior treatment in funding, fund-raising efforts, publicity and promotions, scholarships, facilities,

equipment, coaching, uniforms, practice clothing, awards, and administrative staff and support. During the 1980-81 school year, the year before the trial, the total funding available to the men's athletic programs was $3,017,692, and for the women's programs was $689,757, roughly 23% of the men's. The funds for the men's programs were derived largely from revenues, both gate admissions ($958,503) and media rights, conference revenues, and guaranties ($943,629). Most of these revenues were derived from football ($1,430,554). Of the funding available to the women's programs, most was derived from legislative appropriations ($451,082). Very little came from gate admissions ($10,535). Although the number of participation opportunities for men increased by 115 positions from 1973-74 to 1980-81, the opportunities made available for women decreased nine positions during the same period. The budget for men's scholarships increased from $380,056 to $478,052 during that period; the budget for women's scholarships in 1980-81 was $150,000.

On the basis of numerous findings of fact detailing the inferior treatment of the women's athletic program, the trial court concluded the university had "acted, or failed to act, in the operation of the university's intercollegiate athletics program in a manner that resulted in discriminatory treatment of females . . ." The athletes had "suffered unlawful sex discrimination violative of RCW 49.60 and the State Equal Rights Amendment." The court entered a detailed injunction to remedy the violations. With respect to funding, the court ordered the women's program must receive 37.5% of the university's financial support given to intercollegiate athletics during the year 1982-83. The required minimum percentage for women increased each year by 2% until it corresponded to the percentage of women undergraduates at the university, 44% at the time of the injunction. The trial court provided, however, the level of support for women's athletics was not required to exceed by more than 3% the actual participation rate of women in intercollegiate athletics at the university, excluding football participation from the comparison. The injunction prohibited the total budget for women's athletics ever to be less than the base budget of $841,145 for 1981-82, unless the expenditures for men's athletics were correspondingly reduced.

The injunction also specified the following: In determining the level of university financial support of intercollegiate athletics for purposes of the above calculation, the term "university financial support" shall not include revenue generated by or attributable to any specific sport or program. Such excluded sources of revenue shall specifically include gate receipts, conference revenues, guarantees, sale of media rights, concession and novelty sales at games, coach and athlete work projects, and donations attributable to a sport or program.

The injunction apportioned the funding for athletic scholarships in a similar manner. The women received 37.5% of all money expended for scholarships, excluding funds expended for football scholarships. The percentage increased yearly until it equaled the percentage of women undergraduates. The allocation could not fall below $236,300, the amount allocated for 1982-83, unless matched by a reduction in male scholarships. The court also ordered the university to allow for increased participation opportunities until female participation, again excluding foot-

ball participation from the comparison, reached a level commensurate with the proportion of female undergraduate students. The court noted female participation had increased in recent years and stated in its memorandum opinion, "[t]he change in the last ten years is dramatic, and it seems possible that parity will soon arrive." The court further required the university to take affirmative steps to make opportunities to generate revenue equally available to men's and women's programs, stating, "Because past sex discrimination has afforded women's teams and coaches less opportunity to generate revenue, the university should take affirmative action in providing additional personnel with such knowledge and experience."

The trial court required the university to appoint a committee to monitor the application of the funding formulas and other elements of the injunction. The sex equity committee, composed of students, coaches, and administrators, was also given the mandate to develop recommendations for policies concerning matters affecting sex equity in athletics and recommendations for the promotion of women's athletics. After approval by the provost, the committee's recommendations are to be implemented and administered in an equitable and timely manner. In addition to the injunction, the trial court awarded the plaintiffs monetary damages for certain tangible losses caused by the university's discriminatory policies. The plaintiffs contest the trial court's reduction of the damages award. The trial court held RCW 4.92.110 required the plaintiffs to file a tort claim with the state before bringing a discrimination action under RCW 49.60. The parties had stipulated that if RCW 4.92.110 did apply, the complaint would be deemed filed on September 12, 1980, and any damage award would extend back three years from that date. The court, accordingly, calculated the award based only on injuries since 1977.

The first issue raised by the plaintiffs is whether the trial court abused its discretion in creating an injunctive remedy that excluded football from its calculations for participation opportunities, scholarships, and distribution of nonrevenue funds. We conclude the trial court did abuse its discretion and reverse on this issue. The Equal Rights Amendment and the Law Against Discrimination prohibit such an exclusion.

The Equal Rights Amendment states "Equality of rights and responsibility under the law shall not be denied or abridged on account of sex. The legislature shall have the power to enforce, by appropriate legislation, the provisions of this Article." Const. Art. 31, §§ 1 and 2 (Amend. 61).

The Law Against Discrimination provides "The right to be free from discrimination because of race, creed, color, national origin, sex, or the presence of any sensory, mental, or physical handicap is recognized as and declared to be a civil right. This right shall include, but not be limited to (b) The right to the full enjoyment of any of the accommodations, advantages, facilities, or privileges of any place of public resort, accommodation, assemblage, or amusement . . ." RCW 49.60.030(1)(b).

The recognized purpose of the Equal Rights Amendment is to end special treatment for or discrimination against either sex. This absolute mandate of equality does not, however, bar affirmative governmental efforts to create equality in fact; governmental actions favoring one sex that are intended solely to ameliorate the effects of past discrimination do not implicate the Equal Rights Amendment. Neither party disputes the intercollegiate athletics program at Washington State University is subject to the Equal Rights Amendment and the Law Against Discrimination. The trial court found the operation of the program resulted in discriminatory treatment of women and the women's athletic program in violation of these laws. Football is a large and essential part of intercollegiate athletics at the university. To exclude football, an all male program, from the scope of the Equal Rights Amendment would only serve to perpetuate the discriminatory policies and diminished opportunities for women. The trial court attempted to explain the exclusion of football by stating football was a sport "unique in many respects, the combination of which distinguished it from all other collegiate sports . . ." The court identified such distinguishing characteristics as the number of participants, scholarships, and coaches, amount of equipment and facilities, income generated, media interest, spectator attendance, and publicity generated for

the university as a whole. The court concluded: "Because of the unique function performed by football, it should not be compared to any other sport at the university. Because football is operated for profit under business principles, . . . football should not be included in determining whether sex equity exists. . . ."

We do not believe, however, these or any other characteristics of football justify its exclusion from the scope of the injunction remedying violations of the Equal Rights Amendment. It is stating the obvious to observe the Equal Rights Amendment contains no exception for football. The exclusion of football would prevent sex equity from ever being achieved since men would always be guaranteed many more participation opportunities than women, despite any efforts by the teams, the sex equity committee, or the program to promote women's athletics under the injunction.

The plaintiffs also challenge the portion of the injunction excluding from the division of university financial support the revenue generated by any specific sport or program. The injunction allows each sport to reap the benefit of the revenues it generates. We hold the trial court did not abuse its discretion. Exclusion of sports-generated revenue from the calculations of university financial support is not prohibited under applicable state law and can be supported by several policy considerations. We affirm this portion of the trial court's injunction. The plaintiffs cite no law or authority that would have required the trial court to include sports-generated revenues in its calculations. They cite RCW 28B.10.704 as an indication of legislative support for their position. RCW 28B.10.704 provides in relevant part: "Funds used for purposes of providing scholarships or other forms of financial assistance to students in return for participation in intercollegiate athletics . . . shall include but not be limited to moneys received as contributed or donated funds, or revenues derived from athletic events, including gate receipts and revenues obtained from the licensing of radio and television broadcasts."

The plaintiffs contend this statute indicates a legislative intent to pool sports-generated revenues to make them available for athletic scholarships. The legislative history does not support reading such intent into this provision. The statute, Laws of 1971, 1st Ex.Sess, ch. 28, was enacted following a request for an attorney general opinion regarding the constitutionality of using sports-generated revenues for athletic scholarships. The attorney general had indicated the revenues were state funds and were subject to the provisions of Article 8, § 5, regarding gifts of state funds. After the statute was enacted, the attorney general concluded the statute acted to place such athletic scholarships outside of the boundaries of constitutionally prohibited gifts.

The legislative history supports the contention sports-generated revenues are in fact state funds. We believe it does not, however, support the plaintiffs' assertion this statute should be used to prohibit the trial court's decision, nor is plaintiffs' assertion a necessary inference from the language of the statute. The trial court chose an injunctive remedy neither required nor prohibited by applicable law and acted within its discretion in choosing to create a funding plan allowing each sport to benefit from the revenues it generates. The trial court's funding plan provides incentive for all sports to develop revenue-generating capability of their own. As the trial court stated in its findings of fact and conclusions of law: There is an incentive to coaches and to a lesser extent their athletes to produce as much income as possible from all sources because they are the persons who first benefit from such income. The funding plan encourages the sports to fund their expenses through their own efforts, rather than depend on direct legislative appropriations. The injunction specifically requires the sex equity committee to recommend ways to encourage and promote women's sports to increase their own revenues; the funding plan would further promote such a goal. The plan thus requires the university to create equal opportunity to raise revenue for men's and women's sports.

The funding plan allows disproportionate expenses of any particular sports program to be derived from the program itself. The plan is also gender neutral. It provides a solution that does not violate the Equal Rights Amendment and encourages revenue development for all sports while accommodating the needs of the sports programs incurring the greatest expenses at this time. Our decision upholding the trial court's conclusion regarding sports-generated revenues does not in any way modify the university's obligation to achieve

sex equity under the Equal Rights Amendment. The trial court's minimum requirements for participation opportunities and scholarships, already discussed, must be achieved; the court's guidelines for distribution of nonrevenue funds must be followed, and the remaining portions of the injunction, including promotion and development of women's sports, must be observed.

In addition, our conclusion allowing each sport to use the revenues it generates does not, of course, require the sport to do so. The record reflects the football program was transferring $150,000 or more per year from its revenues to the women's program before the injunction was entered. We encourage such practices to continue, along with other efforts to foster cooperation within the department. We therefore reverse the trial court's exclusion of football from its calculations for participation opportunities and scholarships and affirm the trial court's decision to exclude sports-generated revenues from its distribution of financial support. We emphasize the portion of the injunction requiring additional promotion of women's sports and development of their revenue-generating capability and encourage continued cooperation and efforts to bring the university's intercollegiate athletic program into compliance with the Equal Rights Amendment.

To summarize, the injunctive relief provided it by the trial court is affirmed as modified in this opinion. The football program may not be excluded from the calculations of participation opportunities, scholarships, or distribution of nonrevenue funds. The trial court ruling that plaintiffs must file a claim under RCW 4.92.110 as a condition precedent to bring this suit is affirmed. The issues raised by the university in its cross appeal are affirmed. The entire matter is remanded to the Superior Court to be under its continuing jurisdiction with instructions to take whatever further action is necessary consistent with this opinion.

 For an extended version of the case and review questions to test your understanding of the material, please go to www.HumanKinetics.com/CaseStudiesInSportLaw.

Denis J. O'Connell High School v. The Virginia High School League

581 F.2d 81 (4th Cir. 1978)

The Virginia High School League (the League) appeals from a judgment of the District Court enjoining the League from denying Denis J. O'Connell High School's (O'Connell) application for membership in the League and from barring O'Connell from competing in League-sponsored championship athletic contests.

O'Connell is a state-accredited private nonprofit Catholic high school located in Arlington County, Virginia. In February of 1977, O'Connell applied for admission to the Virginia High School League, Northern Region. The application was denied because the League's Constitution limits membership to public high schools.

The League is an unincorporated association of public high schools in Virginia under the sponsorship of the School of Continuing Education of the University of Virginia. With only one exception, every public high school in Virginia belongs to the League. In 1913 when the League was founded, its constitution included both public and private secondary schools without distinction, but in 1925 the constitution was changed so that only public high schools could be members, and that limitation remains today. The League is maintained by public funds derived in part from the University of Virginia, in part from local school boards, and in part from gate receipts from League-sponsored tournaments.

The League regulates, controls, and governs all athletic, literary, and debating contests between and among its member schools. Private schools are invited by the League to participate as a distinct class in certain statewide tournaments, such as those involving tennis, debating, and speaking. However, the private schools are excluded altogether from League-sponsored tournaments involving such major sports as football, basketball, and baseball.

O'Connell brought suit against the League pursuant to 42 U.S.C. § 1983 and its jurisdictional counterpart, 28 U.S.C. § 1343(3), alleging in its complaint that the League's refusal to admit O'Connell on the sole basis that it is a private

school is an arbitrary classification in violation of the Equal Protection Clause of the Fourteenth Amendment. The complaint further charged that, as a result of this exclusion, O'Connell's students' choice of private education denies them the right to compete on a tournament level in sports such as football, basketball, and baseball, thus placing them in a less favorable competitive position than public high school students to receive athletic scholarships, professional bonuses, and other benefits that accrue to gifted athletes. The League submitted an answer denying the essential allegations of the complaint. Following the court's denial of the league's motion to dismiss and motion for summary judgment, the parties entered into a formal stipulation that was filed with the court prior to trial. The stipulation stated, *inter alia*, that action by the League in supervising interscholastic competition is taken under color of state law and constitutes state action within the meaning of 42 U.S.C. § 1983.

At trial, the League presented three basic arguments in defense of its policy of exclusion. First, the League asserted that because O'Connell had not been deprived of any federally protected right, there was no federal question presented so as to support federal jurisdiction alleged to be founded on 28 U.S.C. § 1343. Second, the League argued that its limitation of membership to public schools is rationally related to the League's interest in enforcing its eligibility rules concerning transfer students. The League presented testimony to the effect that, because public schools draw students only from strictly defined zones whereas private schools are not so limited, the League's transfer rules would be difficult to enforce with respect to private schools. Finally, the League argued that the admission of O'Connell, a parochial school, into the League would violate the Establishment Clause of the First Amendment. The court held that (1) the question whether participation in the League's athletic program can be characterized as a right is not determinative of the constitutional validity of the League's classification, (2) there is nothing in the record to support the asserted bases for the League's exclusion of private schools from League membership, and (3) the activities of the League neither advance nor inhibit religion, and any financial benefits supplied indirectly by the League to O'Connell in the form of surplus proceeds from League-sponsored championship games would not constitute excessive governmental entanglement with religion so as to violate the Establishment Clause. Thus, because the exclusion of O'Connell from the League lacked a rational basis in violation of the Fourteenth Amendment, and because the inclusion of O'Connell in the League would not violate the First Amendment, the court enjoined the League from denying O'Connell membership.

On appeal, the League first contends that the district court erred in holding that jurisdiction exists under 28 U.S.C. § 1343. The League's contention is essentially as follows: Since neither education, nor participation in interscholastic competition, nor the speculative possibility of acquiring an athletic scholarship, professional bonus, or other emolument are rights secured by the constitution or federal law, 28 U.S.C. § 1343 did not provide the district court with jurisdiction over O'Connell's claim. Admittedly, education is not a fundamental right under the Constitution, and, of course, neither is participation in interscholastic athletics such a right. Nor is the speculative possibility of acquiring an athletic scholarship or professional bonus a federally protected property right. The right allegedly abridged, however, is not the right to education or the right to participate in interscholastic athletics; rather, the alleged abridgment is of the right of private school students to be treated similarly as public school students with regard to participation in interscholastic athletics where there is no rational basis for treating the two classes of students differently. That is, O'Connell claims that its students have been denied their right to an equal opportunity to compete in interscholastic competition. A claimed denial of equal protection by state action arises under the Constitution and would normally be within the district court's jurisdiction under § 1343, unless unsubstantial or frivolous. Under the facts of the present case, we cannot

say that the claimed denial of equal protection lacks substance. Therefore, the district court properly took jurisdiction of the claim pursuant to 28 U.S.C. § 1343.

The League next contends that the district court erred in holding that there is no rational basis for the provision of the League's constitution limiting membership to public schools. We agree.

Where, as here, there is no fundamental right or suspect classification involved, the test to determine the validity of state legislation is whether the statutory classification bears some rational relationship to a legitimate state purpose. Furthermore, state legislatures are presumed to have acted within their constitutional power despite the fact that, in practice, their laws result in some inequality. A statutory discrimination will not be set aside if any state of facts reasonably may be conceived to justify it.

The reasons for the League's exclusion of private schools, as established by the statements of two League officials, are as follows: (1) League regulations are not sufficiently defined to determine the area from which private schools, many of which may now draw students from an unlimited geographical area, may draw eligible participants for League activities; (2) the lack of an attendance zone for private schools similar to that of public schools, each of which may draw students only from a specified geographical area, would make the transfer rule difficult to enforce and would give private school students an advantage not enjoyed by public school students; and (3) students eligible to attend private schools could choose to attend private schools or their public school on the basis of athletic programs in violation of the spirit of the League. The transfer rule cited by the League officials states, essentially, that when a student transfers from one high school to another without a corresponding change in district residence by his parents, the student is ineligible to participate in interscholastic competition for one semester at his new school.

In its memorandum opinion, the district court stated that "(t)he only bases asserted by the League for excluding nonpublic high schools from League membership are their ability to draw students from a larger geographical area than the public high schools and the difficulty of enforcing the eligibility rules for transfer students." The court found that neither assertion is supported by the record and no reason was suggested why the League's rules could not be uniformly applied to both private and public high schools.

The court's finding that there is no support in the record for the League's contention that private schools can draw students from a larger geographical area than public schools is based on the failure of the League to introduce actual evidence to that effect. However, it is well-known that many private schools in Virginia suffer no geographical limitation with respect to the areas from which they may draw students. Furthermore, even assuming that there are some Virginia private schools that do draw from strictly defined areas, these schools unlike their public counterparts, are not so limited by state law and could therefore at any time decide to modify or abolish their self-imposed drawing restrictions and recruit students from anywhere. And even assuming that some of these schools chose to continue drawing from strictly defined areas (an assumption the League is not obligated to make), these areas would overlap with the areas from which public schools can draw. Therefore, because the actual and potential disparity in drawing area between public schools and private schools is beyond doubt, the district court should have given credence to the League's assertion that public and private schools lack similar attendance zones.

Given the lack of specifically defined drawing areas with respect to many private schools, it is obvious that the admission into the League of private schools would create difficulties in the enforcement of the transfer rule. Although the difficulty of applying the rule to students transferring from private to public schools might not be affected, surely additional difficulties would arise in applying the rule to students transferring from either private or public schools to zoneless private schools. Since the school to which the student transfers would be lacking a district in which his parents could establish residence, it would seem that any student transferring to a zoneless private school would necessarily be ineligible to participate in that school's athletic programs for one semester even if his parents

moved next door to the school. Thus, any student transferring to a zoneless private school would be victimized by the application of the transfer rule to a situation that it was never meant to cover.

In addition to the problems created by the application of the transfer rule to private schools lacking attendance zones, the League asserted another basis, apparently ignored by the district court, for restricting its membership to public schools. A League official stated that if private schools became members, students eligible to attend such private schools could choose to attend those schools or their public school on the basis of athletic programs in violation of the spirit of the League. Although there was no elaboration by the League official as to exactly what this spirit is, an examination of the League constitution and the League rules and regulations shows that the placing of great emphasis by a student on athletic programs in deciding what school to attend does indeed violate the spirit of the League. Section 6 of the League constitution states that the object of the League is "to foster among the public high schools of Virginia a broad program of supervised competitions and desirable school activities as an aid in the total education of pupils." Rules and Regulations § 26-1-1 states that their purpose is "to protect and preserve the educational values inherent in (interschool) activities." Obviously, the transfer of a student from one school to another solely to participate on the athletic teams of the latter school does not come within the spirit of these two sections. More specifically, § 27-10-1 (Proselyting Rule) states, "no member school or group of individuals representing the school shall subject a student from another school to undue influence by encouraging him to transfer from one school to another for League activities." Section 28-8-3(8) states, "any student who accepts material or financial inducement to attend a school for the purpose of engaging in athletics, regardless of the source of that material or financial inducement, shall be ineligible to represent his school in any interschool athletic contest." The sections quoted above serve to illustrate the League's concern that students not be subjected to pressures by coaches, fans, and other interested parties to attend one school over another. Of course, the objective of the transfer rule, which makes a student ineligible to compete for one semester where his move to a new school is not accompanied by a corresponding change in residence by his parents, is basically the same to deter those who would pressure a student to transfer and to deter the student from succumbing to such pressures by preventing him from becoming immediately eligible to compete at his new school.

All parties to this suit agree that this sort of recruiting of schoolchildren to engage in athletic competition may be considered harmful by the state, and that it may take steps to prevent this harm. Certainly, therefore, reasonable measures taken to reduce or remove the possible temptation to make a choice of schools on the basis of their respective athletic programs are justified.

At present a student who desires to engage in League-sponsored tournaments is not exposed to a potentially tempting choice of schools; of the public schools, he is usually eligible to attend only the one serving the district in which he lives, and private schools are ineligible for League tournament competition. If, however, private schools were admitted to the League, a student eligible to attend such schools could choose to attend any of them or to attend his public school, thus exposing himself to the potential pressures that the League seeks to forestall, and perhaps basing his ultimate choice on athletic considerations in violation of the above-mentioned League spirit. Nor would the transfer rule be effective to deal with such a situation, for that rule applies only to transfers from one secondary school to another, and not to the initial choice of a secondary school. Moreover, the transfer rule would also be inadequate to deal with the situation where a student's residence falls within the district of a private school as well as that of his public school. In such a case, the student could presumably transfer back and forth between the two schools without suffering any ineligibility again, exposing himself to those pressures and temptations against which the League attempts to protect its students.

Against this background, the League's exclusion of private schools must be viewed as one of several reasonable steps taken to combat the serious problem of adolescent students being subjected to and perhaps succumbing to pressures to attend one school over another on the basis of athletic considerations. That there was no evidence presented to establish the existence of such a problem in Virginia is not important, for not only do several provisions of the League's constitution and rules and regulations show clearly the League's concern with the possible occurrence of such activities, but experience elsewhere has shown that this is indeed a problem that needs to be addressed. A statutory discrimination will not be set aside if any state of facts reasonably may be conceived to justify it.

Also inconsequential is the fact that there may be means of addressing the problem other than by blanket exclusion of private schools that may result in less hardship to students at private schools such as O'Connell. The task of the courts in passing on the validity of a classification under the standard Equal Protection test is not to determine if it is the best way, or even a good way, of accomplishing a legitimate state objective. Our task is only to determine whether the classification makes sense in light of the purpose sought to be achieved; beyond that point, the wisdom of the state must be allowed to prevail. Having found that the classification here challenged is rationally related to a legitimate state objective, this court has completed its consideration of the matter.

Because we find that the League may constitutionally exclude private schools from League membership, we do not address League arguments concerning burden of proof, nor do we address the League contention that the admission of a private sectarian school such as O'Connell would violate the Establishment Clause of the First Amendment.

Accordingly, the judgment is reversed.

 For an extended version of the case and review questions to test your understanding of the material, please go to www.HumanKinetics.com/CaseStudiesInSportLaw.

Doe v. Taylor Independent School District

15 F.3d 443 (5th Cir. 1994)

Jane Doe was sexually molested by her high school teacher in Taylor, Texas. Defendant Eddy Lankford, principal of Taylor High, and defendant Mike Caplinger, superintendent of the Taylor Independent School District, were sued in their supervisory capacity by Jane Doe for permitting violations of her substantive due process right to bodily integrity. The district court denied their claim of qualified immunity, and they have filed this interlocutory appeal on that issue. We hold, first, that schoolchildren do have a liberty interest in their bodily integrity that is protected by the Due Process Clause of the Fourteenth Amendment and that physical sexual abuse by a school employee violates that right. Second, we hold that school officials can be held liable for supervisory failures that result in the molestation of a schoolchild if those failures manifest a deliberate indifference to the constitutional rights of that child. Next, we conclude that each of these legal principles was clearly established in 1987, when the violations took place. Finally, in analyzing whether Caplinger and Lankford fulfilled the duty that they owed to Jane Doe, we reverse the district court's denial of immunity to defendant Caplinger, but we affirm its denial of immunity to Lankford.

Defendant Jesse Lynn Stroud, a 20-year veteran of Texas's public education system, was employed by the Taylor Independent School District as a biology teacher and assistant coach from 1981 until 1987. It was no secret within the school community that Coach Stroud behaved inappropriately toward a number of young female students over the course of his employment at Taylor High.

Defendant Eddy Lankford became the principal of Taylor High in August 1983. By the fall semester of 1985, complaints about Stroud's behavior had reached his office through various channels.

All of this behavior occurred before defendant Mike Caplinger ever moved to Taylor or worked for the Taylor Independent School District. Caplinger became the superintendent of the Taylor ISD in July 1986; Lankford did not inform

Caplinger of any problems—real or potential—with Stroud or with his pattern of conduct.

Plaintiff Jane Doe entered Taylor High as a freshman in August 1986; she was a student in Stroud's biology class. Stroud began his seduction of Doe by writing personal—often suggestive—comments on her homework and test papers. The two began exchanging notes and telephoning each other; he often walked her to class. Stroud took Doe and her friends to lunch during the school day and bought alcoholic beverages for them. He did not require Doe to do classwork or to take tests, yet she received high grades in Stroud's class. Not surprisingly, all of this attention flattered Doe, and she developed a "crush" on Stroud. By late fall, Stroud was touching and kissing Jane Doe. In late March or early April 1987, Stroud and Doe had intercourse for the first time. She was 15 years old. Stroud was her first sexual partner.

Their romantic relationship was common knowledge within the Taylor High community, not only among students, but also among the faculty and the parents of many students.

On Stroud's performance evaluation by Lankford for the 1986-87 academic year, however, there was nothing to indicate that Stroud's performance was anything less than fully satisfactory. Indeed, Lankford still had not even informally documented any incident or pattern of conduct relating to Stroud.

Caplinger was by now aware of the rumors about Stroud and Doe and the reports of his favoritism in the classroom. He contacted the school's attorney to discuss the situation concerning Stroud, and, apparently at Caplinger's instruction, Lankford contacted the Texas Education Authority to see if there were any reports about Stroud concerning any inappropriate behavior at the schools where he had previously been employed. Lankford was told that there were no reports specifically naming Stroud, but that the Authority had received an anonymous tip about an inappropriate relationship between a coach and a student at Taylor High.

In July 1987, Doe's parents discovered photographs of Stroud among Doe's possessions. Doe's parents immediately scheduled a meeting with Caplinger. Caplinger confirmed to them that he was aware of rumors concerning Stroud and Doe. After speaking with Doe's parents, Caplinger spoke with Jane Doe privately in his office. He showed her the photographs her parents had just presented to him and inquired about the nature of her relationship with Stroud. Doe suggested that the notes on the photos were just "friendly gestures." She explicitly denied any sexual relations with Stroud.

Caplinger called Lankford after the meeting with the Does, who in turn called Stroud. Upon receiving the message, Stroud sought out Lankford; Stroud vehemently denied any sexual involvement with Doe. For the first time, Lankford spoke of disciplinary consequences. Lankford suggested to Stroud that he resign or take an in-school suspension (which would relieve him of his classroom duties), but Stroud refused. Caplinger and Lankford warned Stroud to keep his distance from Jane Doe, and that he would be fired if something was going on. No further action was taken; however; the meeting that Caplinger had promised to schedule never took place, and Stroud did not hear from either Lankford or Caplinger again until October 6, the day he was suspended from employment. When classes resumed in the late summer of 1987, Stroud's sexual advances toward her resumed as well, and soon thereafter they began having intercourse again. Lankford admits that he watched Stroud no more closely than he previously had. The sexual contact continued into the fall of Jane Doe's sophomore year, until October 5, when Doe's mother found more love letters from Stroud among Jane's possessions. The Does then consulted their family lawyer, who agreed to discuss the matter with Jane. Upon meeting with Jane, the attorney learned the truth about her sexual involvement with Stroud. Doe explained that she had kept the matter a secret because she feared the repercussions of disclosure.

The attorney reported the information to Caplinger at once. Caplinger ordered that Stroud be immediately suspended from employment. Stroud later resigned his position and pled guilty to criminal charges stemming from his molestation of Jane Doe.

Jane Doe brought this section 1983 civil rights lawsuit against Stroud, the school district, Superintendent Caplinger, and Principal Lankford. She charged *inter alia* that these defendants, while acting under color of state law, deprived her of her constitutional rights guaranteed by the Fourteenth Amendment's Due Process and Equal Protection Clauses, in violation of 42 U.S.C. § 1983. Following the denial of their motions for summary judgment on qualified immunity grounds, Caplinger and Lankford filed this appeal. Both contend that they are entitled to qualified immunity because (1) Jane Doe was not deprived of any constitutional right when she was sexually molested by Coach Stroud; (2) even if Doe was deprived of a constitutional right, they owed her no duty in connection with this constitutional violation; (3) even if Doe was deprived of a constitutional right and they owed her a duty with respect to that right, these issues of law were not clearly established in 1987 when the violations took place; and (4) in any event, their response to the situation satisfied any duty that they owed to Doe.

The first step in deciding whether Caplinger and Lankford are entitled to claim qualified immunity from this lawsuit is to determine whether the Constitution, through the Fourteenth Amendment's substantive due process component, protects school-age children attending public schools from sexual abuse inflicted by a school employee. Section 1983 imposes liability for violations of rights protected by the Constitution, not for violations of duties of care arising out of tort law. To state a cause of action under § 1983 for violation of the Due Process Clause, plaintiffs must show that they have asserted a recognized liberty or property interest within the purview of the Fourteenth Amendment, and that they were intentionally or recklessly deprived of that interest, even temporarily, under color of state law. The Supreme Court has expanded the definition of liberty beyond the core textual meaning of that term to include not only the privileges expressly enumerated by the Bill of Rights, but also the fundamental rights implicit in the concept of ordered liberty and deeply rooted in this nation's history and tradition under the Due Process Clause.

The Due Process Clause of the Fourteenth Amendment provides that no state shall deprive a person of life, liberty, or property without due process of law. The Supreme Court has noted that although a literal reading of the clause might suggest that it governs only the procedures by which a state may deprive persons of liberty, for at least 105 years, at least since the clause has been understood to contain a substantive component as well. This substantive component of the Due Process Clause protects individual liberty against certain government actions regardless of the fairness of the procedures used to implement them.

Jane Doe's substantive due process claim is grounded on the premise that schoolchildren have a liberty interest in their bodily integrity that is protected by the Due Process Clause of the Fourteenth Amendment and upon the premise that physical sexual abuse by a school employee violates that right. We have also held that the infliction of corporal punishment in public schools is a deprivation of substantive due process when it is arbitrary, capricious, or wholly unrelated to the legitimate state goal of maintaining an atmosphere conducive to learning.

If the Constitution protects a schoolchild against being tied to a chair or against arbitrary paddlings, then surely the Constitution protects a schoolchild from physical sexual abuse—here, sexually fondling a 15-year-old schoolgirl and statutory rape—by a public schoolteacher. Stroud's sexual abuse of Jane Doe is not contested by the defendants. Thus, Jane Doe clearly was deprived of a liberty interest recognized under the substantive due process component of the Fourteenth Amendment. It is incontrovertible that bodily integrity is necessarily violated when a state actor sexually abuses a schoolchild and that such misconduct deprives the child of rights vouchsafed by the Fourteenth Amendment. Obviously, there is never any justification for sexually molesting a schoolchild, and thus, no state interest, analogous to the punitive and disciplinary objectives attendant to corporal punishment, which might support it.

Having concluded that Stroud's physical sexual abuse of Jane Doe violated her constitutional right to substantive due process, we next must decide whether school officials, like the appellants in this case, owe any duty to a schoolchild when a subordinate violates that child's constitutional rights. Section 1983 provides a claim against anyone who, under color of state law, deprives another of his or her constitutional rights.

This circuit has held that supervisors can be liable for gross negligence or deliberate indifference to violations of their subordinates. Based on these cases, this circuit adopts the following standard:

> A supervisory school official can be held personally liable for a subordinate's violation of an elementary or secondary school student's constitutional right to bodily integrity in physical sexual abuse cases if the plaintiff establishes that (1) the defendant learned of facts or a pattern of inappropriate sexual behavior by a subordinate pointing plainly toward the conclusion that the subordinate was sexually abusing the student, and (2) the defendant demonstrated deliberate indifference toward the constitutional rights of the student by failing to take action that was obviously necessary to prevent or stop the abuse, and (3) such failure caused a constitutional injury to the student.

We must next consider these legal principles in the context of qualified immunity. Under the shield of qualified immunity, Caplinger and Lankford cannot be held liable under section 1983 unless (1) Jane Doe's liberty interest under the substantive due process component of the Fourteenth Amendment and (2) Caplinger's and Lankford's duty with respect to Jane Doe's constitutional right were clearly established at the time these events took place. For a constitutional right to be clearly established, the contours of the right must be sufficiently clear that a reasonable official would understand that what he is doing violates that right. The term "clearly established" does not necessarily refer to commanding precedent that is factually on all-fours with the case at bar, or that holds the very action in question unlawful. Rather, a constitutional right is clearly established if, in the light of preexisting law, the unlawfulness is apparent. Put another way, officials must observe general, well-developed legal principles. Lankford and Caplinger argue, first, that the underlying constitutional right, to be free of sexual abuse, was not clearly established in 1987. Second, they assert that even if the underlying constitutional right was clearly established in 1987, their duty under § 1983 not to be deliberately indifferent to a subordinate's violation of that right was not clearly established.

The contours of a student's substantive due process right to be free from sexual abuse and violations of her bodily integrity were clearly established in 1987. In 1987 this court held that it was clearly established in 1985 that the Due Process Clause protects a schoolchild from being lashed to a chair for the better part of two days for instructional purposes. This case involves similarly egregious and outrageous conduct. Indeed, this much seems crystal clear: No reasonable public school official in 1987 would have assumed that he could, with constitutional immunity, sexually molest a minor student.

Not only was the underlying violation clearly established in 1987, but Lankford's and Caplinger's duty with respect to that violation was also clearly established at that time. Prior cases, although arising under somewhat different circumstances, also acknowledged a duty on the part of supervisors not to be grossly negligent or deliberately indifferent to constitutional violations perpetrated by their subordinates.

In the face of this precedent, Lankford and Caplinger point to no authority from this circuit involving school officials, which would enable them to reasonably believe, in 1987, that they could be deliberately indifferent to their subordinate's violation of a student's constitutional rights and escape supervisory liability under § 1983. Our earlier cases arguably announced a broader duty on the part of school officials than we adopt today. By narrowing the duty that § 1983 imposes on supervisors, the courts have not affected its status as clearly established.

Having established that Jane Doe's constitutional right to bodily integrity and the appellants' duty with respect to that right were clearly established in 1987 when these events occurred, we must determine whether, on the record before us, Lankford and Caplinger have established that they satisfied their duty to Doe, and are thus entitled to summary judgment as a matter of law.

The plaintiff in this case has adduced clear summary judgment evidence of deliberate indifference by defendant Lankford toward her constitutional rights. By 1987, Lankford had certainly received notice of a pattern of inappropriate behavior that had been committed by Stroud that suggested misconduct of a sexual nature. He had spoken with Stroud two years earlier, in 1985, about being too friendly with a particular female student. He had received complaints from parents about Stroud's favoritism toward certain girls

in the classroom. The school librarian reported Stroud's inappropriate behavior with female students to Lankford on two occasions, and at one point described the incident she witnessed as child molestation. More importantly, Lankford received knowledge that Stroud was directing his inappropriate sexual behavior specifically toward Doe. A jury could find that Lankford then received a clear signal that Stroud and Doe were engaged in a sexual relationship when Brittani B. gave him the valentine in February 1987. Later that year, Lankford received reports about Stroud's inappropriate behavior with Doe and learned that Doe's parents had discovered Stroud's autographed photographs in Doe's possession. Thus, under the facts construed in the light most favorable to Jane Doe and considering all the information Lankford received about Stroud's relationship with Doe, she has satisfied the first prong of the test with respect to defendant Lankford—knowledge of facts or a pattern of inappropriate sexual behavior by Stroud pointing plainly toward the conclusion that he was sexually abusing Doe.

Doe has also illustrated, in a manner sufficient to survive a summary judgment motion, that Lankford demonstrated deliberate indifference to the offensive acts by failing to take action that was obviously necessary to prevent or stop Stroud's abuse. When certain parents complained about Stroud's favoritism, Lankford suggested that their children were jealous of the favorite students. Lankford similarly dismissed the librarian's report of child molestation. In perhaps the most striking example of his apathy, he responded to Brittani B.'s presentation of the valentine—which he admitted appeared to bear Stroud's handwriting—by transferring Brittani (not Jane Doe) out of Stroud's class. He never bothered to discuss the valentine incident with Caplinger, Stroud, Doe, or Doe's parents. He did not record any of these complaints of inappropriate conduct in Stroud's personnel file. He did not take the obvious steps of removing Doe from Stroud's class and directing Stroud to stay away from Doe. Both Stroud and Doe stated that they did not begin having sexual intercourse until late March or early April 1987. A jury could reasonably conclude that had Lankford taken actions that were obviously necessary in response to the valentine—indeed, if he had responded at all—the relationship might have been derailed at that point and the violation of Jane Doe's rights would not have been as severe or prolonged. Thus, Jane Doe has, in a manner sufficient to withstand a motion for summary judgment, stated a claim under § 1983 that defendant Lankford was deliberately indifferent to his subordinate's violation of her constitutional right to bodily integrity.

With respect to whether defendant Caplinger is immune from this lawsuit, however, the evidence presented tells a different story. The first time Caplinger heard of any potential misconduct by Stroud was when he received the report from Mickey Miller in February 1987. He promptly notified Lankford and instructed him to speak with Stroud about the incident. There is no evidence that Lankford informed Caplinger at that time about Stroud's past behavior, and it is undisputed that Lankford never documented any of the reports he had received about Stroud. Caplinger did not receive any other reports about Stroud until June 1987, when two parents reported the Corn Festival incident to him. Again, Caplinger promptly responded by contacting the parents of one of the allegedly misbehaving students reportedly at the festival. He was assured that the accused student was not even at the event. We cannot say that Caplinger's decision not to pursue the investigation further, after the parents assured him that their child had not even attended the Corn Festival, exhibited deliberate indifference.

When Doe's parents met with Caplinger concerning the photographs of Stroud in July 1987, Caplinger again responded appropriately, if ineffectively, to the situation. He met with Jane Doe privately and questioned her about her relationship with Stroud. He also met with Stroud, verbally reprimanded him about the inappropriate comments on the photographs, warned him to keep his distance from Jane Doe, and informed him of the consequences if the misconduct continued. Although after the July photograph incident Caplinger had received notice of a pattern of inappropriate sexual behavior sufficient to satisfy the first prong of the test, he certainly did not respond to the misconduct with deliberate indifference. He instructed Lankford to speak with Stroud about the incident at the basketball game; he personally investigated the report concerning the Corn Fes-

tival report; and he met with Stroud immediately after learning of the photographs, reprimanded him for his conduct, and unequivocally warned him of the consequences if any further misconduct was reported. His actions were ineffective, but not deliberately indifferent. Summary judgment should have been granted to defendant Caplinger on the grounds of qualified immunity.

The plaintiff also asserts that Stroud's behavior toward her violated her constitutional rights under the Equal Protection Clause of the Fourteenth Amendment. Doe advances three separate equal protection theories, based on two different sorts of behavior. She first argues that the physical sexual abuse to which Stroud subjected her constituted sexual harassment, which she argues is offensive to the Equal Protection Clause. Second, she contends that Stroud's classroom favoritism toward her also constituted sexual harassment. Finally, she argues that the classroom favoritism constituted the more typical form of disparate gender discrimination, which the Supreme Court has found to be prohibited by the Equal Protection Clause. Following these theories, Doe argues that Caplinger and Lankford should be liable because, as in the case of her due process claim, they were deliberately indifferent to the unconstitutional conduct that caused her injury.

Assuming that Stroud sexually abused Doe, which the defendants do not contest, Stroud violated Doe's substantive due process rights as a matter of law. Doe does not claim that the damages that she could recover from Lankford based on Stroud's alleged violation of her equal protection rights would be any more extensive than the damages that she could recover based on the substantive due process violation. Nor does she argue that, or show how, Caplinger could be supervisorily liable for equal protection violations predicated on Stroud's sexual abuse when he is not supervisorily liable for substantive due process violations involving the same conduct. Consequently, we need not reach the question of whether Doe states an equal protection claim.

The sole question before us is the propriety of the district court's denial of qualified immunity to the appellant school officials. The school officials' main argument that the liability of a school official for ignoring a subordinate's sexual abuse of a 15-year-old student was not clearly established in 1987.

Appellants, however, agree that by 1987 the Constitution clearly protected the most hardened criminal inmate from abuse by his guard and imposed liability on the guard's supervisor who was consciously indifferent to such abuse. Similarly, appellants cannot seriously contest that the § 1983 liability of a police chief was not clearly established in 1987 when the chief was consciously indifferent to his officer's physical abuse of a citizen. In short, supervisory liability for deliberate indifference to constitutional violations committed by subordinates was clearly established when the events in this case occurred. Consequently, the school officials' argument that with constitutional immunity they could ignore the teacher/coach's physical sexual abuse of an impressionable 15-year-old student is, as a practical matter perverse, and, as a legal matter, not supported by the case law. Such an argument neither legally nor logically makes any sense.

For the reasons stated above, we affirm the district court's order denying qualified immunity to defendant Lankford and reverse the district court's order denying qualified immunity to defendant Caplinger. We also remand this case to the district court for further proceedings consistent with this opinion. AFFIRMED in part, REVERSED in part, and REMANDED.

For an extended version of the case and review questions to test your understanding of the material, please go to www.HumanKinetics.com/CaseStudiesInSportLaw.

Hall v. The University of Minnesota

530 F.Supp. 104 (D. Minn. 1982)

This court is presented with a serious and troubling question concerning the academic standing and athletic eligibility of a University of Minnesota varsity basketball player. The plaintiff in this action is a 21-year-old black senior at the defendant University of Minnesota. He is also a formidable basketball player who, up to this season, played for the defendant University of Minnesota men's intercollegiate varsity basketball team. He is before the court seeking an injunction ordering the university to admit him to a degree program, a prerequisite to the athletic eligibility he lost.

The plaintiff was enrolled in a nonbaccalaureate degree program at the defendant University's General College. His program terminated on the accumulation of approximately 90 credits. Once his program terminated, the plaintiff attempted to enroll in a "degree program" at the University Without Walls (hereafter UWW), a college within the defendant University, and at the General College. The plaintiff was denied admission twice at UWW and once at the General College. By failing to enroll in a "degree program," the plaintiff lost his eligibility to play on the defendant university's basketball team according to Charles Liesenfelt, Director of Registration, Records & Scheduling. Liesenfelt contends that in order for the plaintiff to remain eligible to participate on the basketball team, he must be a "candidate for a degree" under Rule 1, § 1, A. Part Two, of the Big Ten Handbook.

The plaintiff does meet the Big Ten eligibility standards with respect to grade point average and credit accumulation, but unless he is enrolled as a "candidate for a degree," he is ineligible to practice or play on the defendant university's basketball team. According to the coach of the university basketball team, the plaintiff is the only player he has known who has met the grade and credit criteria of the Big Ten but has been refused admission into a degree program. The plaintiff filed this action on December 15, 1981, alleging that the defendants rejected his two applications to the UWW without affording him due process and in bad faith in an arbitrary and capricious manner. On December 29, 1981, the plaintiff moved this court for a preliminary injunction compelling his admission to a degree program. Unless the plaintiff is declared eligible for intercollegiate basketball competition on January 4, 1982, he will be ineligible to participate on the basketball team for all of the winter quarter of 1982, which comprises all but two or three games of the remaining season.

According to the evidence, if the plaintiff is accorded the opportunity to represent the University of Minnesota in intercollegiate varsity basketball competition during winter quarter of 1982, his senior year, he will have a significant opportunity to be a second-round choice in the National Basketball Association draft this year, thereby acquiring a probable guarantee of his first year's compensation as a player in the National Basketball Association. If the plaintiff is denied the opportunity to participate in intercollegiate basketball competition on behalf of the University of Minnesota during winter quarter 1982, his chances for a professional career in basketball will be impaired; and it will be extremely unlikely that his compensation as a first-year player in the National Basketball Association will be guaranteed. The evidence indicates that without an opportunity to play during the winter quarter of 1982, the plaintiff would likely be a sixth-round choice in the National Basketball Association draft.

This court has no hesitation in stating that the underlying reason for the plaintiff's desire to be enrolled in a degree program at the defendant University is the enhancement of his chances of becoming a professional basketball player. The plaintiff will probably never attain a degree should he be admitted to a degree program since the National Basketball Association draft occurs in April 1982, well before the plaintiff could accumulate sufficient credits for a degree. The plaintiff was a highly-recruited basketball player out of high school who was recruited to come to the University of Minnesota to be a basketball player and not a scholar. His academic record reflects that he has lived up to those expectations, as do the academic records of many of the athletes presented to this court.

The plaintiff applied for admission to the UWW twice, once in August 1981 and once in October 1981. In each case, the UWW admissions committee determined, based on the plaintiff's application, that he should be admitted to the UWW introductory program. In each case, the directors of the program (further up in the hierarchy of the UWW) intervened in the admissions process and effectively directed the admissions committee to reject plaintiff's application. This interference by the directors never occurred in any other case as to any other student.

Prior to the intervention of the directors, one of the UWW directors contacted Dean Lupton of the General College concerning the plaintiff. The director summarized the information conveyed by Dean Lupton in a confidential memorandum regarding the plaintiff. The memorandum noted that the following factors bore on the plaintiff's application:

1. The "political aspects" of admitting plaintiff
2. Plaintiff's "substantial" travel record (one weekend trip to Chicago in fall quarter 1981)
3. The plaintiff had earned *A*s in courses he was not eligible to be in
4. The General College had found it necessary to monitor plaintiff's work through a Professor Harris
5. The plaintiff improperly turned in work on Regent's letterhead stationery
6. The plaintiff turned in work done by others as his
7. That every W (withdrawal) on plaintiff's transcript was originally an N (equivalent to an F)
8. That within four weeks of the commencement of classes, plaintiff typically had earned a grade of N
9. That plaintiff had put through fake approval forms on more than one occasion

The memorandum further states that Dean Lupton indicated that the plaintiff would not be accepted into a degree program at the General College, even though the plaintiff had not even applied at the time. After receiving the above information, the director contacted another director and they in turn conveyed this information to the admissions committee and effectively instructed the committee to reject the plaintiff's application. Until plaintiff's case arose, the UWW admissions committee decision to admit had been considered final. This memorandum was passed on to a successor director who, after the plaintiff reapplied and was again accepted by the admissions committee, effectively vetoed the decision of the admissions committee.

Opposed to the procedures set forth above used in processing the plaintiff's two applications to the UWW, the UWW distributed a pamphlet explaining the policies and procedures of admission. This pamphlet notes the following:

1. The information you present in your application will determine whether you are admitted to UWW.
2. Admissions decisions are based on your responses to the application form that appears at the back of this booklet.
3. Your application will be reviewed and acted upon by an admissions committee made up of UWW advisors. You will be notified in writing of the committee's decision. If you are not accepted, the reasons for the decision will be explained. . . .
4. The admissions committee will determine which applicants will be admitted for enrollment in the Introductory Period.

With regard to items 1 and 2, the UWW's faculty director testified that these statements were the correct policy with respect to processing UWW admission applications. He further stated that applicants to the UWW are supposed to be judged solely on the basis of their application form.

It seems apparent that the plaintiff was not judged solely on the basis of his applications and the information therein. Each time the admissions committee reviewed the plaintiff's application, they recommended that he be admitted. After the intervention of the directors and the communication of the information outlined in the above-mentioned memorandum, the plaintiff was denied admission. However, in both of the rejection letters sent to the plaintiff, none of the allegations noted in the memorandum were listed as reasons for the plaintiff's failure to gain admission to the UWW.

The plaintiff asserts that he has been denied his right to due process of law arising under the Fourteenth Amendment. Due process protects life, liberty, and property. Protected property interests are usually created and defined by sources such as state laws. A student's interest in attending a university is a property right protected by due process. The defendant asserts that while in cases of expulsion, public education may be a property right, in cases of nonadmission, public education is but a mere privilege. However, the right versus privilege distinction has long been abandoned in the area of due process. And in any event, even though the plaintiff was denied admission, the circumstances of this case make it more like an expulsion case than a nonadmission case. The plaintiff lost existing scholarship rights; he cannot enroll in another college without sitting out one year of competition under athletic rules; and although he has attended the defendant university for several years, he may no longer register for day classes at the defendant university.

But to say that due process applies in the area of a student's interest in attending a university does not finish the analysis. One must answer the question of what process is due. Due process is flexible and calls for such procedural protection as the particular situation demands. Factors balanced to determine what process is due are (1) the private interest affected by the action, (2) the risk of an erroneous deprivation of such interest through the procedures used and the value of additional procedural safeguards, and (3) the government's interest involved, including fiscal and administrative burdens.

The private interest at stake here, although ostensibly academic, is the plaintiff's ability to obtain a no-cut contract with the National Basketball Association. The bachelor of arts, while a mark of achievement and distinction, does not in and of itself assure the applicant a means of earning a living. This applicant seems to recognize this and has opted to use his college career as a means of entry into professional sports as do many college athletes. His basketball career will be little affected by the absence or presence of a bachelor of arts degree. This plaintiff has put all of his eggs into the basket of professional basketball. The plaintiff would suffer a substantial loss if his career objectives were impaired. The government's interest (i.e., the defendant university's interest) is the administrative burden of requiring a hearing or other due process safeguards for every rejection of every student who applies to the university. This burden would be tremendous and this court would not require the defendant university to shoulder it.

The key factor in this case that weighs heavily in the plaintiff's favor is the risk of an erroneous deprivation given the nature of the proceedings used in processing the plaintiff's application. This court is aware that in the area of academic decisions, judicial interference must be minimal. However, an academic decision is based on established academic criteria. In this case, the plaintiff's applications to the UWW were treated very differently than all other applications. The directors intervened in the process and provided the admissions committee with allegations concerning the plaintiff's conduct, a facet of the proceedings that taints this "academic" process and turns it into something much like a disciplinary proceeding. Given this aspect of the proceedings, it would appear that the plaintiff should have at least been notified that allegations had been made regarding his conduct so that he could have presented evidence in his own behalf. Without this safeguard, there exists a chance that the plaintiff may have been wrongfully accused of actions that then form the basis for his rejection.

This is not to say that all applicants who are rejected by the defendant university must be given an opportunity to rebut evidence used in evaluating a college application; however, if the defendant university intends to interject evidence concerning allegations of improper conduct of the applicant into the admissions process, it must provide the applicant an opportunity to give his or her side of the story. Finally, one must consider all that has occurred in light of the standards utilized by the courts in this circuit in evaluating the propriety of issuing a preliminary injunction. Four factors determine whether a preliminary injunction should issue. They are (1) the threat of irreparable harm to the moving party, (2) the state of balance between that harm and the injury that granting the injunction will inflict on other parties, (3) the public interest, and (4) the probability that the movant will succeed on the merits of the claim.

With respect to the first factor, if the plaintiff is not eligible to play basketball by January 4, 1982, he will not play his senior year. This poses a substantial threat to his chances for a no-cut contract in the National Basketball Association, according to his coach, and his overall aspirations regarding a career as a professional basketball player. It would be difficult indeed to measure the loss to the plaintiff in terms of dollars and cents. The

injury is substantial and not really capable of an accurate monetary prediction. Thus, it would be irreparable.

The harm to the other parties (i.e., the defendant university) is difficult to assess. On the one hand, this court doubts that the university men's intercollegiate varsity basketball team and coaching staff would characterize the reinstatement of the plaintiff to the team in terms of "harm." But the defendant university academic wing argues that if this court orders the plaintiff into a degree program, its academic standards and integrity would be undermined. The plaintiff and his fellow athletes were never recruited on the basis of scholarship and it was never envisioned they would be on the Dean's List. Consequently we must view with some skepticism the defendant university's claim regarding academic integrity. This court is not saying that athletes are incapable of scholarship; however, they are given little incentive to be scholars and few persons care how the student athlete performs academically, including many of the athletes themselves. The exceptionally talented student athlete is led to perceive the basketball, football, and other athletic programs as farm teams and proving grounds for professional sports leagues. It well may be true that a good academic program for the athlete is made virtually impossible by the demands of their sport at the college level. If this situation causes harm to the university, it is because they have fostered it, and the institution rather than the individual should suffer the consequence.

It appears from the record that there is a "tug of war" going on over this plaintiff. The academicians are pulling toward higher standards of achievement for all students while the athletic department must tug in the direction of fielding teams who contribute to paying a substantial share of the university's budget. In this tug of war the academic department will suffer substantially no ill effects if it loses. On the other hand, the athletic department, directors, coaches, and personnel under this system are charged with the responsibility of at least maintaining and fielding teams that are capable of competing with the best in their conference or in the nation. This court is not called upon to determine any long-term solution to the dilemma posed. It is called upon to determine if the rights of an individual caught up in the struggle have been violated.

The only perceivable harm to the defendant university would result from the fact that the National Collegiate Athletic Association (NCAA), of which the defendant university is a member, has rules that permit certain sanctions to be leveled upon the defendant university should a player be declared eligible under a court order that is later vacated, stayed, reversed, and so on. This rule defines sanctions including the vacation of the athlete's records for the period for which the athlete played, the forfeiture of games by the team, the declaration of ineligibility of the team for post-season tournaments, to the return of television receipts for games that the athlete played in. However, in this regard, the defendant university's destiny is in its own hands. The university does not have to appeal this order if it is fearful of the sanctions that might be imposed by the NCAA. And the defendant university's lawyer is of the opinion that the NCAA could not force an appeal. Therefore, an appeal with all of the usual uncertainties accompanying it is not mandated. It would be the defendant university's choice whether it wants to risk these sanctions at this time. Presumably, some impartial arbitrator at the defendant university will make the decision of whether the defendant university will risk these potential sanctions.

The public interest is difficult to assess. It depends on whether the public prefers highly-tuned athletes who devote most of their waking hours to honing their athletic skills or whether it wants an individual with the plaintiff's athletic abilities to be required to make substantial scholastic achievement. There is no doubt that the public does have an interest but until the universities themselves clarify their position on the matter, the court must assume that the public interest is equally ambivalent.

The fourth factor concerns the probability that the plaintiff will succeed ultimately on his suit. During the two weeks since this suit was filed, the plaintiff has revealed some disturbing facts regarding the defendant university's handling of the plaintiff's applications to the UWW and the General College. Besides the unusual procedures at the UWW, which forms the basis of this injunction and which has already been discussed, this court has considered the dean of the General College's testimony regarding the plaintiff's application to the General College. Dean Lupton testified that the plaintiff's summer school credits were not good evidence in determining whether the plaintiff has "shown progress" in his academic career because these courses were not General College courses. During the summer of 1981, the plaintiff enrolled in 30 credits of classes at the defendant university and successfully completed 26. The plaintiff received three "As," four "Bs," one "C," and one "satisfactory." Dean Lupton and the defendants' other witnesses were unable to satisfactorily explain to this court why the plaintiff's most recent academic endeavor would not be good evidence in assessing his capabilities and present attitudes or why they did not evidence "progress in his academic career." Although these courses were not the most esoteric in their nature, they were offered for credit by the defendant university. The defendant university academic wing argues that, during the two quarters prior to applying to the General College, the plaintiff only completed 48% of the credits he attempted. If the General College would have considered the plaintiff's summer scholastic activity, his completion rate for the two quarters prior to his application would have been 72%.

This court is of the opinion that the plaintiff has shown a substantial probability of success on at least his claim regarding the UWW. It is conceivable that the UWW may have had reason to deny the plaintiff admission to its degree program. However, the manner in which the UWW processed the plaintiff's application strongly suggests that he has been treated disparately and in a manner violative of due process. The plaintiff was given no notice nor any opportunity to answer the allegations leveled against him by the dean of the General College. It is equally conceivable that the plaintiff would have had a "good answer" to these charges had he been given an opportunity to respond.

Balancing all of the above factors, this court concludes that an injunction should issue requiring the defendant university to admit the plaintiff into a degree program on January 4, 1982, and to declare him eligible to compete in intercollegiate varsity basketball competition.

 For an extended version of the case and review questions to test your understanding of the material, please go to www.HumanKinetics.com/CaseStudiesInSportLaw.

Hill v. National Collegiate Athletic Association

26 Cal.Rptr.2d 834 (Ca. 1994)

The National Collegiate Athletic Association (NCAA) sponsors and regulates intercollegiate athletic competition throughout the United States. Under the NCAA drug-testing program, randomly selected college student athletes competing in postseason championships and football bowl games are required to provide samples of their urine under closely monitored conditions. Urine samples are chemically analyzed for proscribed substances. Athletes testing positive are subject to disqualification.

Plaintiffs, who were student athletes attending Stanford University (Stanford) at the time of trial, sued the NCAA, contending its drug-testing program violated their right to privacy secured by Article I, § 1, of the California Constitution. Stanford intervened in the suit and adopted plaintiffs' position. Finding the NCAA program to be an invasion of plaintiffs' right to privacy, the Superior Court permanently enjoined its enforcement against plaintiffs and other Stanford athletes. The court of appeal upheld the injunction.

By its nature, sports competition demands highly disciplined physical activity conducted in accordance with a special set of social norms. Unlike the general population, student athletes undergo frequent physical examinations, reveal their bodily and medical conditions to coaches and trainers, and often dress and undress in same-sex locker rooms. In so doing, they normally and reasonably forgo a measure of their privacy in exchange for the personal and professional benefits of extracurricular athletics.

A student athlete's already diminished expectation of privacy is outweighed by the NCAA's legitimate regulatory objectives in conducting testing for proscribed drugs. As a sponsor and regulator of sporting events, the NCAA has self-evident interests in ensuring fair and vigorous competition, as well as protecting the health and safety of student athletes. These interests justify a set of drug-testing rules reasonably calculated to achieve drug-free athletic competition.

NCAA rules contain elements designed to accomplish this purpose, including (1) advance notice to athletes of testing procedures and written consent to testing, (2) random selection of athletes actually engaged in competition, (3) monitored collection of a sample of a selected athlete's urine in order to avoid substitution or contamination, and (4) chain of custody, limited disclosure, and other procedures designed to safeguard the confidentiality of the testing process and its outcome. As formulated, the NCAA regulations do not offend the legitimate privacy interests of student athletes.

The NCAA, a private association of more than 1,000 colleges and universities, was created to foster and regulate intercollegiate athletic competition. NCAA rules are made by member institutions, acting collectively and democratically at national conventions. Member institutions and college athletes are required to abide by NCAA rules as a condition to participation in NCAA-sponsored events.

The NCAA prohibits student athlete use of chemical substances in several categories, including (1) psychomotor and nervous system stimulants, (2) anabolic steroids, (3) alcohol and beta blockers (in rifle events only), (4) diuretics, and (5) street drugs. At the time of trial, sympathomimetic amines (a class of substances included in many medications) were also included in the NCAA's list of banned drugs. The NCAA has amended its rules to delete sympathomimetic amines from its list of proscribed substances.

Student athletes seeking to participate in NCAA-sponsored competition are required to sign a three-part statement and consent form. New forms must be executed at the beginning of each year of competition. The first part of the form affirms that the signator meets NCAA eligibility regulations and that he or she has duly reported any known violations of those regulations.

The second part of the form, titled Buckley Amendment Consent, authorizes limited disclosure of the form, the results of NCAA drug tests, academic transcripts, financial aid records, and other information pertaining to NCAA eligibility, to authorized representatives of the athlete's institution and conference, as well as to the NCAA. The items of information to be disclosed are identified in the statement as education records pursuant to the federal Family Educational Rights and Privacy Act of 1974 20 U.S.C. § 1232g.

The final part of the form is a Drug Testing Consent in which the athlete in essence allows the NCAA to drug test. The Drug Testing Consent contains dated signature spaces for the student athlete and, if the student athlete is a minor, a parent. Failure to sign the three-part form, including the Drug Testing Consent, renders the student athlete ineligible to participate in NCAA-sponsored competition.

Drug testing is conducted at NCAA athletic events by urinalysis. All student athletes in championship events or postseason bowl games are potentially subject to testing. Particular athletes are chosen for testing according to plans that may include random selection or other selection criteria such as playing time, team position, place of finish, or suspicion of drug use.

Upon written notice following his or her participation in an athletic event, the selected athlete must report promptly to a collection station. The athlete may choose to be accompanied by a witness-observer. At the collection station, the athlete picks a plastic-sealed beaker with a personal code number. In the presence of an NCAA official monitor of the same sex as the athlete, the athlete supplies a urine specimen of 100 to 200 milliliters. The specimen is identified, documented, and divided into two samples labeled A and B. Both samples are delivered to one of three certified testing laboratories. Chain of custody procedures provide for signed receipts and acknowledgments at each transfer point.

At the laboratory, a portion of sample A is tested by gas chromatography/mass spectrometry—the most scientifically accurate method of analysis available. Positive findings, signifying use of proscribed drugs, are confirmed by testing another portion of sample A, and then reviewed by the laboratory director and reported to the NCAA by code number. The NCAA decodes the reports and relays positive findings to the athletic director of the college or university involved by telephone and overnight letter marked confidential. The institution is required to notify the athlete of the positive finding. Within 24 hours of notice of a positive finding, sample B of the athlete's urine is tested. A positive finding may be appealed to a designated NCAA committee.

A positive test finding results in loss of postseason eligibility. Refusal by a student athlete to follow NCAA-mandated drug-testing procedures yields the same consequence—the offending athlete is barred from competition.

To resolve the dispute between the parties, we address three questions of first impression in this court: (1) Does the Privacy Initiative govern the conduct of private, nongovernmental entities such as the NCAA; (2) if it does, what legal standard is to be applied in assessing alleged invasions of privacy; and (3) under that standard, is the NCAA drug-testing program a violation of the state constitutional privacy right?

Neither plaintiffs nor Stanford assert that the NCAA is an agency or instrumentality of government or a vehicle for state action. Case law generally confirms the status of the NCAA as a private organization, comprised of American colleges and universities, and democratically governed by its own membership.

In its opening attack on the judgment, the NCAA asserts that its private status is dispositive of this action because the Privacy Initiative does not embody a right of action against nongovernmental entities. We disagree.

The Fourth Amendment's search and seizure clause is sometimes referred to as a privacy provision. The Fourth Amendment does not proscribe all searches and seizures, but only those that are unreasonable. Under the Fourth Amendment and the parallel search and seizure clause of the California Constitution (art. I, § 13), the reasonableness of particular searches and seizures is determined by a general balancing test weighing the gravity of the governmental interest or public concern served and the degree to which the challenged government conduct advances that concern against the intrusiveness of the interference with individual liberty.

In summary, outside the separate context of Fourth Amendment searches and seizures, the penumbral federal constitutional right to privacy has generally been applied to intrusions by the government into a narrow and defined class of personal autonomy interests in contraceptive and reproductive decisions. There is at least some prospect that what have been regarded as privacy interests may henceforth be viewed as Fourteenth Amendment liberty interests in federal constitutional analysis. But whatever predictions one might hazard, the murky character of federal constitutional privacy analysis at this stage teaches that privacy interests and accompanying legal standards are best viewed flexibly and in context.

The first essential element of a state constitutional cause of action for invasion of privacy is the identification of a specific, legally protected privacy interest. Whatever their common denominator, privacy interests are best assessed separately and in context. Just as the right to privacy is not absolute, privacy interests do not encompass all conceivable assertions of individual rights. Legally recognized privacy interests are generally of two classes: (1) interests in precluding the dissemination or misuse of sensitive and confidential information (informational privacy), and (2) interests in making intimate personal decisions or conducting personal activities without observation, intrusion, or interference (autonomy privacy).

The second essential element of a state constitutional cause of action for invasion of privacy is a reasonable expectation of privacy on plaintiff's part. The extent of a privacy interest is not independent of the circumstances. Even when a legally cognizable privacy interest is present, other factors may affect a person's reasonable expectation of privacy. For example, advance notice of an impending action may serve to limit an intrusion on personal dignity and security that would otherwise be regarded as serious.

In addition, customs, practices, and physical settings surrounding particular activities may create or inhibit reasonable expectations of privacy. A reasonable expectation of privacy is an objective entitlement founded on broadly-based and widely-accepted community norms. Finally, the presence or absence of opportunities to consent voluntarily to activities impacting privacy interests obviously affects the expectations of the participant.

The third element is the seriousness of the invasion. No community could function if every intrusion into the realm of private action, no matter how slight or trivial, gave rise to a cause of action for invasion of privacy. Complete privacy does not exist in this world except in a desert, and anyone who is not a hermit must expect and endure the ordinary incidents of the community life of which he is a part. Actionable invasions of privacy must be sufficiently serious in their nature, scope, and actual or potential impact to constitute an egregious breach of the social norms underlying the privacy right. Thus, the extent and gravity of the invasion is an indispensable consideration in assessing an alleged invasion of privacy.

Privacy concerns are not absolute; they must be balanced against other important interests. Not every act that has some impact on personal privacy invokes the protections of our Constitution. A court should not play the trump card of unconstitutionality to protect absolutely every assertion of individual privacy.

The diverse and somewhat amorphous character of the privacy right necessarily requires that privacy interests be specifically identified and carefully compared with competing or countervailing privacy and nonprivacy interests in a balancing test. The comparison and balancing of diverse interests is central to the privacy jurisprudence of both common and constitutional law.

Invasion of a privacy interest is not a violation of the state constitutional right to privacy if the invasion is justified by a competing interest. Legitimate interests derive from the legally authorized and socially beneficial activities of government and private entities. Their relative importance is determined by their proximity to the central functions of a particular public or private enterprise. Conduct alleged to be an invasion of privacy is to be evaluated based on the extent to which it furthers legitimate and important competing interests.

Confronted with a defense based on countervailing interests, plaintiff may undertake the burden of demonstrating the availability and use of protective measures, safeguards, and alternatives to defendant's conduct that would minimize the intrusion on privacy interests.

The NCAA is a private organization, not a government agency. Judicial assessment of the relative strength and importance of privacy norms and countervailing interests may differ in cases of private, as opposed to government, action.

First, the pervasive presence of coercive government power in basic areas of human life typically poses greater dangers to the freedoms of the citizenry than actions by private persons. Second, an individual generally has greater choice and alternatives in dealing with private actors than when dealing with the government. Third, private conduct, particularly the activities of voluntary associations of persons, carries its own mantle of constitutional protection in the form of freedom of association. Private citizens have a right, not secured to government, to communicate and associate with one another on mutually negotiated terms and conditions.

Whether a legally recognized privacy interest is present in a given case is a question of law to be decided by the court. Whether plaintiff has a reasonable expectation of privacy in the circumstances and whether defendant's conduct constitutes a serious invasion of privacy are mixed questions of law and fact. If the undisputed material facts show no reasonable expectation of privacy or an insubstantial impact on privacy interests, the question of invasion may be adjudicated as a matter of law.

A defendant may prevail in a state constitutional privacy case by negating any of the three elements just discussed or by pleading and proving, as an affirmative defense, that the invasion of privacy is justified because it substantively furthers one or more countervailing interests. Plaintiff, in turn, may rebut a defendant's assertion of countervailing interests by showing there are feasible and effective alternatives to defendant's conduct that have a lesser impact on privacy interests. Of course, a defendant may also plead and prove other available defenses (e.g., consent, unclean hands) that may be appropriate in view of the nature of the claim and the relief requested.

Plaintiffs correctly assert that the NCAA drug-testing program impacts legally protected privacy interests. First, by monitoring an athlete's urination, the NCAA program intrudes on a human bodily function that by law and social custom is generally performed in private and without observers. Second, by collecting and testing an athlete's urine and inquiring about his or her ingestion of medications and other substances, the NCAA obtains information about the internal medical state of an athlete's body that is regarded as personal and confidential. Observation of urination and disclosure of medical information

may cause embarrassment to individual athletes. The first implicates autonomy privacy—an interest in freedom from observation in performing a function recognized by social norms as private. The second implicates informational privacy—an interest in limiting disclosure of confidential information about bodily condition. But, as we have noted, the identification of these privacy interests is the beginning, not the end, of the analysis.

The observation of urination—a human excretory function—obviously implicates privacy interests. But the reasonable expectations of privacy of plaintiffs and other student athletes in private urination must be viewed within the context of intercollegiate athletic activity and the normal conditions under which it is undertaken.

By its nature, participation in intercollegiate athletics, particularly in highly competitive postseason championship events, involves close regulation and scrutiny of the physical fitness and bodily condition of student athletes. Required physical examinations including urinalysis and special regulation of sleep habits, diet, fitness, and other activities that intrude significantly on privacy interests are routine aspects of a college athlete's life not shared by other students or the population at large. Athletes frequently disrobe in the presence of one another and their athletic mentors and assistants in locker room settings where private bodily parts are readily observable by others of the same sex. They also exchange information about their physical condition and medical treatment with coaches, trainers, and others who have a need to know.

As a result of its unique set of demands, athletic participation carries with it social norms that effectively diminish the athlete's reasonable expectation of personal privacy in his or her bodily condition, both internal and external. The student athlete's reasonable expectation of privacy is further diminished by two elements of the NCAA drug-testing program—advance notice and the opportunity to consent to testing. A drug test does not come as an unwelcome surprise at the end of a postseason match. Full disclosure of the NCAA's banned substances rules and testing procedures is made at the beginning of the athletic season, long before the postseason competition during which drug testing may take place. Following disclosure, the informed written consent of each student athlete is obtained. Thus, athletes have complete information regarding the NCAA drug-testing program and are afforded the opportunity to consent or refuse before they may be selected for testing.

To be sure, an athlete who refuses consent to drug testing is disqualified from NCAA competition. But this consequence does not render the athlete's consent to testing involuntary in any meaningful legal sense. Athletic participation is not a government benefit or an economic necessity that society has decreed must be open to all. Participation in any organized activity carried on by a private, nongovernment organization necessarily entails a willingness to forgo assertion of individual rights one might otherwise have in order to receive the benefits of communal association.

Plaintiffs and Stanford have no legal right to participate in intercollegiate athletic competition. Their ability to do so necessarily depends on their willingness to arrive at and adhere to common understandings with their competitors regarding their mutual sporting endeavor. The NCAA is democratically governed by its member institutions, including Stanford. Acting collectively, those institutions, including Stanford, make the rules, including those regarding drug use and testing. If, knowing the rules, plaintiffs and Stanford choose to play the game, they have, by social convention and legal act, fully and voluntarily acquiesced in the application of those rules. To view the matter otherwise would impair the privacy and associational rights of all NCAA institutions and athletes.

Although diminished by the athletic setting and the exercise of informed consent, plaintiffs' privacy interests are not thereby rendered *de minimis*. Direct observation of urination by a monitor, an intrusive act, appears to be unique to the NCAA program. The NCAA's use of a particularly intrusive monitored urination procedure justifies further inquiry, even under conditions of decreased expectations of privacy.

To justify its intrusion on student athletes' diminished expectations of privacy, the NCAA asserts two countervailing interests: (1) safeguarding the integrity of intercollegiate athletic competition, and (2) protecting the health and safety of student athletes. The central purpose of the NCAA is to promote competitive athletic events conducted pursuant to rules of the game enacted by its own membership. In this way, the NCAA cre-

ates and preserves the level playing field necessary to promote vigorous, high-level, and nationwide competition in intercollegiate sports.

Considered in light of its history, the NCAA's decision to enforce a ban on the use of drugs by means of a drug-testing program is reasonably calculated to further its legitimate interest in maintaining the integrity of intercollegiate athletic competition.

The NCAA also has an interest in protecting the health and safety of student athletes who are involved in NCAA-regulated competition. Contrary to plaintiffs' characterization, this interest is more than a mere naked assertion of paternalism. The NCAA sponsors and regulates intercollegiate athletic events, which by their nature may involve risks of physical injury to athletes, spectators, and others. In this way, the NCAA effectively creates occasions for potential injury resulting from the use of drugs. As a result, it may concern itself with the task of protecting the safety of those involved in intercollegiate athletic competition. This NCAA interest exists for the benefit of all persons involved in sporting events (including not only drug-ingesting athletes but also innocent athletes or others who might be injured by a drug user), as well as the sport itself.

We have been directed to no case imposing on a private organization, acting in a situation involving decreased expectations of privacy, the burden of justifying its conduct as the least offensive alternative possible under the circumstances. Nothing in the language of history of the Privacy Initiative justifies the imposition of such a burden; we decline to impose it.

Moreover, the alternatives posited by plaintiffs—educational programs and suspicion-based drug testing—are different in kind and character from random drug testing. Education may have little effect on persons who are inclined not to listen; competitive pressures or addictive tendencies are likely to prevail over benign attempts at persuasion. Suspicion-based testing assumes reliable visible evidence of drug use and the availability of sufficient resources to make the necessary observations, neither of which finds substantial evidentiary support in the record. It also depends at least in part on the reporting of suspected athletes by their competitors, a situation fraught with conflicts of interest and other difficulties. In light of these factors, the NCAA was not constitutionally compelled to adopt educational or suspicion-based programs to further its interests in the integrity of athletic competition and the health and safety of student athletes.

The closest question presented by this case concerns the method used by the NCAA to monitor athletes as they provide urine samples. A tested athlete's urination is directly observed by an NCAA official of the same sex as the athlete who stands some 5 to 7 feet away. Even the diminished expectations of privacy in a locker room setting do not necessarily include direct and intentional observation of excretory functions. Plaintiffs had a reasonable expectation of privacy under the circumstances; their privacy interest was impacted by the NCAA's conduct. The NCAA was therefore required to justify its use of direct monitoring of urination.

In support of direct monitoring, the NCAA introduced substantial evidence that urine samples can be altered or substituted in order to avoid positive findings and that athletes had actually attempted to do so. The NCAA's interest in preserving the integrity of intercollegiate athletic competition requires not just testing, but effective and accurate testing of unaltered and uncontaminated samples. If direct monitoring is necessary to accomplish accurate testing, the NCAA is entitled to use it.

Notwithstanding plaintiffs' failure of proof in this case, direct monitoring remains a significant privacy issue in athletic and nonathletic drug-testing cases. Social norms validate the distinction between the mere presence of another person in or around an area where urination takes place (such as a bathroom or locker room) and the direct and purposeful observation of the urination act by someone specially commissioned to witness it.

Perhaps because of its greater impact on privacy interests, direct monitoring is not used in all drug-testing programs. With two exceptions, no decided case has upheld direct monitoring, even in the diminished privacy context of athletic competition. The first exception—also in an NCAA drug-testing context—is a later-vacated federal trial court decision containing virtually no analysis of the serious privacy issues. The second involves testing of a probationary police officer after notice and consent. Neither case considers the possibility of less intrusive alternatives to direct monitoring.

There may indeed be less intrusive alternatives to direct monitoring that could nonetheless fully satisfy the tester's objective of ensuring a valid sample. Because we are limited to the record before us, we necessarily leave any further consideration of less intrusive alternatives to direct monitoring initially to the judgment and discretion of the NCAA, and then to future litigation, if any.

As discussed above, plaintiffs' interest in the privacy of medical treatment and medical information is also a protectable interest under the Privacy Initiative. However, the student athlete's reasonable expectation of privacy is similarly diminished because of the nature of competitive athletic activity and the norms under which it is conducted. Organized and supervised athletic competition presupposes a continuing exchange of otherwise confidential information about the physical and medical condition of athletes. Coaches, trainers, and team physicians necessarily learn intimate details of student athletes' bodily condition, including illnesses, medical problems, and medications prescribed or taken. Plaintiffs do not demonstrate that sharing similar information with the NCAA, in its capacity as a regulator of athletic competition in which plaintiffs have voluntarily elected to participate, presents any greater risk to privacy.

Directed and specific inquiries about personal medications (including questions about birth control pills) in the potentially stressful circumstances of a random drug test are undoubtedly significant from a privacy standpoint. Without a correspondingly important reason to know, the NCAA would have no right to demand answers to these kinds of questions. Again, however, the extent of the intrusion on plaintiffs' privacy presented by the question must be considered in light of both the diminished expectations of privacy of athletes in such questions, which are routinely asked and answered in the athletic context.

Drug testing for multiple substances is a complex process. Although both parties acknowledge the NCAA has used and continues to use the best available methods of laboratory analysis, mistakes are possible and false positives can occur. The NCAA's inquiries to athletes about medications and drugs are designed to ensure accuracy in testing. The NCAA maintains that complete and accurate disclosure of these matters by athletes will, in certain instances and with respect to specified substances, serve to explain findings and prevent the embarrassment and distress occasioned by further proceedings. The record supports the NCAA's contentions. These kinds of disclosures are reasonably necessary to further the threshold purpose of the drug-testing program—to protect the integrity of competition through the medium of accurate testing of athletes engaged in competition. The NCAA's interests in this regard adequately justify its inquiries about medications and other substances ingested by tested athletes.

The NCAA follows extensive procedures designed to safeguard test results, including the numbering of urine specimens, chain of custody procedures, and control of disclosures regarding disqualified athletes. Plaintiffs and Stanford offer no serious criticism of the manner in which the NCAA protects the privacy interests of student athletes in the results or the process of drug testing. They point to no instances in which medical data or drug test results were disclosed to persons other than NCAA officials and the athlete's own college or university.

Although plaintiffs plausibly observe that media interest in positive test results is inevitable, the NCAA cannot be held responsible for public curiosity. Under established NCAA procedures, positive drug-testing results are disclosed only to the athlete's school, which, in turn, informs the

athlete. Only those with a need to know learn of positive findings. Plaintiffs fail to identify any other feasible precaution or safeguard. The uncontradicted evidence in the record thus points to a single conclusion: The NCAA carefully safeguards the confidentiality of athlete medical information and drug test data, using the same only to determine eligibility for NCAA athletic competition in accordance with its demonstrated interests. There is no invasion of privacy in the NCAA's procedure.

The NCAA drug-testing program does not violate the state constitutional right to privacy. Therefore, the NCAA is entitled to judgment in its favor. As a result of our disposition, we do not decide whether the recognition of a state constitutional right to privacy in these circumstances would violate the commerce clause of the federal Constitution.

The judgment of the court of appeals affirming the permanent injunction against the NCAA drug-testing program is reversed. This case is remanded with instructions to direct entry of a final judgment in favor of the NCAA. The NCAA shall recover its costs.

 For an extended version of the case and review questions to test your understanding of the material, please go to www.HumanKinetics.com/CaseStudiesInSportLaw.

Jager v. Douglas County School District

862 F.2d 824 (11th Cir. 1989)

This case involves invocations that are delivered prior to public high school football games in Douglas County, Georgia. These football games are school-sponsored activities that are played at a stadium owned by the school system. The schools furnish the equipment used by the participants, and the coaches who supervise these activities are employed by the school system. Taxpayer funds are used to pay the operating costs for the stadium lights and public address system. We hold that the practice of beginning these games with an invocation violates the Establishment Clause of the First Amendment.

In the fall of 1985, Doug Jager, then a member of the Douglas County High School marching band, objected to his school principal about the practice of having pregame invocations delivered at home football games. The invocations often opened with the words "let us bow our heads" or "let us pray" and frequently invoked reference to Jesus Christ or closed with the words "in Jesus' name we pray." These invocations conflict with the Jagers' sincerely held religious beliefs. The Douglas County High School principal informed the band director of Doug Jager's objections to the prayers. The band director proceeded to lecture Doug on Christianity.

On June 2, 1986, Douglas County School Superintendent Kathryn Shehane, the school system attorney, the Jagers and their counsel, and Reverends Jamie E. Jenkins and Donald Mountain of the Douglas County Ministerial Association (DCMA) met and discussed two alternative proposals for modifying the invocation practices: an inspirational wholly secular speech and an equal access plan that would retain some religious content. The Jagers rejected the equal access approach, and notified the school system attorney that the secular inspirational speech was the only feasible alternative to the invocation practice. Upon the Jagers' rejection of the equal access plan, Reverends Jenkins and Mountain drafted a compromise proposal. The stated purpose of the alternative draft was to "perpetuate and regulate the traditional invocation as part of the opening ceremonies of school athletic events." In August 1986, the plaintiffs agreed to reconsider the Jenkins/Mountain version of the equal access plan if prayers voluntarily ceased at football games in the interim.

In September 1986, Superintendent Shehane met with the principals of Douglas County high schools. The group decided to proceed with pregame invocations pursuant to the equal access plan. On September 15, 1986, the high school principals informed their schools that the equal access plan, which the district court found to be coextensive with the Jenkins/Mountain plan, would govern future games, including those scheduled for September 26, 1986.

Under the terms of the equal access plan, all school clubs and organizations can designate club members to give invocations, and any student, parent, or school staff member can seek to deliver an invocation. The plan specifies that the student government will randomly select the invocation speaker, and no ministers will be involved in selecting invocation speakers or in delivering invocations. In addition, the schools will not monitor the content of the invocations.

On September 19, 1986, the Jagers filed a complaint in the United States District Court for the Northern District of Georgia. The district court issued a temporary restraining order enjoining the Douglas County School District (the School District) from conducting or permitting religious invocations prior to any athletic event at the school stadium. The case was tried to the district court

in November 1986. On February 3, 1987, the district court (1) declared the pregame invocations unconstitutional, (2) denied the Jagers' request for a permanent injunction, (3) rejected the Jagers' claim based on the Free Exercise of Religion Clause of the First Amendment, and (4) rejected the Jagers' claim that the School District violated the Georgia Constitution.

After the School District filed a Motion for Clarification, the district court entered an additional order in which it held that the equal access plan was constitutional on its face and did not violate the Establishment Clause. The court expressly declined to determine whether the equal access plan was unconstitutional as applied. The district court denied the Jagers' request for declaratory and injunctive relief relating to the equal access plan.

The district court held that the equal access plan, which involves the random selection of an invocation speaker, was constitutional on its face. The Jagers challenge this holding on appeal.

The Establishment Clause of the First Amendment forbids the enactment of any law or practice respecting an establishment of religion. The religion clauses of the First Amendment require that states pursue a course of complete neutrality toward religion. To determine whether state action embodies the neutrality that comports with the Establishment Clause, this court must apply a three-pronged analysis (*Lemon* test). *Lemon v. Kurtzman*, 403 U.S. 602 (1971). We must ask whether (1) the Douglas County School Superintendent and the school principals had a secular purpose for adopting the equal access plan, (2) the plan's primary effect is one that neither advances nor inhibits religion, and (3) the plan does not result in an excessive entanglement of government with religion. State action violates the Establishment Clause if it fails to meet any of these three criteria.

The School District argues that the *Lemon* test does not apply here. Instead, the School District contends that *Marsh v. Chambers*, 463 U.S. 783, 103 S.Ct. 3330, 77 L.Ed.2d 1019 (1983), provides the standard for determining whether the equal access plan violates the Establishment Clause. In *Marsh*, the Supreme Court upheld Nebraska's practice of commencing state legislative sessions with a prayer delivered by a chaplain employed by the state. In refusing to declare Nebraska's legislative invocation unconstitutional, the court relied on the unique history associated with the practice of opening legislative sessions with a prayer. The practice existed at the time of the adoption of the First Amendment and had continued in many states to the present. Since the Continental Congress and the First Congress opened their sessions with prayers, the *Marsh* court concluded that the drafters of the Establishment Clause undoubtedly perceived no threat from legislative prayer and did not intend to prohibit legislative invocations.

Because *Marsh* was based on more than 200 years of the unique history of legislative invocations, it has no application to the case at bar. The instant case involves the special context of the public elementary and secondary school system, in which the Supreme Court has been particularly vigilant in monitoring compliance with the Establishment Clause. Similarly, the present case does not lend itself to *Marsh's* historical approach because invocations at school-sponsored football games were nonexistent when the Constitution was adopted. Therefore, the *Lemon* test guides this court's analysis in the case at bar.

The first prong of the *Lemon* test asks whether the challenged practice had a secular purpose. In applying the purpose test, it is appropriate to ask whether government's actual purpose is to endorse or disapprove of religion. Clearly, the equal access plan in the case at bar was adopted with the actual purpose of endorsing and perpetuating religion.

The district court found that pregame invocations serve four purposes: (1) to continue a longstanding custom and tradition, (2) to add a solemn and dignified tone to the proceedings, (3) to remind the spectators and players of the importance of sportsmanship and fair play, and (4) to satisfy the genuine, good faith wishes on the part of a majority of the citizens of Douglas County to publicly express support for Protestant Christianity. The School District could serve all of its cited secular purposes by requiring wholly secular inspirational speeches about sportsmanship, fair play, safety, and the values of teamwork and competition. Indeed, the Jagers offered to accept a pregame invocation consisting of a secular inspirational speech. Since the School District rejected this compromise even though it would have fulfilled the three secular purposes of pregame invocations, it is clear that the School

District was most interested in the fourth purpose served by the invocations. That is, the School District wanted to have invocations that publicly express support for Protestant Christianity.

The unmistakable message of the Supreme Court's teachings is that the state cannot employ a religious means to serve otherwise legitimate secular interests. In choosing the equal access plan, the School District opted for an alternative that permits religious invocations, which by definition serve religious purposes, just like all public prayers. The School District's rejection of the alternative of wholly secular invocations makes it very clear that the School District's actual purpose in having pregame invocations was religious. Consequently, the equal access plan fails to survive the *Lemon* test.

The conclusion that an intrinsically religious practice cannot meet the secular purpose prong of the *Lemon* test finds support in other cases. Likewise, the facts in the present case demonstrate that, although the School District emphasized at trial the secular purposes behind the pregame invocations, the pre-eminent purpose behind having invocations was to endorse Protestant Christianity. This is prohibited by the Establishment Clause. In light of the controlling case law and the nature of the challenged practice, we hold that, because the equal access plan fails to satisfy the first prong of the *Lemon* test, the plan violates the Establishment Clause of the First Amendment.

Even assuming, *arguendo*, that the equal access plan survives the first prong of the *Lemon* test, we would still find that the plan is facially unconstitutional because it fails the primary effect prong of the *Lemon* test. The effect prong asks whether, irrespective of government's actual purpose, the practice under review in fact conveys a message of endorsement or disapproval of religion.

In the present case, as noted above, the School District could satisfy its secular objectives by prescribing a strictly secular invocation. The equal access plan, however, permits religious invocations. When a religious invocation is given via a sound system controlled by school principals and the religious invocation occurs at a school-sponsored event at a school-owned facility, the conclusion is inescapable that the religious invocation conveys a message that the school endorses the religious invocation. This message becomes even clearer when the context of these pregame prayers is understood. In the past, pregame invocation speakers at the Douglas County High School, with very few exceptions, have been Protestant Christian ministers. In addition, Protestant Christianity is the majority religious preference in Douglas County. Therefore, the likely result of the equal access plan will be the continuation of Protestant Christian invocations, which have been delivered since 1947. Moreover, the equal access plan places those attending football games in the position of participating in a group prayer. Consequently, the plan violates the primary effect prong of the *Lemon* test.

On the face of the equal access plan, the School District is not entangled with religion at all. The School District does not monitor the content of the invocations, and the DCMA will no longer choose the invocation speakers or deliver the pregame prayers. Nonetheless, the lack of entanglement cannot save the equal access plan because the plan violates the first two prongs of the *Lemon* test.

The School District sets forth several arguments for distinguishing school prayer cases, claiming that these distinctions permit a finding that religious invocations at high school football games are constitutional. The School District first argues that the school prayer cases are not implicated here because pregame invocations occur outside the instructional environment of the classroom. This argument is meritless. Even though not occurring in the classroom, the invocations take place at a school-owned stadium during a school-sponsored event. In *Doe v. Aldine Ind. School Dist.*, 563 F.Supp. 883 (S.D.Tex. 1982), the United States District Court for the Southern District of Texas rejected the argument that the School District asserts here. In *Doe*, a public high school sponsored extracurricular activities at which a prayer was sung. The defendants argued that the prayer did not violate the Establishment Clause because it occurred outside the classroom. The *Doe* court rejected this argument. Their reasoning was that because these extracurricular activities provided a powerful incentive for students to attend and were school sponsored and so closely identified with the school program, the fact that the religious activity took place in a nonreligious setting might create in a student's mind the impression

that the state's attitude toward religion lacks neutrality. The *Doe* court's reasoning applies equally well in the present case.

The School District next contends that football invocations do not invoke the teacher-student relationship, and are directed to a far less impressionable audience of adults and 16- to 18-year-olds. However, the equal access plan does permit teachers to deliver religious invocations, thereby impacting on the teacher-student relationship. Furthermore, to persons of any age who do not believe in prayer, religious invocations permitted by the equal access plan convey the message that the state endorses religions believing in prayer and denigrates those religions that do not. If these prayers are delivered by authority figures, such as teachers, as is possible under the equal access plan, the message endorsing prayer becomes even stronger.

The School District argues further that the invocations are constitutional because they are given at public events at which attendance is entirely voluntary. Courts upholding invocations at graduation ceremonies have stressed that attendance is voluntary. However, the Supreme Court and this court have not held that public prayer becomes constitutional when student participation is purely voluntary. The School District attempts to distinguish these cases on the ground that they involved students who were compelled by law to be in attendance in the classrooms where prayer took place. The School District suggests that, because attendance at football games is voluntary, a constitutional violation is avoided. This argument lacks merit because whether the complaining individual's presence was voluntary is not relevant to the Establishment Clause analysis. The Establishment Clause focuses on the constitutionality of the state action, not on the choices made by the complaining individual.

The School District's final attempt to distinguish the school prayer cases centers on the contention that the invocations constitute a *de minimis* violation of the Establishment Clause because they last 60 to 90 seconds. This approach is flawed. It is no defense to urge that the religious practices here may be relatively minor encroachments on the First Amendment. The Establishment Clause does not focus on the amount of time an activity takes, but rather examines the religious character of the activity.

None of the arguments offered by the School District are persuasive in the present case. Each alleged distinction overlooks the single fact that a state or its subdivision cannot endorse or advance religion. Nor can a state use religious means to achieve secular purposes where, as here, secular means exist to achieve those purposes.

In short, the equal access plan is unconstitutional because it has a religious purpose and a primary effect of advancing religion. By using a purely secular invocation, the School District could avoid any problems of entanglement, fulfill its secular purposes, and not advance religion, thereby complying with the requirements of *Lemon* and its progeny. Because the School District rejected the alternative of a purely secular pregame speech, and instead adopted a plan that fails to satisfy the *Lemon* test, we hold that the equal access plan is unconstitutional on its face.

The district court declared that the pregame invocation system that was in place prior to the adoption of the equal access plan was unconstitutional. The School District contends that the question of the constitutionality of the invocation practices as they existed prior to the equal access plan was moot and, therefore, the district court lacked jurisdiction to make such a declaration. Alternatively, the School District argues that, if the issue was not moot, the district court erroneously declared the prior pregame invocation practice to be unconstitutional.

The School District first raised mootness as a jurisdictional impediment when the district court prepared to award attorneys' fees to the Jagers. The district court rejected the School District's argument because it was not absolutely clear that the prior practice of having religious invocations given by DCMA ministers would not recur.

Ordinarily, the defendant's voluntary cessation of a challenged practice will not moot an action because the defendant is free to return to his old ways.

Under the imminent threat of the Jagers' lawsuit, the School District voluntarily ceased the practice of having pregame religious invocations delivered by Protestant ministers, and it implemented the equal access plan. However, the equal access plan was merely implemented by the school principals. It was not a formal policy adopted by the School District or the Douglas County Board of Education, and the defendants never promised not to resume the prior practice. In fact, the defendants continue to press on appeal that the voluntarily ceased conduct should be declared constitutional. Thus, the controversy concerning the prior invocation practices is not moot.

Conversely, in the present case, there is no indication that the School District will refrain from resuming its 40-year-old practice of having clergy deliver religious invocations before high school football games. Therefore, we will reach the merits of the Jagers' challenge to the pre-equal access plan practices.

The School District appeals the district court's declaration that the practice of having ministers give religious invocations violated the Establishment Clause. However, under the *Lemon* test, this argument is without merit.

First, the invocations were prayers, delivered by ministers, and thus fail the secular purpose prong of the *Lemon* test for the reasons set forth earlier. Second, the primary effect of advancing religion was clear for the reasons given by the district court: One of the effects of the prior practices in regard to invocations was to create the appearance or impression that the school system endorsed Protestant Christianity. The School District labels this finding clearly erroneous, but such a finding is inescapable where the person giving the invocation was identified by name and, frequently, by church affiliation. Third, excessive entanglement occurred because the School District delegated the authority to deliver invocations and to choose invocation speakers to the DCMA, a Protestant ministerial group. We therefore hold that the prior practice violated the Establishment Clause.

In sum, we REVERSE the district court's order declaring the equal access plan constitutional on its face, and we AFFIRM the lower court's order declaring that the pregame invocations were unconstitutional. Because we award relief to the plaintiffs on both of their Establishment Clause claims, we REMAND to the district court to determine the amount of attorneys' fees to be awarded.

 For an extended version of the case and review questions to test your understanding of the material, please go to www.HumanKinetics.com/CaseStudiesInSportLaw.

Menora v. Illinois High School Association

683 F.2d 1030 (7th Cir. 1982)

Interscholastic high school sports in Illinois, including basketball, are conducted under the aegis of the Illinois High School Association, a private association of virtually all of the state's public and private (including parochial) high schools. A rule of the Association forbids basketball players to wear hats or other headwear, with the sole exception of a headband no wider than 2 inches, while playing. The principal concern behind this prohibition is that the headwear might fall off in the heat of play and one of the players might trip or slip on it, fall, and injure himself.

This rule is challenged in the present case as an infringement of the religious freedom of orthodox Jews. According to a stipulation between the parties, orthodox Jewish males are required by their religion "to cover their heads at all times except when they are (a) unconscious, (b) immersed in water, or (c) in imminent danger of loss of life." There is no exception for playing basketball. Orthodox Jews who play basketball comply, or at least try to comply, with this requirement by wearing yarmulkes (small skull caps that cover the crown of the head) fastened to the hair with bobby pins. Ordinarily a yarmulke just perches on the head; the bobby pins are an acknowledgment of the yarmulke's instability on a bobbing head. But bobby pins are not a secure method of fastening; yarmulkes fastened by them fall off in the heat of play with some frequency. The Association has interpreted its rule to forbid the wearing of yarmulkes during play; and the plaintiffs in this lawsuit—two orthodox Jewish high schools in Chicago, the members of their interscholastic basketball teams, and the members' parents—contend that this interpretation forces them to choose between their religious observance and participating in interscholastic basketball, which as it happens is the only interscholastic sport in which the two schools participate.

The district court held that the Association is an arm of the state for purposes of the Fourteenth Amendment, that the hazards posed by yarmulkes are too slight to justify putting the plaintiffs to the choice we have just mentioned, and therefore

that the rule, as applied to prohibit the wearing of yarmulkes while playing basketball, violates the free-exercise clause of the First Amendment, to be applicable to the states by virtue of the due process clause of the Fourteenth Amendment.

The Association no longer contests the finding that it is an arm of the State of Illinois for purposes of the Fourteenth Amendment. Although the Association is nominally a private organization, public high schools comprise the bulk of its membership and dominate its decision-making. Since there is no issue of state action before us, we need not consider the district court's application of the principle of *collateral estoppel* to bar the Association from denying that it is an arm of the state for purposes of the Fourteenth Amendment. Our silence is not to be construed as approval or disapproval of the district court's analysis of this question.

The First Amendment, so far as is relevant to this case, provides that "Congress shall make no law ... prohibiting the free exercise (of religion)." Read literally (after substituting "Illinois High School Association" for "Congress" and "rule" for "law"), this language would not forbid a regulation secular in purpose (the purpose of the no-headwear rule is to promote safety); general in application; not motivated by antipathy to any religious group on which the regulation might bear heavily or by sympathy for a competing group (there is no suggestion of any such motivation here); and that does not actually prohibit a religious observance but merely makes it more costly by forcing the observant to give up some government benefit (here, participation in an interscholastic sport sponsored by an arm of the state).

But whatever the literal or for that matter the original meaning of the free-exercise clause, the Supreme Court has interpreted it to require the government, when it can do so without too much cost or inconvenience, to bend its regulations—even when they are secular, general, nondiscriminatory, and do not forbid but merely burden a religious observance—to spare religious people the painful choice between giving up a part of their religious observance and giving up a valuable government benefit.

This case requires a comparison of two burdens: the burden on the person who is seeking a government benefit of being denied the benefit as the price of observing his religion, and the burden on the government of extending the benefit to someone who fails to meet the usual requirements for eligibility. The more valuable the benefit to the claimant and hence the greater the burden on him of forgoing it in order to continue to observe his religion, the greater must be the burden on the government of relaxing the conditions it places on that benefit for a refusal to make an exception for the claimant to survive a challenge based on the First Amendment. Free exercise of religion does not mean costless exercise of religion, but the state may not make the exercise of religion unreasonably costly.

The benefit that the plaintiffs seek in this case is participation in interscholastic basketball games; for so far as appears, the rules of the Illinois High School Association do not forbid the wearing of headwear in any other sport, and anyway the plaintiffs do not want to participate in any of the other interscholastic sports regulated by the Association. We must also compare the burdens on the states of accommodating their interests to those of the religious claimants. As under any balancing test, each case tends to be *sui generis*, so that the principal value of precedent is to identify the interests that must be weighed and to tell us whether, in weighing them, we should place our thumb on one pan or the other.

But in the view we take of this case we do not have to choose between these formulations, assuming they really are different. A court, before attempting to balance competing interests, must define them as precisely as it can, since in the process of definition it may become apparent that there is no real conflict. The concept of "false conflict," a major theme in the modern scholarship on conflict of laws, has we think, an application to constitutional adjudication in general and to this case in particular. The conflicting claims of church and state are a source of some of the bitterest and most divisive controversies in our society. Weigh them and choose we shall if we must, but we want first to satisfy ourselves that the claims really are irreconcilable.

The parties have argued this case to us as if the religious obligation that was in conflict with state regulation was an obligation while playing basketball to wear a yarmulke fastened to your hair by bobby pins. But that is not what the stipulation says, and while we are not Talmudic scholars we are reasonably confident, and the plaintiffs' counsel acknowledged at oral argument, that the precise nature of the head covering and the method by which it is kept on the head are not specified by Jewish law. The wearing of a yarmulke—which by its size and position is liable to fall off in any activity involving sudden movement—is conventional rather than prescribed; some orthodox Jews prefer to wear an ordinary hat instead. The affixing of the yarmulke to the head (more precisely, the hair) by bobby pins is even more obviously a convention rather than a religious obligation, and it happens to be an inherently insecure method of keeping the yarmulke attached during basketball play.

If the Talmud required basketball players to wear yarmulkes attached by bobby pins, there would be a conflict with the state's interest in safety. But it does not, so it would seem that all the plaintiffs have to do to obviate the state's concern with safety is to devise a method of affixing a head covering that will prevent it from falling off during basketball play. We are not the people to devise the method—to say that yarmulkes should be equipped with chin straps or sewn to headbands or replaced by some form of head covering that fits the head more securely. But we are reasonably sure that a secure head covering exists or can be devised at trivial cost without violating any tenet of orthodox Judaism; that, on the facts of this case at least, bobby pins do not implicate First Amendment values.

The district court thought the fact that the Association once had an exception to its no-headwear rule for "soft barrettes," and repealed it during the course of this litigation, proves that the Association's concern with the safety hazard posed by yarmulkes is spurious. But the exception was not irrational, so even if it was repealed for purely tactical reasons this would not show that the Association has no reason to be concerned about loose yarmulkes. Barrettes, which are worn by girls to keep their hair in place, may fall on the floor, just like yarmulkes, but until they do so they keep the wearer's hair out of her eyes and make it less likely that she will collide with someone or fail to see an obstacle on the floor. Eyeglasses, which also are permitted by the Association's rules though they sometimes fall off, reduce the likelihood of a collision or a fall. A headband, the only form of headwear permitted, prevents sweat from getting in the eyes or falling on the floor and making it slippery. Yarmulkes do not have the safety-enhancing properties of barrettes, headbands, and eyeglasses. That is why, incidentally, the no-headwear rule does not violate the equal protection clause of the Fourteenth Amendment just because glasses and headbands are permitted—the plaintiffs' alternative ground, not addressed by the district court, for upholding that court's judgment. While we are unwilling to dismiss as spurious the safety concern behind the application of the Association's rule to yarmulkes fastened only by bobby pins, we do not think it is great enough to justify the state's placing a heavy burden on religious observance. But virtually by definition it has sufficient substance to outweigh a nonexistent burden on religious observance. And the burden would be nonexistent if the only thing the rule forbade was the wearing of an insecurely mounted yarmulke since, as we said earlier, there appears to be nothing in Jewish law that requires that the head covering take that form. If the plaintiffs can totally allay the state's safety concern at zero, or practically zero, cost to them, they must do so. Otherwise the state's concern, even if relatively slight, will be a compelling interest in relation to the (non)burden on the plaintiffs' religious freedom.

As the plaintiffs had the burden of proving that their First Amendment rights were infringed by the Association's no-headwear rule, we are constrained on this record to conclude that they failed to make out a case and that the judgment in their favor must be vacated. As we have explained, they have no constitutional right to wear yarmulkes insecurely fastened by bobby pins and therefore they cannot complain if the Association refuses to let them do so because of safety concerns that, while not great, are not wholly trivial

either. But it does not follow that the complaint should be dismissed. The district court should retain jurisdiction so that the plaintiffs can have an opportunity to propose to the Association a form of secure head covering that complies with Jewish law yet meets the Association's safety concerns. If the Association refuses to interpret or amend its rule to allow such a head covering to be worn by orthodox Jews, the district court should then proceed to determine, consistently with the analysis in this opinion, the plaintiffs' right to have the rule enjoined as a violation of their religious freedom.

We put the burden of proposing an alternative, more secure method of covering the head on the plaintiffs rather than on the defendants because the plaintiffs know so much more about Jewish law. The stipulation is singularly unilluminating about the content of that law, and because of the importance of avoiding false conflicts in constitutional adjudication we deprecate it as a basis for the decision of this case. Read literally, the stipulation would prevent orthodox Jews from getting haircuts, would require them to wear a hat or yarmulke to bed (though it could be removed after they fell asleep), and might even forbid them to play basketball while wearing yarmulkes fastened only by bobby pins, given the high probability that the yarmulke will fall off at some point during the game (or during the season) and cause—it would seem—a violation of religious law. To the extent that such questions of religious interpretation prove actually relevant to this case they should be addressed, in the first instance at least, by the plaintiffs when they propose to the Association in the further proceedings that we envisage on remand a more secure method of head covering. And if, despite counsel's representation at oral argument, we are incorrect in believing that Jewish religious law permits a more secure head covering than a yarmulke fastened only by bobby pins, this also can be raised on remand.

VACATED AND REMANDED.

 For an extended version of the case and review questions to test your understanding of the material, please go to www.HumanKinetics.com/CaseStudiesInSportLaw.

National Collegiate Athletic Association v. Tarkanian

488 U.S. 179 (1988)

When he became head basketball coach at the University of Nevada, Las Vegas (UNLV), in 1973, Jerry Tarkanian inherited a team with a mediocre 14-14 record. Four years later the team won 29 out of 32 games and placed third in the championship tournament sponsored by the National Collegiate Athletic Association (NCAA), to which UNLV belongs.

Yet in September 1977 UNLV informed Tarkanian that it was going to suspend him. No dissatisfaction with Tarkanian, once described as the winningest active basketball coach, motivated his suspension. Rather, the impetus was a report by the NCAA detailing 38 violations of NCAA rules by UNLV personnel, including 10 involving Tarkanian. The NCAA had placed the university's basketball team on probation for two years and ordered UNLV to show cause why the NCAA should not impose further penalties unless UNLV severed all ties during the probation between its intercollegiate athletic program and Tarkanian.

Facing demotion and a drastic cut in pay, Tarkanian brought suit in Nevada state court, alleging that he had been deprived of his Fourteenth Amendment due process rights in violation of 42 U.S.C. § 1983. Ultimately Tarkanian obtained injunctive relief and an award of attorney's fees against both UNLV and the NCAA. NCAA's liability may be upheld only if its participation in the events that led to Tarkanian's suspension constituted state action prohibited by the Fourteenth Amendment and was performed "under color of" state law within the meaning of section 1983. We granted *certiorari* to review the Nevada Supreme Court's holding that the NCAA engaged in state action when it conducted its investigation and recommended that Tarkanian be disciplined.

In order to understand the four separate proceedings that gave rise to the question we must decide, it is useful to begin with a description of the relationship among the three parties—Tarkanian, UNLV, and the NCAA.

Tarkanian initially was employed on a year-to-year basis but became a tenured professor in 1977. He receives an annual salary with valuable fringe benefits, and his status as a highly successful coach enables him to earn substantial additional income from sports-related activities such as broadcasting and the sponsorship of products.

UNLV is a branch of the University of Nevada, a state-funded institution. The university is organized and operated pursuant to provisions of Nevada's State Constitution, statutes, and regulations. In performing their official functions, the executives of UNLV unquestionably act under color of state law.

The NCAA is an unincorporated association of approximately 960 members, including virtually all public and private universities and four-year colleges conducting major athletic programs in the United States. Basic policies of the NCAA are determined by the members at annual conventions. Between conventions, the Association is governed by its Council, which appoints various committees to implement specific programs.

One of the NCAA's fundamental policies is to maintain intercollegiate athletics as an integral part of the educational program and the athlete as an integral part of the student body, and by so doing, retain a clear line of demarcation between college athletics and professional sports. It has therefore adopted rules, which it calls legislation, governing the conduct of the intercollegiate athletic programs of its members. This NCAA legislation applies to a variety of issues, such as academic standards for eligibility, admissions, financial aid, and the recruiting of student athletes. By joining the NCAA, each member agrees to abide by and to enforce such rules.

The NCAA Bylaws provide that its enforcement program shall be administered by a Committee on Infractions. The Committee supervises an investigative staff, makes factual determinations concerning alleged rule violations, and is expressly authorized to impose appropriate penalties on a member found to be in violation, or recommend to the Council suspension or termination of membership. In particular, the Committee may order a member institution to show cause why that member should not suffer further penalties unless it imposes a prescribed discipline on an employee; it is not authorized, however, to sanction a member institution's employees directly. The bylaws also provide that representatives of member institutions are expected to cooperate fully with the administration of the enforcement program.

Embedded in our Fourteenth Amendment jurisprudence is a dichotomy between state action, which is subject to scrutiny under the Amendment's Due Process Clause, and private conduct, against which the Amendment affords no shield, no matter how unfair that conduct may be. As a general matter the protections of the Fourteenth Amendment do not extend to private conduct abridging individual rights.

In this case Tarkanian argues that the NCAA was a state actor because it misused power that it possessed by virtue of state law. He claims specifically that UNLV delegated its own functions to the NCAA, clothing the Association with authority both to adopt rules governing UNLV's athletic programs and to enforce those rules on behalf of UNLV. Similarly, the Nevada Supreme Court held that UNLV had delegated its authority over personnel decisions to the NCAA. Therefore, the court reasoned, the two entities acted jointly to deprive Tarkanian of liberty and property interests, making the NCAA as well as UNLV a state actor.

These contentions fundamentally misconstrue the facts of this case. In the typical case raising a state-action issue, a private party has taken the decisive step that caused the harm to the plaintiff, and the question is whether the state was sufficiently involved to treat that decisive conduct as state action. This may occur if the state creates the legal framework governing the conduct; if it delegates its authority to the private actor, or sometimes if it knowingly accepts the benefits derived from unconstitutional behavior. Thus, in the usual case we ask whether the state provided a mantle of authority that enhanced the power of the harm-causing individual actor.

This case uniquely mirrors the traditional state-action case. Here the final act challenged by Tarkanian—his suspension—was committed by UNLV. A state university without question is a state actor. When it decides to impose a serious disciplinary sanction on one of its tenured employees, it must comply with the terms of the Due Process Clause of the Fourteenth Amendment to the Federal Constitution. Thus when UNLV notified Tarkanian that he was being separated from all relations with the university's basketball program, it acted under color of state law within the meaning of 42 U.S.C. § 1983.

The mirror image presented in this case requires us to step through an analytical looking glass to resolve the case. Clearly UNLV's conduct was influenced by the rules and recommendations of the NCAA, the private party. But it was UNLV, the state entity, that actually suspended Tarkanian. Thus, the question is not whether UNLV participated to a critical extent in the NCAA's activities, but whether UNLV's actions in compliance with the NCAA rules and recommendations turned the NCAA's conduct into state action.

We examine first the relationship between UNLV and the NCAA regarding the NCAA's rulemaking. UNLV is among the NCAA members and participated in promulgating the Association's rules; it must be assumed, therefore, that Nevada had some impact on the NCAA's policy determinations. Yet the several hundred other public and private NCAA member institutions each similarly affected those policies. Those institutions, the vast majority of which were located in states other than Nevada, did not act under color of Nevada law. It necessarily follows that the source of the legislation adopted by the NCAA is not Nevada but the collective membership, speaking through an organization that is independent of any particular state.

State action nonetheless might lie if UNLV, by embracing NCAA rules, transformed them into state rules and the NCAA into a state actor. UNLV engaged in state action when it adopted NCAA rules to govern its own behavior, but that would be true even if UNLV had taken no part in the promulgation of those rules. Here, UNLV retained the authority to withdraw from the NCAA and establish its own standards. The university alternatively could have stayed in the Association and worked through the Association's legislative process to amend rules or standards it deemed harsh, unfair, or unwieldy. Neither UNLV's decision to adopt the NCAA standards nor its minor role in their formulation is a sufficient reason for concluding that the NCAA was acting under color of Nevada law when it promulgated standards governing athlete recruitment, eligibility, and academic performance.

Tarkanian further asserts that the NCAA's investigation, enforcement proceedings, and consequent recommendations constituted state action because they resulted from a delegation of power by UNLV. UNLV, as an NCAA member, subscribed to the statement in the Association's bylaws that NCAA enforcement procedures are an essential part of the intercollegiate athletic program of each member institution. It is, of course, true that a state may delegate authority to a private party and thereby make that party a state actor. But UNLV delegated no power to the NCAA to take specific action against any university employee. The commitment by UNLV to adhere to NCAA enforcement procedures was enforceable only by sanctions that the NCAA might impose on UNLV itself.

Indeed, the notion that UNLV's promise to cooperate in the NCAA enforcement proceedings was tantamount to a partnership agreement or the transfer of certain university powers to the NCAA is belied by the history of this case. It is quite obvious that UNLV used its best efforts to retain its winning coach—a goal diametrically opposed to the NCAA's interest in ascertaining the truth of its investigators' reports. During the several years that the NCAA investigated the alleged violations, the NCAA and UNLV acted much more like adversaries than like partners engaged in a dispassionate search for the truth. The NCAA cannot be regarded as an agent of UNLV for purposes of that proceeding. It is more correctly characterized as an agent of its remaining members that, as competitors of UNLV, had an interest in the effective and evenhanded enforcement of the NCAA recruitment standards. Just as a state-compensated public defender acts in a private capacity when he or she represents a private client in a conflict against the state, the NCAA is properly viewed as a private actor at odds with the state when it represents the interests of its entire membership in an investigation of one public university.

The NCAA enjoyed no governmental powers to facilitate its investigation. It had no power to subpoena witnesses, to impose contempt sanctions, or to assert sovereign authority over any individual. Its greatest authority was to threaten sanctions against UNLV, with the ultimate sanction being expulsion of the university from membership. Contrary to the premise of the Nevada Supreme Court's opinion, the NCAA did not—indeed, could not—directly discipline Tarkanian or any other state university employee. The express terms of the Confidential Report did not demand the suspension unconditionally; rather, it requested the university to show cause why the NCAA should not impose additional penalties if UNLV declines to suspend Tarkanian. Even the university's vice president acknowledged that the report gave the university options other than suspension: UNLV could have retained Tarkanian and risked additional sanctions, perhaps even expulsion from the NCAA, or it could have withdrawn voluntarily from the Association.

Finally, Tarkanian argues that the power of the NCAA is so great that the UNLV had no practical alternative to compliance with its demands. We are not at all sure this is true, but even if we assume that a private monopolist can impose its will on a state agency by a threatened refusal to deal with it, it does not follow that such a private party is therefore acting under color of state law.

In final analysis the question is whether the conduct allegedly causing the deprivation of a federal right can be fairly attributable to the state. It would be ironic indeed to conclude that the NCAA's imposition of sanctions against UNLV—sanctions that UNLV and its counsel, including the Attorney General of Nevada, steadfastly opposed during protracted adversary proceedings—is fairly attributable to the State of Nevada. It would be more appropriate to conclude that UNLV has conducted its athletic program under color of the policies adopted by the NCAA, rather than that those policies were developed and enforced under color of Nevada law.

The judgment of the Nevada Supreme Court is reversed, and the case is remanded to that court for further proceedings not inconsistent with this opinion.

 For an extended version of the case and review questions to test your understanding of the material, please go to www.HumanKinetics.com/CaseStudiesInSportLaw.

Palmer v. Merluzzi

868 F.2d 90 (3rd Cir. 1989)

This is an appeal from a summary judgment in favor of the defendants, Peter Merluzzi, Superintendent of Schools for the Hunterdon Central High School District, and the Hunterdon Central Board of Education. Plaintiff Dan Palmer, a student and football player at Hunterdon, claims that his Constitutional rights to due process and equal protection were violated when Superintendent Merluzzi suspended him from playing interscholastic football for 60 days.

In September of 1986, Dan Palmer was a senior at Hunterdon Central High School and a starting wide receiver on the high school's football team. He was also enrolled in a high school course called "Careers in Broadcasting Technology." On the evening of September 28, 1986, in order to fill a course requirement, Palmer and three other students were assigned, without faculty supervision, to the school radio station, which is located on the school premises. The next morning, beer stains and a marijuana pipe were discovered at the radio station. Later that day, Palmer, school disciplinarian Dr. Grimm, and Mr. Buckley, Palmer's former football coach, met in Mr. Buckley's office and Palmer was questioned about this discovery. During that meeting, Palmer admitted that the evening before he had smoked marijuana and consumed beer at the radio station.

On September 30, 1986, Dr. Grimm sent Mr. and Mrs. Palmer a letter advising them that their son had been assigned a 10-day out-of-school suspension effective from September 30, 1986 to October 13, 1986. The letter asked the Palmers to call Dr. Grimm if they had additional questions and suggested that they and their son consider counseling. The Palmers took no action to contest the 10-day suspension.

After Dr. Grimm's meeting with Palmer, Superintendent Merluzzi conferred about the appropriateness of additional discipline with Dr. Grimm, Mr. Buckley, assistant principal Dr. Myers, Mr. Kleber, the faculty director of the radio station, and Palmer's current football coach, Mr. Meert. Suspension from extracurricular activities was discussed and all except Dr. Grimm agreed that

such a step was appropriate. No specific number of days for such a suspension was discussed, however.

Thereafter, Merluzzi made telephone calls to two drug-counseling agencies. These agencies suggested 60 days as an average time for the rehabilitation of someone with a minor drug problem, and Merluzzi ultimately decided that 60 days would be an appropriate period for the students concerned to ponder their actions. All students who were involved in the incident at the radio station received the same punishment.

On October 13, the eve of the expiration of the 10-day suspension, the Board of Education met. Palmer's father, James Palmer, hearing "rumors" concerning the possible imposition of additional sanctions on his son, attended the meeting and spoke with Merluzzi shortly before it started. Merluzzi confirmed that he was inclined to impose a 60-day extracurricular suspension, but told James Palmer that he could raise the issue with the Board. James Palmer was accorded half an hour in closed session to present his views; he argued that the additional suspension would adversely affect his son's chances of playing football in college and would also reduce his chances of being awarded college scholarships. The Board declined to intervene and, after the meeting, Merluzzi informed all concerned parents that he was definitely going to impose the 60-day extracurricular suspension.

Subsequent to the imposition of the 60-day extracurricular suspension, Palmer appealed to the New Jersey State Commissioner of Education for a review of the actions of the defendants. On October 20, 1986, an evidentiary hearing was conducted before Administrative Law Judge Bruce R. Campbell. Judge Campbell found that the "ten-day out-of-school suspension was procedurally faultless and consistent with announced policy." With respect to the 60-day football suspension, however, he concluded that Palmer had been denied procedural due process. First Judge Campbell decided that Palmer's interest in participating in the school's football program was such that due process was implicated. Due process was not afforded, according to Judge Campbell, because Palmer was not given notice of the proposed 60-day suspension and afforded a hearing thereon.

On appeal, the Commissioner of Education affirmed the ALJ's finding that "the actions of the Board's agents in suspending [Palmer] from school for 10 days in all respects comports with the due process requirements set forth in *Goss v. Lopez*. . . . The commissioner did not, however, accept the ALJ's conclusion that "the decision to increase the penalty imposed on [Palmer] . . . rises to the level of requiring that the Board provide to him an additional due process proceeding." In the course of reaching this conclusion, the commissioner noted that Palmer "could not or should not have been unaware of the fact that his role as a member of the football team, as well as his status as a student in the school, was in jeopardy when he decided to take the actions he did." The district court granted summary judgment to the defendants, holding that for purposes of due process analysis, Palmer had no property or liberty interest in participating in the school's football program.

Resolution of this appeal does not require that we address the issue found dispositive by the ALJ and the district court—whether procedural due process is required whenever a public school student in New Jersey faces or receives for a breach of discipline solely a suspension from participation in his or her school's athletic program. Palmer did not commit an offense for which athletic suspension was the only potential sanction or the only sanction in fact imposed. Here there was a single proceeding on a single charge that resulted in two sanctions being imposed, a 10-day suspension from school and a 60-day suspension from athletics. The ultimate issue before us is whether the process received by Palmer in that single proceeding was appropriate given the fact that he faced, and ultimately received, both of those sanctions. We conclude that it was.

The threshold issue is whether the interests that could be adversely affected in the proceeding against Palmer were such that the due process clause was implicated. In *Goss v. Lopez*, 419 U.S. 565, 95 S.Ct. 729, 42 L.Ed.2d 725 (1975), the Supreme Court concluded that due process

was required when a student faced a 10-day scholastic suspension.

Having concluded that "some process" was due, we turn to the issue of how much was due. We know from *Goss* what process would have been due if only a 10-day academic suspension had been at stake. After balancing the competing interests involved, the court decided that the student must be given "oral or written notice of the charges against him and, if he denies them, an explanation of the evidence the authorities have and an opportunity to present his side of the story." The court continued, stating that "[t]here need be no delay between the time 'notice' is given and the time of the hearing. . . . We hold only that . . . the student first be told what he is accused of doing and what the basis of the accusation is." The court also stopped short of requiring that the student be given "the opportunity to secure counsel, to confront and cross-examine witnesses supporting the charge, or to call his own witnesses to verify his version of incident." As long as the student "at least ha[s] the opportunity to characterize his conduct and put it in what he deems the proper context," . . . , due process has been satisfied.

Palmer received the process required by *Goss*. The day after the incident at the radio station, in an informal hearing with Dr. Grimm and Mr. Buckley, he was advised of what had been found in the radio station and thus of the character of the offense being investigated. He then admitted his participation in the smoking of marijuana and the drinking of beer at the station. Palmer's involvement in the activities of that evening has never been disputed. During the conference, Palmer had the opportunity to put the events of the prior evening into what he perceived to be their proper context and could have argued for leniency had he so chosen.

Palmer acknowledges that due process would not have been violated if only the 10-day suspension from school had been imposed. Rather, Palmer's argument is that a second notice and a second hearing were required because at the time of his conference with Dr. Grimm he did not have adequate notice that a 60-day athletic suspension might be imposed on him.

We find this argument unpersuasive. The notice required by *Goss* is notice of "what [the student] is accused of doing and what the basis of the accusation is." We have been cited to no authority, and we know of none, suggesting that the notice of the charge and supporting evidence in a *Goss* situation must include a statement of the penalties that could be imposed in the course of the proceeding. We decline to adopt such a requirement in a situation like the one before us, in which the possible sanctions are knowable from previously published materials or are obvious from the circumstances.

In this case, Palmer was advised at the outset that he was suspected of consuming alcohol and a drug on school property. The Student Handbook, which was applicable to all students, specified that "alcohol and/or drug use" would, if a first offense, result in "10 days suspension" from school. The Interscholastic Athletic Program policy statement, which was applicable to Palmer and other students participating in that program, warned that "no student may participate who has not demonstrated good citizenship and responsibility." Based on these provisions, the nature of the offense, and common sense, we, like the New Jersey Commissioner of Education, are confident that Palmer must have realized from the outset that his football eligibility, as well as his status as a student, was at stake. Accordingly, we hold that Palmer's interview with Dr. Grimm and Mr. Buckley provided just as meaningful an opportunity to argue against the athletic suspension as against the scholastic suspension.

Having concluded that Palmer received the process contemplated by *Goss*, we turn to the issue of whether more than that process was required in this case because Palmer faced not only a 10-day suspension from school but a football suspension as well. Palmer urges, as we understand it, that his interest in avoiding an erroneous deprivation of his participation in the football program for 60 days was sufficiently great and that before any decision was made concerning the sanction for his misconduct, he should have been given express notice of the fact that his football eligibility was in jeopardy and that he should have been given the opportunity to secure the advice of an attorney before presenting his defense. Although we acknowledge that the 60-day football suspension had a substantial impact on Palmer, determination of the amount of process due in a given situation involves a balancing of interests and we conclude that, when the balance is struck, the procedure prescribed in *Goss* was sufficient under the circumstances of this case.

Due process is a flexible concept and the process due in any situation is to be determined by weighing (1) the private interests at stake, (2) the governmental interests at stake, and (3) the fairness and reliability of the existing procedures and the probable value, if any, of additional procedural safeguards. In *Goss*, the court described the student's interest as one in avoiding "unfair or mistaken exclusion from the educational process with all its unfortunate consequences." Those consequences include not only the loss of the benefit of the educational process but also potential damage to "the students' standing with their fellow students and their teachers" and potential "interfer[ence] with later opportunities for higher education and employment."

From the school's and the public's point of view, *Goss* recognized the need for maintaining order and discipline in our schools without prohibitive costs and in a manner that will contribute to, rather than disrupt, the educational process. As we have noted, the court concluded that an informal hearing process would reconcile the private and governmental interests and that requiring representation by counsel, cross-examination, and other, more formal procedural safeguards would not sufficiently increase the reliability and fairness of the process to warrant the additional expense and disruption of the educational process.

We accept for present purposes Palmer's contention that, while called an extracurricular activity, the school's football program is an integral part of its educational program. Nevertheless, it is but one part of that program and in terms of lost educational benefit, the loss occasioned by a football suspension is far less than that occasioned by a suspension from school for a comparable period of time. In terms of the student's standing with teachers and peers, we believe the potential loss is likely to be a function of the nature of the offense rather than the penalty; it is therefore unlikely to be affected by the fact that the sanction includes an athletic as well as a school suspension. As a general proposition, we believe the same can be said for the potential for interference with later opportunities for higher education and employment. Indeed, Palmer does not argue otherwise. The loss that he emphasizes is the possible loss of the opportunity to play college football. Although we acknowledge that the loss of the opportunity to impress college scouts with one's senior year play can have a significant adverse effect on one's chances for a college football career, we believe it would be unduly disruptive of a school's educational process to require one disciplinary process for football players and similarly situated athletes and another disciplinary process for other students.

Since the governmental interest at stake here is the same as that in *Goss*, since the incremental efficacy of the process proposed over the process afforded is not materially different than the one in that case, and since we find the student's interest to be only slightly greater, we conclude that the process required by *Goss* was sufficient in the circumstances presented by this case.

Palmer also contends that his suspension violated his right to equal protection under the Fourteenth Amendment. Since participation in extracurricular activities is not a fundamental right under the Constitution and since Palmer's suspension was not based on a suspect classification, . . . we must examine Palmer's argument under the "rational relationship test." We conclude that the disciplinary actions taken by the school were rationally related to a valid state interest. The state has very strong interests in preserving a drug-free environment in its schools and in discouraging drug use by its students. We are unwilling to say that the sanctions imposed on Palmer were not reasonably designed to serve those legitimate interests. Since Palmer's suspensions from school and participation in interscholastic football did not violate any right secured by the Constitution, we will affirm the judgment of the district court.

 For an extended version of the case and review questions to test your understanding of the material, please go to www.HumanKinetics.com/CaseStudiesInSportLaw.

Schaill v. Tippecanoe County School Corporation

864 F.2d 1309 (7th Cir. 1988)

The essential facts of this case are undisputed and can be stated quite briefly. TSC operates Harrison and McCutcheon High Schools in Indiana. In the spring of 1986, based on information concerning possible drug use by athletes on the McCutcheon High School baseball team, the team's coach ordered 16 team members to provide urine samples. Of the 16 students tested, five students' tests produced positive results for the presence of marijuana. Based on these results, other reports of drug use among participants in the TSC athletic program, and their concern over the high incidence of drug abuse among high school students nationwide, the board of trustees of TSC decided to institute a random urine testing program for interscholastic athletes and cheerleaders in the TSC school system.

Under the program, all students desiring to participate in interscholastic athletics and their parent or guardian are required to sign a consent form agreeing to submit to urinalysis if chosen on a random basis. Each student selected for an athletic team is assigned a number. The athletic director and head coach of each athletic team are authorized to institute random urine tests during the athletic season. In order to select individuals to be tested, the number assigned to each athlete is placed in a box and a single number is drawn.

The student selected for testing is accompanied by a school official of the same sex to a bathroom, where the student is provided with an empty specimen bottle. The student is then allowed to enter a lavatory stall and close the door in order to produce a sample. The student is not under direct visual observation while producing the sample; however, the water in the toilet is tinted to prevent the student from substituting water for the sample, the monitor stands outside the stall to listen for normal sounds of urination and the monitor checks the temperature of the sample by hand in order to assure its genuineness. The chain of custody of the sample is designed to ensure the accuracy and anonymity of the testing procedure. The sample is sent to a private testing laboratory, where it is initially tested for the presence of controlled substances or performance-enhancing drugs using the enzyme multiplied immunoassay technique (EMIT). Any sample that tests positive is then retested using the more accurate, and more expensive, gas chromatography/mass spectrometry (GC/MS) method.

If a sample tests positive under both the EMIT and GC/MS analyses, the student and his or her parent or guardian are informed of the results. They then have the opportunity to have the remaining portion of the sample tested at a laboratory of their choice. The student and his or her parent or guardian may also present the athletic director with any evidence that suggests an innocent explanation for the positive result, such as the fact that the athlete legally takes prescription or over-the-counter medication. Barring a satisfactory explanation, the student is then suspended from participation in a portion of the varsity competitions held during the athletic season. A first positive urinalysis test results in a suspension from 30% of the athletic contests, a second positive results in a 50% suspension, a third positive causes a suspension for a full calendar year, and a fourth positive results in the student's being barred from all interscholastic athletic competitions during the remainder of the student's high school career. No other penalties are imposed, and a student may decrease the specified punishment by participating in an approved drug-counseling program.

In the spring of 1987, appellants Darcy Schaill and Shelley Johnson were 15-year-old sophomores at Harrison High School. Shelley had been a member of the varsity swim team as a freshman. Both appellants attended an organizational meeting for students desiring to participate in interscholastic athletics in the fall of 1987, at which time they were first informed of the proposed implementation of the TSC urinalysis program. Both appellants were offended by the thought of having to undergo urinalysis as a condition of participation in interscholastic athletics, and both decided that they would forego the opportunity to compete in interscholastic athletics if required to sign a form consenting to random urine testing. TSC adopted the current version of its drug-testing program on August 28, 1987. Appellants had filed their complaint, which initially challenged a prior version of the program, on August 25, 1987. The district court conducted a trial on the merits of appellants' Fourth Amendment and due process claims on December 7 and 8, 1987. On February 1, 1988, the district court entered its memorandum opinion and order denying appellants' claims for declaratory and injunctive relief. This appeal followed.

As a threshold matter, we must consider whether TSC's random urine testing program involves a "search" as that term is employed in the Fourth Amendment. The Supreme Court has held that "[a] 'search' occurs when an expectation of privacy that society is prepared to consider reasonable is infringed." There can be little doubt that a person engaging in the act of urination possesses a reasonable expectation of privacy as to that act, and as to the urine that is excreted. In our society, it is expected that urination be performed in private, that urine be disposed of in private and that the act, if mentioned at all, be described in euphemistic terms. The fact that urine is voluntarily discharged from the body and treated as a waste product does not eliminate the expectation of privacy that an individual possesses in his or her urine. While urine is excreted from the body, it is not "knowingly expose[d] to the public," . . . ; instead, the highly private manner by which an individual disposes of his or her urine demonstrates that it is not intended to be inspected or examined by anyone.

It is not clear whether, or to what extent, the TSC random urinalysis program's status as a search is affected by the fact that tests will be performed only with respect to students who have previously given their consent. The consent provided in the forms supplied to students is certainly not dispositive of the "search" issue since execution of a consent form is a prerequisite to participation in interscholastic athletics. It is certainly relevant to the ultimate question of constitutionality, however, that the activity to which random testing is attached is participation in an extracurricular activity. Random testing is not, as we discuss later, a condition of a weightier benefit such as employment or school attendance. Nonetheless, since participation in interscholastic athletics is expressly conditioned on a student's waiver of his or her Fourth Amendment rights, the "voluntariness" of a student's submission to urinalysis testing does not alone dispose of the constitutional issues presented by appellants. We must therefore decide whether the searches contemplated by TSC in this case violate the Fourth Amendment.

Having determined that urine testing constitutes a "search" in the constitutional sense, we must consider what level of suspicion is required to authorize urinalysis of any particular student. Appellants first argue that individual student's urine may not be tested unless TSC officials have probable cause to believe that the particular student has consumed the drugs that the test is designed to detect and have obtained a warrant authorizing the test from a neutral and detached judicial officer. Determining the level of suspicion required before the government may conduct a search requires "balanc[ing] the nature and quality of the intrusion on the individual's Fourth Amendment interests against the importance of the governmental interests alleged to justify the intrusion." Unfortunately for appellants, we believe that the Supreme Court has already struck the appropriate balance in the context of school searches and has determined that the probable cause and warrant requirements do not apply.

In *New Jersey v. T.L.O.*, 469 U.S. 325, 105 S.Ct. 733, 83 L.Ed.2d 720 (1985), a school official searched a student's purse, based on a reasonable suspicion that the student had been smoking on school grounds, in violation of school rules. The court therefore held that the warrant and probable cause requirements did not apply; instead, school searches should be judged under the standard of "reasonableness under all the circumstances." The court noted that this standard would "spare teachers and school administrators the necessity of schooling themselves in the niceties of probable cause and permit them to regulate their conduct according to the dictates of reason and common sense."

Appellants argue that where, as here, a search is authorized well in advance of its execution, there is no "special need" to relax the traditional warrant and probable cause requirements. The Supreme Court has ruled that the probable cause and warrant requirements are not applicable to school searches. We therefore reject appellant's broadest attack against the TSC program.

Since the probable cause and warrant requirements are not applicable to the searches involved in this case, we must consider the TSC urinalysis program under the general Fourth Amendment standard of reasonableness. As the Supreme Court recognized in *T.L.O.*, "[t]he fundamental command of the Fourth Amendment is that searches and seizures be reasonable, and although 'both the concept of probable cause and requirement of a warrant bear on the reasonableness of a search, . . . in certain limited circumstances neither is required.'"

In the present case, TSC plans to conduct a search not only without probable cause or a warrant, but in the absence of any individualized suspicion of drug use by the students to be tested. In these circumstances, TSC bears a heavier burden to justify its contemplated actions. However, in several carefully defined situations, the Court has recognized that searches may be conducted in the absence of any grounds to believe that the individual searched has violated the law. The Court has stressed that "[i]n those situations in which the balance of interests precludes insistence upon 'some quantum of individualized suspicion,' other safeguards are generally relied upon to assure that the individual's reasonable expectation of privacy is not 'subject to the discretion of the officer in the field.'" While allowing that "some quantum of individualized suspicion is usually a prerequisite to a constitutional search or seizure," the Court held that "the Fourth Amendment imposes no irreducible requirement of such suspicion."

Nor has individualized suspicion been required in the so-called "administrative search" cases. In these cases, the Court has approved of warrantless, suspicionless searches of commercial premises operating in certain "heavily regulated industries."

The preceding discussion highlights several principles that must inform our decision whether the warrantless, suspicionless searches that TSC proposes are consistent with the Fourth Amendment. First, suspicionless searches are more likely to be permissible in circumstances where an individual has diminished expectations of privacy. An individual's privacy rights vary with the context—whether the individual is at home, at work, in school or in jail, in a car, or on a public sidewalk. Further, in certain pursuits, an individual's expectations of privacy are diminished by a past history of significant governmental regulation.

Second, the governmental interests furthered by a particular search must be weighty, and generally of a nature that alternate, less intrusive means of detection would not sufficiently serve the government's ends. For example, where unlawful conduct or conditions cannot be detected through other means, a warrantless and suspicionless search may be appropriate. That alternative investigative techniques would not deter unlawful conduct to the same extent as the challenged practice may also be a relevant consideration.

The extent to which the examining officer's discretion is limited by the regulatory scheme under which searches are conducted is also an important factor. Confining the enforcement discretion of the officer in the field serves several important functions. First, if individuals are selected for a search based on clearly articulated, objective criteria, the possibility that any particular search is motivated by a desire to harass or intimidate is diminished accordingly. Further, previously enunciated selection criteria assure the individuals searched that the officer is acting in accordance with his or her lawful authority. Objective selection criteria also tend to diminish the subjective intrusiveness of a particular search—the individual is able to understand how and why he or she was selected for search, and need not fear that he or she was "singled out" for improper reasons.

Finally, whether or not the search is intended to discover evidence of criminal activity is of critical importance in assessing the validity of warrantless, suspicionless searches. A search conducted for civil or nonpunitive purposes may be valid in circumstances where a search conducted as part of a criminal investigation would not be permissible. With the foregoing principles in mind, we turn to a more detailed consideration of the urinalysis program proposed in this case.

In general, there is a substantial expectation of privacy in connection with the act of urination. However, the privacy considerations are somewhat mitigated on the facts before us because the provider of the urine sample enters a closed lavatory stall and the person monitoring the urination stands outside listening for the sounds appropriate to what is taking place. The invasion of privacy is therefore not nearly as severe as would be the case if the monitor were required to observe the subject in the act of urination.

We also find great significance in the fact that the drug-testing program in this case is being implemented solely with regard to participants in an interscholastic athletic program. In the first place, in athletic programs in general there is a much diminished expectation of privacy and, in particular, privacy with respect to urinalysis. There is an element of "communal undress" inherent in athletic participation, which suggests reduced expectations of privacy. In addition, physical examinations are integral to almost all athletic programs. In fact, athletes and cheerleaders desiring to participate in the TSC athletic program have long been required to produce a urine sample as part of a mandatory medical examination. This sample is not produced under monitored conditions, is only tested for the presence of sugar in the urine, and is given to the athlete's physician of choice rather than a school official; however, the fact that such samples are required suggests that legitimate expectations of privacy in this context are diminished.

Further, in the case before us, we are dealing with interscholastic athletics. In these programs the Indiana High School Athletic Association has extensive requirements that it imposes on schools and individuals participating in interscholastic athletics. These include minimum grade, residency, and eligibility requirements. In addition to IHSAA regulations, participants in interscholastic athletics are also subject to training rules, including prohibitions on smoking, drinking, and drug use both on and off school premises. Perhaps even more demonstrative of the special characteristics of athletics is the high visibility and pervasiveness of drug testing in professional and collegiate athletics in this country and in the Olympic Games. The suspension and disqualification of prominent athletes on the basis of positive urinalysis results has been the subject of intense publicity all over the world.

The combination of these factors makes it quite implausible that students competing for positions on an interscholastic athletic team would have strong expectations of privacy with respect to urine tests. We can, of course, appreciate that monitored collection and subsequent testing of urine samples may be distasteful, but such procedures can hardly come as a great shock or surprise under present-day circumstances. For this reason, we believe that sports are quite distinguishable from almost any other activity. Random testing of athletes does not necessarily imply random testing of band members or the chess team.

We also note that, as in the "administrative search" cases, there is a strong element of "implied consent" involved in the urinalysis program at issue in this case. These plaintiffs and other athletes must, of course, consent to random urine testing for drugs as a condition of participating in interscholastic athletics. As we have noted, this consent in itself does not render these procedures any the less "searches" subject to the Fourth Amendment. Nonetheless, we must weigh in the balance the fact that these plaintiffs are required to submit to random drug testing only as a condition of participation in an extracurricular activity—athletics. Refusal to submit to these tests will not result in loss of employment, criminal penalties, or any academic penalty whatsoever. No student will be suspended or expelled from school. A student who has a positive urinalysis result will not even be denied participation in the athletic program. He or she will merely be refused participation in 30% of the games.

Although, therefore, there is certainly a burden on these plaintiffs' right to refuse drug testing, that burden is a light one compared with, for example, cases where drug testing is a condition of employment, promotion, or similar job-related interest. Participation in interscholastic athletics is a benefit carrying with it enhanced prestige and status in the student community. It is not unreasonable to couple these benefits with an obligation to undergo drug testing. The fact that students execute consent forms and are fully informed of the manner in which the program will be implemented also provides notice to students that they may be asked to submit to a search. The notice provided by the consent forms significantly diminishes the subjective intrusiveness of the urine testing proposed by TSC. The fact, therefore, that the drug testing involved here is, to the extent indicated, consensual is important to our determination of the constitutionality of the program.

Obviously, TSC's interest in the particular program at issue in this case cannot be gainsaid. In the TSC school system itself, urine tests administered to members of the McCutcheon baseball team in the spring of 1986 produced 5 positive results out of 16 students tested. The incidence of drug use revealed by this test, slightly greater than 31%, is consistent with the national and statewide statistics. Based on this evidence, the district court found that the student athletes involved here used drugs to the same extent as students in the national profile. This is certainly not an established fact, but it is not a wholly unreasonable inference.

The harm done by drug usage by student athletes was the subject of a great deal of testimony in the district court and of findings by the trial judge. At trial, Jacob Burton, the assistant principal and athletic director at McCutcheon High School, testified to three instances in which athletes had admitted that injuries had been caused or exacerbated by drug impairment during athletic contests. In addition, as Judge Sharp found, "[t]he interscholastic athletes of a public school system typically enjoy a unique identity within the school community. . . . The student athlete is generally viewed by the broader community with admiration and respect." Because of their high visibility and leadership roles, it is not unreasonable to single out athletes and cheerleaders for special attention with respect to drug usage. This court may take judicial notice of the fact that in the society at large drug usage by athletes is highly publicized and is a matter of great concern. Drug usage by this widely-admired group is likely to affect the behavior of others and school authorities are within their discretion in conducting a program specifically directed at athletes. We believe that the evidence supports TSC's determination that drug usage among student athletes is a problem with serious implications for students' health and safety. For these reasons, TSC has a substantial interest in enforcement of its proposed random urinalysis program.

The record also contains substantial evidence that alternative methods of investigation would not adequately serve the school's interest in detection and deterrence of drug use. While there was some disagreement between plaintiffs' and defendants' experts regarding the efficacy of trained visual observation, neurobehavioral testing, education programs, or individualized suspicion urine testing, we believe that the evidence of record fully supported the district court's conclusion that the choice made by TSC was reasonable in the circumstances of this case. Among other things, random testing may be particularly effective as a deterrent. Again, we must stress that we are reviewing a decision of school administrators as to how best to deal with a serious threat to the school's learning environment. The school's choice of appropriate means to combat this health and disciplinary problem will not be overturned unless unreasonable in light of available alternatives. Having heard the live testimony of numerous witnesses on this point, the trial court's finding that TSC had made a reasonable decision in implementing its urinalysis program is entitled to considerable deference, and we will not upset this conclusion on appeal.

Where a search is based on general factors rather than individualized suspicion, there is an additional requirement to sustain the constitutionality of the search. The search program must incorporate adequate safeguards to assure that reasonable expectations of privacy are not "subject to the discretion of the official in the field." We believe that this important requirement is met in this case.

The TSC program specifies that athletes will be selected for testing by drawing numbers on a random basis. The officials in charge will not exercise any discretion as to who will be chosen. There are specific provisions for the manner in which the sample is to be obtained, the handling and testing of the sample by a competent laboratory, the confirmation of positive test results, and the consequences of confirmed positive results. We also note that students will be fully advised of the manner in which the program will operate when they are initially asked to sign consent forms, and they will be given a copy of the TSC Drug Program. The information provided will eliminate any element of surprise if and when a particular student is selected for testing, and the student will be able to assure him- or herself that he or she has been selected for testing in a fair and impartial manner. Further, the use of published selection criteria ensures that a student is not stigmatized among his or her peers due to selection for testing.

Finally, we note that the TSC urinalysis program has been instituted in order to enforce the rules of the athletic program and the school. The program is not intended to discover evidence of unlawful activity for use in criminal prosecution. Even in the school setting, the school board has gone to great lengths to emphasize rehabilitation over punishment, as is evidenced both by the progressive nature of the sanctions for a positive test result and by the fact that a student may reduce the length of any suspension imposed by participating in an approved drug-counseling program.

The convergence of several important factors convinces us that the searches involved here take place in one of the relatively unusual environments in which suspicionless searches are permissible: interscholastic athletes have diminished expectations of privacy and have voluntarily chosen to participate in an activity that subjects them to pervasive regulation of off-campus behavior; the school's interest in preserving a drug-free athletic program is substantial and cannot adequately be furthered by less intrusive measures; the TSC program adequately limits the discretion of the officials performing the search; and the information sought is intended to be used solely for noncriminal educational and rehabilitative purposes. Based on a careful and considered weighing of these factors, we conclude that the TSC urinalysis program does not violate the Fourth Amendment.

Appellant's final contention is that the procedures provided in the TSC program for a student to challenge a positive urinalysis test are insufficient under the due process clause of the Fourteenth Amendment. As an initial matter, we note that there is room for doubt whether a student athlete has a constitutionally protected liberty interest in being free of the potential stigma associated with removal from an athletic team. This is especially true where, as here, the plaintiffs have brought a facial challenge to TSC's program. At this point in the implementation of the TSC program, it is highly speculative to assume that the reasons for a student's suspension from athletic competition will become general knowledge, and that the student's reputation will be adversely affected by a suspension. In any event, even assuming that some sort of liberty interest is involved, we believe that the TSC program provides all the process that is due.

Appellants fault the TSC program for placing on the student the burden of proving that the twice-confirmed test result is erroneous, for requiring the student to hire his own toxicologist or testing laboratory to conduct a further evaluation of the TSC urine test, and for allowing the athletic director, who was personally involved in the collection, labeling, and storage of the initial sample, to serve as the adjudicator of the student's claim that the initial result was erroneous.

Given the high degree of accuracy inhering in TSC's testing procedures, we cannot conclude that the school system has violated the due process clause by placing the burden to disprove a confirmed positive result on the student. Further, after providing a confirmatory test using the most accurate technology available at no cost to the student, TSC cannot be faulted for requiring a student to bear the cost of any further testing that the student may desire to perform.

Since TSC's drug-testing program provides for confirmatory testing at no cost to the student and provides the student with notice of the results of the test and an opportunity to rebut a positive result, we cannot find that TSC's drug-testing program violates the due process clause.

In our consideration and decision of this case, we have been mindful of the Supreme Court's admonition that public school students "do not shed their constitutional rights . . . at the schoolhouse gate." In this case, we believe that the Tippecanoe County School Corporation has chosen a reasonable and limited response to a serious evil. In formulating its urinalysis program, the school district has been sensitive to the privacy rights of its students and has sought to emphasize rehabilitation over punishment. We cannot conclude that this approach is inconsistent with the mandates of the Constitution. The judgment of the district court is therefore AFFIRMED.

 For an extended version of the case and review questions to test your understanding of the material, please go to www.HumanKinetics.com/CaseStudiesInSportLaw.

Spring Branch I.S.D. v. Stamos

695 S.W.2d 556 (Tex. 1985)

This is a direct appeal brought by the Attorney General, representing the Texas Education Agency, and others, seeking immediate appellate review of an order of the trial court that held unconstitutional, and enjoined enforcement of, a provision of the Texas Education Code. We hold that the statutory provision is not unconstitutional and reverse the judgment of the trial court.

Chris Stamos and others brought this suit on behalf of Nicky Stamos and others, seeking a permanent injunction against enforcement of the Texas no-pass, no-play rule by the Spring Branch and Alief Independent School Districts. The Texas Education Agency and the University Interscholastic League intervened. The district court issued a temporary restraining order and later, after a hearing, a temporary injunction enjoining all parties from enforcing the rule. This court issued an order staying the district court's order and setting the cause for expedited review.

The Second Called Session of the 68th Legislature adopted a package of educational reforms known as H.B. 72. A major provision of these educational reforms was the so-called no-pass, no-play rule, which generally requires that students maintain a 70 average in all classes to be eligible for participation in extracurricular activities. The rule is incorporated in § 21.920 of the Texas Education Code and provides as follows:

§ 21.920. Extracurricular Activities

(a) The State Board of Education by rule shall limit participation in and practice for extracurricular activities during the school day and the school week. The rules shall, to the extent possible, preserve the school day for academic activities without interruption for extracurricular activities. In scheduling those activities and practices, a district must comply with the rules of the board; (b) A student, other than a mentally retarded student, enrolled in a school district in this state shall be suspended from participation in any extracurricular activity sponsored or sanctioned by the school district during the grade reporting period after a grade reporting period in which the student received a grade lower than the equivalent of 70 on a scale of 100 in any academic class. The campus principal may remove this suspension if the class is an identified honors or advanced class. A student may not be suspended under this subsection during the period in which school is recessed for the summer or during the initial grade reporting period of a regular school term on the basis of grades received in the final grade reporting period of the preceding regular school term; (c) In this section, "mentally retarded" has the meaning assigned by Section 21.503(b)(5) of this code; (d) Subsection (b) of this section applies beginning with the spring semester, 1985.

The sole issue before this court is the constitutionality of the no-pass, no-play rule. The district court held the rule unconstitutional on the grounds that it violated equal protection and due process guarantees. The burden is on the party attacking the constitutionality of an act of the legislature. There is a presumption in favor of the constitutionality of an act of the legislature.

This court has long recognized the important role education plays in the maintenance of our democratic society. Article VII of the Texas Constitution discloses a well-considered purpose on the part of those who framed it to bring about the establishment and maintenance of a comprehensive system of public education, consisting of a general public free school system and a system of higher education. Section 1 of Article VII of the constitution establishes a mandatory duty on the legislature to make suitable provision for the support and maintenance of public free schools. The constitution leaves to the legislature alone the determination of which methods, restrictions, and regulations are necessary and appropriate to carry out this duty, so long as that determination is not so arbitrary as to violate the constitutional rights of Texas' citizens.

Stamos challenges the constitutionality of the no-pass, no-play rule on the ground that it violates the equal protection clause of the Texas Constitution. The first determination this court must make in the context of equal protection analysis is the appropriate standard of review. When the classification created by a state regulatory scheme neither infringes on fundamental rights or interests nor burdens an inherently suspect class, equal protection analysis requires that the classification be rationally related to a legitimate state interest. Therefore, we must first determine whether the rule burdens an inherently suspect class or infringes on fundamental rights or interests.

The no-pass, no-play rule classifies students based on their achievement levels in their academic courses. We hold that those students who fail to maintain a minimum level of proficiency in all of their courses do not constitute the type of discrete, insular minority necessary to constitute a suspect class. Thus, the rule does not burden an inherently suspect class.

Stamos also argues that the rule is subject to strict scrutiny under equal protection analysis because it impinges on a fundamental right (i.e., the right to participate in extracurricular activities). We note that the overwhelming majority of jurisdictions have held that a student's right to participation in extracurricular activities does not constitute a fundamental right.

Stamos cites the case of *Bell v. Lone Oak Independent School District*, 507 S.W.2d 636 (Tex.Civ. App.—Texarkana), writ dism'd, 515 S.W.2d 252 (Tex. 1974), for the proposition that students have a fundamental right to participate in extracurricular activities. In *Bell*, a school regulation prohibited married students from participating in extracurricular activities. Because the regulation impinged on the fundamental right of marriage, the court of appeals held the regulation subject to strict scrutiny and struck it down because the school district had shown no compelling interest to support its enforcement. The presence of a fundamental right (marriage) distinguishes *Bell* from the present cause.

Fundamental rights have their genesis in the express and implied protections of personal liberty recognized in federal and state constitutions. A student's right to participate in extracurricular activities does not rise to the same level as the right to free speech or free exercise of religion, both of which have long been recognized as fundamental rights under our state and federal constitutions. We adopt the majority rule and hold that a student's right to participate in extracurricular activities *per se* does not rise to the level of a fundamental right under our constitution.

Because the no-pass, no-play rule neither infringes on fundamental rights nor burdens an inherently suspect class, we hold that it is not subject to strict or heightened equal protection scrutiny. Rather, the rule must be judged by the standard set forth in *Sullivan v. UIL*. In *Sullivan*, this court struck down on equal protection grounds the UIL's nontransfer rule, which declared all nonseniors ineligible for varsity football and basketball competition for one year following their transfer to a new school. This court emphasized (1) the over-inclusiveness of the rule in light of its intended purpose of discouraging recruitment of student athletes and (2) the irrebuttable presumption created by the rule. In view of these two factors, this court declared that the rule was not rationally related to its intended purpose.

The no-pass, no-play rule distinguishes students based on whether they maintain a satisfactory minimum level of performance in each of their classes. Students who fail to maintain a minimum proficiency in all of their classes are ineligible for participation in school-sponsored extracurricular activities for the following six-week period, with no carryover from one school year to the next. The rule provides a strong incentive for students wishing to participate in extracurricular activities to maintain minimum levels of performance in all of their classes. In view of the rule's objective to promote improved classroom performance by students, we find the rule rationally related to the legitimate state interest in providing a quality education to Texas' public school students. The rule does not suffer from either of the vices found determinative in *Sullivan v. UIL*.

The distinctions recognized in the rule for mentally retarded students and students enrolled in honors or advanced courses likewise do not render the rule violative of the equal protection guarantees of the Texas Constitution. While the statute itself does not deprive students of their right to equal protection of the law, we recognize that the discretion given to school principals in the rule's provision dealing with honors or advanced courses may well give rise to arbitrary or discriminatory application violative of equal protection principles. We are faced with no allegations of discriminatory

application of the rule's honors exception in the present case.

We begin our analysis of the due process arguments in this cause by recognizing that the strictures of due process apply only to the threatened deprivation of liberty and property interests deserving the protection of the federal and state constitutions. The federal courts have made it clear that the federal constitution's due process guarantees do not protect a student's interest in participating in extracurricular activities. We must, then, examine our state constitution to determine whether its due process guarantees extend to a student's desire to participate in school-sponsored extracurricular activities.

A property or liberty interest must find its origin in some aspect of state law. Nothing in either our state constitution or statutes entitles students to an absolute right to participation in extracurricular activities. We are in agreement, therefore, with the overwhelming majority of jurisdictions that students do not possess a constitutionally protected interest in their participation in extracurricular activities. Therefore, the strictures of procedural due process do not apply to the determination by a campus principal, pursuant to § 21.920(b) of the Texas Education Code, as to whether a student who fails an identified honors or advanced course shall be permitted to participate in extracurricular activities.

As stated previously, students have no constitutionally protected interest in participation in extracurricular activities. Because no constitutionally protected interest is implicated by this delegation of authority to school principals, no violation of due process, substantive or procedural, results therefrom.

We do not agree with Stamos' argument that a school principal's exercise of discretion pursuant to the honors exception to the rule is shielded from all review. Arbitrary, capricious, or discriminatory exercise of a school principal's discretion pursuant to subsection 21.920(b) of the Texas Education Code may well give rise to claims based on equal protection grounds. Accreditation audits of schools and school districts may also afford relief against improper utilization of the honors exception. We also note there are no findings of fact before us that any of the student plaintiffs received failing grades in honors or advanced courses.

Finally, Stamos argues that because the no-pass, no-play rule did not become effective until April 5, 1985, it was applied in an *ex post facto* manner to the students involved in this case. We choose not to address this issue, because we have no findings of fact before us relating to the circumstances surrounding the application of the rule to any of the concerned students. We note that the district court has yet to address this issue.

Accordingly, we reverse the district court's judgment with regard to the constitutionality of § 21.920 of the Texas Education Code and dissolve the temporary injunction ordered by the district court.

 For an extended version of the case and review questions to test your understanding of the material, please go to www.HumanKinetics.com/CaseStudiesInSportLaw.

Tinker v. Des Moines Independent Community School District

393 U.S. 503 (1969)

Petitioner John F. Tinker, 15-years-old, and petitioner Christopher Eckhardt, 16-years-old, attended high schools in Des Moines, Iowa. Petitioner Mary Beth Tinker, John's sister, was a 13-year-old student in junior high school. In December 1965, a group of adults and students in Des Moines held a meeting at the Eckhardt home. The group determined to publicize their objections to the hostilities in Vietnam and their support for a truce by wearing black armbands during the holiday season and by fasting on December 16 and New Year's Eve. Petitioners and their parents had previously engaged in similar activities, and they decided to participate in the program.

The principals of the Des Moines schools became aware of the plan to wear armbands. On December 14, 1965, they met and adopted a policy that any student wearing an armband to school would be asked to remove it, and if he refused he would be suspended until he returned without the armband. Petitioners were aware of the regulation that the school authorities adopted.

On December 16, Mary Beth and Christopher wore black armbands to their schools. John Tinker wore his armband the next day. They were all sent home and suspended from school until they would come back without their armbands. They did not return to school until after the planned period for wearing armbands had expired—that is, until after New Year's Day.

This complaint was filed in the United States District Court by petitioners, through their fathers, under § 1983 of Title 42 of the United States Code. It prayed for an injunction restraining the respondent school officials and the respondent members of the board of directors of the school district from disciplining the petitioners, and it sought nominal damages. After an evidentiary hearing the district court dismissed the complaint. It upheld the constitutionality of the school authorities' action on the ground that it was reasonable in order to prevent disturbance of school discipline. The court referred to but expressly declined to follow the Fifth Circuit's holding in a similar case that the wearing of symbols like the armbands cannot be prohibited unless it "materially and substantially interfere(s) with the requirements of appropriate discipline in the operation of the school."

On appeal, the Court of Appeals for the Eighth Circuit considered the case *en banc*. The court was equally divided, and the district court's decision was accordingly affirmed, without opinion. We granted *certiorari*.

The district court recognized that the wearing of an armband for the purpose of expressing certain views is the type of symbolic act that is within the Free Speech Clause of the First Amendment. As we shall discuss, the wearing of armbands in the circumstances of this case was entirely divorced from actually or potentially disruptive conduct by those participating in it. It was closely akin to pure speech, which, we have repeatedly held, is entitled to comprehensive protection under the First Amendment.

First Amendment rights, applied in light of the special characteristics of the school environment, are available to teachers and students. It can hardly be argued that either students or teachers shed their constitutional rights to freedom of speech or expression at the schoolhouse gate. This has been the unmistakable holding of this court for almost 50 years.

In *West Virginia State Board of Education v. Barnette, supra* (*West Virginia State Board of Education v. Barnette,* 319 U.S. 624 [1943]), this court held that under the First Amendment, the student in public school may not be compelled to salute the flag. On the other hand, the court has repeatedly emphasized the need for affirming the comprehensive authority of the states and of school officials, consistent with fundamental constitutional safeguards, to prescribe and control conduct in the schools. Our problem lies in the area where students in the exercise of First Amendment rights collide with the rules of the school authorities.

The problem posed by the present case does not relate to regulation of the length of skirts or the type of clothing, to hair style, or deportment. It does not concern aggressive, disruptive action, or even group demonstrations. Our problem involves direct, primary First Amendment rights akin to pure speech.

The school officials banned and sought to punish petitioners for a silent, passive expression of opinion, unaccompanied by any disorder or disturbance on the part of petitioners. There is here no evidence whatever of petitioners' interference, actual or nascent, with the schools' work or of collision with the rights of other students to be secure and to be let alone. Accordingly, this case does not concern speech or action that intrudes on the work of the schools or the rights of other students.

Only a few of the 18,000 students in the school system wore the black armbands. Only five students were suspended for wearing them. There is no indication that the work of the schools or any class was disrupted. Outside the classrooms, a few students made hostile remarks to the children wearing armbands, but there were no threats or acts of violence on school premises.

The district court concluded that the action of the school authorities was reasonable because it was based on their fear of a disturbance from the wearing of the armbands. But, in our system, undifferentiated fear or apprehension of disturbance is not enough to overcome the right to freedom of expression. Any departure from absolute regimentation may cause trouble. Any variation from the majority's opinion may inspire fear. Any word spoken, in class, in the lunchroom, or on the campus, that deviates from the views of another person may start an argument or cause a disturbance. But our Constitution says we must take this risk, and our history says that it is this sort of hazardous freedom—this kind of openness—that is the basis of our national strength and of the independence and vigor of Americans who grow up and live in this relatively permissive, often disputatious, society.

In order for the state in the person of school officials to justify prohibition of a particular expression of opinion, it must be able to show that its action was caused by something more than a mere desire to avoid the discomfort and unpleasantness that always accompany an unpopular viewpoint. Certainly where there is no finding and no showing that engaging in the forbidden conduct would materially and substantially interfere with the requirements of appropriate discipline in the operation of the school, the prohibition cannot be sustained.

In the present case, the district court made no such finding, and our independent examination of the record fails to yield evidence that the school authorities had reason to anticipate that the wearing of the armbands would substantially interfere with the work of the school or impinge on the rights of other students. Even an official memorandum prepared after the suspension that listed the reasons for the ban on wearing the armbands made no reference to the anticipation of such disruption.

On the contrary, the action of the school authorities appears to have been based on an urgent wish to avoid the controversy that might result from the expression, even by the silent symbol of armbands, of opposition to this nation's part in the conflagration in Vietnam. It is revealing, in this respect, that the meeting at which the school principals decided to issue the contested regulation was called in response to a student's statement to the journalism teacher in one of the schools that he wanted to write an article on Vietnam and have it published in the school paper.

It is also relevant that the school authorities did not purport to prohibit the wearing of all symbols of political or controversial significance. The record shows that students in some of the schools wore buttons relating to national political campaigns, and some even wore the Iron Cross, traditionally a symbol of Nazism. The order prohibiting the wearing of armbands did not extend to these. Instead, a particular symbol—black armbands worn to exhibit opposition to this nation's involvement in Vietnam—was singled out for prohibition. Clearly, the prohibition of expression of one particular opinion, at least without evidence that it is necessary to avoid material and substantial interference with schoolwork or discipline, is not constitutionally permissible.

In our system, state-operated schools may not be enclaves of totalitarianism. School officials do not possess absolute authority over their students. Students in school as well as out of school are persons under our Constitution. They have fundamental rights that the state must respect, just as they themselves must respect their obligations to the state. In our system, students may not be regarded as closed-circuit recipients of only that which the state chooses to communicate. They may not be confined to the expression of those sentiments that are officially approved. In the absence of a specific showing of constitutionally valid reasons to regulate their speech, students are entitled to freedom of expression of their views. As Judge Gewin, speaking for the Fifth Circuit, said, "school officials cannot suppress expressions of feelings with which they do not wish to contend."

The principle of prior cases is not confined to the supervised and ordained discussion that takes place in the classroom. The principal use to which the schools are dedicated is to accommodate students during prescribed hours for the purpose of certain types of activities. Among those activities is personal intercommunication among the students. This is not only an inevitable part of the process of attending school; it is also an important part of the educational process. A student's rights, therefore, do not embrace merely the classroom hours. When he is in the cafeteria, or on the playing field, or on the campus during the authorized hours, he may express his opinions, even on controversial subjects like the conflict in Vietnam, if he does so without materially and substantially interfering with the requirements of appropriate discipline in the operation of the school and without colliding with the rights of others. But conduct by the student, in class or out of it, which for any reason—whether it stems from time, place, or type of behavior—materially disrupts class work or involves substantial disorder or invasion of the rights of others is, of course, not immunized by the constitutional guarantee of freedom of speech.

Under our Constitution, free speech is not a right that is given only to be so circumscribed that it exists in principle but not in fact. Freedom of expression would not truly exist if the right could be exercised only in an area that a benevolent government has provided as a safe haven for crackpots. The Constitution says that Congress and the states may not abridge the right to free speech. This provision means what it says. We properly read it to permit reasonable regulation of speech-connected activities in carefully restricted circumstances. But we do not confine the permissible exercise of First Amendment rights to a telephone booth or the four corners of a pamphlet, or to supervised and ordained discussion in a school classroom.

If a regulation were adopted by school officials forbidding discussion of the Vietnam conflict, or the expression by any student of opposition to it anywhere on school property except as part of a prescribed classroom exercise, it would be obvious that the regulation would violate the constitutional rights of students, at least if it could not be justified by a showing that the students' activities would materially and substantially disrupt the work and discipline of the school. In the circumstances of the present case, the prohibition of the silent, passive witness of the armbands, as one of the children called it, is no less offensive to the Constitution's guarantees.

As we have discussed, the record does not demonstrate any facts that might reasonably have led school authorities to forecast substantial disruption of or material interference with school activities, and no disturbances or disorders on the school premises in fact occurred. These petitioners merely went about their ordained rounds in school. Their deviation consisted only in wearing on their sleeve a band of black cloth, not more than 2 inches wide. They wore it to exhibit their disapproval of the Vietnam hostilities and their advocacy of a truce, to make their views known, and, by their example, to influence others to adopt them. They neither interrupted school activities nor sought to intrude in the school affairs or the lives of others. They caused discussion outside of the classrooms, but no interference with work and no disorder. In the circumstances, our Constitution does not permit officials of the state to deny their form of expression.

We express no opinion as to the form of relief that should be granted, this being a matter for the lower courts to determine. We reverse and remand for further proceedings consistent with this opinion.

 For an extended version of the case and review questions to test your understanding of the material, please go to www.HumanKinetics.com/CaseStudiesInSportLaw.

University of Colorado v. Derdeyn

863 P.2d 929 (Col. 1993)

CU began a drug-testing program in the fall of 1984 for its intercollegiate student athletes. CU has since amended its program in various ways, but throughout the existence of the program participation was mandatory in the sense that if an athlete did not sign a form consenting to random urinalysis pursuant to the program, the student was prohibited from participating in intercollegiate athletics at CU.

CU's drug-testing program originally required a urine test for certain proscribed drugs at each intercollegiate athlete's annual physical and also required random urine tests thereafter. Counseling was mandated following a first positive result. The penalty for a second positive included a seven-day suspension from participation in intercollegiate athletics, and the penalty for a third positive included a minimum one-year suspension. No specific monitoring procedures were prescribed for the collection of the urine samples, and two students testified that during this phase of the program they were not monitored during the act of urination. According to CU's 1984 Form describing the program, all test results were sent to the "Team Physician." The intercollegiate student athletes also were required to give their consent to releasing test results to a variety of University administrators and their parents, legal guardian(s), or spouse. The 1984 Form gave no general or specific assurances of confidentiality.

Sometime thereafter, CU amended its program for the first time. The penalty for a first positive was changed to include suspension for "the current competitive season," and the penalty for a second positive was changed to include permanent suspension from "any activity sponsored by the University of Colorado Athletic Department." Following a first positive, the athlete was also required to successfully complete a substance abuse rehabilitation program as a condition for further participation in intercollegiate athletics. The first amended program also provided that the "collection of the specimen will be observed [sic], and the athlete may be asked to disrobe in order to protect the integrity of the testing procedure." Test results were still sent to the team physician.

CU's third amended program, which became effective August 14, 1988, contained numerous changes. First, it added alcohol, "over-the-counter drugs," and "performance-enhancing substances such as anabolic steroids" to the list of drugs for which students could be tested. Second, the term "athlete" was defined to include "all student participants in recognized intercollegiate sports, including but not limited to student athletes, cheerleaders, student trainers and student managers." Third, random "rapid eye examination (REE)" testing was substituted for random urinalysis, and a urinalysis was performed only after a "finding of reasonable suspicion that an athlete has used drugs," and at the athlete's annual physical examination. Failure to perform adequately on an REE was considered "*prima facie* reasonable suspicion of drug use [except with regard to steroids]," and the student was required to provide a urine specimen for testing purposes if the student did not perform adequately on the REE. In addition, if a student exhibited "physical or behavioral characteristics indicating drug use including, but not limited to tardiness, absenteeism, poor heath [sic] habits, emotional swings, unexplained performance changes, and/or excessive aggressiveness," this was also considered reasonable suspicion of drug use, and the student was required to take a urine test. Fourth, urine samples were to be collected "within the Athletic Department facilities," and athletes were "directed to provide a urine specimen in a private and enclosed area" while a monitor remained outside. The monitor would then receive "the sample from the athlete and check the sample for appropriate color, temperature, specific gravity and other properties to determine that no substitution or tampering has occurred." Fifth, the athletes were required to give their consent to releasing test results to their parent(s) or legal guardian(s) and an expanded list of University administrators. Finally, although CU still gave no general assurances of confidentiality, it did specify in its third amended program that communications between an athlete and physicians at Wardenburg Student Health Center would be confidential.

In October 1986, intercollegiate student athletes at CU filed a class action suit in Boulder County District Court challenging the constitutionality of the drug-testing program as it then existed and seeking declaratory and injunctive relief.

Following a bench trial conducted in August 1989, the trial court entered its written findings of fact, conclusions of law, and order and judgment. The trial court found that "[o]btaining a monitored urine sample is a substantial invasion of privacy." The trial court also found that while the university labels the program as a "Drug Education Program," there is little education. . . . There is no ongoing educational component of the program. Finally, the trial court found that there is no evidence that the university instituted its program in response to any actual drug abuse problem among its student athletes. There is no evidence that any person has ever been injured in any way because of the use of drugs by a student athlete while practicing or playing a sport.

Therefore, the trial court concluded, CU's random urinalysis drug testing of athletes without individualized suspicion violates the Fourth Amendment's guarantee that persons shall be secure against unreasonable searches and seizures conducted by the government.

The fact that CU's athletes signed forms consenting to random drug testing did not alter the trial court's conclusion. Rather, the trial court found that CU failed to demonstrate that the consents given by the athletes were voluntary, and also held that "no consent can be voluntary where the failure to consent results in a denial of the governmental benefit." In addition, the trial court held that "reasonable suspicion" is not the appropriate standard to warrant urinalysis drug testing of athletes by CU, and that such testing is impermissible absent probable cause under either the Fourth Amendment or Article II, § 7, of the Colorado Constitution.

The Colorado Court of Appeals generally affirmed. It held in part IV of its opinion that objective, reasonable, individualized suspicion of drug use could in some circumstances warrant mandatory drug testing of intercollegiate athletes by CU. Accordingly, the court of appeals reversed the order of the trial court only insofar as it prohibited all testing not premised on probable cause.

We granted CU's petition for writ of *certiorari* on the following issues: In the context of the university's drug-testing program, is suspicion-less drug testing constitutionally reasonable? Can student athletes give valid consent to the university's drug-testing program if their consent is a condition of participation in intercollegiate athletics at the University?

The Fourth Amendment to the United States Constitution protects individuals from unreasonable searches conducted by the government, even when the government acts as the administrator of an athletic program in a state school or university. Furthermore, "[b]ecause it is clear that the collection and testing of urine intrudes upon expectations of privacy that society has long recognized as reasonable, these intrusions must be deemed searches under the Fourth Amendment." *Skinner*,

489 U.S. at 617, 109 S.Ct. at 1413. It follows that CU's urinalysis drug-testing program must meet the reasonableness requirement of the Fourth Amendment. A search must usually be supported by a warrant issued on probable cause.

It is clear that CU's drug-testing program is not designed to serve the ordinary needs of law enforcement. We must therefore balance individual student athletes' privacy expectations against CU's governmental interests to determine whether CU's random, warrantless, suspicionless urinalysis-drug-testing program is unreasonable under the Fourth Amendment.

CU argues that its drug-testing program is reasonable under the Fourth Amendment because of the student athletes' diminished expectations of privacy and the compelling governmental interests served by the program. We therefore consider in turn (1) the degree to which CU's drug-testing program intrudes on the reasonable expectations of privacy of student athletes and (2) the magnitude of the governmental interests served by the program. We then balance these factors in order to determine whether CU's drug-testing program is reasonable under the Fourth Amendment.

Although nonvoluntary, random, suspicionless urinalysis drug testing by the government always intrudes on an individual's Fourth Amendment privacy interests, the magnitude of that intrusion can vary from context to context. Some of the factors that courts have taken into account in determining the magnitude of such intrusions include the particular place and manner in which the urine sample is collected; . . . , whether the individual participates "in an industry that is regulated pervasively to ensure safety, a goal dependent, in substantial part, on the health and fitness of covered employees, . . . the operational realities of the workplace in which an individual is subjected to drug testing"; . . . , whether the individual "for whatever reason [is] subject to frequent medical examinations," . . . , and the consequences of refusing to give a urine sample, ..."

CU asserts in its brief that the magnitude of the intrusion of its drug-testing program on its athletes is minimal for a variety of reasons. Specifically, CU asserts that "(a) collection of the urine sample in a closed stall with aural monitoring minimizes any intrusion. CU also asserts

that student athletes' expectations of privacy with regard to urinalysis are diminished because (b) they routinely give urine samples as part of annual, general medical examinations; because (c) they submit to extensive regulation of their on- and off-campus behavior, including maintenance of required levels of academic performance, monitoring of course selection, training rules, mandatory practice sessions, diet restrictions, attendance at study halls, curfews, and prohibitions on alcohol and drug use; because (d) they must submit to the NCAA random urinalysis drug-testing program as a condition of participating in NCAA competition; because (e) the consequences of refusing to provide a urine sample are not severe; and because (f) positive test results are confidential and are not used for the purposes of criminal law enforcement."

CU argues that collection of the urine sample in a closed stall with aural monitoring minimizes any intrusion. We agree that aural monitoring is less intrusive than visual monitoring, but as we have already noted, the trial court found that CU and the other defendants have refused to agree that they will not return to the policy that was initially challenged in this class action (i.e., the policy according to which students were visually monitored while providing a urine sample). In fact, defendants have indicated that there are circumstances under which they would return to that policy.

CU argues that student athletes' expectations of privacy with regard to urinalysis are diminished because they routinely give urine samples as part of an annual, general medical examination, and because they regularly undergo close physical contact with trainers. In this case, however, the trial court heard testimony that samples for random urinalysis drug testing were not collected in a medical environment by persons unrelated to the athletic program. In addition, many people have an annual physical examination, and the fact that CU's athletes have an annual physical would not seem to put them into Dimeo's category of those who must undergo "frequent" medical examinations. Indeed, the trial court heard testimony from one student athlete that "in that I have never been injured, I have been lucky and so the only time I saw the trainers was for a urinalysis."

CU argues that student athletes' expectations of privacy with regard to urinalysis are diminished because they submit to extensive regulation of their on- and off-campus behavior, including maintenance of required levels of academic performance, monitoring of course selection, training rules, mandatory practice sessions, diet restrictions, attendance at study halls, curfews, and prohibitions on alcohol and drug use. In support thereof, CU cites testimony from its athletic director and one student athlete.

Although it is obviously not amenable to precise calculation, it is at least doubtful that the testimony relied on by CU fully supports CU's assertion that its student athletes are "extensively regulated in their on- and off-campus behavior," especially with regard to all of the particulars that CU asserts. More importantly, none of the types of regulation relied on by CU entails an intrusion on privacy interests of the nature or extent involved in monitored collection of urine samples.

CU argues that student athletes' expectations of privacy with regard to urinalysis are diminished because they must submit to the NCAA random urinalysis drug-testing program as a condition of participating in NCAA competition. In this regard, CU's athletic director testified that at NCAA championship events, the NCAA conducts random drug testing of athletes as well as testing of the top three finishers and certain starting players, and evidence in the record suggests that NCAA athletes are required to sign consent forms to such testing. Despite the fact that students might dislike the NCAA drug-testing program, it seems that they must consent to it in order to be NCAA athletes, and submission to one such program could reduce the intrusiveness of having to submit to another. On the other hand, the trial court heard testimony suggesting that part of what is intrusive about the CU program is that it transformed what might otherwise be friendly, trusting, and caring relations between trainers and athletes into untrusting and confrontational relations.

CU argues that student athletes' expectations of privacy with regard to urinalysis are diminished because the consequences of refusing to provide a urine sample are not severe. We appreciate that in comparison to losing one's job, as would be the consequence in some government employee drug-testing cases, not being able to participate in intercollegiate athletics can be regarded as less of a burden. It is, to be sure, only a very small percentage of college athletes whose college "careers" are essential as stepping-stones to lucrative contracts—or to any contract—as professional athletes. On the other hand, however, we must also recognize that many intercollegiate athletes who otherwise could not afford a college education receive athletic scholarships that enable them to obtain a college degree and thereby increase their earning potential. Continuation of such scholarships at CU is dependent on continued participation in the intercollegiate athletic program, which in turn requires consent to the drug-testing program. Furthermore, many intercollegiate athletes pursue professional careers as high school or college coaches, or as administrators in athletic or recreational programs. While having participated in intercollegiate athletics may not be a formal requirement for such jobs, it is commonplace that applicants with experience at the intercollegiate athletic level will not be disadvantaged in seeking such jobs in comparison with those who lack such experience. Also, we recognize that for many student athletes, participation in intercollegiate athletics is an activity highly valued for its own sake. We therefore believe that the consequences of not being able to participate in intercollegiate athletics must be accorded significant weight.

Finally, CU argues that student athletes' expectations of privacy with regard to urinalysis are diminished because positive test results are confidential and are not used for the purposes of criminal law enforcement. It is true that an intrusion by the government outside the context of criminal law enforcement is generally less of an intrusion than one for the purposes of law enforcement. The fact that this is not a criminal matter adds nothing to what we must balance at this point in our analysis. Furthermore, as we have already indicated, CU does not in its written descriptions of its drug-testing programs give any significant specific or general assurances that test results are confidential. There is no evidence at all that CU has ever made available, or ever desired to make available, to the general public any student's urine test results, but the list of people to whom students must consent to the release of drug-test information is substantial, and we are particularly uncertain as to the significance of the fact that in CU's third amended program students must consent to the release of information to "my work supervisor (if applicable)."

Having reviewed the record in light of each of CU's assertions, it is clear that in some places CU seems to overstate its case, while in others, it has a valid point. On balance, however, we are in full agreement with the conclusion of the trial court that CU's random, suspicionless urinalysis drug-testing of athletes is an "intrusion [that] is clearly significant."

CU asserts several interests in maintaining its drug-testing program. These interests are preparing its athletes for drug testing in NCAA championship events, promoting the integrity of its athletic program, preventing drug use by other students who look to athletes as role models, ensuring fair competition, and protecting the health and safety of intercollegiate athletes.

We begin our consideration of these interests by observing that suspicionless urinalysis drug testing by the government has been upheld in numerous cases, and in many of those cases, courts have characterized the relevant government interests as "compelling." However, the Supreme Court has not held that only a "compelling" interest will suffice and some courts have upheld suspicionless urinalysis drug testing by the government without finding a compelling interest. Hence, rather than trying to characterize CU's interests as "compelling," "strong," "substantial," or of some lesser degree of importance, we think it is more instructive simply to compare them with other types of commonly asserted interests that have been held sufficient or insufficient to justify similar intrusions.

We have not been persuaded that CU's athletes have a greatly diminished expectation of privacy, nor are we persuaded that CU's program is not significantly intrusive. In addition, we question whether some of the interests asserted by CU are even significant for Fourth Amendment purposes. For example, although the integrity of its athletic program is, like all the other interests asserted by CU, a valid and commendable one, it does not seem to be very significant for Fourth Amendment purposes. Similarly, although the promotion of fair competition builds character in athletes and enhances the entertainment value of athletic events, CU does not explain why the promotion of fair competition is itself an important governmen-

tal interest, just as it does not explain why preventing the disqualification of its athletes at sporting events is an important governmental interest.

We therefore hold, based on a balancing of the privacy interests of the student athletes and the governmental interests of CU, that CU's drug-testing program is unconstitutional under the Fourth Amendment. More specifically, we hold that random, suspicionless urinalysis drug testing by CU of student athletes is unconstitutional under the Fourth Amendment if that testing is conducted according to the procedures utilized in any of CU's drug-testing programs to the date of trial, or if that testing is conducted in a manner substantially similar to any of the procedures utilized in any of CU's drug-testing programs to the date of trial. Furthermore, because the Colorado Constitution provides at least as much protection from unreasonable searches and seizures as does the Fourth Amendment, CU's drug-testing program is also unconstitutional under Article II, § 7, of the Colorado Constitution.

CU asserts, however, that even if its drug-testing program is not otherwise constitutionally reasonable, there is no constitutional violation because its student athletes voluntarily consent to testing. A warrantless search of an individual is generally reasonable under the Fourth Amendment if the individual has voluntarily consented to it. A voluntary consent to a search is "a consent intelligently and freely given, without any duress, coercion or subtle promises or threats calculated to flaw the free and unconstrained nature of the decision." Whether consent to a search was voluntary "is a question of fact to be determined from all the circumstances. . . ." The government has the burden of proving that consent to a search was voluntarily given, and we must defer to the trial court's findings on the factual issue of voluntariness unless its findings are clearly erroneous.

The fact that participation in intercollegiate sports is not a "right" but a "benefit" does not alter the requirement that any consent be voluntary. It is quite clear that no consent can be voluntary where the failure to consent results in a denial of the governmental benefit. The evidence produced during this trial failed to establish that the consents given by the university's student athletes are voluntary.

It is clear from the record that a student will be denied the opportunity to participate in CU's intercollegiate athletic program in absence of execution of a signed consent. It is equally clear that no athletic scholarship will be available to a student who does not consent to drug testing. The pressure on a prospective student athlete to sign a consent to random, suspicionless drug testing under such circumstances is obvious.

It must be remembered that the consent in question is the consent to an otherwise unconstitutional search, and that to be voluntary such a consent must be "freely given, without any duress, coercion or subtle promises or threats calculated to flaw the free and unconstrained nature of the decision." We conclude that the record supports the trial court's finding that CU failed to bear its burden to prove that consents obtained pursuant

to its random, suspicionless urinalysis drug-testing program for the certified class of intercollegiate student athletes are voluntarily given. We accordingly hold that for the purposes of the Fourth Amendment and Article II, § 7, of the Colorado Constitution, CU's intercollegiate student athletes do not voluntarily consent to being searched pursuant to the drug-testing program.

For the foregoing reasons, we affirm the judgment of the court of appeals.

 For an extended version of the case and review questions to test your understanding of the material, please go to www.HumanKinetics.com/CaseStudiesInSportLaw.

Vernonia School District 47J v. Acton

515 U.S. 646 (1995)

The Student Athlete Drug Policy adopted by School District 47J in the town of Vernonia, Oregon, authorizes random urinalysis drug testing of students who participate in the district's school athletics programs. We granted *certiorari* to decide whether this violates the Fourth and Fourteenth Amendments to the United States Constitution.

Petitioner Vernonia School District 47J (District) operates one high school and three grade schools in the logging community of Vernonia, Oregon. As elsewhere in small-town America, school sports play a prominent role in the town's life, and student athletes are admired in their schools and in the community. Drugs had not been a major problem in Vernonia schools. In the mid-to-late 1980s, however, teachers and administrators observed a sharp increase in drug use. Students began to speak out about their attraction to the drug culture and to boast that there was nothing the school could do about it. Along with more drugs came more disciplinary problems. Between 1988 and 1989 the number of disciplinary referrals in Vernonia schools rose to more than twice the number reported in the early 1980s, and several students were suspended. Students became increasingly rude during class; outbursts of profane language became common.

Not only were student athletes included among the drug users but, as the district court found, athletes were the leaders of the drug culture. This caused the District's administrators particular concern, since drug use increases the risk of sports-related injury. Expert testimony at the trial confirmed the deleterious effects of drugs on motivation, memory, judgment, reaction, coordination, and performance. The high school football and wrestling coach witnessed a severe sternum injury suffered by a wrestler, and various omissions of safety procedures and misexecutions by football players, all attributable in his belief to the effects of drug use.

Initially, the District responded to the drug problem by offering special classes, speakers, and presentations designed to deter drug use. It even brought in a specially trained dog to detect drugs, but the drug problem persisted. At that point, District officials began considering a drug-testing program. They held a parent "input night" to discuss the proposed Student Athlete Drug Policy (Policy), and the parents in attendance gave their unanimous approval. The school board approved the Policy for implementation in the fall of 1989. Its expressed purpose is to prevent student athletes from using drugs, to protect their health and safety, and to provide drug users with assistance programs.

The Policy applies to all students participating in interscholastic athletics. Students wishing to play sports must sign a form consenting to the testing and must obtain the written consent of their parents. Athletes are tested at the beginning of the season for their sport. In addition, once each week of the season the names of the athletes are placed in a "pool" from which a student, with the supervision of two adults, blindly draws the names of 10% of the athletes for random testing. Those selected are notified and tested that same day, if possible.

The student to be tested completes a specimen control form that bears an assigned number. Prescription medications that the student is taking must be identified by providing a copy of the prescription or a doctor's authorization. The student then enters an empty locker room accompanied by an adult monitor of the same sex. Each boy selected produces a sample at a urinal, remaining fully clothed with his back to the monitor, who stands approximately 12 to 15 feet behind the student. Monitors may (though do not always) watch the student while he produces the sample, and they listen for normal sounds of urination. Girls produce samples in an enclosed bathroom stall, so that they can be heard but not observed. After the sample is produced, it is given to the monitor who checks it for temperature and tampering and then transfers it to a vial.

The samples are sent to an independent laboratory, which routinely tests them for amphetamines, cocaine, and marijuana. Other drugs, such as LSD, may be screened at the request of the District, but the identity of a particular student does not determine which drugs will be tested. The laboratory's procedures are 99.94% accurate. The District follows strict procedures regarding the chain of custody and access to test results. The laboratory does not know the identity of the students whose samples it tests. It is authorized to mail written test reports only to the superintendent and to provide test results to District personnel by telephone only after the requesting official recites a code confirming his authority. Only the superintendent, principals, vice-principals, and athletic directors have access to test results, and the results are not kept for more than one year.

If a sample tests positive, a second test is administered as soon as possible to confirm the result. If the second test is negative, no further action is taken. If the second test is positive, the athlete's parents are notified, and the school principal convenes a meeting with the student and his parents, at which the student is given the option of (1) participating for six weeks in an assistance program that includes weekly urinalysis, or (2) suffering suspension from athletics for the remainder of the current season and the next athletic season. The student is then retested prior to the start of the next athletic season for which he or she is eligible. The Policy states that a second offense results in automatic imposition of option (2); a third offense in suspension for the remainder of the current season and the next two athletic seasons.

In the fall of 1991, respondent James Acton, then a seventh grader, signed up to play football at one of the District's grade schools. He was denied participation, however, because he and his parents refused to sign the testing consent forms. The Actons filed suit, seeking declaratory and injunctive relief from enforcement of the Policy on the grounds that it violated the Fourth and Fourteenth Amendments to the United States Constitution and Article I, § 9, of the Oregon Constitution. After a bench trial, the District Court entered an order denying the claims on the merits and dismissing the action. The United States Court of Appeals for the Ninth Circuit reversed, holding that the Policy violated both the Fourth and Fourteenth Amendments and Article I, § 9, of the Oregon Constitution. We granted *certiorari*.

The Fourth Amendment to the United States Constitution provides that the federal government shall not violate "[t]he right of the people to be secure in their persons, houses, papers, and effects, against unreasonable searches and seizures. . . ." We have held that the Fourteenth Amendment extends this constitutional guarantee to searches and seizures by state officers, . . . , including public school officials. As the text of the Fourth Amendment indicates, the ultimate measure of the constitutionality of a governmental search is "reasonableness." At least in a case such as this, where there was no clear practice, either approving or disapproving the type of search at issue, at the time the constitutional provision was enacted, whether a particular search meets the reasonableness standard "is judged by balancing its intrusion on the individual's Fourth

Amendment interests against its promotion of legitimate governmental interests." Where a search is undertaken by law enforcement officials to discover evidence of criminal wrongdoing, this court has said that reasonableness generally requires the obtaining of a judicial warrant. . . . Warrants cannot be issued, of course, without the showing of probable cause required by the Warrant Clause. But a warrant is not required to establish the reasonableness of all government searches; and when a warrant is not required (and the Warrant Clause therefore is not applicable), probable cause is not invariably required either. A search unsupported by probable cause can be constitutional, we have said, "when special needs, beyond the normal need for law enforcement, make the warrant and probable-cause requirement impracticable."

We have found such "special needs" to exist in the public school context. There, the warrant requirement "would unduly interfere with the maintenance of the swift and informal disciplinary procedures [that are] needed," and "strict adherence to the requirement that searches be based upon probable cause" would undercut "the substantial need of teachers and administrators for freedom to maintain order in the schools."

The first factor to be considered is the nature of the privacy interest on which the search here at issue intrudes. The Fourth Amendment does not protect all subjective expectations of privacy, but only those that society recognizes as "legitimate." "What expectations are legitimate varies, of course, with context, . . . , depending, for example, upon whether the individual asserting the privacy interest is at home, at work, in a car, or in a public park. In addition, the legitimacy of certain privacy expectations *vis-à-vis* the state may depend upon the individual's legal relationship with the State." "Central, in our view, to the present case is the fact that the subjects of the Policy are (1) children, who (2) have been committed to the temporary custody of the state as schoolmaster."

Traditionally at common law, and still today, unemancipated minors lack some of the most fundamental rights of self-determination—including even the right of liberty in its narrow sense (i.e., the right to come and go at will). They are subject, even as to their physical freedom, to the

control of their parents or guardians. When parents place minor children in private schools for their education, the teachers and administrators of those schools stand *in loco parentis* over the children entrusted to them. In fact, the tutor or schoolmaster is the very prototype of that status. As Blackstone describes it, a parent "may . . . delegate part of his parental authority, during his life, to the tutor or schoolmaster of his child; who is then *in loco parentis*, and has such a portion of the power of the parent committed to his charge, *viz.* that of restraint and correction, as may be necessary to answer the purposes for which he is employed." 1 W. Blackstone, *Commentaries on the Laws of England* 441 (1769).

Fourth Amendment rights, no less than First and Fourteenth Amendment rights, are different in public schools than elsewhere; the "reasonableness" inquiry cannot disregard the schools' custodial and tutelary responsibility for children. For their own good and that of their classmates, public schoolchildren are routinely required to submit to various physical examinations, and to be vaccinated against various diseases. . . . Particularly with regard to medical examinations and procedures, therefore, "students within the school environment have a lesser expectation of privacy than members of the population generally."

Legitimate privacy expectations are even less with regard to student athletes. School sports are not for the bashful. They require "suiting up" before each practice or event and showering and changing afterwards. Public school locker rooms, the usual sites for these activities, are not notable for the privacy they afford. The locker rooms in Vernonia are typical: No individual dressing rooms are provided; shower heads are lined up along a wall, unseparated by any sort of partition or curtain; not even all the toilet stalls have doors.

There is an additional respect in which school athletes have a reduced expectation of privacy. By choosing to "go out for the team," they voluntarily subject themselves to a degree of regulation even higher than that imposed on students generally. In Vernonia's public schools, they must submit to a preseason physical exam, they must acquire adequate insurance coverage or sign an insurance waiver, maintain a minimum grade point average, and comply with any "rules of conduct, dress, training hours and related matters as may be established for each sport by the head coach and athletic director with the principal's approval." Somewhat like adults who choose to participate in a "closely regulated industry," students who voluntarily participate in school athletics have reason to expect intrusions on normal rights and privileges, including privacy.

Having considered the scope of the legitimate expectation of privacy at issue here, we turn next to the character of the intrusion that is complained of. Under the District's Policy, male students produce samples at a urinal along a wall. They remain fully clothed and are only observed from behind, if at all. Female students produce samples in an enclosed stall, with a female monitor standing outside listening only for sounds of tampering. These conditions are nearly identical to those typically encountered in public restrooms, which men, women, and especially schoolchildren use daily. Under such conditions, the privacy interests compromised by the process of obtaining the urine sample are in our view negligible.

The other privacy-invasive aspect of urinalysis is, of course, the information it discloses concerning the state of the subject's body, and the materials he has ingested. In this regard it is significant that the tests at issue here look only for drugs, and not for whether the student, for example, has epilepsy, is pregnant, or has diabetes. Moreover, the drugs for which the samples are screened are standard, and do not vary according to the identity of the student. And finally, the results of the tests are disclosed only to a limited class of school personnel who have a need to know; and they are not turned over to law enforcement authorities or used for any internal disciplinary function.

Respondents argue, however, that the District's Policy is in fact more intrusive than this suggests, because it requires the students, if they are to avoid sanctions for a falsely positive test, to identify in advance prescription medications they are taking. We agree that this raises some cause for concern. On the other hand, we have never indicated that requiring advance disclosure of medications is *per se* unreasonable. We do not believe this procedure establishes a difference that respondents are entitled to rely on here.

The General Authorization Form that respondents refused to sign, which refusal was the basis for James's exclusion from the sports program, said only (in relevant part), "I . . . authorize the Vernonia School District to conduct a test on a urine specimen which I provide to test for drugs and/or alcohol use. I also authorize the release of information concerning the results of such a test to the Vernonia School District and to the parents and/or guardians of the student." While the practice of the District seems to have been to have a school official take medication information from the student at the time of the test, . . . , that practice is not set forth in, or required by, the Policy, which says simply, "Student athletes who . . . are or have been taking prescription medication must provide verification (either by a copy of the prescription or by doctor's authorization) prior to being tested." It may well be that, if and when James was selected for random testing at a time that he was taking medication, the District would have permitted him to provide the requested information in a confidential manner—for example, in a sealed envelope delivered to the testing lab. Nothing in the Policy contradicts that, and when respondents choose, in effect, to challenge the Policy on its face, we will not assume the worst. Accordingly, we reach the same conclusion as in *Skinner*: that the invasion of privacy was not significant.

Finally, we turn to consider the nature and immediacy of the governmental concern at issue here, and the efficacy of this means for meeting it. In prior cases, we characterized the government interest motivating the search as "compelling." Relying on these cases, the district court held that because the District's program also called for drug testing in the absence of individualized suspicion, the District "must demonstrate a 'compelling need' for the program." The court of appeals appears to have agreed with this view. It is a mistake, however, to think that the phrase "compelling state interest," in the Fourth Amendment context, describes a fixed, minimum quantum of governmental concern so that one can dispose of a case by answering in isolation the question of whether there is a compelling state interest here. Rather, the phrase describes an interest that appears important enough to justify the particular search at hand, in light of other factors that show the search to be relatively intrusive on a genuine expectation of privacy. Whether that relatively high degree of government concern is necessary in this case or not, we think it is met.

That the nature of the concern is important—indeed, perhaps compelling—can hardly be doubted. School years are the time when the physical, psychological, and addictive effects of drugs are most severe. And of course the effects of a drug-infested school are visited not just on the users, but on the entire student body and faculty, as the educational process is disrupted. In the present case, moreover, the necessity for the state to act is magnified by the fact that this evil is being visited not just on individuals at large, but on children for whom it has undertaken a special responsibility of care and direction. Finally, it must not be lost sight of that this program is directed more narrowly to drug use by school athletes, where the risk of immediate physical harm to the drug user or those with whom he is playing his sport is particularly high. Apart from psychological effects, which include impairment of judgment, slow reaction time, and a lessening of the perception of pain, the particular drugs screened by the District's Policy have been demonstrated to pose substantial physical risks to athletes.

As for the immediacy of the District's concerns: We are not inclined to question—indeed, we could not possibly find clearly erroneous—the district court's conclusion that "a large segment of the student body, particularly those involved in interscholastic athletics, was in a state of rebellion," that "[d]isciplinary actions had reached 'epidemic proportions,'" and that "the rebellion was being fueled by alcohol and drug abuse as well as by the student's misperceptions about the drug culture." That is an immediate crisis of great proportions.

As to the efficacy of this means for addressing the problem, it seems to us self-evident that a drug problem largely fueled by the "role model" effect of athletes' drug use, and of particular danger to athletes, is effectively addressed by making sure that athletes do not use drugs. Respondents argue that a "less intrusive means to the same end" was available, namely, "drug testing on suspicion of drug use." We have repeatedly refused to declare that only the "least intrusive" search practicable can be reasonable under the Fourth Amendment. Respondents' alternative entails substantial difficulties—if it is indeed practicable at all. It may be impracticable, for one thing, simply because the parents who are willing to accept random drug testing for athletes are not willing to accept accusatory drug testing for all students,

which transforms the process into a badge of shame. Respondents' proposal brings the risk that teachers will impose testing arbitrarily on troublesome but not drug-likely students. It generates the expense of defending lawsuits that charge such arbitrary imposition, or that simply demand greater process before accusatory drug testing is imposed. And not least of all, it adds to the ever-expanding diversionary duties of schoolteachers the new function of spotting and bringing to account drug abuse, a task for which they are ill-prepared, and which is not readily compatible with their vocation.

Taking into account all the factors we have considered above—the decreased expectation of privacy, the relative unobtrusiveness of the search, and the severity of the need met by the search—we conclude Vernonia's Policy is reasonable and hence constitutional. We caution against the assumption that suspicionless drug testing will readily pass constitutional muster in other contexts. The most significant element in this case is the first we discussed: that the Policy was undertaken in furtherance of the government's responsibilities, under a public school system, as guardian and tutor of children entrusted to its care.

Just as when the government conducts a search in its capacity as employer, . . . , the relevant question is whether that intrusion on privacy is one that a reasonable employer might engage in, so also when the government acts as guardian and tutor the relevant question is whether the search is one that a reasonable guardian and tutor might undertake. Given the findings of need made by the district court, we conclude that in the present case it is.

The Ninth Circuit held that Vernonia's Policy not only violated the Fourth Amendment, but also, by reason of that violation, contravened Article I, § 9, of the Oregon Constitution. Our conclusion that the former holding was in error means that the latter holding rested on a flawed premise. We, therefore, vacate the judgment and remand the case to the court of appeals for further proceedings consistent with this opinion. It is so ordered.

 For an extended version of the case and review questions to test your understanding of the material, please go to www.HumanKinetics.com/CaseStudiesInSportLaw.

3

Contract Law

A contract is a promise, or set of promises, for breach of which the law gives a remedy, or the performance of which the law in some way recognizes a duty. Most contracts are valid if they are in oral form, but there are exceptions to that rule under the legal principle known as the Statute of Frauds. Whether oral or written, a contract should contain certain elements. A contract begins with a promise, a commitment to do something or refrain from doing something. It should have an offer, which contains the parties involved, subject matter of the contract, time and place of performance, and price to be paid. Acceptance must be made in a positive form, can only be made by the party to whom the offer was made, and must mirror the offer's essential terms. Another essential element is consideration. One party must pay a price or suffer a legal detriment. Finally there must be an intent to create a legal relationship.

Contracts in the realm of sports is a subject that has important implications for both players and coaches. For athletes, the issue of contracts often arises when scholarship money is suspended or denied. This was the issue in the case of *Taylor v. Wake Forest* where a college football player had his scholarship terminated. This case alleged breach of contract due to the loss of scholarship money. Other cases involve coaches and the loss of employment. For example, breach of contract was an issue in *Monson v. State* where the head basketball coach at the University of Oregon claimed breach of contract after being removed from his position and *Vanderbilt v. DiNardo* where Vanderbilt alleged breach of contract when the head football coach resigned before the term of his contract had ended. The payment of prerequisites was the primary issue in *Rodgers v. Georgia Tech Athletic Association*. Developing an understanding of contract law and its implications is an integral part of a sport law class. Given the reality of coaching in modern times where tenure is based on performance, contracts are often breached when winning expectations are not met and coaches are removed from their positions. These cases will give the student insight into the practical implications of what happens when a coaching contract is breached. Additionally, the cases provide insight into the breach of contract from the player's perspective where scholarship expectations are not met. The lessons learned from these cases are valuable to the sport manager.

Monson v. State

901 P.2d 904 (Ore. App. 1995)

Plaintiff Don Monson brought this action for breach of contract against defendant State of Oregon, following plaintiff's removal as head men's basketball coach at the University of Oregon. The jury found for the plaintiff, and the State appeals. We reverse.

The material facts are undisputed. In 1978, plaintiff became the head men's basketball coach at the University of Idaho. At that time, he had 17 years of high school coaching experience and two years of assistant coaching at the college level. In March 1983, after the conclusion of the 1982-83 basketball season, plaintiff met with officials of the University of Oregon about becoming the head men's basketball coach. He received a letter from the university's athletic director offering him the position of head basketball coach at a yearly salary of $52,000 plus potential earnings of $10,000 to $12,000 the first year for appearing on radio and television shows and potential additional earnings for running a summer basketball camp. The letter also mentioned other benefits, such as the use of courtesy cars and a complimentary country club membership. The letter specified that the offer was contingent on being ratified by the president of the university. Plaintiff subsequently received a letter from the university's acting vice-president offering an appointment as head men's basketball coach. The offered position was a nontenure faculty appointment as an officer of administration with the rank of professor, for the period from March 23, 1983 through June 30, 1987. The only provision regarding compensation specified a starting annual salary of $52,000. Plaintiff signed the contract.

On January 27, 1986, plaintiff signed a "Notice of Appointment and Contract," appointing him

as an officer of administration, nontenure related, with the rank of professor and title of head men's basketball coach, for the period July 1, 1987 to June 30, 1990, at an annual salary of $60,000. In October 1988, plaintiff signed another "Notice of Appointment and Contract" for the period July 1, 1990 to June 30, 1992. Both contracts provided that "[the] position is subject to the provisions of the Oregon Administrative Rules of the Oregon State Board of Higher Education and to other now existing administrative rules, regulations and policies of the University of Oregon relating to Officers of Administration which are incorporated by reference herein."

In a letter to plaintiff, dated August 6, 1990, Bill Byrne, the university's then athletic director, informed plaintiff that he was doing an outstanding job and that, as a result, the university had agreed to extend his contract by two years through the 1994 basketball season. However, it was later discovered that the appropriate paperwork for the contract extension had never been completed. Dan Williams, the university's vice-president of administration, testified that neither he nor Byrne discovered the oversight until a local newspaper reporter sought to confirm that plaintiff's contract was to expire in 1992. Williams testified that, although plaintiff's removal from the position of basketball coach was already under consideration, he "executed the papers to fulfill that [earlier] promise." Accordingly, on January 24, 1992, plaintiff signed another "Notice of Appointment and Contract" for July 1, 1992, to June 30, 1994, at an annual salary of $79,468. As with the prior two contracts, plaintiff was appointed as an officer of administration, nontenure related, with the rank of professor and title of head men's basketball coach. The contract provided the following: "The position as offered is subject to all applicable provisions of State and Federal law, State administrative rules, and the regulations and policies of the State System of Higher Education and the University of Oregon."

Although none of his notices of appointment and contract mentioned outside income, plaintiff earned additional income during his employment through his summer basketball camp, through outside contracts with equipment sponsors such as Nike and Rawlings Sporting Goods, and through contracts and other agreements involving television and radio companies, including those companies under contract with the university's Oregon Sports Network. Some of the contracts were arranged by the university, but all of the opportunities for outside income made available to plaintiff were in connection with his duties as head men's basketball coach. Plaintiff also was given a complimentary country club membership and, after the first year, the use of two new courtesy cars.

In early February 1992, plaintiff was advised by Byrne that Byrne was going to be inquiring into the financial packages offered to coaches at other schools, in the event of a change at the University of Oregon. Byrne explained that he had not yet decided whether to hire a new coach and that he would not talk to any other coaches before the end of the season, but that he did not want plaintiff to hear through rumors that Byrne was making inquiries. At the time of that discussion, the basketball season was half over. The team had opened the season with a 40-point loss to the University of Montana, a member of the Big Sky conference, which Byrne characterized as "much less significant" and "not comparable to the Pac-10 conference." The university had lost money in men's basketball the previous year, and attendance was down again. Byrne also believed that the team's athletes were of a "lesser caliber than the teams that we were competing against," including opponents that were not in the Pac-10 conference.

Plaintiff met with Byrne again on March 17, 1992, after the basketball season had ended. At that time, Byrne explained that the basketball program was not going in the direction that he wanted and that he was reassigning plaintiff from basketball coach to golf coach. Plaintiff testified that he interpreted Byrne's concerns to be related to the program's finances and the team's win-loss record. Plaintiff told Byrne that he was unwilling to be a golf coach. At trial, plaintiff testified that accepting the position would have been "professional suicide." After his meeting with Byrne, plaintiff left the campus and never returned or attempted to contact the athletic director, the vice-president, or the president of the university.

Shortly after the meeting, plaintiff received a letter from Byrne, dated March 17, 1992, confirming their conversation of that date and formally reassigning plaintiff to head men's golf coach and fund raiser. The letter stated that the university would honor the terms of plaintiff's contract, but that a change in leadership was needed "for the good of the department." In a letter to plaintiff dated April 29, 1992, Byrne offered to reassign plaintiff to a position as the university's compliance coordinator for NCAA rules and regulations. Plaintiff testified that, as with the golf coach position, had he accepted that position, he would have never been able to get back into basketball coaching. After plaintiff failed to accept the new assignment by May 18, 1992, the university considered him to have resigned and paid him no further compensation. Plaintiff testified that, as of that date, he had no unfulfilled contracts or agreements for outside income.

In July 1992, plaintiff filed this breach of contract action. In his complaint, he alleged that he had signed written contracts employing him as head men's basketball coach through June 30, 1994, that he had performed all conditions of the contracts and that "On or about March 18, 1992 the defendant State of Oregon discharged plaintiff as coach at the University of Oregon to plaintiff's damage in the sum of $178,936.92 together with the sum of $221,066.00 as the value of the money and benefits plaintiff would have received from nonpublic sources if he remained in the position as coach, and together with the sum of $25,785.60 for the medical, dental, and retirement benefits included within the contract but which benefits have been terminated, and all for which plaintiff demands judgment against defendant State of Oregon."

Among other defenses raised in its answer, the State asserted that plaintiff was advised that his duties within the Athletic Department were being reassigned, and that plaintiff's reassignment from his position as head basketball coach was authorized under the terms of plaintiff's contract. At the close of plaintiff's evidence, the State moved for directed verdict "on three points": "The first is that the university had a contractual right to reassign plaintiff from his position as men's head basketball coach. The second point is that the university validly exercised that right to reassign. And the third point is that plaintiff has demonstrated no contractual entitlement to receive from the university any of what's been referred to in this case as outside income."

The motion was denied, as was the State's renewed motion for directed verdict at the close of all of the evidence. The jury found for plaintiff and awarded him $292,087.83 in damages.

Although there was some dispute at trial on these matters, the parties now appear to agree that, at the time the dispute arose, the only agreements in force between the State and plaintiff were the Notice of Appointment and Contract expiring in 1992 and the Notice of Appointment and Contract expiring in 1994. The parties also agree that both of those agreements incorporated by reference all State administrative rules, including those pertaining to sanctions and to personnel actions that are not for cause. Finally, the parties agree that the university reassigned plaintiff from his duties as head coach of the men's basketball team.

The State contends that what plaintiff asserts was his contractual "right" to retain the duties of head men's basketball coach was subject to the university's contractual right to reassign personnel. Thus, the State argues that, as a matter of law, the exercise of its right to reassign in a manner consistent with the applicable administrative rules cannot constitute a breach of plaintiff's contract. The university specifically relies on OAR 580-21-318, which, as noted above, the parties agree was incorporated by reference into the contract: "As authorized by statute and by authority delegated to the chancellor and the institution presidents, personnel may be transferred or reassigned within an institution in accordance with the staff needs of the institution or other units. Such personnel action should not be considered sanctions for cause unless they result from actions described in OAR 580-21-325." Under OAR 580-21-325(1)(c), "cause" includes the "[f]ailure to perform the responsibilities of an academic staff member." Evidence to demonstrate

cause under that standard includes evidence of incompetence, gross inefficiency, or intentional or habitual neglect of duty. OAR 580-21-325(2).

OAR 520-21-320 provides that a nontenured academic staff member may be removed from an assigned post and reassigned as a sanction for cause, but that such a sanction must be imposed in accordance with the contested case procedures in OAR 580-21-325 through OAR 580-21-385.

The State contends that plaintiff was reassigned pursuant to OAR 580-21-318. It asserts that the evidence demonstrates that the university decided that plaintiff was no longer the best person for the job of head men's basketball coach and, based on its assessment of its staff needs, the university had the authority, under the rule, to reassign plaintiff to other duties within the athletic department. In support of its position, the State relies on evidence that during plaintiff's last four seasons as head coach, the team had the worst record in the Pac-10 conference, that the players whom plaintiff had recruited were academically and athletically inferior to those of conference and nonconference opponents, that the average home-game attendance figures had dropped, and that the income generated by the basketball program, on which the entire athletic department depends, had declined. The evidence also showed that, based on the recommendations of then Athletic Director Byrne and Vice-President Williams, which included their view that plaintiff could not effectuate a turn-around in the program, University President Myles Brand made the decision to reassign plaintiff's duties, pursuant to OAR 580-21-318. In the letter informing plaintiff of the change, Byrne stated that "for the good of the department we need to make a change in leadership in the men's basketball program."

The trial court's denial of the State's motions for directed verdict appears to have been based, at least in part, on the court's view that the reassignment could not have been in accordance with the "staff needs" of the university because the positions to which plaintiff was to be reassigned were not vacant. The court explained, "If the plaintiff has a burden of disproving that the reassignment from head basketball coach to golf coach thence to rules coordinator, the move was not proper to those positions, the testimony shows that there was a golf coach, at least for the previous season, and no indication that that assignment had been changed or that there was a vacancy and a need to staff that position, even to the extent of transferring the head basketball coach from his position in mid-season to being coach for the golf team. "There's testimony from [plaintiff] that that position was already occupied or that one occupied was never filled by persons of his rank and stature in the athletic department. And similarly, there is testimony that the duties of monitoring and coordinating compliance with NCAA rules had been discharged as only a parcel of the duties of persons assigned to other categories of employment and discharged as part of their duties in those assignments. "Consequently, there is evidence which, if believed by the jury, would leave them to conclude that the transfer, although within the institution, and although done by a person with authority to make the transfer, was not predicated on the staff needs of the institution or some other unit of the institution. That is sufficient to save that issue from a motion to dismiss."

The court also commented that "the only testimony before the jury is that the transfer was to positions already fulfilled or filled by full-time or part-time staff members within the department."

The State argues that the trial court was both factually and legally mistaken in its ruling. We agree. First, contrary to the trial court's summary of the evidence, the only testimony about the golf coach position came from plaintiff, who stated that he did not think there was a golf coach at the time that Byrne reassigned him to that position. Rather, he believed that the position had been vacant for some time, but for less than a year. The undisputed evidence also showed that plaintiff's reassignment occurred at the end of the basketball season, not in "mid-season." More significantly, however, the trial court apparently assumed that "the staff needs of the institution" under OAR 580-21-318 meant only that there is "a vacancy and a need to staff" a particular position. Thus, according to the trial court, evidence showing that the duties of golf coach or compliance officer were being performed by other staff members could support a finding that the reassignment of plaintiff to those positions was not in accordance with the university's "staff needs."

We do not agree with the court's narrow interpretation of the university's authority under the rule. Although this is a breach of contract action, the meaning of the administrative rule at issue here is a question of law for the court. Our task in interpreting a statute or a regulation is to determine the intent of the body that promulgated it; in this case, the State Board of Higher Education. We begin with the language of the regulation, including relevant rules of statutory construction. One such rule is that words of common usage that are not defined in the statute typically are to be given their plain, natural, and ordinary meaning. The critical terms of the rule here, "staff needs," are not defined in the Board of Higher Education's administrative rules. Accordingly, we look to the common usage of those terms. Generally, the noun "need" means "a want of something requisite, desirable, or useful." The adjective "staff" means "of, relating to, or constituting a staff," which, in turn, is defined as "the personnel responsible for the functioning of an institution or the establishment or the carrying out of an assigned task." Thus, in common usage, an institution's "staff needs" are those things that are necessary, useful, or desirable with regards to the group of staff members on which the university depends for its general operation. Examples of an institution's staff needs would include not just an interest in filling vacant positions but also an interest in making the best use of available staff members. Consideration of other rules of the university is also helpful in determining its meaning. It is apparent from the rules that the institution's administration has significant discretion to determine what is necessary, useful, or desirable, in terms of managing its staff. Under OAR 580-21-390, "[a]n academic staff member aggrieved by a president's nondisciplinary personnel decision may appeal such decision" to the Board. Thus, an employee who has been reassigned under the authority of OAR 580-21-318 may request review of that decision. If the Board exercises its discretion to take further action on the personnel decision, the review will include a "fair consideration of the facts," but it "shall not include a *de novo* review on the judgment exercised by the president."

We conclude that, with respect to nontenured faculty members subject to the rule, the university has the authority to reassign individuals based on its assessment of its overall staffing needs. Just as the institution's interest in filling a vacant position may justify reassigning a staff member, so too might the administration's determination that a staff member is no longer the most effective person for a particular position, or a determination that a department would be better served by having a different staff member in that position.

The issue raised by the State's directed verdict motions was whether a reasonable jury could have found that plaintiff's reassignment from his position as head men's basketball coach was inconsistent with the administrative rules governing reassignment. We conclude there was no evidence from which a jury could have made that finding. The essence of plaintiff's argument on appeal is that, because the evidence "suggested that Plaintiff's removal as coach was for 'cause'," it follows that his removal could not have been based on a decision to reassign him under OAR 580-21-318. plaintiff's argument, however, does not defeat a motion for a directed verdict. First, even if the evidence did suggest that plaintiff was reassigned for "cause" from his coaching position, it does not follow that the decision to reassign him was not in accordance with staff needs. The evidence concerning plaintiff's performance, and the effect of that performance on the university's athletic program, is also pertinent to the question of whether a reassignment is consistent with "staff needs."

As discussed above, the assessment of an institution's overall staffing needs includes an evaluation of how best to make use of available staff members. That inquiry requires an assessment of the strengths and abilities of the individual staff members. A determination that an employee's skills are no longer compatible with the changing needs of his or her position does not necessarily mean that that employee is incompetent, grossly inefficient, intentionally or habitually neglecting his or her duty, or in any other way "failing to perform the responsibilities of an academic staff member." Accordingly, the fact that the university's decision to reassign plaintiff was based in part on his performance as head men's basketball coach does not controvert the evidence that the reassignment was "in accordance with the staff needs of the university."

Plaintiff has failed to identify any evidence in the record from which a jury could find that his reassignment from his position as head men's basketball coach was not in accordance with the applicable administrative rules. Accordingly, viewing the evidence in the light most favorable to plaintiff and giving him the benefit of all reasonable inferences, we conclude that a jury could not have found the facts necessary to conclude that the university breached plaintiff's contract. Accordingly, the trial court erred in not directing a verdict in the State's favor. Reversed and remanded for entry of appropriate judgment.

For an extended version of the case and review questions to test your understanding of the material, please go to www.HumanKinetics.com/CaseStudiesInSportLaw.

Rodgers v. Georgia Tech Athletic Association

303 S.E.2d 467 (Ga. App. 1983)

Franklin C. "Pepper" Rodgers brought this breach of contract action against the Georgia Tech Athletic Association to recover the value of certain perquisites that had been made available to him as the head coach of football at the Georgia Institute of Technology. Both parties moved for summary judgment, Rodgers' motion encompassing only the issue of liability under his contract of employment with the Association. The trial court granted the Association's motion and denied Rodgers' motion. The issue presented for resolution by this appeal is whether Rodgers is entitled to recover the value of certain perquisites or "fringe benefits" of his position as head coach of football under the terms of his contract of employment with the Association.

Rodgers was removed from his coaching position by vote of the Association's Board of Trustees on December 18, 1979, notwithstanding a written contract of employment through December 31, 1981. In addition to an annual salary, the contract provided that Rodgers, as an employee of the Association, would be entitled "to various insurance and pension benefits and perquisites" as he became eligible therefor. Rodgers makes no claim for base salary, health insurance, and pension plan benefits, all of which were provided voluntarily by the Association through December 31, 1981, the expiration date of the contract. Rather, his claim is solely for the value of the aforesaid "perquisites," to which he claims entitlement under this employment contract.

Rodgers lists some 29 separate items as such perquisites. In support of his for summary judgment, Rodgers categorized these items into two groups: (1) items provided directly to him by the Association but discontinued when Rodgers was relieved of his duties, and (2) items provided by sources other than the Association by virtue of his position as head coach of football. These items are listed in the appendix to this opinion. The subject contract was in the form of a letter from the Association dated April 20, 1977 offering Rodgers the position of head coach of football for three years at an annual salary plus certain benefits and perquisites. This contract provided that Rodgers could be terminated for illness or other incapacity continuing for three months, death, or "any conduct or activity involving moral turpitude or which in the opinion of [the Board of Trustees] would constitute an embarrassment to the school." Rodgers accepted this contract on April 25, 1977. This contract was extended until January 1, 1982 by a subsequent letter agreement between the parties. At its December 18, 1979 meeting, the Association's Board of Trustees determined that a change should be made in the position of head coach of football.

Rodgers asserts essentially two theories of recovery: (1) breach of contract and (2) appropriation of a "property right." As to the second theory, Rodgers contends that the Association appropriated, that is, took without permission, his position and title as head coach of football at Georgia Tech. . . . We have been cited to no authority, nor are we aware of any, that stands for the proposition that a person has a property right in the position and title of his employment. An employee may not generally obtain specific performance of his contract of employment . . . , his only recourse for breach being damages. That is to say, generally an employer may, rightfully or wrongfully, remove an employee from his employment at any time. The employee's only recourse for wrongful removal is the recovery of damages; he has no right to recover the position and title of his employment. It follows

that an employee has no property right in such position and title.

Rodgers contends that he was terminated or fired from his employment by the Association. However, the evidence of record supports the Association's view that Rodgers was merely relieved of his duties as the head coach of football yet remained an employee of the Association, albeit without any function or duties, for the duration of his contract. In either event, this disassociation of Rodgers from his position and duties was not "for cause" pursuant to the terms of the contract. Therefore, the Association was obligated to pay Rodgers that part of the amount set forth in the contract "which he himself was entitled to receive as compensation for his services."

In addition to a salary, health insurance, and pension benefits, the contract provided that Rodgers, as an employee of the Association, was entitled to "perquisites" as he became eligible therefor. The term "perquisites" is defined as "[e]moluments or incidental profits attaching to an office or official position, beyond the salary or regular fees." The term is also defined as "a privilege, gain, or profit incidental to an employment in addition to regular salary or wages; esp: one expected or promised [e.g.,] the [perquisites] of the college president include a home and car. . . ." Thus, Rodgers was entitled to the perquisites (or their value) for which he was eligible during the duration of his contract. The problem presented here for resolution is to determine whether any of the items listed in the appendix were indeed perquisites to which Rodgers was entitled pursuant to his contract.

First, we must determine the intention of the parties as to the scope of the perquisites to which Rodgers was entitled under the contract. The pertinent language of the contract provides: "You, as Head Coach of Football, will devote your time, attention, skill, and efforts to the performance of your duties as Head Coach under the policies established by the Athletic Board and the Athletic Director, and you will receive compensation at [an] annual rate of $35,175.00 payable in equal monthly installments. In addition, as an employee of the Association, you will be entitled to various . . . perquisites as you become eligible therefor."

The Association contends that the language "as an employee of the Association" limited Rodgers' eligibility for perquisites to those items common to all Association employees. Rodgers argues that he was not only entitled to those perquisites common to all Association employees, but that he was also entitled to additional perquisites for which he became eligible as the head coach of football. Since the contract is susceptible to either construction, it is ambiguous. This ambiguity may be resolved by applying the appropriate rules of construction. "If a contract is so framed as to be susceptible of two constructions, that interpretation which is least favorable to the author . . . should generally be accepted. 'When it is possible to do so without contravening any rule of law, the courts will construe a contract as binding on both the parties, where, from the language of the contract, the conduct of the parties, and all the attendant circumstances, it appears that the intention of the parties was that both should be bound [thereby], and substantial justice requires that the contract be given effect. . . .'"

The subject contract was drafted by the Association. Moreover, the record discloses that Rodgers, during his tenure as head coach of football, did receive perquisites in addition to those received by other Association employees. Accordingly, we conclude that the parties intended that Rodgers would receive perquisites, as he became eligible therefor, based on his position as head coach of football and not merely as an employee of the Association.

We must next determine the nature of the items for which Rodgers seeks damages (i.e., whether the items listed in the appendix are perquisites *vel non*). We will first address ourselves to those items listed in section A of the appendix and address separately those items listed in section B.

The Association asserts that Rodgers was not entitled to any of the items listed in section A because they were expense account items—"tools" to enable him to more effectively execute his duties as head coach of football. Rodgers counters that those items were an integral part of the total compensation package that he received as head coach of football and constituted consideration for his contract of employment. We certainly agree with the Association that Rodgers would be entitled to recover only "compensatory damages that he suffered by reason of the breach of his contract; in other words, that the

proper measure of damages arising from the breach of the contract of employment was actual loss sustained by the breach, and not the gross amount of [his] wages and expenses [under the contract]." However, the evidence offered as to the nature of the items in section A was in considerable dispute. The fact that these items were not reported as taxable income by Rodgers is not conclusive as to their nature . . . , nor is the fact that Rodgers reimbursed the Association for occasional "personal" expenses that it had paid. Thus, with three exceptions, we cannot say as a matter of law either that Rodgers was entitled to the items listed in section A as perquisites of his employment, or that he was not.

The three exceptions to this finding are the services of a secretary, the services of an administrative assistant, and the cost of trips to football conventions, clinics, and so on. The undisputed purpose of the services of the secretary and administrative assistant was to assist Rodgers in fulfilling his duties under the contract. Since Rodgers had been relieved of his duties as head coach of football, and, thus, had no responsibilities under the contract, he had no need for these support services. This is true even though the secretary and administrative assistant may have occasionally provided personal services to Rodgers beyond their duties to him as head coach of football since, as Rodgers admits, their primary functions were to provide services to the head coach of football. Also, since Rodgers had been relieved of his coaching duties, the Association was not obligated to pay his expenses for trips to various football-related activities, these costs clearly being business-related and not in the nature of compensation.

We turn our attention finally to those items in section B of the appendix—items that Rodgers asserts were perquisites he received from sources other than the Association by virtue of his position as head coach of football at Georgia Tech. The Association argues that Rodgers' claim for recovery of these items was in the nature of a tort claim for humiliation and injury to feelings. Rodgers counters that these items were perquisites within the contemplation of the parties that constituted part of the consideration for the contract even though they were provided by sources other than the Association. We do not construe Rodgers' claim for recovery of the items in section B to be in the nature of a personal injury tort.

In the case at bar Rodgers claims that the items in section B were part of the consideration of his contract. No claim for personal injury appears. Furthermore, the State Court of Fulton County, where this case was brought, has no jurisdiction over personal injury claims. Construing Rodgers' complaint to serve his best interests, we hold that the Association's argument here is without merit. Nevertheless, we must now determine whether Rodgers may recover the items in section B under his breach of contract theory. The consideration of a contract need not flow directly from the promisor but may be the promise or undertaking of one or more third persons. Damages growing out of a breach of contract, in order to form the basis of a recovery, must be such as can be traced solely to the breach, must be capable of exact computation, must have arisen naturally and according to the usual course of things from such breach, and must be such as the parties contemplated as a probable result of the breach. As a general rule, a party is entitled to recover profits that would have resulted from a breach of a contract into which he has entered, where the breach is the result of the other party's fault. And while a breach of the original contract will not ordinarily entitle a plaintiff to recover as damages the profits of collateral enterprises or subcontracts, yet where the knowledge of the subcontract is within the contemplation of the parties when the original contract is made, and is known to have been made with reference thereto, anticipated profits shown to be certain, fixed in amount, and the direct fruit of the contract, are recoverable. Profits are excluded only when there are no criteria, definite and certain, upon which an adjudication can be based. They then become speculative and imaginary.

We will apply the foregoing legal principles to the facts of record. Can Rodgers' loss of the items in section B be traced solely to the Association's breach of the contract? Rodgers testified that he received these perquisites as a result of his being head coach of football at Georgia Tech. The record discloses, however, that the items relating to housing and the cost of premiums on a life insurance policy were discontinued several years prior to the Association's breach of contract and were, in fact, not related to the breach. Thus, these items were properly excluded by the

trial court. The remaining items were discontinued as the direct result of Rodgers being relieved of his duties as head coach of football. Are the remaining items in section B capable of exact computation? A "gift" is defined as "[a] voluntary transfer of personal property without consideration." A gift, then, being a voluntary transaction and without consideration, cannot form an enforceable part of the consideration of a contract. Although Rodgers may have received gifts of money and personalty during his tenure as head coach of football, such voluntary contributions to his financial well-being are totally incapable of exact computation, for a gift made in one year is no assurance of a similar gift in the next. In fact, Rodgers concedes that he did not receive these gifts each year. Thus, the item that listed various financial gifts was properly excluded from recovery. The items now remaining are sufficiently capable of computation.

Did these remaining items arise naturally and according to the usual course of things, and were they such as the parties contemplated as a probable result of a breach? There is no evidence of record showing that the Association had any knowledge of Rodgers' free lodging at certain Holiday Inns or of his membership in Terminus International Tennis Club. Thus, the loss of these items could not be such as was contemplated as a probable result of a breach of the contract. The evidence was in dispute as to the remaining items (profits from his television and radio shows and from his summer football camp plus the loss of use of a new automobile and tickets to professional sporting events), whether such items were contemplated by the parties at the time the contract was executed as perquisites or fringe benefits to which Rodgers would be entitled as the result of his position as head coach of football at Georgia Tech. These items are of the type commonly provided to head coaches at major colleges and universities. There was some evidence that the Association knew that Rodgers would receive (and, in fact, did receive) these benefits as the result of his head coaching position and that his removal from that position would result in the loss of these benefits. In fact, some members of the Association assisted Rodgers in obtaining many of these items. Also, there was at least some evidence by which the amount of these items could be fixed. Therefore, summary judgment in favor of the Association as to these items was inappropriate. For these same reasons, summary judgment in favor of Rodgers was properly denied.

In summary, a question of fact remains as to whether Rodgers is entitled to recover those items listed in section A of the appendix not excluded in this opinion and also those items in section B not heretofore excluded, any recovery being subject to proof of the amount of his damages as set forth in this opinion. All items that have been excluded are denoted by asterisks in the appendix. Judgment affirmed in part; reversed in part.

APPENDIX

A. *Benefits and Perquisites Received by Rodgers Directly From the Georgia Tech Athletic Association*

1. Gas, oil, maintenance, repairs, other automobile expenses
2. Automobile liability and collision insurance
3. General expense money
4. Meals available at the Georgia Tech training table
5. Eight season tickets to Georgia Tech home football games during fall of 1980 and 1981
6. Two reserved booths, consisting of approximately 40 seats at Georgia Tech home football games during fall of 1980 and 1981
7. Six season tickets to Georgia Tech home basketball games for 1980 and 1981
8. Four season tickets to Atlanta Falcon home football games for 1980 and 1981
9. Four game tickets to each out-of-town Georgia Tech football game during fall of 1980 and 1981
10. Pocket money at each home football game during fall of 1980 and 1981
11. Pocket money at each out-of-town Georgia Tech football game during fall of 1980 and 1981
12. Parking privileges at all Georgia Tech home sporting events
13. The services of a secretary *
14. The services of an administrative assistant *
15. The cost of admission to Georgia Tech home baseball games during spring of 1980 and 1981
16. The cost of trips to football coaches' conventions, clinics, and meetings and to observe football practice sessions of professional and college football teams *
17. Initiation fee, dues, monthly bills, and cost of membership at the Capital City Club
18. Initiation fee, dues, monthly bills, and cost of membership at the Cherokee Country Club
19. Initiation fee and dues at the East Lake Country Club

B. *Benefits and Perquisites Received by Rodgers From Sources Other Than the Georgia Tech Athletic Association by Virtue of Being Head Coach of Football*

1. Profits from Rodgers' television football show, "The Pepper Rodgers Show," on Station WSB-TV in Atlanta for the fall of 1980 and 1981
2. Profits from Rodgers' radio football show on Station WGST in Atlanta for the fall of 1980 and 1981
3. Use of a new Cadillac automobile during 1980 and 1981
4. Profits from Rodgers' summer football camp, known as the "Pepper Rodgers Football School," for June 1980 and June 1981
5. Financial gifts from alumni and supporters of Georgia Tech for 1980 and 1981 *
6. Lodging at any of the Holiday Inns owned by Topeka Inn Management, Inc. of Topeka, Kansas, for the time period from December 18, 1979 through December 31, 1981 *
7. The cost of membership in Terminus International Tennis Club in Atlanta for 1980 and 1981 *
8. Individual game tickets to Hawk basketball and Braves baseball games during 1980 and 1981 seasons
9. Housing for Rodgers and his family in Atlanta for the period from December 18, 1979 through December 31, 1981 *
10. The cost of premiums of a $400,000 policy on the life of Rodgers for the time period from December 18, 1979 through December 31, 1981 *

 For an extended version of the case and review questions to test your understanding of the material, please go to www.HumanKinetics.com/CaseStudiesInSportLaw.

Taylor v. Wake Forest University

191 S.E.2d 379 (N.C. App. 1972)

This action was instituted for the recovery of educational expenses incurred by George J. Taylor, father, and Gregg F. Taylor, son, after alleged wrongful termination of an athletic scholarship issued to Gregg F. Taylor by Wake Forest University. As early as December 1965, football coaches at Wake Forest were in communication with Gregg Taylor soliciting his enrollment at Wake Forest. As a result of this interest and negotiations, Gregg Taylor and his father, George Taylor, on 27 February 1967, submitted an application entitled, "Atlantic Coast Conference Application For A Football Grant-In-Aid Or A Scholarship."

This application was accepted by Wake Forest on May 24, 1967. It provided in part the following:

> This Grant, if awarded, will be for 4 years provided I conduct myself in accordance with the rules of the Conference, the NCAA, and the Institution. I agree to maintain eligibility for intercollegiate athletics under both Conference and Institutional rules. Training rules for intercollegiate athletics are considered rules of the Institution, and I agree to abide by them. If injured while participating in athletics supervised by a member of the coaching staff, the Grant or Scholarship will be honored; and the medical expenses will be paid by the Athletic Department. This grant, when approved, is awarded for academic and athletic achievement and is not to be interpreted as employment in any manner whatsoever.

At the time of the execution of the agreement between the Taylors and Wake Forest, some of the rules of the NCAA prohibited

> (a) Graduation or cancellation of institutional aid during the period of its award on the basis of a student-athlete's prowess or his contribution to a team's success. (b) Graduation or cancellation of institutional aid during the period of its award because of an injury which prevents the recipient from participating in athletics. (c) Graduation or cancellation of institutional aid during the period of its award for any other athletic reason, except that such aid may be gradated or cancelled if the recipient (1) voluntarily renders himself ineligible for intercollegiate competition, or (2) fraudulently misrepresents any information on his application, letter-of-intent or tender, or (3) engages

in serious misconduct warranting substantial disciplinary penalty. Any such graduation or cancellation of aid is permissible only if (1) such action is taken by the regular disciplinary and/or scholarship awards authorities of the institution, (2) the student has had an opportunity for a hearing, and (3) the action is based on institutional policy applicable to the general student body.

At the time the contract was entered into, Wake Forest did not have a written Grant-In-Aid policy. This policy was not put in writing until January 1969. One of the written policy provisions was to the effect that financial aid could be terminated for "(r)efusal to attend practice sessions or scheduled work-out that are a part of the athletic program or to act in such a manner as to disrupt these sessions." The Wake Forest athletic director set out in an affidavit: "(T)he policy of requiring student athletes to regularly attend practice sessions was in effect at the defendant University when the first scholarship was granted more than 30 years ago." In compliance with the contract entered into, Gregg Taylor enrolled and became a student at Wake Forest at the beginning of the fall session 1967. He participated in the football program during the fall of 1967. At the end of that semester, his grade average was 1.0 out of a possible 4.0. Wake Forest required a 1.35 grade average after freshman year, a 1.65 grade average after sophomore year, and a 1.85 grade average after junior year. The 1.0 grade average received by Gregg Taylor for the first semester of his freshman year in the fall of 1967 was thus below the grade average required by Wake Forest. Gregg Taylor notified the football coach on February 6, 1968 that he would not participate in regular practice sessions of the football team during the spring of 1968 until his grades had improved. For the second semester of his freshman year, which was the spring of 1968, Gregg Taylor obtained a 1.9 grade average. This brought his grade average above what Wake Forest required even after junior year. Despite this improvement in his grade average,

Gregg Taylor decided that he would not further participate in the football program, and in the fall of his sophomore year, which was the fall of 1968, Gregg Taylor attained a 2.4 grade average. Gregg Taylor continued in his refusal to participate in the football program.

Wake Forest notified Gregg Taylor on or about May 1, 1969 that a hearing would be held on May 14, 1969 before the Faculty Athletic Committee as to whether his scholarship should be terminated. At this hearing Gregg Taylor was notified that the Faculty Athletic Committee would recommend to the Scholarship Committee that his scholarship be terminated because of his failure to participate in the football program at Wake Forest. Thereafter, the Scholarship Committee of Wake Forest accepted the recommendation of the Faculty Athletic Committee, and on July 10, 1969, the Scholarship Committee notified Gregg Taylor that his scholarship had been terminated as of the end of the 1968-69 academic year, which was the end of Gregg Taylor's sophomore year. Gregg Taylor continued to attend Wake Forest during the 1969-70 academic year, which was his junior year, and likewise, the academic year of 1970-71, which was his senior year; and he received an undergraduate degree from Wake Forest in June 1971.

As a result of the termination of the scholarship, expenses in the amount of $5,500 were incurred during those two academic years. It is for this sum of $5,500 that this action was instituted. The defendant Wake Forest moved for summary judgment pursuant to Rule 56 of the Rules of Civil Procedure on the ground that there was no genuine issue as to any material fact and that the defendant was entitled to judgment as a matter of law. This motion was allowed, and the plaintiffs appealed.

Plaintiffs contend that there was a genuine issue as to a material fact and that a jury should determine whether Gregg Taylor acted reasonably and in good faith in refusing to participate in the football program at Wake Forest when such participation interfered with reasonable academic progress. The plaintiffs' position depends on a construction of the contractual agreement between plaintiffs and Wake Forest. As stated in the affidavit of George J. Taylor, the position of the plaintiffs is that it was orally agreed between plaintiffs and the representative of Wake Forest that "(I)n the event of any conflict between educational achievement and athletic involvement, participation in athletic activities could be limited or eliminated to the extent necessary to assure reasonable academic progress."

And plaintiffs were to be the judge as to what "reasonable academic progress" constituted.

We do not agree with the position taken by plaintiffs. The scholarship application filed by Gregg Taylor provided that ". . . I agree to maintain eligibility for intercollegiate athletics under both Conference and Institutional rules. Training rules for intercollegiate athletics are considered rules of the Institution, and I agree to abide by them." Both Gregg Taylor and his father knew that the application was for "Football Grant-In-Aid Or A Scholarship," and that the scholarship was "awarded for academic and athletic achievement." It would be a strained construction of the contract that would enable the plaintiffs to determine the "reasonable academic progress" of Gregg Taylor. Gregg Taylor, in consideration of the scholarship award, agreed to maintain his athletic eligibility and this meant both physically and scholastically. As long as his grade average equaled or exceeded the requirements of Wake Forest, he was maintaining his scholastic eligibility for athletics. Participation in and attendance at practice were required to maintain his physical eligibility. When he refused to do so in the absence of any injury or excuse other than to devote more time to studies, he was not complying with his contractual obligations. The record disclosed that Wake Forest fully complied with its agreement and that Gregg Taylor failed to do so. There was no "genuine issue as to any material fact" and summary judgment was proper. We find no error.

 For an extended version of the case and review questions to test your understanding of the material, please go to www.HumanKinetics.com/CaseStudiesInSportLaw.

Vanderbilt University v. DiNardo

174 F.3d 751 (6th Cir. 1999)

Gerry DiNardo resigned as Vanderbilt's head football coach to become the head football coach for Louisiana State University. As a result, Vanderbilt University brought this breach of contract action. The district court entered summary judgment for Vanderbilt, awarding $281,886.43 pursuant to a damage provision in DiNardo's employment contract with Vanderbilt. DiNardo appeals, arguing that the district court erred in concluding (1) that the contract provision was an enforceable liquidated damage provision and not an unlawful penalty under Tennessee law, (2) that Vanderbilt did not waive its right to liquidated damages, (3) that the addendum to the contract was enforceable, and (4) that the addendum applied to the damage provision of the original contract. DiNardo also argues that there are disputed issues of material fact precluding summary judgment.

On December 3, 1990, Vanderbilt and DiNardo executed an employment contract hiring DiNardo to be Vanderbilt's head football coach. Section one of the contract provided the following: "The University hereby agrees to hire Mr. DiNardo for a period of five (5) years from the date hereof with Mr. DiNardo's assurance that he will serve the entire term of this Contract, a long-term commitment by Mr. DiNardo being important to the university's desire for a stable intercollegiate football program. . . ."

The contract also contained reciprocal liquidated damage provisions. Vanderbilt agreed to pay DiNardo his remaining salary should Vanderbilt replace him as football coach, and DiNardo agreed to reimburse Vanderbilt should he leave before his contract expired. Section eight of the contract stated,

> Mr. DiNardo recognizes that his promise to work for the University for the entire term of this 5-year Contract is of the essence of this Contract to the University. Mr. DiNardo also recognizes that the University is making a highly valuable investment in his continued employment by entering into this Contract and its investment would be lost were he to resign or otherwise terminate his employment as Head Football

Coach with the University prior to the expiration of this Contract. Accordingly, Mr. DiNardo agrees that in the event he resigns or otherwise terminates his employment as Head Football Coach (as opposed to his resignation or termination from another position at the University to which he may have been reassigned), prior to the expiration of this Contract, and is employed or performing services for a person or institution other than the University, he will pay to the University as liquidated damages an amount equal to his Base Salary, less amounts that would otherwise be deducted or withheld from his Base Salary for income and social security tax purposes, multiplied by the number of years (or portion(s) thereof) remaining on the Contract.

During contract negotiations, section eight was modified at DiNardo's request so that damages would be calculated based on net, rather than gross, salary. Vanderbilt initially set DiNardo's salary at $100,000 per year. On August 14, 1994, Paul Hoolahan, Vanderbilt's athletic director, . . . offered DiNardo a two-year contract extension. DiNardo told Hoolahan that he wanted to extend his contract, but that he also wanted to discuss the extension with Larry DiNardo, his brother and attorney. Hoolahan telephoned John Callison, deputy general counsel for Vanderbilt, and asked him to prepare a contract extension. Callison drafted an addendum to the original employment contract that provided for a two-year extension of the original contract, specifying a termination date of January 5, 1998. Vanderbilt's chancellor, Joe B. Wyatt, and Hoolahan signed the addendum.

On August 17, Hoolahan returned to Bell Buckle with the addendum. He took it to DiNardo at the practice field where they met in Hoolahan's car. DiNardo stated that Hoolahan did not present him with the complete two-page addendum, but only the second page, which was the signature page. DiNardo asked, "What am I signing?" Hoolahan explained to DiNardo, "[i]t means that your contract as it presently exists will be extended for two years with everything else remaining exactly the same as it existed in the present contract." Before DiNardo signed the addendum, he told Hoolahan, "Larry needs to see a copy before this thing is finalized." Hoolahan agreed, and DiNardo signed the document. DiNardo explained that he agreed to sign the document because he thought the extension was the "best thing" for the football program and that he "knew ultimately, Larry would look at it, and before it would become finalized he would approve it." Hoolahan took the signed document without giving DiNardo a copy.

On August 16, Larry DiNardo had a telephone conversation with Callison. They briefly talked about the contract extension, discussing a salary increase. Larry DiNardo testified that as of that date he did not know that Gerry DiNardo had signed the addendum, or even that one yet existed.

On August 25, 1994, Callison faxed to Larry DiNardo "a copy of the draft Addendum to Gerry's contract." . . . The copy sent was unsigned. . . . On September 27, Callison sent a fax to Larry DiNardo concerning the television and radio contract, and also added "I would like your comments on the contract extension." Larry DiNardo testified that he neither participated in the drafting nor suggested any changes to the addendum. In November 1994, Louisiana State University contacted Vanderbilt in hopes of speaking with DiNardo about becoming the head football coach for LSU. Hoolahan gave DiNardo permission to speak to LSU about the position. On December 12, 1994, DiNardo announced that he was accepting the LSU position.

Vanderbilt sent a demand letter to DiNardo seeking payment of liquidated damages under section eight of the contract. Vanderbilt believed that DiNardo was liable for three years of his net salary: one year under the original contract and two years under the addendum. DiNardo did not respond to Vanderbilt's demand for payment. Vanderbilt brought this action against DiNardo for breach of contract. DiNardo removed the action to federal court, and both parties filed motions for summary judgment. The district court held that section eight was an enforceable liquidated damages provision, not an unlawful penalty, and that the damages provided under section eight were reasonable. The court held that Vanderbilt did not waive its contractual rights under section eight when it granted DiNardo permission to talk to LSU and that the addendum was enforceable and extended the contract for two years. The court entered judgment against DiNardo for $281,886.43. DiNardo appeals.

DiNardo first claims that section eight of the contract is an unenforceable penalty under Tennessee law. DiNardo argues that the provision is not a liquidated damage provision but a "thinly disguised, overly broad non-compete provision," unenforceable under Tennessee law.

Contracting parties may agree to the payment of liquidated damages in the event of a breach. The term "liquidated damages" refers to an amount determined by the parties to be just compensation for damages should a breach occur. Courts will not enforce such a provision, however, if the stipulated amount constitutes a penalty. A penalty is designed to coerce performance by punishing default. In Tennessee, a provision will be considered one for liquidated damages, rather than a penalty, if it is reasonable in relation to the anticipated damages for breach, measured prospectively at the time the contract was entered into, and not grossly disproportionate to the actual damages. When these conditions are met, particularly the first, the parties probably intended the provision to be for liquidated damages. However, any doubt as to the character of the contract provision will be resolved in favor of finding it a penalty.

The district court held that the use of a formula based on DiNardo's salary to calculate liquidated damages was reasonable "given the nature of the unquantifiable damages in the case." The court held that parties to a contract may include consequential damages and even damages not usually awarded by law in a liquidated damage provision provided that they were contemplated by the parties. DiNardo contends that there is no evidence that the parties contemplated that the potential damage from DiNardo's resignation would go beyond the cost of hiring a replacement coach. He argues that his salary has no relationship to Vanderbilt's damages and that the liquidated damage amount is unreasonable and shows that the parties did not intend the provision to be for liquidated damages.

DiNardo's theory of the parties' intent, however, does not square with the record. The contract language establishes that Vanderbilt wanted the five-year contract because "a long-term commitment" by DiNardo was "important to the

University's desire for a stable intercollegiate football program," and that this commitment was of "essence" to the contract. Vanderbilt offered the two-year contract extension to DiNardo well over a year before his original contract expired. Both parties understood that the extension was to provide stability to the program, which helped in recruiting players and retaining assistant coaches. Thus, undisputed evidence, and reasonable inferences therefrom, establish that both parties understood and agreed that DiNardo's resignation would result in Vanderbilt suffering damage beyond the cost of hiring a replacement coach.

This evidence also refutes DiNardo's argument that the district court erred in presuming that DiNardo's resignation would necessarily cause damage to the university. That the university may actually benefit from a coaching change (as DiNardo suggests) matters little, as we measure the reasonableness of the liquidated damage provision at the time the parties entered the contract, not when the breach occurred, . . . , and we hardly think the parties entered the contract anticipating that DiNardo's resignation would benefit Vanderbilt.

The stipulated damage amount is reasonable in relation to the amount of damages that could be expected to result from the breach. As we stated, the parties understood that Vanderbilt would suffer damage should DiNardo prematurely terminate his contract, and that these actual damages would be difficult to measure.

Vanderbilt hired DiNardo for a unique and specialized position, and the parties understood that the amount of damages could not be easily ascertained should a breach occur. Contrary to DiNardo's suggestion, Vanderbilt did not need to undertake an analysis to determine actual damages, and using the number of years left on the contract multiplied by the salary per year was a reasonable way to calculate damages considering the difficulty of ascertaining damages with certainty. The fact that liquidated damages declined each year DiNardo remained under contract is directly tied to the parties' express understanding of the importance of a long-term commitment from DiNardo. Furthermore, the liquidated damages provision was reciprocal and the result of negotiations between two parties, each of whom was represented by counsel.

We also reject DiNardo's argument that a question of fact remains as to whether the parties intended section eight to be a "reasonable estimate" of damages. The liquidated damages are in line with Vanderbilt's estimate of its actual damages. Vanderbilt presented evidence that it incurred expenses associated with recruiting a new head coach of $27,000; moving expenses for the new coaching staff of $86,840; and a compensation difference between the coaching staffs of $184,311. The stipulated damages clause is reasonable under the circumstances, and we affirm the district court's conclusion that the liquidated damages clause is enforceable under Tennessee law.

DiNardo next argues that Vanderbilt waived its right to liquidated damages when it granted DiNardo permission to discuss the coaching position with LSU. Under Tennessee law, a party may not recover liquidated damages when it is responsible for or has contributed to the delay or nonperformance alleged as the breach. Vanderbilt did not waive its rights under section eight of the contract by giving DiNardo permission to pursue the LSU position. First, Hoolahan's permission was quite circumscribed. Hoolahan gave DiNardo permission to talk to LSU about their coaching position; he did not authorize DiNardo to terminate his contract with Vanderbilt. Second, the employment contract required DiNardo to ask Vanderbilt's athletic director for permission to speak with another school about a coaching position, and Hoolahan testified that granting a coach permission to talk to another school about a position was a "professional courtesy." Thus, the parties certainly contemplated that DiNardo could explore other coaching positions, and indeed even leave Vanderbilt, subject to the terms of the liquidated damage provision. Allowing DiNardo to talk to another school did not relinquish Vanderbilt's right to liquidated damages. DiNardo claims that the addendum did not become a binding contract, and therefore, he is only liable for the one year remaining on the original contract, not the three years held by the district court.

DiNardo argues that the addendum did not extend section eight, or that there is at least a question of fact as to whether the addendum extended section eight. Under Tennessee law, the rights and obligations of contracting parties are governed by their written agreements. When the agreement is unambiguous, the meaning is a question of law, and we should enforce the agreement according to its plain terms. DiNardo argues that the original employment contract explicitly provides that section eight is limited to "the entire term of this five-year contract," and the plain, unambiguous language of the addendum did not extend section eight. He points out that the addendum did not change the effective date in section eight, unlike other sections in the contract.

The plain and unambiguous language of the addendum read in its entirety, however, provides for the wholesale extension of the entire contract. Certain sections were expressly amended to change the original contract expiration date of January 5, 1996, to January 5, 1998, because those sections of the original contract contained the precise expiration date of January 5, 1996. The district court did not err in concluding that the contract language extended all terms of the original contract.

DiNardo also claims that the addendum never became a binding contract because Larry DiNardo never expressly approved its terms. DiNardo contends that, at the very least, a question of fact exists as to whether the two-year addendum is an enforceable contract. The district court concluded that the addendum was enforceable as a matter of law because the parties acted as though the contract had been extended and because Larry DiNardo never objected to the addendum. Under Tennessee law, parties may accept terms of a contract and make the contract conditional upon some other event or occurrence. DiNardo argues that the addendum is not enforceable because it was contingent on Larry DiNardo's approval. Vanderbilt responds that the undisputed facts establish that there was no condition precedent to the addendum's enforceability. Vanderbilt first points out that DiNardo did not make this argument until late in the litigation, and more importantly did not make this argument when Vanderbilt initially requested payment from DiNardo in January 1995. Vanderbilt also contends that if Larry DiNardo found any of the language in the simple two-page addendum objectionable, he should have objected immediately. Finally,

Vanderbilt argues that if we decide that Larry DiNardo's approval was a condition precedent to enforceability, the condition was satisfied by Larry DiNardo's failure to object.

Viewing the evidence in the light most favorable to DiNardo, as we must, we are convinced that there is a disputed question of material fact as to whether the addendum is enforceable. There is a factual dispute as to whether Larry DiNardo's approval of the contract was a condition precedent to the addendum's enforceability. Gerry DiNardo testified that he told Hoolahan that the contract extension was not "final" until Larry DiNardo looked at it. Hoolahan's testimony on this point was consistent with DiNardo's: "He [Gerry DiNardo] said that he wanted to discuss the matter with you [Larry DiNardo], which I said certainly." Furthermore, although Callison's version of Larry DiNardo's role in the preparation of the contract extension differs from DiNardo's, it is undisputed that on August 25, nine days after Gerry DiNardo signed the addendum, Callison sent Larry DiNardo an unsigned copy of the "draft addendum." The cover sheet on a fax sent by Callison to DiNardo on September 27 closes with "I would like your comments on the contract extension." From these facts, a jury could conclude that Larry DiNardo's approval was required before the addendum became a binding contract.

Of course, there is evidence that the addendum was not contingent on Larry DiNardo's approval. Gerry DiNardo told others that he was happy with his contract extension, and Larry DiNardo never objected to the addendum. This evidence, however, does not carry the day, because we view the evidence on summary judgment in the light most favorable to DiNardo and resolve all factual disputes in his favor.

Likewise, Larry DiNardo's failure to object to the addendum may have constituted acceptance of the addendum's terms . . . , but on this record, we cannot resolve the issue on summary judgment. There is evidence from which a jury could find that Larry DiNardo's failure to object did not amount to acceptance of the Addendum. First, . . . , there is evidence explaining DiNardo's delay. The parties were primarily negotiating the radio and television contract during the fall of 1994. Callison testified that he could not recall whether he had any conversations with DiNardo in September about the contract extension. He explained, "The hot issue, if you will, was the radio and television contract. That was what was on my mind." It is not unreasonable to infer that the parties had not completely negotiated the details of the contract extension; the original contract did not expire for another year. On September 27, Callison asked Larry DiNardo for "his comments" on the contract extension. A jury could conclude from this solicitation that even Vanderbilt did not believe that the addendum had been approved and was enforceable as of that time. We cannot say that Larry DiNardo's failure to object by December 12, 1994, constitutes an acceptance of the addendum as a matter of law.

Accordingly, we affirm the district court's judgment that the contract contained an enforceable liquidated damage provision, and we affirm the portion of the judgment reflecting damages calculated under the original five-year contract. We reverse the district court's judgment concluding that the addendum was enforceable as a matter of law. We remand for a resolution of the factual issues as to whether Larry DiNardo's approval was a condition precedent to the enforceability of the addendum and, if so, whether the condition was satisfied by Larry DiNardo's failure to object. We affirm in part, reverse in part, and remand the case to the district court for further proceedings consistent with this opinion.

David A. Nelson, Circuit Judge, concurring in part and dissenting in part.

My principal reasons for viewing section eight as a penalty are these: (1) although the damages flowing from a premature resignation would normally be the same whether or not Coach DiNardo took a job elsewhere, section eight does not purport to impose liability for liquidated damages unless the coach accepts another job; (2) the section eight formula incorporates other variables that bear little or no relation to any reasonable approximation of anticipated damages; and (3) there is no evidence that the parties were attempting, in section eight, to come up with a reasonable estimate of the university's probable loss if the coach left. Section eight does not make Coach DiNardo liable for any liquidated damages at all, interestingly enough, unless, during the unexpired term of his contract, he "is employed or performing services for a person or institution other than the University. . . ." The logical inference, therefore, would seem to be that section eight was intended to penalize the coach for taking another job, and was not intended to make the university whole by liquidating any damages suffered as a result of being left in the lurch. This inference is strengthened, as I see it, by a couple of other anomalies in the stipulated damages formula. First, I am aware of no reason to believe that damages arising from the need to replace a prematurely departing coach could reasonably be expected to vary in direct proportion to the number of years left on the coach's contract. Second, the use of a "take-home pay" measuring stick suggests that the function of the stick was to rap the coach's knuckles and not to measure the university's loss. Finally, the record before us contains no evidence that the contracting parties gave any serious thought to attempting to measure the actual effect that a premature departure could be expected to have on the university's bottom line. On the contrary, the record affirmatively shows that the university did not attempt to determine whether section eight formula would yield a result reasonably approximating anticipated damages.

 For an extended version of the case and review questions to test your understanding of the material, please go to www.HumanKinetics.com/CaseStudiesInSportLaw.

4

Employment Law

When we speak of employment law, we are often addressing issues such as hiring and firing, and employee evaluations. In the world of sport, coaches often stand in the unenviable position of having very little job security. Many of the cases in employment law involving sports arise from situations where a coach or teacher is either released before the contract expires or the contract is not renewed. Coaches are often fired early in their tenure at a university where expectations are high and the win-loss record falls below what is expected. This has been the subject of much commentary, debate, and legal action. Employment contracts are therefore critical for coaches who might be forced to leave the job early.

The process of terminating an employee is difficult, and knowing how to avoid or prepare for lawsuits is important for the sport manager. The justification or reason for firing a coach and/or teacher is the central issue in many lawsuits brought by an aggrieved plaintiff. In some cases, it is alleged by plaintiffs that they were fired due to an act of retaliation by their boss after they had fought for their rights in some manner (e.g., brought a sexual harassment claim or age or gender discrimination claim). The cases provided in this chapter are diverse and useful from a practical standpoint in that they pose the different types of situations where employment-related issues may arise.

This chapter contains cases and questions involving junior high, high school, and college coaches and teachers. The issue of employee termination in the junior high school setting arose in *Burkey v. Marshall County* where a female junior high school teacher and coach was fired from her coaching position after she had filed sex discrimination charges. In the high school setting, the issue of employee termination arose in *Hegener v. Board of Education of City of Chicago*. In Hegener, a high school teacher was fired based upon alleged conduct unbecoming a teacher.

In the college setting, the cases selected for this section are *Moore v. Notre Dame* where a coach alleged age discrimination upon termination from his position, and *Perdue v. City University of New York* and *Stanley v. USC* where a coach brought a gender discrimination claim after the university decided not to renew her employment contract. The cases are interesting and illustrate the diversity of issues involved in employment cases.

Burkey v. Marshall County Board of Education

513 F.Supp. 1084 (D.C. W.Va. 1981)

Mrs. Burkey is a 1970 graduate of West Liberty State College, where she was a member of four different school athletic teams, including girls' basketball, volleyball, softball, and field hockey. In 1976, Mrs. Burkey received a master's degree in physical education from West Virginia University and thereafter she completed 15 additional graduate credit hours beyond her master's degree. Since July 1, 1970, to date, Burkey has been employed as a teacher by the defendant Marshall County Board of Education ("the Board"). After successfully completing a three school year probationary period, Mrs. Burkey achieved tenure within the Marshall County School District and has taught since the 1973-74 school year under a continuing contract with the Board. She has a permanent teaching certificate from the State of West Virginia. From 1971 until her transfer to the Washington Lands Elementary School in 1976, she coached girls' basketball at Moundsville Junior High School. Coaching appointments or contracts are made on a one school year basis and no teacher employed by the Board achieves tenure as a coach.

Prior to the 1971-72 school year no interscholastic sports program existed for girls at any of the junior high schools within the Marshall County School District. Opportunity to coach such sports was, therefore, limited to male teachers and opportunity to compete was limited to boys. During the 1971-72 school year Linda Burkey was responsible for forming an interscholastic girls' basketball team at Moundsville Junior High School. She continued to coach this team until the 1975-76 school year, during which time her teams won 31 games, lost four,

and forfeited one game. On March 24, 1975, the Moundsville City Council passed a unanimous resolution congratulating her for coaching the team to the 1975 county championship. During her employment in the Marshall County School District, Mrs. Burkey has received written letters of recommendation from three principals who have directly supervised her work. These letters, from defendant Robert Eaton (letter of January 3, 1973), David Gill (letter of May 27, 1977), and James Loew (letter of December 22, 1978), were uniformly favorable and described Mrs. Burkey as an "excellent teacher."

Defendant Marshall County Board of Education is ultimately responsible for the supervision and control of the Marshall County School District and the employment of its personnel. Defendant Donald A. Haskins is and has been superintendent of the Marshall County Board of Education since July 1, 1972.

Defendant Robert R. Eaton is and has been assistant superintendent of the Marshall County Board of Education since July 1, 1972. In those capacities, Haskins and Eaton were responsible for recommending and approving the transfer of Burkey as a teacher from Moundsville Junior High School to Washington Lands Elementary School and the termination of Burkey from her coaching position at Moundsville Junior High School at the conclusion of the 1975-76 school year. The defendant James P. Lydon is and has been principal of Moundsville Junior High School since July 1, 1972. In that capacity he was responsible for initiating the recommendation for transfer of Burkey as a teacher from Moundsville Junior High School and her removal or termination from her coaching position. All defendants were sued in their official capacities and as individuals.

Prior to the 1973-74 school year women were not paid for coaching girls' junior high school athletics, although males were paid $380 for coaching boys' junior high school athletics. In the 1973-74 through 1975-76 school year all women coaches of girls' junior high school sports, save one, were uniformly paid one-half (1/2) of the salary that male coaches of comparable or identical boys' junior high school sports were paid. Two men who coached girls' junior high school sports were paid at the same salary level as women coaches of girls' sports were paid. Prior to October 1973, no official policies existed for the administration of girls' interscholastic athletic programs in the Marshall County Schools. The "Policies Governing Marshall County Junior High School Athletic Programs," . . . , were approved by the Board in June 1969, but were explicitly limited to boys' interscholastic athletics.

In October 1973, the defendant Board adopted a statement of "Policies of Marshall County Girls Athletic Program." These policies governed only girls' athletics at junior and senior high schools within the Marshall County School District during the 1973-74 school year, while boys' athletics at junior high schools within the District were governed during that school year by the "Governing Policies of Marshall County Junior High Athletic Programs," as revised July 11, 1973.

In the 1975-76 school year defendants abolished the separate policy statements for girls' and boys' sports and consolidated the school district's athletic policies into a document titled "Policies Marshall County Athletic Program." Despite this consolidation of policy statement, female coaches of junior high school athletics, including Linda Burkey, were still uniformly paid one-half (1/2) of the salary that male coaches were paid to coach identical or comparable sports during the 1975-76 school year.

On September 11, 1973, after discussing their concerns with Carl F. Norman, their principal, Linda Burkey, Linda Campbell, and Victoria Lavenski, the women physical education teachers at Moundsville Junior High School, wrote a letter to defendant Haskins concerning the payment of women coaches of girls' athletics at Moundsville Junior High School. Defendant Haskins ignored the requested action and made no response to the letter. On April 1, 1974, Mrs. Burkey and Mrs. Campbell filed a grievance with the defendant Board challenging the discrimination against women coaches and girl athletes in the athletic policies and practices of the Marshall County School District.

Pursuant to the contract between the defendant Board and the Marshall County Education Association, the grievance of Mrs. Burkey and Mrs. Campbell was processed. This process involved and included meetings between Mrs. Burkey and Mrs. Campbell and Carl F. Norman, their principal, Paul C. Crago, general supervisor of the Marshall County School District, and defendant Haskins. The grievance was ultimately denied by a unanimous decision of the defendant Board on June 28, 1974.

On September 19, 1975, Linda Burkey filed a charge with the West Virginia Human Rights Commission that alleged that defendants were, and had been, unlawfully discriminating against her on the basis of sex in regard to her coaching duties. This charge was cross-filed with the Equal Employment Opportunity Commission (EEOC), which assumed jurisdiction of the charge on November 24, 1975 (EEOC charge Number 034-60412-7).

On March 17, 1976, Mrs. Burkey filed an additional complaint with the West Virginia Human Rights Commission protesting these retaliatory practices. On May 23, 1976, Mrs. Burkey filed a second charge with the EEOC, alleging that defendants had retaliated against her for the filing of her initial EEOC charge by transferring her from her teaching position and removing her from her coaching position at Moundsville Junior High School. In the fall of 1976 the EEOC consolidated Mrs. Burkey's May 23, 1976, charge of sex discrimination and retaliation with her September 19, 1975, charge of sex discrimination. On November 8, 1976, the EEOC acted on this consolidated charge and found reasonable cause to believe the defendants had retaliated against Linda Burkey for the filing of her September 19, 1975, charge of sex discrimination. On November 15, 1977, the EEOC issued a determination on reconsideration as to consolidated charge 034-61644-1, finding reasonable cause that defendants had discriminated against Linda Burkey on the basis of her sex in the payment of compensation for her coaching duties and that defendants had retaliated against her for the filing of her September 19, 1975, charge. Defendants nevertheless refused to rectify the instances of illegal conduct found to exist by the EEOC, and on January 16, 1978, the Department of Justice issued to Linda Burkey a right to sue letter on this consolidated charge.

On August 12, 1977, Mrs. Burkey filed a third charge with the EEOC, alleging that defendants had retaliated against her for the filing of her two earlier charges by denying her positions as a coach and teacher at John Marshall High School for the 1977-78 school year. On September 12, 1976, Linda Burkey filed a complaint with the Department of Health, Education, and Welfare, alleging that defendants were illegally discriminating against women coaches and girl students on the basis of their sex in the operation of the athletic programs of the Marshall County School District. After a four-day investigation of the Marshall County School District, the Department of Health, Education, and Welfare on August 19, 1977, issued a finding that the district's operation of its girls' athletic program violated the rights of both female coaches, including Linda Burkey, and girl students under Title IX of the Education Amendments Act of 1972, 20 U.S.C. §§ 1681-86. Defendants have not changed to date policies found to be violative of the law in respect to male and female coaching positions and boys and girls athletic programs.

Only after five years of attempts to obtain a resolution of her sex discrimination complaints from within the Marshall County School District and from state and federal administrative agencies had proved unsuccessful did Linda Burkey, on April 6, 1978, file her complaint in this action. Plaintiff has exhausted available administrative remedies.

Defendants Haskins, Eaton, and Lydon have never recommended, and the defendant Board has never hired, transferred, or otherwise assigned, a female teacher to coach boys' sports in the Marshall County School District. During the time since Linda Burkey has been in the employ of the Marshall County Board of Education defendants have maintained, and continue to maintain, an unwritten policy that female teachers cannot coach boys' sports. Linda Burkey is qualified to coach boys' basketball and track and possesses

qualifications equal, or superior, to most of the males who coach and have coached these sports in the Marshall County School District while she has taught there. Linda Burkey has also worked with, and taught, boys, as well as girls, the fundamentals of basketball and track and field in her physical education classes. There was no evidence adduced or assertion made by defendants that there was any bonafide occupational qualification or other reason that would prevent qualified women from coaching male teams in the school district.

In 1973-74, Burkey was paid two hundred dollars ($200) annually to coach girls' basketball while all male coaches coaching boys' junior high basketball were paid four hundred dollars ($400) annually. In 1974-75, she was paid two hundred twenty dollars ($220) annually, while male coaches received four hundred forty dollars ($440). In 1975-76, she received two hundred thirty dollars ($230) annually while male coaches received four hundred sixty dollars ($460). Prior to the 1976-77 school year defendants maintained the policy, as expressed in the Board's salary indexes, . . . , of paying the female coaches of girls' junior high school sports one-half of the salary paid to male coaches for coaching the same junior high school sports. This policy was uniformly applied to all female junior high school coaches, regardless of the sport coached.

Linda Burkey's position as coach of the girls' basketball team at Moundsville Junior High School during the 1973-74 through 1975-76 school years required work, skill, effort, and responsibility equal to that required of the male coaches of boys' basketball at Moundsville Junior High School during those years. As were the male coaches of boys' basketball, Mrs. Burkey was responsible for selecting, training, and coaching in interscholastic competition a junior high school basketball team. Such responsibilities necessitated a knowledge of the rules of girls' junior high school basketball, which were and are identical with the rules of boys' junior high school basketball, as well as a knowledge of the proper techniques of coaching and teaching student athletes. As did the male coaches of the boys' junior high school basketball teams, Mrs. Burkey held daily practice sessions with her team over a basketball season of substantially the same length of time as the boys' season, traveled with her teams to away games, and was responsible for scheduling games for her teams.

The only areas of difference between Linda Burkey's coaching responsibilities and those of the male coaches of boys' basketball were insubstantial. To the extent that any such differences may have existed, they were based solely on defendants' policy of discriminating against women coaches on the basis of their sex in the opportunities provided to them to coach and to have their teams participate in an identical number of interscholastic games over the same season as did the teams coached by male teachers. The difference in salary between what Linda Burkey was paid to coach girls' sports and what men were paid to coach boys' sports during the same years was based solely on her sex and was not based on any factor other than sex.

After a four-day investigation of the Marshall County School District, the Department of Health, Education, and Welfare, on August 19, 1977, issued a finding that the district's operation of its girls' athletic program violated the rights of women coaches and female students under Title IX of the Education Amendments Act of 1972, 20 U.S.C. §§ 1681-86. In its November 15, 1977, determination on reconsideration, the EEOC found reasonable cause to believe that defendants' coaching salary practices and policies constituted unlawful discrimination against Linda Burkey because of her sex.

In March of 1976, defendants Haskins, Eaton, and Lydon recommended and approved Linda Burkey's transfer from Moundsville Junior High School and removal from her coaching position at that school. At the Board's March 23, 1976, meeting Linda Burkey was also removed from the position of coaching the girls' basketball team at Moundsville Junior High School, which she had held for five years. Mrs. Burkey is the only coach of girls' sports ever to have been removed from such a coaching position. She was removed from her position simultaneously with defendants' creation of a second coaching position for girls' basketball at Moundsville Junior High School.

Although defendant Eaton initially cited "economy measures" as a reason for Linda Burkey's transfer from Moundsville Junior High School to the Consolidated Washington Lands Elementary School, this alleged reason

was merely pretextual. Linda Burkey's transfer could have resulted in no monetary savings to the school district since at the time the Board transferred her it intended to refill her teaching position at the junior high school. Defendants originally announced that they intended to fill Mrs. Burkey's teaching position at Moundsville Junior High School by transferring Joanne Kutrovac, a special education teacher with no previous coaching experience, from another school to fill that position. Instead, both Linda Burkey's teaching and coaching positions were filled by the hiring of a new teacher, Josette Wilson, who was less qualified by education and experience than plaintiff Burkey.

Defendant Eaton also assigned a "personality conflict" between plaintiff and defendant Lydon as a basis for Burkey's transfer and removal from coaching. . . . The assertion of "personality conflict" as a reason for transfer is pretextual. Subsequent to plaintiff Burkey's transfer and removal from the coaching position, defendants contended that these personnel actions were taken for yet another reason. They asserted she was transferred for insubordination to Lydon in regard to the scheduling of a game with a non-school "club" girls' team from Shadyside, Ohio. Although this incident may have provided a reasonable basis for some form of discipline, when viewed with totality of evidence this assigned basis for transfer is also pretextual. The court finds that plaintiff Burkey would not have been transferred and removed from the coaching position but for her assertion of charges against the defendants and her continued requests and demand for sex equality regarding compensation, terms, and conditions of employment and working conditions.

During the time in which Linda Burkey has been employed by the defendant Board, several other teachers in the Marshall County School District have coached athletic teams at schools other than the school at which they taught. Linda Burkey was one of only two teachers to be removed from all of his or her coaching assignments by the Board at its March 23, 1976, meeting. Defendants retaliated against Linda Burkey for her filing of a charge with the EEOC by transferring her from the teaching position that she had held for six years at Moundsville Junior High

School and removing her from the coaching position that she had held at that school for five years. After being advised of their obligations as employers under Title VII and the Equal Pay Act and being made subject of complaints and charges under those laws and others, defendants persisted in willful disregard of plaintiff's rights. Defendants acted or refused to act in regard to plaintiff's rights willfully and in bad faith.

Coaching contracts awarded by boards of education in West Virginia are, by law and practice, one-year contracts and nontenured. A board of education has extensive discretion under statute in West Virginia to transfer teachers and employees, W.Va. Code, 1931, § 18A-2-7, as amended. A teacher has no personal right or property right under the United States Constitution to a limited, nontenured coaching contract, where state law provides none, and no cause of action may be implied by the court where Congress has been given the power to enforce constitutional provisions by appropriate legislation.

Defendants Cassis, Dobbs, Logston, Wilson, Barger, Anderson, Gould, Haskins, Eaton, and Lydon are all "persons" within the meaning of 42 U.S.C. § 1983. In West Virginia, a county board of education is not a local unit of government. A county board of education in West Virginia is a state agency and as such is entitled to sovereign immunity under West Virginia Constitution, Article VI, § 35. A state and its agencies are absolutely immune from 42 U.S.C. § 1983 under the Eleventh Amendment because a state is not a person within the meaning of 42 U.S.C. § 1983. Because a state is immune under the Eleventh Amendment, a county board of education in West Virginia is not subject to a teacher's claim for back pay or an award of damages over it in a § 1983 action. The defendant Marshall County Board of Education is not a person within the meaning of 42 U.S.C. § 1983.

Actions seeking remedies of prospective relief against state officials and county officials for violations of the Fourteenth Amendment or statutes in aid thereof are not prevented by the Eleventh Amendment. The Eleventh Amendment provides no shield for a state official or county board member who is confronted by a claim that he has deprived another of a federal right under color of state law. The county board

member or school official is, in that case, stripped of his official or representative character and is subjected in his person to the consequences of his individual conduct. County board members and school officials may be subject to a § 1983 action, although the board is not, because the officials' actions were taken under color of state law. Members and former members of a board of education in West Virginia and supervising officials employed by the board are entitled to raise the defense of qualified good faith immunity against a § 1983 action for discretionary acts performed in the course of their official conduct. Members and former members of the Marshall County Board of Education and supervising officials employed by the Board are entitled to raise the defense of qualified immunity from personal monetary liability as individuals. If the defendant Board members and school officials are found to be liable in their individual capacities, the measure of damages would not be the equitable one of back pay but instead the value of the contract defendants wrongfully broke. Where monetary damages are sought, the general doctrine of *respondeat superior* does operate to affix responsibility; the plaintiff must prove personal involvement of a defendant to recover from him.

Defendant Marshall County Board of Education is an employer within the meaning of Title VII and the Equal Pay Act. A state instrumentality does not have an Eleventh Amendment defense to either Title VII or the Equal Pay Act. Defendants Cassis, Dobbs, Logston, Wilson, Barger, Gould, Anderson, as board members and/or former board members, and Haskins, as the Superintendent of the Board, are employers within the meaning of Title VII and the Equal Pay Act, since they "control" Linda Burkey's employment. Defendants' policy of restricting coaching positions for boys' sports to male teachers constitutes, and has constituted, illegal discrimination against Linda Burkey on the basis of her sex, and operates, and has operated, to deny her the rights accorded her by Title VII and 42 U.S.C. § 1983.

Linda Burkey was and is as qualified to coach boys' athletics as most of the males who have and are coaching boys' athletics within the Marshall County School District. Defendants' refusal to permit Linda V. Burkey to coach boys' sports solely because of her sex constitutes an unlawful employment practice under Title VII and 42 U.S.C. § 1983. Defendants paid Linda V. Burkey less than male coaches were paid for the same or comparable work solely because of her sex. Defendants' policy of not compensating Linda V. Burkey for coaching girls' basketball (prior to 1973-74) or for compensating her at only one-half (1/2) of the salary paid to the male coaches of basketball constituted illegal discrimination against Linda V. Burkey on the basis of her sex and has operated to deny her the rights accorded her by Title VII, 42 U.S.C. § 1983 and the Equal Pay Act, 29 U.S.C. § 206(d) (1). Defendants' refusal to pay Linda V. Burkey a salary for coaching basketball, equal to the salary paid male coaches for coaching

basketball constitutes an unlawful employment practice under Title VII and 42 U.S.C. § 1983. Defendants transferred Linda V. Burkey from her teaching position at Moundsville Junior High School and removed her from her coaching position at that school in retaliation for her filing of a sex discrimination charge with the EEOC. Defendants' retaliation against Linda V. Burkey for filing a charge of sex discrimination with the EEOC violated rights accorded her by Title VII and 42 U.S.C. § 1983.

 For an extended version of the case and review questions to test your understanding of the material, please go to www.HumanKinetics.com/CaseStudiesInSportLaw.

Hegener v. Board of Education of City of Chicago

567 N.E.2d 566 (Ill. App. 1 Dist. 1991)

Plaintiff, Rosemary Hegener, a tenured high school teacher, appeals from the trial court's order, on administrative review, affirming the decision of the Illinois State Board of Education (hereafter State Board) to dismiss her as a teacher for the Chicago Board of Education (hereafter Chicago Board) because of "conduct unbecoming a teacher." She contends that the conduct in question did not constitute sufficient "cause" for dismissal. She also contends that even if the conduct would have been sufficient cause, it was remediable and, because she was not given the proper written warning, her dismissal was improper.

On July 18, 1984, the Chicago Board initiated proceedings to dismiss plaintiff as a teacher in the Chicago Public School system, charging her with "conduct unbecoming a teacher," including having improper sexual contacts with one former and one current student. . . . Charging that this conduct was "irremediable," the Chicago Board served notice on plaintiff, without first providing the written warning that would have been required had the conduct been deemed remediable, and suspended her from teaching until a hearing could be held by the State Board on her dismissal.

Commencing October 3, 1984, a hearing was conducted by a hearing officer appointed by the State Board. The evidence at the hearing disclosed that plaintiff, a married woman with two sons, was a tenured physical education teacher who first began working for the Chicago Board in 1962. . . . While at Lucy Flower High School, she received an "excellent" teaching rating for each of her first four years and a "superior" rating, the highest possible rating in the Chicago Public School system, for each of the remaining years up until the date of her suspension. The conduct that formed the bases of the charge against plaintiff allegedly occurred from 1982 to 1984.

Prior to receiving notice of the charge involved in this case, plaintiff was never advised that any of these relationships were inappropriate or unprofessional. As indicated, the relationships that were the bases for the charge for which plaintiff was dismissed developed while she was a teacher at Lucy Flower High School.

Plaintiff's relationship with L.R., though later in time than her relationship with A.P., triggered the investigation that led to the charge of "conduct unbecoming a teacher" and therefore will be described first. The formal investigation concerning plaintiff's relationship with L.R. was precipitated by a November 29, 1983 letter, prepared by Phyllis Banks, a physical education teacher at Lucy Flower, accusing plaintiff of engaging in lesbian conduct with L.R.

Plaintiff testified that she continued to press Hortense Bright, the principal, to stop the rumors being spread by Banks and S.W., which were ruining her reputation, ... After receipt of the November 29, 1983 letter, Bright contacted the District Superintendent regarding the charge and formal proceedings commenced.

Thus the hearing officer rejected the improper sexual contact charges as unproven and unbelievable.

The hearing officer explicitly stated in his findings that the charges regarding the alleged November 29, 1982 incident, like the charges regarding the alleged June 15, 1983 incident with L.R., were not sufficiently supported by the evidence. Thus, here as with respect to L.R., the hearing officer found insufficient evidence to support any improper sexual contact. The hearing officer found this conduct to be inappropriate and unprofessional because plaintiff had used her professional position to develop an intense and intimate relationship with a student.

After reviewing the evidence presented, the hearing officer concluded that there was sufficient impropriety in plaintiff's conduct to constitute cause even though the charges of sexual improprieties were not proven. The hearing officer further concluded that plaintiff's conduct was irremediable because it: (1) covered a long period of time, (2) was deliberate and calculated, and (3) caused severe damage to A.P., L.R., and the school generally.

It should be noted that for purposes of this appeal, the defendants have totally abandoned any charges of sexually improper contact that were rejected by the hearing officer and stand only on the lesser charges left standing by the hearing officer. Plaintiff initially contends that the hearing officer's conclusion that her relationships with A.P. and L.R. constituted cause for her dismissal was against the manifest weight of the evidence and should have been reversed by the trial court. Specifically, she argues that her relationship with A.P. before her high school graduation was entirely proper and further that her conduct with

A.P. after graduation when A.P. ceased being a student, while in point of fact remaining proper, became irrelevant. She also contends that her conduct and interaction with L.R., while entirely proper, occurred essentially outside of school grounds, and further that she should not be penalized for false rumors regarding that relationship that spread as a result of totally fabricated accusations concerning the alleged June 15, 1983 incident. She further contends that even if cause were present, it was remediable and first required a written warning.

In order to encourage experienced and able teachers to remain within the educational system and to ensure that rehiring decisions will be based on merit and not on political, partisan, or capricious reasons, the School Code provides for the removal of tenured teachers only for cause. Though the School Code does not define cause, §§ 10-22.4 of the Code do provide some guidance by providing for dismissals of teachers for "incompetency, cruelty, negligence, immorality, or other sufficient cause." Additional guidance may be found in case law that has defined cause as "some substantial shortcoming which render[s] continuance in office or employment in some way detrimental to the discipline and efficiency of the service and something which the law and a sound public opinion recognize as good cause for not longer occupying the place." Case law further requires that the conduct that forms the basis for claiming cause must bear some relationship to a teacher's ability to perform her job. The school board has the right, in the first instance, to determine what constitutes cause, using the best interest of the school as a "guiding star."

Our duty on review is to examine the entire record to determine whether the school board's findings and conclusions are against the manifest weight of the evidence. If they are not against the manifest weight of the evidence, we must affirm. However, when conduct that forms the basis for the dismissal of a tenured teacher is remediable, the School Code requires that a school board first give the teacher "reasonable warning in writing, stating specifically the causes which, if not removed, may result in charges.". . . A failure to provide such a written warning warrants a reversal. Accordingly, we must first consider the administrative finding below with respect to the existence of cause. If we conclude, as we do, that the administrative finding with respect to cause was not contrary to the manifest weight of the evidence, we must and shall then consider whether such cause was remediable.

Even though the hearing officer disbelieved the evidence to support the more serious charges against plaintiff, namely, the charges involving sexual contact and interaction between the plaintiff and A.P., we cannot say that his conclusion that the remaining lesser charges pertaining to plaintiff's relationship with A.P. constituted cause was against the manifest weight of the evidence. We find sufficient evidence in the record to support the hearing officer's conclusion that plaintiff had used her professional position to develop a personal relationship with A.P. This evidence, cumulatively, if not individually, would suffice to support the hearing officer's findings of cause with respect to plaintiff's relationship with A.P.

Plaintiff argues that she should not be held to account for her conduct with A.P. after A.P. graduated even if that conduct were improper, which she denies. There is considerable merit to this argument since after graduation there was no longer a teacher-student relationship to be maintained with the commensurate duties and responsibilities that a school and faculty share towards matriculating students. Moreover, none of the aspects of plaintiff's conduct toward A.P. after graduation occurred on school premises but was totally private. Nor was any evidence introduced to bring into focus whether any of this postgraduation conduct would render her unfit to teach ongoing students. But, on balance, we hesitate to hold the hearing officer's conclusion to consider this postgraduation conduct in his assessment of cause to be against the manifest weight of the evidence, since this conduct followed closely the relationship that started while A.P. was still plaintiff's student at Lucy Flower, albeit late in the final semester of her senior year. As with A.P., even though the hearing officer disbelieved the evidence to support the most damaging charges against plaintiff, involving the accusations of sexual contact or interaction between plaintiff and L.R., we find sufficient evidence in the record to support the hearing officer's conclusion that plaintiff had sought out, encouraged, and participated in an inappropriate personal relationship with L.R. on school grounds. Granted the relationship with L.R. differed from the one with A.P. in that L.R. was never plaintiff's student and the relationship itself had been expressly endorsed by L.R.'s parent. However, it too, as in A.P.'s case, was a relationship that can be held to have developed as a result of plaintiff's misdirected use of her professional position as a member of the school faculty to develop a personal relationship with a student at that school even though L.R. was not plaintiff's personal student. Plaintiff argues that her activities with L.R. occurred outside of school for the most part and are therefore protected private conduct. The record, however, belies that argument. Much of the conduct with L.R. occurred on school grounds or close enough to school grounds as to become known to members of the school community.

Plaintiff also argues that her conduct with L.R. on school premises should not constitute cause for dismissal because (1) there were no written rules against it, (2) other teachers at Lucy Flower did many of the same things she did without any disciplinary action resulting therefrom, and (3) she was being unfairly penalized for false rumors regarding her relationship with L.R. Though the fact that there were no written rules against engaging in personal friendships with current students is a mitigating factor . . . , it does not completely condone plaintiff's conduct. As an experienced teacher, plaintiff should have been able to recognize the professional standards that must guide a teacher's conduct without requiring written rules.

Nonetheless, a teacher must be able to draw the line between conduct that is necessary for the proper performance of her educative function and that which is or which degenerates into one that is primarily for her own emotional gratification. In the present case, there is sufficient evidence to support the finding that this line was clearly traversed.

Plaintiff next contends that even if her personal relationships with A.P. and L.R. constituted cause, it was remediable cause and the State Board had no jurisdiction to dismiss her because she had not been given the statutorily required written warning to allow her an opportunity to correct her conduct. She argues that she was entitled to a written warning because there was no showing that her conduct caused damage to either A.P. or L.R., the faculty, or the school and, even if it did cause some damage, it was clearly correctable. We agree.

As previously noted, when conduct that forms the basis for the dismissal of a tenured teacher is remediable, the School Code requires that a school board give the teacher written warning of the causes. Conduct is deemed remediable if (1) the conduct has not damaged the students, faculty, or school; or (2) the conduct could have been corrected had the teacher received the written warning. The degree of required damage is damage that is so severe as to justify dismissal absent service of a warning notice. Conduct that is initially remediable can become irremediable if continued over a long period of time. Where conduct is remediable and the board has not given the required statutory warning to a teacher, a dismissal of that teacher is properly reversed because the board lacked jurisdiction to take such action. A reviewing court, however, will not overturn a school board's determination of irremediability unless "the Board has acted in an arbitrary or capricious manner or the reasons formulated for the dismissal were against the manifest weight of the evidence." We find that the hearing officer's determination of irremediability was against the manifest weight of the evidence because there was an insufficient showing that any of plaintiff's proven conduct significantly damaged either A.P. or L.R., the faculty, or the school.

The defendant, Chicago Board, argues that damage was established by A.P.'s testimony on how she felt about her relationship with plaintiff, the testimony of A.P.'s parents regarding her condition after the alleged but unproven November 29, 1982 incident, the testimony of L.R. about how she felt concerning the rumors, the testimony of Dr. Moore, and testimony from various witnesses regarding the rumors that spread throughout Lucy Flower after the alleged but unproven June 15, 1983 incident. This evidence failed for various reasons to prove that plaintiff's conduct caused any of the claimed damage. There also is no evidence of damage to L.R. resulting from her relationship with plaintiff. She did not testify that she

was damaged and no other witness testified that she, in fact, was damaged. Moreover, L.R.'s testimony regarding how she reacted to the rumors at school, including her need to ultimately transfer to another high school, fails to show any damage attributable to any wrongful conduct of the plaintiff. Absent any testimony that she was adversely affected by that relationship, it cannot be said that plaintiff's conduct caused her harm.

The defendant, Chicago Board, however, maintains that plaintiff's continued relationship with L.R. exacerbated the existent, albeit false, rumors concerning her. No explicit evidence of any such exacerbation was introduced. Moreover, if one is to speculate on the question of exacerbation, we must equally speculate that if plaintiff had ceased any relationship with L.R. in the face of the rumors, her cessation would have been viewed as an admission that she had engaged in an improper relationship and thus lent added credibility to the charges.

Aside from the dearth of evidence to establish any exacerbation of already existent rumors regarding the unproven June 15 incident, the pivotal question is whether plaintiff's conduct with L.R. not only contributed to the rumors, but also, the extent to which such exacerbation would have damaged the school. It is not enough to show that some damage occurred. The damage must be significant before the conduct causing the damage can be declared irremediable. We find no basis in the record for reaching such a conclusion. There is no evidence in this case that plaintiff's proven conduct caused significant damage to the school. . . . Though we are mindful of the deference to be given to an administrative body on findings, . . . , we cannot say that the hearing officer's finding of damage is supported by the manifest weight of the evidence. Aside from Dr. Moore's opinions, which could not show actual adverse effect on A.P. or L.R. and which are premised on hypotheticals containing serious, unsubstantiated accusations, there was no other evidence of significant damage that can fairly be attributable to plaintiff's conduct.

The defendant, Chicago Board, argues a variation of the principle that once remediable conduct may become irremediable if continued over a long period of time by stating that this conduct was irremediable because plaintiff admitted it was no different than other relationships she had with numerous other students over the years. In considering this argument, we must point out that the mere continuation of conduct for a period of years does not make once remediable conduct irremediable. Under the facts of the present case, there are two problems with defendant's argument. First, plaintiff was not charged with unprofessional or inappropriate conduct involving any other students. The charges that were brought dealt solely with A.P. and L.R. If defendant is now arguing that plaintiff also should be charged with engaging in unprofessional and inappropriate conduct with other students, then the charges as stated would be insufficient because they do not fairly apprise her of the claimed deficiencies so that she can refute them.

Second, even if plaintiff had been advised that these other relationships with other students were part of her claimed deficiency, cases that deal with the principle of once remediable conduct becoming irremediable conduct require some continuing warning that the conduct in question was inappropriate. We also find the conduct remediable because defendants have failed to meet their burden of showing that even if there was damage, plaintiff's conduct was not correctable. Defendants have failed to demonstrate that plaintiff could not stop engaging in personal relationships with students even if given the proper written warning. They argue that the fact that she has for many years engaged in these personal relationships with students suggests that a warning would be futile. The statute requiring such a warning (Ill.Rev.Stat.1987, ch. 122, par. 34-85) makes no exception for instances where the school board deems such warning "futile." However, even if futility would obviate the need to warn, there is no basis to assume that a written warning would have no impact. It is precisely because such conduct was longstanding and widely

practiced at the school by other teachers as well that the conclusion of futility is unwarranted. Never until plaintiff's confrontation with Banks was any attempt made at the school to check such conduct. Surely it is by no means plausible that under these circumstances a written warning from the school board would be unheeded.

Defendant, Chicago Board, also argues that the fact that plaintiff did not change her relationship with L.R. after her September 1983 meeting with Hortense Bright indicates that a warning would be futile. We note that Bright merely addressed the charges arising out of the alleged June 15, 1983 and November 29, 1982 incidents at that meeting, without even going into the details regarding the latter incident. Since the hearing officer found insufficient evidence of these charges, plaintiff cannot be charged with continuing that which the evidence did not support as ever having occurred. A warning would appear to be particularly appropriate in this case where the Board is apparently taking a new position on relatively widespread conduct of which it previously had tacitly approved or to which it had apparently turned a blind eye.

As previously indicated, the State Board was justified in finding that plaintiff's personal relationships with L.R. and A.P. constituted cause. Nonetheless, since there was insufficient proof of any significant damage resulting from her conduct and, moreover, that any was correctable, plaintiff, as a tenured teacher, was entitled to the statutory written warning to correct, if she could, her remediable conduct. Having not received such a warning, she could not be dismissed. For the foregoing reasons, we reverse the order of the Circuit Court of Cook County.

 For an extended version of the case and review questions to test your understanding of the material, please go to www.HumanKinetics.com/CaseStudiesInSportLaw.

Moore v. University of Notre Dame

22 F.Supp. 2d 896 (N.D. Ind. 1998)

This cause is before this court on plaintiff's Motion for Award of Reinstatement/Front Pay and plaintiff's Bill of Costs. Plaintiff, Joseph R. Moore (Moore), filed a claim in this court against The University of Notre Dame (Notre Dame) alleging age discrimination, retaliation, and defamation. Only the age discrimination claim survived summary judgment. The case went to trial in Lafayette on July 9, 1998. On July 15, 1998, the jury found that Notre Dame had violated the Age Discrimination in Employment Act (ADEA) and awarded Moore back pay in the amount of $42,935.28. Additionally, because the jury determined that Notre Dame's violation of ADEA was willful, plaintiff also was awarded liquidated damages in the additional amount of $42,935.28. Judgment must and now does enter in favor of the plaintiff, Joseph E. Moore, and against the defendant, Notre Dame, in the amount of $85,870.56. Accordingly, the court now considers Moore's posttrial motions.

The remedial scheme for a discriminatory discharge is designed to make a plaintiff who has been the victim of discrimination whole through the use of equitable remedies. When confronted with a violation of the ADEA, a district court is authorized to afford relief by means of reinstatement, backpay, injunctive relief, declaratory judgment, and attorney's fees. Additionally, in the case of a willful violation of the Act, the ADEA authorizes an award of liquidated damages equal to the backpay award. Moore now asks the court to reinstate him in his former coaching position, or to award five year's front pay in lieu of reinstatement. Notre Dame contends that Moore has received all relief to which he was entitled and therefore asks this court to deny Moore's Motion for Reinstatement/Front Pay.

Although reinstatement is the preferred remedy in a discrimination case, it is not always appropriate. The factors that should be considered when determining its propriety include hostility in the past employment relationship and the absence of an available position for the plaintiff. Additionally, under ADEA, when a

period for reinstatement is relatively short, such that plaintiff is close to retirement, the strong preference in favor of reinstatement is neutralized by the increased certainty of potential loss of pay permitting consideration of a front pay award.

The decision to reinstate a discriminatorily terminated employee is consigned to the sound discretion of the district court, which should not grant reinstatement "where the result would be undue friction and controversy." Evidence that hostility developed between the employer and employee during litigation may also be considered, but is not dispositive. In the present case, Moore's reinstatement would cause significant friction as well as disruption of the current football program. Moore and Davie, his direct supervisor, are no longer on speaking terms. During trial, sufficient evidence was presented to infer that Moore and Davie would be unable to engage in a workable relationship. Reinstatement in this instance is impracticable. Moreover, even if hostility and undue friction were not a problem, reinstatement is not appropriate in this case.

The Seventh Circuit has also held that reinstatement can reasonably be denied when "someone else currently occupies the employee's former position." Other circuits hold similarly. The law is clear. Even if this court determined that reinstatement is warranted, it is not an appropriate remedy in this case as there is no available position to which Moore could return. Therefore, the court turns to the more difficult issue of whether front pay is warranted.

Plaintiff is incorrect in stating that "if the Court rejects Moore's request for reinstatement, it must award him front pay." Front pay is an available remedy under ADEA, however, such an award remains discretionary with court. The Seventh Circuit has defined front pay as "a lump sum . . . representing the discounted present value of the difference between the earnings (an employee) would have received in his old employment and the earnings he can be expected to receive in his present and future, and by hypothesis, inferior, employment." *McKnight v. General Motors Corp.*, 908 F.2d 104, 116. Such a remedy may especially be indicated when the plaintiff has no reasonable prospect of obtaining comparable employment or when the time period for which front pay is to be awarded is relatively short. The court determines the amount of front pay to award depending on whether (1) the plaintiff has a reasonable prospect of obtaining comparable employment, (2) the time period for the award is relatively short, (3) the plaintiff intends to work or is physically capable of working, and (4) liquidated damages have been awarded. Front pay is awarded for a reasonable period of time, until a date by which the plaintiff, using reasonable diligence, should have found comparable employment. Moreover, an award must be grounded in available facts, acceptable to a reasonable person and not highly speculative. It cannot be based simply on a plaintiff's own stated intentions with regard to how long he or she would have worked.

Notre Dame contends that Moore is not entitled to front pay because (1) evidence acquired by Notre Dame after Moore's discharge would have led to his discharge based on legitimate, nondiscriminatory reasons, (2) Moore's award of liquidated damages has already made him whole, and (3) Moore has failed to make reasonable efforts to mitigate his damages.

The fact that Moore is entitled to damages based on the jury's finding of a willful violation does not conclusively preclude front pay. Front pay may be less appropriate when liquidated damages are awarded. Authority clearly states that liquidated damages is one factor to be considered in awarding front pay and does not stand for the proposition that front pay and liquidated damages may never be awarded to the same plaintiff. Furthermore, an award of front pay, constituting an estimate of what the employee might have earned had he been reinstated at the conclusion of trial, is necessarily speculative; this speculative aspect should not deter courts from fashioning awards that accomplish ADEA's goal of making a wronged employee whole.

In the present case, Notre Dame argues that Moore's jury award of $42,935.28 and liquidated damages award of $42,935.28 make him whole and that further compensation would "be a total award greater than the statute contemplates." The court disagrees. Moore's 1996-97 annual salary was $79,552.08. Assuming an annual increase of 4%, his 1997-98 salary would have been $82,734.16

and his 1998-99 salary $86,043.53. In addition to loss of salary, Moore also lost several benefits. It is unlikely he will be able to duplicate the benefits and prestige the Notre Dame position provided him. Moreover, as Moore is at or near retirement age, it is unlikely he will find comparable employment at the salary level he enjoyed while at Notre Dame. The evidence showed that Moore had coached at Notre Dame for nine years and intended to continue in that position until retirement. Moore has been unable to replace his Notre Dame position with a comparable one. He is currently earning $46,600 and working three jobs. In this court's opinion, the jury award has not "made him whole" and front pay may be appropriate.

Notre Dame also asserts that Moore is not entitled to front pay because Notre Dame administrators made it clear that had they known of Moore's alleged physical and verbal abuse of players, they would have terminated him immediately. Notre Dame argues that evidence of the alleged abuse was "after acquired" and therefore precludes both front pay and reinstatement. What sets an after-acquired evidence case apart from a mixed-motives case . . . , or a pretext case . . . is that the articulated "legitimate" reason for terminating the employee was nonexistent at the time of the adverse decision and could not possibly have motivated the employer to the slightest degree. Where an employer seeks to rely upon after-acquired evidence of wrongdoing, it must first establish that the wrongdoing was of such severity that the employee in fact would have been terminated on those grounds alone if the employer had known of it at the time of discharge. It is this court's opinion that Notre Dames' argument fails on both points.

First, the after-acquired evidence doctrine does not bar front pay to a discharged employee whose alleged wrongdoing was known to the employer at the time of the discharge and was asserted as being a reason for the discharge. It is this court's opinion that defendant's knowledge of Moore's coaching behavior does not fall within the ambit of after-acquired evidence as set forth in McKennon. Moore coached football at Notre Dame for nine years. Davie knew of, and in fact, argued that Moore's behavior was one of the reasons for his termination. The record is replete with such evidence. The jury apparently rejected this argument. Based on its defense at trial, Notre Dame cannot now claim that this "legitimate" reason was nonexistent at the time of the adverse decision and could not possibly have motivated it to the slightest degree.

Notre Dame has also failed to establish that Moore's alleged wrongdoing was of such severity that he in fact would have been terminated on those grounds alone. Football is an aggressive sport. Coaching a winning team requires a degree of "killer instinct." Notre Dame's blanket assertion that if certain administrators had known of Moore's alleged abuse of players, Moore would have been immediately fired is insufficient to prove that such would have actually occurred. This assertion is nothing more than an excuse made after the fact. Additionally, this court will not speculate, like defendant does, as to the reason the jury did not award a large amount of back pay. An award of back pay less than requested does not necessarily mean the jury concluded Moore would have been terminated for nondiscriminatory reasons and it does not therefore preclude front pay. Accordingly, this court finds defendant's after-acquired evidence argument without merit.

Notre Dame finally argues that Moore is not entitled to front pay because he failed to undertake reasonable efforts to mitigate his damages. This court disagrees. Generally, an ADEA plaintiff satisfies the mitigation of damages requirement that he use "reasonable diligence in attempting to secure employment" by demonstrating his commitment to seeking active employment and by remaining ready, willing, and able to work. However, a plaintiff's duty to mitigate his damages is not met by using reasonable diligence to obtain any employment, rather the employment must be comparable employment. The Seventh Circuit has defined "comparable work" as a position that affords "virtually identical promotional opportunities, compensation, job responsibilities, working conditions, and status" as the previous position. The goal of mitigation is to prevent the plaintiff from remaining idle and doing nothing. Furthermore, an employee is not required to go to heroic lengths in attempting to mitigate his damages, but only to take reasonable steps to do so. Furthermore, a claimant has no obligation to accept lesser employment . . . or relocate to a new community.

When evaluating the reasonableness and duration of a job search a court may consider the plaintiff's background and individual characteristics. Moreover, it is the defendant's burden to prove that a plaintiff has failed to discharge his duty. In the present case, Notre Dame has not met this burden. Moore sought and obtained employment shortly after his discharge. He currently works at three different jobs. The fact that he did not accept a position at Cornell does not indicate a failure to mitigate. That position offered a $40,000 salary, significantly less than Moore's former salary, and involved a tenuous situation where the head coach was seeking other employment. Nor does the fact that Moore did not apply for certain positions mentioned by defendant indicate a failure to mitigate. Moore is presently 66-years-old. The options available to him are not as great as those available to someone younger. Moore has demonstrated his willingness to work, but, the chances of finding "comparable work" as defined by the Seventh Circuit, *supra*, are slim. It is this court's opinion that Moore used reasonable diligence in attempting to obtain employment.

The purpose of front pay under the Age Discrimination in Employment Act is to ensure that a person who has been discriminated against on the basis of age is made whole, not to guarantee every claimant who cannot mitigate damages by finding comparable work and annuity to age 70. Furthermore, the risk of noncontinuity of future employment in a "volatile" field must be considered in determining an award of front pay, . . . , and the court has considered this fact. Defendant's argument that front pay is too speculative when the plaintiff's profession has a high turnover rate does not preclude a front pay award. In this case, such an award is not "highly speculative." The court has solid evidence concerning Moore's annual salary and the number of years he hoped to continue his employment. While Moore asserts that five years front pay is warranted, this court disagrees. The evidence presented at trial establishes that Moore expressed a desire to work two more years and then retire. There was no guarantee that Davie would remain at Notre Dame longer than his current contract or that Moore would indefinitely remain in Davie's employ. The evidence also suggests that Moore and Davie had philosophical differences that may have led to a parting of the ways. With all evidence considered, the court finds an award of two years' front pay sufficient. The front pay is calculated as follows: Had Moore remained at Notre Dame his total 1998 salary would have been $84,388.84. Subtracted from this amount is Moore's annual salary from his present employment. Moore testified that he currently earns $1,600 for his services as assistant football coach at Cathedral Preparatory School, $15,000 for his work with the Baltimore Ravens, and $30,000 from his work with Tollgrade Communications. His total current yearly earning amount is therefore $46,600. The difference between Moore's Notre Dame salary and his current salary is $37,788.84 per year. This amount is multiplied by a period of two years and yields a total of $75,577.68. Because the court is not including an additional amount for lost benefits and is not factoring in any increase for the second year, no discounting of the front pay award is warranted. Thus, the total front pay award equals $75,577.68 plus postjudgment interest.

For the preceding reasons it is hereby ordered that plaintiff's Motion for Reinstatement is DENIED. Plaintiff's Motion for Award of Front Pay is GRANTED. Plaintiff is awarded front pay in the amount of $75,577.68 plus postjudgment interest. It is further ordered that plaintiff's Motion for Costs and Fees is GRANTED in part as modified herein. Plaintiff is awarded costs in the total amount of $9,672.45. Plaintiff is also awarded attorney fees and expenses in the total amount of $394,865.74. Finally, pursuant to jury verdict, the plaintiff is awarded $42,935.28 in back pay and an additional $42,935.28 in liquidated damages.

 For an extended version of the case and review questions to test your understanding of the material, please go to www.HumanKinetics.com/CaseStudiesInSportLaw.

Perdue v. City University of New York

13 F.Supp.2d 326 (E.D.N.Y. 1998)

Plaintiff, Molly Perdue (Perdue), the former women's basketball coach and women's sports administrator at Brooklyn College, brought suit against Brooklyn College, the City University of New York (collectively, except as otherwise indicated, referred to as CUNY), and the individually-named defendants, alleging violations of the Equal Pay Act (EPA), 29 U.S.C. § 206(d); Title VII of the Civil Rights Act of 1964 (Title VII), 42 U.S.C. §§ 2000e *et seq.*; the Civil Rights Act of 1871, 42 U.S.C. § 1983; Title IX of the Education Amendments of 1972 (Title IX), 20 U.S.C. §§ 1681 *et seq.*; and the New York Human Rights Law, New York Executive Law §§ 296 *et seq.* Perdue alleged that the defendants discriminated against her on the basis of her gender during her employment. By order of the court (Gershon, J.) dated July 11, 1997, the complaint was dismissed in its entirety as to the individually-named defendants, and Perdue's § 1983 and New York State Human Rights Law claims against CUNY were dismissed.

On August 28, 1997, the jury returned a verdict in favor of Perdue for willful violation of the EPA

for the period from September 1, 1990 through July 9, 1992, and on her intentional discrimination claim. It rejected Perdue's remaining claims. The jury awarded Perdue $85,000 in compensatory damages for CUNY's intentional discrimination. The parties agreed that the court should determine back pay.

There are four postverdict matters now before the court: (1) whether within the purview of preverdict Rule 50(a) and postverdict Rule 50(b) motions, CUNY is entitled to judgment as a matter of law for insufficiency of the evidence regarding the EPA and Title VII intentional discrimination verdicts and/or excessiveness of the compensatory damages award; (2) in the alternative, whether a new trial should be granted pursuant to Rule 59(a), or a remittitur pursuant to Rule 59(e); (3) if the EPA verdict stands, the amount of back pay that the court should award, and other relevant remedial issues; and (4) the amount of attorneys' fees and expenses to be awarded pursuant to 42 U.S.C. §§ 2000e-5(k) and 29 U.S.C. § 216(b).

For the reasons that follow, the court (1) denies CUNY's motions for judgment as a matter of law and for a new trial or remittitur; (2) awards Perdue $134,829 in back wages, $5,262 in unpaid retirement benefits, and $134,829 in liquidated damages, in addition to the $85,000 in compensatory damages, for a total of $359,920, plus rejudgment interest on the back pay and compensatory damages in the sum of $83,264.94 through May 31, 1998, and $43.25 per diem to the date that judgment is entered; and (3) awards Perdue attorneys' fees in the amount of $339,399.60 and expenses in the amount of $16,982.19, to be divided as set forth below between her former counsel, Marcus Montgomery P.C. (MM), and her current counsel, Freeman Forrest & Chenetz LLP (FFC).

Pursuant to 29 U.S.C. § 206(d), the EPA is violated if an employer of a covered employee, such as Perdue, pays wages to that employee: "(1) at a rate less than the rate at which he pays wages to employees of the opposite sex . . . ; (2) for equal work on jobs the performance of which requires equal skill, effort, and responsibility, and (3) which are performed under similar working conditions. . . ." In other words, "[a] violation occurs when an employer pays lower wages to an employee of one gender than to substantially equivalent employees of the opposite gender in similar circumstances." To show a violation of the EPA, a plaintiff need not prove that an intention to discriminate on the basis of gender motivated the pay disparity.

Where there is a willful violation of the EPA, the resulting compensatory award should be doubled as liquidated damages. A violation of the EPA is willful if "the employer either knew or showed reckless disregard for the matter of whether its conduct was prohibited by the statute." It is not necessary for a plaintiff to show that an employer acted with intent to discriminate or in bad faith.

In its jury charge, the court instructed that in order to sustain her burden of proof in this case that she was discriminated against on the basis of sex in her pay, Perdue must prove each of the following by a preponderance of the evidence: (1) that CUNY paid different wages to Perdue's claimed male counterparts; (2) that Perdue and her claimed male counterpart performed equal work on jobs requiring equal skill, effort, and responsibility; and (3) that the jobs were performed under similar working conditions.

In regard to CUNY's contention that the evidence does not establish that Perdue satisfied all three elements of her EPA claim for the time period from September 1, 1990 through July 9, 1992, and that CUNY did not prove its affirmative defense, the court notes, preliminarily, that CUNY's Rule 50(a) trial motion was seemingly restricted to its contention that Perdue did not have comparable work experience to either Reiner or Kestenbaum, in contradistinction to the more pervasive concerns on which an EPA claim must be evaluated. Nonetheless, the court will view CUNY's 50(a) preverdict motion as questioning whether there was sufficient evidence to permit the jury to determine that Perdue's work during that time period was equal in skill, effort, and responsibility to Kestenbaum's and Reiner's, and was performed under similar working conditions for, admittedly, less pay.

Perdue provided extensive testimony regarding her responsibilities and duties as women's basketball coach and women's sports administrator. With regard to her responsibilities as coach, Perdue testified that she and the men's basketball team coach, Kestenbaum, coached "basically" the same season, the same number of games, the same number of players, and the same number of practices. Perdue further testified that she and Kestenbaum were "both responsible [for] organizing and putting a team together that is going to become successful. . . . [R]ecruiting is a big responsibility of both positions." Moreover, they both managed their team's budgets, scholarships, assistant coaches, scouting of opponents, game preparation, and ordering of equipment. Perdue also testified that they both were responsible for the supervision, guidance, and counseling of athletes, and for team conduct. Finally, Perdue and Kestenbaum were accountable to the same person.

Contrary to CUNY's contention, the testimony was also sufficient to permit the jury to determine that Perdue performed the same duties as women's sports administrator as Reiner did as men's sports administrator during this time period. Descriptions of their respective sports administrator jobs, as Perdue pointed out, state that they "were both in charge of organizing, he with the men, the men's programs, me with the women." In fact, according to the job descriptions, Perdue and Reiner had the same 11 duties, and Perdue had the extra duty of "being available for guidance of all female student athletes." Perdue and Reiner were both responsible for the daily operations of sports, game scheduling, organizing team budgets, organizing student orientation, and administering the athletic program. In addition, Perdue and Reiner both reported to the same individual.

Thus, CUNY's 50(a) EPA motion as well as that branch of its 50(b) motion challenging the jury's determination regarding the underlying elements of Perdue's EPA claim are denied.

In any event, the record provides ample evidence to support the jury's determination that CUNY's prohibited conduct was willful. The Presidential Advisory Committee reviewed and approved salaries of athletic personnel. Thus, the jury could have appropriately concluded that CUNY was aware of the salary discrepancies between Perdue and her counterparts. Furthermore, Perdue testified that she complained to her superiors about her working conditions. Perdue also testified that she complained to her superiors about conflicts of practice time between the men's and women's basketball teams, . . . , the fact that she had to clean the gym before the women's basketball team's games, . . . , and the general disparities between the men's and women's basketball teams. In addition, despite the fact that the Office of Civil Rights found that CUNY had committed multiple Title IX violations, there was testimony that CUNY did not implement the modifications promised in its detailed assurances.

Finally, statements by other members of CUNY indicate that not only was CUNY aware of the disparities, but that CUNY was not willing to take steps to make improvements. For example, Perdue testified that when the Title IX subcommittee presented its report on Brooklyn College's women's sports at a meeting of the Presidential Advisory Committee, Len Roitman stated, "Let the women sue." This evidence is clearly sufficient to support the jury's finding that CUNY's violation was willful.

Title VII provides the following: "[i]t shall be an unlawful employment practice for an employer . . . to discharge any individual, or otherwise to discriminate against any individual with respect to his [or her] compensation, terms, conditions, or privileges of employment, because of such individual's . . . sex. . . ." In order to establish a claim of gender-based discrimination under Title VII, Perdue was required to prove "she was treated less favorably than comparable male employees in circumstances from which a gender-based motive could be inferred." A plaintiff need not prove discrimination through direct evidence, rather, "a plaintiff charging discrimination against an employer is usually constrained to rely on the cumulative weight of circumstantial evidence." After a plaintiff has met her burden of proving a *prima facie* case of discrimination, the burden shifts to the defendant to put forth nondiscriminatory reasons that motivated its decisions with respect to the plaintiff. Once the defendant puts forth a nondiscriminatory reason, the plaintiff has the opportunity to "demonstrate that defendant's articulated reason for its decision is in fact a pretext for discrimination," and has the "ultimate burden of persuasion to demonstrate . . . that the challenged employment decision was the result of intentional discrimination."

In addition to the $85,000 compensatory damages award, Perdue seeks back wages in the amount of $140,200, consisting of (1) $22,750 for the period from September 1, 1990 through December 31, 1990; (2) $72,844 for the period from January 1, 1991 through December 31, 1991; and (3) $44,786 for the period from January 1, 1992 through July 9, 1992. Perdue also seeks employer matching retirement benefits, which she does not characterize as "back wages," in the amount of $1,119 for 1990, $3,435 for 1991, and $1,657 for 1992, and summer camp wages for 1991 in the amount of $3,500. Furthermore, Perdue claims that the back wages of $140,200 should be doubled as liquidated damages as a result of the jury's finding of willfulness. Finally, Perdue seeks prejudgment interest.

In opposition to Perdue's application for damages, CUNY argues that the State's Eleventh Amendment immunity bars monetary recovery under the EPA. Alternatively, CUNY contends that (1) Perdue's damages should be calculated with reference to Kestenbaum only, (2) Perdue is not entitled to summer camp wages, (3) Perdue is not entitled to liquidated damages, and (4) Perdue is not entitled to employer matching retirement benefits.

The issue of Eleventh Amendment immunity was initially raised in this litigation *sua sponte* by Judge Gershon on July 9, 1997, when she requested both parties to brief the question of whether the Supreme Court's decision in *Seminole Tribe of Florida v. Florida*, 517 U.S. 44, 116 S.Ct. 1114, 134 L.Ed.2d 252 (1996), bars suit under the EPA against the State. In denying CUNY's pretrial motion to dismiss the EPA claim, she resolved this issue, without comment, against CUNY. During the trial, CUNY again raised the issue, stating, "We believe that pursuant to Seminole, the Equal Pay Act does not abrogate [Eleventh] Amendment . . . immunity." In response, this Court stated, "That has been ruled on by Judge Gershon, that you can proceed against the state on the equal pay [act] notwithstanding the [Eleventh] Amendment. Seminole has been construed in this case as permitting that. I agree with Judge Gershon's rulings as to the law[.] [T]hat will go forward. . . . [T]hat issue is preserved."

The Eleventh Amendment provides that "The Judicial power of the United States shall not be construed to extend to any suit in law or equity, commenced or prosecuted against one of the United States by Citizens of another State, or by Citizens or Subjects of any Foreign State." The Eleventh Amendment bars suits for monetary damages by all persons against a State in Federal Court. This immunity also applies to entities, such as CUNY, that are considered to be governmental in nature or "arms of the state."

Immunity under the Eleventh Amendment does not apply in two situations: (1) a State may consent to be sued in federal court, and (2) Congress may abrogate sovereign immunity. Since CUNY has not consented to be sued in federal court under the EPA, the court must decide whether in enacting the EPA Congress has abrogated the States' sovereign immunity in respect to claims arising under that act. This determination is governed by application of the two-part test articulated by the Supreme Court in Seminole Tribe: "[F]irst, whether Congress has 'unequivocally express[ed] its intent to abrogate the immunity' . . . and second, whether Congress has acted 'pursuant to a valid exercise of power.'"

The Equal Pay Act, Pub.L. No. 88-38 (codified at 29 U.S.C. § 206(d)), was initially enacted by Congress in 1963 as an amendment to the Fair Labor Standards Act ("FLSA"), 29 U.S.C. §§ 201-219, and was extended to the States in 1974. The Second Circuit recently was called upon in *Close v. State of New York*, 125 F.3d 31 (2d Cir. 1997), to determine whether a suit can be maintained against the State for its failure to pay overtime compensation in violation of 29 U.S.C. § 207(a) of the FLSA. Applying the requisite two-prong test of Seminole, the court held, in regard to the first prong, that Congress clearly intended to abrogate the States' sovereign immunity in respect to the FLSA. However, in regard to the second prong of the Seminole inquiry, the Second Circuit, noting that the FLSA was enacted pursuant to Congress' power under the Interstate Commerce Clause, held on the strength of the Supreme Court's over-ruling of *Union Gas in Seminole*, that Congress could not, therefore, be deemed to have acted pursuant to a valid exercise of power in seeking to abrogate the States' sovereign immunity by enactment of the FLSA. Consequently, New York could not be sued for its alleged failure to pay overtime compensation. Since the EPA is part of the FLSA, a broad reading of *Close* would bar suits bottomed on the EPA against the States. In this court's opinion, however, it would be improper to do so.

The concept underlying the remedial scheme in employment discrimination cases is to make the plaintiff whole. In employment discrimination cases, "district courts have broad discretion to fashion a wide range of remedies." In accordance with these principles, the court will proceed to fashion a full remedy. The EPA authorizes back pay as a remedy to compensate for unlawful disparate salaries. The regulations promulgated pursuant to the EPA state that, for purposes of this statute, wages "include all payments made to [or on behalf of] an employee as remuneration for employment. The term includes all forms of compensation irrespective of the time of payment . . . whether called wages, salary, profit sharing . . . or some other name. Fringe benefits are deemed to be remuneration for employment." They include "retirement benefits; . . . leave; and other such concepts." Retirement benefits are properly included in calculating damages owed to an individual who has been discriminated against in violation of the EPA. Since a plaintiff is entitled to liquidated damages in an amount equal to back wages where there is a willful violation of the EPA, in light of the jury's finding of willfulness, Perdue is entitled to an additional $134,829 as liquidated damages.

For the foregoing reasons, CUNY's motions for judgment as a matter of law, or alternatively for a new trial and/or a remittitur, are denied. Judgment shall be entered in favor of Perdue

against CUNY and Brooklyn College, jointly and severally, in the total sum of $799,566.73, plus per diem interest at the rate of $43.25 from June 1, 1998, to the date of entry.

 For an extended version of the case and review questions to test your understanding of the material, please go to www.HumanKinetics.com/CaseStudiesInSportLaw.

Stanley v. University of Southern California

178 F.3d 1069 (9th Cir. 1999)

Appellant Marianne Stanley appeals from the district court's order granting summary judgment in favor of defendants University of Southern California and Michael Garrett on Stanley's claims of discrimination and breach of employment contract.

Marianne Stanley was hired as head coach of the women's basketball team for the University of Southern California (USC) in 1989. Her initial contract, signed in July of that year, was for a four-year term, expiring June 30, 1993. The contract provided that she would make a base salary of $60,000 per year. This base salary was increased to $62,000 per year in 1992. The women's basketball program at USC enjoyed much success during Stanley's tenure.

Defendant Michael Garrett is the athletic director at USC. On April 20, 1993, two months prior to the expiration of Stanley's contract, Stanley and Garrett had an initial meeting to negotiate a new contract. The parties disagree over what took place at this meeting. Stanley contends that on that date she entered into a contract for a salary equivalent to that of George Raveling, the USC men's basketball coach. It is undisputed that Garrett expressly stated that USC could not pay her that salary, but that he would make her a formal offer in writing shortly after that meeting.

On April 27, 1993, Garrett offered Stanley, in writing, a three-year contract providing $80,000 in year one, $90,000 in year two, and $100,000 in year three, with a $6,000 per year housing allowance for each of the three years. The parties met again

on May 27, 1993, at which point Garrett claims that Stanley rejected the April 27 offer because she insisted that her compensation should be equivalent to Raveling's. Stanley argues that she never rejected this offer, but simply disagreed as to the amount of compensation, because the April 27 offer was inconsistent with the April 20 offer—for Raveling's salary level—that she already had accepted.

On June 7, 1993, Stanley proposed a three-year contract providing $96,000 per year for the first 18 months, and a salary equivalent to that of Raveling for the remainder of the term. Garrett rejected this offer. Stanley then retained an attorney who, on June 18, 1993, proposed to Garrett a three-year contract with an automatic two-year renewal provision, and total compensation of $88,000 for year one, $97,000 for year two, and $112,000 for year three, plus additional incentives. Garrett rejected this offer and withdrew the April 27 offer.

On June 21, 1993, Garrett sent to Stanley's attorney a written offer for a one-year contract for $96,000. Stanley's existing contract expired on June 30, 1993, but Stanley continued to perform her duties. On July 13, while on a recruiting trip, Stanley asked Garrett if he would still offer her a multiyear contract. He indicated that his June 21 one-year contract offer was USC's final offer, and that Stanley would have to accept or reject it by the end of the day. Stanley did not respond, but sent a memo to Garrett on July 14 requesting additional time to consider the offer. On July 15 Garrett revoked the offer, informed Stanley that he was seeking a new coach for the team, and requested that Stanley perform no further services for USC.

On August 5, 1993, Stanley initiated this action in Los Angeles County Superior Court, making claims of sex discrimination and retaliatory discharge. On August 6, 1993, the Superior Court granted Stanley's request for a temporary restraining order reinstating Stanley as head coach of the women's team at $96,000 per year pending the hearing on Stanley's motion for preliminary injunction. On that same day, defendants removed the action to federal court on the ground that the complaint stated claims arising under federal law.

On August 30, 1993, the district court denied the motion for preliminary injunction, and Stanley appealed. This court affirmed the denial of the preliminary injunction in an opinion filed January 6, 1994. Between September 1993 and February 1994, Stanley amended her complaint several times, and defendants' motions to dismiss were granted as to several claims. Stanley's Third Amended Complaint alleges the following causes of action: (1) violation of the Equal Pay Act, 29 U.S.C. § 206(d)(1) and California Fair Employment and Housing Act (FEHA); (2) violation of Article I, § 8 of the California Constitution; (3) violation of Title IX of the Civil Rights Act of 1972, 20 U.S.C. § 1681; (4) retaliation; (5) wrongful discharge in violation of public policy; (6) breach of express contract; (7) breach of implied-in-fact contract; and (8) breach of implied covenant of good faith and fair dealing. Stanley sought reinstatement, declaratory relief, injunctive relief preventing USC from further discriminating against her, back pay, $3 million in compensatory damages, and $5 million in punitive damages.

On October 17, 1994, defendants filed a motion for summary judgment. After Stanley was allowed additional time to conduct discovery, on March 10, 1995, the district court granted summary judgment for USC and Garrett. This appeal followed.

The Equal Pay Act provides in relevant part that "No employer having employees subject to any provisions of this section shall discriminate, within any establishment in which such employees are employed, between employees on the basis of sex by paying wages to employees . . . at a rate less than the rate at which he pays wages to employees of the opposite sex in such establishment for equal work on jobs the performance of which requires equal skill, effort, and responsibility, and which are performed under similar working conditions. . . ." 29 U.S.C. § 206(d)(1).

In an Equal Pay Act case, the plaintiff has the burden of establishing a *prima facie* case of discrimination by showing that employees of the opposite sex were paid different wages for equal work. The *prima facie* case is limited to a comparison of the jobs in question, and does not involve a comparison of the individuals who hold the jobs. To make out a *prima facie* case, the plaintiff bears the burden of showing that the jobs being compared are "substantially equal." Significantly, under the Act, the plaintiff need not demonstrate that the jobs in question are identical; she must show only that the jobs are substantially equal.

Because we are reviewing an appeal from the grant of summary judgment, the question is whether, viewing the evidence in the light most favorable to Stanley, and resolving all inferences in her favor, a genuine issue of material fact exists regarding the substantial equality of the jobs. Circuit courts employ a two-step "substantially equal" analysis in Equal Pay Act cases. In *Brobst v. Columbus Srvs. Int'l*, 761 F.2d 148, 156 (3d Cir. 1985), the Third Circuit described this approach, writing that "[t]he crucial finding on the equal work issue is whether the jobs to be compared have a 'common core' of tasks, i.e. whether a significant portion of the two jobs is identical." When a plaintiff establishes such a "common core of tasks," the court must then determine whether any additional tasks, incumbent on one job but not the other, make the two jobs "substantially different."

Here, we may assume that the men's and women's coaching jobs share a common core of tasks. Garrett—USC's athletic director and a defendant in this case—has acknowledged that the women's and men's coaches "have the same basic responsibilities" with regard to recruiting athletes and administering the basketball programs. In his declaration, Garrett also stated: "Both the women's and men's head basketball coaches have the following general duties and responsibilities: basketball program; coaching and discipline of team members; general supervision over the personal and academic lives of the student athletes; and supervision over assistant coaches, part-time coaches and other athletic department personnel involved in the women's and men's basketball programs."

The parties are in serious dispute, however, as to whether the additional responsibilities borne by the men's coach, but not by the women's coach, suffice to make the two jobs "substantially different." The defendants point out that the men's coach bears greater revenue generating responsibilities, that he is under greater media and spectator pressure to produce a winning program, and that he actually generates more revenue for the university.

Stanley claims that the differences between the two jobs are attributable to previous gender-based decisions on the part of the university. Essentially, Stanley claims that the differences between the two jobs result from the university's historically disparate treatment of male and female teams; namely, its decisions to invest in and promote the men's program more than the women's program. She then claims that because the differences between the jobs derive from previous gender-based decisions on the part of the university, the differences cannot be relied on to determine that the jobs are "substantially different."

The university, on the other hand, argues that the differences between the two jobs are not attributable to anything it has done or failed to do in the past. According to USC, the reason that women's basketball does not generate the same amount of revenue as men's basketball, and that the women's coach is not under the same pressure as the men's coach, is that there simply is not a sufficient spectator or media market for women's basketball games. Accordingly, it contends that the differences in responsibilities in the two jobs legitimately suffice to make them "substantially different."

We need not decide which party is correct regarding the reason for the differences that exist. Even assuming that Stanley has succeeded in raising a genuine issue of fact as to this question, the university is entitled to summary judgment on other grounds. A defendant may rebut a *prima facie* case by showing that the disparity in pay is a "differential based on any . . . factor other than sex." Defendants here assert an affirmative defense (that is, a nondiscriminatory reason for the pay differential) based on Stanley's and Raveling's markedly disparate levels of experience and qualifications. The record convincingly supports their claim. When Raveling began coaching at USC, he had 31 years of coaching experience. He had been the coach of the men's Olympic basketball team. He had been twice named national coach of the year, and twice named PAC-10 coach of the year. On top of his coaching experience, Raveling also had nine years of marketing and promotional experience, and was the author of several books on basketball. When Stanley started coaching at USC, three years after Raveling became head coach of the men's team, she had 17 years of experience coaching basketball, or 14 years less experience than Raveling. She never coached an Olympic team. She had no marketing or promotional experience other than what she gained as a coach. She had never published a book about basketball.

The EEOC Notice cited above, on which the plaintiff relies extensively, recognizes this type of affirmative defense, stating that "[s]uperior experience, education, and ability may justify pay disparities if distinctions based on these criteria are not gender based." In *Stanley I*, moreover, we wrote that "[e]mployers may reward professional experience and education without violating the EPA." Coaches with substantially more experience and significantly superior qualifications may, of course, be paid more than their less experienced and qualified counterparts, even when it is the male coach who has the greater level of experience and qualifications. By alleging that the pay differential at issue here was due to Stanley's and Raveling's markedly different levels of experience and qualifications, the defendants have proffered a factor "other than sex," to explain the difference in pay.

Where the defendant demonstrates that a pay differential was based on a factor other than sex, the employee may prevail by showing that the employer's proffered nondiscriminatory reason is a "pretext for discrimination." On this appeal, Stanley bears the burden of demonstrating a material fact regarding pretext in order to survive summary judgment. Stanley's pretext argument, however, fails to meet even this minimal burden. In her briefs, Stanley disputes that Raveling had greater qualifications and experience than she. Stanley has conspicuously failed, moreover, to present any meaningful evidence in support of her claim that she and Raveling had comparable levels of experience.

In the end, therefore, we are left with these undisputed facts: Stanley had far less relevant experience and qualifications than Raveling. She had 14 years less experience as a basketball coach. She, unlike Raveling, never coached the Olympic team. She had no marketing experience outside coaching. She had never written any books on basketball. Accordingly, Stanley has failed to raise a genuine issue of fact as to Raveling's markedly "superior experience," and qualifications. In short, she has failed to raise a genuine issue of fact as to the university's nondiscriminatory reason for paying Raveling a higher salary. Accordingly, we affirm the district court's decision to grant the defendants' motion for summary judgment on the Equal Pay Act claim.

Stanley contends that USC breached an implied covenant of good faith and fair dealing when USC failed to pay her a salary equal to Raveling's, when it failed to negotiate in good faith to renew the contract, and when it refused to reduce to writing the "contract" that Garrett entered into on USC's behalf at the April 20, 1993 meeting. However, a claim for breach of an implied good faith covenant depends on the existence of a valid contract. Thus, because Stanley had no valid contract based on the April 20, 1993 meeting, her claim fails with respect to that alleged contract.

Moreover, the record evidence does not support Stanley's claim that USC acted in bad faith with respect to the written contract that expired June 30, 1993. USC paid Stanley according to the terms of that contract, and no rational fact finder could conclude that USC acted in bad faith during negotiations for a new contract. Indeed, USC offered Stanley a new contract at a substantially higher salary than her previous contract provided, and engaged in repeated negotiations in an attempt to reach an agreement. Bad faith cannot be inferred from the mere fact that Stanley was unhappy with USC's proposed terms. Summary judgment was properly granted. We affirm the district court's grant of summary judgment in favor of USC and Garrett and its denial of the motion for disqualification. However, we remand its denial of the motion to retax costs. We deny appellees' motions for sanctions. Each side shall bear its own costs on appeal.

 For an extended version of the case and review questions to test your understanding of the material, please go to www.HumanKinetics.com/CaseStudiesInSportLaw.

5

Intellectual Property

Intellectual property law encompasses both copyright and trademark issues. The purpose of this area of law is to protect the creative endeavors of individuals and organizations. Copyright law provides protection for authors of written works, musical works and performances, and movies and other audiovisual works. Television and radio broadcasts of live sporting events are also covered under copyright law. *National Football League v. McBee & Bruno's* is a case presented here that deals with a violation of the copyright law when a sports bar is found showing NFL telecasts blacked out in their region.

Trademark law is another aspect addressed under intellectual property. The Lanham Act of 1946 and the Trademark Antidilution law of 1996 govern trademark law. Of the six cases presented in this section, five deal with situations involving trademark infringement. The *Boston Athletic Association v. Sullivan* case is a classic case of trademark infringement involving the consumer confusion of promotional goods. The *Dallas Cowboys Cheerleaders, Inc. v. Pussycat Cinema, Ltd.* case illustrates how the combination of colors and the location of decorations on uniforms can be eligible for trademark protection when they have acquired secondary meaning. The *Lyons Partnership v. Giannoulas* case illustrates the role that a parody plays in trademark infringement. Use of the word "Olympic" by San Francisco Arts & Athletics, Inc. was the primary issue in *San Francisco Arts & Athletics, Inc. v. United States Olympic Committee.* Finally, in *University of Pittsburgh v. Champion Products, Inc.,* the concepts of likelihood of confusion, functionality of goods, secondary meaning, and unfair competition were demonstrated.

Boston Athletic Association v. Sullivan

867 F.2d 22 (1st Cir. 1989)

In this service mark infringement case, Boston Athletic Association (BAA) and Image Impact, Inc. (Image) appeal the denial of their motion for summary judgment and the concurrent granting of the defendants', Mark Sullivan d/b/a Good Life (Sullivan) and Beau Tease, Inc. (Beau Tease), motion for summary judgment. This case arises out of the sale by the defendants of T-shirts (hereinafter called shirts) and other wearing apparel with designs alleged to infringe on BAA's service marks "Boston Marathon," "BAA Marathon," and its unicorn logo.

BAA is a charitable organization whose principal activity has been conducting the Boston Marathon since it was first run in 1897. The race is run annually from Hopkinton to Boston on Patriots' Day, the third Monday in April. In recent years, a day or two prior to the race an exposition has been put on by Conventures, Inc. under BAA's sponsorship. At the exposition, various businesses set up booths and sell shirts, running apparel, and sports items. The registered runners also pick up their numbers and official materials from the BAA booth.

Defendant Sullivan, a resident of Hopkinton, Massachusetts, retails wearing apparel under the name "Good Life" at a store in Hopkinton. Defendant Beau Tease, Inc. is a Massachusetts corporation doing business in Cambridge. It imprints and distributes merchandise, including shirts, to the trade.

In an effort to defray the costs of the race, BAA began an active campaign to market its name via licensing agreements. It registered the names "Boston Marathon" and "BAA Marathon" and its unicorn logo in Massachusetts in 1983 and "Boston Marathon" in the United States Patent and Trademark Office in 1985. As early as 1978, the defendants were imprinting and selling shirts with the name "Boston Marathon" and various other terms including the year on them. In 1984, defendant Sullivan negotiated an agreement under which Beau Tease sold to BAA a large quantity of shirts, which BAA gave away to the athletes and volunteers during the 1985 race. In

1986, Image, through its president, Mickey Lawrence, entered into an exclusive license with BAA for the use of BAA's service marks on wearing apparel including shirts. Starting in 1986, Image and BAA gave notice to imprinters, wholesalers, and retailers that Image was the exclusive licensee of the BAA and that any unauthorized use on merchandise of the name "Boston Marathon," or a similar name or a colorable imitation thereof, would violate the exclusive rights of BAA and its licensee.

BAA brought suit in Massachusetts Superior Court against the current defendants, and others, alleging that the above design infringed on its marks. The superior court denied its request for a preliminary injunction; the denial was affirmed by a single justice of the Massachusetts Court of Appeals. The action was discontinued without prejudice; the parties reserved their right to assert their positions in any future action.

In 1987, the exposition was held on Saturday, April 18, and the race on Monday, April 20. On April 1, 1987, BAA and Image filed suit in the United States District Court for the District of Massachusetts alleging that defendants' 1986 and 1987 shirts, with the logos described above, infringed BAA's marks. The complaint alleged confusion in violation of the Lanham Act, 15 U.S.C. § 1114, and a similar provision in Mass.Gen.Laws Ann. ch. 110B, § 11. The complaint also included additional state law counts for dilution, Mass.Gen.Laws Ann. ch. 110B, § 12, sale of counterfeits and imitations, Mass.Gen.Laws Ann. ch. 110B, § 13, and unauthorized use of a name, Mass.Gen.Laws Ann. ch. 214, § 3A. Along with the complaint, plaintiffs filed a motion for a preliminary injunction, seeking to stop the manufacture and sale of any article bearing the name "Boston Marathon" or any similar name.

On April 8, 1987, the district court held a hearing at which it consolidated the preliminary injunction hearing with a trial on the merits; the defendants were deemed to have made a general denial. Judgment for the defendants was entered and the preliminary injunction was dissolved. This appeal followed.

Defendants argue that they should prevail because BAA's marks are entitled to no protection for two reasons: (1) "Boston Marathon" has become a generic term inasmuch as it now refers to both the race and the services rendered by BAA, and (2) defendants' use of "Boston Marathon" on shirts from 1978 constitutes a prior usage.

In 1984, Congress amended § 14(c) of the Lanham Act, 15 U.S.C. § 1064(c). The amendment added the following to the section:

A registered mark shall not be deemed to be the common descriptive name of goods or services [i.e., a generic] solely because such mark is also used as a name of or to identify a unique product or service. The primary significance of the registered mark to the relevant public rather than purchaser motivation shall be the test for determining whether the registered mark has become the common descriptive name of goods or services in connection with which it has been used.

The burden of proof is on the party seeking to have a registered mark declared a generic to show that it has become so under the above test. Here, the defendants have introduced no evidence on the issue of "primary significance" and thus, have failed to meet the burden of proof.

With respect to prior usage, it is axiomatic that "registration does not create the underlying right in a trademark. That right, which accrues from the use of a particular name or symbol, is essentially a common law property right." Therefore, BAA's failure to register its marks until the mid-1980s is not dispositive. Furthermore, a mark provides protection not only for the product or service to which it is originally applied but also to related items or services.

Here, the uncontradicted evidence, consisting mainly of media references to the race, especially newspaper and magazine articles, shows that (1) the race was originally called the Boston Athletic Association or Boston A.A. Marathon; (2) since 1917, the race has also been called the Boston Marathon; and (3) since at least 1977, a year before defendants' prior usage, BAA used the names "B.A.A. Marathon" and "Boston Marathon" interchangeably. This use by BAA undercuts defendants' prior use claim as to the words *per se*. As for the use of the words on shirts and other running apparel, such apparel is related to the service provided by BAA, the race, and BAA is entitled to enjoin use of its marks on such items. We agree with the district court that BAA has had valid and enforceable marks for the entire relevant time frame.

Having held that BAA has enforceable rights in its marks, we turn to the central issue in this and most infringement cases: the likelihood of confusion. Claims for infringement of a registered trademark are governed by § 32(1) of the Lanham Act, 15 U.S.C. § 1114(1), which provides, in pertinent part:

Any person who shall, without the consent of the registrant—

(a) use in commerce any reproduction, counterfeit, copy, or colorable imitation of a registered mark in connection with the sale, offering for sale, distribution, or advertising of any goods or services on or in connection with which such use is likely to cause confusion or to cause mistake, or to deceive shall be liable in a civil action by the registrant for the remedies hereinafter provided.

In order to determine whether defendants' shirts are likely to cause confusion, we must first ask, confusion as to what? In the typical trademark infringement case, the likelihood of confusion inquiry centers on whether members of the purchasing public are likely to mistake defendants' products or services for plaintiffs' protected products or services within the same category. One question before us is whether members of the purchasing public are likely to mistake defendants' shirts for those of plaintiffs. This was the main issue that was addressed and decided below.

There is, however, a distinct but inseparably related issue, not adverted to directly below, that is involved in this case. Defendants are using the Boston Marathon sponsored and operated by the BAA to promote the sale of goods that are adorned so as to capitalize on the race. This implicates what is called a promotional goods issue. Under this issue, the likelihood of confusion inquiry focuses on whether the purchasing public is likely to believe that the sponsor of the Boston Marathon produces, licenses, or otherwise endorses defendants' shirts.

The First Circuit has identified eight factors to be weighed in assessing likelihood of confusion: (1) the similarity of the marks, (2) the similarity of the goods, (3) the relationship between the parties' channels of trade, (4) the relationship between the parties' advertising, (5) the classes of prospective purchasers, (6) evidence of actual confusion, (7) the defendant's intent in adopting its mark, and (8) the strength of the plaintiff's mark. *Astra v. Beckman Instruments*, 718 F.2d 1201, 1205; *Pignons v. Polaroid Corp.*, 657 F.2d 482, 487. Examining the evidence favorable as it applies to defendants, we must determine on the whole whether there is any genuine issue as to likelihood of confusion. No one factor is necessarily determinative, but each must be considered.

Similarity is determined on the basis of the total effect of the designation, rather than a comparison of the individual features. Meaning alone, without reference to appearance and sound, may be sufficiently close to constitute similarity.

It is evident that defendants' logos refer specifically to the "Boston Marathon." There is but one Boston marathon race; defendants' logos use the term "Marathon" and depicts runners. It is run annually; defendants' logos refer to a specific year implying an annual event. The race begins at Hopkinton and ends in Boston; defendants' logos include these cities. Despite this, defendants have introduced no evidence showing that they have taken steps to turn their similarly marked products into dissimilar ones by clearly distinguishing their products, and their lack of BAA sponsorship, from those sold by plaintiffs. When one uses a mark similar to one already in use, there is generally an affirmative duty to avoid the likelihood of confusion.

The district court's holding that plaintiffs' rights did not sweep any further than their actual marks is not a correct application of trademark law. Such a rule would eviscerate trademark law because few would be stupid enough to make exact copies of another's mark or symbol. It has been well said that the most successful form of copying is to employ enough points of similarity to confuse the public with enough points of difference to confuse the courts.

Here, the meaning of the two marks is more than similar, it is identical. This overcomes any difference in appearance between them.

The parties offer virtually the same goods: shirts and other wearing apparel. Thus, under this factor, there is a strong likelihood of confusion.

The parties sell their shirts predominantly in Boston-area retail shops, at the exposition, and along the race course. Sales are largely seasonal, centering on the race date. The parties use the same general method of advertising: displays in store windows, in booths at the exposition, and along the race course. Prospective purchasers are drawn from the public at large. The shirts involved here retailed for about $7 to $10 and were sometimes sold under hectic conditions. Inexpensive items, bought by the casual purchaser, are not likely to be bought with great care. Courts have found less likelihood of confusion where goods are expensive and purchased after careful consideration.

The virtual identity between the parties' sales outlets and advertising methods, as well as the purchasing public's lack of opportunity to exercise discrimination in making such purchases, all point toward a likelihood of confusion.

Before we move to the sixth factor, we must first address the district court's initial division of the purchasing public into two classes. In fashioning its preliminary injunction, the court split the purchasing public into a class of those interested enough in racing to attend the exposition and all others. It found that only the former were likely to connect BAA with the Boston Marathon, and thus, were the only ones likely to infer sponsorship of defendants' products by BAA. In its summary judgment decision, the court stated that there was a genuine issue as to the public's knowledge of BAA's sponsorship of the Marathon but that this issue was not material because resolution of the issue would not alter the outcome.

Distinctions based on expertise can be useful in analyzing likelihood of confusion, but we find no reason for such a distinction here. It is the general public that is the market for shirts commemorating the Boston Marathon. In making its distinction, the court appears to have reasoned as follows: defendants' logos mean "Boston Marathon"; Boston Marathon shirts imply sponsorship by someone; the public (as opposed to those who attend the exposition) does not know that BAA sponsors the Marathon; therefore, the public cannot infer that BAA sponsors defendants' shirts.

The key step in this reasoning—the public's lack of knowledge of BAA's sponsorship of the race—is not supported in the record. Indeed, the evidence is to the contrary. Plaintiffs submitted voluminous, uncontradicted evidence, in the form of numerous newspaper and magazine articles dating back to 1897, videotapes of television broadcasts, and encyclopedia entries, all showing that the public was continually exposed to the fact of BAA's sponsorship of the Boston Marathon.

Defendants argue that the plaintiffs' evidence is not sufficient to show the public's knowledge because a public poll was not conducted. The lack of survey data, however, does not fatally undercut plaintiffs' claims. The defendants offered no evidence tending to contradict plaintiffs' assertions. Plaintiffs were not bound to a particular form of evidence. A poll might have been more accurate, but the lack of one does not nullify the evidence plaintiffs did introduce.

We find that no genuine issue of fact exists as to the public's general awareness of BAA's sponsorship of the Boston Marathon; there was, therefore, no reason to divide the purchasing public into two classes.

While not as accurate as a survey might have been, this evidence shows that some people were actually confused as to who sponsored defendants' shirts. This factor, then, weighs in favor of a likelihood of confusion.

The facts can only be interpreted to mean that defendants sought to profit from BAA's sponsorship of the Boston Marathon. The defendants chose designs that obviously referred to the Marathon, put those designs on the same types of clothing sold by the plaintiffs, sold those shirts at the same time and in the same manner as the plaintiffs to the same general purchasing public. Defendants' actions clearly show their intent to trade on BAA's sponsorship and management of the Boston Marathon.

"The distinctiveness and reknown [sic] of a trademark determine its relative strength or weakness, which, in turn, defines the scope of protection to be accorded the mark against others which are confusingly similar." We have found the following factors useful in determining a trademark's relative strength: the length of time a mark has been used and the plaintiff's relative renown in its field, the strength of the mark in plaintiff's field of business, especially by looking at the number of similar registered marks; and the plaintiff's actions in promoting its mark.

Here, although BAA has only relatively recently registered its marks, it used them for a long period of time before registration. The Boston Marathon is one of the oldest and most prestigious marathons in this country. BAA, as a charitable organization, does not have the same impetus to advertise that a for-profit company would have. Nonetheless, its broad media exposure serves a similar purpose; it makes known to the public the BAA's sponsorship of the Boston Marathon. Finally, no evidence was introduced that others have obtained, or have not been able to obtain, registration of similar marks in the United States Patent and Trademark Office or its Massachusetts counterpart. The strength factors militate in favor of a finding that the mark held by BAA in "Boston Marathon" is a strong one. Therefore, broad protection of the mark is warranted.

Based on the undisputed facts and the pertinent law, plaintiffs have proved that the purchasing public are likely to confuse defendants' shirts with those of plaintiffs.

The question with the promotional goods issue is whether the purchasing public is likely to believe that the sponsor of the Boston Marathon, produces, licenses, or endorses defendants' shirts. Whether or not purchasers happen to know that the sponsor of the Boston Marathon is an organization called the "Boston Athletic Association" is irrelevant to this likelihood of confusion analysis. In order to establish infringement in a promotional goods case, it has traditionally been the plaintiff's burden to show that prospective purchasers are in fact likely to be confused or misled into thinking that the defendant's product was produced, licensed, or otherwise sponsored by the plaintiff.

There can be no doubt that the language and design on defendant's shirts intentionally call attention to an event that has long been sponsored and supported by the BAA—an event that is, in fact, the subject of its registered mark. Defendants' shirts are clearly designed to take advantage of the Boston Marathon and to benefit from the good will associated with its promotion by plaintiffs. Defendants thus obtain a free ride at plaintiffs' expense. In the oft quoted words of the Supreme Court in *International News Service v. Associated Press*, 248 U.S. 215, 39 S.Ct. 68, 63 L.Ed. 211 (1918), because the Boston Marathon has achieved its renown as a result of BAA's expenditure of labor, skill, and money, such unlicensed use of BAA's mark would permit defendants to reap where they have not sown. Like Rosie Ruiz, a notorious imposter in the 1980 Boston Marathon, defendants would be given a medal without having run the course. Under these facts, the plaintiffs have to prove, of course, that the defendants are trading on plaintiffs' mark and goodwill. We do not think, however, that plaintiffs also have to prove that members of the public will actually conclude that defendants' product was officially sponsored by the Marathon's sponsor whoever that sponsor may be. One difficulty with presenting such proof is that few people, other than legal specialists, could venture an informed opinion on whether someone using the logo of the sponsor of a sporting event is required to have the permission of the event's sponsor. Lacking such knowledge, the question of approval is pure guesswork. To ask a fact finder to determine whether the public would think that defendants' shirts were authorized or official shirts is to ask it to resolve a confusing and, in many contexts, virtually meaningless question.

In the present case, we adopt a similar presumption. Given the undisputed facts that (1) defendants intentionally referred to the Boston Marathon on its shirts, and (2) purchasers were likely to buy the shirts precisely because of that reference, we think it fair to presume that purchasers are likely to be confused about the shirt's source or sponsorship. We presume that, at the least, a sufficient number of purchasers would be likely to assume—mistakenly—that defendants' shirts had some connection with the official sponsors of the Boston Marathon. In the absence of any evidence that effectively rebuts this presumption of a likelihood of confusion, we hold that plaintiffs are entitled to enjoin the manufacture and sale of defendants' shirts.

In the present case, the facts clearly show that defendants intentionally referred to the Boston Marathon on their shirt in order to create an identification with the event and, thus, to sell their shirts. This evidence is itself sufficient to raise the inference of a likelihood of confusion. Given this presumption in favor of plaintiffs and the fact that defendants offered no evidence that would rebut the presumption, there is no genuine issue of material fact about the likelihood of confusion.

We acknowledge that a trademark, unlike a copyright or patent, is not a right in gross that enables a holder to enjoin all reproductions. In Justice Holmes's words, "When the mark is used in such a way that does not deceive the public we see no such sanctity in the word as to prevent it being used to tell the truth. It is not taboo." *Prestonettes, Inc. v. Coty,* 264 U.S. 359. But when a manufacturer intentionally uses another's mark as a means of establishing a link in consumers' minds with the other's enterprise, and directly profits from that link, there is an unmistakable aura of deception. Such a use is, by its very nature, likely to cause confusion, or to cause mistake, or to deceive. Unless the defendant can show that there is in fact no likelihood of such confusion or deception about the product's connection to the trademark holder, such a use can be enjoined.

Applying the pertinent law to the facts as considered in the light most favorable to defendants, we hold as follows: (1) there is no genuine issue of fact with respect to the likelihood of confusion of goods; nor is there any genuine issue of fact that the purchasing public will likely believe that the sponsor of the Boston Marathon produces, licenses, or otherwise endorses defendants' shirts and other goods with logos referring to the Boston Marathon. These two findings stem from the same set of facts; (2) the plaintiff, BAA, owns the name "Boston Marathon" and the defendants' shirts imprinted with logos suggesting that event constitute an infringement of BAA's mark. This includes the design "Boston; runner/s; 19xx," which was the subject of plaintiffs' amended complaint submitted on February 4, 1988; (3) The judgment of the district court is reversed. Judgment shall issue for the plaintiffs, which shall include the following permanent injunction:

The defendants, Mark Sullivan d/b/a/ Good Life and Beau Tease, Inc., and all persons and entities acting in concert or in participation with them, are hereby enjoined from manufacturing or selling goods displaying the name "Boston Marathon" or any other design that is confusingly similar to or a colorable imitation of "Boston Marathon," including goods that are imprinted with "19xx Marathon; runners; Hopkinton—Boston," or with "Boston; [runner/s]; 1988." Costs awarded to appellants.

 For an extended version of the case and review questions to test your understanding of the material, please go to www.HumanKinetics.com/CaseStudiesInSportLaw.

Dallas Cowboys Cheerleaders, Inc. v. Pussycat Cinema, Ltd.

604 F.2d 200 (2nd Cir. 1979)

This is an appeal from orders of the United States District Court for the Southern District of New York granting plaintiff's motions for a preliminary injunction prohibiting Pussycat Cinema, Ltd., and Michael Zaffarano from distributing or exhibiting the motion picture *Debbie Does Dallas*. On March 14 this court granted defendants' motion to stay the injunction and ordered an expedited appeal. The case was argued before us on April 6, following which we dissolved the stay and reinstated the preliminary injunction.

Plaintiff in this trademark infringement action is Dallas Cowboys Cheerleaders, Inc., a wholly-owned subsidiary of the Dallas Cowboys Football Club, Inc. Plaintiff employs 36 women who perform dance and cheerleading routines at Dallas Cowboys football games. The cheerleaders have appeared frequently on television programs and make commercial appearances at such public events as sporting goods shows and shopping center openings. In addition, plaintiff licenses others to manufacture and distribute posters, calendars, T-shirts, and the like depicting Dallas Cowboys Cheerleaders in their uniforms. These products have enjoyed nationwide commercial success, due largely to the national exposure the Dallas Cowboys Cheerleaders have received through the news and entertainment media. Moreover, plaintiff has expended large amounts of money to acquaint the public with its uniformed cheerleaders and earns substantial revenue from their commercial appearances.

At all the football games and public events where plaintiff's cheerleaders appear and on all commercial items depicting the cheerleaders, the women are clad in plaintiff's distinctive uniform. The familiar outfit consists of white vinyl boots, white shorts, a white belt decorated with blue stars, a blue bolero blouse, and a white vest decorated with three blue stars on each side of the front and a white fringe around the bottom. In this action plaintiff asserts that it has a trademark in its uniform and that defendants have infringed and diluted that trademark in advertising and exhibiting *Debbie Does Dallas.*

Pussycat Cinema, Ltd., is a New York corporation that owns a movie theater in New York City. In November 1978, the Pussycat Cinema began to show *Debbie Does Dallas,* a gross and revolting sex film whose plot, to the extent that there is one, involves a cheerleader at a fictional high school, Debbie, who has been selected to become a "Texas Cowgirl." In order to raise enough money to send Debbie, and eventually the entire squad, to Dallas, the cheerleaders perform sexual services for a fee. The movie consists largely of a series of scenes graphically depicting the sexual escapades of the "actors." In the movie's final scene Debbie dons a uniform strikingly similar to that worn by the Dallas Cowboys Cheerleaders and for approximately 12 minutes of film footage engages in various sex acts while clad or partially clad in the uniform. Defendants advertised the movie with marquee posters depicting Debbie in the allegedly infringing uniform and containing such captions as "Starring Ex Dallas Cowgirl Cheerleader Bambi Woods" and "You'll do more than cheer for this X Dallas Cheerleader." Similar advertisements appeared in the newspapers.

Plaintiff brought this action alleging trademark infringement under § 43(a) of the Lanham Act (15 U.S.C. § 1125(a)), unfair competition, and dilution of trademark in violation of § 368-d of the New York General Business Law. The district court, in its oral opinion of February 13, 1979, found that "plaintiff ha(d) succeeded in proving by overwhelming evidence the merits of each one of its contentions." Defendants challenge the validity of all three claims.

A preliminary issue raised by defendants is whether plaintiff has a valid trademark in its cheerleader uniform. Defendants argue that the uniform is a purely functional item necessary for the performance of cheerleading routines and that it therefore is not capable of becoming a trademark. We do not quarrel with defendants' assertion that a purely functional item may not become a trademark. However, we do not agree that all of the characteristics of plaintiff's uniform serve only a functional purpose or that, because an item is in part incidentally functional, it is necessarily precluded from being designated as a trademark. Plaintiff does not claim a trademark in all clothing designed and fitted to allow free movement while performing cheerleading routines, but claims a trademark in the particular combination of colors and collocation of decorations that distinguish plaintiff's uniform from those of other squads. It is well established that, if the design of an item is nonfunctional and has acquired secondary meaning, the design may become a trademark even if the item itself is functional. Moreover, when a feature of the construction of the item is arbitrary, the feature may become a trademark even though it serves a useful purpose. Thus, the fact that an item serves or performs a function does not mean that it may not at the same time be capable of indicating sponsorship or origin, particularly where the decorative aspects of the item are nonfunctional. In the instant case the combination of the white boots, white shorts, blue blouse, and white star-studded vest and belt is an arbitrary design that makes the otherwise functional uniform trademarkable.

Having found that plaintiff has a trademark in its uniform, we must determine whether the depiction of the uniform in *Debbie Does Dallas* violates that trademark. The district court found that the uniform worn in the movie and shown on the marquee closely resembled plaintiff's uniform and that the public was likely to identify it as plaintiff's uniform. Our own comparison of the two uniforms convinces us that the district court was correct, and defendants do not seriously contend that the uniform shown in the movie is not almost identical with plaintiff's. Defendant's contention is that, despite the striking similarity of the two uniforms, the public is unlikely to be confused within the meaning of § 43(a) of the Lanham Act.

Defendants assert that the Lanham Act requires confusion as to the origin of the film, and they contend that no reasonable person would believe that the film originated with plaintiff. In order to be confused, a consumer need not believe that the owner of the mark actually produced the item and placed it on the market. The public's belief that the mark's owner sponsored or otherwise approved the use of the trademark satisfies the confusion requirement. In the instant case, the uniform depicted in *Debbie Does Dallas* unquestionably brings to mind

the Dallas Cowboys Cheerleaders. Indeed, it is hard to believe that anyone who had seen defendants' sexually depraved film could ever thereafter disassociate it from plaintiff's cheerleaders. This association results in confusion that has "a tendency to impugn (plaintiff's services) and injure plaintiff's business reputation. . . ."

Plaintiff expects to establish on trial that the public may associate it with defendants' movie and be confused into believing that plaintiff sponsored the movie, provided some of the actors, licensed defendants to use the uniform, or was in some other way connected with the production. The trademark laws are designed not only to prevent consumer confusion but also to protect "the synonymous right of a trademark owner to control his product's reputation." The district court did not err in holding that plaintiff had established a likelihood of confusion within the meaning of the Lanham Act sufficient to entitle it to a preliminary injunction and that plaintiff had a right to preliminary relief on its claims of unfair competition and dilution.

Defendants assert that the copyright doctrine of "fair use" should be held applicable to trademark infringement actions and that we should apply the doctrine to sanction their use of a replica of plaintiff's uniform. Fair use is "a 'privilege in others than the owner of a copyright to use the copyrighted material in a reasonable manner without his consent. . . .'" The fair use doctrine allows adjustments of conflicts between the First Amendment and the copyright laws, . . . , and is designed primarily to balance "the exclusive rights of a copyright holder with the public's interest in dissemination of information affecting areas of universal concern, such as art, science and industry." It is unlikely that the fair use doctrine is applicable to trademark infringements; however, we need not reach that question. Although, as defendants assert, the doctrine of fair use permits limited copyright infringement for purposes of parody, defendants' use of plaintiff's uniform hardly qualifies as parody or any other form of fair use.

Nor does any other First Amendment doctrine protect defendants' infringement of plaintiff's trademark. That defendants' movie may convey a barely discernible message does not entitle them to appropriate plaintiff's trademark in the process of conveying that message. Plaintiff's trademark is in the nature of a property right and as such it need not "yield to the exercise of First Amendment rights under circumstances where adequate alternative avenues of communication exist." Because there are numerous ways in which defendants may comment on "sexuality in athletics" without infringing plaintiff's trademark, the district court did not encroach on their First Amendment rights in granting a preliminary injunction.

For similar reasons, the preliminary injunction did not constitute an unconstitutional "prior restraint." This is not a case of government censorship, but a private plaintiff's attempt to protect its property rights. The propriety of a preliminary injunction where such relief is sought is so clear that courts have often issued an injunction without even mentioning the First Amendment. The prohibition of the Lanham Act is content neutral and therefore does not arouse the fears that trigger the application of constitutional "prior restraint" principles.

The district court's issuance of a preliminary injunction is reversible only for abuse of discretion. A preliminary injunction is proper where the plaintiff establishes possible irreparable harm and either (1) probable success on the merits or (2) sufficiently serious questions going to the merits to make them a fair ground for litigation and a balance of hardships tipping decidedly in the movant's favor. Plaintiff has established a probability of success at trial, and the confusion engendered by defendants' movie would result in irreparable harm to plaintiff were defendants not enjoined from its distribution and exhibition. Accordingly, we affirm the orders of the district court.

 For an extended version of the case and review questions to test your understanding of the material, please go to www.HumanKinetics.com/CaseStudiesInSportLaw.

Lyons Partnership v. Giannoulas

179 F.3d 384 (5th Cir. 1999)

Lyons Partnership LP (Lyons), the owners of the rights to the children's caricature Barney, sued Ted Giannoulas, the creator of a sports mascot—The Famous Chicken (the Chicken)—because the Chicken had incorporated a Barney look-alike in its act. The district court granted summary judgment to Giannoulas and awarded attorneys' fees.

On appeal, Lyons raises six issues, the most important of which is whether the district court erred when it determined that there was insufficient evidence that Giannoulas's use of the Barney trademark caused consumer confusion under the Lanham Act.

This case involves a dispute over the use of the likeness of "Barney," a children's character who appears in a number of products marketed to children. Barney, a 6-foot tall purple "tyrannosaurus rex," entertains and educates young children. His awkward and lovable behavior, good-natured disposition, and renditions of songs like "I love you, you love me," have warmed the hearts and captured the imaginations of children across the United States.

According to Lyons, the owner of the intellectual property rights for Barney and the plaintiff in the suit below, the defendants—Giannoulas d/b/a The Famous Chicken and TFC, Inc. (TFC), the owner of the intellectual property rights to the Chicken—sought to manipulate Barney's wholesome image to accomplish their own nefarious ends.

The Chicken, a sports mascot conceived of and played by Giannoulas, targets a more grown-up audience. While the Chicken does sell marketing merchandise, it is always sold either by direct order or in conjunction with one of the Chicken's appearances. Thus, the Chicken's principal means of income could, perhaps loosely, be referred to as "performance art." Catering to the tastes of adults attending sporting events, most notably baseball games, the Chicken is renowned for his hard hitting satire. Fictional characters, celebrities, ball players, and, yes, even umpires, are all targets for the Chicken's levity.

And so, perhaps inevitably, the Chicken's beady glare came to rest on that lovable and carefree icon of childhood, Barney. Lyons argues that the Chicken's motivation was purely mercenary. Seeing the opportunity to hitch his wagon to a star, the Chicken incorporated a Barney look-alike into his acts. The character, a person dressed in a costume (sold with the title "Duffy the Dragon") that had a remarkable likeness to Barney's appearance, would appear next to the Chicken in an extended performance during which the Chicken would flip, slap, tackle, trample, and generally assault the Barney look-alike.

The sketch would begin with the Chicken disco dancing. The Barney character would join the Chicken on the field and dance too, but in an ungainly manner that mimicked the real Barney's dance. The Chicken would then indicate that Barney should try to follow the Chicken's dance steps (albeit, by slapping the bewildered dinosaur across the face). At this point, Barney would break character and out-dance the Chicken, to the crowd's surprise. The Chicken would then resort to violence, tackling Barney and generally assaulting Barney. Barney would ultimately submit to the Chicken and they would walk off the field apparently friends, only for the Chicken to play one last gag on the back-in-character naive and trusting Barney. The Chicken would flip Barney over a nearby obstacle, such as a railing.

Lyons ultimately filed a suit against Giannoulas and TFC, alleging trademark infringement, false association, unfair competition, and trademark dilution under the Lanham Act, copyright infringement, and other claims. The district court granted the defendants' motion for summary judgment. In addition, the district court awarded attorneys' fees to the defendants based on provisions in the Copyright Act. Lyons has filed a timely appeal with respect to the Lanham Act claims, the Copyright Act claims, and the award of attorneys' fees.

A trademark is a word, name, symbol, or device adopted and used by a manufacturer to identify the source of goods. To establish a trademark violation, Lyons must establish that Giannoulas has used in commerce a mark confusingly similar to Lyons's. The district court held that there was no likelihood of consumer confusion. In reaching this decision, the district court relied on its finding that the Chicken's performance was clearly meant to be a parody.

Lyons makes two arguments with respect to its trademark confusion claim. First, Lyons argues that Giannoulas's use of Barney was not intended as a parody. Because Lyons continues to contest this issue on appeal, we first address whether there are any genuine issues of material fact regarding whether Giannoulas was engaged in parodying Barney. Lyons's second argument is that the district court accorded too much weight to its finding that Giannoulas's use was a parody.

In general, a parody is defined "as an artistic work that imitates the characteristic style of an author or a work for comic effect or ridicule." In general, a reference to a copyrighted work or trademark may be permissible if the use is purely for parodic purposes. To the extent the original work must be referenced in order to accomplish the parody, that reference is acceptable. Giannoulas claims that his use of a Barney look-alike clearly qualifies as a parody. He used the minimum necessary to evoke Barney—while he used a character dressed like Barney that danced like Barney, he did not make any other references to the mythical world in which Barney resides. He did not, for instance, incorporate any of Barney's other "friends" into his act, have the character imitate Barney's voice, or perform any of Barney's songs. According to Giannoulas, Barney was clearly the butt of a joke and he referenced the Barney character only to the extent necessary to conjure up the character's image in his audience's mind.

Lyons argues that the conduct was not a parody but simply the use of Barney. To support this claim, Lyons points to two kinds of proffered evidence. First, Lyons notes that Giannoulas himself admits that he did not have a definite plan when he incorporated Barney into the act. Lyons argues that this creates an issue of fact regarding whether Giannoulas really intended to parody Barney or simply intended to profit from incorporating the Barney character into his act.

This argument is meritless. Clearly, in the context in which Giannoulas intended to insert a reference to the Barney character, the humor came from the incongruous nature of such an appearance, not from an attempt to benefit from Barney's goodwill. This point is clearly established by the fact that the Chicken's actions toward Barney seem to have always been antagonistic. Although the performance may have evolved into a far more sophisticated form of commentary, even at its inception, it was clearly meant as a parody.

The second argument made by Lyons is that the audience could not have understood the performance to be a parody. Lyons assumes that the target audience here is children and that children would clearly believe that the caricature actually was Barney. Although Lyons is correct that the intended audience is an important factor in determining whether a performance qualifies as a parody, Lyons presented no credible evidence that a significant portion of the audience at evening sporting events are children. Even if young children—like the 2-year-old who had such a traumatic reaction to the down-trodden Barney—are in attendance, we would expect them to be supervised by parents who could explain the nature of the parody. We therefore agree with the district court that Giannoulas's use of the caricature clearly qualifies as a parody. We note that Lyons's insistence that the Chicken's act is not a parody is, in our view, a completely meritless argument.

In order to understand Giannoulas's second argument, we must first review our own precedent with respect to consumer confusion under the Lanham Act. Our case law has set out a long list of nonexclusive, nondispositive factors to consider when determining whether a use can result in confusion. These factors are referred to as the digits of confusion. In determining whether a likelihood of confusion exists, this court considers the following non-exhaustive list of factors: (1) the type of trademark allegedly infringed, (2) the similarity between the two marks, (3) the similarity of the products or services, (4) the identity of the retail outlets and purchasers, (5) the identity of the advertising media used, (6) the defendant's intent, and (7) any evidence of actual confusion. The Fifth Circuit has held that confusion resulting from a parody is not an affirmative defense to a trademark infringement claim but is instead an additional factor that should be considered.

The district court relied on its finding that the conduct was a parody when considering each of the remaining factors or digits described in a prior case. Giannoulas's argument is that the relevance of the conduct being a parody is only one digit to be considered among the digits of confusion. Lyons argues the district court erred by relying on the conduct being a parody to conclude that the other factors did not indicate a risk of confusion. The crux of Lyons's argument is that, when considering whether conduct is likely to cause consumer confusion, even if there is overwhelming evidence that the conduct is a parody, the other digits of confusion must still be considered separately, without reference to whether the conduct is a parody. If, after conducting this analysis, there are factors that support the plaintiff's claim, he argues that the plaintiff should be permitted to proceed to trial.

We find this analysis absolutely absurd. Such an approach would all but require a trial for any trademark suit where the conduct was a parody. A brief consideration of only one of the digits of confusion makes this point clear.

The first digit, that is, the type of trademark allegedly infringed, questions whether the trademark is so distinctive that a consumer encountering the defendant's mark would be likely to assume that the source of a product or service is the owner of the trademark. Thus, under the traditional analysis, the stronger the trademark, the more likely that this factor would weigh in favor of the plaintiff. However, as the district court correctly noted in this case, when a consumer encounters the use of a trademark in a setting that is clearly a parody, the strength of the mark may actually make it easier for the consumer to realize that the use is a parody. Therefore, a strong mark is not as relevant a factor when the use is that of parody.

It seems reasonable to us to expect that most comedians will seek to satirize images or figures who will be widely recognized by their audiences. It therefore seems unlikely that comedians will target trademarks that do not have significant strength. If the district court were not able to consider the relevance that parody plays in this analysis, the district court would almost always have to conclude that this digit of confusion weighed in favor of the plaintiff. Such a result would effectively tie the district court's hands unnecessarily and prevent the district court from applying common sense to determine whether a particular factor is actually likely to lead to confusion.

Simply put, although the fact that conduct is a parody is not an affirmative defense to trademark infringement, a parody should be treated differently from other uses that infringe on a trademark. While it is only one factor to consider, it is a factor that must be considered in conjunction with all of the other digits of confusion. When, as here, a parody makes a specific, ubiquitous trademark the brunt of its joke, the use of the trademark for satirical purposes affects our analysis of the factors to consider when determining whether the use is likely to result in consumer confusion.

We therefore conclude that the district court did not err in considering the other digits of confusion in the light of its finding that the Chicken's performance is a parody. In doing so, we hold that, when we stated in *Elvis* that use as parody was a relevant factor, we did not intend for the nature of the use to be considered separately from the other digits of confusion. The district court ably considered the other digits of confusion in this respect, and we find no error in its conclu-

sion that there is insufficient evidence to support a violation under the Lanham Act.

In this case, Lyons argued that Giannoulas's use of a Barney caricature violated the Copyright Act and the Lanham Act. The district court disagreed and a review of the record indicates that the district court did not err in doing so. On appeal, we address only the argument related to the relevance that parodic conduct has on determining the likelihood of confusion in a trademark infringement case. We note that in this case the conduct was, without doubt, a parody. Having made that finding, the district court did not err in concluding that the nature of Giannoulas's use is relevant when analyzing the other digits of confusion to determine likelihood of confusion. For the foregoing reasons, the ruling of the district court is AFFIRMED.

 For an extended version of the case and review questions to test your understanding of the material, please go to www.HumanKinetics.com/CaseStudiesInSportLaw.

National Football League v. McBee & Bruno's, Inc.

792 F.2d 726 (8th Cir. 1986)

This lawsuit, brought by the National Football League (NFL) and the St. Louis Football Cardinals (Cardinals), alleges that defendants, the owners of several St. Louis restaurants, violated federal copyright and communications law by showing Cardinals' home games that had been blacked out in the St. Louis area. According to plaintiffs, defendants picked up the signals for such games by means of satellite dish antennae. The district court, which had already issued a temporary restraining order and a preliminary injunction, entered a permanent injunction against defendants after a trial on the merits. The decision was based on the Copyright Act of 1976, 17 U.S.C. §§ 101 *et seq.*, and the Federal Communications Act, § 705 (formerly § 605). In the main, we affirm.

The Cardinals, a professional football team, is one of 28 teams composing the NFL, an unincorporated nonprofit association through which the member clubs schedule games and manage their

affairs as a group, including contracts with the three major television networks. One provision of those television contracts is that games that are not sold out within 72 hours of game time are to be blacked out, that is, not broadcast within a 75-mile radius of the home team's playing field. Officials of the league and club testified at trial that such a rule boosts team revenue directly by increasing ticket sales and indirectly because a full stadium contributes to a more exciting television program and therefore makes the right to broadcast games more valuable.

Witnesses also described the process by which a live football game is telecast by the networks, in this case CBS. As television cameras capture the visual portion of the game, announcers describe and discuss the action from a sound booth of some kind. Those simultaneous audio and video signals are combined at an earth station outside the stadium. This signal—called an uplink—is transmitted up to a satellite, which then sends the signal back—called a downlink—to a network control point on Long Island. Because that signal contains no images other than those from the stadium, this stage is referred to as a clean feed. The signal is then sent by cable to CBS studios in New York; commercials and other interruptions, such as station breaks, are inserted, and it is now described as a dirty feed. There is another uplink to the satellite, and then a downlink to local affiliates, who insert local material and finally put the live broadcast on the air. The process apparently takes far longer to describe than to occur; at argument, counsel for the NFL called the procedure simultaneous, instantaneous, and said that the delay between the action on the field and the broadcast by local affiliates was considerably less than two seconds.

The defendants are owners, corporate or individual, of St. Louis bar-restaurants within 75 miles of Busch Stadium, the Cardinals' home field. All defendants have satellite dish antennae that enable them to receive transmissions in the so-called C-band frequency, approximately 3200-4200 megahertz, in which the satellite sends and receives transmissions. There is no question that prior to November 19, 1984, all defendants but two picked up the clean feed (from the satellite to CBS) and thereby showed blacked-out home games of the Cardinals. On that date, plaintiffs requested and the district court entered a temporary restraining order, preventing defendants from intercepting and showing the home game scheduled for the following Sunday; after a hearing, the court issued a preliminary injunction in basically the same terms, dealing with the last home game of the season. The district court found that the telecasts were copyrightable under § 102 of the Copyright Act, that the plaintiffs were owners of those copyrights, and that display of the clean feed transmissions of those telecasts violated plaintiffs' exclusive right of display and performance under § 106 of the Act, as well as § 705 of the Communications Act. A permanent injunction issued on September 13, 1985, prohibiting the defendants from intercepting and showing plaintiffs' programming, whether in the form of the clean or dirty feed transmissions.

The owners of the defendant restaurants challenge the district court's Copyright Act decision on a variety of grounds: that the evidence presented by plaintiffs to show irreparable injury was too speculative to support the issuance of a permanent injunction; that defendants' display of blacked-out home games falls under statutory limitations on exclusive rights of a copyright owner; that defendants did not infringe on plaintiffs' copyright because they intercepted the clean feed rather than the dirty feed, which was the transmission actually fixed under the Copyright Act and registered with the Copyright Office; and that under 17 U.S.C. § 411, no permanent injunction can issue concerning works that are not already in existence. Although some of these arguments have more substance than others, we consider all to be ultimately without merit.

Defendants first allege that plaintiffs have not shown that either the League or the local team will suffer the sort of irreparable injury necessary to justify a permanent injunction. Instead, say the restaurant owners, the plaintiffs' evidence is mere bluster, insufficient to make out a claim of copyright infringement under *Sony Corp. of America v. Universal City Studios, Inc.*, 464 U.S. 417, 104 S.Ct. 774, 78, L.Ed.2d 514 (1984), which they say requires factual evidence of harm.

Copyright law has long held that irreparable injury is presumed when the exclusive rights of the holder are infringed. The only limitation *Sony* placed on that principle was to require that if the unauthorized use of copyright material is for a noncommercial purpose, the likelihood of future harm must be demonstrated. However, if the intended use is for commercial gain, that likelihood may be presumed. The record in this case clearly shows that defendants did far better business on those days when they exhibited the blacked-out Cardinals' games, and the district court so found. Any claim that *Sony* changes the standard of proof required under these circumstances is simply incorrect.

Although the district court recognized this presumption of irreparable harm, it also stated that more persons attend the games if a televised showing is not available than if it is, noting that a full stadium translates into greater ticket sales and a more exciting—and therefore more marketable—television entertainment program. This finding is not clearly erroneous.

Defendants' second and most considerable argument is that their display of plaintiffs' blacked-out games falls into the category of non-infringing acts under § 110(5) of the Copyright Act. Under that provision, no copyright liability can be imposed for communication of a transmission embodying a performance by the public reception of the transmission on a single receiving apparatus of a kind commonly used in private homes. The district court rejected this argument, finding that satellite dish antennae, which in the United States are outnumbered by television sets by more than 100-to-1, were outside the statutory exemption.

According to the defendants, this ruling ignores their theory that how the signal was captured by the antenna outside the premises is irrelevant. Instead, they argue, the key to § 110(5) is whether an alleged infringer uses commercial equipment to enhance the sound or visual quality of the performance as it is perceived inside the premises. This interpretation ignores both the plain language of the statute and its obvious intent.

The home-use exemption was included in the 1976 Copyright Act specifically in response to the Supreme Court's decision in *Twentieth Century Music Corp. v. Aiken*, 422 U.S. 151, 95 S.Ct. 2040, 45 L.Ed.2d 84 (1975). Aiken held that the owner of a small fried-chicken restaurant was not performing copyright works when he played a conventional radio through four in-the-ceiling speakers for the benefit of customers and employees. According to the legislative history of the 1976 Act, an act such as Aiken's would be considered a performance; to decide whether an infringement had occurred, the critical question instead would be the type of equipment used by the putative infringer.

Common sense alone says that it does not matter how well speakers amplify a performance if a receiver cannot pick up the signal in the first place. Moreover, both the legislative history and the plain language of the statute—which speaks of a receiving set—contemplate that how the signal is captured will be as much at issue under the exemption as how good the captured signal sounds or looks. There is no indication that the portion of a system that receives should be considered separately from that which displays.

The factors listed in the legislative history do speak of the size of the area where the transmission will be played and the extent to which the receiving apparatus is altered for the purpose of improving the aural or visual quality of the performance. And it is true, as defendants argue, that most of the cases involving the § 110(5) exemption deal with the enhancement factor. The reason, however, is that these cases have to do not with interception of blacked-out television programming, where the difficulty is in intercepting a signal, but with the playing of music for which no royalties have been paid. In this sort of case, the question as a practical matter is whether the defendant establishment is of the size and kind that Congress would expect to obtain a license through a subscription music service.

In the present case, however, the NFL and Cardinals are not saying the bar owners can display their programs if a license fee is paid; these plaintiffs intend that their work not be performed at all outside their aegis, making the fact of reception rather than just its quality the primary consideration. The question in this instance, therefore, is how likely the average patron who watches a blacked-out Cardinals game at one of the defendant restaurants is to have the ability to watch the same game at home? If it is likely—that is, if such systems are the kind commonly used in private homes—then the § 110(5) exemption applies.

Given these facts, the court's finding that satellite dishes are not commonly found in private homes is not clearly erroneous. There was testimony that the number of such receivers has been growing rapidly, and while some day these antennae may be commonplace, they are not now.

The Copyright Act protects original works of authorship fixed in any tangible medium, including motion pictures and other audiovisual works. As for live broadcasts, such as the football games at issue here, the Act states that a work consisting of sounds, images, or both, that are being transmitted, is fixed if a fixation of the work is being made simultaneously with its transmission; to transmit is defined as to communicate by any device or process whereby images or sounds are received beyond the place from which they are sent. The defendants claim that no infringement took place because they intercepted the clean feed, and it was the dirty feed that was fixed under the Act and for which the plaintiffs sought copyright protection. In making the argument that the clean and dirty feeds represent separate works, defendants depend on the quoted definitions, as well as a third provision of § 101 that states that each draft version of a work prepared over a period of time constitutes a separate work. The district court rejected this theory on two grounds. Not only could the argument rule out any protection for live broadcasting by satellite transmission but, the court said, it also ignored the fact that the game, and not the inserted commercials and station breaks, constituted the work of authorship.

We agree. Plaintiffs testified copyright protection was obtained for the game, the game action . . . the noncommercial elements of the game. More important, the legislative history demonstrates a clear intent on the part of Congress to resolve, through the definition of fixation, the status of live broadcasts, using—coincidentally but not insignificantly—the example of a live football game. We have already discussed the near-instantaneous nature of the picture's journey from stadium to viewer; Congress surely was aware that the images and sounds from a live broadcast do not go directly from camera or microphone to a home television or radio. To hold that this transmission process nevertheless represents the performance of separate works would gut the plain purpose of the fixation definition, as well as distort the concept of a work prepared over a period of time.

Defendants' final argument is that, under § 411(b) of the Copyright Act, the district court could not issue a permanent injunction regarding works not yet in existence. This provision allows the copyright owner of a live broadcast to institute an action either before or after fixation only if the alleged infringer has received notice between 10 and 30 days before the broadcast. By its terms, say defendants, this eliminates the possibility of permanent injunctive relief in the present case.

We disagree, and hold that permanent injunctive relief was an appropriate remedy in this situation. Defendants' argument reads § 411(b) in a vacuum, ignoring the general grant of remedial authority in § 502(a) of the Copyright Act, which permits a court to grant temporary and final injunctions on such terms as it may deem reasonable to prevent or restrain infringement of a copyright.

The other two defendants, however, Jerrald Guttmann and Frank & Frank, Inc., have not violated the Copyright Act. Nor has Frank & Frank, owner of Sandrina's bar and restaurant, done anything that even arguably violates the Communications Act, so far as we can tell. Customers watched the games as

broadcast by the CBS affiliate in Cape Girardeau, Missouri, which is more than 75 miles from Busch Stadium. There was evidence that on December 9, 1984, approximately 45 persons watching the game upstairs in Sandrina's did view a signal captured by satellite dish, but the district court made no finding to that effect, apparently not crediting this evidence. Plaintiffs concede that on the previous occasion, when Sandrina's picked up a game from Cape Girardeau, it did not infringe a copyright or violate the Communications Act. We therefore see no basis for permanent injunctive relief against Sandrina's, at least in the absence of further findings by the district court, and the injunctive relief granted with respect to this defendant will be vacated.

The situation as to Guttmann's is somewhat different. There, a signal was received by satellite dish, but because only four people, including Guttmann and three friends, watched the game, no public performance in violation of the Copyright Act took place. The legal possibility remains open that this incident did involve a violation of the Communications Act. The key question is whether such an interception of the clean feed, on its way from St. Louis to Long Island by way of the satellite, was an unauthorized interception in violation of the Communications Act. We believe the special facts of the present case make it inappropriate for a court of equity to reach this issue. Guttmann's, as we have already noted, does not have a Sunday liquor license and is not open for business on Sundays, the day when most NFL games are played. It is conceivable that the owner and a few friends may gather again on an occasional Sunday and use the satellite dish, but even if they do so, no injury will result to plaintiffs different from the arguable injury they sustain from the few satellite dishes installed at private homes. This sort of injury has never been the focus of the present lawsuit, and there is no evidence that, standing alone, it would work a sufficient irreparable harm to justify injunctive relief. We therefore hold that it was not appropriate to enter permanent injunctive relief against Guttmann's, and the district court's order will be vacated in respect of this defendant as well.

 For an extended version of the case and review questions to test your understanding of the material, please go to www.HumanKinetics.com/CaseStudiesInSportLaw.

San Francisco Arts & Athletics, Inc. v. United States Olympic Committee

483 U.S. 522 (1987)

In this case, we consider the scope and constitutionality of a provision of the Amateur Sports Act of 1978, 36 U.S.C. §§ 371-396, that authorizes the United States Olympic Committee to prohibit certain commercial and promotional uses of the word "Olympic."

Petitioner San Francisco Arts & Athletics, Inc. (SFAA), is a nonprofit California corporation. The SFAA originally sought to incorporate under the name "Golden Gate Olympic Association," but was told by the California Department of Corporations that the word "Olympic" could not appear in a corporate title. After its incorporation in 1981, the SFAA nevertheless began to promote the Gay Olympic Games, using those words on its letterheads and mailings and in local newspapers.

Section 110 of the Amateur Sports Act (Act), 92 Stat. 3048, 36 U.S.C. § 380, grants respondent United States Olympic Committee (USOC) the right to prohibit certain commercial and promotional uses of the word "Olympic" and various Olympic symbols. In late December 1981, the executive director of the USOC wrote to the SFAA, informing it of the existence of the Amateur Sports Act, and requesting that the SFAA immediately terminate use of the word "Olympic" in its description of the planned games. The SFAA at first agreed to substitute the word "Athletic" for the word "Olympic," but, one month later, resumed use of the term. The USOC became aware that the SFAA was still advertising its games as Olympic through a newspaper article in May 1982. In August, the USOC brought suit in the Federal District Court for the Northern District of California to enjoin the SFAA's use of the word "Olympic." The district court granted a temporary restraining order and then a preliminary injunction. The Court of Appeals for the Ninth Circuit affirmed. After further proceedings, the district court granted the USOC summary judgment and a permanent injunction.

The court of appeals affirmed the judgment of the district court. It found that the Act granted the USOC exclusive use of the word "Olympic" without requiring the USOC to prove that the unauthorized use was confusing and without regard to the defenses available to an entity sued for a trademark violation under the Lanham Act, 60 Stat.427, as amended, 15 U.S.C. §§ 1051 *et seq.* The court also found that the USOC's property right in the word Olympic and its associated symbols and slogans can be protected without violating the First Amendment. We granted *certiorari*, to review the issues of statutory and constitutional interpretation decided by the court of appeals. We now affirm.

The SFAA contends that the court of appeals erred in interpreting the Act as granting the USOC anything more than a normal trademark in the word "Olympic." The starting point in every case involving construction of a statute is the language itself. Section 110 of the Act provides:

> Without the consent of the USOC, any person who uses, for the purpose of trade, to induce the sale of any goods or services, or to promote any theatrical exhibition, athletic performance, or competition, the words "Olympic," "Olympiad," "Citius Altius Fortius," or any combination or simulation thereof tending to cause confusion, to cause mistake, to deceive, or to falsely suggest a connection with the USOC or any Olympic activity shall be subject to suit in a civil action by the USOC for the remedies provided in the Lanham Act. 36 U.S.C. § 380(a).

This legislative history demonstrates that Congress intended to provide the USOC with exclusive control of the use of the word "Olympic" without regard to whether an unauthorized use of the word tends to cause confusion. The SFAA further argues that the reference in § 110 to Lanham Act remedies should be read as incorporating the traditional trademark defenses as well. This argument ignores the clear language of the section. Also, this shorthand reference to remedies replaced an earlier draft's specific list of remedies typically available for trademark infringement (e.g., injunctive relief, recovery of profits, damages, costs, and attorney's fees). This list contained no reference to trademark defenses. Moreover, the USOC already held a trademark in the word "Olympic." Under the SFAA's interpretation, the Act would be largely superfluous. In sum, the language and legislative history of § 110 indicate clearly that Congress intended to grant the USOC exclusive use of the word "Olympic" without regard to whether use of the word tends to cause confusion, and that § 110 does not incorporate defenses available under the Lanham Act.

This court has recognized that "national protection of trademarks is desirable because . . . trademarks foster competition and the maintenance of quality by securing to the producer the benefits of good reputation." In the Lanham Act, 15 U.S.C. §§ 1051 *et seq.*, Congress established a system for protecting such trademarks. Section 45 of the Lanham Act defines a trademark "as any word, name, symbol, or device or any combination thereof adopted and used by a manufacturer or merchant to identify and distinguish his goods, including a unique product, from those manufactured or sold by others." Under § 32 of the Lanham Act, the owner of a trademark is protected from unauthorized uses that are "likely to cause confusion, or to cause mistake, or to deceive." Section 33 of the Lanham Act grants several statutory defenses to an alleged trademark infringer.

The protection granted to the USOC's use of the Olympic words and symbols differs from the normal trademark protection in two respects: the USOC need not prove that a contested use is likely to cause confusion, and an unauthorized user of the word does not have available the normal statutory defenses. The SFAA argues, in effect, that the differences between the Lanham Act and § 110 are of constitutional dimension. First, the SFAA contends that the word "Olympic" is a generic word that could not gain trademark protection under the Lanham Act. The SFAA argues that this prohibition is constitutionally required and thus that the First Amendment prohibits Congress from granting a trademark in the word "Olympic." Second, the SFAA argues that the First Amendment prohibits Congress from granting exclusive use of a word absent a requirement that the authorized user prove that an unauthorized use is likely to cause confusion. This court has recognized that words are not always fungible, and that the suppres-

sion of particular words runs a substantial risk of suppressing ideas in the process. The SFAA argues that this principle prohibits Congress from granting the USOC exclusive control of uses of the word "Olympic," a word that the SFAA views as generic. Yet this recognition always has been balanced against the principle that when a word acquires value as the result of organization and the expenditure of labor, skill, and money by an entity, that entity constitutionally may obtain a limited property right in the word.

There is no need in this case to decide whether Congress ever could grant a private entity exclusive use of a generic word. Congress reasonably could conclude that the commercial and promotional value of the word "Olympic" was the product of the USOC's "own talents and energy, the end result of much time, effort, and expense." The USOC, together with respondent International Olympic Committee (IOC), have used the word "Olympic" at least since 1896, when the modern Olympic Games began. Baron Pierre de Coubertin of France, acting pursuant to a government commission, then proposed the revival of the ancient Olympic Games to promote international understanding. De Coubertin sought to identify the "spirit" of the ancient Olympic Games that had been corrupted by the influence of money and politics. De Coubertin thus formed the IOC, that has established elaborate rules and procedures for the conduct of the modern Olympics. In addition, these rules direct every national committee to protect the use of the Olympic flag, symbol, flame, and motto from unauthorized use. Under the IOC Charter, the USOC is the national Olympic committee for the United States with the sole authority to represent the United States at the Olympic Games. Pursuant to this authority, the USOC has used the Olympic words and symbols extensively in this country to fulfill its object under the Olympic Charter of ensuring the development and safeguarding of the Olympic movement and sport.

The history of the origins and associations of the word "Olympic" demonstrates the meritlessness of the SFAA's contention that Congress simply plucked a generic word out of the English vocabulary and granted its exclusive use to the USOC. Congress reasonably could find that since 1896, the word "Olympic" has acquired what in trademark law is known as a secondary meaning—"it has become distinctive of the USOC's goods in commerce." The right to adopt and use such a word "to distinguish the goods or property of the person whose mark it is, to the exclusion of use by all other persons, has been long recognized." Because Congress reasonably could conclude that the USOC has distinguished the word "Olympic" through its own efforts, Congress' decision to grant the USOC a limited property right in the word "Olympic" falls within the scope of trademark law protections, and thus certainly within constitutional bounds.

Congress also acted reasonably when it concluded that the USOC should not be required to prove that an unauthorized use of the word "Olympic" is likely to confuse the public. To the extent that § 110 applies to uses "for the purpose of trade or to induce the sale of any goods or services," its application is to commercial speech. Commercial speech "receives a limited form of First Amendment protection." Section 110 also allows the USOC to prohibit the use of "Olympic" for promotion of theatrical and athletic events. Although many of these promotional uses will be commercial speech, some uses may go beyond the "strictly business" context. In this case, the SFAA claims that its use of the word "Olympic" was intended to convey a political statement about the status of homosexuals in society. Thus, the SFAA claims that in this case § 110 suppresses political speech.

By prohibiting the use of one word for particular purposes, neither Congress nor the USOC has prohibited the SFAA from conveying its message. The SFAA held its athletic event in its planned format under the names "Gay Games I" and "Gay Games II" in 1982 and 1986, respectively. Nor is it clear that § 110 restricts purely expressive uses of the word "Olympic." Section 110 restricts only the manner in which the SFAA may convey its message. The restrictions on expressive speech properly are characterized as incidental to the primary congressional purpose of encouraging and rewarding the USOC's activities. The appropriate inquiry is thus whether the incidental restrictions on First Amendment freedoms are greater than necessary to further a substantial governmental interest.

One reason for Congress to grant the USOC exclusive control of the word "Olympic," as with other trademarks, is to ensure that the USOC receives the benefit of its own efforts so that the USOC will have an incentive to continue to produce a "quality product," that, in turn, benefits the public. But in the special circumstance of the USOC, Congress has a broader public interest in promoting, through the activities of the USOC, the participation of amateur athletes from the United States in the great four-yearly sport festival, the Olympic Games. The USOC's goal under the Olympic Charter, Rule 24(B), is to further the Olympic movement, that has as its aims: "to promote the development of those physical and moral qualities which are the basis of sport"; "to educate young people through sport in a spirit of better understanding between each other and of friendship, thereby helping to build a better and more peaceful world"; and "to spread the Olympic principles throughout the world, thereby creating international goodwill." Congress' interests in promoting the USOC's activities include these purposes as well as those specifically enumerated in the USOC's charter. Section 110 directly advances these governmental interests by supplying the USOC with the means to raise money to support the Olympics and encourages the USOC's activities by ensuring that it will receive the benefits of its efforts.

The restrictions of § 110 are not broader than Congress reasonably could have determined to be necessary to further these interests. Section 110 primarily applies to all uses of the word "Olympic" to induce the sale of goods or services. Although the Lanham Act protects only against confusing uses, Congress' judgment respecting a certain word is not so limited. Congress reasonably could conclude that most commercial uses of the Olympic words and symbols are likely to be confusing. It also could determine that unauthorized uses, even if not confusing, nevertheless may harm the USOC by lessening the distinctiveness and thus the commercial value of the marks.

In this case, the SFAA sought to sell T-shirts, buttons, bumper stickers, and other items, all emblazoned with the title "Gay Olympic Games." The possibility for confusion as to sponsorship is obvious. Moreover, it is clear that the SFAA sought to exploit the "commercial magnetism," of the word given value by the USOC. There is no question that this unauthorized use could undercut the USOC's efforts to use, and sell the right to use, the word in the future, since much of the word's value comes from its limited use. Such an adverse effect on the USOC's activities is directly contrary to Congress' interest. Even though this protection may exceed the traditional rights of a trademark owner in certain circumstances, the application of the Act to this commercial speech is not broader than necessary to protect the legitimate congressional interest and therefore does not violate the First Amendment.

Section 110 also extends to promotional uses of the word "Olympic," even if the promotion is not to induce the sale of goods. Under § 110, the USOC may prohibit purely promotional uses of the word only when the promotion relates to an athletic or theatrical event. The USOC created the value of the word by using it in connection with an athletic event. Congress reasonably could find that use of the word by other entities to promote an athletic event would directly impinge on the USOC's legitimate right of exclusive use. The SFAA's proposed use of the word is an excellent example. The "Gay Olympic Games" were to take place over a nine-day period and were to be held in different locations around the world. They were to include a torch relay, a parade with uniformed athletes of both sexes divided by city, an "Olympic anthem" and "Olympic Committee," and the award of gold, silver, and bronze medals, and were advertised under a logo of three overlapping rings. All of these features directly parallel the modern-day Olympics, not the Olympic Games that occurred in ancient Greece. The image the SFAA sought to invoke was exactly the image carefully cultivated by the USOC. The SFAA's expressive use of the word cannot be divorced from the value the USOC's efforts have given to it. The mere fact that the SFAA claims an expressive, as opposed to a purely commercial, purpose does not give it a First Amendment right to "appropriat[e] to itself the harvest of those who have sown." The USOC's right to prohibit use of the word "Olympic" in the promotion of athletic events is at the core of its legitimate property right.

The SFAA argues that even if the exclusive use granted by § 110 does not violate the First Amend-

ment, the USOC's enforcement of that right is discriminatory in violation of the Fifth Amendment. The fundamental inquiry is whether the USOC is a governmental actor to whom the prohibitions of the Constitution apply. The USOC is a "private corporatio[n] established under Federal law." In the Act, Congress granted the USOC a corporate charter, § 371, imposed certain requirements on the USOC, and provided for some USOC funding through exclusive use of the Olympic words and symbols, § 380, and through direct grants.

The fact that Congress granted it a corporate charter does not render the USOC a government agent. All corporations act under charters granted by a government, usually by a State. They do not thereby lose their essentially private character. Even extensive regulation by the government does not transform the actions of the regulated entity into those of the government. Nor is the fact that Congress has granted the USOC exclusive use of the word "Olympic" dispositive. All enforceable rights in trademarks are created by some governmental act, usually pursuant to a statute or the common law. The actions of the trademark owners nevertheless remain private. Moreover, the intent on the part of Congress to help the USOC obtain funding does not change the analysis. The government may subsidize private entities without assuming constitutional responsibility for their actions.

This court also has found action to be governmental action when the challenged entity performs functions that have been traditionally the exclusive prerogative of the federal government. Certainly the activities performed by the USOC serve a national interest, as its objects and purposes of incorporation indicate. The fact that a private entity performs a function that serves the public does not make its acts governmental action. The Amateur Sports Act was enacted "to correct the disorganization and the serious factional disputes that seemed to plague amateur sports in the United States." The Act merely authorized the USOC to coordinate activities that always have been performed by private entities. Neither the conduct nor the coordination of amateur sports has been a traditional governmental function.

Most fundamentally, this court has held that a government "normally can be held responsible for a private decision only when it has exercised coercive power or has provided such significant encouragement, either overt or covert, that the choice must in law be deemed to be that of the [government]." The USOC's choice of how to enforce its exclusive right to use the word "Olympic" simply is not a governmental decision. There is no evidence that the federal government coerced or encouraged the USOC in the exercise of its right. At most, the federal government, by failing to supervise the USOC's use of its rights, can be said to "exercise [m]ere approval of or acquiescence in the initiatives" of the USOC. This is not enough to make the USOC's actions those of the government. Because the USOC is not a governmental actor, the SFAA's claim that the USOC has enforced its rights in a discriminatory manner must fail.

 For an extended version of the case and review questions to test your understanding of the material, please go to www.HumanKinetics.com/CaseStudiesInSportLaw.

University of Pittsburgh v. Champion Products, Inc.

566 F.Supp. 711 (W.D. Pa. 1983)

This case is before us on remand from the United States Court of Appeals for the Third Circuit. The Court of Appeals reversed only to the extent that it held that Pitt's claim for prospective injunctive relief was not barred by laches. The court of appeals remanded the case for disposition of all the remaining issues. The court of appeals specifically affirmed our findings of historical facts.

We now specifically reaffirm our original Findings of Fact 1-37 made January 7, 1982. Findings of Fact 5-6 and 36-37 will require further explanation because of the additional issues present on remand.

We find, as a matter of fact, that there is no likelihood of confusion, whether of source, origin, sponsorship, endorsement, or any other nature, between the soft goods of defendant, Champion Products, Inc. (Champion), emblazoned with Pitt insignia, and with the plaintiff, Pitt. This finding rests on, *inter alia*, the following facts: (1) Champion's long-standing sales of the Pittsburgh insignia soft goods in commerce without any instances of actual confusion; (2) the total absence of any other probative evidence of consumer attitudes or reactions; (3) Champion's efforts to indicate the actual source, origin, sponsor, and endorser (i.e., Champion) of the Pitt insignia soft goods at issue; (4) the lack of any evidence that Champion has ever done anything to indicate or represent that the Pitt insignia on its soft goods amounted to an indicator of source, origin, sponsorship, or endorsement; and (5) the fact that there was no historical custom or practice in the soft goods industry treating the school, college, or university insignia prominently emblazoned on the outside of soft goods as an indicator of source, origin, sponsorship, or endorsement.

From in or about 1936 to the present, Champion's sales were continuous and substantial, with two minor exceptions, Champion has sold soft goods bearing Pitt insignia in each year since 1946 to entities not affiliated with Pitt. From about 1936 to 1960, Champion sold its soft goods bearing the Pitt insignia to the main university bookstore located on the Pitt campus. During that same period of time, Champion sold Pitt insignia software continuously to others not affiliated with Pitt.

Despite these 47 years of continuous and substantial sales, Pitt has failed to provide a convincing instance of actual confusion involving these goods (i.e., an instance in which a consumer has purchased or attempted to purchase Champion Pitt insignia soft goods in the erroneous belief that Pitt was the source, origin, sponsor, or endorser thereof).

Pitt pointed to only two incidents of supposed consumer confusion. Indeed, assuming that both of these alleged incidents did amount to consumer confusion, such instances of confusion would be so infrequent as to create a presumption against likelihood of confusion in the future.

Pitt has not introduced any poll, survey, or study, or any other evidence, probative of consumer attitudes or reaction to Pitt-insignia soft goods.

Champion's labels and packaging clearly identify Champion as the source and origin of the goods. Champion's trademarks are well-known and the goodwill connected therewith has been built up over the years of Champion's existence. For many years Champion's marketing of soft goods containing insignia or other identification of colleges or universities has been presented as a total line. Champion has built up substantial goodwill in the business of selling soft goods bearing college or university insignia. Champion has a sales force of between 100 and 125 salesmen who serve more than 10,000 accounts. Champion's products all conspicuously bear the Champion label on the neck.

For the reasons stated in our previous Findings 28-31, we find that Champion has made reasonable efforts to indicate that the true source, origin, sponsor, and endorser of Champion's Pitt-insignia soft goods is Champion.

Champion has for many years sold its product with the Pitt insignia through the Pitt bookstore (except for the period 1960-1970). Champion has marketed its goods with the Pitt insignia openly and notoriously in the Pittsburgh area, and there is no evidence of intent to confuse the public as to source or origin. Champion has marketed its goods at trade shows sponsored by the National Association of College Stores, which the Director of Pitt's bookstore attended.

For the reasons stated in our previous Findings 32-35, we find that Champion has never done anything to indicate that the Pitt insignia emblazoned on Champion's Pitt-insignia soft goods constituted an indication of source, origin, sponsorship, or endorsement.

From about 1936 to 1960, Champion sold its soft goods bearing the Pitt insignia to the main university bookstore located on the Pitt campus. During that same period of time, Champion sold Pitt insignia software continuously to others not affiliated with Pitt. Sam Friedland, a salesman for Champion, sold soft goods in the Pittsburgh area from about 1936 until his retirement in 1968.

Prior to or about 1946, while still selling to the on-campus bookstore and to others, Champion began selling soft goods bearing the Pitt insignia

to the Shea Sporting Goods (Shea), a retail store that is located close to the Pitt campus but is not affiliated with Pitt. Shea, in turn, marketed these goods to the general public. In or about 1960, Pitt representatives told Mr. Friedland that soft goods, including Champion's products, would no longer be sold in the campus bookstore. Rather, the bookstore was restricting its sales to products directly tied to Pitt's educational program. This policy continued at least until 1970. Pitt now sells to the order of individual customers T-shirts that are decorated through the application of heat transfers.

Relying on Pitt's cessation of the sale of soft goods at the bookstore in 1960, Champion through Mr. Friedland, increased its efforts to find, and was successful in finding, new retailers, not affiliated with Pitt, in the Pittsburgh metropolitan area.

Based on the foregoing evidence, we find that there never has been any significant period of time during which the university was the sole or exclusive source for Pitt-insignia soft goods.

There was evidence in the record that the historical custom and practice regarding soft goods bearing the insignia of other schools, colleges, or universities was similar to that present in the instant case. That is, as a matter of custom or practice, the schools, colleges, or universities were not the sole or exclusive source of soft goods bearing their insignia. We have noted, there is no proof that any consumers erroneously believe that Pitt was either the source, origin, sponsor, or endorser of Champion's Pitt-insignia soft goods. There is utterly no evidence in the record that any consumers attached any importance to the question whether Pitt was the source, origin, sponsor, or endorser of such soft goods. The burden of proof of likelihood of confusion is on Pitt, the plaintiff, as an element of its case.

The Pitt insignia, as used by Champion prominently emblazoned on soft goods, are functional. These insignia perform the function of allowing the wearer to express identity, affiliation, or allegiance to Pitt. This functional feature is an essential feature of the product. The product could not perform this function unless it bore the Pitt insignia. The Pitt insignia prominently emblazoned on the Champion Pitt-insignia soft goods is therefore essential to the use or purpose of the articles.

The Pitt insignia emblazoned on the front of soft goods do not indicate to the consumer at the time of purchase that Pitt is the source, origin, or sponsor of the soft goods.

Based on our previous Findings 28-31, we find that Champion has taken reasonable steps to designate itself as the true source, origin, sponsor, and endorser of its Pitt-insignia soft goods. Pitt-insignia as used by Champion on its soft goods are prominent features of each item so as to be visible to others when worn, allowing the wearers publicly to express their allegiance to Pitt.

There is no evidence that Champion has ever designated its Pitt-insignia merchandise as official or otherwise affirmatively indicated sponsorship by Pitt. Pitt was unable to show any likelihood of customer confusion about the origin, sponsorship, or endorsement of Champion's soft goods, or that it had ever received any complaints about Champion's soft goods.

The evidence suggested that other merchants sold unlicensed Pitt-insignia goods, implying that consumers did not ordinarily purchase soft goods from only official sources.

As noted below, we believe that as a matter of law the burden of proving functionality—or more properly, nonfunctionality—is on Pitt, as plaintiff, seeking to establish the existence of an enforceable trademark.

Because the evidence is essentially uncontradicted, we would reach the same findings of ultimate fact on the issue of functionality even if the burden were shifted to Champion as defendant.

Although there may be some evidence in the record that would tend to suggest that the Pitt insignia have taken on a secondary meaning for the provision of educational and athletic services, there is simply no evidence that the Pitt insignia ever have had a secondary meaning for soft goods.

While we did find that Pitt had used goods bearing the Pitt insignia prior to 1936, there is no evidence that Pitt either sold such goods or otherwise introduced them into commerce prior to 1936.

The plaintiff's claims in this suit have four sources: common law trademark infringement, common law unfair competition, the Pennsylvania Trademark Act, 73 Pa.Stat.Ann. § 23 (Purdon's) (repealed in 1982 and replaced by similar language at 54 Pa.C.S.A. § 1123), and § 43(a) of the Lanham Act, 15 U.S.C. § 1125(a).

On all of its claims, Pitt, as plaintiff, bears the burden of proving four elements essential to a successful unfair competition case: (a) likelihood of confusion, (b) nonfunctionality, (c) secondary meaning, and (d) prior use, by a fair preponderance of the evidence. All four elements present questions of fact for us to resolve. Because we have found that Pitt has failed to meet its burden of proving any of these elements, we conclude that Pitt's complaint must fail. Since each of these four elements is essential to Pitt's claim, the failure of Pitt to prevail on any one of these four elements would be adequate to support our ultimate judgment.

Likelihood of confusion on the part of the consuming public is the case issue in any trademark infringement case. Proof of this element is the *sine qua non* of any such case. Throughout the nation, trademark law seeks not to protect trademarks, but to protect the consuming public from confusion.

Pitt, as plaintiff, bears the burden of proving likelihood of confusion. Pitt has totally failed to meet this burden of proof, or indeed provide any real evidence of likelihood of confusion. Pitt has in contrast failed to make any real showing of likelihood of confusion. Pitt undertook no survey of any sort to demonstrate likelihood of confusion of source, authorization, or sponsorship.

The two supposed incidents of actual confusion demonstrated by Pitt were so vague and infrequent as to imply not only that there is no likelihood of confusion but indeed little chance of any confusion whatever. Pitt has simply failed to provide any evidence from which we could find likelihood of consumer confusion as to source, origin, authorization, or sponsorship. The soft goods products at issue here are clearly marked as made by Champion. They are not advertised, described, or denominated as official or in any way sanctioned by Pitt. There being no likelihood of confusion of any sort, Pitt's claims must fail in their entirety.

Features of a product that are functional are not protected either by the Lanham Act or by state unfair competition law.

The Supreme Court has defined functionality as follows:

> "In general terms, a product feature is functional if it is essential to the use or purpose of the article or if it affects the cost or quality of the article." *Inwood Laboratories,* 102 S.Ct. at 2186 n. 10.

The burden of proof on functionality, or more precisely, the burden of proving nonfunctionality, is on Pitt, as plaintiff.

The question of whether or not a product feature is functional is one that we must decide only after a careful evaluation of all the evidence. Having done so, we conclude that the Pitt insignia as used by Champion are functional characteristics of the soft goods in question. Consequently, Pitt's claims would fail even if the university could show a likelihood of confusion.

By any standard, Champion has made a prominent disclosure of the soft goods' true source. We do not believe, however, that the use of Pitt's name on soft goods has acquired any special significance beyond allowing the garment's wearer to display his or her support for the school and its athletic teams. The insignia on these soft goods thus serve a real, albeit aesthetic, function for the wearer. We do not believe that anyone could seriously argue that the soft goods at issue here are, in any realistic way, in competition with similar, unadorned soft goods. The relevant product market for the consumer in this case is soft goods that allow the consumer to show his or her allegiance to Pitt. There is no evidence that the consumer cares who has made the soft goods or whether they were made under license. Because the Pitt insignia on soft goods serve a functional purpose and largely define a sub market of some size, granting Pitt the relief it seeks would give Pitt a perpetual monopoly over that sub market, precluding any competition in the Pitt insignia soft goods market. We know of no legal theory that would countenance such a result.

In order to make out a trademark claim, Pitt, which is primarily in the business of providing educational services, needed to prove that the Pitt insignia had taken on a secondary meaning in the soft goods market prior to the time when Champion entered that market.

The Supreme Court has observed that:

> To establish secondary meaning, a manufacturer must show that, in the minds of the public, the primary significance of a product feature or term is to identify the source of the product rather than the product itself. *Inwood Laboratories, Inc. v. Ives Laboratories, Inc.*, 102 S.Ct. at 2186 n. 11.

As noted earlier, we have found that the relevant market is the market for soft goods, that Champion entered that market in 1936, and that Pitt has failed to prove that the Pitt insignia had taken on a secondary meaning in the market for soft goods prior to 1936, or, indeed, at any time since.

Our finding of no secondary meaning is closely linked to our earlier finding of no likelihood of confusion. In order to prove secondary meaning, Pitt would have had to show a substantial association in the public's mind between the use of Pitt insignia on soft goods and a sense that Pitt was in some way affiliated with the source of the products. Pitt made no such showing.

As a necessary element for either a trademark infringement or unfair competition claim against Champion, Pitt had to prove not only that it had priority of use of the Pitt insignia as against Champion, but also that it had priority of trademark use in commerce.

We believe that the use of the Pitt insignia on the soft goods in question was strictly ornamental. We have already noted that the Pitt insignia were functional and, indeed, defined a sub market within the larger market for soft goods. We see no inconsistency between our finding of functionality and our finding that the insignia were ornaments. Ornaments may well be functional in certain contexts, they simply may not be afforded trademark protection.

Because we have found as a matter of fact that Pitt was not using its insignia as trademarks for soft goods prior to 1936, when Champion entered the market, Pitt does not have priority over Champion in this market.

Pitt has failed to prove any of the essential elements of its case. It has produced no real evidence of confusion on the part of the buying public. It has essentially conceded the functionality of Champion's use of Pitt insignia by admitting that such products are not really in competition with generic soft goods. Pitt has also failed to produce any evidence that its insignia have taken on a secondary meaning. Finally, in the commercial use of the insignia on soft goods, Champion's use was clearly prior to that of Pitt.

In this case, the Pitt insignia are being used for essentially decorative purposes, with neither the intent to confuse the buying public nor any likelihood of accidentally doing so.

For the foregoing reasons, we will enter judgment in favor of the defendant.

 For an extended version of the case and review questions to test your understanding of the material, please go to www.HumanKinetics.com/CaseStudiesInSportLaw.

6

Products Liability

Products liability falls under the auspices of tort law and involves the responsibility of manufacturers and retailers to provide quality products as well as to compensate buyers, users, and in some cases, bystanders for injuries caused by their products. A key concept of products liability is a theory known as strict liability, which is defined as liability without fault. The concept of strict liability in tort law was founded on the premise that when a manufacturer or retailer presents her goods to the public for sale, she represents the product as suitable for its intended use. The rationale for this extension of liability held that providers of products and services—chiefly manufacturers and corporations—were almost always in a better position than consumers to prevent accidents and to provide insurance for those accidents that could not be prevented. In other words, the main theme of strict liability revolved around placing the loss of an accident where it would be felt the least and could be carried most easily. A manufacturer may have implemented top-rated methods of quality control but would still be held liable if the product that emerged from the manufacturing process was defective.

There are four common causes of action under which products liability claims generally fall: improper design, manufacturing defect, failure to warn, and breach of warranty. Eight cases are presented in this section illustrating the application of these causes of action. The improper design cause of action illustrated by two cases, *Dudley Sports Company v. Schmitt*, and *Everett v. Warren* while *Byrns v. Riddell* illustrates a manufacturing defect. The key to both of these causes of action is to show the defect (whether caused by poor design or manufacturing) makes the product unreasonably dangerous to the user or consumer. The *Pell* and *Rawlings* cases provide classic examples of the failure to warn cause of action. Finally, the *Filler, Hauter,* and *Hemphill* cases illustrate the breach of warranty cause of action, where the manufacturers failed to back up their claims of performance by their products.

Byrns v. Riddell, Inc.

550 P.2d 1065 (Ariz. 1976)

On October 2, 1970, the appellant, Kevin Byrns, received an "on-side" kick while playing football as a member of the Alhambra High School varsity football team. He fell to the ground and was thereafter struck by at least one member of the opposing team. As a result of the injuries received during that play, appellant commenced this action. A trial by jury was held in Maricopa County Superior Court. At the close of appellant's case, the court granted appellee's motion for a directed verdict and denied appellants' motion for a new trial. An appeal was then taken to the court of appeals. We granted the petition for review in this matter. The decision of the court of appeals is vacated.

In their first amended complaint, appellant alleges that the helmet manufactured by appellee, a corporation involved in the manufacture and sale of football helmets nationally, was defective by design and manufacture and by reason of such defects was inherently dangerous to the user. The appellant also charged appellee with the failure to provide a warning of the defects.

Fred Rappleayea, a witness, was produced by appellant in order to prove the existence of a defect in the Riddell TK-2 helmet worn by appellant, Kevin Byrns. Rappleayea stated that the helmet was defective and unreasonably dangerous insofar as it "bottoms out" or transmits the energy of the blow to the head of the wearer without absorbing a sufficient amount of energy within the helmet cushioning system itself.

Testimony by appellant's physicians revealed that the injury to appellant's head consisted of a swelling of the right temporal lobe of the brain. One doctor testified that such an injury would result from a blow in front of the right ear and behind the right eye, or from a blow to the opposite side of the head. Rappleayea testified that the front and back portions of the TK-2 helmet were tested and did not meet a crash helmet standard known as Z90.1, which he felt was applicable to a football helmet when the application was limited to the test's impact standard. Another of appellant's witnesses, Anderson Irving, testified that the TK-2 failed the Z90.1 impact test in terms of energy-absorbing characteristics in the forehead, rear, and temporal areas of the helmet.

Appellee presented evidence relating to the inapplicability of the Z90.1 standard to the testing of football helmets. Gerald Morgan, chairman of the board of the appellee corporation, stated that the Z90.1 standard is inapplicable since the test conditions do not simulate the results of an impact to the human skull. Appellee further established on cross-examination that the top of the TK-2 helmet had not been tested by appellant's experts. Mr. Rappleayea concluded that the top of the helmet was the best place to be hit from the point of view of rating the effectiveness of the suspension system. The relevancy of the focus on the effectiveness of the top of the helmet with respect to its energy-absorbing characteristics was developed by appellee in its analysis of a moving picture film of the game, which includes shots of the accident.

Appellee argued on its motion for a directed verdict that there was no proof of a defect in the TK-2 helmet, nor was there proof that a defect in the helmet caused the injury. Support for these arguments was provided by means of the game film and the testimony of Coach Hakes. Appellee argued that the game film shows a clear top-of-helmet to top-of-helmet impact. Coach Hakes testified that the two players hit "head-to-head." Appellee concludes that since the top of the helmet is not defective and since the film shows a blow to the top of the head, it is clear that the injury was not caused by a defect in the helmet.

The trial court found that the film clearly demonstrated that the impact was not a frontal impact, nor was it at the base, nor was it over the ears. Thus, the court stated reasonable minds could not differ as to the place of impact. In its conclusion, the trial court further held that since the strongest (top) portion of the helmet was not tested, it would be mere speculation on the part of the jury to determine that the top of the helmet was defective. The trial court therefore directed a verdict for appellee.

This court adopted the theory of strict liability set forth in Restatement (Second) of Torts § 402A (1965). In view of the steady growth in this area of the law, coupled with the singularity of the facts in this case, a further review and analysis of the law of strict liability in tort are necessary.

The term "unreasonably dangerous" has been considered by many courts in the jurisdictions that have adopted § 402A. A recent survey of cases that considered the concept of an "unreasonably dangerous" defect states that this concept is especially effective as a means of limiting the strict tort liability doctrine "in cases in which the issue is the nature of the duty of a manufacturer with respect to safe design, or in situations in which injury does not follow as a matter of course from the defect, and in which there are serious questions as to the effect to be given harm producing conduct or misuse on the part of the injured person."

The United States District Court, Eastern District of Pennsylvania, adopted the following test of "unreasonable danger": "whether a reasonable manufacturer would continue to market his product in the same condition as he sold it to the plaintiff with knowledge of the potential dangerous consequences the trial just revealed." The court went on to state: "And in measuring the likelihood of harm one may consider the obviousness of the defect since it is reasonable to assume that the user of an obviously defective product will exercise special care in its operation, and consequently the likelihood of harm diminishes."

Comment (i) Restatement (Second) of Torts § 402A further defines the element of an unreasonably dangerous defect from the viewpoint of the consumer in the following language:

> The article sold must be dangerous to an extent beyond that which would be contemplated by the ordinary consumer who purchases it, with the ordinary knowledge common to the community as to its characteristics. The obviousness of the defect is only one factor to be considered in the determination of whether the defect is unreasonably dangerous.

The court in *Dorsey v. Yoder Co.*, 331 F.Supp.753 (E.D. Pa. 1971), subscribed to the following factor analysis prepared by Dean Wade to determine if a defect is unreasonably dangerous:

> (1) the usefulness and desirability of the product, (2) the availability of other and safer products to meet the same need, (3) the likelihood of injury and its probable seriousness, (4) the obviousness of the danger, (5) common knowledge and normal public expectation of the danger (particularly for established products), (6) the avoidability of injury by care in use of the product (including the effect of instructions or warnings), and (7) the ability to eliminate the danger without seriously impairing the usefulness of the product or making it unduly expensive.

We must add a note of caution at this point. No all-encompassing rule can be stated with respect to the applicability of strict liability in tort to a given set of facts. Each case must be decided on its own merits. The foregoing analysis is offered as an approach to the question of whether a defect is unreasonably dangerous.

The facts in this case as presented by appellant establish the possibility of a defect in the sling design of the TK-2 suspension system. This defect is established by the testimony of Irving and Rappleayea regarding a series of tests conducted by them and measured by a standard known as the Z90.1 impact test. Rappleayea further established the defect based on his experience in testing the TK-2 while employed by appellee. This evidence is sufficient to raise the likelihood that reasonable men may reach different conclusions on the issue of an unreasonably dangerous defect in the sling design of the TK-2 helmet. The "bottoming out" defect might be of a type that a reasonable consumer would not contemplate. There is a question of fact as to the place of impact, with a resulting question of causation in terms of the relationship between the impact and the injury. There is also a question as to the possibility of a substantial change in condition caused by the addition of a facemask manufactured and installed by someone other than appellee.

"(P)laintiff has the burden of proving that the defective condition of the injury producing product was in being at the time it left the hands of the seller. The plaintiffs must be permitted to rely on circumstantial evidence alone." *Reader v. General Motors Corp.*, 483 P.2d 1388, 1393. Plaintiff must also prove the relationship between the defect and the injury. "Thus, if there is . . . (expert) evidence of the possibility of the existence of the causal relationship together with other evidence or circumstances indicating such relationship, the finding that the accident caused the injury will be sustained." *Kennecott Copper Corp. v. McDowell*, 413 P.2d 749, 754. We hold that appellant established the presence of a defect in the helmet at the time it left the hands of the seller to the extent that reasonable minds could reach different conclusions as to that question of fact. Furthermore, we hold that appellant provided sufficient proof that a defect caused appellant's injury. The issue of causation is one of fact for the jury to decide. It was error for the trial court to direct a verdict in favor of appellee. Reversed and remanded for further proceedings not inconsistent with this opinion.

For an extended version of the case and review questions to test your understanding of the material, please go to www.HumanKinetics.com/CaseStudiesInSportLaw.

Dudley Sports Co. v. Schmitt

279 N.E.2d 266 (Ind. App. 2 Dist. 1972)

This is an appeal of a personal injury products liability case (baseball pitching machine) by the defendant-appellant, Dudley Sports Co., Inc. of New York (Dudley), from a jury verdict awarding $35,000 to the plaintiff-appellee, Lawrence Schmitt (Schmitt).

On March 24, 1965, Danville High School (the High School) purchased an automatic baseball pitching machine (the machine), purportedly designed and manufactured by Dudley, from Em-Roe Sporting Goods Company of Indianapolis, Indiana (Em-Roe). Dudley's name, "Dudley Automatic Pitching Machine Dudley Sports Co., Inc.," was affixed to the machine by a metal tag, but the machine was manufactured by Commercial Mechanisms, Inc., of Kansas City, Missouri, under a written agreement by which Dudley was to be the exclusive distributor. However, none of Dudley's advertising material or the metal tag on the machine discloses this arrangement.

The machine consists of a frame and an open extended metal throwing arm. No protective shield guards the throwing arm, which operates in a clockwise cycle, triggered by a large coiled spring at the base of the machine. A ball rack at the top of the machine loads the arm when it is in a horizontal 9 o'clock position. When the arm reaches a 10 o'clock energized position, after receiving a ball, energy is released from the coiled spring and transmitted to the arm by tension on a steel cable running between the coiled spring and the arm, causing the arm to pass through a clockwise pitching cycle at a high rate of speed, coming to rest in a 4 o'clock position. The arm

can then be returned to the 10 o'clock energized position by using the electric motor (located near the base of the machine) to rewind the spring, or by deliberate manual operation of the arm to that position. The only purpose of the electric motor is to automatically rewind the spring, which eliminates the necessity of manually returning the throwing arm to the energized 10 o'clock position. Thus, the machine is still capable of delivering a powerful blow when in the 10 o'clock position even though it is unplugged.

Evidence showed that if the throwing arm is in the 10 o'clock energized position, it can be set off by any slight vibration or a change in atmospheric conditions. If it is between the 4 o'clock rest position and the 10 o'clock dead center (unstable) position, the machine is "stable" and it will not go off spontaneously. The danger of triggering the arm increases as it moves in a counterclockwise position toward 10 o'clock.

On receipt of the machine by the High School, it was uncrated by the vice principal, Glenden Gibbs (Gibbs), and the baseball coach, John Trotter (Trotter). In addition to the machine, the crate also included a parts list, assembly instructions, and a tool to deactivate the coiled spring. The only warning instructions found in the crate was a general warning tag that said: "Warning! Safety First! Read Instructions Before Rotating Machine Either Electrically or Manually! Stay Clear of Throwing Arm at All Times! Don't Remove This Packing Block Until You Fully Understand the Operation of the Arm and the Danger Involved." However, no operating instructions were included in the crate.

Moreover, no information was supplied as to the use of the tool that deactivates the coiled spring (energy source).

The machine was then tested by Gibbs and Trotter for one-half hour. They found that the throwing arm was bent, so minor adjustments were required to improve the accuracy of the machine. Trotter testified that he put the arm in the resting 6 o'clock position and stored the machine, unplugged, behind locked doors in locker room No. 2. However, the two adjoining locker rooms, with inside entrances to locker room No. 2, were not locked from their outside hallway entrance. It would have been possible to enter the unlocked doors of rooms No. 1 or No. 3 to gain access to locker room No. 2.

The next day, Schmitt, who was a student at the High School, was sweeping in locker room No. 2 as he had done several times in the past at the request of the coaching staff. He said that as he approached the front of the machine, he heard a whistling noise and a pop. He could not remember whether his broom touched the machine, but the next thing he knew was that he had been hit in the face by the throwing arm, causing extensive facial injuries. These injuries consisted of deep cuts and lacerations on Schmitt's upper lip, nose, and above his right eyebrow, a partially severed nose, a crushed left sinus cavity, skull bone exposure, and two chipped teeth. Four surgical operations were subsequently required to remedy these facial injuries, leaving Schmitt with permanent facial scars.

Schmitt brought an action against the High School, Em-Roe, and Dudley, alleging negligence in design, manufacturing, and storage of the machine. Schmitt in his Complaint alleged that Dudley was negligent in designing and manufacturing the machine with no protective shield or guard around the arm and in failing to supervise and control its agent, Em-Roe. A verdict of $35,000 was rendered by the jury in favor of Schmitt, and Dudley now appeals.

ISSUE 1. Is a vendor of a product who holds himself out as the manufacturer of that product and labels the product as such, to be held to the same standard of care in the design, manufacture, and sale of that product as the manufacturer?

It is our opinion that a vendor who holds himself out as the manufacturer of a product and labels the product as such must be held to the same standard of care as if he were in fact the manufacturer. This is a question of first impression in Indiana. The discernible emerging trend is that one who labels a product with his own name and represents the product to be his own will be held to the same standard of care as if he had manufactured it. We adopt as the law of Indiana what appears to be the prevailing modern rule and in doing so we look to an abundance of well-reasoned authority, particularly the Restatement of Torts (2d) § 400, which flatly states, "One who puts out as his own product a chattel manufactured by another is subject to the same liability as though he were its manufacturer." Thus, a vendor is liable not only for his own negligence but also for any negligence on the part of the actual manufacturer, even though the vendor could not reasonably discover the defect.

The reason for imposing such liability is not hard to find. When a vendor puts his name exclusively on a product, in no way indicating that it is the product of another, the public is induced to believe that the vendor was the manufacturer of the product. This belief causes the public to rely on the skill of the vendor. When products are held out in this manner, the ultimate purchaser has no available means of ascertaining who is the true manufacturer. By this act of concealment, the vendor vouches for the product and assumes the manufacturer's responsibility as his own.

The mechanism manufactured by Commercial Mechanisms, Inc., of Kansas City, Missouri, bore Dudley's name only, as did advertising material. The caption contained in Dudley's catalog, entered as Plaintiff's Exhibit No. 59, reads "Dudley 'Olympia' Automatic Baseball Pitching Machine." The catalog also includes Dudley's New York address, telephone number, and a discussion of the machine's characteristics but makes no reference to Commercial Mechanisms. The record discloses no revelation on the part of Dudley in the advertising, distribution, and sale of the machine that Commercial Mechanisms, Inc. was the manufacturer.

While Dudley never positively states that it is the manufacturer, no reasonable grounds exist to believe otherwise. The only implication is that Dudley is the manufacturer and therefore should be held to the same standard of care as a manufacturer.

ISSUE 2. Was the evidence sufficient to support the jury's conclusion that Dudley was negligent in the design, manufacture, and sale of the machine?

It is our opinion that the evidence most favorable to Schmitt was sufficient for the jury to conclude that Dudley was negligent in the design, manufacture, and sale of the machine. Schmitt contends that Dudley was negligent for failing to provide a shield around the pitching arm; for failing to provide a lock or catch mechanism on the machine by which the pitching arm could be locked; and for failing to give specific instructions as to the operation of the machine. Dudley replies that a manufacturer is under no duty to design an accident-proof product; that their duty was limited only to the use of reasonable care; that the danger from the lack of a protective shield around the throwing arm was an obvious danger, and therefore no warning was necessary.

While we recognize the validity of the argument that a manufacturer may not be liable for obvious dangers, it is also the law that a manufacturer and vendor are bound to avoid hidden defects or concealed dangers in their products. Their products must not be traps for the unwary.

The lack of a guard around the arm was probably obvious to all potential users of the machine. But the extent of the hazards involved from the lack of a guard was not apparent. The potential risks of harm to the users of this machine lie first in its ability to deliver a swift, crippling blow even though unplugged. Secondly, whether connected or disconnected, if the throwing arm is in the 10 o'clock position, a slight vibration or even a change in atmospheric conditions will trigger the throwing arm. This ability to operate while unplugged as a result of even a slight vibration is a latent danger that could only be discovered through an examination of the machine combined with knowledge of the engineering principles that produce the action of the machine. Such knowledge is not ordinarily possessed by a 16-year-old high school boy who had never seen the machine before.

In spite of these concealed dangers, Dudley asserts that placing a screen around the throwing arm would create a false sense of security, thereby attracting curious persons to place their fingers inside the screen. We are not persuaded by this argument. The utilization of such a protective screen would, in fact, be actual notice of the danger. Those placing their fingers inside the screen would do so at their own risk, as would one who touches the blade of a power saw. Without a screen, however, there is no notice of, or protection from, the inherent dangers of this machine. As a result, the false sense of security is created when there is no screen.

There was reasonable evidence of probative value sufficient to support a conclusion by the jury that this machine is a potentially dangerous mechanism capable of inflicting injury to life or limb to those unaware of its hazards. Dudley was bound to provide a machine reasonably safe for its intended use. Because this machine was recommended for high school use, we think that the jury could reasonably have concluded that it was not safe for use by high school students.

The law requires a supplier of an imminently dangerous chattel to warn all who may come in contact with the chattel of any concealed danger, regardless of privity of contract. Although a manufacturer or vendor is under no duty to warn of apparent dangers, this court has adopted the rule, which held that "in cases dealing with a manufacturer's liability for injuries to remote users, the stress has always been upon the duty of guarding against hidden defects and of giving notice of concealed dangers."

Dudley argues that because a general warning tag was sent to the High School, no liability can be attached to Dudley for Schmitt's injuries. Dudley did include a general warning tag in the shipping crate cautioning the High School to read the operating instructions before using the machine. However, this general warning tag merely conveyed an implication that the machine would only be dangerous when in operation. No warning was given of the latent dangers of this machine. Nothing was mentioned about its triggering capabilities while unplugged. Thus, a more specific warning was required to fulfill Dudley's duty to warn. The specific operating instructions referred to by the general warning tag were not included in the crate. Presumably, these instructions would have informed the purchaser as to the various positions of the throwing arm, the positions that were dangerous, that the machine was capable of being triggered even though unplugged, and that triggering the machine only required a slight vibration or change in atmospheric conditions.

A prying tool to deactivate the coiled spring was included in the crate sent to the High School. This prying tool was evidently the safety feature of this machine. But there was no information on how to use this tool or any indication what it was. The missing operating instructions could also be expected to include the information regarding this tool.

Although a manufacturer may assume that the purchaser will properly use the product and avoid obvious dangers, such reliance is improper if the product contains latent dangers and no notice is given thereof. Because no specific operating instructions were sent to the High School and no warning was given as to the specific latent dangers of the machine, it was reasonably forseeable that a high school student might be the victim of such negligence. Thus, it was reasonable for the jury to find from the evidence before them that Schmitt's injuries were the natural and probable consequence of Dudley's negligence.

There is no vitality in Dudley's argument that the machine was in keeping with modern scientific advancement in the baseball pitching machine industry and that it was an advancement when compared to the other models on the market. The fact that a particular product meets or exceeds the requirements of its industry is not conclusive proof that the product is reasonably safe. In fact, standards set by an entire industry can be found negligently low if they fail to meet the test of reasonableness.

Likewise, the fact that experts testified that the machine was reasonably safe is not conclusive proof that it was in fact a reasonably safe machine. The weight to be given expert testimony is for the jury to decide. They are not bound by an expert's opinion and they may even disregard it if they so desire. The jury could well have found that Dudley violated its duty to notify the High School, and ultimately Schmitt, of the machine's inherent dangers.

Dudley stresses the fact that Trotter testified he stored the pitching machine behind locked doors in locker room No. 2 with the pitching arm in the 6 o'clock resting position. Schmitt and his two friends testified that they did not disturb the pitching arm. Therefore, Dudley concludes that the pitching arm was in the 6 o'clock position when Schmitt was injured, and since the arm cannot be triggered from the 6 o'clock position, Schmitt's theory of the accident is contrary to physical facts and scientific principles. On this basis, Dudley asserts that the jury's decision was contrary to the evidence presented.

This position has a marshmallow-like quality. Dudley overlooks the fact that Trotter also testified he only locked the hallway door to locker room No. 2, while leaving the hallway doors to adjacent locker rooms Nos. 1 and 3, with inside entrances to No. 2, unlocked. Therefore, it was possible for an interloper to enter either locker room No. 1 or No. 3 and use inside entrances to gain access to locker room No. 2. The other weakness of this position is that the credibility of a witness is for the jury to decide. The jury may refuse to believe any testimony, even when it is uncontradicted, so long as such refusal is not arbitrary. Obviously they did not believe Mr. Trotter.

Dudley seeks refuge from liability by resort to the doctrine of intervening cause. If the machine was not secured under lock and key, someone must have taken the arm out of the 6 o'clock position that Trotter stored it in. Therefore, an intervening cause arose relieving Dudley of any liability. Assuming a mysterious stranger tampered with the machine (which there is no evidence to support), Dudley would still be liable for Schmitt's injuries. Where harmful consequences are brought about by intervening and independent forces, the operation of which should have been foreseen, the chain of causation extending from the original wrongful act to the injury is not broken by the intervening and independent force. The original wrongful act will still be treated as the proximate cause of the accident. It could have been foreseen that the High School, bereft of knowledge of the latent dangers involved in this machine, might not store it properly and that such a mechanism could attract the attention of curious individuals, thereby inducing them to tamper with the machine. The chain of causation is not broken in this state of affairs.

In conclusion, we believe that the jury properly found that Dudley was negligent in the design, manufacture, and sale of an imminently dangerous mechanism containing latent defects of which Schmitt had no proper warning. The decision of the trial court is therefore affirmed.

 For an extended version of the case and review questions to test your understanding of the material, please go to www.HumanKinetics.com/CaseStudiesInSportLaw.

Everett v. Bucky Warren, Inc.

380 N.E.2d 653 (Mass. 1978)

In this case the plaintiff seeks damages from the suppliers of a protective helmet he was wearing when, while playing in a hockey game, he was struck in the head by a puck and was seriously injured. The question before us is whether, on the various counts brought under both negligence and strict liability theories, the evidence was sufficient to support the verdicts for the plaintiff.

The controversies in this case revolve around the design of the protective helmet worn by the plaintiff when he was injured. It is described as a three-piece helmet because its protective components are three sections of high-impact plastic lined on the inside with shock foam. One piece covers the back of the head, extending from the nape up about 6 inches, and running horizontally between positions slightly behind each ear; the second piece, approximately 2 inches wide, rings the front of the head from the same positions, thus covering the forehead; and the third piece joins the tops of these two sections and covers the top of the head. This top piece is loosely connected to the other two sections by six strips of leather, each 1-1/2 to 1-3/4 inches in width and 1-1/2 to 2 inches in length. The side pieces are linked by a 3/4 inch wide elastic strap, whose length is adjustable. The result of this three-piece design and loose method of linking the sections is that there are gaps within the helmet where no plastic piece covers. The gap between the top piece and the two side pieces ranges from 1/2 to 3/4 of an inch. The gaps between the two side pieces vary with the size of the wearer's head and the tension with which the elastic straps are adjusted, and range from 0 to 3/4 of an inch. This three-piece design, characterized by the internal gaps, was somewhat unique, and there were available at the time of the plaintiff's injury and for some time prior thereto helmets designed as one-piece units without such gaps.

When the injury occurred the plaintiff was a postgraduate student and a member of the hockey team at the defendant New Preparatory School (New Prep) in Cambridge, Massachusetts. On January 10, 1970, the New Prep team went to Providence, Rhode Island, to play the Brown University freshman team. During the game the plaintiff, a defense man, attempted to block the shot of a Brown player by throwing himself into a horizontal position on the ice, about 10 to 15 feet in front of the shooting player and perpendicular to the intended line of flight of the puck. The puck struck the plaintiff above and slightly back from his right ear, and penetrated into the gap of the helmet formed where the three helmet sections came together. As a result of this penetration the puck hit his head and caused a fracture of the skull. This serious injury subsequently required that a plate be inserted in the plaintiff's skull, and caused the plaintiff to have headaches that will continue indefinitely.

The helmet was being worn by the plaintiff on the night of his injury as a result of its being supplied to him through the following process. The helmet was manufactured by J.E. Pender (Pender), a proprietorship engaged in the manufacture of sporting goods and represented in this action by the defendant George Whittie, executor of the will of James E. Pender. In 1967 through 1969 Pender sold at least 14 helmets of the type worn by the plaintiff to the defendant Bucky Warren, Inc. (Bucky Warren), a retailer in sporting goods, which in turn sold them to New Prep. The helmets had been specially ordered by Owen Hughes, the coach of the New Prep team, who was the person authorized by the school to make such purchases. Each player on the plaintiff's team was supplied with one of these helmets for practice and game use, although Hughes's testimony indicated that, had a player so wished, he could have worn a different helmet of his own choosing. Rather than purchasing his own helmet, the plaintiff chose to wear the one supplied to him by the school authorities.

The plaintiff brought this action claiming that, because of the gaps, the Pender helmet was defectively designed, and that therefore all three defendants, Pender, Bucky Warren, and New Prep, were liable to him in negligence for supplying him the helmet, and that the defendants Pender and Bucky Warren were also liable to him in tort on a strict liability theory. At trial, motions for directed verdicts were denied, and 14 special questions were submitted to the jury. The jury found that all three defendants were negligent, that the helmet was not in a reasonably safe condition when sold by Pender and Bucky Warren, that the plaintiff's injury was caused by the condition of the helmet and the negligence of the defendants, and that the plaintiff himself neither assumed the risk of the injury nor was contributorily negligent. The plaintiff was awarded $85,000 in damages. After proper motions the judge, notwithstanding the jury verdicts, entered judgments in favor of all defendants on the negligence counts, holding that, as matter of law, the plaintiff assumed the risk of his injury. He entered judgment for the plaintiff for $85,000 on the strict liability counts, however, on the ground that assumption of the risk was not a defense to this cause of action. Appeals and cross appeals were claimed, and we granted an application for direct appellate review.

The issues raised here are whether there was sufficient evidence for the jury to find that (a) the defendants Pender and New Prep were negligent, (b) the plaintiff was not negligent and did not assume the risk of his injury, and (c) the helmet was defective and unreasonably dangerous as sold by Pender and Bucky Warren. Additionally, we address certain evidentiary and procedural matters raised by the defendants.

A manufacturer is under a duty to use reasonable care to design a product that is reasonably safe for its intended use. The Pender helmet was designed by James E. Pender, who possessed no engineering background. It was intended to protect the vital areas of the head, the temples and cranium. It was designed in three pieces, however, not for safety reasons, but to facilitate adjustment. Pender indicated in his deposition that the helmet was consciously designed so that there would be gaps between its sections when it was properly adjusted; the larger the head of the wearer, the larger would be the gaps. The jury could reasonably have concluded from the examination of the helmet that Pender knew, or should have known, that a puck could penetrate between the sections

and cause serious injury to the wearer. Pender was aware that other manufacturers were producing helmets of a one-piece design, but he nevertheless failed to make any tests of his own helmet to determine its safety. We hold that this evidence was sufficient to support the answer of the jury that Pender was negligent in the design of the helmet.

We reach a similar conclusion with regard to the defendant New Prep. As stated in its brief, the issue with regard to New Prep is whether "it was bad practice for a hockey coach to supply the (p)laintiff with the helmet in question and (whether) the supplying of said helmet to the (p)laintiff was causally related to his injuries." As to the claim of lack of causation we see no serious question; the jury could clearly have concluded that the presence of the gaps in the helmet was the cause of his injury. The more substantial issue here is whether the jury was warranted in finding that New Prep, through its agent, Coach Owen Hughes, was negligent in supplying the helmet to the plaintiff. As a supplier New Prep was required to exercise reasonable care not to provide a chattel that it knew or had reason to know was dangerous for its intended use. Hughes, as a person with substantial experience in the game of hockey, may be held to a higher standard of care and knowledge than would an average person. Since many of the teams that New Prep played prior to 1970 wore one-piece helmets, the jury could have found that Hughes knew, or should have known, of their availability. He conceded in his testimony that the one-piece helmets were safer than the Pender model since the gaps in the latter would allow for the penetration of a puck. There was sufficient evidence to permit the jury to decide whether, in these circumstances, the supplying of the helmet to the plaintiff was negligent conduct.

Having determined that the jury was warranted in finding negligence on the parts of the defendants, we turn now to a consideration of the defenses of assumption of the risk and contributory negligence. Unlike contributory negligence, assumption of the risk involves a subjective standard, keyed not to the knowledge or understanding of the hypothetical reasonable man, but to what the particular plaintiff in fact sees, knows, understands, and appreciates.

In order to rule that a plaintiff assumed the risk of his injury as matter of law, the facts must be so plain that reasonable men could draw only one inference. The facts here are not so plain. The plaintiff testified that he did not know of any dangers that he was exposed to by wearing the helmet. He believed that it would protect his head from injury. The helmet had been supplied to him by a person with great knowledge and experience in hockey, a person whose judgment the plaintiff had reason to trust, and it was given to him for the purpose implied, if not expressed, of protecting him. On the other hand, the obviousness of the gaps in the helmet would support an inference that he was actually aware of the risks he ran. It was on this basis that on the negligence counts the judge entered judgments for the defendants notwithstanding the verdicts for the plaintiff. But we do not think that these gaps were so large or so obvious as to require the conclusion, as matter of law, that the plaintiff possessed the awareness necessary to support an assumption of the risk defense. Rather it was the function of the jury to balance the obviousness of the helmet design against the plaintiff's testimony and the circumstances in which he received the helmet in order to arrive at a conclusion as to what the plaintiff knew at the time of the injury. That he knew that the game of hockey carries with it certain other risks, such as being hit in his unprotected face, is not relevant to this issue; the question is whether the plaintiff appreciated the risk of the injury that befell him.

The defendant Pender alone argues that this court should rule that the plaintiff was contributorily negligent as matter of law. Pender's brief, however, provides us with little factual or legal support for this claim. We note simply that the question of contributory negligence is rarely to be taken from the jury and decided as matter of law, and we find no exceptional circumstances in this case that would justify such an action.

The plaintiff claims that the three-piece design of the Pender helmet, with the gaps in it, was defective and unreasonably dangerous as defined in the Restatement, and therefore that the manu-facturer and retailer are liable to him. We hold that there was sufficient evidence to reach the jury on this theory. For a product to be in a defective condition it does not have to be the result of errors made during the manufacturing process; it is defective as well "when it is properly made according to an unreasonably dangerous design" and does not meet a consumer's reasonable expectation as to its safety. The focus is on the design itself, not on the manufacturer's conduct. Factors that should be weighed in determining whether a particular product is reasonably safe include "the gravity of the danger posed by the challenged design, the likelihood that such danger would occur, the mechanical feasibility of a safer alternative design, the cost of an improved design, and the adverse consequences to the product and to the consumer that would result from an alternative design." *Back v. Wickes Corp.*, 378 N.E.2d 964, 970. In this case the gravity of the danger posed by the three-piece design was demonstrated by the injuries to the plaintiff. There was substantial evidence that tended to show that helmets of the one-piece design were safer than the Pender model, that these one-piece helmets were in manufacture prior to the plaintiff's injury, and that, while more expensive than the Pender helmets, they were not economically unfeasible. This evidence provided a sufficient basis for the jury's finding that the helmet was "unreasonably dangerous."

The defendants also argue that the plaintiff is barred from recovery on the strict liability counts because he assumed the risk of injury. In view of our holding earlier in this opinion that the jury was warranted in finding that the plaintiff had not assumed the risk, we need not decide whether assumption of the risk would be a defense to a strict liability claim under Rhode Island law.

The judgments on the strict liability counts are affirmed. The judgments on the negligence counts are reversed with instructions that judgments be entered on the verdicts.

 For an extended version of the case and review questions to test your understanding of the material, please go to www.HumanKinetics.com/CaseStudiesInSportLaw.

Filler v. Rayex Corporation

435 F.2d 336 (7th Cir. 1970)

In this diversity action, Michael Filler sued to recover damages for the loss of his right eye, and his mother, Barbara Mitchell, sought to recover her expenses for his hospitalization, artificial eye, and physician's services.

When his injury occurred, Michael Filler was a 16-year-old student at Oak Hill High School, near Marion, Indiana. While he was practicing for a varsity baseball game in the late afternoon of June 10, 1966, fungoes were being lofted to him by a fellow player. Filler lost a fly ball in the sun, although he was wearing flipped-down "baseball sunglasses" manufactured by defendant. After tipping the top of his baseball glove, the ball struck the right side of the sunglasses, shattering the right lens into sharp splinters that pierced his right eye, necessitating its removal nine days later.

Filler's coach was Richard Beck, an experienced ballplayer whose first baseball season at Oak Hill was in 1965. During that season, Beck would not allow his players to use sunglasses, considering them too dangerous. However, before the 1966 season, he read the following advertisement of defendant in *Sporting News*: "PLAY BALL and Flip for Instant Eye Protection with RAYEX Baseball SUNGLASSES Professional FLIP-SPECS." The advertisement also stated: "Scientific lenses protect your eyes with a flip from sun and glare anywhere—baseball, beach, boat, driving, golfing, fishing—just perfect for Active and Spectator Sports—World's finest sunglasses!"

After seeing this material, Beck decided to buy six pairs of defendant's flip-type baseball sunglasses for use by his outfielders and second basemen. Each pair of sunglasses was in a cardboard box labeled "Baseball Sunglasses—Professional Flip-Specs," stating "Simply flip for instant eye protection." The guarantee inside each box provided: "Rayex lenses are guaranteed for life against breakage. If lens breakage occurs mail glasses and 50 cents (Postage Handling Charge) for complete repair service. Rayex Sunglasses are guaranteed to:

1. Eliminate 96% of harmful ultraviolet and infrared rays.

2. Protect your eyes against reflected glare from smooth surfaces, roads, water, snow, etc.

3. Retain clear, undistorted vision."

Except for the flip feature and elastic tape at the rear of the frame, the glasses resembled ordinary sunglasses. The thinness of the lenses was shielded by the frames and therefore not obvious to users. These glasses were stored in the glove compartment of coach Beck's car, and in accordance with the custom of his teammates, Filler removed a pair of the sunglasses from the coach's car and was using them at the time of his injury. Neither Filler, nor Beck, nor indeed even defendant's president knew the lenses would shatter into sharp splinters when hit by a baseball.

After a bench trial, the district judge awarded Filler $101,000 damages and his mother $1,187.75 for her consequential damages. In an unreported memorandum opinion, the district judge supported this result on three independent grounds: implied warranty, strict liability, and negligence. Under any of those theories, privity between the manufacturer and plaintiff is not required by controlling Indiana law. We agree that defendant is liable for breach of an implied warranty of fitness for a particular purpose. Indiana has adopted the implied warranty provision of the Uniform Commercial Code dealing with fitness for a particular purpose:

> Implied Warranty—Fitness for particular purpose. Where the seller at the time of contracting has reason to know any particular purpose for which the goods are required and that the buyer is relying on the seller's skill or judgment to select or furnish suitable goods, there is unless excluded or modified under the next section an implied warranty that the goods shall be fit for such purpose.

These sunglasses were advertised as baseball sunglasses that would give "instant eye protection." Although they were intended for use by baseball fielders, the thickness of the lenses ranged only from 1.2 mm to 1.5 mm, so that shattering into exceedingly sharp splinters would occur on their breaking. Since they lacked the safety features of plastic or shatterproof glass, the sunglasses were in truth not fit for baseball playing, the particular purpose for which they were sold. Therefore, breach of that implied warranty was properly found.

Indiana has adopted the doctrine of strict liability of sellers of products "in a defective condition unreasonably dangerous to the user," as provided in § 402A of the Restatement of Torts Second. Here the thinness of the lenses made them unreasonably dangerous to users, so that the doctrine of strict liability is applicable. However, defendant argues against strict liability, on the ground that the sunglasses were "unavoidably unsafe products" within the exception of Comment k to § 402A. Even assuming *arguendo* that the state of the art is not capable of producing a shatter-resistant or splinter-free baseball sunglass as defendant claims, Comment k furnishes no shelter from liability in this case. The exception applies only when the product is "accompanied by proper warning," which defendant's product lacked.

Finally, we also agree that defendant was liable for negligence. Defendant knew that these glasses shattered readily, for a hundred were returned daily for lens replacements. At least it had constructive knowledge that the impact of a baseball would shatter these lenses into sharp splinters, since it must anticipate the reasonably foreseeable risks of the use of the product. Moreover, despite the obviously physical stresses to which these glasses would be put, inadequate tests were made concerning their physical properties. Accordingly, even if defendant is not liable for negligence in production and sale of a poorly constructed product, it was properly held liable for its negligent failure to warn users of the danger of its product. Judgment is affirmed.

 For an extended version of the case and review questions to test your understanding of the material, please go to www.HumanKinetics.com/CaseStudiesInSportLaw.

Hauter v. Zogarts

534 P.2d 377 (Cal. 1975)

Defendants manufacture and sell the "Golfing Gizmo" (hereinafter Gizmo), a training device designed to aid unskilled golfers to improve their games. Defendants' catalogue states that the Gizmo is a "completely equipped backyard driving range." In 1966, Louise Hauter purchased a Gizmo from the catalogue and gave it to Fred Hauter, her 13-1/2-year-old son, as a Christmas present. The Gizmo is a simple device consisting of two metal pegs, two cords—one elastic, one cotton—and a regulation golf ball. After the pegs are driven into the ground approximately 25 inches apart, the elastic cord is looped over them. The cotton cord, measuring 21 feet in length, ties to the middle of the elastic cord. The ball is attached to the end of the cotton cord. When the cords are extended, the Gizmo resembles the shape of a large letter "T," with the ball resting at the base.

The user stands by the ball in order to hit his practice shots. The instructions state that when

hit correctly, the ball will fly out and spring back near the point of impact; if the ball returns to the left, it indicates a right-hander's "slice"; a shot returning to the right indicates a right-hander's "hook." If the ball is "topped," it does not return and must be retrieved by the player. The label on the shipping carton and the cover of the instruction booklet urge players to "drive the ball with full power" and further state, "COMPLETELY SAFE BALL WILL NOT HIT PLAYER."

On July 14, 1967, Fred Hauter was seriously injured while using defendants' product. Thereafter, plaintiffs filed the instant suit on his behalf, claiming false representation, breach of express and implied warranties, and strict liability in tort. Fred Hauter testified at trial that prior to his injury, he had practiced golf 10 to 20 times at driving ranges and had played several rounds of golf. His father instructed him in the correct use of the Gizmo. Fred had read the printed instructions that accompany the product and had used the

Gizmo about a dozen times. Before the accident, Fred set up the Gizmo in his front yard according to the printed instructions. The area was free of objects that might have caused the ball to ricochet, and no other persons were nearby. Fred then took his normal swing with a seven iron. The last thing he remembers was extreme pain and dizziness. After a period of unconsciousness, he staggered into the house and told his mother that he had been hit on the head by the ball. He suffered brain damage and, in one doctor's opinion, is currently an epileptic.

George Peters, a safety engineer and an expert on the analysis and reconstruction of accidents, testified for plaintiffs. In Peters' opinion, Fred Hauter had hit underneath the ball and had caught the cord with his golf club, thus drawing the cord upwards and toward him on his follow-through. The ball looped over the club producing a "bolo" effect and struck Fred on the left temple. Peters, an expert on the cause of accidents, concluded that the Gizmo is a "major hazard."

Ray Catan, a professional golfer, also testified for plaintiffs. He added that even if the club had hit the lower part of the ball, the same result probably would have occurred. He personally tested the Gizmo, intentionally hitting low shots, and found that his club became entangled in the cord, bringing the ball back toward him as he completed his swing. Describing Fred Hauter as a beginner, Catan stated that since such a golfer's swing usually is very erratic, he rarely hits the ball solidly.

Defendants did not dispute plaintiffs' version of the accident. The manufacturer merely stated that he bought the rights to manufacture and distribute the Gizmo from a former professional golfer in 1962 and that the product had been on the market since that time.

Following a unanimous jury verdict for defendants on each cause of action, the trial judge granted plaintiffs' motion for judgment notwithstanding the verdict and plaintiffs' alternative motion for a new trial. Defendants have limited their appeal to the order granting judgment notwithstanding the verdict.

As a matter of law, plaintiffs should recover on their cause of action for false representation. Plaintiffs' claim of false representation relies on common law tort principles reflected in § 402B of the Restatement Second of Torts. For plaintiffs to recover under this section, defendants' statement "COMPLETELY SAFE BALL WILL NOT HIT PLAYER" must be a misrepresentation of material fact on which plaintiffs justifiably relied. If defendants' assertion of safety is merely a statement of opinion—mere "puffing"—they cannot be held liable for its falsity. Defendant's statement is so broad, however, that it properly falls within the ambit of § 402B. The assertion that the Gizmo is completely safe, that the ball will not hit the player, does not indicate the seller's subjective opinion about the merits of his product but rather factually describes an important characteristic of the product. Courts have consistently held similar promises of safety to be representations of fact.

These decisions evidence the trend toward narrowing the scope of "puffing" and expanding the liability that flows from broad statements of manufacturers as to the quality of their products. Courts have come to construe unqualified statements such as the instant one liberally in favor of injured consumers. Furthermore, the illustrations in the Restatement indicate that the assertion "COMPLETELY SAFE BALL WILL NOT HIT PLAYER" constitutes a factual representation. Moreover, the materiality of defendants' representation can hardly be questioned; anyone learning to play golf naturally searches for a product that enables him to learn safely. Fred Hauter's testimony that he was impressed with the safety of the item demonstrates the importance of defendants' statement. That Fred's injury occurred while he used the Gizmo as instructed proves the inaccuracy of the assertion on the carton.

Defendants, however, maintain that plaintiffs' reliance on the assurance of safety is not justifiable. Alluding to the danger inherent to the sport, defendants argue that the Gizmo is a "completely safe" training device only when the ball is hit squarely. Defendants repeatedly state that an improperly hit golf shot exposes the player, as well as others nearby, to a serious risk of harm; they point to testimony recounting how an experienced player once hit a shot so poorly that the ball flew between his legs. As a result, contend defendants, plaintiffs cannot reasonably expect the Gizmo to be "completely safe" under all circumstances, particularly those in which the player hits beneath the ball.

Defendants' argument does not withstand analysis. Fred Hauter was not "playing golf." He was home on his front lawn learning to play the game with the aid of defendants' supposedly danger-free training device. By practicing in an open, isolated area apart from other golfers and free of objects off which a poorly hit shot could ricochet, Fred Hauter eliminated most of the dangers present during a normal round of play. Moreover, even though certain dangers are inherent in playing golf, the risk that the golfer's own ball will wrap itself around his club and strike the golfer on the follow-through is not among those dangers. Fred Hauter's injury stemmed from a risk inherent in defendants' product, not a risk inherent in the game of golf.

Additionally, defendants' analysis would render their representation of safety illusory. Were we to adopt their analysis, the words "COMPLETELY SAFE BALL WILL NOT HIT PLAYER" would afford protection to consumers only in relatively infrequent instances in which the "duffers" using the Gizmo managed to hit the ball solidly. Yet defendants' instructions supplied with the Gizmo clearly indicate that defendants anticipated the users of their product would "hook," "slice" and "top" the ball. They expected their customers to commit the errors that normally plague beginning golfers. Thus, when they declared their product "completely safe," the only reasonable inference is that the Gizmo was a safe training device for all golfers, regardless of ability and regardless of how squarely they hit the ball.

Although defendants claim they did not intend their statement to cover situations such as the one at bar, subjective intent is irrelevant. The question is not what a seller intended, but what the consumer reasonably believed. The rule "is one of strict liability for physical harm to the consumer, resulting from a misrepresentation of the character or quality of the chattel sold, even though the misrepresentation is an innocent one, and not made fraudulently or negligently." We conclude that Fred Hauter reasonably believed he could use the Gizmo with safety and agree with the trial court that plaintiffs established all the elements of a cause of action for misrepresentation.

Defendants breached their express warranty that the Golfing Gizmo ball was "completely safe" and would "not hit player," as well as their implied warranty of merchantability. As an alternative cause of action, plaintiffs claim that defendants breached both an express warranty and an implied warranty of merchantability. The crucial issue here is not whether defendants created a warranty—as explained below, they clearly did. Rather, the bone of contention is whether they can escape liability by impliedly limiting the scope of their promise.

We first treat the claim for breach of express warranty, which is governed by California Commercial Code § 2313. The key under this section is that the seller's statements—whether fact or opinion—must become "part of the basis of the bargain." The basis of the bargain requirement represents a significant change in the law of warranties. Whereas plaintiffs in the past have had to prove their reliance on specific promises made by the seller . . . , the Uniform Commercial Code requires no such proof. According to Official Comment 3 to the Uniform Commercial Code following § 2313, "no particular reliance . . . need be shown in order to weave (the seller's affirmations of fact) into the fabric of the agreement. Rather, any fact which is to take such affirmations, once made, out of the agreement requires clear affirmative proof."

Fred Hauter's testimony shows that he read and relied on defendants' representation; he was impressed by "something on the cover dealing with the safety of the item." More importantly, defendants presented no evidence that could remove their assurance of safety from the basis of the bargain. The trial court properly concluded, therefore, that defendants expressly warranted the safety of their product and are liable for Fred Hauter's injuries, which resulted from a breach of that warranty.

The trial court also held for plaintiffs on the theory of breach of an implied warranty of merchantability. Unlike express warranties, which are basically contractual in nature, the implied warranty of merchantability arises by operation of law. "Into every mercantile contract of sale the law inserts a warranty that the goods sold are merchantable, the assumption being that the parties themselves, had they thought of it, would specifically have so agreed." Consequently, defendants' liability for an implied warranty does not depend on any specific conduct or promise on their part, but instead turns on whether their product is merchantable under the code.

Merchantability has several meanings, two of which are relevant to the instant case: the product must "(c)onform to the promises or affirmations of fact made on the container or label"..., and must be "fit for the ordinary purposes for which such goods are used." The Gizmo fails in both respects. As already explained, it does not live up to the statement on the carton that it is "COMPLETELY SAFE BALL WILL NOT HIT PLAYER." Furthermore, as explained below, the evidence shows that the Gizmo is not fit for the ordinary purposes for which such goods are normally used.

The Gizmo is designed and marketed for a particular class of golfers—"duffers"—who desire to improve their technique. Such players rarely hit the ball solidly. When they do, testified the golf pro, "it would be sort of a mistake, really." The safety expert classed the Gizmo as a major safety hazard. Furthermore, defendants admit that when a person using the Gizmo hits beneath the ball as Fred Hauter apparently did, he stands a substantial chance of seriously injuring himself. Defendants nevertheless seek to avoid liability by limiting the scope of their warranties. They claim that the box containing the Gizmo and the instructions pertaining to its use clarified that the product was "completely safe" only when its user hit the ball properly. They point to no language expressing such a limitation but instead claim that a drawing in the instructions depicting a golfer "correctly" using their product implies the limitation. As we explained above in discussing the false representation claim, defendants' argument is wholly without merit. Furthermore, they fail to meet the stern requirements of California Uniform Commercial Code § 2315, which governs disclaimer and modification of warranties. Although § 2316 has drawn criticism for its vagueness, its purpose is clear. No warranty, express or implied, can be modified or disclaimed unless a seller clearly limits his liability. "This section is designed principally to deal with those frequent clauses in sales contracts which seek to exclude 'all warranties, express or implied.'" It seeks to protect a buyer from unexpected and unbargained language of disclaimer by denying

effect to such language when inconsistent with language of express warranty and permitting the exclusion of implied warranties only by conspicuous language or other circumstances that protect the buyer from surprise.

Because a disclaimer or modification is inconsistent with an express warranty, words of disclaimer or modification give way to words of warranty unless some clear agreement between the parties dictates the contrary relationship. At the very least, § 2316 allows limitation of warranties only by means of words that clearly communicate that a particular risk falls on the buyer. Moreover, any disclaimer or modification must be strictly construed against the seller. Although the parties are free to write their own contract ..., the consumer must be placed on fair notice of any disclaimer or modification of a warranty and must freely agree to the seller's terms. "A unilateral nonwarranty cannot be tacked onto a contract containing a warranty."

In the instant case, defendants do not point to any language or conduct on their part negating their warranties. They refer only to a drawing on the box and to the notion that golf is a dangerous game; based on that meager foundation, they attempt to limit their explicit promise of safety. Such a showing does not pass muster under the code, which requires clear language from anyone seeking to avoid warranty liability. We conclude, therefore, that the trial court properly granted plaintiffs judgment notwithstanding the verdict with regard to the warranty causes of action.

Plaintiffs are entitled to recover as a matter of law on the cause of action based on strict liability. They claim that the Gizmo is defectively designed, a fact which, if proven, renders defendants strictly liable in tort for Fred's injuries. To prevail on this theory, plaintiffs need only prove that the product is defective, and need not show that the user was unaware of the defect. In the instant case the trial court ruled that the Gizmo was defectively designed as a matter of law, a conclusion that is firmly supported by the record. At trial, plaintiffs demonstrated how a person using the Gizmo under normal conditions is likely to injure himself by entangling his club in the cord attached to the ball, a significant danger not inherent in the game of golf. The evidence further shows that the risk of harm built into the Gizmo is greatest when the product is being used by its intended user, a player of limited ability. Defendants introduced no evidence whatsoever to rebut this showing.

On this state of the record, the court properly found that the Gizmo was defectively designed as a matter of law, and that the defect was the proximate cause of the injuries in question.

We affirm the order of the trial court granting judgment notwithstanding the verdict and remand the case to the trial court for the purpose of ascertaining damages.

 For an extended version of the case and review questions to test your understanding of the material, please go to www.HumanKinetics.com/CaseStudiesInSportLaw.

Hemphill v. Sayers

552 F.Supp. 685 (S.D. Ill. 1982)

Before the court are motions to dismiss filed by each defendant. They argue that plaintiff's complaint should be dismissed for failure to state claims on which relief can be granted.

These defendants, sued in their individual capacities, argue that they are immune from suit under the Eleventh Amendment. In the alternative, they argue that plaintiff's warranty and strict liability claims should be dismissed as to them. Defendants Sayers, Dempsey, and Schulz argue that at all relevant times, they were agents of the State of Illinois, and that Chapter V, § D.11, Indemnification Policy of the Policies of the Board of Trustees, Southern Illinois University is applicable. That section provides that each employee

> shall be indemnified by the Board of Trustees of Southern Illinois University against all costs and expenses reasonably incurred by or imposed upon him . . . in connection with or resulting from an action, suit, proceeding, claim, or investigation, civil or criminal, to which he . . . shall or may be made a party . . . by reason, directly, or indirectly, of his action or omission to act in the scope of his appointment as a trustee, officer, or employee of the university. . . .

On the basis of this provision, defendants Sayers, Dempsey, and Schulz argue that any judgment against them will be paid out of the state treasury, and thus this suit is barred by the Eleventh Amendment. It is submitted that any tort claim against them must be filed in the Illinois Court of Claims pursuant to Ill. Rev. Stat., ch. 37, § 439.8. The court disagrees.

As noted, Counts II and III allege breach of warranties. Count II is governed by § 2-315. At issue is whether these defendants can be liable under this section. Simply stated, since these defendants are not sellers, § 2-315 does not apply to them.

For the same reason, plaintiff's § 2-314 theory in Count III fails against these defendants. Defendants Sayers, Dempsey, and Schulz do not qualify as merchants. It is clear that plaintiff's warranty theories do not apply to these defendants, and that Counts II and III should be dismissed as to them.

Count IV alleges that defendants Sayers, Dempsey, and Schulz are strictly liable in tort to plaintiff. This count must also fail as to these defendants. These defendants are not part of the original producing and marketing chain. Liability will not be imposed on a defendant who is not a part of the original producing and marketing chain. The rationale for that qualification was explained in *Keene v. Dominick's Finer Foods, Inc.*, 364 N.E.2d 502 (1st Dist. 1977):

> [I]t becomes apparent that the cornerstone of liability rests on the defendant's active participation in placing the product into commerce for use and consumption by others. One of the underlying reasons for imposing strict liability is to ensure that losses are borne and subsequently reaped the profit of marketing the allegedly defective product.

This rationale underscores why defendants Sayers, Dempsey, and Schulz cannot be held strictly liable in tort for the allegedly defective football helmet. They did not create the risk and reap the profits. Accordingly, Count IV must be dismissed as to these defendants.

Defendant Riddell argues that plaintiff's warranty theories under Ill. Rev. Stat., ch. 26, §§ 2-314 and 2-315 should be dismissed because no privity exists. As for plaintiff's strict liability theory, defendant Riddell submits that critical elements are missing from plaintiff's pleading. These arguments will be considered separately.

Defendant Riddell argues that because it lacks contractual privity with plaintiff, it cannot be held liable for breaching the implied warranty of merchantability, § 2-314, or the implied warranty of fitness for a particular purpose, § 2-315. Although direct contractual privity is not always necessary for an implied warranty theory, the court agrees with defendant Riddell that plaintiff cannot succeed under either §§ 2-314 and 2-315, and Counts II and III should be dismissed.

The court in *Slate Printing Company v. Metro Envelope Co.*, 532 F.Supp. 431 (N.D. Ill. 1982), analyzing state law, found that a plaintiff must satisfy at least one of three possibilities before bringing a warranty action: (1) there must be privity of contract between the plaintiff and the defendant, . . . ; (2) the plaintiff must be in a position equivalent to that of a third-party beneficiary of the defendant's sales contract; or (3) the plaintiff must otherwise be able to sustain a tort action against the defendant. At issue is whether plaintiff falls into any of these categories. In the court's opinion, he does not. Analysis must begin with § 2-318. That section defines the scope of the statutory warranties:

> A seller's warranty whether express or implied extends to any natural person who is in the family or household of his buyer or who is a guest in his home if it is reasonable to expect that such person may use, consume or be affected by the goods and who is injured in person by breach of the warranty. A seller may not exclude or limit the operation of this section. Ill.Rev. Stat., Ch. 26, § 2-318.

This language defines the classes of persons who may benefit from implied warranties who stand in "horizontal" nonprivity to the last buyer in the distributive chain. A horizontal nonprivity plaintiff has been defined as not a buyer in the distributive chain but one who uses or is otherwise affected by the product. In contrast, a "vertical" nonprivity plaintiff is a buyer in the distributive chain who did not purchase from the defendant. Subsection 3 of the Official Comment to § 2-318 indicates that the class of vertical nonprivity plaintiffs entitled to warranty protection may be expanded by judicial fiat:

> This section expressly includes as beneficiaries within its provisions the family, household, and any guests of the purchaser. Beyond this, the section is neutral and is not intended to enlarge or restrict the developing case law on whether the seller's warranties, given to his buyer who resells, extend to other persons in the distributive chain.

The text of § 2-318 and its Official Comment 3 have been interpreted to mean that although the class of vertical nonprivity buyers entitled to warranty protection may be judicially expanded and contracted, the class of horizontal nonprivity plaintiffs entitled to such protection has been statutorily limited to "natural persons" in the "family or household of the buyer and to his guests" where it is "reasonable to expect that such persons may use, consume or be affected by the goods." A horizontal nonprivity plaintiff not within the language of § 2-318 is not entitled to warranty protection.

This conclusion is buttressed by considering alternative versions of § 2-318 which the General Assembly rejected:

> Alternative B. A seller's warranty whether express or implied extends to natural person who may reasonably be expected to use, consume or be affected by the goods and who is injured in person by breach of the warranty. A seller may not exclude or limit the operation of this section.

> Alternative C. A seller's warranty whether express or implied extends to any person who may reasonably be expected to use, consume or be affected by the goods and who is injured by breach of the warranty. A seller may not exclude or limit the operation of this section with respect to injury to the person of an individual to whom the warranty extends.

These alternatives obviously contemplate a much more expansive class of horizontal nonprivity plaintiffs entitled to warranty protection. The court agrees that "the legislature consciously chose to limit a seller's liability for breach of warranty to the specific classes enumerated therein." If this court chose to exceed the express limitations of § 2-318, the judgment of the legislature would be substituted.

The recognized exceptions to the privity requirement in warranty actions have developed in Illinois according to Official Comment 3, which contemplates that the class of vertical nonprivity plaintiffs may be determined judicially. Those exceptions include: (1) a plaintiff standing in a third-party beneficiary relationship to the seller's sales contract, and (2) a plaintiff who may otherwise sustain a tort action against the seller. Illinois case law reflects that these two departures from the privity requirement were developed as an expansion of the class of vertical nonprivity plaintiffs, as contemplated by Official Comment 3.

Cases involving horizontal nonprivity plaintiffs have adhered to the express limitations of § 2-318. As noted, that provision "was meant to act as a limitation only upon a seller's liability for breach of warranty to those who stand in horizontal [non-]privity. . . ." Plaintiff is a user outside the distributive chain. He was supplied the football helmet by Southern Illinois University, the last buyer in the distributive chain. As discussed, it would be inappropriate for the Court to afford him warranty protection pursuant to Official Comment 3. At issue is whether plaintiff falls within the express language of § 2-318. In the court's opinion, he does not.

As noted, § 2-318 extends warranty protection to "any natural person who is in the family or household of his buyer or who is a guest in his home if it is reasonable to expect that such person may use, consume or be affected by the goods and who is injured in person by breach of the warranty." Plaintiff is neither a household member or a guest. The court declines to amend § 2-318 to extend warranty protection to family members, guests, "or their functional equivalents." Accordingly, Counts II and III should be dismissed as to defendant Riddell.

Defendant Riddell argues that Count IV fails to allege (1) the nature, character, or description of the product's condition making it unreasonably dangerous; and (2) that the product's allegedly dangerous condition existed at the time it left the manufacturer. Defendant Riddell suggests Count IV should be dismissed with leave to refile. The court agrees.

In Illinois, products liability plaintiffs must "prove that their injury or damage resulted from a condition of the product, that the condi-

tion was an unreasonably dangerous one and that the condition existed at the time it left the manufacturer's control." The dangerous condition may be a result of a defect in design as well as one of manufacture. Plaintiff has not properly alleged his product liability claim. Even given the liberal notice pleading standard, plaintiff's allegation of the condition of the helmet is insufficient. Presumably, paragraph 4 of plaintiff's Count IV contains why the helmet was unreasonably dangerous: "That the said helmet was defective and in an unreasonable dangerous condition for use as protective headwear for football games in that it suddenly and unexpectedly failed to protect plaintiff's cervical spine when put to the use intended. . . ." This language explains what the helmet allegedly did without describing the condition rendering it unreasonably dangerous. It is impossible to infer what type of defect is alleged. Further, plaintiff alleges that "said defective and unreasonably dangerous helmet was in substantially the same condition at the time of Mark Hemphill's injury as it had been when sold, furnished, manufactured, placed in commerce or supplied by defendants to plaintiff." The court agrees with defendant Riddell that this language is not the same as alleging that the unreasonably dangerous condition existed at the time the product left the manufacturer's control. Count IV should be dismissed with leave to refile a third amended complaint that cures these defects.

Defendant Bleyer argues that plaintiff's warranty theories, in Counts II and III, should be dismissed because privity is lacking. Count V should be dismissed, it is argued, because it is unintelligible. The court has already decided that Count V should be dismissed with leave to refile. As to plaintiff's warranty theories, the reasoning applicable to defendant Riddell applies with full force to defendant Bleyer. Plaintiff remains in horizontal nonprivity and does not qualify as a family member or guest under § 2-318. The implied warranties of §§ 2-314 and 2-315 do not benefit plaintiff. To avoid confusion, the court states that it believes that plaintiff does not and could not assert his strict liability in tort theory against defendant Bleyer. Defendant Bleyer has stipulated that defendant Riddell is the helmet's manufacturer. By operation of Ill. Rev. Stat., ch. 110, § 801 *et seq.*, the certifying defendant cannot be held strictly liable in tort. Accordingly, Counts II and II should be dismissed; Count V, if it purports to state a claim against defendant Bleyer, should be dismissed with leave to refile.

The court finds as follows:

1. Defendants Sayers', Dempsey's, and Schulz' Motion to Dismiss is hereby GRANTED in part and DENIED in part.
2. Defendant Riddell's Motion to Dismiss is hereby GRANTED.
3. Defendant Bleyer's Motion to Dismiss is hereby GRANTED.
4. Counts II and III are hereby DISMISSED as to all defendants.
5. Count IV is hereby DISMISSED as to defendants Sayers, Dempsey, Schulz, and Bleyer.
6. Count IV is hereby DISMISSED as to defendant Riddell, with leave to refile a third amended Count IV only against defendant Riddell, within ten (10) days of this order. Said amended complaint shall cure the defects discussed in this order.
7. Count V is hereby DISMISSED with leave to refile. Plaintiff is GRANTED leave to file a third amended Count V, which indicates that defendants are charged, and corresponds enumerated acts with the respective defendant, within ten (10) days of this order.

 For an extended version of the case and review questions to test your understanding of the material, please go to www.HumanKinetics.com/CaseStudiesInSportLaw.

Pell v. Victor J. Andrew High School

462 N.E.2d 858 (Ill. App. 1 Dist. 1984)

This is an appeal by defendant AMF, Inc. ("AMF") from the entry of judgment in the circuit court of Cook County on a jury verdict for plaintiff Lauren M. Pell for permanent injuries plaintiff sustained during gym class while performing a somersault off a trampoline manufactured by AMF. Prior to trial, plaintiff and defendants School District 230 and Victor J. Andrew High School entered into a settlement agreement for $1.6 million. Thereafter, the jury awarded plaintiff $5 million against AMF on the theory of strict liability, which amount was set off by the $1.6 million settlement figure and resulted in a final judgment against AMF for $3.4 million.

On appeal, AMF contends that the trial court erroneously failed to direct a verdict in its favor or to grant its motion for judgment notwithstanding the verdict because (1) AMF cannot be held liable for failure to provide warnings and instructional materials to either of the other defendants, (2) because the proximate cause of plaintiff's injury was the school district's willful and wanton misconduct in failing to properly instruct and supervise plaintiff in the use of the trampoline, and (3) because plaintiff's knee condition was

the proximate cause of her injury. AMF contends further that the trial court erred in (4) refusing to allow AMF to present evidence on the issue of plaintiff's comparative negligence, (5) admitting exhibits that dealt with full-size trampolines, (6) refusing to admit two of AMF's exhibits, and (7) finding that plaintiff's settlement with the school district was made in good faith.

On December 29, 1980, plaintiff, a 16-year-old sophomore and beginner gymnast at Victor J. Andrew High School, was injured as the result of a somersault she performed on a product manufactured by AMF, called a mini-trampoline or trampolette (mini-tramp). This equipment consists of a 37-inch, square-shaped metal frame holding a "bed" of polypropylene fabric with rubber cables that lace the "bed" to the frame. Two adjustable metal leg sections can be used to set the frame at any angle or to fold the equipment flat. The mini-tramp was sold to School District 230 with a heat-laminated caution label affixed to the bed that stated:

Caution. Misuse and abuse of this trampoline is dangerous and can cause serious injuries. Read instructions before using this trampoline. Inspect before using and replace any worn, defective, or missing parts. Any activity involving motion or height creates the possibility of accidental injuries. This unit is intended for use only by properly trained and qualified participants under supervised conditions. Use without proper supervision can be dangerous and should not be undertaken or permitted.

When the mini-tramp was assembled by a faculty member at the high school, the bed was placed so that the caution label was on the bottom, facing the floor, as opposed to the top where it would be visible to a performer. There were printed warnings also on the frame of the mini-tramp; however, they were covered by frame pads on each of the four sides. On the day of the injury, plaintiff had first performed two somersaults off the mini-tramp. Both of the school's coaches, Charlene Nutter, the varsity gymnastics coach, and Cathi Miles, were present in the gymnasium. Miles witnessed plaintiff's third somersault from a distance of approximately 10 feet. Plaintiff testified that she took a few running steps up to the mini-tramp and jumped onto the bed. When she went into the air, at the point when her feet were straight up and down above her, plaintiff said she felt a sharp pain in her knee and was unable to properly complete her somersault. She collapsed onto a nearby mat, severing her spine.

Plaintiff then filed a cause of action against Victor J. Andrew High School, School District 230, Crown Mats, Inc., and AMF. Counts III, IV, VII, and VIII of plaintiff's complaint alleged that AMF's mini-tramp was not reasonably safe for its intended use; that AMF failed to adequately warn or advise plaintiff that use without a harness, safety belt, and supervision by a trained instructor would result in severe injury and that AMF carelessly and negligently failed to provide a support harness or restraining device to prevent improper landing. Plaintiff further alleged that as a direct and proximate result of the defect in the mini-tramp, plaintiff landed on her neck, severed her spine, and was permanently paralyzed.

In reply, AMF filed affirmative defenses asserting that (1) plaintiff had assumed the risk of injury because she knew of the condition of the mini-tramp and the dangers involved in using it, and (2) that any verdict against AMF must be reduced by the percentage of plaintiff's contributory negligence.

Plaintiff then filed a motion *in limine* to preclude AMF from presenting evidence that her conduct contributed to cause her injury. Granting the motion, the court reasoned that although it would allow AMF to offer evidence of plaintiff's negligence, it would "wait and see what happens" before deciding whether to give a comparative negligence instruction to the jury. The jury returned a verdict against AMF and assessed plaintiff's damages at $5 million. Following the entry of judgment on this verdict, AMF appealed.

Initially, AMF maintains that the trial court erred in failing to direct a verdict in its favor or to grant its motion for a judgment notwithstanding the verdict because it cannot be held liable, as a matter of law, for failing to provide warnings and instructional materials for using the mini-tramp since the school district as well as the high school had all of the appropriate instructional materials. We find this reasoning unpersuasive, however, because it misstates the central issue presented to the trier of fact, which was the unreasonably dangerous condition of the mini-tramp that, plaintiff alleged, existed because AMF failed to adequately warn of the equipment's propensity to cause severe spinal cord injuries if used for somersaulting without a safety device operated by a trained instructor. Warnings must be adequate to perform their intended function of risk reduction. Warnings may be inadequate, however, if they (1) do not specify the risk presented by the product, (2) are inconsistent with how a product would be used, (3) if they do not provide the reason for the warnings, or (4) if they do not reach foreseeable users.

Considering these principles, in our opinion there was sufficient evidence in the instant case from which the jury could conclude that AMF's warnings were ineffective. First, the warnings did not specify the risk of severe spinal cord injury that would result in permanent paralysis during somersaulting off the mini-tramp if performed without a spotter or safety harness. Charlene Nutter, head coach at the high school, testified that she did not know that the mini-tramp had any more risk involved in it than did any other gymnastic equipment and had she known, she would have taken precautions.

Coach Cathi Miles was also unaware of any rule that somersaults should not be performed on a mini-tramp without a spotter or overhead mechanical safety belt, although she had used the safety harness with a larger (full-size) trampoline as well as the mini-tramp. In addition, the jury could have reasonably determined that the warnings were inadequate because their location was inconsistent with the equipment's use. Plaintiff presented evidence that the assembly instructions failed to specify that the warning label should be placed in such a manner that it would be clearly visible to a gymnast. As a result, the warning label on the "bed" was placed underneath, facing the floor. The warnings on the sides of the metal frame were also ineffective because they were covered by frame pads.

In addition, because there was evidence that AMF had regularly participated in the United States Gymnastic Safety Association (USGSA), the jury could have easily concluded that AMF was familiar with the warnings that that association recommended, which were that the labels should explain the reason for a warning and should be clearly visible to a mini-tramp user. AMF, however, failed to present evidence that anyone from the high school had attended a trampoline safety certification clinic. Thus, the jury in this case, which examined the mini-tramp from a distance of a few feet, was able to determine whether AMF's warnings were adequate. We are convinced that this determination was correct.

AMF next contends that the trial court erred in failing to issue a directed verdict or judgment notwithstanding the verdict because the proximate cause of plaintiff's injury was the school district's failure to provide plaintiff with proper gymnastic instructions in the safe use of the mini-tramp. We cannot agree. In a strict liability action, a manufacturer may remain a contributing cause of an injury if the intervening acts or omissions of others were foreseeable. Foreseeability means that which is objectively reasonable to expect, not what might conceivably occur. Liability will also attach if the defendant's conduct contributed in whole or in part to the injury, so long as it was one of the proximate causes.

In the case before us, there was sufficient evidence to support a finding that it was objectively foreseeable that mini-tramp users such as plaintiff would not always be under the direct supervision of a coach and that neither a gymnast nor a coach would have sufficient knowledge of the dangers of the mini-tramp because the warnings were inadequate. As we have previously explained, plaintiff submitted ample evidence that strongly suggested that AMF's warnings were inadequate.

Additionally, the record shows that both Larry Fie and Mike Jacki testified that coaches were not "told to put the kids in harnesses if they're using a mini-tramp to avoid crippling injuries from doing a somersault." In our judgment, therefore, the trial court could not have directed a verdict for AMF since the evidence, when viewed in a light most favorable to the nonmovant, plaintiff, demonstrated that (1) the absence of direct supervision was reasonably foreseeable, and (2) that AMF's failure to adequately warn of the risk of serious injury was a proximate cause of plaintiff's injury. Accordingly, the trial court's denial of AMF's motion will not be disturbed.

Next, as an alternative to the preceding argument, AMF maintains that plaintiff's "idiosyncratic" knee condition was the proximate cause of her injury and that because this condition was unforeseeable, AMF did not have a duty to warn or to protect plaintiff against the danger of performing on the mini-tramp with such a condition. In the case at bar, however, plaintiff testified that her knee had never been such a problem for her that she could not practice gymnastics, although it had been "locking up" on her during her diving (swimming) practice in her freshman year. Thus, even if AMF had known of plaintiff's "knee condition," it would not be absolved of the duty to adequately warn users of the high risk of injury associated with the mini-tramp.

AMF next contends that the trial court's refusal to give several of its jury instructions improperly precluded the jury from considering the percentage of contributory negligence attributed to plaintiff. It maintains that because plaintiff was aware of her knee condition and knew that a safety harness and spotters were available to assist her, the jury could have found that plaintiff's failure to request her coach's permission to somersault without a spotter or harness was a proximate cause of her injury. The court's failure to give a comparative negligence instruction precluded the jury from making this determination, AMF asserts. This contention cannot prevail.

In *Coney v. J.L.G. Industries, Inc.* (1983), 97 Ill.2d 104, 73 Ill.Dec. 337, 454 N.E.2d 197, our Supreme Court upheld the principle that contributory negligence is not a defense in a strict product liability tort action. Comparative fault is applicable to strict liability cases, the court determined, but only insofar as the defenses of misuse and assumption of risk are concerned. Moreover, these defenses no longer preclude recovery in such actions. Thus, once a defendant's liability is established, and where both the defective product and the plaintiff's misconduct contribute to cause the damages, the comparative fault principle will operate to reduce the plaintiff's recovery by that amount that the trier of fact finds him at fault.

In the case at bar, AMF failed to establish that plaintiff's alleged negligence rose to the level of misuse of the mini-tramp or that she assumed the risk of injury. Rather, we are of the opinion that the evidence showed that because the warnings as well as any other information AMF provided about the mini-tramp were ineffective and failed to warn that use of the equipment without a safety device and proper supervision could result in permanent injury, plaintiff was unaware that somersaulting off of this product could result in serious injury. Furthermore, because there was no evidence that plaintiff had used the mini-tramp for a purpose that was neither intended nor reasonably foreseeable, AMF's allegation of misuse of the product will be rejected.

We reject this contention since permitting the ordinary contributory negligence of a plaintiff to reduce damages in strict liability actions would frustrate the policy considerations underlying this tort theory. In such actions, the focus is on the design and performance of the product and the plaintiff is relieved of the burden of proving negligence. Moreover, a consumer's unobservant or inattentive failure to discover or guard against a defect is not a damage reducing factor. The trial court's ruling, which denied AMF's

request for a contributory negligence instruction, will therefore prevail.

Next, it is urged that the trial court erroneously admitted evidence pertaining to full-size trampolines. A mini-tramp differs from a full-size trampoline in size, purpose, and function, AMF contends, even though the definition of both pieces of equipment are the same. (A "bed," secured on a metal frame, suspended by springs with pads that cover the springs and frame.) We cannot agree. Because there was conflicting evidence throughout the trial of this case as to whether the definition of a full-size trampoline also applied to a mini-tramp, it was well within the court's discretion to admit relevant evidence concerning both kinds of equipment as such evidence clearly showed that neither the ASTM nor AMF in its equipment catalogue specifically defined a mini-tramp. As far as the other exhibits pertaining to full-size trampolines that the trial court admitted, which included instructions for proper display of trampoline cautionary statements and trampoline care and maintenance, for the foregoing reasons we do not believe that the court's decision was in error. Moreover, if in any instance AMF was harmed, it was not prejudiced thereby and neither was the outcome of the case unduly affected.

We cannot agree with AMF's contention. Accordingly, for all of the foregoing reasons, the judgment of the circuit court of Cook County will be affirmed.

 For an extended version of the case and review questions to test your understanding of the material, please go to www.HumanKinetics.com/CaseStudiesInSportLaw.

Rawlings Sporting Goods Company, Inc. v. Daniels

619 S.W.2d 435 (Tex. Civ. App. — Waco 1981)

This is an appeal by defendant Rawlings from $1.5 million judgment against it in favor of plaintiff Daniels in a products liability and negligence case. Plaintiff Daniels sued defendant Rawlings alleging plaintiff sustained injuries on August 20, 1974 during football practice; that plaintiff was wearing a Rawlings helmet when he was in collision with another player; that the helmet

rather than deflecting the blow and absorbing the shock, caved in, causing massive head and brain injuries to plaintiff; that the helmet as manufactured by defendant was defective; and exposed plaintiff to an unreasonable risk of harm. Plaintiff further alleged defendant was negligent in failing to warn of the protective limitations of the helmet, which was a proximate cause of plaintiff's injuries. Plaintiff sought damages of $750,000. Plaintiff additionally alleged defendant was grossly negligent in failing to warn users and the public of the limitations on the protective capabilities of its helmet, for which he sought exemplary damages.

Trial was to a jury, which found that

1. the injury to plaintiff resulting in subdural hematoma occurred August 20, 1974,
2. at the time plaintiff received the injury he was wearing a helmet manufactured by defendant,
3. the helmet as manufactured by defendant was defectively manufactured,
4. such defective condition was a producing cause of plaintiff's injuries,
5. the failure of defendant to warn that the helmet would not protect against subdural hematomas exposed plaintiff to an unreasonable risk of harm,
6. the failure of defendant to warn that the helmet would not protect against subdural hematomas was a producing cause of plaintiff's injuries,
7. the failure of defendant to warn that the helmet would not protect against subdural hematomas was negligence,
8. such negligence was a proximate cause of the event in question,
9. the failure of defendant to warn that the helmet would not protect against subdural hematomas was gross negligence,
10. fixed plaintiff's damage at $750,000,
11. fixed exemplary damage at $750,000.

Plaintiff was quarterback on the Franklin High School football team. On August 20, 1974, while participating in team practice, he was involved in a "head-to-head" collision with a teammate. The collision caused an indentation in plaintiff's helmet. Plaintiff turned the helmet into the coach and continued with practice. The next day, August 21, plaintiff returned to practice. While participating in such practice he passed out. He was taken to a Bryan hospital, and then to a Houston hospital, where his condition was diagnosed as a subdural hematoma. After the subdural hematoma had been surgically evacu-

ated he returned to school on September 14, 1974. Plaintiff's injury resulted in severe permanent brain damage drastically reducing his abilities.

Point 1 asserts that Finding 2 is against the great weight and overwhelming preponderance of the evidence. Finding 2 found the helmet plaintiff was wearing was a helmet manufactured by defendant. The school owned four to six helmets manufactured by defendant; 15 to 18 McGregor helmets; and 15 to 20 B & B helmets. Some of the helmets had been reconditioned by a company in San Antonio. The McGregors, purchased in 1973, were the newest. Plaintiff had lettered in 1973 and had worn a McGregor helmet in 1973. Once a letterman chose a helmet he usually kept it throughout the remainder of his playing career. After the accident on August 20, plaintiff turned his helmet into the coach who placed it in his office where it remained for about a year and then disappeared.

Coach Hedrick testified he had only seen one dented helmet in his experience; that it was his recollection that the helmet brought to his office was a Rawlings HC20 helmet; that "there is (no) question in (his) mind but what the helmet that was dented and kept in his office was a Rawlings helmet." We think the evidence ample to sustain Finding 2, and that such finding is not against the great weight and preponderance of the evidence.

Points 2 through 6 assert there is no evidence to support Findings 3 and 4, and that such findings are against the great weight and overwhelming preponderance of the evidence. Finding 3 found the helmet defectively manufactured; Finding 4 found such defective condition was a producing cause of plaintiff's injuries. Defendant asserts there is no finding or evidence that the helmet was defective at the time it left the hands of Rawlings, and that plaintiff has failed to trace the defect to the manufacturer's hands.

The helmet worn by plaintiff was manufactured by defendant. Franklin High School purchased the helmet between 1967 and 1969. Defendant puts no limit of years or use limit on its helmets. There is evidence that some helmets owned by the school had been sent to a firm in San Antonio for reconditioning, but such evidence is at best a *scintilla*. The coach who testified to the foregoing did not remember whether such occurred before August 1974 or later (trial was in April 1980). And he further testified that helmets sent for reconditioning were returned with "Alamo Athletic" stamped on them. There is no evidence that the helmet worn by plaintiff was so stamped. Another coach testified that some helmets had been sent to Alamo for reconditioning, but he did not recall whether any were sent between 1967 and 1974 or not. Plaintiff was wearing the helmet manufactured by defendant when he had the head-to-head collision. The helmet indented inward some 1-1/2 to 2 inches. There is evidence that if a helmet receives a blow and doesn't deflect it, but instead indents in, that the helmet was defective; and defendant's own witnesses testified that if a helmet indented 1-1/2 inches and came in contact with the wearer's skull that considerable force was transmitted to and focused on the wearer's skull at that point. There is other evidence that the indenting of the helmet on collision does not reflect defective manufacture. All the evidence is that the purpose of the helmet was to protect the wearer's head from injury. There is evidence that if a football helmet indents it is not performing its function, that it is "defective headgear."

It is our view there is ample evidence from which the jury could conclude that the indented helmet was defective because it failed to perform its intended purpose, to protect the wearer from head injuries, and that Finding 3 is not against the great weight and preponderance of the evidence. It is our further view that the evidence is ample to sustain Finding 4, that such defective condition was a producing cause of plaintiff's injury; and that Finding 4 is not against the great weight and preponderance of the evidence.

Points 7 through 10 assert: (1) The trial court erred in submitting Issues 5 and 7 because defendant had no duty to warn that its helmet would not protect against subdural hematomas; 2) there is no evidence to support Findings 5, 6, 7, and 8; and (3) such findings are against the great weight and preponderance of the evidence.

Issue 5 found the failure of defendant to warn that its helmet would not protect against subdural hematomas exposed plaintiff to an unreasonable risk of harm; Issue 6 found the failure to warn was a producing cause of plaintiff's injury; Issues 7 and 8 found the failure to warn was negligence and a proximate cause of the plaintiff's injury. All the evidence is that the primary purpose of a football helmet is to protect against "head" or "brain" injuries of the wearer of

the helmet. Defendant has known for a long time that a helmet will not protect against brain injury and against subdural hematoma; that almost all fatal football injuries result from head and neck injuries; and that when a person uses a football helmet for its intended purpose of protecting the head while playing football, that there is still a significant risk of brain injury. In spite of this knowledge defendant made an election, a conscious decision, not to warn users that the helmet would not protect the brain from this type of injury. Every manufacturer has a duty to warn of dangers in the use of its product of which it knows or should know.

We think defendant had a duty to warn that its helmet would not protect against head and brain injuries. Where there is no warning, as here, the presumption is that the user would have read an adequate warning. And plaintiff's father affirmatively testified he would not have consented to plaintiff's playing had he been aware the helmet would not have protected against brain injury. The danger to plaintiff was not inherent in the helmet, but in the use of the helmet. We think liability arises when a product is manufactured and marketed for protection of the consumer, the consumer buys the product, relying on it for his protection, while engaged in a generally dangerous activity, the manufacturer fails to warn of known limitations in the protective abilities of its product with which the user is not equally familiar, and as a result, the consumer is injured while using the product.

The rationale supporting a duty to warn is clear. The consumer is encouraged to participate in dangerous activity because of his confidence in the protective ability of the product. The manufacturer on the other hand, has superior knowledge of the limitations of the product. Where it is foreseeable that a consumer will rely on the product, thus exposing himself to a risk he might have avoided had he known the limitations, there is a duty to warn. Here the failure to warn was negligence. A product that does not include a warning is dangerously defective. In the instant case the jury was authorized to believe that a proximate cause of plaintiff's injury was the absence of a warning of the limitations of his helmet sufficient to prevent his reliance on its protective capacities. The evidence is ample to sustain Findings 5, 6, 7, and 8, and such findings are not against the great weight and preponderance of the evidence.

Points 11 and 12 assert there is no evidence of gross negligence, and that Findings 9 and 11 are against the great weight and preponderance of the evidence. Issue 9 found that defendant's failure to warn that the helmet would not protect against subdural hematomas was gross negligence; and Issue 11 awarded $750,000 exemplary damages.

Defendant admitted that it never made any attempt to warn potential users of the limitations of its helmets; that it had known for a long time that the helmets will not protect against brain injuries; that it made the "conscious decision" not to tell people the helmet would not protect against subdural hematomas; that the company "elected" not to warn that the helmets would not protect against head injuries, in spite of the knowledge that laymen believe that the purpose of the helmet is to protect the head. A witness for defendant testified that 30 to 40 deaths occur each year from subdural hematomas received in football; that parents do not have this detailed knowledge, and that "it is the responsibility of the manufacturer to explain that." Defendant asserts that it exercised care in manufacturing the helmet; but there is no evidence of any care whatsoever being exercised in the matter of failure to warn of the helmet's limitation.

The trial court defined gross negligence: "Gross negligence means the entire want of care which would raise a belief that the act or omission complained of was the result of conscious indifference to the rights or welfare of persons to be affected by it." The Texas Supreme Court in *Burk Royalty Co. v. Sally K. Walls, Ind.*, 616 S.W.2d 911 (Tex. 1981) (596 S.W.2d 932), in its latest expression addressing the question of gross negligence, and after an exhaustive review of its history, states:

> The essence of gross negligence is not the neglect which must, of course, exist. What lifts ordinary negligence into gross negligence is the mental attitude of the defendant; that is what justifies the penal nature of the imposition of exemplary damages. The plaintiff must show that the defendant was consciously, i.e., knowingly, indifferent to his rights, welfare and safety. In other words, the plaintiff must show that the defendant knew about the peril, but his acts or omissions demonstrated that he didn't care. Such conduct can be active or passive in nature.

In determining whether there is some evidence of the jury's finding of gross negligence, the reviewing court must look to all of the surrounding facts, circumstances, and conditions, not just individual elements or facts. A mental state may be inferred from actions. All actions or circumstances indicating a state of mind amounting to a conscious indifference must be examined in deciding if there is some evidence of gross negligence.

In the instant case, defendant fully understood the dangers that were incidental to the use of its helmets. Testimony of defendant's own witnesses revealed defendant knew (1) a practical helmet could not be designed that would prevent all head injuries; (2) there are limitations on the protection capabilities of any helmet; (3) it has been known for a long time that helmets will not protect against all brain injuries; (4) defendant's helmets would not protect against all subdural hematomas; (5) laymen believe the purpose of the helmet is to protect the head; (6) almost all fatal football injuries are related to head and neck injuries; (7) 200,000 to 4 million football players are injured each year; (8) you can receive a brain injury while in a helmet that performs all the functions that it was designed to perform; (9) the helmet has severe limitations on protecting the brain; it will not protect against subdural hematomas; (10) total football deaths are between 30 and 40 a year from subdural hematoma; and (11) parents of high school players don't have this detailed knowledge of the dangers of subdural hematoma.

There is evidence that since 1960 almost all fatal injuries from playing football have been as a result of head or neck injuries; that in spite of the helmets being worn, the injury sustained by plaintiff, subdural hematoma, can occur, and that the foregoing was well known to defendant. In spite of all the facts known to defendant, it made a conscious business decision not to warn of this grave danger.

Viewing all the circumstances in this case, and the entire record, we think the jury authorized to find defendant grossly negligent in answering Issues 9 and 11 as they did. We think the evidence ample to sustain such findings, and that they are not against the great weight and preponderance of the evidence. All defendant's points and contentions have been considered and are overruled.

 For an extended version of the case and review questions to test your understanding of the material, please go to www.HumanKinetics.com/CaseStudiesInSportLaw.

7

Statutory Law

Statutes are laws enacted by the legislature at the state and federal level that mandate, direct, enable, or declare a course of action. Statutes used in the sport context may be directly designed to address sport issues or be of a more general nature and have application in the sport context given the circumstances of a particular case. For example, several of the cases in this section address non-sport-specific laws with implications for sport such as discrimination issues under the Americans with Disabilities Act (ADA) and sexual harassment under Title VII of the Civil Rights Act of 1964. The Americans with Disabilities Act was at issue in *Pottgen v. Missouri SHSAA* where a high school student who had repeated two grades in elementary school due to an undiagnosed learning disability was declared ineligible to play on his high school baseball team because he was too old by the time he wanted to play. Another case involving the ADA is *Sandison v. Michigan HSAA, Inc.*, where two students who sought to run on the cross-country team were declared ineligible due to their age and brought lawsuits. Similar to the facts in *Pottgen*, they suffered from a learning disability, and before reaching high school each fell behind the typical school grade for children of their age (they were 19 entering their senior year of high school). *Concerned Parents v. City of West Palm Beach* revolved around the reduction of leisure services provided in the city's recreation program to the disabled.

Title VII has also seen application in the sport and recreation context. An example is *Faragher v. City of Boca Raton,* which involved a sexual harassment lawsuit brought against a beach lifeguard. Other cases involve a determination of whether statutory authority was exceeded. *DeFrantz v. USOC*, for example, addressed the issue of whether statutory powers were exceeded when Olympic athletes were denied participation in the 1980 Moscow Olympics.

> *Cook v. Colgate University* was a Title IX case that was decided on the issue of mootness because all of the named plaintiffs had graduated by the time the case came to trial. In *Bunger v. Iowa HSAA*, the plaintiff challenged the validity of a rule by the IHSAA prohibiting the use of alcohol and drugs. The issues in the cases presented in this section are interesting, diverse, and applicable to a wide range of sport activities.

Bunger v. Iowa High School Athletic Association

197 N.W.2d 555 (Iowa 1972)

This case involves the validity of a rule of the Iowa High School Athletic Association (which we will refer to as IHSAA or the Association). IHSAA is an unincorporated association in charge of boys' interscholastic athletic events in Iowa, including tournaments. Waverly-Shell Rock Community School District is a member of IHSAA, as are all other high schools in Iowa except the school at Kalona. Member schools agree to abide by the constitution and bylaws of IHSAA, which may be amended by referendum of the members. A board of control is in charge of the affairs of IHSAA and may interpret its rules. The board consists of six individuals elected by the members of IHSAA, a seventh appointed by the Iowa Association of School Boards, and an eighth (ex officio) appointed by the State Board of Public Instruction. IHSAA has, in addition, a representative council that consists of 25 individuals elected by high school administrators. An executive secretary manages the affairs of IHSAA. A portion of the gate receipts of tournaments plus membership fees of $2 each support the association. Under the constitution and bylaws, a member school cannot allow an athlete who is known to be ineligible to engage in interscholastic athletic events. Nor can a member school engage in such events with a nonmember school. A member school violating the constitution or bylaws is subject to probation, suspension, or expulsion.

The member schools strongly oppose the use of alcoholic beverages by athletes. In recent years, the drinking problem has increased, particularly the drinking of beer. Attempts by individual school boards to deal with the problem proved unsatisfactory. School boards and administrators were sometimes under local pressure to play outstanding athletes notwithstanding infractions, and different boards had varying rules relating to similar violations.

Largely at the behest of the schools themselves, a committee of IHSAA studied the problem and proposed rules that were adopted by a substantial majority vote of the membership. Pertinent to this case is § 20 of those rules. This section is known as the Good Conduct Rule and Item 2 of it is known as the "beer rule." Purporting to interpret the beer rule, the board of control adopted the following ruling (which we will refer to as "the interpretation" or "the rule"):

> A boy shall lose at least 6 weeks of interscholastic competition if he is found guilty of possession, consumption or transportation of alcoholic beverages or dangerous drugs, or if he admits to a school administrator, the coach or an officer of the law that he has possessed or consumed such beverages or drugs. A boy is also subject to the same loss of eligibility if he is in a vehicle stopped by a law officer and alcoholic beverages and/or dangerous drugs are found in the vehicle. However, if he reports this incident to his superintendent, principal, athletic director or coach the next day of school or prior to the next scheduled contest, whichever occurs first, and then following the boy's answers to six basic questions and completion of investigation, the school administration is convinced that the boy had no knowledge of such beverages or drugs in the vehicle, the administrator shall then file a report to the Board of Control on a form provided by the Association, that the boy has lost no eligibility and is therefore remaining eligible. The six basic questions are: (a) Did the boy have knowledge that there was alcoholic beverages and/or dangerous drugs in the vehicle? (b) Were there any open containers of

alcoholic beverages or dangerous drugs in the vehicle? (c) Had anyone in the vehicle been consuming beverages or drugs found in the vehicle? (d) When did the athlete become aware that there were beverages or drugs in the vehicle? (e) What did the law officer observe? (f) Has the boy been in violation of the Good Conduct Rule before? If following the investigation the administration finds that the boy has been in violation, he shall be ineligible. It shall not be a violation when an athlete is stopped in a vehicle with his father, mother, brother or sister who is twenty-one years of age or older.

The State Department of Public Instruction approved the Good Conduct Rule and the interpretation of it and IHSAA disseminated that rule and the interpretation among its members. The members made the rule and interpretation known to athletes, including plaintiff William Hal Bunger. William is a 16-year-old football player of ability on the outstanding Waverly-Shell Rock team.

On the evening of June 7, 1971, William and three other minors were riding in a car containing a case of beer. An Iowa highway patrolman stopped the four minors, discovered the beer, and issued summonses to all four for possession of beer as minors. Three pleaded guilty. William pleaded not guilty, and the charges against him were subsequently dismissed by the county attorney. On June 10, 1971, William reported the beer incident to his school athletic director and stated he knew at the time that the beer was in the car. Thereupon, the school officials declared William ineligible for six weeks commencing with the opening of the fall football season.

William brought the present suit to enjoin enforcement of the rule. The trial court upheld the rule, and William appealed. William levels a number of charges against the rule. We think, however, that we need not consider all of his claims, for two basic questions control the case. First, does IHSAA have authority to promulgate the rule in question? Second, is the rule valid on its merits? We confine ourselves to the rule before us rendering ineligible an athlete who occupies a car with knowledge of the presence of beer that is found by a law officer.

In our scheme of things, authority to provide for the educational interests of the state is confided in the General Assembly. Pursuant to that authority, the legislature has provided for school districts, to be under the control of elected district directors. Can a school board redelegate its rule-making power regarding pupils to some other organization? Several courts have considered this question to more or less extent, although under statutes or facts distinguishable from the present ones.

Rule making by school boards involves the exercise of judgment and discretion. The legislature has delegated rule making to those boards, and the general principle is that while a public board or body may authorize performance of ministerial or administrative functions by others, it cannot redelegate matters of judgment or discretion.

A school board must clearly understand the difference between the exercise of judgment and discretion and the performance of administrative or ministerial duties. The courts have held quite consistently that the board of education cannot delegate its powers unless they are of administrative or ministerial nature.

But IHSAA contends the rule in question is actually a rule of each individual school board, in that each board agrees to abide by the rules of IHSAA when it joins the association. By joining the association, IHSAA says, each board promulgates IHSAA's rules as its own.

We think this contention is inconsonant with the realities of the situation. The rules are actually association rules. A rule is initially adopted by majority vote of the association members. Bearing in mind that a school board cannot redelegate its rule-making power, how can we say that a school that votes against a proposed rule has itself promulgated that rule? Again, a school that joins IHSAA after a number of rules have been adopted has no choice as to the rules it will accept. It must take them all and abdicate its nondelegable responsibility to select the rules it wishes to have. Then what about a member school that becomes dissatisfied with a rule? It has no power to repeal the rule. To say the school can withdraw from IHSAA is no answer. If it leaves IHSAA voluntarily, or involuntarily for violating the rule, its boys' interscholastic athletic program is at an end—except for playing Kalona. Its hands are tied. The power is actually in the association, not in each school board where the statute places it.

What we have here, in fact, is an association that started out arranging interschool games and tournaments and grew into an organization above individual schools, regulating all manner of affairs relating to athletes. The association did not usurp the regulatory functions of individual schools; the schools turned over those functions to the association. IHSAA also contends that a statute has been enacted that makes the rule valid in two separate ways—by authorizing schools to delegate their rule-making power to an association, and by authorizing the association itself to make rules subject to the approval of the State Board of Public Instruction.

In 1968 IHSAA adopted the Good Conduct Rule and the interpretation of it and reported them to the State Department of Public Instruction, which approved them. But the State Board did not promulgate them as its own rules or put them through chapter 17A procedure.

IHSAA's first contention, that § 257.25(10) authorizes school boards to redelegate to it their rule-making authority, overextends the statute. The language of § 257.25(10) is that public schools shall not allow students to participate in an interscholastic contest or competition "which is sponsored or administered by an organization as defined in this subsection" unless the organization registers and files financial statements with the State Department of Public Instruction and complies with the Board's rules. An "organization" is defined to include an association such as IHSAA. This language of § 257.25(10) clearly means that schools may participate in interscholastic events sponsored by qualifying organizations, and we think it also means, inferentially, that schools may belong to such organizations. But the language cannot be stretched to mean that schools may turn over their statutory rule-making authority to such organizations.

IHSAA's second contention that § 257.25(10) authorizes IHSAA itself to promulgate rules if approved by the State Department of Public Instruction is contrary to the language of the statute. Subsection 10 permits schools to allow students to participate in interscholastic events sponsored by organizations that are, among other things, "in compliance with rules and reg-

ulations which the State board of public instruction shall adopt for the proper administration, supervision, operation, eligibility requirements, and scheduling of such extracurricular interscholastic contests and competitions. . . ." Thus the eligibility rule-making authority, so far as § 257.25(10) is concerned, is in the State Board, not in IHSAA. Moreover, since promulgation of eligibility rules involves judgment and discretion, we think the State Board cannot redelegate its rule-making authority under § 257.25(10) any more than a school board can redelegate its rule-making authority under § 279.8. And since eligibility rules are of general application and do not merely relate to the internal operation of the State Department, such rules by the Board must undergo chapter 17A procedure.

The rule before us is, in fact, a rule of IHSAA and not of the Waverly-Shell Rock Board of Education or of the State Board. Neither of the latter public bodies could redelegate its rule-making authority. We hold that the rule is invalid for want of authority in IHSAA to promulgate it.

The conclusion just stated disposes of the case, but the parties ask us to deal with the rule on its merits for guidance in promulgation of rules by proper authority. This involves William's charge against the rule on its merits, which we now proceed to consider.

In approaching this charge we emphasize that we have no intention of eroding the statutory powers of duly-constituted state and local school authorities. However, the courts do intervene if the action of school officials involves "a plain case of exceeding the power conferred." The first main principle involved in considering the validity of a school rule is that the rule must pertain to conduct "which directly relates to and affects management of the school and its efficiency." School authorities operate in a narrower area than do, say, city councils. The latter may ordain laws covering a variety of acts in the community. The former are only concerned, however, with the school and its proper operation, and their authority is correspondingly more circumscribed.

Student misconduct in the classroom obviously affects the operation of the school; misbehavior of a child at home within the family clearly is beyond the concern of the school. Between those extremes lie the cases that more or less affect the operation of the school, and the task is to determine on which side of the line particular conduct falls. In a given case, the particular circumstances must be examined. The present case involves the advantages and enjoyment of an extracurricular activity provided by the school, a consideration that we believe extends the authority of a school board somewhat as to participation in that activity. The influence of the students involved is an additional consideration. Standout students, whether in athletics, forensics, dramatics, or other interscholastic activities, play a somewhat different role from the rank and file. Leadership brings additional responsibility. These student leaders are looked up to and emulated. They represent the school and depict its character. We cannot fault a school board for expecting somewhat more of them as to eligibility for their particular extracurricular activities.

We have no doubt that school authorities may make a football player ineligible if he drinks beer during football season. No doubt such authorities may do likewise if the player drinks beer at other times during the school year, or if he then possesses, acquires, delivers, or transports beer. Probably a player shown to have actually violated beer laws during summer vacation, whether convicted in criminal court or not, can be rendered ineligible by school rule. All of these situations have direct bearing on the operation of the school, although the bearing becomes progressively less direct. But we are inclined to think the nexus between the school and a situation like the present one is simply too tenuous: outside of football season, beyond the school year, no illegal or even improper use of beer. We cannot find a "direct" effect on the school here. School authorities in reaching out to control beer in cases like this one are entering the sphere of the civil authorities. We hold that the rule in question is invalid as beyond the permissible scope of school rules.

The other main principle involved in considering the validity of a school rule is reasonableness. The general requirement that a rule promulgated by a governmental subdivision or unit be reasonable applies to school board rules. Much of what we have said as to the scope of the rule-making power of school authorities applies to the issue of the reasonableness of a rule itself. In dealing with ineligibility for extracurricular activities as contrasted to expulsion from school altogether, and with students who represent the school in interscholastic activities as contrasted to less active students, school rules may be broader and still be reasonable.

Is the instant rule within the bounds of reason? The rule does not require violation of the criminal law for an infraction to occur, but school rules need not be confined to crimes. To some extent at least, school authorities may base disciplinary measures on immoral acts or on acts definitely contrary to current mores. This particular rule is not confined to the consumption of beer or even to the acquisition, disposition, possession, or transportation of beer. It imposes ineligibility for mere occupation of a car containing beer with knowledge of the presence of the beer, when the beer is discovered by an officer. School authorities may make reasonable beer rules, but we think this rule is too extreme. Some closer relationship between the student and the beer is required than mere knowledge that the beer is there. The rule as written would even prohibit a student from accepting a ride home in a car by an adult neighbor who had a visible package of beer among his purchases. We realize that the rule has been made broad in an effort to avoid problems of proving a connection between the student and the beer, but rules cannot be so extended as to sweep in the innocent in order to achieve invariable conviction of the guilty.

We hold the rule in question is invalid as unreasonable. Reversed.

For an extended version of the case and review questions to test your understanding of the material, please go to www.HumanKinetics.com/CaseStudiesInSportLaw.

Concerned Parents to Save Dreher Park Center v. City of West Palm Beach

846 F.Supp. 986 (S.D. Fla. 1994)

Concerned Parents to Save Dreher Park Center is an unincorporated association of over 50 parents and volunteers organized in response to the elimination of certain recreational programs for persons with disabilities, which had previously been provided by the defendant City of West Palm Beach (the City). The other named plaintiffs are individuals with disabilities who had been participating in these programs prior to their elimination, or parents or guardians of such participants.

In 1986, the City conducted a needs assessment to determine the need for leisure services for persons with physical and/or mental disabilities of West Palm Beach. The City determined that West Palm Beach had a significant disabled population in need of such services. As a result, and since that time, the City has made available a variety of recreational and social programs and activities for individuals with disabilities and their families at the Dreher Park Center.

During Fiscal Year 1992-93 approximately 300 disabled persons participated in the Dreher Park Center programs. The 1992-93 budget for the entire Department of Leisure Services was $6,573,550. Of this amount, the Special Populations section was allotted $384,560 for their budget. Of the $384,560, the Dreher Park Center's share of the budget was $170,694.

In the fall of 1993, as a result of budget constraints the City made various cuts to the 1993-94 budget, including those for programs in the Department of Leisure Services. The entire budget of the Department of Leisure Services was reduced from $6,573,550 in Fiscal Year 1992-93 to $5,919,731 in Fiscal Year 1993-94. The budget for the Special Populations section was reduced from $384,560 to $82,827. The remaining $82,827 is apparently specifically designated for the salary and benefits for one staff member (a Special Population Supervisor) and for utilities and maintenance of the Howard Park Senior Citizens Center building and liability insurance. Three other positions in the Special Populations section (those for personnel at

the Dreher Park Center) were eliminated, as was maintenance for the Dreher Park Center facility. The effective result was that all previously existing programs for persons with disabilities were completely eliminated.

Plaintiffs instituted this action for injunctive relief in the Court of Fifteenth Judicial Circuit alleging violation of the Americans with Disabilities Act, 42 U.S.C. §§ 12101, *et seq.* (the "ADA") and Article I, § 2 of the Florida Constitution. The action was removed from state court and this court has jurisdiction pursuant to 28 U.S.C. § 1331 and § 1441 and the ADA.

To prevail in a motion for preliminary injunction, the movant must show: (1) a substantial likelihood that the movant will ultimately prevail on the merits, (2) that the movant will suffer irreparable injury if the injunction is not issued, (3) that the threatened injury to the movant outweighs the potential harm to the opposing party, and (4) that the injunction, if issued, would not be adverse to the public interest.

The ADA became effective on July 26, 1992, and there is relatively little case law interpreting the reach of the statute. Neither party has directed the court to any case that applies Title II (relating to public services) of the ADA to city-sponsored recreational programs, nor has this court been able to locate any cases directly applicable. However, the statute and regulations promulgated thereunder are clear enough to decide this particular case of first impression.

Title II of the ADA provides that no qualified individual with a disability shall, by reason of such disability, be excluded from participation in or be denied the benefits of the services, programs, or activities of a public entity, or be subjected to discrimination by any such entity. 42 U.S.C. § 12132. Thus, to show a violation of Title II, a plaintiff must show: (1) that he is, or he represents, the interests of a qualified individual with a disability; (2) that such individual was either excluded from participation in or denied the benefits of some public entity's services, programs, or activities or was otherwise discriminated against; and (3) that such exclusion, denial of benefits, or discrimination was by reason of the plaintiff's disability.

First, there is no dispute that plaintiffs or those whose interests plaintiffs represent are qualified individuals with disabilities. The definition of the term is an individual with a disability who, with or without reasonable modifications to rules, policies, or practices meets the essential eligibility requirements for the receipt of services or the participation in programs or activities provided by a public entity. 28 C.F.R. § 35.104.

There is no dispute as to the fact that plaintiffs are individuals with disabilities. However, although defendant has not raised it, the court considered the issue of whether plaintiffs were qualified individuals with disabilities. It could be argued that in many recreational/athletic activities a threshold level of physical and mental abilities constitutes essential eligibility requirements that disabled persons may not meet. As a paradigmatic scenario, it may be the case that there are wheelchair-bound children who cannot meet the essential requirements for a soccer team because they cannot run or cannot kick a ball. However, such an analysis would be persuasive only if the full and entire extent of the City's recreational program was one soccer team. An essential eligibility requirement of a soccer team may be the ability to run and kick, but the only essential eligibility requirement of the City's recreational program (which is the sum of a variety of individual recreational, social, and educational activities and programs) is the request for the benefits of such a program. Therefore, the only essential eligibility requirement that plaintiffs must meet is to request the benefits of a recreational program.

Further, even if certain physical or mental abilities were considered to be essential eligibility requirements, the same nonqualifying disabled individuals may be able to meet such requirements when reasonable modifications to the program are made. Thus, if the City's recreational program is not merely one athletic or other activity but rather an entire network of individual activities and services, a creation of a wheelchair soccer team or something of comparable recreational value may be a reasonable modification of the City's recreational program. The physical ability requirements for wheelchair soccer, obviously, are different than for nondisabled soccer and may be met by the same disabled persons disqualified for regular soccer.

Second, the elimination of the Dreher Park Center programs has the effect of denying persons with disabilities the benefits of the City's recreational programs. The City emphasizes that none of the City's recreational programs are closed to individuals with disabilities, and in this round-about way the City seems to be arguing that because no discriminatory animus exists, there is no Title II violation. Certainly intentional discrimination is banned by Title II. But further, actions that have the effect of discriminating against individuals with disabilities likewise violate the ADA. The most directly applicable part of the regulations under Title II provides that a public entity may not, directly or through contractual or other arrangements, utilize criteria or methods of administration that have the effect of subjecting qualified individuals with disabilities to discrimination on the basis of disability or that have the purpose or effect of defeating or substantially impairing accomplishment of the objectives of the public entity's program with respect to individuals with disabilities. 28 C.F.R. § 35.130(b) (3).

Thus, although the City is not required to offer to the public (disabled or nondisabled) any type of recreational or leisure programs in the first place, when it does provide and administer such programs, it must use methods or criteria that do not have the purpose or effect of impairing its objectives with respect to individuals with disabilities.

The complete elimination of the Dreher Park Center programs clearly has the effect of impairing the Leisure Services Department's self-professed mission statement to provide comprehensive and quality recreation services and entertainment with respect to plaintiffs and other disabled persons. There are no equivalent programs provided by the County of Palm Beach or any other neighboring municipal or private entities (which are also facing shrinking budgets) that can fill the void left by the elimination of these programs. While it is true that there is no evidence of deliberate exclusion of disabled persons from the general recreational programs offered by the City, it is clear that many of the general programs are unable to offer the benefits of recreation to individuals with disabilities because of the nature of the recreational activities and the physical and other limitations of persons with disabilities. Although the ADA contemplates that public entities will provide integrated settings for services and programs, the requirement is for the most integrated setting appropriate to the needs of qualified individuals with disabilities. Therefore, the ADA contemplates that different or separate benefits or services be provided if they are necessary to provide qualified individuals with disabilities with aids, benefits, or services that are as effective as those provided to others. It appears from the evidence that the City had offered the Dreher Park Center programs precisely because they were needed to give equal benefits of recreation to persons with disabilities. When these programs were eliminated, plaintiffs were denied the benefits of the City's leisure services in contravention of Title II.

Lastly, there is strong evidence that the denial of the benefits of recreation was by reason of plaintiffs' disabilities. The City argues that there is no discriminatory intent against the disabled population, but rather that fiscal concerns dictated the elimination of the Dreher Park Center programs. However, at oral argument the City was unable to account for the extreme disparity between the extent of the budget cuts for the disabled population and the nondisabled, nor has any evidence of any other legitimate reason been presented. This is a significant failure of proof because while Title II does not require any particular level of services for persons with disabilities in an absolute sense, it does require that any benefits provided to nondisabled persons must be equally made available for disabled persons. Therefore, had the City cut their entire budget for the Department of Leisure Services, effectively eliminating recreational programs for disabled and nondisabled alike, the ADA would not be implicated because both groups would be equally affected. However, if the City chooses to provide leisure services to nondisabled persons, the ADA requires that the City provide equal opportunity for persons with disabilities to receive comparable benefits.

The court accordingly holds that plaintiffs have shown a substantial likelihood of prevailing on the merits of the ADA claim because there

is persuasive evidence for and a lack of any evidence against the finding that the complete elimination of the Dreher Park Center programs denies the plaintiffs of an equal access to recreational services provided by the City on account of plaintiffs' disabilities.

The court finds that plaintiffs are suffering irreparable injury in the absence of the kinds of programs previously offered by the City, which cannot be remedied by monetary damages. These City-sponsored programs are of great importance in the lives of individuals with disabilities. Indeed, they are even more essential to disabled than to nondisabled persons because various factors (i.e., the limited access to leisure activities, the need for greater supervision, need for trained personnel, physical and other impairments) make it much more difficult for individuals with disabilities to create their own recreational opportunities. The elimination of the Dreher Park Center programs creates irreparable harm because these social, athletic, and other leisure programs present opportunities for recreation that are not being otherwise offered. These programs, prior to their elimination, were contributing to a sense of emotional and psychological well-being, the injury for which injunctive relief is appropriately granted.

The court also finds that irreparable harm suffered by plaintiffs outweighs the potential harm to the City. The City argues that the public purpose of fiscal integrity and maintaining a balanced budget outweighs the injury to plaintiffs. First, the expenditure of funds cannot be considered a harm if the law requires it. Further, some $170,000 in the context of a $6.5 million budget does not create any real issues of fiscal integrity nor presents a threat to an otherwise balanced budget.

Although there is a substantial public interest in balancing the City's budget, as discussed above this interest is not disserved to any significant extent by the continued funding of the Dreher Park Center programs. Further, beyond the interests of the 300 plus disabled individuals that participate in the programs offered by the City, the public also has an interest in meeting the recreational needs of people with disabilities, as well as in upholding the principle of equal rights for individuals with disabilities. The equality of all persons is the underlying principle of the ADA, and one that the public has a strong interest in promoting.

THE COURT has considered the Motion and the pertinent portions of the record, and being otherwise fully advised in the premises, it is ORDERED AND ADJUDGED that the said Motion be, and the same is hereby GRANTED. It is further ORDERED AND ADJUDGED as follows:

1. The City of West Palm Beach shall immediately take all necessary steps to afford the benefits of the City's recreational program to persons with disabilities in full compliance with Title II of the ADA. The City shall submit to this Court within fifteen (15) days of this Order its plan for compliance herewith.

2. The City shall immediately begin to take steps to comply with and conclude with all due speed its compliance with the requirements of 28 C.F.R. §§ 35.105, 35.106, and 35.107, relating to self-evaluation, notice, and designation of responsible employee and adoption of grievance procedures. The City shall submit to this Court within thirty (30) days of this Order its plan and estimated timetable for compliance therewith.

 For an extended version of the case and review questions to test your understanding of the material, please go to www.HumanKinetics.com/CaseStudiesInSportLaw.

Cook v. Colgate University

992 F.2d 17 (2nd Cir. 1993)

Colgate University appeals from a judgment entered in the United States District Court for the Northern District of New York (David N. Hurd, Magistrate Judge) ordering it to elevate its women's club ice hockey team to varsity status and to provide equal funding and benefits to its men's and women's ice hockey programs.

Colgate, a private university, has a male varsity ice hockey team and a female club ice hockey team. Plaintiffs Jennifer Baldwin Cook, Melissa Ehlers, Christine Price, Thayer Jaques, and Julie Wolff are either current or former Colgate students and all are former members of Colgate's women's club ice hockey team.

The athletic department at Colgate sponsors men's and women's sports teams at both the club and varsity levels. The differences between a varsity team and a club team at Colgate are as one might expect. Because of their greater status and visibility, varsity teams generally receive more university recognition, encouragement, and financial support than club teams. Club teams are generally less formal, student-run organizations, with inferior facilities and less financial support. By the same token, club teams provide more opportunity than varsity

teams to students seeking introductory or intermediate level experience in the sport. Although Colgate sponsors a men's varsity ice hockey team, its women's team has remained at the club level.

Any Colgate club team that seeks an upgrade to varsity status may apply as often as once every two years to Colgate's Committee on Athletics. If approved by the Committee, the application wends its way through the bureaucracy up to the President of the University for final approval. Colgate's women's club ice hockey team applied for such an upgrade in 1979, 1983, 1986, and 1988 without success.

Frustrated by Colgate's continual reluctance to elevate the women's club team to varsity status, plaintiffs filed this suit on April 10, 1990, alleging that Colgate's failure to provide a comparable ice hockey program to men and women students violated Title IX of the Education Amendments of 1972, 20 U.S.C. §§ 1681-1688 (1990), the regulations of the Department of Education, as well as the Fifth and Fourteenth Amendments to the Constitution. For its part, Colgate denied any discrimination and argued that its compliance with the mandates of Title IX should be measured by its overall athletic program, not by a sport-by-sport comparison.

Following a three-day bench trial, Magistrate Judge Hurd agreed with the plaintiffs that Colgate's disparate treatment of men and women ice hockey players violated Title IX. Focusing on the disparities between their respective ice hockey programs, he found that Colgate treated its women ice hockey players less favorably than its men ice hockey players, and that it did this without sufficient justification. As a remedy, he ordered Colgate to upgrade the women's club ice hockey team to varsity status starting with the 1993-94 academic year and to provide equal athletic opportunities for women ice hockey players.

Colgate now appeals, arguing, among other things, that the action has become moot because this year's ice hockey season ended on February 28, 1993, and each of the plaintiffs will graduate before commencement of 1993-94 academic year. At oral argument, counsel for the plaintiffs confirmed that Jennifer Baldwin Cook, Melissa Ehlers, and Christine Price have already graduated, and that Thayer Jaques and Julie Wolff, who are now seniors, are scheduled to graduate this May.

It is commonplace that jurisdiction of federal courts is limited to cases and controversies. Hence, litigants are required to demonstrate a "personal stake" or "legally cognizable interest in the outcome" of their case. While the standing doctrine evaluates this personal stake as of the outset of the litigation, the mootness doctrine ensures that the litigant's interest in the outcome continues to exist throughout the life of the lawsuit, including the pendency of the appeal. Accordingly, a case that is "live" at the outset may become moot "when it becomes impossible for the courts, through the exercise of their remedial powers, to do anything to redress the injury."

We agree with Colgate that the end of the ice hockey season and the graduation of the last of the plaintiffs render this action moot. None of the plaintiffs can benefit from an order requiring equal athletic opportunities

for women ice hockey players. The only two plaintiffs with arguable standing are Thayer Jaques and Julie Wolff, both presently seniors at Colgate. However, the district court's order requiring Colgate to upgrade the status of its women's club ice hockey team does not take effect until the 1993-94 academic year. Because Jaques and Wolff will have graduated by then, nothing that we decide could affect their rights *vis-à-vis* Colgate.

Plaintiffs maintain that this action falls within the exception to the mootness doctrine for those situations "capable of repetition, yet evading review." In the absence of a class action, however, that exception is unavailable unless "(1) the challenged action [is] in its duration too short to be fully litigated prior to its cessation or expiration, and (2) there [is] a reasonable expectation that the same complaining party would be subjected to the same action again." *Weinstein v. Bradford*, 423 U.S. 147, 149. Both prongs of the exception must be present and here the plaintiffs fail to satisfy the second.

The last of the complaining parties will graduate before the district court's order can affect them, and there has been no suggestion that Colgate's policies will be visited on any one of them in the future. Accordingly, these plaintiffs may not litigate the claims of students unnamed and unrepresented in this action. We have suggested that a student's claim may not be rendered moot by graduation if he or she sued in a "representational capacity" as the leader of a student organization. However, the complaint herein sought damages and injunctive relief solely on behalf of the plaintiffs individually, not as representatives of the women's ice hockey club team or other "similarly situated" individuals.

The judgment of the district court is vacated and the matter remanded to the district court with instructions to dismiss the action as moot.

 For an extended version of the case and review questions to test your understanding of the material, please go to www.HumanKinetics.com/CaseStudiesInSportLaw.

DeFrantz v. United States Olympic Committee

492 F.Supp. 1181 (D.C. Cir. 1980)

Plaintiffs, 25 athletes and one member of the Executive Board of defendant United States Olympic Committee (USOC), have moved for an injunction barring defendant USOC from carrying out a resolution, adopted by the USOC House of Delegates on April 12, 1980, not to send an American team to participate in the Games of the XXIInd Olympiad to be held in Moscow in the summer of 1980. Plaintiffs allege that in preventing American athletes from competing in the Summer Olympics, defendant has exceeded its statutory powers and has abridged plaintiffs' constitutional rights.

For the reasons discussed below, we find that plaintiffs have failed to state a claim on which relief can be granted. Accordingly, we deny plaintiffs' claim for injunctive and declaratory relief and dismiss the action.

In essence, the action before us involves a dispute between athletes who wish to compete in the Olympic Games to be held in Moscow this summer, and the United States Olympic Committee, which has denied them that opportunity in the wake of the invasion and continued occupation of Afghanistan by Soviet military forces. Because this dispute confronts us with questions concerning the statutory authority of the USOC, its place and appropriate role in the international Olympic movement, and its relationship to the United States Government and with certain United States officials, we begin with a brief discussion of the organizational structure of the Olympic Games and the facts that have brought this action before us. These facts are not in dispute.

According to its rules and bylaws, the International Olympic Committee (IOC) governs the Olympic movement and owns the rights of the Olympic Games. IOC Rules provide that National Olympic Committees (NOC) may be established as the sole authorities responsible for the representation of the respective countries at the Olympic Games, so long as the NOC's rules and regulations are approved by the IOC. The USOC is one such National Olympic Committee.

The USOC is a corporation created and granted a federal charter by Congress in 1950. Pub.L. No. 81-805, 64 Stat. 899. This charter was revised by the Amateur Sports Act of 1978, Pub.L. No. 95-606, 92 Stat. 3045, 36 U.S.C. §§ 371 *et seq.* Under this statute, defendant USOC has exclusive jurisdiction and authority over participation and representation of the United States in the Olympic Games.

The routine procedure initiating the participation of a national team in Olympic competition is the acceptance by the NOC of an invitation from the Olympic Organizing Committee for the particular games. In accordance with this routine procedure under IOC Rules, the Moscow Olympic Organizing Committee extended an invitation to the USOC to participate in the Summer Games. Recent international and domestic events, however, have made acceptance of this invitation, which must come on or before May 24, 1980, anything but routine.

On March 21, 1980, President Carter told members of the Athletes Advisory Council, an official body of the USOC, that American athletes will not participate in the Moscow Summer Games. On April 8, 1980, the President sent a telegram to the president and officers of the USOC and to its House of Delegates, urging the USOC to vote against sending an American team to Moscow. In an April 10th speech, the President said, "if legal actions are necessary to enforce (my) decision not to send a team to Moscow, then I will take those legal actions." On April 10 and 11, 1980, the 13-member Administrative Committee of the USOC met in Colorado Springs and voted to support a resolution against sending a team to Moscow. Only Anita DeFrantz, a plaintiff in this action, dissented.

Plaintiffs state three causes of action in their complaint. The first, a statutory claim, is that defendant violated the Amateur Sports Act of 1978. Plaintiffs' second cause of action, a constitutional claim, alleges that defendant's action constituted governmental action that abridged plaintiffs' rights of liberty, self-expression, personal autonomy, and privacy guaranteed by the First, Fifth, and Ninth Amendments to the United States Constitution. Plaintiffs' third cause of action is that the USOC has violated its constitution, bylaws, and governing statute, injuring the USOC and violating the rights of plaintiff Shaw, a member of the USOC's Executive Board, and that defendant is subject to an action to compel compliance with its constitution, bylaws, and governing statute.

Plaintiffs allege that unredressed, these violations will result in great and irreparable injury to the athletes. Many would lose a once-in-a-lifetime opportunity to participate in the Olympic Games, and the honor and prestige that such participation affords. Most of the class members are at or near their physical peaks at the present time and will not physically be capable of reaching the same or higher levels at a later period of their lives.

In summary, plaintiffs ask this court to declare the April 12, 1980 resolution of the USOC House of Delegates null and void because it violated statutory authority and constitutional provisions and to permanently enjoin the USOC from carrying out that resolution.

Defendant and the government have moved to dismiss pursuant to Rule 12(b) (6), Fed. R. Civ. P. and argue for dismissal of this action on several grounds. They contend that the Amateur Sports Act of 1978 has not been violated by defendant, that the Act does not deny the USOC the authority to decide not to send an American team to the Moscow Games, that the Act does not grant plaintiffs a right to compete in the Olympics if the USOC decides not to enter a team, and that plaintiffs lack a cause of action under the Act to maintain this lawsuit. As for the constitutional claims, they argue that the decision of the USOC was not state action and therefore, that plaintiffs have no cognizable constitutional claims. They further argue that even if the action of the USOC could be considered state action, no rights guaranteed to plaintiffs under the Constitution were abridged.

Plaintiffs allege in their complaint that by its decision not to send an American team to compete in the Summer Olympic Games in Moscow, defendant USOC has violated the Amateur Sports Act of 1978, *supra*, (The Act) in at least six respects. Reduced to their essentials, these allegations are that the Act does not give, and that Congress intended to deny, the USOC the authority to decide not to enter an American team in the Olympics, except perhaps for sports-related reasons, and that the Act guarantees to certain athletes a right to compete in the Olympic Games, which defendant denied them.

The United States Olympic Committee was first incorporated and granted a federal charter in 1950. Pub.L. No. 81-805, *supra*. However, predecessors to the now federally-chartered USOC have existed since 1896, and since that time, they have exercised the authority granted by the International Olympic Committee to represent the United States as its National Olympic Committee in matters pertaining to participation in Olympic Games. It is unquestioned by plaintiffs that under the International Olympic Committees Rules and Bylaws, the National Olympic Committees have the right to determine their nation's participation in the Olympics. IOC Rule 24B provides that NOCs shall be the sole authorities responsible for the representation of the respective countries at the Olympic Games and chapter 5, paragraph 7 of the bylaws to Rule 24 provides that representation covers the decision to participate. Nothing in the IOC Charter, Rules, or Bylaws requires a NOC, such as the USOC, to accept an invitation to participate in any particular Olympic contest and the President of the IOC has said that participation in the Olympic Games is entirely voluntary. As defendant has argued, an invitation to participate is just that, an invitation, which may be accepted or declined.

Because defendant USOC clearly has the power under IOC Rules to decide not to enter an American team in Olympic competition, the question then becomes whether the Amateur Sports Act of 1978, which rewrote the USOC's charter, denies the USOC that power. Plaintiffs emphatically argue that it does, and defendant and the government just as emphatically argue that it does not.

Plaintiffs' argument is simple and straightforward: The Act by its terms does not expressly confer on the USOC the power to decline to participate in the Olympic Games, and if any such power can be inferred from the statute, the power must be exercised for sports-related reasons. Defendant and the government respond that the

Act gives the USOC broad powers, including the authority to decide not to accept an invitation to send an American team to the Olympics.

The principal substantive powers of the USOC are found in § 375(a) of the Act. In determining whether the USOC's authority under the Act encompasses the right to decide not to participate in an Olympic contest, we must read these provisions in the context in which they were written. In writing this legislation, Congress did not create a new relationship between the USOC and the IOC. Rather, it recognized an already long-existing relationship between the two and statutorily legitimized that relationship with a federal charter and federal incorporation. The legislative history demonstrates Congressional awareness that the USOC and its predecessors, as the National Olympic Committee for the United States, have had a continuing relationship with the IOC since 1896. Congress was necessarily aware that a National Olympic Committee is a creation and a creature of the International Olympic Committee, to whose rules and regulations it must conform. The NOC gets its power and its authority from the IOC, the sole proprietor and owner of the Olympic Games.

In view of Congress' obvious awareness of these facts, we would expect that if Congress intended to limit or deny to the USOC powers it already enjoyed as a National Olympic Committee, such limitation or denial would be clear and explicit. No such language appears in the statute. Indeed, far from precluding this authority, the language of the statute appears to embrace it. For example, the objects and purposes section of the Act speaks in broad terms, stating that the USOC shall exercise exclusive jurisdiction over all matters pertaining to the participation of the United States in the Olympic Games. We read this broadly stated purpose in conjunction with the specific power conferred on the USOC by the Act to represent the United States as its National Olympic Committee in relations with the International Olympic Committee, and in conjunction with the IOC Rules and Bylaws, which provide that representation includes the decision to participate. In doing so, we find a compatibility and not a conflict between the Act and the IOC Rules on the issue of the authority of the USOC to decide whether or not to accept an invita-

tion to field an American team at the Olympics. The language of the statute is broad enough to confer this authority, and we find that Congress must have intended that the USOC exercise that authority in this area, which it already enjoyed because of its long-standing relationship with the IOC. We accordingly conclude that the USOC has the authority to decide not to send an American team to the Olympics.

Plaintiffs next argue that if the USOC does have the authority to decide not to accept an invitation to send an American team to the Moscow Olympics, that decision must be based on sports-related considerations. In support of their argument, plaintiffs point to §§ 392(a) (5) and (b) of the Act, which plaintiffs acknowledge are not in terms applicable to the USOC, but rather concern situations in which national governing bodies of various sports, which are subordinate to the USOC, are asked to sanction the holding of international competitions below the level of the Olympic or Pan American Games in the United States or the participation of the United States athletes in such competition abroad. These sections provide that a national governing body may withhold its sanctions only on clear and convincing evidence that holding or participating in the competition would be detrimental to the best interests of the sport. Plaintiffs argue by analogy that a similar sports-related limitation must attach to any authority the USOC might have to decide not to participate in an Olympic competition. We cannot agree.

The provision on which plaintiffs place reliance by analogy is specifically concerned with eliminating the feuding between various amateur athletic organizations and national governing bodies that for so long characterized amateur athletics. As all parties recognize, this friction, such as the well-publicized power struggles between the NCAA and the AAU, was a major reason for passage of the Act, and the provisions plaintiffs cite, among others, are aimed at eliminating this senseless strife, which the Senate and House Committee Reports indicate had dramatically harmed the ability of the United States to compete effectively in international competition. In order to eliminate this internecine squabbling, the Act elevated the USOC to a supervisory role over the various amateur athletic organizations, and provided that the USOC establish procedures for the swift and equitable settlement of these disputes. As indicated above, it also directed that the national governing bodies of the various sports could only withhold their approvals of international competition for sports-related reasons. Previously, many of these bodies had withheld their sanction of certain athletic competitions in order to further their own interests at the expense of other groups and to the detriment of athletes wishing to participate.

In brief, this sports-related limitation is intimately tied to the specific purpose of curbing the arbitrary and unrestrained power of various athletic organizations subordinate to the USOC not to allow athletes to compete in international competition below the level of the Olympic Games and the Pan American Games. This purpose has nothing to do with a decision by the USOC to exercise authority granted by the IOC to decide not to participate in an Olympic competition.

We therefore conclude that the USOC not only had the authority to decide not to send an American team to the Summer Olympics, but also that it could do so for reasons not directly related to sports considerations.

Plaintiffs argue that the Act provides, in express terms, an Athlete's Bill of Rights, pointing to the following provisions in the Act's objects and purposes section, which directs that the USOC shall provide for the swift resolution of conflicts and disputes involving amateur athletes, national governing bodies, and amateur sports organizations, and protect the opportunity of any amateur athlete, coach, trainer, manager, administrator, or official to participate in amateur athletic competition. 36 U.S.C. § 374(8). A similar provision is contained in § 382b, which provides that the USOC shall establish and maintain provisions for the swift and equitable resolution of disputes involving any of its members and relating to the opportunity of an amateur athlete, coach, trainer, manager, administrator, or official to participate in the Olympic Games or other such protected competition as defined in such constitution and bylaws.

Plaintiffs argue that the Report of the President's Commission on Olympic Sports, which was the starting point for the legislation proposed, and the legislative history supports their

argument that the statute confers an enforceable right on plaintiffs to compete in Olympic competition. Again, we are compelled to disagree with plaintiffs.

The legislative history and the statute are clear that the right to compete, which plaintiffs refer to, is in the context of the numerous jurisdictional disputes between various athletic bodies, such as the NCAA and the AAU, which we have just discussed, and which was a major impetus for the Amateur Sports Act of 1978.

The Senate Report makes clear that the language relied on by plaintiffs is not designed to provide any substantive guarantees, let alone a Bill of Rights. Further, to the extent that any guarantees of a right to compete are included in the USOC Constitution as a result of this provision, they do not include a right that amateur athletes may compete in the Olympic Games despite a decision by the USOC House of Delegates not to accept an invitation to enter an American team in the competition. This provision simply was not designed to extend so far. Rather, it was designed to remedy the jurisdictional disputes among amateur athletic bodies, not disputes between athletes and the USOC itself over the exercise of the USOC's discretion not to participate in the Olympics.

Plaintiffs argue that they have a private cause of action under the Amateur Sports Act of 1978 to maintain an action to enforce their rights under that Act. This argument assumes (1) the existence of a right, and (2) the capability of enforcing that right by a private cause of action. As the foregoing discussion establishes, we have found that the statute does not guarantee plaintiffs a right to compete in the Olympics if the USOC decides not to send an American team to the Olympic Games and we have found that defendant has violated no provision of the Act. Thus, the right the plaintiffs seek to enforce under the Act simply does not exist. Under these circumstances, we cannot find that plaintiffs have an implied private right of action under the Amateur Sports Act to enforce a right that does not exist.

Plaintiffs have alleged that the decision of the USOC not to enter an American team in the Summer Olympics has violated certain rights guaranteed to plaintiffs under the First, Fifth, and Ninth Amendments to the United States Constitution. This presents us with two questions: (1)

whether the USOC's decision was governmental action (state action), and, assuming state action is found; and (2) whether the USOC's decision abridged any constitutionally-protected rights.

Although federally chartered, defendant is a private organization. Because the Due Process Clause of the Fifth Amendment, on which plaintiffs place great reliance, applies only to actions by the federal government, plaintiffs must show that the USOC vote is a governmental act (i.e., state action). In defining state action, the courts have fashioned two guidelines. The first involves an inquiry into whether the state has so far insinuated itself into a position of interdependence with (the private entity) that it must be recognized as a joint participant in the challenged activity. *Burton v. Wilmington Parking Authority*, 365 U.S. 715, 725, 81 S.Ct. 856, 862, 6 L.Ed.2d 45 (1961).

Here, there is no such intermingling, and there is no factual justification for finding that the federal government and the USOC enjoyed the symbiotic relationship that courts have required to find state action. The USOC has received no federal funding and it exists and operates independently of the federal government. Its chartering statute gives it exclusive jurisdiction over all matters pertaining to the participation of the United States in the Olympic Games. To be sure, the Act does link the USOC and the federal government to the extent it requires the USOC to submit an annual report to the President and Congress. But this hardly converts such an independent relationship to a joint participation.

The second guideline fashioned by the courts involves an inquiry of whether there is a sufficiently close nexus between the state and the challenged action of the regulated entity so that the action of the latter may be fairly treated as that of the state itself. *Jackson v. Metropolitan Edison Co.*, 419 U.S. 345, 351, 95 S.Ct. 449, 453, 42 L.Ed.2d 477 (1974).

In the instant case, there was no requirement that any federal government body approve actions by the USOC before they become effective. Plaintiffs clearly recognize this, but they argue that by the actions of certain federal officials, the federal government initiated, encouraged, and approved of the result reached (i.e., the vote of the USOC not to send an American team to the Summer Olympics). Plaintiffs advance a novel theory.

Essentially, their argument is that the campaign of governmental persuasion, personally led by President Carter, crossed the line from governmental recommendation, which plaintiffs find acceptable and presumably necessary to the operation of our form of government, into the area of affirmative pressure that effectively places the government's prestige behind the challenged action, and thus, results in state action. We cannot agree.

Here there is no such control. The USOC is an independent body, and nothing in its chartering statute gives the federal government the right to control that body or its officers. Furthermore, the facts here do not indicate that the federal government was able to exercise any type of *de facto* control over the USOC. The USOC decided by a secret ballot of its House of Delegates. The federal government may have had the power to prevent the athletes from participating in the Olympics even if the USOC had voted to allow them to participate, but it did not have the power to make them vote in a certain way. All it had was the power of persuasion. We cannot equate this with control. To do so in cases of this type would be to open the door and usher the courts into what we believe is a largely nonjusticiable realm, where they would find themselves in the untenable position of determining whether a certain level, intensity, or type of Presidential or administration or political pressure amounts to sufficient control over a private entity so as to invoke federal jurisdiction.

We accordingly find that the decision of the USOC not to send an American team to the Summer Olympics was not state action, and therefore, does not give rise to an actionable claim for the infringements of the constitutional rights alleged.

Assuming *arguendo* that the vote of the USOC constituted state action, we turn briefly to plaintiffs' contention that by this action they have been deprived of their constitutional rights to liberty, to self-expression, to travel, and to pursue their chosen occupation of athletic endeavor. Were we to find state action in this case, we would conclude that defendant USOC has violated no constitutionally-protected right of plaintiffs.

Plaintiffs have been unable to draw our attention to any court decision that finds that the rights allegedly violated here enjoy constitutional protection, and we can find none. Plaintiffs would expand the constitutionally-protected scope of liberty and self-expression to include the denial of an amateur athlete's right to compete in an Olympic contest when that denial was the result of a decision by a supervisory athletic organization acting well within the limits of its authority.

Defendant has not denied plaintiffs the right to engage in every amateur athletic competition. Defendant has not denied plaintiffs the right to engage in their chosen occupation. Defendant has not even denied plaintiffs the right to travel, only the right to travel for one specific purpose. We can

find no justification and no authority for the expansive reading of the Constitution that plaintiffs urge. To find as plaintiffs recommend would be to open the floodgates to a torrent of lawsuits.

The courts have correctly recognized that many of life's disappointments, even major ones, do not enjoy constitutional protection. This is one such instance.

For an extended version of the case and review questions to test your understanding of the material, please go to www.HumanKinetics.com/CaseStudiesInSportLaw.

Faragher v. City of Boca Raton

524 U.S. 775 (1998)

This case calls for identification of the circumstances under which an employer may be held liable under Title VII of the Civil Rights Act of 1964, 78 Stat. 253, as amended, 42 U.S.C. §§ 2000e *et seq.*, for the acts of a supervisory employee whose sexual harassment of subordinates has created a hostile work environment amounting to employment discrimination.

Between 1985 and 1990, while attending college, petitioner Beth Ann Faragher worked part time and during the summers as an ocean lifeguard for the Marine Safety Section of the Parks and Recreation Department of respondent, the City of Boca Raton, Florida (City). During this period, Faragher's immediate supervisors were Bill Terry, David Silverman, and Robert Gordon. In June 1990, Faragher resigned.

In 1992, Faragher brought an action against Terry, Silverman, and the City, asserting claims under Title VII, Rev. Stat. §1979, 42 U.S.C. § 1983, and Florida law. So far as it concerns the Title VII claim, the complaint alleged that Terry and Silverman created a "sexually hostile atmosphere" at the beach by repeatedly subjecting Faragher and other female lifeguards to "uninvited and offensive touching," by making lewd remarks, and by speaking of women in offensive terms. The complaint contained specific allegations that Terry once said that he would never promote a

woman to the rank of lieutenant, and that Silverman had said to Faragher, "Date me or clean the toilets for a year." Asserting that Terry and Silverman were agents of the City, and that their conduct amounted to discrimination in the "terms, conditions, and privileges" of her employment, Faragher sought a judgment against the City for nominal damages, costs, and attorney's fees.

Following a bench trial, the United States District Court for the Southern District of Florida found that throughout Faragher's employment with the City, Terry served as chief of the Marine Safety Division, with authority to hire new lifeguards (subject to the approval of higher management), to supervise all aspects of the lifeguards' work assignments, to engage in counseling, to deliver oral reprimands, and to make a record of any such discipline. Silverman was a Marine Safety lieutenant from 1985 until June 1989, when he became a captain. Gordon began the employment period as a lieutenant and at some point was promoted to the position of training captain. In these positions, Silverman and Gordon were responsible for making the lifeguards' daily assignments and for supervising their work and fitness training.

The lifeguards and supervisors were stationed at the city beach and worked out of the Marine Safety Headquarters, a small one-story building containing an office, a meeting room, and a single, unisex locker room with a shower. Their work routine was structured in a "paramilitary configuration," . . . , with a clear chain of command. Lifeguards reported to lieutenants and captains, who reported to Terry. He was supervised by the recreation superintendent, who in turn reported to a director of Parks and Recreation, answerable to the city manager. The lifeguards had no significant contact with higher city officials like the Recreation superintendent.

In February 1986, the City adopted a sexual harassment policy, which it stated in a memorandum from the city manager addressed to all employees. In May 1990, the City revised the policy and reissued a statement of it. Although the City may actually have circulated the memos and statements to some employees, it completely failed to disseminate its policy among employees of the Marine Safety Section, with the result that Terry, Silverman, Gordon, and many lifeguards were unaware of it.

From time to time over the course of Faragher's tenure at the Marine Safety Section, between four and six of the 40 to 50 lifeguards were women. During that five-year period, Terry repeatedly touched the bodies of female employees without invitation, would put his arm around Faragher, with his hand on her buttocks, and once made contact with another female lifeguard in a motion of sexual simulation. He made crudely demeaning references to women generally, and once commented disparagingly on Faragher's shape. During a job interview with a woman he hired as a lifeguard, Terry said that the female lifeguards had sex with their male counterparts and asked whether she would do the same.

Silverman behaved in similar ways. He once tackled Faragher and remarked that, but for a physical characteristic he found unattractive, he would readily have had sexual relations with her. Another time, he pantomimed an act of oral sex. Within earshot of the female lifeguards, Silverman made frequent, vulgar references to women and sexual matters, commented on the bodies of female lifeguards and beachgoers, and at least twice told female lifeguards that he would like to engage in sex with them.

Faragher did not complain to higher management about Terry or Silverman. Although she

spoke of their behavior to Gordon, she did not regard these discussions as formal complaints to a supervisor but as conversations with a person she held in high esteem. Other female lifeguards had similarly informal talks with Gordon, but because Gordon did not feel that it was his place to do so, he did not report these complaints to Terry, his own supervisor, or to any other City official. Gordon responded to the complaints of one lifeguard by saying that "the City just [doesn't] care."

In April 1990, however, two months before Faragher's resignation, Nancy Ewanchew, a former lifeguard, wrote to Richard Bender, the City's personnel director, complaining that Terry and Silverman had harassed her and other female lifeguards. Following investigation of this complaint, the City found that Terry and Silverman had behaved improperly, reprimanded them, and required them to choose between a suspension without pay or the forfeiture of annual leave.

On the basis of these findings, the district court concluded that the conduct of Terry and Silverman was discriminatory harassment sufficiently serious to alter the conditions of Faragher's employment and constitute an abusive working environment. The district court then ruled that there were three justifications for holding the City liable for the harassment of its supervisory employees. First, the court noted that the harassment was pervasive enough to support an inference that the City had "knowledge, or constructive knowledge" of it. Next, it ruled that the City was liable under traditional agency principles because Terry and Silverman were acting as its agents when they committed the harassing acts. Finally, the court observed that Gordon's knowledge of the harassment, combined with his inaction, "provides a further basis for imputing liability on [sic] the City." The district court then awarded Faragher $1 in nominal damages on her Title VII claim.

A panel of the Court of Appeals for the Eleventh Circuit reversed the judgment against the City. We granted *certiorari*, and now reverse the judgment of the Eleventh Circuit and remand for entry of judgment in Faragher's favor.

Under Title VII of the Civil Rights Act of 1964, "[i]t shall be an unlawful employment practice for an employer . . . to fail or refuse to hire or to discharge any individual, or otherwise to discriminate against any individual with respect to his compensation, terms, conditions, or privileges of employment, because of such individual's race, color, religion, sex, or national origin." We have repeatedly made clear that although the statute mentions specific employment decisions with immediate consequences, the scope of the prohibition "is not limited to 'economic' or 'tangible' discrimination." . . .

We explained that in order to be actionable under the statute, a sexually objectionable environment must be both objectively and subjectively offensive, one that a reasonable person would find hostile or abusive, and one that the victim in fact did perceive to be so. We directed courts to determine whether an environment is sufficiently hostile or abusive by "looking at all the circumstances," including the "frequency of the discriminatory conduct; its severity; whether it is physically threatening or humiliating, or a mere offensive utterance; and whether it unreasonably interferes with an employee's work performance." Most recently, we explained that Title VII does not prohibit "genuine but innocuous differences in the ways men and women routinely interact with members of the same sex and of the opposite sex." A recurring point in these opinions is that "simple teasing," . . . , offhand comments, and isolated incidents (unless extremely serious) will not amount to discriminatory changes in the "terms and conditions of employment." These standards for judging hostility are sufficiently demanding to ensure that Title VII does not become a "general civility code." Properly applied, they will filter out complaints attacking "the ordinary tribulations of the workplace, such as the sporadic use of abusive language, gender-related jokes, and occasional teasing." We have made it clear that conduct must be extreme to amount to a change in the terms and conditions of employment, and the courts of appeals have heeded this view.

While indicating the substantive contours of the hostile environments forbidden by Title VII, our cases have established few definite rules for determining when an employer will be liable for a discriminatory environment that is otherwise actionably abusive. Given the circumstances

of many of the litigated cases, including some that have come to us, it is not surprising that in many of them, the issue has been joined over the sufficiency of the abusive conditions, not the standards for determining an employer's liability for them.

The court of appeals identified, and rejected, three possible grounds drawn from agency law for holding the City vicariously liable for the hostile environment created by the supervisors. It considered whether the two supervisors were acting within the scope of their employment when they engaged in the harassing conduct. The court then inquired whether they were significantly aided by the agency relationship in committing the harassment, and also considered the possibility of imputing Gordon's knowledge of the harassment to the City. Finally, the court of appeals ruled out liability for negligence in failing to prevent the harassment. Faragher relies principally on the latter three theories of liability.

A "master is subject to liability for the torts of his servants committed while acting in the scope of their employment." This doctrine has traditionally defined the "scope of employment" as including conduct "of the kind [a servant] is employed to perform," occurring "substantially within the authorized time and space limits," and "actuated, at least in part, by a purpose to serve the master," but as excluding an intentional use of force "unexpectable by the master." Courts of appeals have typically held, or assumed, that conduct similar to the subject of this complaint falls outside the scope of employment. In so doing, the courts have emphasized that harassment consisting of unwelcome remarks and touching is motivated solely by individual desires and serves no purpose of the employer. For this reason, courts have likened hostile environment sexual harassment to the classic "frolic and detour" for which an employer has no vicarious liability. Here it is enough to recognize that their disparate results do not necessarily reflect wildly varying terms of the particular employment contracts involved, but represent differing judgments about the desirability of holding an employer liable for his subordinates' wayward behavior.

The proper analysis here, then, calls not for a mechanical application of indefinite and malleable factors set forth in the Restatement, *see*, e.g., §§ 219, 228, 229, but rather an inquiry into the reasons that would support a conclusion that harassing behavior ought to be held within the scope of a supervisor's employment, and the reasons for the opposite view. The Restatement itself points to such an approach, as in the commentary that the "ultimate question" in determining the scope of employment is "whether or not it is just that the loss resulting from the servant's acts should be considered as one of the normal risks to be borne by the business in which the servant is employed."

It is by now well recognized that hostile environment sexual harassment by supervisors (and, for that matter, coemployees) is a persistent problem in the workplace. An employer can, in a general sense, reasonably anticipate the possibility of such conduct occurring in its workplace, and one might justify the assignment of the burden of the untoward behavior to the employer as one of the costs of doing business, to be charged to the enterprise rather than the victim.

Two things counsel us to draw the contrary conclusion. First, there is no reason to suppose that Congress wished courts to ignore the traditional distinction between acts falling within the scope and acts amounting to what the older law called frolics or detours from the course of employment. Such a distinction can readily be applied to the spectrum of possible harassing conduct by supervisors. First, a supervisor might discriminate racially in job assignments in order to placate the prejudice pervasive in the labor force. Instances of this variety of the heckler's veto would be consciously intended to further the employer's interests by preserving peace in the workplace. Next, supervisors might reprimand male employees for workplace failings with banter, but respond to women's shortcomings in harsh or vulgar terms. A third example might be the supervisor who, as here, expresses his sexual interests in ways having no apparent object whatever of serving an interest of the employer. If a line is to be drawn between scope and frolic, it would lie between the first two examples and

the third, and it thus makes sense in terms of traditional agency law to analyze the scope issue, in cases like the third example, just as most federal courts addressing that issue have done, classifying the harassment as beyond the scope of employment.

The second reason goes to an even broader unanimity of views among the holdings of district courts and courts of appeals thus far. Those courts have held not only that the sort of harassment at issue here was outside the scope of supervisors' authority, but, by uniformly judging employer liability for co-worker harassment under a negligence standard, they have also implicitly treated such harassment as outside the scope of common employees' duties. If, indeed, the cases did not rest, at least implicitly, on the notion that such harassment falls outside the scope of employment, their liability issues would have turned simply on the application of the scope-of-employment rule.

It is quite unlikely that these cases would escape efforts to render them obsolete if we were to hold that supervisors who engage in discriminatory harassment are necessarily acting within the scope of their employment. The rationale for placing harassment within the scope of supervisory authority would be the fairness of requiring the employer to bear the burden of foreseeable social behavior, and the same rationale would apply when the behavior was that of co-employees. The employer generally benefits just as obviously from the work of common employees as from the work of supervisors; they simply have different jobs to do, all aimed at the success of the enterprise. As between an innocent employer and an innocent employee, if we use scope-of-employment reasoning to require the employer to bear the cost of an actionably hostile workplace created by one class of employees (i.e., supervisors), it could appear just as appropriate to do the same when the environment was created by another class (i.e., co-workers).

The answer to this argument might well be to point out that the scope of supervisory employment may be treated separately by recognizing that supervisors have special authority enhancing their capacity to harass, and that the employer can guard against their misbehavior more easily because their numbers are by definition fewer than the numbers of regular employees. But this answer happens to implicate an entirely separate category of agency law, which imposes vicarious liability on employers for tortious acts committed by use of particular authority conferred as an element of an employee's agency relationship with the employer. Since the virtue of categorical clarity is obvious, it is better to reject reliance on misuse of supervisory authority (without more) as irrelevant to scope-of-employment analysis.

The court of appeals also rejected vicarious liability on the part of the City insofar as it might rest on the concluding principle set forth in § 219(2)(d) of the Restatement, that an employer "is not subject to liability for the torts of his servants acting outside the scope of their employment unless . . . the servant purported to act or speak on behalf of the principal and there was reliance on apparent authority, or he was aided in accomplishing the tort by the existence of the agency relation." Faragher points to several ways in which the agency relationship aided Terry and Silverman in carrying out their harassment. She argues that in general offending supervisors can abuse their authority to keep subordinates in their presence while they make offensive statements, and that they implicitly threaten to misuse their supervisory powers to deter any resistance or complaint. Thus, she maintains that power conferred on Terry and Silverman by the City enabled them to act for so long without provoking defiance or complaint.

The City, however, contends that § 219(2)(d) has no application here. It argues that the second qualification of the subsection, referring to a servant "aided in accomplishing the tort by the existence of the agency relation," merely "refines" the one preceding it, which holds the employer vicariously. But this narrow reading is untenable; it would render the second qualification of § 219(2)(d) almost entirely superfluous (and would seem to ask us to shut our eyes to the potential effects of supervisory authority, even when not explicitly invoked). The illustrations accompanying this subsection make clear that it covers not only cases involving the abuse of apparent authority, but also cases in which tortious conduct is made possible or facilitated by the existence of the actual agency relationship.

We therefore agree with Faragher that in implementing Title VII it makes sense to hold an employer vicariously liable for some tortious conduct of a supervisor made possible by abuse of his supervisory authority, and that the aided-by-agency-relation principle embodied in § 219(2)(d) of the Restatement provides an appropriate starting point for determining liability for the kind of harassment presented here. Several courts, indeed, have noted what Faragher has argued, that there is a sense in which a harassing supervisor is always assisted in his misconduct by the supervisory relationship. The agency relationship affords contact with an employee subjected to a supervisor's sexual harassment, and the victim may well be reluctant to accept the risks of blowing the whistle on a superior. When a person with supervisory authority discriminates in the terms and conditions of subordinates' employment, his actions necessarily draw on his superior position over the people who report to him, or those under them, whereas an employee generally cannot check a supervisor's abusive conduct the same way that she might deal with abuse from a co-worker. When a fellow employee harasses, the victim can walk away or tell the offender where to go, but it may be difficult to offer such responses to a supervisor, whose "power to supervise—[which may be] to hire and fire, and to set work schedules and pay rates—does not disappear . . . when he chooses to harass through insults and offensive gestures rather than directly with threats of firing or promises of promotion." Recognition of employer liability when discriminatory misuse of supervisory authority alters the terms and conditions of a victim's employment is underscored by the fact that the employer has a greater opportunity to guard against misconduct by supervisors than by common workers; employers have greater opportunity and incentive to screen them, train them, and monitor their performance.

Although Title VII seeks "to make persons whole for injuries suffered on account of unlawful employment discrimination," . . . its "primary objective," like that of any statute meant to influence primary conduct, is not to provide redress but to avoid harm. As long ago as 1980, the EEOC, charged with the enforcement of Title VII, adopted regulations advising employers to "take all steps necessary to prevent sexual harassment from occurring, such as . . . informing employees of their right to raise and how to raise the issue of harassment," and in 1990 the EEOC issued a policy statement enjoining employers to establish a complaint procedure "designed to encourage victims of harassment to come forward [without requiring] a victim to complain first to the offending supervisor." It would therefore implement clear statutory policy and complement the government's Title VII enforcement efforts to recognize the employer's affirmative obligation to prevent violations and give credit here to employers who make reasonable efforts to discharge their duty. Indeed, a theory of vicarious liability for misuse of supervisory power would be at odds with the statutory policy if it failed to provide employers with some such incentive.

In order to accommodate the principle of vicarious liability for harm caused by misuse of supervisory authority, as well as Title VII's equally basic policies of encouraging forethought by employers and saving action by objecting employees, we adopt the following holding in this case. An employer is subject to vicarious liability to a victimized employee for an actionable hostile environment created by a supervisor with immediate (or successively higher) authority over the employee. When no tangible employment action is taken, a defending employer may raise an affirmative defense to liability or damages, subject to proof by a preponderance of the evidence, *see* Fed. Rule Civ. Proc. 8(c). The defense comprises two necessary elements: (a) that the employer exercised reasonable care to prevent and correct promptly any sexually harassing behavior, and (b) that the plaintiff employee unreasonably failed to take advantage of any preventive or corrective opportunities provided by the employer or to avoid harm otherwise. While proof that an employer had promulgated an antiharassment policy with complaint procedure is not necessary in every instance as a matter of law, the need

for a stated policy suitable to the employment circumstances may appropriately be addressed in any case when litigating the first element of the defense. And while proof that an employee failed to fulfill the corresponding obligation of reasonable care to avoid harm is not limited to showing an unreasonable failure to use any complaint procedure provided by the employer, a demonstration of such failure will normally suffice to satisfy the employer's burden under the second element of the defense. No affirmative defense is available, however, when the supervisor's harassment culminates in a tangible employment action, such as discharge, demotion, or undesirable reassignment.

It is undisputed that these supervisors "were granted virtually unchecked authority" over their subordinates, "directly controll[ing] and supervis[ing] all aspects of [Faragher's] day-to-day activities." It is also clear that Faragher and her colleagues were "completely isolated from the City's higher management." The City did not seek review of these findings.

While the City would have an opportunity to raise an affirmative defense if there were any serious prospect of its presenting one, it appears from the record that any such avenue is closed. Under such circumstances, we hold as a matter of law that the City could not be found to have exercised reasonable care to prevent the supervisors' harassing conduct. Unlike the employer of a small workforce, who might expect that sufficient care to prevent tortious behavior could be exercised informally, those responsible for city operations could not reasonably have thought that precautions against hostile environments in any one of many departments in far-flung locations could be effective without communicating some formal policy against harassment, with a sensible complaint procedure.

The judgment of the Court of Appeals for the Eleventh Circuit is reversed, and the case is remanded for reinstatement of the judgment of the district court.

 For an extended version of the case and review questions to test your understanding of the material, please go to www.HumanKinetics.com/CaseStudiesInSportLaw.

Pottgen v. The Missouri State High School Activities Association

40 F.3d 926 (8th Cir. 1994)

The Missouri State High School Activities Association (hereinafter MSHSAA) appeals the issuance of a preliminary injunction that restrains it from enforcing its age limit for interscholastic sports against Edward Leo Pottgen. Pottgen repeated two grades in elementary school due to an undiagnosed learning disability. By his senior year, this delay in completing his education made him too old to play interscholastic baseball under MSHSAA eligibility standards. In district court, Pottgen challenged the age limit as violating § 504 of the Rehabilitation Act of 1973, Title II of the Americans with Disabilities Act, and § 1983.

After Pottgen repeated two grades in elementary school, the school tested him to see whether he needed special classroom assistance. When the school discovered that Pottgen had several learning disabilities, it placed him on an individualized program and provided him with access to special services. With these additional resources, Pottgen progressed through school at a normal rate. It is not clear from the evidence whether he attempted to make up the lost time through summer school or other remedial activities.

Pottgen was active in sports throughout junior high and high school. He played interscholastic baseball for three years in high school and planned to play baseball his senior year as well. However, because he had repeated two grades, Pottgen turned 19 shortly before July 1 of his senior year. Consequently, MSHSAA Bylaws rendered Pottgen ineligible to play. The MSHSAA Bylaw states, in relevant part, that "A student shall not have reached the age of nineteen prior to July 1 preceding the opening of school. If a student reaches the age of nineteen on or following July 1, the student may be considered eligible for interscholastic sports during the ensuing school year."

Pottgen petitioned MSHSAA for a hardship exception to the age limit since he was held back due to his learning disabilities. MSHSAA determined that waiving the requirement violated the intent of the age eligibility rule.

Pottgen then brought this suit, alleging MSHSAA's age limit violated the Rehabilitation Act of 1973 (the Rehabilitation Act), the Americans with Disabilities Act (the ADA), and § 1983. The district court granted a preliminary injunction enjoining MSHSAA from (i) preventing Pottgen from competing in any Hancock High School baseball games or district or state tournament games, and (ii) imposing any penalty, discipline, or sanction on any school for which or against which [Pottgen] competes in these games.

MSHSAA appeals the district court's finding that Pottgen could potentially prevail under the Rehabilitation Act. MSHSAA contends Pottgen is not an otherwise qualified individual under § 504 of the Rehabilitation Act. Section 504 states that no otherwise qualified individual with a disability shall, solely by reason of her or his disability, be excluded from the participation in, be denied the benefits of, or be subjected to discrimination under any program or activity receiving federal financial assistance. In *Southeastern Community College v. Davis*, 442 U.S. 397, 406, 99 S.Ct. 2361, 2367, 60 L.Ed.2d 980 (1979), the Supreme Court defined an otherwise qualified individual as one who is able to meet all of a program's requirements in spite of his handicap. Courts cannot apply the *Davis* test to all the requirements; if they did, no reasonable requirement could ever violate § 504, no matter how easy it would be to accommodate handicapped individuals who cannot fulfill it. Rather, individuals with disabilities need only meet a program's necessary or essential requirements.

The district court found Pottgen to be an otherwise qualified individual because, except for the age limit, Pottgen meets all MSHSAA's eligibility requirements. The court framed the issue as not whether Pottgen meets all of the eligibility requirements, but rather whether reasonable accommodations existed. We disagree. A Rehabilitation Act analysis requires the court to determine both whether an individual meets all of the essential eligibility requirements and whether reasonable modifications exist.

Here, Pottgen cannot meet all the baseball program's requirements in spite of his disability. He is too old to meet the MSHSAA age limit. This failure to meet the age limit does not keep Pottgen from being otherwise qualified unless the age limit is an essential or necessary eligibility requirement.

We find that MSHSAA has demonstrated that the age limit is an essential eligibility requirement in a high school interscholastic program. An age limit helps reduce the competitive advantage flowing to teams using older athletes; protects younger athletes from harm; discourages student athletes from delaying their education to gain athletic maturity; and prevents over-zealous coaches from engaging in repeated red-shirting to gain a competitive advantage. These purposes are of immense importance in any interscholastic sports program.

Even though Pottgen cannot meet this essential eligibility requirement, he is otherwise qualified if reasonable accommodations would enable him to meet the age limit. Reasonable accommodations do not require an institution to lower or to effect substantial modifications of standards to accommodate a handicapped person. Accommodations are not reasonable if they impose undue financial and administrative burdens or if they require a fundamental alteration in the nature of the program.

Since Pottgen is already older than the MSHSAA age limit, the only possible accommodation is to waive the essential requirement itself. Although Pottgen contends an age limit waiver is a reasonable accommodation based on his disability, we disagree. Waiving an essential eligibility standard would constitute a fundamental alteration in the nature of the baseball program. Other than waiving the age limit, no manner, method, or means is available that would permit Pottgen to satisfy the age limit. Consequently, no reasonable accommodations exist.

Since Pottgen can never meet the essential eligibility requirement, he is not an otherwise qualified individual. Section 504 was designed only to extend protection to those potentially able to meet the essential eligibility requirements of a program or activity. As a result, the district court erred by granting the injunction based on Pottgen's Rehabilitation Act claim.

MSHSAA also appeals the district court's ruling that Pottgen would likely prevail on his ADA claim. MSHSAA contends Pottgen is not a qualified individual with a disability under Title II of the ADA.

Title II prohibits discrimination by public entities against individuals with disabilities. Congress intended Title II to be consistent with § 504 of the Rehabilitation Act. This desire for consistency is evident from the ADA statutory scheme itself. Enforcement remedies, procedures, and rights under Title II are the same as under § 504. In addition, regulations interpreting Title II must be consistent with regulations relating to § 504 of the Rehabilitation Act. Consequently, our § 504 analysis necessarily affects our Title II analysis.

Title II provides that no qualified individual with a disability shall, by reason of such disability, be excluded from participation in or be denied the benefits of the services, programs, or activities of a public entity, or be subjected to discrimination by any such entity. Unlike § 504 of the Rehabilitation Act, the ADA's text itself defines qualified individual with a disability. It states that a qualified individual with a disability means an individual with a disability, who, with or without reasonable modifications to rules, policies, or practices meets the essential eligibility requirements for the participation in programs or activities provided by a public entity.

To determine whether Pottgen was a qualified individual for ADA purposes, the district court conducted an individualized inquiry into the necessity of the age limit in Pottgen's case. Such an individualized inquiry is inappropriate at this stage. Instead, to determine whether Pottgen is a qualified individual under the ADA, we must first determine whether the age limit is an essential eligibility requirement by reviewing the importance of the requirement to the interscholastic baseball program. If this requirement is essential, we then determine whether Pottgen meets this requirement with or without modification. It is at this later stage that the ADA requires an individualized inquiry.

The dissent disagrees with this holding and would impose an individualized essential eligibility requirement inquiry at the first stage. We think this is not required, and for good reason. A public entity could never know the outer boundaries of its services, programs, or activities. A requirement could be deemed essential for one person with a disability but immaterial for another similarly, but not identically, situated individual.

MSHSAA's interscholastic baseball program demonstrates this proposition. The dissent admits that the age requirement is admittedly salutary but believes it must fall away for Pottgen because an individualized fact-finding inquiry found him not appreciably larger than the average 18-year-old and not a threat to the safety of others. If this is the query, MSHSAA would need to establish a fact-finding mechanism for each individual seeking to attack a program requirement. At that time, MSHSAA would have to show the essential nature of each allegedly offending program requirement as it applies to the complaining individual. The dissent's approach requires thorough

evidentiary hearings at each stage of the process. Clearly the ADA imposes no such duty.

Consistent with our Rehabilitation Act analysis, we find MSHSAA has demonstrated that the age limit is an essential eligibility requirement of the interscholastic baseball program. Again, Pottgen alleges he can meet the eligibility requirement if MSHSAA waives it for him. In conformity with our previous finding, we conclude that this is not a reasonable modification.

Thus, we find that Pottgen is not a qualified individual under the ADA. The district court erred in granting a preliminary injunction based on recovery under this Act.

 For an extended version of the case and review questions to test your understanding of the material, please go to www.HumanKinetics.com/CaseStudiesInSportLaw.

Sandison v. Michigan High School Athletic Association, Inc.

64 F.3d 1026 (6th Cir. 1995)

Ronald Sandison and Craig Stanley, two recent graduates of Michigan public high schools, filed this action against their respective high schools and the Michigan High School Athletic Association (MHSAA) alleging claims under, *inter alia*, the Rehabilitation Act of 1973, 29 U.S.C. § 794, and Titles II and III of the Americans with Disabilities Act (ADA), 42 U.S.C. §§ 12132, 12182. Each student suffers from a learning disability, and before reaching high school each fell behind the typical school grade for children of his age. The plaintiffs started their senior years in fall 1994, but by then had turned 19-years-old. The MHSAA, of which the plaintiffs' high schools are members, prohibits students who turn 19 by September 1 of the school year to compete in interscholastic high school sports. In the district court, the plaintiffs won preliminary injunctive relief.

Sandison started ungraded kindergarten at age six, rather than at the usual age of five, and it was not until age seven that Sandison was considered a student in graded kindergarten. This two-year

delay placed Sandison two school grades behind his age group. With the help of special education support, Sandison attended Rochester Adams High School in regular classrooms and graduated in June 1995. Sandison ran on Adams's cross-country and track teams during his first three years of high school. He turned 19-years-old in May 1994, a few months before starting his senior year.

Due to a learning disability in mathematics, Craig Stanley repeated kindergarten and then spent five years in a special education classroom. Stanley made the transition into regular classrooms by entering the fourth grade, rather than the fifth grade, after those five years in special education. Accordingly, Stanley is two school grades behind his age group. With the help of special education support, Stanley has attended Grosse Pointe North High School in regular classrooms and graduated in June 1995. Stanley ran on his high school's cross-country and track teams during the first three years. He turned

19-years-old in May 1994, a few months before starting his senior year.

Like most high schools in Michigan, Rochester Adams and Grosse Pointe North are members of the MHSAA. Members of the MHSAA agree to adopt the MHSAA's rules governing interscholastic sports. MHSAA Regulation I § 2 forbids students over 19-years-old from playing interscholastic sports.

On August 18, 1994, the plaintiffs sued the Rochester and Grosse Pointe school systems, and the MHSAA, under the Rehabilitation Act of 1973, 29 U.S.C. § 794; the Americans with Disabilities Act, 42 U.S.C. §§ 12132, 12182; the federal Constitution, 42 U.S.C. § 1983; and the Michigan Handicappers' Civil Rights Act, Mich. Comp. Laws Ann. §§ 37.1101-1607. Sandison and Stanley alleged that excluding them from playing interscholastic sports amounted to unlawful disability discrimination. In late August 1994, the district court granted the plaintiffs a temporary restraining order permitting the students to run in immediately upcoming interscholastic cross-country races. The plaintiffs then moved in early September for a preliminary injunction, which the district court entered.

First, the district court restrained all three defendants from preventing the plaintiffs from participating in interscholastic cross-country and track competition. Second, the district court enjoined the MHSAA from sanctioning Rochester Adams and Grosse Pointe North for permitting the plaintiffs to participate in interscholastic meets. The district court explained that it relied only on the Rehabilitation Act and the ADA to support the preliminary injunction.

The district court first reasoned that two titles of the ADA, as well as the Rehabilitation Act, applied to the claim against the MHSAA. The district court held that, by managing interscholastic athletic events, the MHSAA operated places of education and places of entertainment under Title III of the ADA, §§ 12181-89, which generally prohibits disability discrimination in places of public accommodation. In addition, the district court relied on Michigan law and the MHSAA's membership to conclude that the MHSAA was a public entity under Title II of the ADA, §§ 12131-34. Finally, the district court held that the MHSAA indirectly received federal financial assistance under the Rehabilitation Act, § 794.

As for the remaining elements of a disability discrimination claim under the Rehabilitation Act and the ADA, the district court held that the plaintiffs were disabled, otherwise qualified, and discriminated against solely on the basis of their disabilities. The MHSAA does not dispute the finding of disability on appeal. The district court concluded that the plaintiffs were otherwise qualified because permitting the plaintiffs to participate would not thwart the purposes of the age restriction. The district court reasoned that the age limit had two purposes: (1) to safeguard other athletes against injuries arising from competing against overage, and thus oversized, athletes; and (2) to prevent overage athletes from gaining an unfair competitive advantage. Accordingly, waiver of the age limit for Sandison and Stanley was a reasonable accommodation because the plaintiffs played a noncontact sport and were not star players. The MHSAA appealed the issuance of the preliminary injunction. However, neither Rochester Adams nor Grosse Pointe North appealed; both schools have supported the plaintiffs' position from the start.

We review the district court's issuance of a preliminary injunction for abuse of discretion. In determining whether the district court abused its discretion, we review the district court's findings of fact for clear error and its legal conclusions *de novo*. A legal or factual error may be sufficient to determine that the district court abused its discretion. However, absent such an error, the district court's weighing and balancing of the equities is overruled only in the rarest of cases.

We consider four factors in determining whether the district court abused its discretion in issuing the preliminary injunction: (1) whether the movant has a strong likelihood of success on the merits, (2) whether the movant would otherwise suffer irreparable injury, (3) whether issuance of a preliminary injunction would cause substantial harm to others, and (4) whether the public interest would be served by issuance of a preliminary injunction. It is important to recognize that the four considerations applicable to preliminary injunctions are factors to be balanced and not prerequisites that must be satisfied. These factors simply guide the discretion of the court; they are not meant to be rigid and unbending requirements.

We first discuss the plaintiffs' claim under § 504 of the Rehabilitation Act of 1973. In its current form, the section provides in pertinent part that "no otherwise qualified individual with a disability in the United States shall, solely by reason of his or her disability, be excluded from the participation in, be denied the benefits of, or be subjected to discrimination under any program or activity receiving Federal financial assistance." 29 U.S.C. § 794(a) (as amended 1992).

A cause of action under § 504 comprises four elements: (1) the plaintiff is a handicapped [disabled] person under the Act; (2) the plaintiff is otherwise qualified for participation in the program; (3) the plaintiff is being excluded from participation in, being denied the benefits of, or being subjected to discrimination under the program solely by reason of his handicap [disability]; and (4) the relevant program or activity is receiving federal financial assistance.

In this case, the plaintiffs are unlikely to succeed on the merits of the second and third elements.

Taking the latter element to start, we hold that the plaintiffs are not, in the words of the statute, "being excluded from the participation in any program or activity solely by reason of his disability." Few cases explain the meaning of the term "solely by reason of" disability, but we garner guidance from one of the Supreme Court's earliest § 504 cases, *Southeastern Community College v. Davis*, 442 U.S. 397, 99 S.Ct. 2361, 60 L.Ed.2d 980 (1979), to interpret statutory language similar to "solely by reason of." In *Davis*, the plaintiff applied for entry into a state college's nursing degree program, completion of which would qualify her for certification as a registered nurse. However, the plaintiff's severe hearing disability prevented her from successfully understanding oral communication unless she could use her lipreading skills. The college denied admission into the nursing program, relying on the conclusion of the state nursing board's executive director that the plaintiff could not safely participate in the clinical training program. The district court too found that the plaintiff could not safely perform registered nursing duties in situations precluding lipreading, such as when physicians and other nurses wore surgical masks.

In holding that § 504 did not mandate that the college provide the plaintiff with individual faculty supervision or to dispense certain required

courses entirely, the Court explained that § 504 does not require affirmative action, that is, substantial changes, such as a fundamental alteration in the nature of a program or changes imposing undue financial and administrative burdens. Rather, § 504 demands evenhanded treatment of qualified handicapped persons.

Similarly, under a natural reading of § 504, the MHSAA's disqualification of students who reach 19 years of age by the specified date cannot readily be characterized as a decision made, solely by reason of each student's respective learning disability. Regulation I § 2 is a neutral rule—neutral, that is, with respect to disability—and as far as the record shows, is neutrally applied by the MHSAA. Throughout the plaintiffs' first three years of high school, Regulation I § 2 did not bar the students from playing interscholastic sports, yet the students were of course learning disabled during those years. It was not until they turned 19 that Regulation I § 2 operated to disqualify them. Accordingly, we must conclude that the age regulation does not exclude students from participating solely by reason of their disability. The plain meaning of § 504's text does not cover the plaintiffs' exclusion.

Nevertheless, it remains, for example, an open question whether § 504 forbids recipients of federal financial assistance from engaging in conduct that has an unjustifiable disparate impact on the disabled.

Moreover, we are also aware that we have considered several cases in which the solely by reason of disability element was presumably not implicated, and yet the allegedly violative conduct was simply the application of a facially neutral requirement to an individual whose disability prevented him from meeting that requirement.

In this case, however, absent their respective learning disability, Sandison and Stanley still fail to satisfy Regulation I § 2. The plaintiffs' respective learning disability does not prevent the two students from meeting the age requirement; the passage of time does. We hold that, under § 504, the plaintiffs cannot meet the age requirement solely by reason of their dates of birth, not solely by reason of disability.

Finally, we briefly note and reject the plaintiffs' contention that the MHSAA's age requirement violates a Department of Education regulation purporting to implement § 504. The Department's regulation prohibits recipients from discriminating on the basis of handicap in athletic programs and mandates that recipients offering interscholastic sports programs "shall provide to qualified handicapped students an equal opportunity" to participate. If we were to read § 104.37(c)(1) as forbidding the MHSAA's age restriction, then the short answer to the plaintiffs' reliance on the regulation is that we have already read § 504 as not plausibly covering the age restriction. The Department's unreasonable interpretation of § 504 would yield to the statutory section. But the terms of § 104.37(c) (1) do not even cover the MHSAA age restriction; the restriction does not discriminate on the basis of handicap and the MHSAA does provide an equal opportunity to participate. Again, the age restriction disqualifies an overage nondisabled student just as it disqualifies the overage disabled plaintiffs.

We also hold that the district court clearly erred by finding that the plaintiffs are likely to show that they are otherwise qualified to participate in interscholastic track and cross-country competition. Specifically, after finding that the plaintiffs are not star players and are not an injury risk to other competitors, the district court found that the MHSAA must waive Regulation I § 2 as to Sandison and Stanley in order to reasonably accommodate the plaintiffs. We disagree.

Under § 504, a disabled individual is otherwise qualified to participate in a program if, with reasonable accommodation, the individual can meet the necessary requirements of the program.

Aside from the necessity of the program's requirement, the other question in the otherwise qualified inquiry is whether some reasonable accommodation is available to satisfy the legitimate interests of both the grantee and the handicapped person. And since it is part of the otherwise qualified inquiry, our precedent requires that the reasonable accommodation question be decided as an issue of fact. Generally, an accommodation is not reasonable if it either imposes undue financial and administrative burdens on a grantee or requires a fundamental alteration in the nature of the program.

We hold that the district court did not clearly err in finding that Regulation I § 2 is necessary. In defending against the preliminary injunction

motion, the MHSAA proffered testimony from an expert in physical growth and development. The testimony supports the district court's conclusions that the age restriction advances two purposes: (1) safeguards against injury to other players, and (2) prevents any unfair competitive advantage that older and larger participants might provide. The age restriction is a necessary requirement of the interscholastic sports program.

But the district court erred in finding that waiver of Regulation I § 2 constituted a reasonable accommodation. Due to the usual ages of first-year high school students, high school sports programs generally involve competitors between 14 and 18 years of age. Removing the age restriction injects into competition students older than the vast majority of other students, and the record shows that the older students are generally more physically mature than younger students. Expanding the sports program to include older students works a fundamental alteration.

Second, although the plaintiffs assert that introducing their average athletic skills into track and cross-country competition would not fundamentally alter the program, the record does not reveal how the MHSAA, or anyone, can make that competitive unfairness determination without an undue burden. The MHSAA's expert explained that five factors weigh in deciding whether an athlete possessed an unfair competitive advantage due to age: chronological age, physical maturity, athletic experience, athletic skill level, and mental ability to process sports strategy. It is plainly an undue burden to require high school coaches and hired physicians to determine whether these factors render a student's age an unfair competitive advantage. The determination would have to be made relative to the skill level of each participating member of opposing teams and the team as a unit. And of course each team member and the team as a unit would present a different skill level. Indeed, the determination would also have to be made relative to the skill level of the would-be athlete whom the older student displaced from the team. It is unreasonable to call on coaches and physicians to make these near-impossible determinations.

Finally, we note that there is a significant peculiarity in trying to characterize the waiver of the age restriction as a reasonable accommodation of the plaintiffs' respective learning disability. Ordinarily, an accommodation of an individual's disability operates so that the disability is overcome and the disability no longer prevents the individual from participating. In this case, although playing high school sports undoubtedly helped the plaintiffs progress through high school, the waiver of the age restriction is not directed at helping them overcome learning disabilities; the waiver merely removes the age ceiling as an obstacle.

Accordingly, we conclude that the plaintiffs are unlikely to succeed in pursuing their § 504 claim. The plaintiffs are excluded from participating in interscholastic track and cross-country competition solely by reason of age, not disability. Furthermore, waiver of the necessary age restriction does not constitute a reasonable accommodation.

Our analysis of the plaintiffs' ADA claim closely tracks our § 504 analysis. We decline to decide whether the MHSAA is a public entity covered by Title II, § 12131(1) (A), (B), because it is unnecessary to do so, and proceed directly to the other elements of Title II. However, we first emphasize that we do hold that the MHSAA is not covered by Title III of the ADA.

Generally stated, Title III of the ADA, 42 U.S.C. §§ 12181-89, prohibits discrimination on the basis of disability in public accommodations operated by private entities. Section 12182(a) provides a general rule in that no individual shall be discriminated against on the basis of disability in the full and equal enjoyment of the goods, services, facilities, privileges, advantages, or accommodations of any place of public accommodation by any person who owns, leases (or leases to), or operates a place of public accommodation. In order to define public accommodation, § 12181(6) first explains that private entity means any entity other than a public entity (as defined in § 12131(1) of this title).Then, § 12181(7) provides that the following private entities are considered public accommodations for purposes of this subchapter, if the operations of such entities affect commerce, and lists numerous facilities, including places of public gathering, places of recreation, and gymnasiums.

The Attorney General's regulations implementing Title III take a more straightforward path in defining place of public accommodation. The definition regulation introduces the long list of covered facilities by stating that a place of public accommodation means a facility, operated by a private entity, whose operations affect commerce and fall within at least one of the following categories.

We conclude that the district court erred in holding that Title III covers the MHSAA. The text of §§ 12181-82 and § 36.104 compel the conclusion that the applicability of Title III turns not so much on who is covered. Any person leasing or operating a place of public accommodation is covered. The critical inquiry will typically be the nature of the place to which the disabled individual alleges unequal access. Title III protects disabled individuals from unequal enjoyment of places of public accommodation. And § 12181(7) and § 36.104 make clear that public accommodations are operated by private entities, not public entities. The plaintiffs complain that the MHSAA age eligibility rule precludes them from equally participating in track events held on public school grounds or, presumably for cross-country events, in public parks. Public school grounds and public parks are of course operated by public entities, and thus cannot constitute public accommodations under Title III. Accordingly, we conclude that no place of public accommodation is implicated here and Title III does not apply.

Section 12132 provides that subject to the provisions of this subchapter, no qualified individual with a disability shall, by reason of such disability, be excluded from participation in or be denied the benefits of the services, programs, or activities of a public entity, or be subjected to discrimination by any such entity. Unlike the Rehabilitation Act, Title II expressly provides a statutory definition of qualified individual with a disability; however, the statutory definition bears some similarity to the case law definition. The term "qualified individual with a disability" means an individual with a disability who, with or without reasonable modifications to rules, policies, or practices, meets the essential eligibility requirements for the receipt of services or the participation in programs or activities provided by a public entity.

Accordingly, a plaintiff proceeding under Title II of the ADA must, similar to a § 504 plaintiff, prove that the exclusion from participation in the program was solely by reason of disability. We again conclude that Sandison and Stanley were excluded by reason of age, not disability. Absent their respective learning disability, the plaintiffs still would not meet the age restriction. The plaintiffs are unlikely to succeed in establishing this element of the Title II claim.

Nor are the plaintiffs likely to succeed in showing that they are qualified individuals under §§ 12131(2), 12132. Our earlier conclusion that the age restriction is a necessary requirement under § 504 foreordains our conclusion now that Regulation I § 2 is an essential eligibility requirement under § 12131(2). We also find that waiver of the age restriction does not constitute a reasonable modification under § 12131(2). The daunting task of determining whether an older student possesses an unfair competitive advantage is not a reasonable modification, just as the task is not a reasonable accommodation. We add only that the word "modification" connotes moderate change, and nothing in the context or structure of Title II suggests otherwise. Requiring waiver of the age restriction under the facts of this case would fundamentally change the currently bright-line age restriction.

Finally, the plaintiffs again rely on regulations to support their contention that waiver is required: A public entity shall make reasonable modifications when the modifications are necessary to avoid discrimination on the basis of disability, unless the public entity can demonstrate that making the modifications would fundamentally alter the nature of the service, program, or activity and a public entity shall not impose or apply eligibility criteria that screen out or tend to screen out an individual with a disability from fully and equally enjoying any service, program, or activity, unless such criteria can be shown to be necessary for the provision of the service, program, or activity being offered.

The first subsection does not alter our conclusion because the plaintiffs are not subjected to discrimination on the basis of disability, and waiver is not in this case a reasonable modification. Furthermore, the age restriction does not prevent the plaintiffs from fully and equally enjoying the interscholastic sports program. Lastly, although § 35.130(b)(8) might interpret Title II to recognize a class-based disparate impact claim, the plaintiffs here did not present this theory at all, and the record contains no hint that the age restriction disproportionately excludes members of the class of disabled students.

Accordingly, the plaintiffs are unlikely to succeed on the merits of their § 504 and ADA claims. We DISMISS as moot the appeal from that portion of the preliminary injunction ordering that the high schools and the MHSAA permit the plaintiffs to run on the cross-country and track teams; and we REVERSE that portion of the preliminary injunction ordering the MHSAA to refrain from entering penalties for the plaintiffs' performance.

 For an extended version of the case and review questions to test your understanding of the material, please go to www.HumanKinetics.com/CaseStudiesInSportLaw.

8

Title IX

The courts have struggled with gender participation issues related to sports for many years and the decisions have not been consistent. Even with the advances that society has made over the past few decades in breaking down gender barriers, attitude bias still exists. Females are sometimes denied participation in the sports of their choice. Title IX of the Education Amendments Act was passed to guarantee that the interests and abilities of the underrepresented gender, which in most instances is female, would be appreciably developed and met in both work and athletic settings in the United States. The primary focus of case law dealing with gender discrimination in athletics is on whether institutions have complied with Title IX. The key compliance issues are whether or not institutions or organizations fall within the court's recommended proportionality range of percentage of opportunities versus percentage of total population for a given gender. The courts have examined the following factors (addressed by the selected cases) when determining whether an institution has complied with Title IX. These factors include: (1) accommodating the interests and abilities of both sexes when selecting sports; (2) the provision of equipment and supplies; (3) game and practice time; (4) travel and per diem allowances; (5) coaching and academic tutoring; (6) compensation of coaches and scholarships for players; (7) access to and quality of locker rooms and game and practice facilities; (8) access to and quality of medical and training facilities and services; (9) provision for housing and dining facilities; (10) publicity opportunities; and (11) recruiting budgets. These factors are addressed in *Cohen v. Brown, Favia v. IUP, Kelley v. Board,* and *Roberts v. Colorado State Board of Agriculture.*

Other types of Title IX cases address a school district's indifference to allegations of gender discrimination within the school district. *Davis v. Monroe County* involved a situation in which an elementary-age student was harassed by one of her peers. *Franklin v. Gwinnett County* and *Gebser v. Lago Vista ISD* both addressed student–teacher relationships. A key issue addressed by these cases involves determining an equitable remedy or monetary damages for the aggrieved party. The cases are interesting, extremely relevant, and important in today's sports environment.

Cohen v. Brown University

101 F.3d 155 (1st Cir. 1996)

This is a class action lawsuit charging Brown University, its president, and its athletics director (collectively Brown) with discrimination against women in the operation of its intercollegiate athletics program, in violation of Title IX of the Education Amendments of 1972, 20 U.S.C. §§ 1681-1688 (Title IX), and its implementing regulations, 34 C.F.R. §§ 106.1-106.71. The plaintiff class comprises all present, future, and potential Brown University women students who participate, seek to participate, and/or are deterred from participating in intercollegiate athletics funded by Brown.

This suit was initiated in response to the demotion in May 1991 of Brown's women's gymnastics and volleyball teams from university-funded varsity status to donor-funded varsity status. Contemporaneously, Brown demoted two men's teams, water polo and golf, from university-funded to donor-funded varsity status. As a consequence of these demotions, all four teams lost, not only their university funding, but most of the support and privileges that accompany university-funded varsity status at Brown.

The district court determined after a lengthy bench trial that Brown's intercollegiate athletics program violates Title IX and its supporting regulations. The district court ordered Brown to submit within 120 days a comprehensive plan for complying with Title IX, but stayed that portion of the order pending appeal. The district court subsequently issued a modified order, requiring Brown to submit a compliance plan within 60 days. Finding that Brown's proposed compliance plan was not comprehensive and that it failed to comply with the opinion and order of *Cohen III*, the district court rejected the plan and

ordered in its place specific relief consistent with Brown's stated objectives in formulating the plan. The court's remedial order required Brown to elevate and maintain at university-funded varsity status the women's gymnastics, fencing, skiing, and water polo teams. The district court entered final judgment on September 1, 1995, and on September 27, 1995, denied Brown's motion for additional findings of fact and to amend the judgment. This appeal followed.

As a Division I institution within the National Collegiate Athletic Association (NCAA) with respect to all sports but football, Brown participates at the highest level of NCAA competition. Brown operates a two-tiered intercollegiate athletics program with respect to funding: although Brown provides the financial resources required to maintain its university-funded varsity teams, donor-funded varsity athletes must themselves raise the funds necessary to support their teams through private donations.

Brown's decision to demote the women's volleyball and gymnastics teams and the men's water polo and golf teams from university-funded varsity status was apparently made in response to a university-wide cost-cutting directive. The district court found that Brown saved $62,028 by demoting the women's teams and $15,795 by demoting the men's teams, but that the demotions "did not appreciably affect the athletic participation gender ratio." Plaintiffs alleged that, at the time of the demotions, the men students at Brown already enjoyed the benefits of a disproportionately large share of both the university resources allocated to athletics and the intercollegiate participation opportunities afforded to student athletes. Thus, plaintiffs contended, what appeared to be the even-handed demotions of two men's and two women's teams, in fact, perpetuated Brown's discriminatory treatment of women in the administration of its intercollegiate athletics program.

In the course of the preliminary injunction hearing, the district court found that, in the academic year 1990-91, Brown funded 31 intercollegiate varsity teams, 16 men's teams and 15 women's teams, and that, of the 894 undergraduate students competing on these teams, 63.3% (566) were men and 36.7% (328) were women. During the same academic year, Brown's undergraduate enrollment comprised 52.4% (2,951) men and 47.6% (2,683) women. The district court also summarized the history of athletics at Brown, finding, *inter alia*, that, while nearly all of the men's varsity teams were established before 1927, virtually all of the women's varsity teams were created between 1971 and 1977, after Brown's merger with Pembroke College. The only women's varsity team created after this period was winter track, in 1982.

In the course of the trial on the merits, the district court found that, in 1993-94, there were 897 students participating in intercollegiate varsity athletics, of which 61.87% (555) were men and 38.13% (342) were women. During the same period, Brown's undergraduate enrollment comprised 5,722 students, of which 48.86% (2,796) were men and 51.14% (2,926) were women. The district court found that, in 1993-94, Brown's intercollegiate athletics program consisted of 32 teams, 16 men's teams and 16 women's teams. Of the university-funded teams, 12 were men's teams and 13 were women's teams; of the donor-funded teams, three were women's teams and four were men's teams. At the time of trial, Brown offered 479 university-funded varsity positions for men, as compared to 312 for women; and 76 donor-funded varsity positions for men, as compared to 30 for women. In 1993-94, then, Brown's varsity program—including both university- and donor-funded sports—afforded over 200 more positions for men than for women.

Accordingly, the district court found that Brown maintained a 13.01% disparity between female participation in intercollegiate athletics and female student enrollment, . . . , and that "[a]lthough the number of varsity sports offered to men and women are equal, the selection of sports offered to each gender generates far more individual positions for male athletes than for female athletes."

In computing these figures, the district court counted as participants in intercollegiate athletics for purposes of Title IX analysis those athletes who were members of varsity teams for the majority of the last complete season. Brown argued at trial that "there is no consistent measure of actual participation rates because team size varies throughout the athletic season," and that "there is no consistent measure of actual participation rates because there are alternative definitions of 'participant' that yield very different participation totals." Reasoning that "[w]here both the athlete and coach determine that there is a place on the team for a student, it is not for this Court to second-guess their judgment and impose its own, or anyone else's, definition of a valuable or genuine varsity experience," the district court concluded that "[e]very varsity team member is therefore a varsity 'participant.'" Thus, the district court held that the "participation opportunities" offered by an institution are measured by counting the actual participants on intercollegiate teams. The number of participants in Brown's varsity athletic program accurately reflects the number of participation opportunities Brown offers because the university, through its practices "predetermines" the number of athletic positions available to each gender.

The district court found from extensive testimony that the donor-funded women's gymnastics, women's fencing, and women's ski teams, as well as at least one women's club team, the water polo team, had demonstrated the interest and ability to compete at the top varsity level and would benefit from university funding. The district court did not find that full and effective accommodation of the athletics interests and abilities of Brown's female students would disadvantage Brown's male students.

Title IX provides that "[n]o person in the United States shall, on the basis of sex, be excluded from participation in, be denied the benefits of, or be subjected to discrimination under any education program or activity receiving Federal financial assistance." As a private institution that receives federal financial assistance, Brown is required to comply with Title IX. Title IX also specifies that its prohibition against gender discrimination shall not "be interpreted to require any educational institution to grant preferential or disparate treatment to the members of one sex on account of an imbalance which may exist" between the total number or percentage of persons of that sex participating in any federally-supported program or activity, and "the total number or percentage of persons of that sex in any community, State, section, or other area." Subsection (b) also provides, however, that it "shall not be construed to prevent the consideration in any . . . proceeding under this chapter of statistical evidence tending to show that such an imbalance exists with respect to the participation in, or receipt of the benefits of, any such program or activity by the members of one sex."

Applying § 1681(b), the prior panel held that Title IX "does not mandate strict numerical equality between the gender balance of a college's athletic program and the gender balance of its student body." The panel explained that, while evidence of a gender-based disparity in an institution's athletics program is relevant to a determination of noncompliance, "a court assessing Title IX compliance may not find a violation solely because there is a disparity between the gender composition of an educational institution's student constituency, on the one hand, and its athletic programs, on the other hand." Title IX was passed with two objectives in mind: "to avoid the use of federal resources to support discriminatory practices," and "to provide individual citizens effective protection against those practices." To accomplish these objectives, Congress directed all agencies extending financial assistance to educational institutions to develop procedures for terminating financial assistance to institutions that violate Title IX.

The agency responsible for administering Title IX is the United States Department of Education (DED), through its Office for Civil Rights (OCR). Congress expressly delegated to DED the authority to promulgate regulations for determining whether an athletics program complies with Title IX. The regulations specifically address athletics at 34 C.F.R. §§ 106.37(c) and 106.41.

In the first appeal, this court held that an institution's failure effectively to accommodate

both genders under § 106.41(c)(1) is sufficient to establish a violation of Title IX. In 1978, several years after the promulgation of the regulations, OCR published a proposed "Policy Interpretation," the purpose of which was to clarify the obligations of federal aid recipients under Title IX to provide equal opportunities in athletics programs. The Policy Interpretation establishes a three-part test, a two-part test, and factors to be considered in determining compliance under 34 C.F.R. § 106.41(c)(1). At issue in this appeal is the proper interpretation of the first of these, the so-called three-part test, which inquires as follows:

> (1) Whether intercollegiate level participation opportunities for male and female students are provided in numbers substantially proportionate to their respective enrollments; or

> (2) Where the members of one sex have been and are underrepresented among intercollegiate athletes, whether the institution can show a history and continuing practice of program expansion which is demonstrably responsive to the developing interest and abilities of the members of that sex; or

> (3) Where the members of one sex are underrepresented among intercollegiate athletes, and the institution cannot show a continuing practice of program expansion such as that cited above, whether it can be demonstrated that the interests and abilities of the members of that sex have been fully and effectively accommodated by the present program. 44 Fed.Reg. at 71,418.

Brown contends that the district court misconstrued and misapplied the three-part test. Specifically, Brown argues that the district court's interpretation and application of the test are irreconcilable with the statute, the regulation, and the agency's interpretation of the law, and effectively renders Title IX an "affirmative action statute" that mandates preferential treatment for women by imposing quotas in excess of women's relative interests and abilities in athletics.

Brown asserts, in the alternative, that if the district court properly construed the test, then the test itself violates Title IX and the United States Constitution.

We reject Brown's kitchen-sink characterization of the Policy Interpretation and its challenge to the substantial deference accorded that document by the district court. The Policy Interpretation represents the responsible agency's interpretation of the intercollegiate athletics provisions of Title IX and its implementing regulations. It is well settled that, where, as here, Congress has expressly delegated to an agency the power to "elucidate a specific provision of a statute by regulation," the resulting regulations should be accorded "controlling weight unless they are arbitrary, capricious, or manifestly contrary to the statute." It is also well established "that an agency's construction of its own regulations is entitled to substantial deference." As the Supreme Court has explained, "[b]ecause applying an agency's regulation to complex or changing circumstances calls on the agency's unique expertise and policymaking prerogatives, we presume that the power authoritatively to interpret its own regulations is a component of the agency's delegated lawmaking powers."

We hold that the district court did not err in the degree of deference it accorded the regulation and the relevant agency pronouncements.

As previously noted, the district court held that, for purposes of the three-part test, the intercollegiate athletics participation opportunities offered by an institution are properly measured by counting the number of actual participants on intercollegiate teams. The Policy Interpretation was designed specifically for intercollegiate athletics. Because the athletics regulation distinguishes between club sports and intercollegiate sports, under the Policy Interpretation, "club teams will not be considered to be intercollegiate teams except in those instances where they regularly participate in varsity competition." Accordingly, the district court excluded club varsity teams from the definition of "intercollegiate teams" and, therefore, from the calculation of participation opportunities, because the evidence was inadequate to show that the club teams regularly participated in varsity competition.

Brown contends that an athletics program equally accommodates both genders and complies with Title IX if it accommodates the relative interests and abilities of its male and female students. This "relative interests" approach posits that an institution satisfies prong three of the three-part test by meeting the interests and abilities of the underrepresented gender only to

the extent that it meets the interests and abilities of the overrepresented gender.

Brown maintains that the district court's decision imposes on universities the obligation to engage in preferential treatment for women by requiring quotas in excess of women's relative interests and abilities. With respect to prong three, Brown asserts that the district court's interpretation of the word "fully" "requires universities to favor women's teams and treat them better than men's [teams]. . . . forces them to eliminate or cap men's teams. . . . [and] forces universities to impose athletic quotas in excess of relative interests and abilities."

Brown's interpretation of full and effective accommodation is "simply not the law." We agree with the prior panel and the district court that Brown's relative interests approach "cannot withstand scrutiny on either legal or policy grounds," because it "disadvantages women and undermines the remedial purposes of Title IX by limiting required program expansion for the underrepresented sex to the status quo level of relative interests." After *Cohen II*, it cannot be maintained that the relative interests approach is compatible with Title IX's equal accommodation principle as it has been interpreted by this circuit.

Brown argues that the district court's interpretation of the three-part test requires numerical proportionality, thus imposing a gender-based quota scheme in contravention of the statute. The three-part test is, on its face, entirely consistent with § 1681(b) because the test does not require preferential or disparate treatment for either gender. Neither the Policy Interpretation's three-part test, nor the district court's interpretation of it, mandates statistical balancing; "[r]ather, the policy interpretation merely creates a presumption that a school is in compliance with Title IX and the applicable regulation when it achieves such a statistical balance."

The test is also entirely consistent with § 1681(b) as applied by the prior panel and by the district court. The panel then carefully delineated the burden of proof, which requires a Title IX plaintiff to show, not only "disparity between the gender composition of the institution's student body and its athletic program, thereby proving that there is an underrepresented gender," but also "that a second element—unmet interest—is present," meaning that the underrepresented gender has not been fully and effectively accommodated by the institution's present athletic program. Only where the plaintiff meets the burden of proof on these elements and the institution fails to show as an affirmative defense a history and continuing practice of program expansion responsive to the interests and abilities of the underrepresented gender will liability be established.

The law requires that, absent a demonstration of continuing program expansion for the underrepresented gender under prong two of the three-part test, an institution must either provide athletics opportunities in proportion to the gender composition of the student body so as to satisfy prong one, or fully accommodate the interests and abilities of athletes of the underrepresented gender under prong three.

We think it clear that neither the Title IX framework nor the district court's interpretation of it mandates a gender-based quota scheme. In our view, it is Brown's relative interests approach to the three-part test, rather than the district court's interpretation, that contravenes the language and purpose of the test and of the statute itself. To adopt the relative interests approach would be, not only to overrule *Cohen II*, but to rewrite the enforcing agency's interpretation of its own regulation so as to incorporate an entirely different standard for Title IX compliance. This relative interests standard would entrench and fix by law the significant gender-based disparity in athletics opportunities found by the district court to exist at Brown, a finding we have held to be not clearly erroneous. According to Brown's relative interests interpretation of the equal accommodation principle, the gender-based disparity in athletics participation opportunities at Brown is due to a lack of interest on the part of its female students, rather than to discrimination, and any attempt to remedy the disparity is, by definition, an unlawful quota. This approach is entirely contrary to "Congress's unmistakably clear mandate that educational institutions not use federal monies to perpetuate gender-based discrimination," and makes it virtually impossible to effectuate Congress's intent to eliminate sex discrimination in intercollegiate athletics.

Brown also claims error in the district court's failure to apply Title VII standards to its analysis of whether Brown's intercollegiate athletics program complies with Title IX. The district court rejected the analogy to Title VII, noting that, while Title VII "seeks to determine whether gender-neutral job openings have been filled without regard to gender[,] Title IX . . . was designed to address the reality that sports teams, unlike the vast majority of jobs, do have official gender requirements, and this statute accordingly approaches the concept of discrimination differently from Title VII."

It does not follow from the fact that § 1681(b) was patterned after a Title VII provision that Title VII standards should be applied to a Title IX analysis of whether an intercollegiate athletics program equally accommodates both genders, as Brown contends. While this court has approved the importation of Title VII standards into Title IX analysis, we have explicitly limited the crossover to the employment context.

It is imperative to recognize that athletics presents a distinctly different situation from admissions and employment and requires a different analysis in order to determine the existence *vel non* of discrimination. While the Title IX regime permits institutions to maintain gender-segregated teams, the law does not require that student athletes attending institutions receiving federal funds must compete on gender-segregated teams; nor does the law require that institutions provide completely gender-integrated athletics programs. To the extent that Title IX allows institutions to maintain single-sex teams and gender-segregated athletics programs, men and women do not compete against each other for places on team rosters. Accordingly, and notwithstanding Brown's protestations to the contrary, the Title VII concept of the "qualified pool" has no place in a Title IX analysis of equal opportunities for male and female athletes because women are not "qualified" to compete for positions on men's teams, and vice-versa. In addition, the concept of "preference" does not have the same meaning, or raise the same equality concerns, as it does in the employment and admissions contexts.

Brown's approach fails to recognize that, because gender-segregated teams are the norm in intercollegiate athletics programs, athletics differs from admissions and employment in analytically material ways. In providing for gender-segregated teams, intercollegiate athletics programs necessarily allocate opportunities separately for male and female students, and, thus, any inquiry into a claim of gender discrimination must compare the athletics participation opportunities provided for men with those provided for women. For this reason, and because recruitment of interested athletes is at the discretion of the institution, there is a risk that the institution will recruit only enough women to fill positions in a program that already underrepresents women, and that the smaller size of the women's program will have the effect of discouraging women's participation.

In this unique context, Title IX operates to ensure that the gender-segregated allocation of athletics opportunities does not disadvantage either gender. Rather than create a quota or preference, this unavoidably gender-conscious comparison merely provides for the allocation of athletics resources and participation opportunities between the sexes in a nondiscriminatory manner. We find no error in the district court's refusal to apply Title VII standards in its inquiry into whether Brown's intercollegiate athletics program complies with Title IX. We conclude that the district court's application of the three-part test does not create a gender-based quota and is consistent with Title IX, 34 C.F.R. § 106.41, the Policy Interpretation, and the mandate of *Cohen II*.

Brown has contended throughout this litigation that the significant disparity in athletics opportunities for men and women at Brown is the result of a gender-based differential in the level of interest in sports and that the district court's application of the three-part test requires universities to provide athletics opportunities for women to an extent that exceeds their relative interests and abilities in sports. Thus, at the heart of this litigation is the question whether Title IX permits Brown to deny its female students equal opportunity to participate in sports, based on its unproven assertion that the district court's finding of a significant disparity in athletics opportunities for male and female students reflects, not discrimination in Brown's intercollegiate athletics program, but a lack of interest on the part of its female students that is unrelated to a lack of opportunities.

We view Brown's argument that women are less interested than men in participating in inter-collegiate athletics, as well as its conclusion that institutions should be required to accommodate the interests and abilities of its female students only to the extent that it accommodates the interests and abilities of its male students, with great suspicion. To assert that Title IX permits institutions to provide fewer athletics participation opportunities for women than for men, based on the premise that women are less interested in sports than are men, is (among other things) to ignore the fact that Title IX was enacted in order to remedy discrimination that results from stereotyped notions of women's interests and abilities.

Interest and ability rarely develop in a vacuum; they evolve as a function of opportunity and experience. The Policy Interpretation recognizes that women's lower rate of participation in athletics reflects women's historical lack of opportunities to participate in sports. Thus, there exists the danger that, rather than providing a true measure of women's interest in sports, statistical evidence purporting to reflect women's interest instead provides only a measure of the very discrimination that is and has been the basis for women's lack of opportunity to participate in sports. Prong three requires some kind of evidence of interest in athletics, and the Title IX framework permits the use of statistical evidence in assessing the level of interest in sports.

Nevertheless, to allow a numbers-based lack-of-interest defense to become the instrument of further discrimination against the underrepresented gender would pervert the remedial purpose of Title IX. We conclude that, even if it can be empirically demonstrated that, at a particular time, women have less interest in sports than do men, such evidence, standing alone, cannot justify providing fewer athletics opportunities for women than for men. Furthermore, such evidence is completely irrelevant where, as here, viable and successful women's varsity teams have been demoted or eliminated. On these facts, Brown's failure to accommodate fully and effectively the interests and abilities of the underrepresented gender is clearly established. Under these circumstances, the district court's finding that there are interested women able to compete at the university-funded varsity level, is clearly correct.

Brown's relative interests approach is not a reasonable interpretation of the three-part test. This approach contravenes the purpose of the statute and the regulation because it does not permit an institution or a district court to remedy a gender-based disparity in athletics participation opportunities. Instead, this approach freezes that disparity by law, thereby disadvantaging further the underrepresented gender. Had Congress intended to entrench, rather than change, the status quo—with its historical emphasis on men's participation opportunities to the detriment of women's opportunities—it need not have gone to all the trouble of enacting Title IX.

In the first appeal, this court rejected Brown's Fifth Amendment equal protection challenge to the statutory scheme. Here, Brown argues that its challenge is to the decision of the district court. In rejecting Brown's equal protection claim, the *Cohen II* panel stated, "It is clear that Congress has broad powers under the Fifth Amendment to remedy past discrimination."

Therefore, we review the constitutionality of the district court's order requiring Brown to comply with Title IX by accommodating fully and effectively the athletics interests and abilities of its women students. Because the challenged classification is gender-based, it must be analyzed under the intermediate scrutiny test.

Under intermediate scrutiny, the burden of demonstrating an exceedingly persuasive justification for a government-imposed, gender-conscious classification is met by showing that the classification serves important governmental objectives, and that the means employed are substantially related to the achievement of those objectives. Applying that test, it is clear that the district court's remedial order passes constitutional muster. We find that the first part of the test is satisfied. The governmental objectives of "avoid[ing] the use of federal resources to support discriminatory practices," and "provid[ing] individual citizens effective protection against those practices," are clearly important objectives. We also find that judicial enforcement of federal antidiscrimination statutes is at least an important governmental objective.

Applying the second prong of the intermediate scrutiny test, we find that the means employed by the district court in fashioning relief for the statu-

tory violation are clearly substantially related to these important objectives. Intermediate scrutiny does not require that there be no other way to accomplish the objectives, but even if that were the standard, it would be satisfied in the unique context presented by the application of Title IX to athletics. As explained previously, Title IX as it applies to athletics is distinct from other antidiscrimination regimes in that it is impossible to determine compliance or to devise a remedy without counting and comparing opportunities with gender explicitly in mind. Even under the individual rights theory of equal protection, the only way to determine whether the rights of an individual athlete have been violated and what relief is necessary to remedy the violation is to engage in an explicitly gender-conscious comparison. Accordingly, even assuming that the three-part test creates a gender classification that favors women, allowing consideration of gender in determining the remedy for a Title IX violation serves the important objective of "ensur[ing] that in instances where overall athletic opportunities decrease, the actual opportunities available to the underrepresented gender do not." In addition, a gender-conscious remedial scheme is constitutionally permissible if it directly protects the interests of the disproportionately burdened gender.

Under Brown's interpretation of the three-part test, there can never be a remedy for a violation of Title IX's equal opportunity mandate. In concluding that the district court's interpretation and application of the three-part test create a quota, Brown errs, in part, because it fails to recognize that (i) the substantial proportionality test of prong one is only the starting point, and not the conclusion, of the analysis; and (ii) prong three is not implicated unless a gender-based disparity with respect to athletics participation opportunities has been shown to exist. Where such a disparity has been established, the inquiry under prong three is whether the athletics interests and abilities of the underrepresented gender are fully and effectively accommodated, such that the institution may be found to comply with Title IX, notwithstanding the disparity. Of course, a remedy that requires an institution to cut, add, or elevate the status of athletes or entire teams may impact the genders differently, but this will be so only if there is a gender-based disparity with respect to athletics opportunities to begin with, which is the only circumstance in which prong three comes into play. Here, however, it has not been shown that Brown's men students will be disadvantaged by the full and effective accommodation of the athletics interests and abilities of its women students.

The district court itself pointed out that Brown may achieve compliance with Title IX in a number of ways:

> It may eliminate its athletic program altogether, it may elevate or create the requisite number of women's positions, it may demote or eliminate the requisite number of men's positions, or it may implement a combination of these remedies. I leave it entirely to Brown's discretion to decide how it will balance its program to provide equal opportunities for its men and women athletes. I recognize the financial constraints Brown faces; however, its own priorities will necessarily determine the path to compliance it elects to take.

With these precepts in mind, we first examine the compliance plan Brown submitted to the district court in response to its order. We then consider the district court's order rejecting Brown's plan and the specific relief ordered by the court in its place. Brown's proposed compliance plan stated its goal as follows:

> The plan has one goal: to make the gender ratio among University-funded teams at Brown substantially proportionate to the gender ratio of the undergraduate student body. To do so, the University must disregard the expressed athletic interests of one gender while providing advantages for others. The plan focuses only on University-funded sports, ignoring the long history of successful donor-funded student teams.

The general provisions of the plan may be summarized as follows: (i) maximum squad sizes for men's teams will be set and enforced, (ii) head coaches of all teams must field squads that meet minimum size requirements, (iii) no additional discretionary funds will be used for athletics, (iv) four new women's junior varsity teams—basketball, lacrosse, soccer, and tennis—will be university-funded, and (v) Brown will make explicit a *de facto* junior varsity team for women's field hockey. The plan sets forth nine steps for its implementation and concludes that "if the Court determines that this plan is not sufficient to reach proportionality, phase two will be the elimination of one or more men's teams."

The district court found Brown's plan to be "fatally flawed" for two reasons. First, despite the fact that 76 men and 30 women participated on donor-funded varsity teams, Brown's proposed plan disregarded donor-funded varsity teams. Second, Brown's plan "artificially boosts women's varsity numbers by adding junior varsity positions on four women's teams." As to the propriety of Brown's proposal to come into compliance by the addition of junior varsity positions, the district court held: "Positions on distinct junior varsity squads do not qualify as 'intercollegiate competition' opportunities under the Policy Interpretation and should not be included in defendants' plan. As noted in *Cohen*, 879 F.Supp. at 200, 'intercollegiate' teams are those that 'regularly participate in varsity competition.' Junior varsity squads, by definition, do not meet this criterion. Counting new women's junior varsity positions as equivalent to men's full varsity positions flagrantly violates the spirit and letter of Title IX; in no sense is an institution providing equal opportunity if it affords varsity positions to men but junior varsity positions to women."

The district court found that these two flaws in the proposed plan were sufficient to show that Brown had "not made a good faith effort to comply with this Court's mandate." In criticizing another facet of Brown's plan, the district court pointed out that "[a]n institution does not provide equal opportunity if it caps its men's teams after they are well-stocked with high-caliber recruits while requiring women's teams to boost numbers by accepting walk-ons. A university does not treat its men's and women's teams equally if it allows the coaches of men's teams to set their own maximum capacity limits but overrides the judgment of coaches of women's teams on the same matter."

The district court ordered Brown to "elevate and maintain women's gymnastics, women's water polo, women's skiing, and women's fencing to university-funded varsity status." The court stayed this part of the order pending appeal and further ordered that, in the interim, the preliminary injunction prohibiting Brown from eliminating or demoting any existing women's varsity team would remain in effect.

We agree with the district court that Brown's proposed plan fell short of a good faith effort to meet the requirements of Title IX as explicated by this court in *Cohen II* and as applied by the district court on remand. Indeed, the plan is replete with argumentative statements more appropriate for an appellate brief. It is obvious that Brown's plan was addressed to this court, rather than to offering a workable solution to a difficult problem.

It is clear, nevertheless, that Brown's proposal to cut men's teams is a permissible means of effectuating compliance with the statute. Thus, although we understand the district court's reasons for substituting its own specific relief under the circumstances at the time, and although the district court's remedy is within the statutory margins and constitutional, we think that the district court was wrong to reject out-of-hand Brown's alternative plan to reduce the number of men's varsity teams. After all, the district court itself stated that one of the compliance options available to Brown under Title IX is to "demote or eliminate the requisite number of men's positions." Our respect for academic freedom and reluctance to interject ourselves into the conduct of university affairs counsel that we give universities as much freedom as possible in conducting their operations consonant with constitutional and statutory limits.

Brown therefore should be afforded the opportunity to submit another plan for compliance with Title IX. The context of the case has changed in two significant respects since Brown presented its original plan. First, the substantive issues have been decided adversely to Brown. Brown is no longer an appellant seeking a favorable result in the court of appeals.

Second, the district court is not under time constraints to consider a new plan and fashion a remedy so as to expedite appeal. Accordingly, we remand the case to the district court so that Brown can submit a further plan for its consideration. In all other respects the judgment of the district court is affirmed. The preliminary injunction issued by the district court in *Cohen I* will remain in effect pending a final remedial order.

Affirmed in part, reversed in part, and remanded for further proceedings.

 For an extended version of the case and review questions to test your understanding of the material, please go to www.HumanKinetics.com/CaseStudiesInSportLaw.

Davis v. Monroe County Board of Education

526 U.S. 629 (1999)

Petitioner brought suit against the Monroe County Board of Education and other defendants, alleging that her fifth-grade daughter had been the victim of sexual harassment by another student in her class. Among petitioner's claims was a claim for monetary and injunctive relief under Title IX of the Education Amendments of 1972 (Title IX), 86 Stat. 373, as amended, 20 U.S.C. §§ 1681 *et seq*. The district court dismissed petitioner's Title IX claim on the ground that "student-on-student," or peer harassment provides no ground for a private cause of action under the statute. The Court of Appeals for the Eleventh Circuit, sitting *en banc*, affirmed. We consider here whether a private damages action may lie against the school board in cases of student-on-student harassment. Petitioner's minor daughter, LaShonda, was allegedly the victim of a prolonged pattern of sexual harassment by one of her fifth-grade classmates at Hubbard Elementary School, a public school in Monroe County, Georgia. According to petitioner's complaint, the harassment began in December 1992, when the classmate, G.F., attempted to touch LaShonda's breasts and genital area and made vulgar statements such as "I want to get in bed with you" and "I want to feel your boobs." Similar conduct allegedly occurred on or about January 4 and January 20, 1993. LaShonda reported each of these incidents to her mother and to her classroom teacher, Diane Fort. Petitioner, in turn, also contacted Fort, who allegedly assured petitioner that the school principal, Bill Querry, had been informed of the incidents. Petitioner contends that, notwithstanding these reports, no disciplinary action was taken against G.F. as his conduct allegedly continued for many months.

The string of incidents finally ended in mid-May, when G.F. was charged with, and pleaded guilty to, sexual battery for his misconduct. The complaint alleges that LaShonda had suffered during the months of harassment, however; specifically, her previously high grades allegedly dropped as she became unable to concentrate on her studies, and, in April 1993, her father discovered that she had written a suicide note. The complaint further alleges that, at one point, LaShonda told petitioner that she "didn't know how much longer she could keep [G.F.] off her." Nor was LaShonda G.F.'s only victim; it is alleged that other girls in the class fell prey to G.F.'s conduct. At one point, in fact, a group composed of LaShonda and other female students tried to speak with Principal Querry about G.F.'s behavior. According to the complaint, however, a teacher denied the students' request with the statement, "If [Querry] wants you, he'll call you."

Petitioner alleges that no disciplinary action was taken in response to G.F.'s behavior toward LaShonda. In addition to her conversations with Fort and Pippen, petitioner alleges that she spoke with Principal Querry in mid-May 1993. When petitioner inquired as to what action the school intended to take against G.F., Querry simply stated, "I guess I'll have to threaten him a little bit harder." Yet, petitioner alleges, at no point during the many months of his reported misconduct was G.F. disciplined for harassment. Indeed, Querry allegedly asked petitioner why LaShonda "was the only one complaining." Nor, according to the complaint, was any effort made to separate G.F. and LaShonda. On the contrary, notwithstanding LaShonda's frequent complaints, only after more than three months of reported harassment was she even permitted to change her classroom seat so that she was no longer seated next to G.F. Moreover, petitioner alleges that, at the time of the events in question, the Monroe County Board of Education (Board) had not instructed its personnel on how to respond to peer sexual harassment and had not established a policy on the issue.

On May 4, 1994, petitioner filed suit in the United States District Court for the Middle District of Georgia against the Board, Charles Dumas, the school district's superintendent, and Principal Querry. The complaint alleged that the Board is a recipient of federal funding for purposes of Title IX, that "[t]he persistent sexual advances and harassment by the student G.F. upon [LaShonda] interfered with her ability to attend school and perform her studies and activities," and that "[t]he deliberate indifference by Defendants to the unwelcome sexual advances of a student upon LaShonda created an intimidating, hostile, offensive and abus[ive] school environment in violation of Title IX." The complaint sought compensatory and punitive damages, attorney's fees, and injunctive relief.

The defendants (all respondents here) moved to dismiss petitioner's complaint under Federal Rule of Civil Procedure 12(b)(6) for failure to state a claim on which relief could be granted, and the District Court granted respondents' motion. With regard to petitioner's claims under Title IX, the court dismissed the claims against individual defendants on the ground that only federally-funded educational institutions are subject to liability in private causes of action under Title IX. As for the Board, the court concluded that Title IX provided no basis for liability absent an allegation "that the Board or an employee of the Board had any role in the harassment."

Petitioner appealed the district court's decision dismissing her Title IX claim against the Board, and a panel of the Court of Appeals for the Eleventh Circuit reversed. Borrowing from Title VII law, a majority of the panel determined that student-on-student harassment stated a cause of action against the Board under Title IX: "[W]e conclude that as Title VII encompasses a claim for damages due to a sexually hostile working environment created by co-workers and tolerated by the employer, Title IX encompasses a claim for damages due to a sexually hostile educational environment created by a fellow student or students when the supervising authorities knowingly fail to act to eliminate the harassment." The Eleventh Circuit panel recognized that petitioner sought to state a claim based on school "officials' failure to take action to stop the offensive acts of those over whom the officials exercised control," and the court concluded that petitioner had alleged facts sufficient to support a claim for hostile environment sexual harassment on this theory.

The Eleventh Circuit granted the Board's motion for rehearing *en banc* and affirmed the district court's decision to dismiss petitioner's Title IX claim against the Board. The *en banc* court relied, primarily, on the theory that Title IX was passed pursuant to Congress' legislative authority under the Constitution's Spending Clause, U.S. Const., Art I, § 8, cl. 1, and that the statute therefore must provide potential recipients of federal education funding with "unambiguous notice of the conditions they are assuming when they accept" it. Title IX, the court reasoned, provides recipients with notice that they must stop their employees from engaging in discriminatory conduct, but the statute fails to provide a recipient with sufficient notice of a duty to prevent student-on-student harassment. We granted *certiorari* in order to resolve a conflict in the Circuits over whether, and under what circumstances, a recipient of federal educational funds can be liable in a private damages action arising from student-on-student sexual harassment.

Title IX provides, with certain exceptions not at issue here, that "[n]o person in the United States shall, on the basis of sex, be excluded from participation in, be denied the benefits of, or be subjected to discrimination under any education program or activity receiving Federal financial assistance." 20 U.S.C. § 1681(a). Congress authorized an administrative enforcement scheme for Title IX. Federal departments or agencies with the authority to provide financial assistance are entrusted to promulgate rules, regulations, and orders to enforce the objectives of § 1681, *see* § 1682, and these departments or agencies may rely on "any . . . means authorized by law," including the termination of funding, to give effect to the statute's restrictions. There is no dispute here that the Board is a recipient of federal education funding for Title IX purposes. Nor do respondents support an argument that student-on-student harassment cannot rise to the level of "discrimination" for purposes of Title IX. Rather, at issue here is the question whether a recipient of federal education funding may be liable for damages under Title IX under any circumstances for discrimination in the form of student-on-student sexual harassment.

Petitioner urges that Title IX's plain language compels the conclusion that the statute is intended to bar recipients of federal funding from permitting this form of discrimination in their programs or activities. She emphasizes that the statute prohibits a student from being "subjected to discrimination under any education program or activity receiving Federal financial assistance." It is Title IX's "unmistakable focus on the benefited class," rather than the perpetrator, that, in petitioner's view, compels the conclusion that the statute works to protect students from the discriminatory misconduct of their peers.

Here, however, we are asked to do more than define the scope of the behavior that Title IX proscribes. We must determine whether a district's failure to respond to student-on-student harassment in its schools can support a private suit for money damages. This Court has indeed recognized an implied private right of action under Title IX and we have held that money damages are available in such suits. Because we have repeatedly treated Title IX as legislation enacted pursuant to Congress' authority under the Spending Clause, however, private damages actions are available only where recipients of federal funding had adequate notice that they could be liable for the conduct at issue. When Congress acts pursuant to its spending power, it generates legislation "much in the nature of a contract: in return for federal funds, the States agree to comply with federally imposed conditions." In interpreting language in spending legislation, we thus "insis[t] that Congress speak with a clear voice," recognizing that "[t]here can, of course, be no knowing acceptance [of the terms of the putative contract] if a State is unaware of the conditions [imposed by the legislation] or is unable to ascertain what is expected of it."

Respondents urge that Title IX provides no notice that recipients of federal educational funds could be liable in damages for harm arising from student-on-student harassment. Respondents contend, specifically, that the statute only proscribes misconduct by grant recipients, not third parties. Respondents argue, moreover, that it would be contrary to the very purpose of Spending Clause legislation to impose liability on a funding recipient for the misconduct of third parties, over whom recipients exercise little control. We agree with respondents that a recipient of federal funds may be liable in damages under

Title IX only for its own misconduct. The recipient itself must "exclud[e] [persons] from participation in, . . . den[y] [persons] the benefits of, or . . . subjec[t] [persons] to discrimination under" its "program[s] or activit[ies]" in order to be liable under Title IX. The government's enforcement power may only be exercised against the funding recipient, and we have not extended damages liability under Title IX to parties outside the scope of this power.

We disagree with respondents' assertion, however, that petitioner seeks to hold the Board liable for G.F.'s actions instead of its own. Here, petitioner attempts to hold the Board liable for its own decision to remain idle in the face of known student-on-student harassment in its schools. In *Gebser*, we concluded that a recipient of federal education funds may be liable in damages under Title IX where it is deliberately indifferent to known acts of sexual harassment by a teacher. We recognized that the scope of liability in private damages actions under Title IX is circumscribed by *Pennhurst*'s requirement that funding recipients have notice of their potential liability. We also recognized, however, that this limitation on private damages actions is not a bar to liability where a funding recipient intentionally violates the statute. Accordingly, we rejected the use of agency principles to impute liability to the district for the misconduct of its teachers. In addition, rather than imposing negligence standards, we concluded that the district could be liable for damages only where the district itself intentionally acted in clear violation of Title IX by remaining deliberately indifferent to acts of teacher-student harassment of which it had actual knowledge.

We consider here whether the misconduct identified—deliberate indifference to known acts of harassment—amounts to an intentional violation of Title IX, capable of supporting a private damages action, when the harasser is a student rather than a teacher. We conclude that, in certain limited circumstances, it does. As an initial matter, in *Gebser* we expressly rejected the use of agency principles in the Title IX context, noting the textual differences between Title IX and Title VII. Additionally, the regulatory scheme surrounding Title IX has long provided funding recipients with notice that they may be liable for

their failure to respond to the discriminatory acts of certain non-agents. The Department of Education requires recipients to monitor third parties for discrimination in specified circumstances and to refrain from particular forms of interaction with outside entities that are known to discriminate. The common law, too, has put schools on notice that they may be held responsible under state law for their failure to protect students from the tortious acts of third parties. In fact, state courts routinely uphold claims alleging that schools have been negligent in failing to protect their students from the torts of their peers.

This is not to say that the identity of the harasser is irrelevant. On the contrary, both the "deliberate indifference" standard and the language of Title IX narrowly circumscribe the set of parties whose known acts of sexual harassment can trigger some duty to respond on the part of funding recipients. Deliberate indifference makes sense as a theory of direct liability under Title IX only where the funding recipient has some control over the alleged harassment. A recipient cannot be directly liable for its indifference where it lacks the authority to take remedial action.

If a funding recipient does not engage in harassment directly, it may not be liable for damages unless its deliberate indifference "subject[s]" its students to harassment. That is, the deliberate indifference must, at a minimum, "cause [students] to undergo" harassment or "make them liable or vulnerable" to it. Moreover, because the harassment must occur "under" "the operations of" a funding recipient, the harassment must take place in a context subject to the school district's control.

These factors combine to limit a recipient's damages liability to circumstances wherein the recipient exercises substantial control over both the harasser and the context in which the known harassment occurs. Only then can the recipient be said to "expose" its students to harassment or "cause" them to undergo it "under" the recipient's programs. Here, the misconduct occurs during school hours and on school grounds—the bulk of G.F.'s misconduct, in fact, took place in the classroom—the misconduct is taking place "under" an "operation" of the funding recipient. In these circumstances, the recipient retains substantial control over the context in which the harassment occurs. More importantly, however, in this setting the Board exercises significant control over the harasser. On more than one occasion, this Court has recognized the importance of school officials' "comprehensive authority . . . , consistent with fundamental constitutional safeguards, to prescribe and control conduct in the schools." The common law, too, recognizes the school's disciplinary authority. We thus conclude that recipients of federal funding may be liable for "subject[ing]" their students to discrimination where the recipient is deliberately indifferent to known acts of student-on-student sexual harassment and the harasser is under the school's disciplinary authority. Our conclusion here—that recipients may be liable for their deliberate indifference to known acts of peer sexual harassment—does not mean that recipients can avoid liability only by purging their schools of actionable peer harassment or that administrators must engage in particular disciplinary action.

School administrators will continue to enjoy the flexibility they require so long as funding recipients are deemed "deliberately indifferent" to acts of student-on-student harassment only where the recipient's response to the harassment or lack thereof is clearly unreasonable in light of the known circumstances. The dissent consistently mischaracterizes this standard to require funding recipients to "remedy" peer harassment, . . . , and to "ensur[e] that . . . students conform their conduct to" certain rules. Title IX imposes no such requirements. On the contrary, the recipient must merely respond to known peer harassment in a manner that is not clearly unreasonable.

The requirement that recipients receive adequate notice of Title IX's proscriptions also bears on the proper definition of "discrimination" in the context of a private damages action. Having previously determined that "sexual harassment" is "discrimination" in the school context under Title IX, we are constrained to conclude that student-on-student sexual harassment, if sufficiently severe, can likewise rise to the level of discrimination actionable under the statute. Students are not only protected from discrimination, but also specifically shielded from being "excluded from participation in" or "denied the benefits of" any "education program or activity receiving Federal financial assistance." The stat-

ute makes clear that, whatever else it prohibits, students must not be denied access to educational benefits and opportunities on the basis of gender. We thus conclude that funding recipients are properly held liable in damages only where they are deliberately indifferent to sexual harassment, of which they have actual knowledge, that is so severe, pervasive, and objectively offensive that it can be said to deprive the victims of access to the educational opportunities or benefits provided by the school.

The district's knowing refusal to take any action in response to such behavior would fly in the face of Title IX's core principles, and such deliberate indifference may appropriately be subject to claims for monetary damages. It is not necessary, however, to show physical exclusion to demonstrate that students have been deprived by the actions of another student or students of an educational opportunity on the basis of sex. Rather, a plaintiff must establish sexual harassment of students that is so severe, pervasive, and objectively offensive, and that so undermines and detracts from the victims' educational experience, that the victimized students are effectively denied equal access to an institution's resources and opportunities. Courts, moreover, must bear in mind that schools are unlike the adult workplace and that children may regularly interact in a manner that would be unacceptable among adults. Indeed, at least early on, students are still learning how to interact appropriately with their peers. It is thus understandable that, in the school setting, students often engage in insults, banter, teasing, shoving, pushing, and gender-specific conduct that is upsetting to the students subjected to it. Damages are not available for simple acts of teasing and name-calling among school children, however, even where these comments target differences in gender. Rather, in the context of student-on-student harassment, damages are available only where the behavior is so severe, pervasive, and objectively offensive that it denies its victims the equal access to education that Title IX is designed to protect.

Moreover, the provision that the discrimination occur "under any education program or activity" suggests that the behavior be serious enough to have the systemic effect of denying the victim equal access to an educational program or activity. Although, in theory, a single instance of sufficiently severe one-on-one peer harassment could be said to have such an effect, we think it unlikely that Congress would have thought such behavior sufficient to rise to this level in light of the inevitability of student misconduct and the amount of litigation that would be invited by entertaining claims of official indifference to a single instance of one-on-one peer harassment. By limiting private damages actions to cases having a systemic effect on educational programs or activities, we reconcile the general principle that Title IX prohibits official indifference to known peer sexual harassment with the practical realities of responding to student behavior, realities that Congress could not have meant to be ignored.

Applying this standard to the facts at issue here, we conclude that the Eleventh Circuit erred in dismissing petitioner's complaint. Petitioner alleges that her daughter was the victim of repeated acts of sexual harassment by G.F. over a five-month period, and there are allegations in support of the conclusion that G.F.'s misconduct was severe, pervasive, and objectively offensive.

The harassment was not only verbal; it included numerous acts of objectively offensive touching, and, indeed, G.F. ultimately pleaded guilty to criminal sexual misconduct. Further, petitioner contends that the harassment had a concrete, negative effect on her daughter's ability to receive an education. The complaint also suggests that petitioner may be able to show both actual knowledge and deliberate indifference on the part of the Board, which made no effort whatsoever either to investigate or to put an end to the harassment. On this complaint, we cannot say "beyond doubt that [petitioner] can prove no set of facts in support of [her] claim which would entitle [her] to relief." Accordingly, the judgment of the United States Court of Appeals for the Eleventh Circuit is reversed, and the case is remanded for further proceedings consistent with this opinion.

 For an extended version of the case and review questions to test your understanding of the material, please go to www.HumanKinetics.com/CaseStudiesInSportLaw.

Favia v. Indiana University of Pennsylvania

812 F.Supp. 578 (W.D. Pa. 1993)

Before the Court is a class action lawsuit brought by women students at Indiana University of Pennsylvania (IUP) alleging systemic discrimination on the basis of gender in IUP's intercollegiate athletic program. The action is brought on behalf of the women athletic program participants and all present and future IUP women students or potential students who participate, seek to participate, or are deterred from participating in intercollegiate athletics sponsored by IUP. The named plaintiffs had been members of the women's gymnastics and field hockey teams. The school, the school's president, Dr. Lawrence Pettit, and the director of athletics, Frank Cignetti, are the named defendants. Pursuant to Rule 65, Fed. R. Civ. P., the plaintiffs seek a preliminary injunction to have the two teams reinstated and to prohibit the defendants from eliminating any more women's teams. This case arises out of Title IX of

the Education Amendments of 1972, 20 U.S.C. §§ 1681 *et seq.* and the equal protection clause of the Fourteenth Amendment. But plaintiffs here rely solely on alleged Title IX violations as the basis for their preliminary injunction motion. They contend that IUP fostered disparities in athletic participation opportunities on the basis of gender by providing disparate levels of support to male and female athletes and by allocating athletic scholarships in a gender discriminatory way.

IUP is a university within the Pennsylvania State System of Higher Education. It is federally funded and thus subject to the mandates of Title IX. In 1990-91, IUP had 10,793 students, 4790 men and 6003 women. Thus, about 55.61% of the IUP student population was female at the time of the decision to cut intercollegiate athletic teams.

In 1991, IUP was faced with a budget crisis. There were substantial reductions in both state and federal aid to the school, and as a result, the university administration advised its various departments that they had to reduce their budgets, including the Department of Athletics, which was instructed to reduce its budget by $350,000. In August 1991, an announcement was made that the women's gymnastics and field hockey teams and the men's soccer and tennis teams were going to be eliminated beginning with the 1992-93 school year. Prior to the 1991 cutback, IUP had a total of 503 athletes on its intercollegiate teams, 313 male and 190 female. The percentage of female athletes was 37.77%, compared to the entire female student population percentage of 55.61%. After these program cutbacks, including normal attrition on the football team, roughly 397 students were participating in interscholastic athletics, 248 males and 149 females, or 36.51% females.

IUP has three categories of sports teams: (1) intercollegiate varsity teams, which belong to the National Collegiate Athletic Association (NCAA) and bring the school the most money and prestige of the three categories; (2) club teams, which are informal, basically student-run organizations; and (3) intramural teams, which are open to all students. Varsity teams, the "official" representative of the university, have full- and part-time coaches, designated schedules, rules, and regulations. Varsity teams also have access to ice, water, storage and locker space, and have professional athletic trainers and a traveling budget for away games. They also have more funding and coaches than the intramural or club teams. At the time of the 1991 cutbacks, IUP had roughly 18 varsity sports (half male and half female as far as numbers of teams), 18 club sports, and 44 intramural sports (19 female, 5 coed, and 20 male). Before the cutbacks, IUP had nine men's and nine women's intercollegiate athletic teams. Because of the elimination of the four teams, IUP now has seven teams per gender.

Apparently, Mr. Frank Cignetti, the athletic director, believed that it was best to eliminate equal numbers of men's and women's teams, recommended this to the Athletic Policy Committee, which in turn recommended the cuts to IUP's previous president. These teams were eliminated because they were no longer viable, according to the witnesses for IUP. Dr. David DeCoster, vice-president of student affairs, cited

a declining national trend in women's gymnastics and field hockey, but testified that the popularity of women's soccer is increasing. He, Mr. Cignetti, and others testified that it was the intent of the university to replace the women's gymnastic and field hockey teams with a women's varsity soccer team at sometime in the future when there was less of a financial crunch at the university.

The statistics speak for themselves and make a strong case for the women plaintiffs. We find that while the number of female students greatly exceeds the number of male students at IUP, roughly 55% to 45%, the percentage of female versus male athletes is quite the opposite. In 1991-92, 37% of all athletes were female and 63% were males. With the elimination of the two women's teams the percentage of women athletes dropped to 36% and the men increased to 64%.

We heard considerable testimony about the general state of IUP athletics for women. Ruth Podbielski, former associate director of athletics at IUP, retired in 1987 after 31.5 years at IUP. The first women's varsity team, she said, was formed in 1970. Prior to that all women's teams were club teams. When Frank Cignetti, the athletic director, came to IUP in 1982 there were 10 varsity women's teams. This subsequently dropped to nine, and with the cuts under consideration here there are only seven. According to Ms. Podbielski, the women athletes and teams have generally been behind the men's in terms of priorities. She felt that Mr. Cignetti was well motivated toward all athletes and athletics (and so do we), and he made some very constructive improvements when he came to the university in 1982, but with the budget problems, the situation has deteriorated.

Although retired, Ms. Podbielski wrote a letter to the president of IUP, spoke to Dr. David DeCoster, vice-president of student affairs (who was also a witness), and to Frank Cignetti about the situation and warned them that she felt that the cuts were a violation of Title IX. She cited a number of inequities at IUP. The scholarships for football and men's basketball are higher than in other sports, and this affects participation. The baseball field (for men) is kept in much better shape than the softball field (for women).

Ms. Podbielski was succeeded by another woman, Vivian Fuller (also a witness) as associate athletic director. Ms. Fuller left in August 1992, and because of the budget problems, there are no plans to replace her. This leaves Mr. Cignetti and another male, who is an associate athletic director, as the two holding the top positions in the department.

Ms. Christine Grant testified as an expert in the area of equity in sports. She had been president of the AIAW and since 1973 has been the director of the Women's Athletic Program at the University of Iowa. Her conclusions, after studying the situation at IUP, were that IUP should (i) reallocate resources, (ii) appoint a committee to draw up a five-year plan for athletics, and (iii) immediately reinstate the women's gymnastics and field hockey teams. Ms. Grant also testified that it was good for student athletes to compete in championship meets no matter who sponsored them, or how prestigious they might be, and that whether or not it was the NCAA that sponsored them should not be a factor. We note that she had been president of the AIAW, and this may have had something to do with her disdain for the NCAA, but nevertheless, we were impressed with Ms. Grant's background, abilities, and testimony. In terms of student scholarships the women also fall well behind the men; in 1990-91 the university awarded $314,178 in scholarships. Of this amount, $246,755 went to men and only $67,423 to women, or 21% to women and 79% to men.

The thrust of the testimony of the witnesses for the university was that the cuts were necessitated by the budget problems, that the university had maintained equality by cutting two men's teams as well as two women's teams, and that it intended to elevate women's soccer to varsity status as soon as the budget would permit. Unfortunately, however, Title IX does not provide for any exception to its requirements simply because of a school's financial difficulties. In other words, a cash crunch is no excuse.

In ruling on a motion for a preliminary injunction, we must consider four factors: (1) the likelihood that plaintiffs will prevail on the merits of their claims, (2) the extent to which plaintiffs are being irreparably harmed, (3) the extent to which defendants will suffer irreparable harm if the preliminary injunction is issued, and (4) whether the public interest favors the entry of the preliminary injunction. Only if plaintiffs produce evidence

sufficient to convince us that all four factors favor preliminary relief should a preliminary injunction issue. Plaintiffs have the burden of proof.

By cutting the women's gymnastics and field hockey teams, IUP has denied plaintiffs the benefits to women athletes who compete interscholastically: they develop skill, self-confidence, learn team cohesion and a sense of accomplishment, increase their physical and mental well-being, and develop a lifelong healthy attitude. The opportunity to compete in undergraduate interscholastic athletics vanishes quickly, but the benefits do not. We believe that the harm emanating from lost opportunities for the plaintiffs is likely to be irreparable.

We do not believe that the defendants will be irreparably harmed if the women's field hockey and gymnastics teams are reinstated. The budget, while shrinking, has space for reallocation and cutbacks in other areas.

Next, we must consider whether plaintiffs have shown that they have a reasonable probability of success on the merits of their Title IX claim. Our decision to grant the preliminary injunction is legally only a prediction about the merits of plaintiffs' case. We hasten to add, however, that in view of the statistical evidence produced at the preliminary injunction hearing, there is little doubt as to the outcome of any additional hearings on these issues.

We believe that plaintiffs have proved their case. Title IX provides a cause of action to battle discrimination based on gender by educational institutions that receive federal funding and was intended to prevent the use of federal resources to support gender discrimination. We must look to the language of Title IX of the Education Amendments of 1972: "No person in the United States shall, on the basis of sex, be excluded from participation in, be denied the benefits of, or be subjected to discrimination under any education program or activity receiving Federal financial assistance." 20 U.S.C. § 1681(a). Federal enforcement of the statute and its regulation is within the jurisdiction of the Department of Education's Office for Civil Rights (OCR). OCR's Policy Interpretation deserves our great deference. The Office of Civil Rights Regulations applies Title IX to interscholastic, intercollegiate, club, and intramural athletics. Title IX and the implementing regulations can be violated without showing a specific intent on the part of the educational institution to discriminate against women.

The OCR Policy Interpretation sets out a three-pronged test for whether an educational institution complies with the duty to provide equality in its opportunities to participate in intercollegiate athletics. We must consider:

1. Whether intercollegiate level participation opportunities for male and female students are provided in numbers substantially proportionate to their respective enrollments; or

2. Where the members of one sex have been and are underrepresented among intercollegiate athletics, whether the institution can show a history and continuing practice of program expansion which is demonstrably responsive to the developing interests and abilities of the members of that sex; or

3. Where the members of one sex are underrepresented among intercollegiate athletes, and the institution cannot show a continuing practice of program expansion such as that cited above, whether it can be demonstrated that the interests and abilities of the members of that sex have been fully and effectively accommodated by the present program. 44 Fed.Reg. 71418 (Dec. 11, 1979).

Defendants bear the burden of proof with respect to the second and third prongs. IUP is in violation of Title IX if all three prongs are answered in the negative. We find that plaintiffs have established their claim that IUP has discriminated against women athletes on the basis of gender.

We agree with the plaintiffs that IUP has failed to provide women students with opportunities to participate in intercollegiate athletics proportionate to the percentage of women in the undergraduate student body. Before the 1991 cuts, 37.77% of the intercollegiate athletes were women, but 55.61% of the students were women. Once the gymnastics and field hockey teams were cut (41 women), and men's tennis, soccer, and football team attrition is factored in, the percentage of women intercollegiate athletes dropped to 36.51%. We believe that the pre-1991 status of women's proportionality requires remedial action to correct the discriminatory effects of IUP's policies. The 1991 cuts simply exacerbated an already existing Title IX violation.

Defendants have failed to override the proportionality requirement by not showing a history of expanding its athletic opportunities to respond to the developing interest of its women students. In the years before the 1991 cuts, IUP may be congratulated for some expansion of women's sports, but as the statistics show, in 1992 they have regressed. The levels of opportunities for women to compete went from low to lower, and the 1991 cuts were not responsive to the needs, interests, and abilities of women students. Women's athletic expenditures in 1991 were $2.75 for each $8.00 spent on men's programs, women athletes received 21.46% of IUP's athletic scholarship funds (compared to 35% women participating), while only 36.51% of intercollegiate athlete positions were filled by women. Although it may at sometime in the future, IUP has not elevated its popular women's club soccer to varsity status. You can't replace programs with promises. Defendants' counsel urges us to look to other schools' proportionality statistics, cited in numerous OCR investigations. But these cases are nonpersuasive because the universities under investigation had not cut back on women's teams. IUP has.

Although the university has continued to honor its scholarship commitments to women athletes whose teams have been eliminated and offered to assist athletes in transferring to other schools, defendants have not shown that this fully and effectively accommodates the interests and abilities of women at IUP. Nor does the promise of a women's varsity soccer team at some indeterminate future time meet the interests and abilities of female athletes. We are not persuaded by IUP's defenses. "[F]inancial concerns alone cannot justify gender discrimination." Men's athletics have reaped the benefits of favoritism. Defendants also claim that because the NCAA sponsors no gymnastics championship, the elimination of gymnastics was justified. We disagree.

The gymnastic team had plenty of quality competition, as did the field hockey team. Although the field hockey team had a poor win-loss record, this probably stems from a tough conference, but even more likely is the negative effect of lack of funding, scholarships, and staff. The testimony of the named plaintiffs clearly showed an interest and commitment to their respective sports, and IUP has now denied the plaintiffs participation in their sports. Finally, our decision to grant plaintiffs' motion for a preliminary injunction must factor in the public interest in the granting of the preliminary injunction. The public has a strong interest in the prevention of any violation of constitutional rights.

In summary, the women plaintiffs merely seek what the law requires, equal athletic opportunities. We understand the fiscal constraints placed on IUP's Athletic Department, but new monies or reallocation of funds to reinstate these teams is the least the Athletic Department can do in light of its legal violations.

 For an extended version of the case and review questions to test your understanding of the material, please go to www.HumanKinetics.com/CaseStudiesInSportLaw.

Franklin v. Gwinnett County Public Schools

503 U.S. 60 (1992)

This case presents the question whether the implied right of action under Title IX of the Education Amendments of 1972, 20 U.S.C. §§ 1681-1688 (Title IX), which this Court recognized in *Cannon v. University of Chicago*, 441 U.S. 677, 99 S.Ct. 1946, 60 L.Ed.2d 560 (1979), supports a claim for monetary damages.

Petitioner Christine Franklin was a student at North Gwinnett High School in Gwinnett County, Georgia, between September 1985 and August 1989. Respondent Gwinnett County School District operates the high school and receives federal funds. According to the complaint filed on December 29, 1988, in the United States District Court for the Northern District of Georgia, Franklin was subjected to continual sexual harassment beginning in the autumn of her tenth grade year (1986) from Andrew Hill, a sports coach and teacher employed by the district. The complaint further alleges that though they became aware of and investigated Hill's sexual harassment of Franklin and other female students, teachers and administrators took no action to halt it and discouraged Franklin from pressing charges against Hill. On April 14, 1988, Hill resigned on the condition that all matters pending against him be dropped. The school thereupon closed its investigation.

In this action, the district court dismissed the complaint on the ground that Title IX does not authorize an award of damages. The court of appeals affirmed. The court noted that analysis of Title IX and Title VI of the Civil Rights Act of 1964, 42 U.S.C. §§ 2000d *et seq.* (Title VI), has developed along similar lines. Accordingly, it held that an action for monetary damages could not be sustained for an alleged intentional violation of Title IX, and affirmed the district court's ruling to that effect.

Because this opinion conflicts with a decision of the Court of Appeals for the Third Circuit, we granted *certiorari*. We reverse.

In *Cannon*, the Court held that Title IX is enforceable through an implied right of action. We have no occasion here to reconsider that decision. Rather, in this case we must decide what remedies are available in a suit brought pursuant to this implied right. As we have often stated, the question of what remedies are available under a statute that provides a private right of action is analytically distinct from the issue of whether such a right exists in the first place. Thus, although we examine the text and history of a statute to determine whether Congress intended to create a right of action, we presume the availability of all appropriate remedies unless Congress has expressly indicated otherwise. This principle has deep roots in our jurisprudence.

Where legal rights have been invaded, and a federal statute provides for a general right to sue for such invasion, federal courts may use any available remedy to make good the wrong done. From the earliest years of the Republic, the Court has recognized the power of the Judiciary to award appropriate remedies to redress injuries actionable in federal court, although it did not always distinguish clearly between a right to bring suit and a remedy available under such a right. In *Marbury v. Madison*, 5 U.S. (1 Cranch) 137, 163, 2 L.Ed. 60 (1803), for example, Chief Justice Marshall observed that our government has been emphatically termed a government of laws, and not of men. It will certainly cease to deserve this high appellation, if the laws furnish no remedy for the violation of a vested legal right. This principle originated in the English common law, and Blackstone described it as a general and indisputable rule, that where there is a legal right, there is also a legal remedy, by suit or action at law, whenever that right is invaded. 3 W. Blackstone, *Commentaries* 23 (1783).

Respondents and the United States as *amicus curiae*, however, maintain that whatever the traditional presumption may have been, it has disappeared in succeeding decades. We do not agree. In *J.I. Case Co. v. Borak*, 377 U.S. 426, 84 S.Ct. 1555, 12 L.Ed.2d 423 (1964), the Court adhered to the general rule that all appropriate relief is available in an action brought to vindicate a federal right when Congress has given no indication of its purpose with respect to remedies.

That a statute does not authorize the remedy at issue in so many words is no more significant than the fact that it does not in terms authorize execution to issue on a judgment. Subsequent cases have been true to this position.

The United States contends that the traditional presumption in favor of all appropriate relief was abandoned by the Court in *Davis v. Passman*, 442 U.S. 228, 99 S.Ct. 2264, 60 L.Ed.2d 846 (1979). The United States quotes language in *Davis* to the effect that the question of who may enforce a statutory right is fundamentally different from the question of who may enforce a right that is protected by the Constitution. The government's position, however, mirrors the very misunderstanding over the difference between a cause of action and the relief afforded under it that sparked the confusion we attempted to clarify in *Davis*. Whether Congress may limit the class of persons who have a right of action under Title IX is irrelevant to the issue in this lawsuit. To reiterate, the question whether a litigant has a cause of action is analytically distinct and prior to the question of what relief, if any, a litigant may be entitled to receive. *Davis*, therefore, did noth-

ing to interrupt the long line of cases in which the Court has held that if a right of action exists to enforce a federal right and Congress is silent on the question of remedies, a federal court may order any appropriate relief.

The general rule, therefore, is that absent clear direction to the contrary by Congress, the federal courts have the power to award any appropriate relief in a cognizable cause of action brought pursuant to a federal statute.

We now address whether Congress intended to limit application of this general principle in the enforcement of Title IX. Because the cause of action was inferred by the Court in *Cannon*, the usual recourse to statutory text and legislative history in the period prior to that decision necessarily will not enlighten our analysis. Respondents and the United States fundamentally misunderstand the nature of the inquiry, therefore, by needlessly dedicating large portions of their briefs to discussions of how the text and legislative intent behind Title IX are silent on the issue of available remedies. Since the Court in *Cannon* concluded that this statute supported no express right of action, it is hardly surprising that Congress also said nothing about the applicable remedies for an implied right of action.

During the period prior to the decision in *Cannon*, the inquiry in any event is not basically a matter of statutory construction, as the United States asserts. Rather, in determining Congress' intent to limit application of the traditional presumption in favor of all appropriate relief, we evaluate the state of the law when the Legislature passed Title IX. In the years before and after Congress enacted this statute, the Court followed a common-law tradition and regarded the denial of a remedy as the exception rather than the rule. This has been the prevailing presumption in our courts since at least the early 19th century. In *Cannon*, the majority upheld an implied right of action in part because in the decade immediately preceding enactment of Title IX in 1972, this Court had found implied rights of action in six cases. Wholly apart from the wisdom of the *Cannon* holding, therefore, the same contextual approach used to justify an implied right of action more than amply demonstrates the lack of any legislative intent to abandon the traditional presumption in favor of all available remedies.

In the years after the announcement of *Cannon*, on the other hand, a more traditional method of statutory analysis is possible, because Congress was legislating with full cognizance of that decision. Our reading of the two amendments to Title IX enacted after *Cannon* leads us to conclude that Congress did not intend to limit the remedies available in a suit brought under Title IX. In the Rehabilitation Act Amendments of 1986, 100 Stat. 1845, 42 U.S.C. §§ 2000d-7, Congress abrogated the states' Eleventh Amendment immunity under Title IX, Title VI, § 504 of the Rehabilitation Act of 1973, and the Age Discrimination Act of 1975. This statute cannot be read except as a validation of *Cannon's* holding. A subsection of the 1986 law provides that in a suit against a state, "remedies including remedies both at law and in equity are available for such a violation to the same extent as such remedies are available for such a violation in the suit against any public or private entity other than a State." 42 U.S.C. § 2000d-7(a)(2). While it is true that this saving clause says nothing about the nature of those other available remedies, absent any contrary indication in the text or history of the statute, we presume Congress enacted this statute with the prevailing traditional rule in mind.

In addition to the Rehabilitation Act Amendments of 1986, Congress also enacted the Civil Rights Restoration Act of 1987, Pub.L. 100-259, 102 Stat. 28. Without in any way altering the existing rights of action and the corresponding remedies permissible under Title IX, Title VI, § 504 of the Rehabilitation Act, and the Age Discrimination Act, Congress broadened the coverage of these antidiscrimination provisions in this legislation. In seeking to correct what it considered to be an unacceptable decision on our part in *Grove City College v. Bell*, 465 U.S. 555, 104 S.Ct. 1211, 79 L.Ed.2d 516 (1984), Congress made no effort to restrict the right of action recognized in *Cannon* and ratified in the 1986 Act or to alter the traditional presumption in favor of any appropriate relief for violation of a federal right. We cannot say, therefore, that Congress has limited the remedies available to a complainant in a suit brought under Title IX.

Respondents and the United States nevertheless suggest three reasons why we should not apply the traditional presumption in favor of appropriate relief in this case.

First, respondents argue that an award of damages violates separation of powers principles because it unduly expands the federal courts' power into a sphere properly reserved to the Executive and Legislative Branches. In making this argument, respondents misconceive the difference between a cause of action and a remedy. Unlike the finding of a cause of action, which authorizes a court to hear a case or controversy, the discretion to award appropriate relief involves no such increase in judicial power. Federal courts cannot reach out to award remedies when the Constitution or laws of the United States do not support a cause of action. Indeed, properly understood, respondents' position invites us to abdicate our historic judicial authority to award appropriate relief in cases brought in our court system. It is well to recall that such authority historically has been thought necessary to provide an important safeguard against abuses of legislative and executive power, as well as to ensure an independent Judiciary. Moreover, selective abdication of the sort advocated here would harm separation of powers principles in another way, by giving judges the power to render inutile causes of action authorized by Congress through a decision that no remedy is available.

Next, consistent with the court of appeals' reasoning, respondents and the United States contend that the normal presumption in favor of all appropriate remedies should not apply because Title IX was enacted pursuant to Congress' Spending Clause power. We disagree. The point of not permitting monetary damages for an unintentional violation is that the receiving entity of federal funds lacks notice that it will be liable for a monetary award. This notice problem does not arise in a case such as this, in which intentional discrimination is alleged. Unquestionably, Title IX placed on the Gwinnett County Public Schools the duty not to discriminate on the basis of sex, and when a supervisor sexually harasses a subordinate because of the subordinate's sex, that supervisor discriminates on the basis of sex. We believe the same rule should apply when a teacher sexually harasses and abuses a student. Congress surely did not intend for federal moneys to be expended to support the intentional actions it sought by statute to proscribe. Moreover, the notion that Spending Clause statutes do not authorize monetary awards for intentional violations is belied by our unanimous holding in *Darrone*. *See* 465 U.S., at 628, 104 S.Ct., at 1251. Respondents and the United States characterize the backpay remedy in *Darrone* as equitable relief, but this description is irrelevant to their underlying objection: that application of the traditional rule in this case will require state entities to pay monetary awards out of their treasuries for intentional violations of federal statutes.

Finally, the United States asserts that the remedies permissible under Title IX should nevertheless be limited to backpay and prospective relief. In addition to diverging from our traditional approach to deciding what remedies are available for violation of a federal right, this position conflicts with sound logic. First, both remedies are equitable in nature, and it is axiomatic that a court should determine the adequacy of a remedy in law before resorting to equitable relief. Under the ordinary convention, the proper inquiry would be whether monetary damages provided an adequate remedy, and if not, whether equitable relief would be appropriate. Moreover, in this case the equitable remedies suggested by respondent and the federal government are clearly inadequate. Backpay does nothing for petitioner, because she was a student when the alleged discrimination occurred. Similarly, because Hill—the person she claims subjected her to sexual harassment—no longer teaches at the school and she herself no longer attends a school in the Gwinnett system, prospective relief accords her no remedy at all.

The government's answer that administrative action helps other similarly situated students in effect acknowledges that its approach would leave petitioner remediless.

In sum, we conclude that a damages remedy is available for an action brought to enforce Title IX. The judgment of the court of appeals, therefore, is reversed, and the case is remanded for further proceedings consistent with this opinion.

 For an extended version of the case and review questions to test your understanding of the material, please go to www.HumanKinetics.com/CaseStudiesInSportLaw.

Gebser v. Lago Vista Independent School District

524 U.S. 274 (1998)

The question in this case is when a school district may be held liable in damages in an implied right of action under Title IX of the Education Amendments of 1972, 86 Stat. 373, as amended, 20 U.S.C. §§ 1681 *et seq.* (Title IX), for the sexual harassment of a student by one of the district's teachers.

In the spring of 1991, when petitioner Alida Star Gebser was an eighth-grade student at a middle school in respondent Lago Vista Independent School District (Lago Vista), she joined a high school book discussion group led by Frank Waldrop, a teacher at Lago Vista's high school. Lago Vista received federal funds at all pertinent times. During the book discussion sessions, Waldrop often made sexually suggestive comments to the students. Gebser entered high school in the fall and was assigned to classes taught by Waldrop in both semesters. Waldrop continued to make inappropriate remarks to the students, and he began to direct more of his suggestive comments toward Gebser, including during the substantial amount of time that the two were alone in his classroom. He initiated sexual contact with Gebser in the spring, when, while visiting her home ostensibly to give her a book, he kissed and fondled her. The two had sexual intercourse on a number of occasions during the remainder of the school year. Gebser did not report the relationship to school officials, testifying that while she realized Waldrop's conduct was improper, she was uncertain how to react and she wanted to continue having him as a teacher.

In October 1992, the parents of two other students complained to the high school principal about Waldrop's comments in class. The principal arranged a meeting, at which, according to the principal, Waldrop indicated that he did not believe he had made offensive remarks but apologized to the parents and said it would not happen again. The principal also advised Waldrop to be careful about his classroom comments and told the school guidance counselor about the meeting, but he did not report the parents' complaint to Lago Vista's superintendent, who was the district's Title IX coordinator.

A couple of months later, in January 1993, a police officer discovered Waldrop and Gebser engaging in sexual intercourse and arrested Waldrop. Lago Vista terminated his employment, and subsequently, the Texas Education Agency revoked his teaching license. During this time, the district had not promulgated or distributed an official grievance procedure for lodging sexual harassment complaints; nor had it issued a formal antiharassment policy.

Gebser and her mother filed suit against Lago Vista and Waldrop in state court in November 1993, raising claims against the school district under Title IX, Rev. Stat. § 1979, 42 U.S.C. § 1983, and state negligence law, and claims against Waldrop primarily under state law. They sought compensatory and punitive damages from both defendants. After the case was removed, the United States District Court for the Western District of Texas granted summary judgment in favor of Lago Vista on all claims, and remanded the allegations against Waldrop to state court. In rejecting the Title IX claim against the school district, the court reasoned that the statute was enacted to counter policies of discrimination in federally-funded education programs, and that only if school administrators have some type of notice of the gender discrimination and fail to respond in good faith can the discrimination be interpreted as a policy of the school district. Here, the court determined, the parents' complaint to the principal concerning Waldrop's comments in class was the only one Lago Vista had received about Waldrop, and that evidence was inadequate to raise a genuine issue on whether the school district had actual or constructive notice that Waldrop was involved in a sexual relationship with a student.

Petitioners appealed only on the Title IX claim. The Court of Appeals for the Fifth Circuit affirmed, relying in large part on two of its recent decisions. The court first declined to impose strict liability on school districts for a teacher's

sexual harassment of a student, reiterating its conclusion in a prior case that strict liability is inconsistent with the Title IX contract. The court then determined that Lago Vista could not be liable on the basis of constructive notice, finding that there was insufficient evidence to suggest that a school official should have known about Waldrop's relationship with Gebser. Finally, the court refused to invoke the common law principle that holds an employer vicariously liable when an employee is aided in accomplishing a tort by the existence of the agency relation, explaining that application of that principle would result in school district liability in essentially every case of teacher-student harassment.

The court concluded its analysis by reaffirming its holding that school districts are not liable in tort for teacher-student sexual harassment under Title IX unless an employee who has been invested by the school board with supervisory power over the offending employee actually knew of the abuse, had the power to end the abuse, and failed to do so, and ruling that petitioners could not satisfy that standard. The Fifth Circuit's analysis represents one of the varying approaches adopted by the courts of appeals in assessing a school district's liability under Title IX for a teacher's sexual harassment of a student. We granted *certiorari* to address the issue, and we now affirm.

Title IX provides in pertinent part that "no person shall . . . on the basis of sex, be excluded from participation in, be denied the benefits of, or be subjected to discrimination under any education program or activity receiving Federal financial assistance." The express statutory means of enforcement is administrative: The statute directs federal agencies that distribute education funding to establish requirements to effectuate the nondiscrimination mandate, and permits the agencies to enforce those requirements through "any means authorized by law," including ultimately the termination of federal funding. We subsequently established in *Franklin v. Gwinnett County Public Schools*, 503 U.S. 60, 112 S.Ct. 1028, 117 L.Ed.2d 208 (1992), that monetary damages are available in the implied private action. *Franklin* thereby establishes that a school district can be held liable in damages in cases involving a teacher's sexual harassment of a student; the decision, however, does not purport to define the contours of that liability.

We face that issue squarely in this case. Petitioners, joined by the United States as *amicus curiae*, would invoke standards used by the courts of appeals in Title VII cases involving a supervisor's sexual harassment of an employee in the workplace. Petitioners and the United States submit that, in light of *Franklin*'s comparison of teacher-student harassment with supervisor-employee harassment, agency principles should likewise apply in Title IX actions.

Specifically, they advance two possible standards under which Lago Vista would be liable for Waldrop's conduct. First, relying on a 1997 Policy Guidance issued by the Department of Education, they would hold a school district liable in damages under Title IX where a teacher is aided in carrying out the sexual harassment of students by his or her position of authority with the institution, irrespective of whether school district officials had any knowledge of the harassment and irrespective of their response on becoming aware. That rule is an expression of *respondeat superior* liability (i.e., vicarious or imputed liability under which recovery in damages against a school district would generally follow whenever a teacher's authority over a student facilitates the harassment). Second, petitioners and the United States submit that a school district should at a minimum be liable for damages based on a theory of constructive notice (i.e., where the district knew or should have known about harassment but failed to uncover and eliminate it). Both standards would allow a damages recovery in a broader range of situations than the rule adopted by the court of appeals, which hinges on actual knowledge by a school official with authority to end the harassment.

In this case, moreover, petitioners seek not just to establish a Title IX violation but to recover damages based on theories of *respondeat superior* and constructive notice. It is that aspect of their action, in our view, that is most critical to resolving the case. Unlike Title IX, Title VII contains an express cause of action and specifically provides for relief in the form of monetary damages. Congress therefore has directly addressed the subject of damages relief under Title VII and has set out the particular situations in which damages are available as well as the maximum amounts recoverable. With

respect to Title IX, however, the private right of action is judicially implied, and there is thus no legislative expression of the scope of available remedies, including when it is appropriate to award monetary damages. In addition, although the general presumption that courts can award any appropriate relief in an established cause of action, coupled with Congress' abrogation of the states' Eleventh Amendment immunity under Title IX, led us to conclude in *Franklin* that Title IX recognizes a damages remedy, we did so in response to lower court decisions holding that Title IX does not support damages relief at all. We made no effort in *Franklin* to delimit the circumstances in which a damages remedy should lie.

Because the private right of action under Title IX is judicially implied, we have a measure of latitude to shape a sensible remedial scheme that best comports with the statute. That endeavor inherently entails a degree of speculation, since it addresses an issue on which Congress has not specifically spoken. To guide the analysis, we generally examine the relevant statute to ensure that we do not fashion the scope of an implied right in a manner at odds with the statutory structure and purpose.

Those considerations, we think, are pertinent not only to the scope of the implied right, but also to the scope of the available remedies. We suggested as much in *Franklin*, where we recognized the general rule that all appropriate relief is available in an action brought to vindicate a federal right, but indicated that the rule must be reconciled with congressional purpose. The general rule yields where necessary to carry out the intent of Congress or to avoid frustrating the purposes of the statute involved.

Applying those principles here, we conclude that it would frustrate the purposes of Title IX to permit a damages recovery against a school district for a teacher's sexual harassment of a student based on principles of *respondeat superior* or constructive notice (i.e., without actual notice to a school district official). Because Congress did not expressly create a private right of action under Title IX, the statutory text does not shed light on Congress' intent with respect to the scope of available remedies. Instead, we attempt to infer how the [1972] Congress would have addressed the issue had the action been included as an express provision in the statute.

As a general matter, it does not appear that Congress contemplated unlimited recovery in damages against a funding recipient where the recipient is unaware of discrimination in its programs. When Title IX was enacted in 1972, the principal civil rights statutes containing an express right of action did not provide for recovery of monetary damages at all, instead allowing only injunctive and equitable relief. It was not until 1991 that Congress made damages available under Title VII, and even then, Congress carefully limited the amount recoverable in any individual case, calibrating the maximum recovery to the size of the employer. Adopting petitioners' position would amount, then, to allowing unlimited recovery of damages under Title IX where Congress has not spoken on the subject of either the right or the remedy, and in the face of evidence that when Congress expressly considered both in Title VII it restricted the amount of damages available.

Congress enacted Title IX in 1972 with two principal objectives in mind: To avoid the use of federal resources to support discriminatory practices and to provide individual citizens effective protection against those practices. The statute was modeled after Title VI of the Civil Rights Act of 1964, which is parallel to Title IX except that it prohibits race discrimination, not sex discrimination, and applies in all programs receiving federal funds, not only in education programs. The two statutes operate in the same manner, conditioning an offer of federal funding on a promise by the recipient not to discriminate, in what amounts essentially to a contract between the government and the recipient of funds.

That contractual framework distinguishes Title IX from Title VII, which is framed in terms not of a condition but of an outright prohibition. Title VII applies to all employers without regard to federal funding and aims broadly to eradicate discrimination throughout the economy. Title VII, moreover, seeks to make persons whole for injuries suffered through past discrimination. Thus, whereas Title VII aims centrally to compensate victims of discrimination, Title IX focuses more on protecting individuals from discriminatory practices carried out by recipients of federal funds. That might explain why, when the Court first recognized the implied right under Title IX in the opinion referred to injunctive or equitable relief in a private action, but not to a damages remedy.

Title IX's contractual nature has implications for our construction of the scope of available remedies. When Congress attaches conditions to the award of federal funds under its spending power as it has in Title IX and Title VI, we examine closely the propriety of private actions holding the recipient liable in monetary damages for noncompliance with the condition. Our central concern in that regard is with ensuring that the receiving entity of federal funds has notice that it will be liable for a monetary award. If a school district's liability for a teacher's sexual harassment rests on principles of constructive notice or *respondeat superior*, it will likewise be the case that the recipient of funds was unaware of the discrimination. It is sensible to assume that Congress did not envision a recipient's liability in damages in that situation.

Most significantly, Title IX contains important clues that Congress did not intend to allow recovery in damages where liability rests solely on principles of vicarious liability or constructive notice. Title IX's express means of enforcement—by administrative agencies—operates on an assumption of actual notice to officials of the funding recipient. The statute entitles agencies who disburse education funding to enforce their rules implementing the nondiscrimination mandate through proceedings to suspend or terminate funding or through other means authorized by law. Significantly, however, an agency may not initiate enforcement proceedings until it has advised the appropriate person or persons of the failure to comply with the requirement and has determined that compliance cannot be secured by voluntary means. The administrative regulations implement that obligation, requiring resolution of compliance issues by informal means whenever possible, 34 C.F.R. § 100.7(d) (1997), and prohibiting commencement of enforcement proceedings until the agency has determined that voluntary compliance is unobtainable and the recipient has been notified of its failure to comply and of the action to be taken to effect compliance.

In the event of a violation, a funding recipient may be required to take such remedial action as is deemed necessary to overcome the effects of the discrimination. While agencies have conditioned continued funding on providing equitable relief to the victim, the regulations do not appear to contemplate a condition ordering payment of monetary damages, and there is no indication that payment of damages has been demanded as a condition of finding a recipient to be in compliance with the statute.

Presumably, a central purpose of requiring notice of the violation to the appropriate person and an opportunity for voluntary compliance before administrative enforcement proceedings can commence is to avoid diverting education funding from beneficial uses where a recipient was unaware of discrimination in its programs and is willing to institute prompt corrective measures. The scope of private damages relief proposed by petitioners is at odds with that basic objective. When a teacher's sexual harassment is imputed to a school district or when a school district is deemed to have constructively known of the teacher's harassment, by assumption the district had no actual knowledge of the teacher's conduct. Nor, of course, did the district have an opportunity to take action to end the harassment or to limit further harassment.

It would be unsound, we think, for a statute's express system of enforcement to require notice to the recipient and an opportunity to come into voluntary compliance while a judicially implied system of enforcement permits substantial liability without regard to the recipient's knowledge or its corrective actions on receiving notice. Moreover, an award of damages in a particular case might well exceed a recipient's level of federal funding. Where a statute's express enforcement scheme hinges its most severe sanction on notice and unsuccessful efforts to obtain compliance, we cannot attribute to Congress the intention to have implied an enforcement scheme that allows imposition of greater liability without comparable conditions.

Because the express remedial scheme under Title IX is predicated on notice to an appropriate person and an opportunity to rectify any violation we conclude, in the absence of further direction from Congress, that the implied damages remedy should be fashioned along the same lines. An appropriate person under § 1682 is, at a minimum, an official of the recipient entity with authority to take corrective action to end the discrimination. Consequently, in cases like this one that do not involve official policy of the recipient entity, we hold that a damages remedy will not lie under Title IX unless an official who at a minimum has authority to address the alleged discrimination and to institute corrective measures on the recipient's behalf has actual knowledge of discrimination in the recipient's programs and fails adequately to respond.

We think, moreover, that the response must amount to deliberate indifference to discrimination. The administrative enforcement scheme presupposes that an official who is advised of a Title IX violation refuses to take action to bring the recipient into compliance. The premise, in other words, is an official decision by the recipient not to remedy the violation. That framework finds a rough parallel in the standard of deliberate indifference. Under a lower standard, there would be a risk that the recipient would be liable in damages not for its own official decision but instead for its employees' independent actions. Comparable considerations led to our adoption of a deliberate indifference standard for claims under § 1983 alleging that a municipality's actions in failing to prevent a deprivation of federal rights was the cause of the violation.

Applying the framework to this case is fairly straightforward, as petitioners do not contend they can prevail under an actual notice standard. The only official alleged to have had information about Waldrop's misconduct is the high school principal. That information, however, consisted of a complaint from parents of other students charging only that Waldrop had made inappropriate comments during class, which was plainly insufficient to alert the principal to the possibility that Waldrop was involved in a sexual relationship with a student. Lago Vista, moreover, terminated Waldrop's employment on learning of his relationship with Gebser. Justice STEVENS points out in his dissenting opinion that Waldrop of course had knowledge of his own actions. Where a school district's liability rests on actual notice principles, however, the knowledge of the wrongdoer himself is not pertinent to the analysis.

Petitioners focus primarily on Lago Vista's asserted failure to promulgate and publicize an effective policy and grievance procedure for sexual harassment claims. They point to Department of Education regulations requiring each funding recipient to adopt and publish grievance procedures providing for prompt and equitable resolution of discrimination complaints and to notify students and others that it does not discriminate on the basis of sex in the educational programs or activities that it operates. Lago Vista's alleged failure to comply with the regulations, however, does not establish the requisite actual notice and deliberate indifference. And in any event, the failure to promulgate a grievance procedure does not itself constitute discrimination under Title IX. Of course, the Department of Education could enforce the requirement administratively: Agencies generally have authority to promulgate and enforce requirements that effectuate the statute's nondiscrimination mandate even if those requirements do not purport to represent a definition of discrimination under the statute. We have never held, however, that the implied private right of action under Title IX allows recovery in damages for violation of those sorts of administrative requirements.

The issue in this case, however, is whether the independent misconduct of a teacher is attributable to the school district that employs him under a specific federal statute designed primarily to prevent recipients of federal financial assistance from using the funds in a discriminatory manner. Our decision does not affect any right of recovery that an individual may have against a school district as a matter of state law or against the teacher in his individual capacity under state law or under 42 U.S.C. § 1983. Until Congress speaks directly on the subject, however, we will not hold a school district liable in damages under Title IX for a teacher's sexual harassment of a student absent actual notice and deliberate indifference. We therefore affirm the judgment of the court of appeals.

 For an extended version of the case and review questions to test your understanding of the material, please go to www.HumanKinetics.com/CaseStudiesInSportLaw.

Kelley v. Board of Trustees

35 F.3d 265 (7th Cir. 1994)

On May 7, 1993, the University of Illinois announced that it intended to terminate four varsity athletic programs, including the men's swimming program, effective July 1, 1993. On May 25, 1993, the plaintiffs, all members of the University of Illinois' men's swimming team prior to its termination, brought suit against the Board of Trustees of the University, its chancellor, athletic director, and associate athletic director (defendants), alleging that defendants violated Title IX of the Education Amendments of 1972 (20 U.S.C. § 1681) and the Equal Protection Clause of the Fourteenth Amendment. Plaintiffs' complaint sought damages, as well as an injunction prohibiting the defendants from terminating the men's swimming program, under 42 U.S.C. § 1983 and 42 U.S.C. § 1985(3). In response, defendants filed a motion to dismiss, which the parties agreed to convert to a motion for summary judgment. Plaintiffs moved for a preliminary injunction. After hearing

testimony in support of plaintiffs' request for a preliminary injunction and receiving affidavits in support of defendants' motion for summary judgment, the district court granted summary judgment in favor of the defendants and found that the request for a preliminary injunction was therefore moot. Plaintiffs now appeal.

Title IX of the Education Amendments of 1972 (20 U.S.C. § 1681 (1988)) provides that no person shall, on the basis of sex, be excluded from participation in, be denied the benefits of, or be subjected to discrimination under any education program or activity other than those specifically described in the Act receiving Federal financial assistance.

In 1974, Congress requested that the Secretary of the Department of Health, Education, and Welfare prepare and publish regulations implementing the provisions of Title IX, including, with respect to intercollegiate athletic activities, reasonable provisions considering the nature of particular sports. Promulgated the following year, the pertinent regulation allows schools to field single-sex teams in certain circumstances but requires that they provide equal athletic opportunity for both sexes. 34 C.F.R. § 106.41(c). Section 106.41(c) sets out the factors to be examined in determining whether a school provides equal athletic opportunity. Chief among these, and of primary concern here, is whether the selection of sports and levels of competition effectively accommodate the interests and abilities of members of both sexes. Although § 106.41(c) lists nine other factors, an institution may violate Title IX solely by failing to accommodate effectively the interests and abilities of student athletes of both sexes.

In 1979, the Department of Health, Education, and Welfare, in an effort to encourage self-policing, issued a policy interpretation providing guidance on what constitutes compliance with the law. According to the policy interpretation, an institution has effectively accommodated the interests of its male and female students if it satisfies any of three benchmarks:

> (1) whether intercollegiate level participation opportunities for male and female students are provided in numbers substantially proportionate to their respective enrollments; or (2) where the members of one sex have been and are underrepresented among intercollegiate athletes, whether the institution can show a history and continuing practice of program expansion that is demonstrably responsive to the developing interest and abilities of the members of that sex; or (3) where members of one sex are underrepresented among intercollegiate athletes, and the institution cannot show a continuing practice of program expansion, whether it can be demonstrated that the interests and abilities of the members of that sex have been fully and effectively accommodated by the present program. 44 Fed.Reg. 71,418 (1979).

In 1982, the Office of Civil Rights of the United States Department of Education determined that the University of Illinois had denied its female students equal athletic opportunities. Relying on the university's representations that it would remedy the disparity within a reasonable period of time, the Office of Civil Rights concluded that the school was not in violation of Title IX. A decade later, however, female participation in intercollegiate athletics at the University of Illinois continued to be disproportionate to female undergraduate enrollment. Thus in 1993, for example, while women comprised 44% of the student body of the university, they accounted for only 23.4% of the school's intercollegiate athletes.

It was against this backdrop that the decision to cut the men's swimming program was made. Faced with a significant deficit in its athletic budget—$600,000 before the receipt of substantial, unanticipated income from a college football bowl game—the university determined that it would need to reduce athletic costs significantly. Determined to field only teams capable of competing for championships in the Big Ten Conference, the athletic conference to which the university belongs, and the National Collegiate Athletic Association, the university concluded that it would have to discontinue certain intercollegiate teams in order to eliminate its deficit.

While the university's decision to reduce its athletic offerings was motivated by budget considerations, other considerations—including the need to comply with Title IX—influenced the selection of particular programs to be terminated. The final selection of the teams to be eliminated was made by defendant Morton Weir, then chancellor of the university's Urbana-Champaign Campus. In reaching his decision, Chancellor Weir relied on the recommendation of the Athletic Board of Control, a body that advises the chancellor on athletic issues. The Athletic Board of Control, in turn, relied on advice from the university's athletic director, defendant Ronald Guenther. In making his recommendation, Guenther evaluated all 19 sports offered by the university against seven criteria: (1) whether or not the Big Ten Conference and the National Collegiate Athletic Association sponsored a championship in the sport, (2) the tradition of success of the sport at the university, (3) the level of interest and participation in the sport at the high school level, (4) the adequacy of the university's facilities for the sport, (5) the level of spectator interest in the sport, (6) gender and ethnic issues, and (7) the cost of the sport. Guenther recommended that four teams—men's swimming, men's fencing, and men's and women's diving—be cut, a recommendation adopted by Chancellor Weir.

Men's swimming was selected for termination because, among other things, the program was historically weak, swimming is not a widely offered athletic activity in high schools, and it does not have a large spectator following. The university did not eliminate the women's swimming program because the school's legal counsel advised that such action would put the university at risk of violating Title IX.

The university's decision not to terminate the women's swimming program was—given the requirements of Title IX and the applicable regulation and policy interpretation—extremely prudent. The percentage of women involved in intercollegiate athletics at the University of Illinois is substantially lower than the percentage of women enrolled at the school. If the university had terminated the women's swimming program, it would have been vulnerable to a finding that it was in violation of Title IX. Female participation would have continued to be substantially disproportionate to female enrollment, and women with a demonstrated interest in an intercollegiate athletic activity and demonstrated ability to compete at the intercollegiate level would be left without an opportunity to participate in their sport. The university could, however, eliminate the men's swimming program without violating Title IX since even after eliminating the program, men's participation in athletics would continue to be more than substantially proportionate to their presence in the university's student body. And as the case law makes clear, if the percentage of student athletes of a particular sex is substantially proportionate to the percentage of students of that sex in the general student population, the athletic interests of that sex are presumed to have been accommodated. The university's decision to retain the women's swimming program—even though budget constraints required that the men's program be terminated—was a reasonable response to the requirements of the applicable regulation and policy interpretation.

Plaintiffs contend, however, that the applicable regulation, 34 C.F.R. § 106.41, and Policy Interpretation, 44 Fed.Reg. 71,418 (1979), pervert Title IX. Title IX, plaintiffs contend has through some alchemy of bureaucratic regulation been transformed from a statute that prohibits discrimination on the basis of sex into a statute that mandates discrimination against males. Or, as plaintiffs put it later: "If a university is required by Title IX to eliminate men from varsity athletic competition, then the same Title IX should require the university to eliminate women from the academic departments where they are over-represented and men from departments where they have been over-represented. Such a result would be ridiculous."

We agree that such a result would be ridiculous. But Congress itself recognized that addressing discrimination in athletics presented a unique set of problems not raised in areas such as employment and academics. Congress therefore specifically directed the agency in charge of administering Title IX to issue, with respect to intercollegiate athletic activities, regulations containing reasonable provisions considering the nature of particular sports. And where Congress has specifically delegated to an agency the responsibility to articulate standards governing a particular area, we must accord the ensuing regulation considerable deference.

The regulation at issue here is neither arbitrary nor manifestly contrary to the statute. The regulation provides that notwithstanding Title IX's requirement that "no person shall, on the basis of sex, be excluded from participation in any activity," a school may "sponsor separate teams for members of each sex where selection for such teams is based upon competitive skill or the activity involved is a contact sport." Such a provision is not at odds with the purpose of Title IX and we do not understand plaintiffs to argue that it is. And since 34 C.F.R. § 106.41 is not manifestly contrary to the objectives of Title IX, this court must accord it deference.

Plaintiffs, while they concede the validity of 34 C.F.R. § 106.41, argue that the substantial proportionality test contained in the agency's Policy Interpretation of that regulation establishes a gender-based quota system, a scheme they allege is contrary to the mandates of Title IX. But the Policy Interpretation does not, as plaintiffs suggest, mandate statistical balancing. Rather the Policy Interpretation merely creates a presumption that a school is in compliance with Title IX and the applicable regulation when it achieves such a statistical balance. Even if substantial proportionality has not been achieved, a school may establish that it is in compliance by demonstrating either that it has a continuing practice of increasing the athletic opportunities of the underrepresented sex or that its existing programs effectively accommodate the interests of that sex.

Moreover, once it is agreed Title IX does not require that all teams be co-ed—a point the plaintiffs concede—and that 34 C.F.R. § 106.41 is therefore a valid regulation, schools must be provided some means of establishing that despite offering single-sex teams, they have provided equal athletic opportunities for both sexes. Undoubtedly the agency responsible for enforcement of the statute could have required schools to sponsor a women's program for every men's program offered and vice versa. Requiring parallel teams would certainly have been the simplest method of ensuring equality of opportunity—and plaintiffs would doubtless have preferred this approach since, had it been adopted, the men's swimming program would likely have been saved. It was not unreasonable, however, for the agency to reject this course of action. Requiring parallel teams is a rigid approach that denies schools the flexibility to respond to the differing athletic interests of men and women. It was perfectly acceptable, therefore, for the agency to chart a different course and adopt an enforcement scheme that measures compliance by analyzing how a school has allocated its various athletic resources.

This court must defer to an agency's interpretation of its regulations if the interpretation is reasonable, a standard the Policy Interpretation at issue here meets. Measuring compliance through an evaluation of a school's allocation of its athletic resources allows schools flexibility in meeting the athletic interests of their students and increases the chance that the actual interests of those students will be met. And if compliance with Title IX is to be measured through this sort of analysis, it is only practical that schools be given some clear way to establish that they have satisfied the requirements of the statute. The substantial proportionality contained in Benchmark 1 merely establishes such a safe harbor.

Since the Policy Interpretation maps out a reasonable approach to measuring compliance with Title IX, this court does not have the authority to condemn it. Plaintiffs' claim that the University of Illinois violated Title IX when it terminated the men's swimming program is, therefore, rejected. The university's actions were consistent with the statute and the applicable regulation and policy interpretation. And despite plaintiffs' assertions to the contrary, neither the regulation nor the policy interpretation run afoul of the dictates of Title IX.

Plaintiffs' final argument is that the defendants' decision to eliminate the men's swimming program while retaining the women's program denied them equal protection of law as guaranteed by the Fourteenth Amendment. We do not agree.

First, the record makes clear that the university considered gender solely to ensure that its actions did not violate federal law. And insofar as the university actions were taken in an attempt to comply with the requirements of Title IX, plaintiffs' attack on those actions is merely a collateral attack on the statute and regulations and is therefore impermissible.

To the extent that plaintiffs' argument is that Title IX and the applicable regulation—rather than the actions of the defendants—are unconstitutional, it is without merit. While the effect of Title IX and the relevant regulation and policy interpretation is that institutions will sometimes consider gender when decreasing their athletic offerings, this limited consideration of sex does not violate the Constitution. Congress has broad powers under the Due Process Clause of the Fifth Amendment to remedy past discrimination. Even absent a specific finding that discrimination has occurred, remedial measures mandated by Congress are constitutionally permissible to the extent that they serve important governmental objectives and are substantially related to achievement of those ends. There is no doubt but that removing the legacy of sexual discrimination—including discrimination in the provision of extracurricular offerings such as athletics—from our nation's educational institutions is an important governmental objective. We do not understand plaintiffs to argue otherwise.

Plaintiffs' complaint appears, instead, to be that the remedial measures required by Title IX and the applicable regulation and policy interpretation are not substantially related to their purported goal. Plaintiffs contend that the applicable rules allow the university to improve its statistics without adding any opportunities for women, an outcome they suggest is unconstitutional. But to survive constitutional scrutiny, Title IX need not require—as plaintiffs would have us believe—that the opportunities for the underrepresented group be continually expanded. Title IX's stated objective is not to ensure that the athletic opportunities available to women increase. Rather its avowed purpose is to prohibit educational institutions from discriminating on the basis of sex. And the remedial scheme established by Title IX and the applicable regulation and policy interpretation are clearly substantially related to this end. Allowing a school to consider gender when determining which athletic programs to terminate ensures that in instances where overall athletic opportunities decrease, the actual opportunities available to the underrepresented gender do not. And since the remedial scheme here at issue directly protects the interests of the disproportionately burdened gender, it passes constitutional muster.

Since the district court correctly determined that the University of Illinois decision to terminate the men's swimming program did not violate Title IX or the Equal Protection Clause, its decision is affirmed.

 For an extended version of the case and review questions to test your understanding of the material, please go to www.HumanKinetics.com/CaseStudiesInSportLaw.

Roberts v. Colorado State Board of Agriculture

998 F.2d 824 (10th Cir. 1993)

The Colorado State Board of Agriculture (SBA or defendant) appeals the decision of the district court finding that it violated Title IX of the Education Amendments of 1972, 20 U.S.C. §§ 1681-1688, and ordering it to reinstate the women's fast pitch softball team at Colorado State University (CSU) with all of the incidental benefits of a varsity team.

Plaintiffs, CSU students and former members of the fast pitch softball team, brought suit in their individual capacities against SBA and CSU in June 1992 after CSU announced that it was discontinuing the varsity fast pitch softball program. In February of this year the district court found that SBA and CSU had violated Title IX and issued a permanent injunction reinstating the softball program. Approximately three weeks later, the district court held a status conference and amplified its earlier orders to require defendant to hire a coach promptly, recruit new members for the team, and organize a fall season. This court denied a motion for a stay but expedited the appeal.

Plaintiffs first contest our jurisdiction to hear these appeals. On the merits, defendant contends that the district court erred in finding a Title IX violation. Defendant also maintains that even if the verdict was correct, the district court abused its discretion when it ordered reinstatement of the softball team and required defendant to follow specific directions in effecting that reinstatement rather than affording defendant the opportunity to present a plan that would bring it into compliance with Title IX.

Defendant maintains that, as a matter of law, it did not violate Title IX. Title IX provides that: "no person in the United States shall, on the basis of sex, be excluded from participation in, be denied the benefits of, or be subjected to discrimination under any education program or activity receiving federal financial assistance." Since 1988, Title IX has applied to recipients of federal funds in all of their operations. The statute delegated to the Secretary of Health, Education and Welfare (now the Secretary of Education) the responsibility to promulgate regulations implementing Title IX, including specifically intercollegiate athletic activities. Title 34, § 106.41, of the Code of Federal Regulations applies Title IX to college athletics.

This controversy concerns one subpart of the regulations implementing Title IX. Subparagraph c of § 106.41 provides that a recipient that operates or sponsors interscholastic, intercollegiate, club, or intramural athletics shall provide equal athletic opportunity for members of both sexes.

In determining whether equal opportunities are available the Director of the Office for Civil Rights will consider, among other factors, whether the selection of sports and levels of competition effectively accommodate the interests and abilities of members of both sexes. Although § 106.41(c) goes on to list nine other factors that enter into a determination of equal opportunity in athletics, an institution may violate Title IX simply by failing to accommodate effectively the interests and abilities of student athletes of both sexes.

In 1979, the Department of Health, Education, and Welfare issued a policy interpretation explaining the ways in which institutions may effectively accommodate the interests and abilities of their student athletes. The Policy Interpretation delineates three general areas in which the OCR will assess compliance with the effective accommodation section of the regulation: (a) the determination of athletic interests and abilities of students, (b) the selection of sports offered, and (c) the levels of competition available including the opportunity for team competition.

Despite some similar and overlapping language in the Policy Interpretation's discussion of these three broad policy areas, a close reading of the application sections immediately following this initial statement of policy reveals that plaintiffs' claim concerns their opportunity to participate in team competition. The OCR assesses effective accommodation with respect to opportunities for intercollegiate competition by determining

> (1) Whether intercollegiate level participation opportunities for male and female students are provided in numbers substantially proportionate to their respective enrollments; or
>
> (2) Where the members of one sex have been and are underrepresented among intercollegiate athletes, whether the institution can show a history and continuing practice of program expansion that is demonstrably responsive to the developing interest and abilities of the members of that sex; or
>
> (3) Where the members of one sex are underrepresented among intercollegiate athletes, and the institution cannot show a continuing practice of program expansion such as that cited above, whether it can be demonstrated that the interests and abilities of the members of that sex have been fully and effectively accommodated by the present program.

In effect, substantial proportionality between athletic participation and undergraduate enrollment provides a safe harbor for recipients under Title IX. In the absence of such gender balance, the institution must show that it has expanded and is continuing to expand opportunities for athletic participation by the underrepresented gender, or else it must fully and effectively accommodate the interests and abilities among members of the underrepresented gender.

In addition to assessing whether individuals of both sexes have the opportunity to compete in intercollegiate athletics, the OCR also examines whether the quality of competition provided to male and female athletes equally reflects their abilities. This will depend on whether, program wide, the competitive schedules of men's and women's teams afford proportionally similar numbers of male and female athletes equivalently advanced competitive opportunities, or whether the institution can demonstrate a history and continuing practice of upgrading the competitive opportunities available to the historically disadvantaged sex as warranted by developing abilities among the athletes of that sex. However, institutions are not required to upgrade teams to intercollegiate status or otherwise develop intercollegiate sports absent a reasonable expectation that intercollegiate competition in that sport will be available within the institution's normal competitive regions.

The district court found that plaintiffs met their burden of showing that defendant could not take shelter in the safe harbor of substantial proportionality. The district court reviewed a substantial quantity of statistical data, and made the undisputed finding that following the termination of the varsity softball program, the disparity between enrollment and athletic participation for women at CSU is 10.5%. Defendant maintains that, as a matter of law, a 10.5% disparity is substantially proportionate.

The OCR has instructed its Title IX compliance investigators that there is no set ratio that constitutes substantially proportionate or that, when not met, results in a disparity or a violation. However, the Manual (Title IX Athletics Investigators Manual 7 [1990]) suggests that substantial proportionality entails a fairly close relationship between athletic participation and undergraduate enrollment. Furthermore, in a Title IX compliance review completed in 1983, the OCR found that CSU's athletic participation opportunities for men and women were not substantially proportionate to their respective enrollments. During the three years that were the subject of that review, the differences between women enrolled and women athletes were 7.5%, 12.5%, and 12.7%. The district court relied on these sources, as well as expert testimony that a 10.5% disparity is statistically significant, in concluding that CSU could not meet this first benchmark. Without demarcating further the line between substantial proportionality and disproportionality, we agree with the district court that a 10.5% disparity between female athletic participation and female undergraduate enrollment is not substantially proportionate. The fact that many or even most other educational institutions have a greater imbalance than CSU does not require a different holding.

The district court also found that defendant could not prove a history and continuing practice of expansion in women's athletics at CSU. Defendant argues that the district court should have given greater weight to its dramatic expansion of women's athletic opportunities during the 1970s. In essence, defendant suggests reading the words "continuing practice" out of this prong of the test. In support of this position, defendant offers anecdotal evidence of enforcement at other institutions, and the OCR's 1983 finding of compliance for CSU, which was contingent on CSU's fulfilling the provisions of a plan that CSU never met.

Although CSU created a women's sports program out of nothing in the 1970s, adding 11 sports for women during that decade, the district court found that women's participation opportunities declined steadily during the 1980s. Furthermore, although budget cuts in the last 12 years have affected both men and women athletes at CSU, the district court found that women's participation opportunities declined by 34%, whereas men's opportunities declined by only 20%. The facts as found by the district court (and largely undisputed by defendant) can logically support no other conclusion than that, since adding women's golf in 1977, CSU has not maintained a practice of program expansion in women's athletics, and indeed has since dropped three women's sports.

We recognize that in times of economic hardship, few schools will be able to satisfy Title IX's effective accommodation requirement by continuing to expand their women's athletics programs. Nonetheless, the ordinary meaning of the word "expansion" may not be twisted to find compliance under this prong when schools have increased the relative percentages of women participating in athletics by making cuts in both men's and women's sports programs. Financially strapped institutions may still comply with Title IX by cutting athletic programs such that men's and women's athletic participation rates become substantially proportionate to their representation in the undergraduate population.

The district court found that defendant could not demonstrate that CSU's athletic program fully and effectively accommodated the interests and abilities of women athletes. Because a Title IX violation may not be predicated solely on a disparity between the gender composition of an institution's athletic program and the gender composition of its undergraduate enrollment, plaintiff must not only show that the institution fails on the first benchmark of substantial proportionality but also that it does not fully and effectively accommodate the interests and abilities of its women athletes. Further, an institution would be hard-pressed to establish the full and effective accommodation of the interests and abilities of its women athletes in the abstract. The ultimate burden must lie with the plaintiffs to show that they have been excluded from participation in or denied the benefits of an athletic program on the basis of sex. However, if plaintiffs establish that their interests and abilities are not being accommodated by the university's athletic program, the institution may still decline to upgrade or create an intercollegiate team if there is no reasonable expectation of competition for that team within the institution's normal competitive region.

In the case before us the district court made extensive findings concerning the unmet abilities and interests of the plaintiff softball players, and the feasibility of their organizing a competitive season of play. The district court credited the plaintiffs' testimony regarding their commitment to softball, the recognition they have achieved both as a team and as individuals, and the substantial interest in softball among first-year CSU students who are participating in a club team. The district court also credited testimony that softball is increasing in popularity among high school students in Colorado. Although CSU's traditional rivals do not field softball teams, there is no dispute that before the CSU softball team was terminated it played a competitive schedule within its athletic conference. Because the record is more than adequate in this regard, we are able to consider the question of effective accommodation, placing the burden of proof on the plaintiffs.

The heart of the controversy is the meaning of the phrase "full and effective accommodation of interests and abilities." Defendant maintains that even if there is interest and ability on the part of women athletes at CSU, the university is obliged to accommodate them only to the extent it accommodates men. Thus, the argument goes, plaintiffs cannot be heard to complain because both women's softball and men's baseball were eliminated in the last round of cuts and there are more disappointed male than female athletes at CSU. This benchmark sets a high standard: it demands not merely some accommodation, but full and effective accommodation. If there is sufficient interest and ability among members of the statistically underrepresented gender, not slaked by existing programs, an institution necessarily fails this prong of the test.

Based on the district court's subsidiary findings of fact, we conclude that plaintiffs met the burden of showing that CSU has not accommodated their interests and abilities fully and effectively. Questions of fact under this third prong will be less vexing when plaintiffs seek the reinstatement of an established team rather than the creation of a new one. Here, plaintiffs were members of a successful varsity softball team that played a competitive schedule as recently as the spring of 1992. Although apparently four plaintiffs have transferred and one has been dismissed, seven or eight plaintiffs remain at CSU for at least part of the 1993-94 school year and would be eligible to play on a reinstated team. We agree with the district court that CSU fails the third prong of effective accommodation test.

Finally, defendant argues that the district court erred in holding that plaintiffs were not required to show discriminatory intent. Defendant reasons that because Title IX was modeled on Title VI of the Civil Rights Act of 1964, 42 U.S.C. §§ 2000d to 4a, and because discriminatory intent is required to prove a violation of Title VI, proof of a Title IX violation must therefore also require intentional discrimination.

Although Title VI itself requires proof of discriminatory intent, the administrative regulations under Title VI incorporating a disparate-impact standard are valid. Plaintiffs' complaint alleges violations both of Title IX and of the implementing regulations. If we accept defendant's analogy to Title VI, then this prior holding would permit us to find a violation of Title IX's regulations without proof of discriminatory intent. Further, despite the fact that Title IX was explicitly modeled on Title VI, this court has held that Title VII of the Civil Rights Act of 1964, 42 U.S.C. §§ 2000e to 17, is the most appropriate analogue when defining Title IX's substantive standards, including the question of whether disparate impact is sufficient to establish discrimination under Title IX. Because it is well settled that Title VII does not require proof of overt discrimination, the district court did not err here in failing to require proof of discriminatory intent.

Defendant makes two broad objections to the relief ordered by the district court. First, it maintains that plaintiffs have an adequate remedy at law and therefore injunctive relief is inappropriate. Second, defendant argues that it should have been afforded the opportunity to present a plan to the court that would have brought it into compliance with Title IX, rather than ordered to reinstate the softball program and required to take other specific actions with respect to its management of the team.

Defendant's second argument has more substance. Defendant contends that the district court abused its discretion by prescribing the precise manner in which it must comply with Title IX. Defendant objects to the specificity of the district court's order because it believes the district court has ordered it to maintain a softball team in perpetuity, and because it believes it is entitled to devise a plan for its own compliance. Were this a class action, there might be some power to defendant's argument that an order specifically requiring an institution to maintain a softball team goes further than is necessary to correct a violation of Title IX. In a class action case a more appropriate remedy for violation might be to enjoin CSU's conduct of men's varsity competition until defendant presented a plan that would bring CSU into compliance with Title IX. This is, however, an action for relief to individual plaintiffs, brought in their individual capacities.

The district court's order of relief directly responds to the harms plaintiffs have sustained, and the relief they have requested, as individuals. Plaintiffs are former members of a terminated varsity program, seeking reinstatement of their team because of defendant's failure to comply with Title IX. The Supreme Court has recognized that in reaching Title IX's goal of protecting private citizens against discriminatory practices, there are situations in which it makes little sense to impose on an individual, whose only interest is in obtaining a benefit for herself, the burden of demonstrating that an institution's practices are so pervasively discriminatory that a complete cutoff of federal funding is appropriate.

This is such a situation. The award of individual relief to a private litigant who has prosecuted her own suit is not only sensible but is also fully consistent with—and in some cases even necessary to—the orderly enforcement of Title IX. The district court correctly provided plaintiffs with individual relief. Had the district court allowed defendant to devise its own plan for Title IX compliance, it would, in effect have been forcing plaintiffs to become unwilling representatives in a class action suit they chose not to bring.

Only the CSU softball players have established that their athletic interests and abilities are not being accommodated effectively under Title IX. Therefore, relief is appropriate only for them. Moreover, because this relief runs to plaintiffs individually, defendant is incorrect in its assumption that CSU must sustain a softball team indefinitely. To the contrary, once all the plaintiffs in this case have transferred or gradu-

ated, defendant could return to court and seek to have the injunction dissolved.

Further, because the reinstatement of the softball team is predicated on defendant's Title IX violation, if that violation were remedied in accordance with either of the other two benchmarks of the effective accommodation test defendant would then no longer be obligated to maintain its softball program. If, for example, defendant chose to cut its athletic programs in such a way as to meet the substantial proportionality benchmark, plaintiffs would have no basis for asserting their right to play softball. The district court acknowledged this in its order: "The underlying mandate of this opinion is that CSU may not continue to operate an intercollegiate athletic program that provides a disproportionate amount of participation opportunities to male athletes where there is no evidence of continuing program expansion or effective accommodation of the interests and abilities of its female students." If defendant decided to operate CSU's athletic program in compliance with the underlying mandate of the district court's opinion, plaintiffs' entitlement to individual relief would evaporate.

Finally, we turn to the specifics of the district court's order. Defendant alleges that aspects of the injunction amount to the district court's micromanaging CSU's softball program. In one respect, we agree. Under the broad sweep of Title IX, the district court has the power to ensure that the reinstated softball program receives all the incidental benefits of varsity status. Thus, we find ample support for the district court's insistence that defendant promptly hire a softball coach (equal opportunity in athletics includes the opportunity to receive coaching), prepare a field for the softball team's use (practice and competitive facilities), and provide equipment and uniforms (equipment and supplies). The district court also emphasized that defendant must recruit members for its reinstated team, although it did not require defendant to offer scholarships to new recruits. Clearly the district court was concerned that reinstatement of the softball team was not to be done in a slipshod manner. However, insofar as recruiting is integral to team development, it is a core coaching function. Under the Title IX regulations, defendant would not be permitted to hobble a coach's efforts to improve his or her team. Because the district court clearly did not order defendant to offer scholarships, we interpret its order regarding recruiting as part and parcel of its order to hire a coach. Any suggestion that this coach must recruit top flight varsity players, is merely precatory.

The district court did exceed its authority in demanding that the softball team play a fall 1993 exhibition season. The district court's apparent rationale for ordering a fall season, which had not previously been a regular practice at CSU, was to ensure that CSU would be able to field a competitive team the following spring. Nothing in Title IX requires an institution to create a top flight varsity team, nor is it within the district court's power, once it reinstates the softball program with all the incidental benefits of varsity status, to make sure they have a good season. Because a fall season is not required to effect the appropriate remedy, we hold that the district court overstepped its authority in ordering it.

The decision of the district court is AFFIRMED in part and REVERSED in part. The cause is REMANDED with instructions that the injunction be modified consistent with this opinion.

 For an extended version of the case and review questions to test your understanding of the material, please go to www.HumanKinetics.com/CaseStudiesInSportLaw.

9

Tort Law

Tort law is a dynamic area of law for which the fundamental issue is determining when losses from an injury should be shifted from the victim to the individual or organization causing the injury. Tort law is defined as a civil wrong suffered by one person as a result of another's intentional or unintentional conduct. Intentional torts include claims of assault, battery, and defamation while unintentional torts primarily involve negligence. Sports are full of torts resulting in major concerns for recreation and sport managers at all levels and settings of sport. This section presents 29 cases each illustrating a slightly different perspective of tort law related to four different settings: recreational, high school, college, and professional sport.

Tort Law in a Recreational Setting

Injuries incurred in recreational sport activities typically occur as a result of the normal risks associated with participation in the sport. *Knight v. Jewett* and *Dilger v. Moyles* illustrate the assumption of risk doctrine and how it applies to sport situations. *Miller v. United States* demonstrates how recreational use statutes and warnings can be used as a defense. Yet, there have been a growing number of documented incidents where injuries did occur as a consequence of arguably tortuous behavior by coparticipants in a recreational sport program. It is for these situations the courts have been called upon to determine the proper standard of care for injuries between coparticipants, or in other words, what is considered an accepted part of the game and what action deserves redress. In *Baugh v. Redmond,* the plaintiff was assaulted and battered by a player. *Crawn v. Campo, Dotzler v. Tuttle, Jaworski v. Kiernan, Lestina v. West Bend Mutual Insurance Company,* and *Nabozny v. Barnhill* illustrate different standards of care between coparticipants. The duty of care owed a participant by a facility operator or owner is the primary issue in *Maussner v. Atlantic City Country Club, Inc.* and *Sallis v. City of Bossier City.*

Tort Law in a High School Setting

Tort law cases in high school settings often involve injuries received by a student involved in a physical education class or high school athletics as demonstrated by *Mogabgab v. Orleans Parish School Board* and *Vargo v. Svitchan.* While the fundamental application of tort law remains the same as for other settings, the supervisory role of the school as well as the fact that students are minors create a unique perspective upon the outcome of these types of cases. Transportation of student athletes, coaches, cheerleaders, and fans is another activity commonly sponsored by high schools in connection with their sports programs. Transportation is a liability exposure for any institution and creates risk management issues administrators must address. Use of an independent contractor for transportation was the determining factor in *Lofy v. Joint School District #2.*

Tort Law in a College Setting

Negligence is an unintentional tort and an ordinary cause of action consisting of a duty, breach of duty, proximate cause, and damages. Negligent conduct is defined as that which falls below the standard established by law for the protection of others against an unreasonable risk of harm. There are numerous cases involving negligence and its application to a collegiate sports environment. For example, *Benjamin v. State, Eddy v. Syracuse University, Rispone v. Louisiana State University,* and *Schiffman v. Spring* focus specifically upon the institution's duty to provide safe facilities for participants and spectators in sport activities. *Gillespie v. Southern Utah State College* and *Kleinknecht v. Gettysburg College* illustrate the duty of an institution to provide medical care to its athletes injured in practices or games. The question of participant-to-participant duty was the allegation in *Hanson v. Kynast.* Assumption of risk was a successful defense used by the defendant university when a student died in a university-sponsored road race in *Gehling v. St. George's University School of Medicine, Ltd.* Duties of supervision and instruction are yet more issues evoking litigation. *DeMauro v. Tusculum College, Inc.* provides a good illustration of the responsibility instructors have toward students receiving instruction in their courses. Negligent supervision of spectators was an issue in *Bearman v. University of Notre Dame* and *Hayden v. University of Notre Dame.* Finally, *Foster v. Board of Trustees of Butler County Community College* provides insight into the court's perspective of *respondeat superior* in regard to the duty of a university in recruiting prospective athletes.

Tort Law in a Professional Sport Setting

When a participant at the professional sports level consents to play in a sport, physical contact with other participants involving injury, yet within the rules of the game, is rarely litigated. These cases often deal with intentional torts, which can best be defined as intentional, harmful, and/or offensive contact by one person to another. Litigation of intentional tort cases is challenging because of the difficulty of establishing intent to harm and for the plaintiff to prove lack of consent. *Averill, Jr. v. Lutrell* illustrates a situation involving an intentional act and the implications involving the professional baseball team for which he played.

Tort law cases at the professional sport level more often than not deal with spectators rather than participants. Professional venue owners and operators must have a good understanding of who their users will be, how to best utilize their staff in recognizing potential hazards to the users, how best to supervise activities, and how to deal with unusual conditions that could threaten the safety of spectators at their facilities. *Friedman v. Houston Sports Association* and *Lowe v. California League of Professional Baseball* both illustrate the responsibility of stadium owners and their respective professional sports teams in providing a safe environment for spectators.

Averill, Jr. v. Luttrell

311 S.W.2d 812 (Tenn. App. 1958)

In this action the plaintiff, Lyle Luttrell, a professional baseball player with the Chattanooga Baseball Club, sued the defendants, Nashville Baseball Club, a corporation, and Earl Averill, Jr., one of its players, for damages for an assault and battery committed by Averill on plaintiff during the playing of one of the regularly scheduled games between these two teams at Engel Stadium, in Chattanooga, Tennessee, on the night of August 20, 1955. Plaintiff's declaration alleges in substance that the defendant, Earl Averill, Jr., without reasonable cause or justification, struck plaintiff from behind with such force and violence that he not only suffered a fractured jaw but was rendered unconscious from the blow, and that said defendant was at the time "acting within the scope of his employment as the agent, servant, or employee of the Nashville Baseball Club, and in furtherance of its said business," and plaintiff sued said defendants for both compensatory and punitive damages.

The trial resulted in a jury verdict for the plaintiff against both defendants for $5,000, and motions for a new trial having been made and overruled, only the defendant Nashville Baseball Club has appealed. By assignments of error it is urged on behalf of the Nashville Baseball Club that the trial court should have sustained its motion for a directed verdict made at the conclusion of plaintiff's

proof, because plaintiff introduced no evidence that the assault committed by Averill was within the scope of his employment, or in the prosecution and furtherance of the business of this defendant.

According to the undisputed proof the assault occurred during the sixth inning of the game while the plaintiff, who played the position of shortstop for the Chattanooga Lookouts, was batting for his team. Pitching for the Nashville Vols was Gerry Lane, a resident of Chattanooga, and catching was the defendant Averill. The contest between the teams was keen and the players as well as the fans were tense with excitement, some of which was probably due to Lane's pitching against his home town team. Lane had made three pitches known as curves or sliders, called by the umpire as "balls," and on each Luttrell had stepped forward to meet the ball before the break or curve started. These balls barely missed Luttrell, who had to dodge, and his teammates and the crowd got the impression that he was being, in baseball parlance, "dusted off" by Lane, who on his fourth pitch hit Luttrell on the seat of his pants.

It appears that immediately after, Luttrell threw his bat in the direction of the pitcher's mound that Averill, without any warning whatsoever, stepped up behind Luttrell and struck him a hard blow on the side or back of the head with his fist. The force of the blow rendered Luttrell unconscious, and on falling face first to the ground he sustained a fractured jaw. Thereafter the players and the fans generally, who rushed out on the field, engaged in what was described as a "free for all" until the police arrived in sufficient force to restore order, after which the game was continued. Meantime Luttrell was removed by ambulance to the hospital, and Averill, who was put out of the game by the umpire, was arrested. It was undisputed that there was no previous "animosity or malice" between Averill and Luttrell, who testified that when they spoke "it was on friendly terms." Nor was there any proof showing that Averill had ever committed a similar act, or that his employer should have anticipated his unwarranted assault.

It was conceded that the assault made by Averill "was no part of the ordinary risks expected to be encountered in sportsmanlike play." Nor was there any proof showing that the assault was other than a willful independent act on Averill's part, entirely outside the scope of his duties. The assault was neither incident to nor in the furtherance of his employer's business, and under the circumstances we think that the Nashville Baseball Club would not be liable under the doctrine of *respondeat superior*, and that the learned trial judge should have sus-

tained the defendant's motion for a directed verdict made at the conclusion of the plaintiff's proof.

It seems to be the rule generally that a master is not liable for the willful acts of his servant who steps aside from his master's business and commits an act wholly independent and foreign to the scope of his employment. The applicable rule is stated in 57 C.J.S., as follows: "It is not ordinarily within the scope of a servant's authority to commit an assault on a third person, and, in the absence of a nondelegable duty, such as that imposed by the relationship of carrier and passenger, or hotel and guest, if the assault committed by the servant was outside the scope of his employment and was made in a spirit of vindictiveness or to gratify personal animosity, or to carry out an independent purpose of his own, the master is not liable, unless the servant's conduct is ratified by the master." § 575, p. 341.

Accordingly, for reasons indicated, the judgment against the Nashville Baseball Club will be reversed, and the suit as to this defendant will be dismissed at plaintiff's costs.

 For an extended version of the case and review questions to test your understanding of the material, please go to www.HumanKinetics.com/CaseStudiesInSportLaw.

Baugh v. Redmond

565 So.2d 953 (La. App. 2 Cir. 1990)

In this action for damages as the result of a battery, defendant, Maurice Redmond, appealed the judgment of the trial court in favor of plaintiff, Jimmie Baugh, and defendant's insurer, Aetna Casualty and Surety Company. On appeal, defendant presents the following assignments of error: (1) the trial court erred in finding plaintiff had proven by a preponderance of the evidence that defendant intended to commit a battery, (2) the trial court erred in failing to mitigate the general damage award as plaintiff's actions precipitated and provoked the incident, (3) the trial court erred in failing to acknowledge the applicability of comparative fault in an intentional tort case, and (4) the trial court erred in finding the insurer was

not liable based on a provision excluding liability for bodily injury that was expected or intended from the standpoint of the insured.

On May 20, 1987, plaintiff was umpiring an adult softball game between teams from the Ouachita Parish Sheriff's Department and Ouachita Electric Service, Inc., a Redmond corporation, which sponsored the team. During the game, plaintiff called a Ouachita Electric Service player out for leaving a base early on a fly ball and defendant became enraged by plaintiff's call. Throughout the remainder of the game, defendant verbally harassed plaintiff and defendant's team eventually lost the game. Following the game, plaintiff and defendant had a confrontation on exiting the field in which heated words were exchanged and eventually resulted in defendant striking plaintiff in the face. As a result of the blow, plaintiff's eyeglasses were knocked off his face and he incurred a bloody mouth with extensive damage to his teeth.

On August 21, 1987, plaintiff instituted this action for damages naming as defendants Maurice Redmond and Ouachita Electric Service, Inc. Ouachita Electric Service, Inc. was later dismissed from the litigation. In his petition, plaintiff alleged defendant had punched him in the face without provocation, knocking him to the ground, breaking his eyeglasses, and causing extensive damage to plaintiff's teeth and bones in his mouth necessitating extensive dental treatment and oral surgery.

Defendant filed an amending and supplemental answer in which he alleged plaintiff was guilty of contributory negligence that partially contributed to the incident and therefore his recoverable damages should be reduced in proportion to the degree or percentage of fault attributed to him. In the event the court deemed contributory negligence inapplicable, defendant alleged that any damages awarded should be mitigated due to the conduct of plaintiff in escalating the confrontation.

After the trial on the merits, the trial court found in favor of plaintiff and third-party defendant. In its written opinion, the trial court reviewed the testimony of the parties and witnesses as to the confrontation and found that the evidence established that defendant had allowed himself to become outraged at plaintiff over the call made against his team. His anger rekindled at losing the game and he confronted plaintiff inside the playing area where he had no reason to be and there, without any legal justification or provocation, committed a battery on plaintiff by striking him in the mouth, causing the injuries and damages sustained by him. The court found plaintiff had proven the battery by a preponderance of the evidence. The court noted the medical testimony established that the blow to plaintiff's mouth was consistent with and caused significant trauma to six upper teeth requiring four root canals as well as other oral surgery. The court observed that plaintiff's injuries were quite painful and plaintiff had missed work and lost wages due to his dental treatments that began immediately after

the battery and continued until January 1988. As general damages for plaintiff's pain and suffering, the court found the sum of $20,000 was fair and adequate under the circumstances. The court further awarded plaintiff special damages in the amount of $4,812.80 for past medical expenses and lost wages incurred as a result of the battery. The trial court found that as this matter was an intentional tort, contributory and/or comparative negligence was not applicable. The court further stated it had considered all the evidence in light of defendant's request for mitigation of damages and declined to grant the same. The court found that defendant's conduct after the game was unnecessary and his actions toward plaintiff were deliberate and intentional.

On defendant's motion for a new trial, the trial court agreed it should have applied the principles of comparative fault to this matter. However, on reviewing all of the testimony and the factors to be considered in apportioning fault, the trial court found the testimony did not establish by a preponderance of the evidence that plaintiff was at fault in causing or contributing to his injuries. Rather, the evidence established there was unprovoked battery committed by defendant when plaintiff was only trying to exit the playing field.

A battery is any intentional and unpermitted contact with the plaintiff's person or anything attached to it or practically identified with it. In order to recover for a battery, plaintiff must prove by a preponderance of the evidence that his damages resulted from an unprovoked attack by defendant. The intention of the defendant need not be malicious nor need it be an intention to inflict actual damage. It is sufficient if the actor intends to inflict either a harmful or physical contact without the other's consent. Liability for a battery depends on the facts and circumstances of each case. Where the defendant relies on provocation as justification for a battery, he must prove some conduct or action by the plaintiff sufficient to provoke and arouse defendant to the point of physical retaliation. Louisiana's aggressor doctrine precludes tort recovery by plaintiff if the evidence establishes he was at fault in provoking the difficulty in which he was injured, unless the person retaliating has used excessive force to repel the aggression.

On appeal, defendant argues the trial court erred in finding plaintiff had proven by a preponderance of the evidence that defendant intended to commit a battery on the plaintiff. We disagree. The record shows that defendant had become angry with plaintiff during the game and verbally harassed plaintiff periodically throughout the remainder of the game. After the game concluded defendant proceeded to his team's dugout and confronted plaintiff as he was proceeding through the dugout area, which was his [plaintiff's] normal practice at the end of each game. Defendant verbally harassed plaintiff about his authority to eject defendant from the park if disruptive during a game. The evidence established that plaintiff continued to walk through the dugout toward the concession stand and was followed closely behind by defendant who was apparently intent on provoking a confrontation with plaintiff through verbal harassment. There was no evidence that plaintiff pushed or made any threatening moves toward defendant in any manner so as to cause defendant to believe it was necessary to defend himself. Rather, it is clear that the blow to plaintiff was completely unexpected and unprovoked. Considering all the circumstances surrounding this incident, it appears clear that defendant did intend to strike plaintiff and the trial court was not manifestly erroneous in this determination.

Contributory negligence is conduct on the part of plaintiff that falls below the standard to which he should conform for his own safety and protection, that standard being that of a reasonable man under like circumstances. *Harris v. Pineset*, 499 So.2d 499 (La. App. 2d Cir. 1986). La.C.C.Art. 2323 provides that a plaintiff whose negligence contributes to his own injuries for which he seeks damages shall have his claim reduced in proportion to his degree of fault. The determination and apportionment of fault are factual matters and the trial court's findings in this regard should not be disturbed by a reviewing court unless they are erroneous.

In assessing comparative fault the trial court must consider the nature of each party's conduct and the extent of the causal relationship between the conduct and the damages claimed. Relevant factors concerning the nature of each party's conduct include (1) whether the conduct resulted from inadvertence or involved an awareness of the danger, (2) how great a risk was created by the conduct, (3) the significance of what was sought by the conduct, (4) the capacities of the actor, whether superior or inferior, and (5) any extenuating circumstances that might require the actor to proceed in haste, without proper thought.

It is well-settled that it is within the trial court's discretion to mitigate a general damage award when plaintiff's conduct helps create the circumstances giving rise to the injury. Mere words, even though designed to excite or irritate, cannot excuse a battery. However, words that are calculated to provoke and arouse to the point of physical retaliation may mitigate damages in a civil action. How and when damages are mitigated are determinations that are within the discretion of the trial court.

Since the adoption of comparative fault, this court has held that the principles of La.C.C.Art. 2323 are a more appropriate approach rather than the concept of mitigation of damages. Where the words or actions of the plaintiff in a civil battery action are sufficient to establish provocation that would warrant a mitigation of damages, the court should apply comparative fault principles based on the facts and circumstances of the case. Defendant argues the trial court erred in failing to mitigate the general damage award as plaintiff's actions precipitated and provoked the incident and further the trial court erred in failing to acknowledge the applicability of comparative fault in an intentional tort case. This argument is without merit.

The record shows that when defendant began his attempts to confront plaintiff following the conclusion of the game, plaintiff attempted to avoid such a confrontation by walking ahead of defendant and toward the concession stand. Defendant continued to walk behind plaintiff and to verbally harass him as to his authority to eject defendant from the park. There was no evidence that plaintiff acted verbally or physically to escalate the situation but rather was attempting to avoid any type of confrontation when struck unexpectedly by defendant. Under these circumstances we find plaintiff was not guilty of any comparative fault so as to reduce his recovery for injuries sustained by him.

For these reasons, the judgment of the trial court in favor of plaintiff and against defendant is AFFIRMED. The judgment dismissing the third-party demand is REVERSED, and there is judgment in favor of the third-party plaintiff, Maurice Redmond, and against the third-party defendant, Aetna Casualty and Surety Company, for the amount of the judgment on the main demand against defendant, and for attorney fees in the sum of $3,000.

 For an extended version of the case and review questions to test your understanding of the material, please go to www.HumanKinetics.com/CaseStudiesInSportLaw.

Bearman v. University of Notre Dame

453 N.E.2d 1196 (Ind. App. 3 Dist. 1983)

Christenna Bearman suffered a broken leg when she was knocked down by a drunk as she was returning to her car after a Notre Dame football game. Bearman and her husband sued the University of Notre Dame for damages resulting from that injury. After the close of all evidence, the trial court granted Notre Dame's motion for judgment on the evidence. Bearman appeals, raising one issue: Whether Notre Dame had a duty to protect Mrs. Bearman from injury caused by the acts of third persons.

The evidence and inferences most favorable to Bearman show that on October 27, 1979, Mr. and Mrs. Bearman attended a football game at the University of Notre Dame. The Bearmans left the game shortly before it ended. As they were walking through a parking lot toward their car, they observed two men who appeared to be drunk. The men were fighting, one of them fell down, and then they walked away from each other. One of the men walked past the Bearmans. A few moments later, the man fell into Mrs. Bearman from behind, knocking her to the ground. Mrs. Bearman suffered a broken leg from the fall. There were no ushers or security people in the area when the incident occurred.

Bearman argues that she was a business invitee of the University of Notre Dame; therefore, Notre Dame owed to her a duty to protect her from injury caused by the acts of other persons on the premises. On the other hand, Notre Dame argues that absent notice or knowledge of any particular danger to a patron, the university cannot be held liable for the acts of third persons. It is axiomatic that the conduct of a person will give rise to an action for negligence only if that person owed a duty to the plaintiff to conform his actions to the standard of care. The existence of such a duty is a question of law. Generally, the operator of a place of public entertainment owes a duty to keep the premises safe for its invitees. This duty includes a duty to provide a safe and suitable means of ingress and egress, and a duty to exercise ordinary and reasonable care to protect a patron from injury caused by third persons. However, the invitor is not the insuror of the invitee's safety.

Before liability may be imposed on the invitor, it must have actual or constructive knowledge of the danger.

The Restatement of Torts (Second) § 344 (1965) sets forth the applicable rule:

> A possessor of land who holds it open to the public for entry for his business purposes is subject to liability to members of the public while they are on the land for such a purpose, for physical harm caused by the accidental, negligent, or intentionally harmful acts of third persons or animals, and by the failure of the possessor to exercise reasonable care to (a) discover that such acts are being done or are likely to be done, or (b) give a warning adequate to enable the visitors to avoid the harm, or otherwise to protect them against it.

Comment (f) of this section is particularly pertinent to this case:

> f. Duty to police premises. Since the possessor is not an insurer of the visitor's safety, he is ordinarily under no duty to exercise any care until he knows or has

reason to know that the acts of the third person are occurring, or are about to occur.

He may, however, know or have reason to know, from past experience, that there is a likelihood of conduct on the part of third persons in general which is likely to endanger the safety of the visitor, even though he has no reason to expect it on the part of any particular individual. If the place or character of his business, or his past experience, is such that he should reasonably anticipate careless or criminal conduct on the part of third persons, either generally or at some particular time, he may be under a duty to take precautions against it, and to provide a reasonably sufficient number of servants to afford a reasonable protection.

The university is aware that alcoholic beverages are consumed on the premises before and during football games. The university is also aware that "tailgate" parties are held in the parking areas around the stadium. Thus, even though there was no showing that the university had

reason to know of the particular danger posed by the drunk who injured Mrs. Bearman, it had reason to know that some people will become intoxicated and pose a general threat to the safety of other patrons. Therefore, Notre Dame is under a duty to take reasonable precautions to protect those who attend its football games from injury caused by the acts of third persons.

The questions whether the protective measures employed by Notre Dame were inadequate and, if so, whether such inadequacy contributed to Mrs. Bearman's injury are questions for the jury. Therefore, we reverse the judgment of the trial court and remand this case for proceedings consistent with this opinion.

 For an extended version of the case and review questions to test your understanding of the material, please go to www.HumanKinetics.com/CaseStudiesInSportLaw.

Benjamin v. State

453 N.Y.S.2d 329 (N.Y. Ct. Cl. 1982)

In the evening of November 16, 1979, Thomas Benjamin, age 11 years, was struck and injured by a puck while watching a hockey game at the Romney Arena, a state facility, located on the campus of the State University of New York at Oswego. Alleging that the State negligently failed to provide adequate protection for the safety of spectators seated in its arena, Thomas now seeks compensation for his injuries.

Romney Arena, as it was laid out by the State for hockey, consisted of an oblong shaped rink that ran lengthwise in a north/south direction. It was enclosed by a dasher board that was approximately 3-1/2 feet in height. Two players' benches had been placed along the easterly sidelines. Elevated spectator bleachers surrounded the remainder of the rink. Goals were placed at both the north and south end. To the rear of each goal and along the sidelines, a protective fence, measuring 6 feet and 3 feet in height, respectively, was mounted atop the dasher board. The fence,

however, was not continuous. In front of each players' bench, a distance of approximately 20 feet, no protective fencing had been installed. Except for the dasher board, this area remained essentially open.

Thomas, accompanied by his brother and friends, had gone to the arena that evening to see a college hockey double header. They had paid their admission and had taken seats in the bleachers behind the south goal. Near the end of the first game, they left the area and proceeded to a concession stand that was located at the opposite end of the arena. After they purchased a drink, and while they were returning to their seats, they decided to view the remainder of the game from the sidelines. They found seats in the second or third row of the bleachers and sat down. When seated, they were behind the protective fence, 10 to 15 feet north of the nearest players' bench. While there, an errant puck found its way through the open area in front of the players' bench, passed behind the protective fence, and struck Thomas on the left side of his forehead.

The State, like any other owner or occupier of land, is only under a duty to exercise "reasonable care under the circumstances" to prevent injury to those who come to watch games played at its facilities. In the present case, the State argues that due care required it only to provide protective seating behind the goal where the danger was the greatest. Having done so, it argues that Thomas should have remained in his protected seat behind the goal and by choosing to do otherwise, he assumed the risk of being hit by a puck. The State's reasoning is somewhat flawed, however, since it undertook to provide spectators with protected seating along the sidelines, as well. In doing so, it was under a duty to make certain that such an area was reasonably safe for its intended purpose.

In determining whether the State fulfilled its duty here, the court is somewhat guided by the uncontradicted testimony of the claimant's expert, who testified to a structural defect. He testified that in similar facilities, it was the usual and customary practice to protect the area around the players' bench. Absent such protection, it was the usual and customary practice to restrict seating to an area without the zone of danger. Since neither course of action was chosen, he opined that the State failed to provide Thomas with adequate protection that evening.

When viewing the evidence in its totality, the court finds that the absence of a fence in front of the players' bench constituted a dangerous condition that presented a foreseeable risk of injury to those spectators, including Thomas, who were seated in the protected seating area adjacent thereto. The lack of any evidence that an accident of the same kind had happened before is of no moment, since such an accident was reasonably to be anticipated. In sum, the court finds that the failure of the State to provide for the safety of Thomas in the protected seating area constituted negligence and that such negligence was a substantial factor in bringing about Thomas' injuries.

In addition, the court finds that the accident and the injuries sustained by Thomas were not attributable to any culpable conduct on his part. When he took his seat in the protected area on the sidelines, he had the right to assume that every reasonable care had been taken for his safety. Although he admits to being aware that the area in front of the players' bench was unprotected, it cannot be said that a reasonably prudent person of Thomas' years, intelligence, degree of development, would have fully appreciated the danger and, hence, could have been said to have assumed the risk. Nor can it be said that such a reasonably prudent person should have been aware of the risk so as to be guilty of contributory negligence. When struck, Thomas felt numb all over. He did not, however, lose consciousness. He was administered first aid at the facility and later taken to a local hospital where he was examined and then discharged. The following morning he awoke feeling nauseous and began to vomit. His parents immediately contacted a pediatrician, who advised them that he be taken to the Upstate Medical Center in Syracuse, New York. On his arrival at Upstate, he was again examined and X-ray studies of his skull were ordered. The examination revealed a palpable depression in the left frontal area. The films confirmed that Thomas sustained, as a result of being struck by a puck, a 4 millimeter depressed skull fracture supralateral to the left orbit on the frontoparietal bone.

Following his discharge, he spent the next two weeks in bed. He then was allowed to get out of bed for brief periods of time. At the end of one month, he returned to school. During the period he was home, he complained of pain and it was noted that he was having difficulty with his equilibrium. When Thomas returned to school, his activities were somewhat limited. He was compelled to wear a protective helmet from time to time, especially when taking gym. He complained of intermittent headaches. In all, his disability continued for almost a year. Except for a surgical scar, measuring 4 inches in length (2-1/2 inches outside of hairline), there are no permanent residuals.

In view of the foregoing, the court finds that Thomas has been damaged in the sum of $24,000 (all compensatory) and an award is made accordingly.

 For an extended version of the case and review questions to test your understanding of the material, please go to www.HumanKinetics.com/CaseStudiesInSportLaw.

Crawn v. Campo

643 A.2d 600 (N.J. 1994)

Plaintiff was playing catcher in a pickup softball game and was injured when defendant, attempting to score from second base, either slid or ran into him at home plate. Plaintiff sued to recover for his personal injuries. The critical issue in this action turns on the nature of a player's duty to avoid inflicting physical injury on another player. The issue is directly posed by the competing perspectives of the lower courts. The Law Division determined that the applicable standard governing players engaged in informal sports activity is to avoid injurious conduct that is reckless or intentional. By contrast, the Appellate Division concluded that the appropriate standard of care is to avoid conduct that would constitute negligence under the circumstances. We conclude that the trial court was correct. We now hold that the duty of care applicable to participants in informal recreational sports is to avoid the infliction of injury caused by reckless or intentional conduct.

The game took place on May 1, 1988. The teams were not associated with any league and the games were played without independent umpires or referees. The parties agree that the game was played under the general rules of softball. They disagree, however, whether the group had a rule prohibiting sliding.

Plaintiff's witnesses testified that the group played with a no-slide rule. They were uncertain about when the players first agreed to the rule, but they were certain that by the time the group began playing its weekly game, everyone understood that sliding was prohibited. In fact, whenever a player did slide, the other team invoked the rule. Plaintiff's witnesses were equivocal about the exact scope of the no-slide rule. Plaintiff's witnesses did agree that the purpose of the rule was to prevent injury. In sharp contrast, defendant's witnesses, including defendant himself, insisted that no rule governed sliding at all.

Defendant was a runner on first base. The batter hit a ground ball to the shortstop, who flipped the ball to the second baseman to get the force-out on defendant. Defendant slid into second base, taking the legs out from beneath the second baseman. Plaintiff's witnesses testified that after that play, the other players reminded defendant that sliding was prohibited. Defendant, according to those witnesses, acknowledged the rule and indicated his willingness to abide by it. Defendant, however, disputed that version of events, testifying that his slide into second base did not result in any warning about sliding.

With defendant now on second, the next batter hit a ball to right field. As the outfielder relayed the ball to the first baseman, defendant rounded third and headed for home. As defendant approached the plate, he lowered his body and barreled into plaintiff's left side. Plaintiff reeled backwards and defendant ended up on top of plaintiff's lower leg. Plaintiff heard a pop in his leg and then felt severe pain. Because he was off to the first-base side of the plate, plaintiff claims that defendant had ample room to run past him and touch home plate without making contact. He argues that defendant's motive in deliberately running into him was to dislodge the ball from plaintiff's glove to avoid the out. Defendant, however, testified that when he approached home plate, plaintiff was straddling the plate with a foot on either side. Defendant believed that the only way to reach home plate and to avoid a tag was to slide. He slid feet first into plaintiff's left leg. Although plaintiff later tried to resume play, his left leg collapsed under him when he attempted to run. He was taken from the field to a hospital, where it was determined that he had suffered a torn knee ligament, which required surgery.

Plaintiff brought this action seeking recovery for his personal injuries. The jury returned a verdict for plaintiff, finding that defendant's conduct had been reckless and that plaintiff had not assumed the risk of reckless conduct. Defendant brought a motion for a new trial.

Defendant filed a motion to the court for leave to appeal the Appellate Division decision on the standard-of-care issue and the need for expert testimony. Plaintiff filed a motion for leave to cross appeal on the affirmance of the grant of a new trial. We granted those motions.

The majority of jurisdictions that have considered the issue of a person's duty to exercise care to avoid injury when engaged in a sports activity have concluded that to constitute a tort, conduct must exceed the level of ordinary negligence. Most courts have determined that the appropriate duty players owe to one another is not to engage in conduct that is reckless or intentional. "The preference for a standard of care that exceeds negligent conduct is driven by the perception that the risk of injury is a common and inherent aspect of informal sports activity. . . . In some situations, . . . the careless conduct of others is treated as an 'inherent risk' of a sport."

The imposition of a recklessness standard is primarily justified by two policy reasons. One is the promotion of vigorous participation in athletic activities. The other reason is to avoid a flood of litigation.

Anytime a court raises the standard of care that defines the legal duty that is owed for the safety of others, it implicitly immunizes a part of the conduct that otherwise would be considered tortious and actionable. As the Appellate Division here noted, New Jersey tolerates immunities only for important reasons of public policy and in relatively exceptional situations, and therefore strongly endorses a standard of care based on ordinary negligence. Recognition of a duty of care, ultimately, rests on considerations of public policy and on notions of fairness. That multifaceted analysis, focusing on personal relationships, the nature of risks, and considerations of public policy and fairness, is one that must inform our determination of this case. Based on that analysis, we conclude that liability arising out of mutual, informal, recreational sports activity should not be based on a standard of ordinary negligence but on the heightened standard of recklessness or intent to harm.

We concur substantially in the Appellate Division's determination that considerations of public policy and notions of fairness do not impel a protection of sports activity in the form of a broad tort immunity. Concededly, informal athletic and recreational sports activities are quite important, as evidenced by their universal popularity in all walks and in all stages of life. To that extent a societal interest is served by encouraging the vigorous participation in sports activity. That societal interest, however, does not itself demand that wrongful conduct by the participants in such activity that foreseeably results in injury to others should be totally removed from the law of torts. That kind of sweeping immunity, we are satisfied, is not justified.

The more perplexing inquiry is whether informal recreational sports activity, given its societal importance, should be accorded a partial immunity that effectively exempts from liability conduct that is simply negligent, unreasonable, or careless, and sanctions liability only for behavior that is more egregious. Arguably, considerations of public policy and fairness as evidenced, at least indirectly, by legislative policy, support such a limited or partial immunity.

The concerns that focus on the relationship among participants and the nature of the risks that surround informal sports activity are equally germane to defining the appropriate duty of care. Participation in recreational sports activities has unique aspects that separate such sports from other common activities. In many recreational sports, softball included, some amount of physical contact is expected. Physical contact is an inherent or integral part of the game in many sports. The degree of physical contact allowed varies from sport to sport and even from one group of players to another. In addition, the physicality of sports is accompanied by a high level of emotional intensity.

Our analysis is further complicated by the wide variation in expectations regarding the physical contact and emotional intensity that are appropriate from sport to sport and from game to game. Nevertheless, other courts and commentators have acknowledged that violations of rules, even of rules imposed for safety reasons, are often a "part of the game." Despite those factors, which both typify and complicate informal recreational sports activity, the Appellate Division felt that a standard of care based on negligence would suffice as a basis for liability. It believed that courts could adequately evaluate sports conduct and make clear to juries that "[a] co-participant who creates only risks that are 'normal' or 'ordinary' to the sport acts as a 'reasonable [person] of ordinary prudence under the circumstances.'"

The problem with the court's analysis lies in the extraordinary difficulty in judging conduct that is based on limitless variables with respect to how the same game is played among different groups of people. The relationship among sports participants is derived from a consensual arrangement that involves both articulated and unarticulated rules, obvious and obscure conventions, and clear and not-so-clear expectations. Some rules are broken, yet their transgression is tolerated. Certain practices are customary yet others are followed inconsistently. Some conventions are well understood, others are not always known or appreciated by all participants. Each player's expectations are often subjective, and may not be shared or experienced by others in the same way.

The reasonableness of conduct that occurs within a consensual relationship can be fairly evaluated only by reference to the nature of the consent and mutual understanding of the persons in the relationship and to the common expectations that serve to identify what conduct is acceptable among those persons. Prior cases indicate that if acceptable conduct cannot be recognized except by looking to the highly subjective understandings between persons in a special relationship, the standard of general reasonableness is not truly workable. That is because conduct that is highly subjective cannot be reliably equated with the conduct of an average person under like circumstances.

Realistically, complete agreement among the 18 or 20 persons engaged in playing a softball game covering the limitless kinds of physical contact that can occur in the course of the game can rarely, if ever, be found. That consideration indicates that a legal duty of care based on the standard of what, objectively, an average reasonable person would do under the circumstances is illusory, and is not susceptible to sound and consistent application on a case-by-case basis. Accordingly, we hold that the duty of care in establishing liability arising from informal sports activity should be based on a standard that requires, under the circumstances, conduct that is reckless or intentional.

Our conclusion that a recklessness standard is the appropriate one to apply in the sports context is founded on more than a concern for a court's ability to discern adequately what constitutes reasonable conduct under the highly varied circumstances of informal sports activity. The heightened standard will more likely result in affixing liability for conduct that is clearly unreasonable and unacceptable from the perspective of those engaged in the sport yet leaving free from the supervision of the law the risk-laden conduct that is inherent in sports and more often than not assumed to be "part of the game."

One might well conclude that something is terribly wrong with a society in which the most commonly-accepted aspects of play—a traditional source of a community's conviviality and cohesion—spurs litigation. The heightened recklessness standard recognizes a commonsense distinction between excessively harmful conduct and the more routine rough-and-tumble of sports that should occur freely on the playing fields and should not be second-guessed in courtrooms.

The judgment of the Appellate Division is modified and, as modified, is affirmed.

 For an extended version of the case and review questions to test your understanding of the material, please go to www.HumanKinetics.com/CaseStudiesInSportLaw.

DeMauro v. Tusculum College, Inc.

603 S.W.2d 115 (Tenn. 1980)

This case involves an action by a student against a private college for personal injuries sustained while she was receiving instruction in a physical education class. Plaintiff, a freshman and a beginner at golf, was struck by a golf ball driven by a senior student who was majoring in physical education and who was taking a course designated as "Teaching Assistant." The jury returned a verdict for the plaintiff, appellant here, which was approved by the trial judge. The court of appeals, in a split decision, reversed and dismissed, holding that there was no material evidence of causative negligence. The court held that while the accident was "an unfortunate occurrence" it was, as a matter of law, one for which the educational institution could not be held responsible.

After careful consideration, we are of the opinion that the court of appeals was in error in this regard and that a jury issue was presented as to the liability of the defendant. On the other hand, we find that there was error in certain jury instructions that were given and in the failure to give other instructions that were properly requested. There was a disputed issue as to the status of the senior student whose golf ball inflicted the injuries. Plaintiff insisted that he was a servant or representative of the college in instructing an introductory course in golf, while the defendant insisted that he was simply a fellow student, somewhat more advanced, and that he was a person for whose negligence the college was not legally responsible. We are of the opinion that differing inferences could have been drawn from the proof offered on that subject. The trial judge, however, instructed the jury, as a matter of law, that the senior student was a servant or agent of the school and that it would be legally responsible for any negligence on his part. We find that this instruction, to which proper exceptions were taken, was erroneous. The status of that student was an important issue to one of the theories of liability asserted. We think that the jury should have been permitted to determine whether the senior was or was not an authorized representative of the school. Also, omitted from

the instructions, despite proper requests, were the subjects of assumption of risk and of unavoidable accident, as to both of which some evidence had been introduced.

Plaintiff, Donna DeMauro, was 18-years-old at the time of the accident on March 31, 1977. She was entering the third quarter of her freshman year at Tusculum College, a private liberal arts college located near Greeneville, Tennessee. She was required to take courses in physical education during her first year, including one course each quarter in "Activities." During the spring quarter she had elected to take a course designated as Physical Education No. 171, entitled "Golf." The college provided a member of its staff, a Dr. Shasby, as the instructor for the course. Plaintiff had never played golf before, nor had she ever received any instruction in the sport.

Prior to the date of the accident, there had been a few sessions of the class. One of these was held in the gymnasium, where students were given some general instructions by Dr. Shasby and where they had practiced using golf clubs with plastic balls. Although it is not clear from the record, we infer that the students used golf clubs and equipment furnished by the college both at the gymnasium and later on the golf course. There is some reference in the testimony to the students' having been taken by Dr. Shasby to a driving range on one occasion prior to the date of the accident. On Thursday, March 31, 1977, the students went to the golf course for the first time to engage in practice consisting of actual play on a regular course. Plaintiff was a member of a foursome, consisting of three other freshmen girls, only one of whom appears to have had any substantial previous playing experience. Dr. Shasby was not with the foursome, which included the plaintiff at the time of the accident.

In his place and stead a senior student, James Hunter, accompanied the four girls. Hunter was attending Tusculum College on an athletic scholarship in basketball. Golf was not his major sport. He had taken an introductory course in golf at a junior college a few years previously and had occasionally played the game, but the jury could easily infer from the testimony that he was by no means an expert in the sport. Hunter, who was 22 years of age, testified that he was majoring in physical education and that he took for credit during the spring quarter a course designated as Physical Education No. 400, entitled "Teaching Assistant." The college catalogue, which was introduced in evidence, described this course as follows: "Offered as needed. Students will be expected to assist in all aspects of the instruction of an activity course and, on occasion, to conduct the class. Prerequisites: Senior or junior P.E. major status only, approval of the instructor and of the division chairperson." Hunter described his duties as follows: "Get the clubs, take over if Dr. Shasby wasn't there, and helping with the class."

Hunter was not paid for his services, and it is clear that these services were a part of his own course of instruction in becoming a physical education teacher. Although the phrase was not used in the record, at oral argument it was stated that he might be considered as a sort of "practice teacher." He had assisted in a tennis class during the previous quarter but had never before assisted in instruction in golf. He testified that he had not played "a lot of golf" on his own since taking freshman instruction in the sport as previously mentioned. Plaintiff testified that she was not aware that Hunter "had little or no experience," that she knew he was a "student assistant" and thought "Jim perhaps knew about the game." Hunter accompanied plaintiff and three other freshmen girls to the No. 5 tee on the Twin Creeks Golf Course near Greeneville. This was a 425-yard hole, bordered on the left by a creek. The rules of the course stated that a stroke to the left of the creek was out of bounds. As one faced the fairway, the green was to the left around a "dog-leg." A large tree was situated at the turn in the fairway. It would have been possible for a person driving from the men's tee, as Hunter undertook to do, to drive to the left of this tree in a straight line toward the green. The usual method of playing the hole, however, was to drive straight down the center of the fairway to the right of the tree. It is unclear from the record which way Hunter intended to drive, although he thought that he probably meant to drive to the right of the tree.

Hunter was a left-handed golfer. He approached the men's tee with the girls standing at about a 90° angle opposite him and several yards away. All of them testified that they had generally been instructed to stand in this position. An instruction book in golf, which the students purchased, generally confirmed that this was the correct area for players to stand and watch in safety, or at least the jury could so conclude from the evidence. There is little testimony in the record as to the manner or method in which Hunter struck the ball or as to what he actually did, except that he apparently "shanked" the shot, striking the ball with the toe of his driver. The ball veered off at an angle of about 90° from the fairway, and it struck the plaintiff in the face. She received severe and painful injuries from which she suffered extensive bleeding and for which she had to undergo at least two different surgical operations about a year apart. She was given immediate first aid and assistance by Hunter and other persons. The degree and extent of her injuries and the amount of the jury award are not involved in this appeal.

The jury could infer from the evidence that Dr. Shasby had placed Hunter in charge of the group that included plaintiff. They could also have concluded that Hunter was acting as a golfing instructor, although he was admittedly an inexperienced player. Obviously he improperly struck the ball and injured one of the very persons whom he was supposed to be instructing in the game. It seems to us that reasonable persons might find that Dr. Shasby, and through him the college, was negligent in placing a person of Hunter's experience in a position of sole responsibility and that Hunter's lack of experience was at least a factor that made injury to one of the students foreseeable. Regardless of whether Hunter himself was or was not negligent in the way he struck the ball, we are of the opinion that the court of appeals was in error in directing a verdict for the defendant college. The jury could have found that the likelihood of accidental injury was enhanced by placing such an inexperienced person in charge of the instruction.

A private school is not the insurer of the safety of its students. This has been held in numerous cases in many jurisdictions throughout the country. The failure of proper supervision of students is not sufficient to fix liability on the school unless it is shown that failure was the proximate cause of the plaintiff's injuries. This proposition has been announced in numerous cases in a number of jurisdictions. In the *Stehn* case the court noted that there were a number of factual issues regarding the nature of the instruction given, the understanding of the students, the number of students involved, the number of instructors, and so on.

We are of the opinion that the same may be said here. The status of the student, Hunter, was ambiguous, and a trier of fact might, as the defendant insists, conclude that he was only a fellow student playing a few holes of golf with other adult students in a situation where the college had no legal responsibility. On the other hand, a trier of fact might conclude that the plaintiff, a beginner and a novice at the sport, was receiving instructions as to how golf should be played. She was observing Hunter as he attempted to drive the ball and was then expecting to drive for the first time under actual playing conditions. The regular instructor was absent and the duty of supervision that the school legally owed under these circumstances had apparently been delegated to Hunter. A jury might conclude that the latter was the instructor or was standing in the place and stead of an instructor who had a non-delegable responsibility. Negligence could have been found, predicated not so much on Hunter's improperly addressing the ball, as on breach of the duty of supervision and instruction that the school owed to the student.

It could be inferred from the proof that the defendant felt that some supervision and instruction in the game of golf were needed, at least for beginning players. On the other hand, golf perhaps is not as high-risk sport as some others, and the reasonableness of the conduct of defendant commensurate with the risks involved, in our opinion, was for the trier of fact to determine. The case does not turn entirely, however, on whether Hunter's own stroke of the ball was or was not "a negligent act," as concluded by the court of appeals, nor solely on whether he was or was not a servant of the college.

It is entirely possible that under proper instructions, a trier of fact would conclude that the accident was completely unavoidable, as insisted by appellee. Certain risks, obviously, inhere in any sport or physical educational activity. In connection with golf, such risks include that of a ball being driven on an unintended path. There is testimony that plaintiff was aware of that risk, and we are of the opinion, as previously stated, that there was sufficient evidence to justify a charge to the jury on assumption of risk.

Since the plaintiff was standing in an area where she had been instructed to stand, however, and in which the evidence indicates an observer properly should stand, she could not be said, as a matter of law, to have necessarily assumed the risk that her own instructor would strike the ball in such a way as to injure her. We are of the opinion that all of the issues, including that of unavoidable accident, should have been submitted to the jury under proper instructions and that these instructions should have delineated the nature of the duty of a private school toward its students as above indicated.

There are numerous cases in which educational institutions have been held liable for negligence in furnishing inadequate or improper instruction or supervision. It is insisted by appellee that it would have had no duty or responsibility whatever to appellant had she simply been struck by a fellow student while engaged in a game of golf. Under some circumstances, of course, this may be correct. It is also true that participants in sporting activities occupy a somewhat different legal position from mere observers or passers-by. Where, however, students are novices and are receiving courses of instruction in sports held out and offered for credit by an educational institution, a duty of supervision and instruction arises from the relationship that is not terminated or abrogated merely by reason of the fact that one student participant injures another.

Each case of this nature turns on all of the facts and circumstances. Hard and fast criteria are difficult to establish. Frequently expert testimony is helpful to show what the accepted standards and practices are in a particular sport. There may indeed be many instances where a directed verdict is proper. Where, however, different and varied conclusions could be drawn from the proof, a jury issue is usually presented. We are convinced that such is the present case and that neither party was entitled to a directed verdict on any issue on the trial record. Of course a different situation may be presented on re-trial.

The judgment of the court of appeals is reversed and the cause is remanded for a new trial under more complete and appropriate jury instructions consistent with the issues presented.

 For an extended version of the case and review questions to test your understanding of the material, please go to www.HumanKinetics.com/CaseStudiesInSportLaw.

Dilger v. Moyles

63 Cal.Rptr.2d 591 (Cal. App. 1 Dist. 1997)

Dorothy Dilger (appellant) was struck on the golf course by a ball hit by another golfer, David Moyles (respondent), whom she sued. She appeals the trial court's entry of summary judgment in his favor.

On the morning of April 26, 1994, appellant and two companions were golfing at Sky West Golf Course in Hayward. After teeing off on the fifth tee, appellant, who was 78-years-old at the time, drove her golf cart to where her ball had landed—approximately 95 yards down the fairway. She stopped her cart on the left side of the fairway, which borders the fairway of the sixth hole. After stopping her cart, appellant was struck in the mouth by a ball hit by respondent from the sixth fairway. At the time he hit the ball, respondent was standing behind a row of trees that separated the fifth and sixth fairways. Respondent claimed these trees blocked the line of sight to where appellant was located. Whether or not respondent yelled "fore" when he hit his errant shot was disputed.

Appellant argues that the doctrine of assumption of risk is inappropriate as a defense for golfers. The California Supreme Court has found that participants generally do not have a duty to protect other participants against risks inherent in an active sport.

While golf may not be as physically demanding as other more strenuous sports such as basketball or football, risk is nonetheless inherent in the sport. Hitting a golf ball at a high rate of speed involves the very real possibility that the ball will take flight in an unintended direction. If every ball behaved as the golfer wished, there would be little sport in the sport of golf. That shots go awry is a risk that all golfers, even the professionals, assume when they play.

Holding participants liable for missed hits would only encourage lawsuits and deter players from enjoying the sport. Golf offers many healthful advantages to both the golfer and the community. The physical exercise in the fresh air

with the smell of the pines and eucalyptus renews the spirit and refreshes the body. The sport offers an opportunity for recreation with friends and the chance to meet other citizens with like interests. A foursome can be a very social event, relieving each golfer of the stresses of business and everyday urban life. Neighborhoods benefit by the scenic green belts golf brings to their communities, and wildlife enjoy and flourish in a friendly habitat. Social policy dictates that the law should not discourage participation in such an activity whose benefits to the individual player and to the community at large are so great.

By eliminating liability for unintended accidents, the doctrine of primary assumption of risk ensures that the fervor of athletic competition will not be chilled by the constant threat of litigation from every misstep, sharp turn, and sudden stop. On a larger scale, participation in amateur athletics is a socially desirable activity that improves the mental and physical well-being of its participants. The freedom to enjoy such activity is preserved through application of the doctrine of primary assumption of the risk. While golf and sailing may involve less strenuous activity than touch football, and the risk of injury thus may be less, risk of injury is still a real possibility; therefore, golfers assume this risk on stepping up to the first tee, just as do sailors on boarding or football players at kickoff.

Golf etiquette requires that a player whose shot may endanger another warn the other by shouting "fore." But golf etiquette does not necessarily rise to the level of a duty. If no duty was owed, the defense of primary assumption of risk completely bars recovery. Whether a duty exists depends on whether the activity in question was an inherent risk of the sport. The Fourth Appellate District has found that missed hits are an inherent risk of golf.

When the activity involved is an inherent risk of a sport, a participant owes no duty to coparticipants unless he intentionally injures another player or engages in reckless conduct that is totally outside the range of the ordinary activity involved in the sport. We do not believe the failure to yell "fore" is that reckless or intentional conduct contemplated by the *Knight* court. Similarly, in the case at bench, respondent's failure to warn appellant of his errant shot, while possibly negligent, did not breach a legal duty to appellant. Whether or not the golfer yells "fore" does not alter the inherent risk of the sport—being struck by a golf ball.

The grant of summary judgment is affirmed.

 For an extended version of the case and review questions to test your understanding of the material, please go to www.HumanKinetics.com/CaseStudiesInSportLaw.

Dotzler v. Tuttle

449 N.W.2d 774 (Neb. 1990)

Plaintiff, Joseph Dotzler, sued the defendant, Bruce Tuttle, for injuries arising out of a collision between them during a "pickup" basketball game. The trial court sustained defendant's demurrer as to plaintiff's cause of action for negligence; the jury returned a verdict in favor of the defendant on the cause of action involving an allegation of recklessness. Plaintiff appeals.

Plaintiff assigns as error the actions of the trial court in (1) sustaining defendant's demurrer as to plaintiff's cause of action in negligence; (2) sustaining defendant's motion *in limine* excluding the testimony of plaintiff's expert witness; (3) instructing the jury that plaintiff, in order to meet his burden of proof, must establish that defendant acted with intent; (4) failing to instruct the jury that intent was not a part of plaintiff's burden of proof; (5) giving an instruction defining negligence and explaining the relationship between negligence and recklessness without defining intent; and (6) instructing that contributory negligence is a defense to recklessness.

Plaintiff and defendant were playing on opposing teams in a pickup basketball game during the noon hour at the Omaha Southwest YMCA on December 28, 1984. The two parties were not acquainted and had not played basketball against each other before. It was plaintiff's testimony that he had just made a shot at the basket and moved back to play defense. He stated that he was standing near the top of the key when he saw a blur and felt a shove or push on his chest. The force of the collision sent him flying backward 19 or 20 feet, causing him to land near the baseline. Reaching back to break his fall, he fractured both of his wrists when he landed on the floor.

Plaintiff contends that the trial court erred in sustaining the demurrer to his negligence cause of action. At issue is whether an individual participating in a contact sport has a cause of action against another participant because of injuries sustained as a result of ordinary negligence on the part of that other participant. The majority of jurisdictions that have addressed this issue have held that suit by the injured participant, if not based on intentional infliction of injury, must be based on reckless disregard of safety; an allegation of negligence is not sufficient to state a cause of action. The majority of jurisdictions that have considered this issue have concluded that personal injury cases arising out of an athletic event must be predicated on reckless disregard of safety.

Adopting the rationale of the majority rule, we hold that a participant in a game involving a contact sport such as basketball is liable for injuries in a tort action only if his or her conduct is such that it is either willful or with a reckless disregard for the safety of the other player, but is not liable for ordinary negligence. The allegation as to ordinary negligence did not state a cause of action, and the trial court was correct in sustaining defendant's demurrer.

We next deal with assignments of error Nos. 3, 4, and 5, dealing generally with the court's instructions relating to the definition of recklessness. The trial court instructed the jury on the issue of recklessness in the following manner:

You are instructed that the standard for Defendant's conduct is recklessness—a reckless disregard for the safety of the other player, i.e., the Plaintiff. The term "recklessness" is conduct amounting to more than negligence. It is needlessness [sic] or indifference to the rights of others or of the consequences of one's act. It indicates an indifferent disregard for the rights of others or of the consequences.

The Defendant's conduct was in reckless disregard of the safety of the Plaintiff if he does an act or intentionally fails to do an act which it is his duty to the other to do, knowing or having reason to know of facts which would lead a reasonable man to realize, not only that his conduct creates an unreasonable risk of physical harm to another, but also that such risk is substantially greater than that which is necessary to make his conduct negligent.

Reckless misconduct differs from negligence, in that the latter consists of mere inadvertence [sic], lack of skillfulness or failure to take precautions, while reckless misconduct involves a choice or adoption of a course of action either with knowledge of the danger or with knowledge of facts which would disclose this danger to a reasonable man. Recklessness also differs in that it consists of intentionally doing an act with knowledge not only that it contains a risk of harm to others as does negligence, but that it actually involves a risk substantially greater in magnitude than is necessary in the case of negligence.

We therefore adopt the following as a definition of recklessness:

Recklessness is the disregard for or indifference to the safety of another or for the consequences of one's act. Conduct is in reckless disregard to the safety of another if the actor intentionally does an act, or intentionally fails to do an act which it is his or her duty to another to do, knowing or having reason to know of facts which would lead a reasonable person to realize not only that his or her conduct creates an unreasonable risk of physical harm to another, but also that such risk is substantially greater than that which is necessary to make his or her conduct negligent. Recklessness differs from intentional wrongdoing in that while the act must be intended by the actor in order to be considered reckless, the actor does not intend to cause the harm which results from the act.

The judgment of the district court is reversed, and the cause is remanded for a new trial.

 For an extended version of the case and review questions to test your understanding of the material, please go to www.HumanKinetics.com/CaseStudiesInSportLaw.

Eddy v. Syracuse University

433 N.Y.S.2d 923 (N.Y.A.D. 1980)

Defendant appeals from a judgment awarding damages for personal injuries sustained by plaintiff on March 27, 1977, in a gymnasium on defendant's campus. Defendant offered no proof at trial and argues here, as it did before the trial court, that as a matter of law the facts do not support a finding of negligence, and that plaintiff's assumption of risk in playing in the gymnasium in the manner he did was the proximate cause of the accident. Plaintiff, a student from Harpur College, was injured while playing in a game called "ultimate frisbee" between a Harpur team and one from Syracuse University.

The two teams were admitted to the gymnasium building by a person believed by plaintiff to have been the janitor. The players changed clothes in a locker room, entered the gymnasium, and thereupon established the game's playing area to run the length of the gymnasium, using as the goal lines the outermost sidelines of two basketball courts that were laid out across the width of the gymnasium. The west goal line thus established was located approximately 5 to 8 feet from the gymnasium's west wall, which was of masonry construction with glass doors in the center. Plaintiff, running toward the west wall and looking back over his shoulder for a thrown frisbee, was unable to stop before striking one of the doors. He turned and saw the door, however, in time to raise his right arm in an attempt to protect himself. His body struck the handlebar across the door but because the door was locked, it did not open. The glass shattered and as plaintiff's upper torso went through the door his right arm was severely lacerated.

Plaintiff acknowledged that he was aware of the presence of the walls and the doors when he participated in the game. He also testified that such frisbee games are played on an "informal" basis; and there was no proof that the Syracuse team was officially recognized or sponsored by defendant. In support of its assertion that the evidence was insufficient to submit the case to the jury, defendant argues that it did not authorize the use of the gymnasium; had no foreknowledge of plaintiff's use; could not foresee the manner in which it would be used and, finally, that the gymnasium was not defective in its construction or design, nor was it unsuited for its ordinary purposes.

Common law classifications of the status of one injured when on the land of another are no longer determinative in assessing the duty of care owed by the landowner, and it is now well established that the duty owed is one of "reasonable care under the circumstances (with) foreseeability (as) a measure of liability." The injured party's status remains relevant, however, in assessing the foreseeability of his presence on the land and the probability that he might suffer injury. In determining whether the evidence is sufficient to submit to the jury, the court must examine the facts to ascertain "whether the foreseeability of the presence of an entrant on land is too remote, given the nature of the risk and the burdens that would be imposed on the landowner to guard against it." Additionally, the court should weigh "the probability of harm, the gravity of the harm against the burden of precaution, and other relevant and material considerations from which it can determine whether reasonable persons can differ as to whether the defendant was negligent." It is only when the court concludes that there is no reasonable view of the evidence on which to assess liability that the issue should be decided as one of law. Where varying inferences are possible, however, the issue is one for the jury.

Applying those principles, we conclude that it was proper here for the court to submit the issue of negligence to the jury. Surely the jury could have concluded that defendant should reasonably have foreseen plaintiff's presence in the gymnasium, located as it is on the campus of a large university, and that some of its students, and their guests, might use the facility without express permission. Also properly left to the jury was the question of whether the glass doors, located as they were in a building intended to be used for strenuous physical activity, constituted a dangerous condition. The close proximity of the doors to the basketball court sideline could be found to present a danger to a player in a hotly-contested basketball game. That danger is enhanced, of course, with the playing of a running game employing the length of the gymnasium. Thus, the question arises of whether defendant should have foreseen that students might use the gymnasium for the playing of games other than those for which the basketball courts had been laid out. Here, again, because of the propensity of college students to engage in novel games, a jury question was presented, and if such foreseeability was found, the probability and gravity of harm was readily apparent.

The jury could also reasonably have found that the risk presented by the glass doors could have been obviated without imposing an undue burden on defendant. The obvious danger could have been protected against, for example, by replacement of the glass with a solid material, or by placing a metal grill or a strong wire mesh over the glass. The court properly presented the issues to the jury in a charge that was rendered without request or exception by either party. Implicit in the jury verdict is its finding that defendant had a duty to protect users of the gymnasium, including plaintiff, from the dangers of the glass and that the breach of that duty was the proximate cause of the accident. Finally, we note that the jury was correctly instructed on the law of comparative negligence and assumption of risk. Judgment unanimously affirmed, with costs.

 For an extended version of the case and review questions to test your understanding of the material, please go to www.HumanKinetics.com/CaseStudiesInSportLaw.

Foster v. Board of Trustees of Butler County Community College

771 F.Supp. 1122 (D. Kan. 1991)

This matter is before the court on the motions for new trial filed by defendant Douglas S. Pringle, Special Administrator for the Estate of George D. Johnson ("Pringle") and defendants Board of Trustees of Butler County Community College, Butler County Community College, and Randy Smithson (collectively, the BCCC defendants).

This case arose out of a motor vehicle collision occurring at the intersection of Airport/Yoder Road and U.S. Highway 50 in Reno County, Kansas, on March 22, 1987. Plaintiff Christopher Foster was a passenger in a car driven by George Johnson. Johnson failed to stop at the stop sign on Airport Road and collided with the tractor-trailer rig driven by plaintiff Clark. Johnson died as a result of the injuries he received in the accident.

Foster, a native of Ohio, was a high school senior at the time of the accident. He was visiting Kansas on a recruiting visit at the request of defendant Randy Smithson, the head coach of the BCCC basketball team. Johnson picked Foster up at the Wichita airport at Smithson's request. Smithson had previously taken several other recruits to Hutchinson for the National Junior College Basketball Tournament. Contrary to the instructions given by Smithson, Johnson took Foster to Hutchinson to watch the game. Johnson telephoned Smithson from Hutchinson just prior to the collision. Smithson told Johnson to bring Foster to El Dorado. Johnson was en route to El Dorado when the collision occurred.

At the close of the evidence, the court directed a verdict in favor of the plaintiffs on the issue of *respondeat superior*, ruling that Johnson was the servant or employee of the BCCC defendants and was acting within the scope of his authority at the time of the accident. On February 27, 1991, the jury returned a verdict finding plaintiff Clark 10% at fault and defendants 90% at fault. Damages in the amount of $2,257,000 were awarded to plaintiff Foster and in the amount of $302,000 to plaintiff Clark. After reducing the judgment by Clark's 10% fault, the court entered judgment in the amount of $2,031,300 in favor of Foster and

$271,800 in favor of Clark. These motions for new trial followed.

Defendant Pringle raises the following issues in his motion for new trial: (1) the verdict is contrary to the evidence, (2) the amount of damages awarded is so excessive as to appear to have been based on passion and prejudice, (3) the evidence is insufficient to sustain the verdict, and (4) the court improperly allowed the jury to consider testimony regarding Johnson's lack of liability insurance. Defendant Pringle filed a memorandum in support of his motion out of time but with leave of court. The BCCC defendants raise the following issues: (1) the verdict is contrary to the evidence, (2) the amount of damages awarded is so excessive as to appear to have been based on passion and prejudice, (3) the court improperly allowed the jury to consider testimony regarding Johnson's lack of liability insurance coverage and evidence regarding the proof of insurance that must be provided by a student who is operating his own automobile in connection with a school function, (4) the court improperly refused to submit to the jury the questions of whether Johnson was the employee of BCCC and whether Johnson was operating within the scope of his employment at the time of the accident, (5) the court improperly refused to submit the issue of plaintiff Foster's comparative negligence to the jury, and (6) the court improperly refused to allow testimony concerning plaintiff Clark's opinion that he considered the intersection where the accident occurred to be a dangerous one. In the alternative, the BCCC defendants move for remittitur. The BCCC defendants did not file a memorandum or brief in support of their motion.

At trial, plaintiffs introduced evidence that the BCCC defendants were negligent in selecting Johnson as a gratuitous employee. An employer may be liable for injuries to a third person that are a direct result of the incompetence or unfitness of his employee when the employer was negligent in employing the employee or in retaining him in employment when the employer knew or should have known of such incompetence or unfitness. Johnson was unfit to drive a basketball recruit since he lacked a driver's license and liability insurance and his vehicle was not registered. The BCCC defendants could have discovered Johnson's unfitness for the task had any investigation been conducted. The evidence introduced by the plaintiffs was relevant to show the BCCC defendants' negligence. The evidence of Johnson's lack of liability insurance was relevant to show that the BCCC defendants failed to use due care in selecting Johnson to perform the task of transporting Foster.

In connection with the direct negligence claim and the evidence of Johnson's lack of insurance, the plaintiffs offered evidence of BCCC policies regarding use of college and personal vehicles. The BCCC Policies and Procedures Manual provides in pertinent part:

College Vehicle Policy:

College vehicles. All persons, included students, employees, and noncollege personnel, must have a driving record review and clearance. Requests for students and noncollege employees to drive college vehicles must be approved by the Director of Buildings and Grounds. These requests must be in writing and forwarded through the Business Office.

Personal vehicles. In cases when a college vehicle has been officially requested and is not available, the person making the request may be reimbursed for mileage if using a personal vehicle. In cases when an instructor or sponsor is not able to drive a college vehicle, a student with proof of current liability insurance may be permitted to use his/her car and be reimbursed for mileage with prior approval from the Director of Buildings and Grounds. The BCCC Athletic Policies and Procedures Manual provides that "School transportation must be used whenever possible. Private cars should be used only with permission of the athletic director."

While these policies were not directly applicable since Johnson was not officially a coach, they indicated a general school policy of requiring an inquiry before allowing a teacher or coach to drive a BCCC vehicle and proof of liability insurance before allowing a student to use a personal vehicle for BCCC business. It was undisputed that Smithson did not obtain the permission of the athletic director before arranging for Johnson to transport Foster. This evidence was relevant to plaintiffs' claim

that the BCCC defendants were directly negligent in appointing Johnson as a gratuitous employee charged with the duty of transporting Foster.

At the close of the evidence, the court directed a verdict on two issues: (1) Johnson was the servant or employee of BCCC, and (2) Johnson was acting within the scope of his authority at the time of the accident. The BCCC defendants challenge this ruling.

The issue of the existence of an agency relationship is normally a question of fact for the jury. On appellate review, what constitutes agency and whether there is competent evidence reasonably tending to prove the relationship is a question of law. While the determination of what constitutes agency and whether there is any evidence tending to prove its existence is a question of law, the weight to be given the evidence and the resolution of conflicts therein are functions of the trier of fact. When there is no material conflict in the evidence, the terms of the contract are not ambiguous or disputed, and only one inference may be drawn, the question of whether the relation of employer and employee exists is one of law for the court; otherwise it is one of fact for the jury. Under Kansas law, the controlling test in determining the existence of agency, so that the doctrine of *respondeat superior* would apply, is the right to control the purported employee. When agency relationship is in issue, the party relying on the existence of an agency relationship to establish his claim has the burden of establishing the existence of the relationship by clear and satisfactory evidence.

An employer is not liable for a tortious act committed by his employee, unless the act is done by authority of the employer, either express or implied, or unless the act is done by the employee in the course or within the scope of his employment. Under Kansas law, an employee is acting within the scope of his authority when he is performing services for which he has been employed, or when he is doing anything which is reasonably incidental to his employment. The test is not necessarily whether the specific conduct was expressly authorized or forbidden by the employer, but whether such conduct should have been fairly foreseen from the nature of the employment and the duties relating to it. Whether an act is within the employee's scope of employment ordinarily presents a question to be determined by the jury. The liability of the employer for the acts of the employee depends on whether the employee, when he did the wrong, was acting in the prosecution of the employer's business and within the scope of his authority or whether he had stepped aside from the business and had done an individual wrong.

The determination of whether an employee was acting within the scope of his employment involves a consideration of the individual factual setting of each case, including objective as well as subjective considerations. Several factors are relevant to the determination of scope of employment. First, the key consideration in determining whether an employee is acting within the scope of employment is the purpose of the employee's act rather than the method of performance. This calls for consideration of the objective circumstances of the incident as well as the subjective thoughts of the employee. Second, the court must examine whether the employee has express or implied authority to do the acts in question, although in certain situations, an employer may be liable for the acts of the employee, even if the acts are done in excess of the authority conferred. Third, the determination of whether an employee's acts are incidental to his employment involves a consideration of whether the employee's acts were reasonably foreseeable by the employer. Finally, the time at which the agent commits the alleged wrongful act is a factor to be considered, although it is not accorded great weight.

Defendants have not argued that Smithson lacked the authority to hire Johnson to assist in Smithson's recruiting duties. Johnson could be an employee or servant even though no compensation was paid or expected. Whether compensation was paid or not paid is not determinative. Additionally, it is not necessary that there be a formal employment contract. The evidence that Johnson was acting as the employee of Smithson and was acting within the scope of his authority came from the testimony of defendant Smithson. Smithson had the right to control and indeed exercised significant control over Johnson. Smithson testified that he instructed Johnson on what to do that evening. Smithson testified that he instructed Johnson to pick up Foster from the airport, get him something to eat, take him to the motel in El Dorado and await Smithson's return from Hutchinson. Smithson gave Johnson $20 to pay for dinner. Smithson further testified that when Johnson called late that evening from Hutchinson, Smithson told Johnson to bring Foster back to El Dorado as quickly and as safely as possible. Smithson gave Johnson directions on the two routes available from Hutchinson to El Dorado, via Highway 96 or via Airport Road/Highway 50. Smithson indicated that he used the Airport Road/Highway 50 route. Smithson told Johnson to ask for directions to Airport Road from where Johnson was located.

Plaintiff's Exhibit 25 (Smithson's statement) indicates that Smithson initially intended Johnson to bring Foster to the basketball game in Hutchinson. Later, Smithson decided to have Johnson instead take Foster directly to the motel in El Dorado. Given this background, it would be foreseeable that Johnson might take Foster to Hutchinson instead of El Dorado. Driving to Hutchinson would therefore be within the scope of the employment. Assuming that Johnson had deviated from the scope of his employment by going to Hutchinson, Johnson re-entered the scope of his employment after he talked to Smithson. Smithson specifically directed Johnson to return to El Dorado. Johnson was performing the service for which he had been employed, in the manner in which he had been instructed, when the accident occurred. The purpose of Johnson's acts was to return Foster to El Dorado. Johnson had express authority to drive Foster back to El Dorado. It was (or should have been) reasonably foreseeable to Smithson that Johnson could become involved in an automobile accident on the way to El Dorado. Johnson committed the negligent act while he was performing the task that was appointed to him—taking Foster to El Dorado.

Defendants argued at trial that Johnson was only doing a favor for Smithson. Viewing the facts most favorably to the BCCC defendants, Johnson was a volunteer. He was doing a favor for Smithson. However, the fact that this undertaking was gratuitous is not fatal to the existence of an employer-employee relationship.

Defendants also argued that the phone call was a "red herring." If the telephone conversation between Johnson and Smithson never occurred, the court would be faced with a different set of facts. But, those are not the facts of this case. The phone call was a key fact indicating that, if Johnson had deviated from the scope of his employment by going to Hutchinson, he reentered the scope of his employment by seeking and obtaining instructions from Smithson on his future course of action.

Construing the evidence in the light most favorable to the BCCC defendants, the evidence points only one way. There were no conflicts in the evidence. There was no evidence from which a reasonable mind could conclude that Johnson either was not the employee of BCCC or was not acting within the scope of his authority at the time of the collision. There was no evidence on which the jury could properly find for the BCCC defendants on the issue of employment and scope. Defendants have pointed to no such evidence in the record.

The BCCC defendants argue that the court erred in refusing to allow the jury to consider the comparative negligence of plaintiff Foster. These defendants assert that Foster was negligent in riding in a vehicle that allegedly was operating without its lights on during the dark of night on an unlit county road.

The court gave a standard instruction that Johnson's negligence would not be imputed to Foster. Under Kansas law, a passenger may be liable for negligence when: (1) he failed to use due care for his own safety as a passenger in an automobile, or (2) under a joint enterprise, the negligence of the driver would be imputed to him. The court did not understand the BCCC defendants' position to be that Johnson's negligence should be imputed to Foster under a joint enterprise theory. The BCCC defendants alleged at trial that Foster was independently negligent for riding in a car that had its lights off. The defendants did not dispute that it was their burden to show that either of the plaintiffs were negligent. As for plaintiff Clark, defendants presented testimony of an expert accident reconstructionist who opined that Clark had

been speeding. On the issue of plaintiff Foster's negligence, defendants seek to rely on Clark's testimony that he (Clark) did not see any lights.

Defendants seek to use this testimony as evidence that the Johnson vehicle indeed did not have its lights on. From this, defendants conclude that Foster was negligent for allowing himself to be driven in a car that had its lights off and, apparently, for his alleged failure to warn Johnson to turn his lights on. At most, Clark's testimony that he saw no lights is evidence that Clark may have been inattentive. The jury did find him 10% at fault. There was no evidence that Johnson was driving with his lights off and, therefore, no question of fault on the part of Foster to submit to the jury.

Having reviewed the evidence presented at trial, the court finds that the amount of the award to plaintiff Clark was not excessive. The amount was supported by the evidence. The court shall not grant a remittitur. IT IS BY THE COURT THEREFORE ORDERED that defendant Pringle's motion for a new trial (Doc. 152) is hereby denied as to plaintiff Clark and is moot as to plaintiff Foster. IT IS FURTHER ORDERED that defendants Board of Trustees of Butler County Community College, Butler County Community College, and Randy Smithson's motion for a new trial (Doc. 153) is hereby denied as to plaintiff Clark and is moot as to plaintiff Foster.

 For an extended version of the case and review questions to test your understanding of the material, please go to www.HumanKinetics.com/CaseStudiesInSportLaw.

Friedman v. Houston Sports Association

731 S.W.2d 572 (Tex. App. — Houston [1st Dist.] 1987)

This is an appeal from a judgment *n.o.v.* involving a baseball injury at the Astrodome. The jury found that the appellee was negligent in failing to warn of the danger of being struck by a baseball behind the first base dugout, and that this was the proximate cause of Karen Friedman's injury. The trial judge granted the appellee's motion for judgment *n.o.v.* with respect to these two findings. The jury also found that Karen

Friedman and her father, Robert Friedman, were not negligent, that the plexiglass cover of the first base dugout was not an attractive nuisance, and that the appellee was not negligent in failing to place protection in front of the first base dugout. The jury awarded Karen Friedman $50,000 in actual damages, and her father $5,000 in actual damages. The jury also awarded $125,000 in punitive damages.

The record reveals that 11-year-old Karen Fried-man attended the Astros game on July 14, 1978. Karen was seated with her father and two family friends, Melvin Weiss and his daughter Penny. Karen and her father did not elect to sit in the screened area behind home plate that the appellee had provided for the protection of spectators. The record indicates that seats were available in this area. Instead, the appellants chose to sit several rows behind the first base dugout. In the bottom of the ninth inning, Karen and Penny left their seats, and walked down behind the first base dugout. Karen was hit near her right eye by a line-drive foul ball.

In the appellants' first, second, and third points of error, they argue that there was sufficient evidence to uphold the jury's verdict that the appellee was negligent in failing to warn of the danger of being struck by a baseball behind the first base dugout, and that this negligence was the proximate cause of Karen's injury. The trial court granted the appellee's motion for judgment *n.o.v.*, but did not specify its reasons. It is, therefore, the appellants' burden to discredit each ground in the appellee's motion.

One of the grounds asserted by the appellee in its motion for a judgment *n.o.v.* is that there is no duty on the part of the owner of a baseball stadium to warn spectators of the open and obvious risk of injury from baseballs. This proposition is well settled as a matter of law in Texas. These cases do not eliminate the stadium owner's duty to exercise reasonable care under the circumstances to protect patrons against injury. However, they define that duty so that once the stadium owner has provided "adequately screened seats" for all those desiring them, the stadium owner has fulfilled its duty of care as a matter of law.

The appellants argue that these Texas cases no longer apply because of the present comparative negligence statute. *Tex.Civ.Prac. & Rem.Code Ann.* §§ 33.001-33.017 (Vernon 1986). The appellants mis-construe the purpose of comparative negligence. Comparative negligence does not create a duty; it simply allows partial recovery for a plaintiff who is no more than 50% at fault. The appellants in this case still have the burden to prove that the appellee owed them a duty to warn. Virtually all jurisdictions have adopted the limited duty of stadium owners to screen certain seats, and have held that where there is a screened area for the protection of spectators,

and a fan elects to sit in an unscreened area, liability will be precluded even though injury arises.

We find that a stadium owner has no duty to warn spectators of the danger of foul balls. The stadium owner's duty is to provide "adequately screened seats" for all those desiring them. The appellants' first, second, and third points of error are overruled. In point of error four, the appel-lants challenge the jury's finding that the appellee was not negligent in failing to place protection behind the first base dugout. In point of error five, the appellants challenge the jury's finding that the plexiglass top of the first base dugout was not an attractive nuisance.

We hold that the appellants have waived both their "no evidence" and insufficient evidence points of error. The appellants' fourth and fifth points of error are overruled. The judgment of the trial court is affirmed.

Cohen, Justice, concurring.
Our courts have held that the danger from foul balls at baseball games is so well known that it may be judicially noticed. It may be a good rule when applied to adults. I am not convinced, however, that it is the rule, and certainly not a good rule, to apply this principle, as a matter of law, in a case involving an 11-year-old child as a plaintiff. Some 11-year-olds will know the dangers of baseball, and some will not. I cannot say, as a matter of law in every case and without exception, that those 11-year-olds who do not know of baseball's dan-gers lack the minimum level of "neighborhood knowledge" that society demands. In my opinion, a landowner who invites an unsupervised 11-year-old child to its premises should not be surprised if a court imposes liability on finding that the child is less aware of some particular danger, and thus more in need of warning, than its parents or older siblings. Juries are well suited to make such dis-tinctions, and we owe considerable deference to their verdicts when reviewing judgments *n.o.v.*

I nevertheless join the court's decision because I believe that any failure to warn this 11-year-old was excused, since she was accompanied by an adult responsible for her welfare. The law holds that there is no duty to warn adults. When a young minor enters a premises with a responsible adult, the landowner has a right to rely on the adult to protect the minor from dangers that are within the adult's "neighborhood knowledge." Thus the neighborhood knowledge that the law requires of Robert Friedman is imputed through him to Karen Friedman. In fact, Karen was generally warned about baseballs on the night of the accident by Melvin Weiss, and was told not to try to catch foul balls and to be careful when she approached the dugout.

The jury refused to find that Robert Friedman was negligent in failing to warn Karen about foul balls, in selecting seats behind the dugout, or in allowing Karen to leave her assigned seat. Yet Texas law holds, notwithstanding the jury's verdict, that Robert Friedman assumed this risk for Karen by allowing her to be at the place where she was injured. Although uncomfortable with this rule, as an intermediate appellate court justice, I am bound to follow it. This does not mean that a duty to warn could never arise. An unsupervised 11-year-old invited into the stadium, despite his lack of "neighborhood knowledge," might be owed a warning, although his parents might be negligent for allowing him to attend without supervision.

 For an extended version of the case and review questions to test your understanding of the material, please go to www.HumanKinetics.com/CaseStudiesInSportLaw.

Gehling v. St. George's University School of Medicine, Ltd.

705 F.Supp. 761 (E.D.N.Y. 1989)

This is the second chapter of a case that arose from the collapse of Earl Gehling after crossing the finish line while participating in a "road race" on the Island of Grenada on April 18, 1982. Gehling was a student at St. George's University School of Medicine (SGU). Rose Gehling, decedent's mother, instituted this action as administratrix of her son's estate, on her own behalf, and also on behalf of her deceased husband's estate. The case was originally brought in Pennsylvania and those actions now before this court concern events occurring solely in Grenada. This court has previously determined that the plaintiff has waived all rights to a jury trial by failing to demand same.

Following the Order in the prior case of October 12, 1988, there remained before this court the issues of (1) negligence in the conduct of the road race, (2) medical malpractice and negligence at the race site and at the Grenada General Hospital, and (3) negligence in the context of an unauthorized autopsy. The court has considered all of the evidence offered at trial, including eyewitness testimony, expert testimony by several doctors, and testimony from student sponsors. Predicated on the evidence and the law the court makes the following findings of fact and conclusions of law, and accordingly dismisses the remaining causes of action.

On April 18, 1982, Earl Gehling ran in a race of approximately 2.5 miles on the Island of Grenada, West Indies, which began on a public road in front of the "True Blue" campus of the St. George's University Medical School and finished on the "Grand Anse" campus of the same school. Most of the territory covered by the race was on public roads in between the two campuses. The race took place in the late afternoon when the temperature was hot, approximately 80-85° Fahrenheit and the humidity was high.

SGU's business administrator, Gary Sollin, followed the runners in a school vehicle equipped with oxygen and was prepared to pick up runners who faltered. Approximately half way through the race, water was available to runners at a spigot alongside the road. The race itself was a regular SGU event, . . . and it was organized by several students at SGU with SGU's full knowledge and consent. The road race had taken place twice a year for at least two, perhaps three, years prior to the date in question.

SGU did not organize, supervise, or control the road race. The race was organized, supervised, and controlled by students at SGU on their own initiative. No doctor or ambulance or provisions including ice and towels were furnished by SGU at the finish line. However, at the finish line there was water, ice, and towels soaked in cold water provided by the students. In addition, medical students who had been trained as physician's assistants were stationed at the finish line. At the time of the race Gehling was 25-years-old, stood 5'10" tall and was approximately 75 pounds overweight. He suffered from high blood pressure, also known as hypertension, and the left ventricle of his heart was hypertrophied, or enlarged. A person with hypertension that is not being treated is at great risk of developing fatal left ventricular hypertrophy, which can lead to a heart attack. Gehling was athletic, participating in many sports activities including basketball and weight lifting, and he practiced jogging before the race. These activities were done under similar weather conditions as existed at the time of the race at issue. According to the toxicological report prepared in Pennsylvania after the race, Gehling had taken, before the race, ephedrine, which is an amphetamine-like substance that speeds the heart rate.

The race began about 4 p.m. and ended around 5 p.m. It took Gehling approximately 1/2 hour to finish the race. After he crossed the finish line on the Grand Anse campus he collapsed and lost control, becoming combative, irrational, and refusing the assistance offered him. He fell and then struggled up and fell again. He was then moved into shade where ice and wet towels were applied to his body in an attempt to cool him down. At the finish line a blood pressure cuff was also available and used. Those in attendance attempted to give Gehling oxygen. After 15 to 20 minutes in the shade near the finish line Gehling was carried by several students to the nearby office of Dr. Davidheiser in the anatomy laboratory, which was air conditioned. Efforts to cool Gehling were continued. After approximately 15 to 20 minutes in Dr. Davidheiser's office Gehling was transferred by ambulance to St. George's General Hospital (Hospital). The ride in the ambulance to the Hospital took 15 minutes. At the Hospital, Gehling's treatment included ice packs to bring down his body temperature, valium to control his convulsions, intravenous fluids to cool his body, EKGs to monitor his heart, and, as a last attempt to revive him, epinephrine was injected directly into his heart. Gehling was comatose from shortly after his collapse until his death.

Under New York law it is well-established that a defendant may be found liable for negligence only if a duty exists, the breach of which is the proximate cause of the plaintiff's injury. There is a distinction between sponsoring an event and being responsible for any actions that take place. In this instance, medical students of SGU were the sponsors of the race and responsible for its conduct. SGU was only a sponsor of the race, not responsible for the conduct thereof.

Although it knew of the race, SGU did not control, monitor, or supervise any aspect of the road race. Nor did it owe Gehling a duty to control, monitor, or supervise the race. Even if SGU did "sponsor" the race, for liability to attach, SGU must have had "sufficient control over the event to be in a position to prevent negligence." This it did not have. As the owner and/or occupier of the land on which the race began and ended, SGU had a duty to exercise reasonable care under the circumstances and to prevent injury to people on its property. This it did. The race was run in part on SGU's property with its knowledge and approval. SGU funded the purchase of T-shirts and trophies, and some of its employees participated in the race. SGU was responsible to exercise the necessary care to see that nothing on its property, at the beginning or the end of the race, could cause an injury to the runners. There was no evidence that the property was dangerous or not in a safe condition. The students who organized the race were responsible to exercise due care under the circumstances during the entire race including the end of the race. SGU was not.

In a short race of 2.5 miles run in tropical environmental conditions some type of assistance should be provided for the runners at the end of the race, in this instance, primarily by the students of SGU. The availability of water, ice, oxygen, and wet towels at the finish line, coupled with the stationing there of medical students with some emergency training, was sufficient to satisfy this duty of care. In view of the short distance of the race it was not necessary to have a doctor and special provisions for emergency, such as intravenous capability, at the Grand Anse campus.

None of the persons who rendered medical treatment to Gehling following his collapse was an employee or agent of SGU. Accordingly, SGU is not vicariously liable for any medical malpractice or negligence of such persons nor is there any evidence of the same. Plaintiff has failed to meet its burden of proving by a preponderance of the evidence that there was any negligence on the part of SGU in the conduct of the race.

Moreover, even if SGU had a duty to control, monitor, or otherwise supervise the race its failure to do so would not be the proximate cause of Gehling's death. Plaintiff has failed to meet its burden of proving by a preponderance of the evidence that SGU was guilty of any medical malpractice or negligence. It is also true that the negligence or malpractice, if any, of SGU or any of the persons who treated Gehling prior to his removal by ambulance was not the proximate cause of any of his injuries. Gehling's death was caused by his physical condition—his being overweight, having hypertension, taking ephedrine, and his hypertrophied left ventricle—and the circumstances under which the race was run.

New York has enacted a pure comparative negligence statute. But assumption of risk is still relevant as a factor to be taken into account in determining the proportion of culpable conduct. A university that undertakes to be responsible for or to control an athletic event has the duty to exercise reasonable care under the circumstances to prevent injury to those who engage in the athletic event that it controls. "Intramural sporting activities involve inherent dangers to participants. This claimant, in electing to play, assumed the dangers

of the game. . . . The State was required only to act reasonably in providing a field of play for claimant." So here Gehling entered the race voluntarily and assumed the dangers of the race.

In assessing liability a court may take into account that prior sporting events had taken place at the scenario without incident and also the age of the university students. The decedent, being a sixth semester medical student, is charged with knowledge of his own condition and of the tropical conditions of the Island, and by entering the race he assumed the risk of thermal injury under the circumstances including the risk of suffering heat prostration and/or heat stroke.

In sum, the court finds that (1) in connection with the race there was no negligence on the part of SGU; (2) Gehling's death was not caused by any negligence on the part of SGU, but was caused by Gehling's voluntarily entering the race while in poor physical condition; (3) he assumed the risk of his own death; and (4) SGU was not guilty of any malpractice in connection with the treatment of Gehling at the end of the race or at the Hospital. Judgment to be entered accordingly.

 For an extended version of the case and review questions to test your understanding of the material, please go to www.HumanKinetics.com/CaseStudiesInSportLaw.

Gillespie v. Southern Utah State College

669 P.2d 861 (Utah 1983)

This is an action to recover damages for personal injuries to the plaintiff Rickey Gillespie and for emotional injuries to, and loss of educational and employment opportunities by, the plaintiff Ghislaine Gillespie, Rickey's wife. At the conclusion of the plaintiffs' case, the trial court dismissed Ghislaine's cause of action. In addition, after the entry of the jury's special verdict finding that the defendant Southern Utah State College (hereafter College) was not negligent, the trial court also dismissed Rickey's cause of action. We affirm.

Rickey was attending the College on a basketball scholarship for the 1977-78 school year. On January 4, 1978, Rickey sprained his ankle in a practice scrimmage. The basketball coach turned the treatment of Rickey's injury over to David Slack, a student trainer for the College. The treatment applied by Mr. Slack consisted of spraying the ankle with a tape adherent, applying a prewrap to prevent the tape from coming into contact with the skin, and then taping it. After taping the ankle, Mr. Slack instructed Rickey to immerse his ankle in a bucket of ice water for 10 to

15 minutes, then to remove it and walk on it for 3 to 5 minutes, and to repeat this cycle two to three more times. Rickey followed this procedure for the remainder of the practice scrimmage and then continued it for two hours at home. Later that evening, Mr. Slack brought a bag of ice to Rickey's apartment, helped Rickey into bed, elevated his foot, and put the bag of ice on his ankle. The ice lasted approximately two hours.

On January 5, 1978, the morning after the injury, Mr. Slack made arrangements for Rickey to see the third-party defendant Dr. Scott L. Brown that afternoon. Dr. Brown noted in passing that due to the swelling the tape was difficult to remove. Dr. Brown took an X-ray of Rickey's ankle that revealed that it was not fractured, only sprained. When queried regarding the treatment that Mr. Slack had prescribed for Rickey's ankle, Mr. Slack replied that he had been "icing" it. Dr. Brown assumed that "icing" meant applying ice packs. Dr. Brown instructed Rickey and Mr. Slack to continue wrapping and "icing" Rickey's ankle for a period not to exceed 72 hours from the time of injury and prescribed codeine for pain.

After leaving Dr. Brown's office, Rickey and Mr. Slack went to the training room where Rickey's ankle was retaped with a pressure bandage to allow for swelling and the ice water immersion treatments were continued. That evening, Mr. Slack brought a bag of ice to Rickey's apartment and told Rickey to continue the ice water immersion treatments. There was testimony indicating that Rickey slept that night with his ankle submerged in a bucket of ice water.

Late in the afternoon on January 9, 1978, the basketball coach and/or Mr. Slack started Rickey on warm whirlpool treatments. That evening, Mr. Slack visited Rickey at his home and found him using the ice water immersion treatment because Rickey said that it made his foot feel better. Mr. Slack immediately called Dr. Brown, who instructed Mr. Slack to stop the ice water treatment, to wrap Rickey's foot with Atomic Balm, which created heat, and to have Rickey sleep with his foot elevated.

On the morning of January 10, 1978, six days after the injury, Rickey visited Dr. Brown, who sent Rickey to the Valley View Hospital to be admitted and treated for the injury to his foot. Rickey was diagnosed as suffering from thrombophlebitis and as having apparent frostbite of the fourth and fifth

toes along with smaller areas on the bottom of his foot and heel. On January 23, 1978, Rickey was discharged from the Valley View Hospital for further treatments at a hospital nearer to his home in Milwaukee, Wisconsin. Dr. Rydlewicz, who treated Rickey in Milwaukee, rated Rickey's right lower extremity as being 90% disabled due to amputation of a gangrenous toe, removal of some tissue and muscle of the right foot, and osteomyelitis of the right foot. During his testimony at trial, Dr. Rydlewicz also expressed his concern as to whether Rickey's foot could be saved because of the osteomyelitis and said that a below the knee amputation may be necessary at some future time.

On March 2, 1979, Rickey and Ghislaine filed suit against the College claiming that the basketball coach and Mr. Slack were negligent in their treatment of Rickey's injury. At trial, at the conclusion of the plaintiffs' case, the trial court dismissed Ghislaine's cause of action. The jury subsequently returned a special verdict in which it found that (1) Rickey was 100% negligent and such negligence was the proximate cause of his injuries, and (2) the College and Dr. Brown were not negligent. Based on the jury's special verdict, the trial court also dismissed Rickey's cause of action.

On appeal, Rickey claims that the jury verdict should be set aside because the jury's finding of no negligence by the College was contrary to the evidence and an abuse of the jury's deliberative process. Rickey also claims that the trial court erred in the instruction that it gave to the jury regarding the standard of care for an athletic trainer. Ghislaine claims that the trial court erred in dismissing her cause of action.

Rickey contends that the jury's verdict that the College was not negligent is contrary to the uncontroverted evidence and therefore should be set aside. Rickey claims that the evidence is uncontroverted that Mr. Slack's taping of Rickey's ankle on January 4, 1978, which did not allow for swelling, was negligent. While some of the physicians and trainers that testified at trial stated that Mr. Slack's tight taping of Rickey's ankle might, in conjunction with the ice immersion treatments and the failure to elevate the ankle, have contributed to Rickey's injuries, there was other testimony to the contrary.

Rickey also claims that the trial court erred in the instruction that it gave to the jury regarding the standard of care required of an athletic trainer.

Rickey's argument is that the instruction was improper because (1) Mr. Slack is not a physician nor a professional, and (2) by providing treatment to an injury that would have healed by itself if left alone, Mr. Slack became a "guarantor" of good results. These arguments are without merit. Even if the giving of the instruction was error, it was harmless in this case because it held Mr. Slack to the higher standard of care that governs physicians and surgeons rather than the lower standard that may be applicable to laymen or athletic trainers. Furthermore, the second argument cannot prevail because it would mean that anyone, including physicians and surgeons, who treated an ordinary sprained ankle or another injury that would heal by itself if left unattended would be "strictly" liable without fault for any adverse consequences resulting from the treatment. No authority has been cited, nor has our research revealed any, that supports such an extension of tort law. Thus, the trial court did not err in giving the instruction regarding an athletic trainer's standard of care. Affirmed. No costs awarded.

 For an extended version of the case and review questions to test your understanding of the material, please go to www.HumanKinetics.com/CaseStudiesInSportLaw.

Hanson v. Kynast

526 N.E.2d 327 (Oh. App. 5 Dist. 1987)

On May 1, 1982, Hanson sustained paralyzing injuries while playing in a lacrosse game for Ohio State University (OSU) against Ashland University. With some four minutes remaining in the game, at Ashland, Roger Allen, an OSU teammate of Hanson, intercepted a pass and scored a goal. As Allen was scoring, he was "body-checked" from behind by an Ashland defender Kynast. Allen fell and Kynast allegedly lingered over Allen, taunting him. Hanson, apparently unobserved by Kynast, grabbed Kynast from the side or back and held him in a bear hug. Kynast immediately twisted and flipped Hanson over his (Kynast's) back, with Hanson's head striking the ground. The evidence is undisputed that appellant Hanson sustained his injury on impact with the ground.

On December 13, 1983, Hanson filed an amended complaint in the Court of Common Pleas of Ashland County against Kynast, Ashland University, Bachrach-Rasin, Inc., and Stall & Dean Manufacturing Company, Inc. Ashland University filed a motion for summary judgment that was granted on November 16, 1984. The trial court held that no agency relationship existed between Kynast and Ashland University, and that the university did not have a legal duty to have an ambulance at the game. In a split decision filed June 3, 1985, this court reversed the judgment of the trial court, stating that genuine issues of fact existed as to the university's potential liability. The Ohio Supreme Court reversed this court in a July 2, 1986 opinion, holding the trial court correctly granted summary judgment in favor of Ashland University.

On October 8, 1986, the trial court issued a lengthy opinion granting summary judgment to Kynast. The basis of the trial court's opinion was that Hanson had assumed the risk of any possible injury to himself when he grabbed Kynast, ... Appellant Hanson now raises the following four assignments of error:

Under this assigned error, appellant argues that the thrust of the trial court's opinion is that no cause of action exists when an individual participant in a sporting event is injured by another participant. What the trial court is saying is that an athlete is not immune from liability for an intentional tort. That is what the court is describing when it states "a specific and perverse intent to cause physical injury." Put another way, this court understands the trial court to be saying the duty not to commit an intentional tort against another remains intact, even in the heat of battle in a spirited body-contact sport such as lacrosse. By his own characterization, as reflected in his appellate brief, appellant's first assigned error is "limited to the question of whether a cause of action exists as a matter of legal doctrine in Ohio where one participant in a sporting activity is injured by another."

We believe that a cause of action does exist in such a situation, but only for an intentional tort (i.e., an intentionally inflicted injury not arising out of the ongoing conduct of the sport itself) as herein. For example, if Kynast, five minutes after the game was over, had run across the field and thrown a body block at Hanson, or if Hanson had done the same to Kynast, then an obvious cause of action would exist. However, the facts as presented to the trial court show no element of intent to injure on the part of Kynast. Everyone agrees, including all three courts that have reviewed this tragic injury, that Kynast's action was reflexive and instinctive. This assignment of error is not well-taken and it is overruled.

Our holding is briefly this: Construing the evidence most strongly in Hanson's favor, we must conclude that no ascertainable duty was breached giving rise to a cause of action. The evidence is not sufficient to support a viable cause of action for an intentional tort and this assignment of error must be overruled.

By this assignment of error, appellant repeats his attack on the trial court's summary judgment in favor of appellee Kynast. We believe that the trial court found no genuine issue of material fact and said so both in its opinion and judgment entry. This court concurs with the lower court in that regard. Also, we cannot improve on the statement in appellee's appellate brief that Hanson has been unable "to meet that burden (of showing breach of duty) on a factual basis and a review of the law pertinent to the manner in which this judgment was rendered would support the trial court's ruling unequivocally." This assignment of error is overruled.

For the above reasons all four of appellant's assignments of error are overruled and the judgment of the Court of Common Pleas of Ashland County is affirmed. Judgment affirmed.

Milligan, Presiding Judge, concurring separately.
To defeat a motion for summary judgment in a negligence case the plaintiff must show that

1. Defendant owed a duty to plaintiff.
2. Defendant breached that duty.

3. Plaintiff suffered injuries.
4. Defendant's breach of duty proximately caused plaintiff's injuries.

The first hurdle in this analysis is the issue of the existence, nature, and scope of duty. There can be no liability for negligence absent a duty owed to a particular plaintiff. The initial question is whether, under the facts and circumstances of the instant case, such a relationship existed between the parties that the law will impose a legal duty on one or the other. Courts have avoided adopting a negligence standard in such cases because the standard would simply place unreasonable burdens on the "free and vigorous participation in sports." Paradoxically, courts have found a duty based on intentional or recklessness standard. The majority herein fails to specifically identify precise standards of duty that recognize a balance between clearly objectionable athletic misconduct and conduct generally recognized as either an integral or collateral part of the athletic contest involved. Courts considering this problem have given little consideration to a precise definition of the requisite intent in the context of conduct on the athletic field.

"Intent" denotes "that the actor desires to cause [the] consequences of his act, or that he believes that the consequences are substantially certain to result from it." Thus, an intentional tort is characterized by the intentional act of an actor to cause the specific harm suffered by the victim. The actor is certain, or substantially certain, that the desired consequences will result from his intentional act. In the context of athletic competition, an intentional tort characterizes the conduct of an athlete whereby he or she intentionally acts to cause a specific harm or injury. Such acts must be reasonably unforeseeable in the context of the particular athletic event engaged in.

Recklessness, on the other hand, involves a lesser degree of substantial certainty that the specific injury will result from the intentional act. . . . This nebulous continuum has led courts to use various formulations to define reckless conduct. Thus, reckless misconduct results when a person, with no intent to inflict the particular harm, intentionally performs an act so unreasonably dangerous that he knows or should reasonably know that it is highly probable that harm will result. In the context of athletic contests, "recklessness" will vary depending on the nature of the particular athletic event or sport.

The *quid pro quo* of an "assumed greater risk" is a diminished duty. Thus participants in bodily contact games such as basketball (and lacrosse) owe a lesser duty to each other than golfers and others involved in non-physical contact sports. However, injuries that result from conduct on the playing field that are not reasonably foreseeable are of a different nature. The focus is on the reasonable foreseeability of the conduct, and not on the particular injury. Naturally, this foreseeability is dependent on such factors as the nature of the sport involved, the rules and regulations that govern the sport, the customs and practices that are generally accepted and that have evolved with the development of the sport, and the facts and circumstances of the particular case. Another factor is whether or not the sport is played professionally.

Such a standard is intended to strike a delicate balance between allowing the free and uninhib-ited participation and development of sports, and curbing the excessive violence sometimes extant in certain sports.

Defenses may be raised in such cases that directly impact the nature and extent of the duty owed. The law provides, under assumption of risk, that one assumes only those risks that are reasonably foreseeable. Contributory negligence focuses on the conduct of the plaintiff and leaves unaffected the characterization of the conduct of the tortfeasor. Thus, a player consents as a matter of law to assume the risk of injuries resulting from reasonably foreseeable conduct by other players. Such reasonable foreseeability is determined by the rules and regulations of the particular game, and the customs and practices generally accepted as a part of the game.

 For an extended version of the case and review questions to test your understanding of the material, please go to www.HumanKinetics.com/CaseStudiesInSportLaw.

Hayden v. University of Notre Dame

716 N.E.2d 603 (Ind. App. 1999)

William and Letitia Hayden appeal from the trial court's grant of the University of Notre Dame's (Notre Dame) motion for summary judgment, presenting one issue for review: Whether the trial court erred in concluding that Notre Dame did not owe a duty to Letitia Hayden to protect her from the criminal acts of a third party. We reverse.

On September 16, 1995, William and Letitia Hayden attended a football game on the Notre Dame campus. During the second quarter of the game, one of the teams kicked the football toward the goal. The net behind the goalposts did not catch the ball, and it landed in the stands close to Letitia Hayden's seat. Several people from the crowd lunged for the ball in an effort to retrieve it for a souvenir. One of them struck Letitia Hayden from behind, knocking her down and causing an injury to her shoulder.

The Haydens brought suit against Notre Dame for failing to exercise care to protect Letitia Hayden. Notre Dame moved for summary judgment, arguing that it did not have a legal duty to protect Letitia Hayden from the intentional criminal acts of an unknown third person. The trial court granted Notre Dame's motion. The Haydens now appeal. The Haydens claim that Notre Dame was negligent in failing to protect Letitia Hayden. In order to prevail on a claim of negligence, a plaintiff must prove (1) a duty owed to the plaintiff by the defendant, (2) a breach of that duty by the defendant, and (3) injury to the plaintiff proximately caused by that breach. The only element at issue here is whether Notre Dame owed Letitia Hayden a duty under the circumstances. Whether a duty exists is generally a question of law for the court to determine.

The Haydens argue that this case is governed by premises liability principles and that the relevant standard of care is determined by Letitia Hayden's status as an invitee. The parties do not dispute that Letitia Hayden was a business invitee of Notre Dame. Nonetheless, Notre Dame argues that it owed no duty to protect Letitia Hayden from a third party's criminal act. It contends that the third party's action was unforeseeable, and that it therefore owed no duty to anticipate it and protect Letitia Hayden, a business invitee.

Our supreme court recently decided several cases that articulated the test for determining when a landowner's duty to its invitees extends to protecting them against the criminal actions of third parties that occur on its land. In *Delta Tau Delta v. Johnson*, 712 N.E.2d 968 (Ind. 1999), the court adopted a "totality of the circumstances" test for determining when such a duty arises. This test "requires landowners to take reasonable precautions to prevent foreseeable criminal actions against invitees." The court explained that, "[u]nder the totality of the circumstances test, a court considers all of the circumstances surrounding an event, including the nature, condition, and location of the land, as well as prior similar incidents, to determine whether a criminal act was foreseeable." "A substantial factor in the determination is the number, nature, and location of prior similar incidents, but the lack of prior similar incidents will not preclude a claim where the landowner knew or should have known that the criminal act was foreseeable."

Applying this test to the case before us, we find that the totality of the circumstances establishes that Notre Dame should have foreseen that injury would likely result from the actions of a third party in lunging for the football after it landed in the seating area. As a result, it owed a duty to Letitia Hayden to protect her from such injury. The Haydens were seated in Notre Dame's stadium to watch a football game. Notre Dame well understands and benefits from the enthusiasm of the fans of its football team. It is just such enthusiasm that drives some spectators to attempt to retrieve a football to keep as a souvenir. There was evidence that there were many prior incidents of people being jostled

or injured by efforts of fans to retrieve the ball. Letitia Hayden testified that she and her husband had attended Notre Dame football games for many years, and that she witnessed footballs land in the seating area around her many times. On numerous occasions, she saw people jump to get the ball. She testified that she witnessed another woman injured a number of years earlier when people in the crowd attempted to retrieve a football, and that she was knocked off her seat earlier in the game by crowd members attempting to retrieve the ball prior to the incident in which she was injured.

William Hayden testified that the net behind the goalpost caught the ball only about 50% of the time that it was kicked. The other half of the time, the ball would fall in the seating area around his seat, and people would try desperately to retrieve the ball. He stated that a few years prior to this incident, he had been knocked off his feet and thrown into the next row by fans eager to retrieve a football, and that he had been jostled a number of times. He stated that Notre Dame ushers witnessed fans being jostled in scrambles for the ball, but did not make aggressive attempts to recover the balls. He testified that in prior years, student managers, who were Notre Dame employees, would aggressively attempt to retrieve balls from fans and were usually successful in returning the balls to the playing field. The managers, however, no longer tried to retrieve the balls and stayed on the playing field.

Based on the totality of the circumstances, we hold that Notre Dame owed Letitia Hayden a duty to take reasonable steps to protect her from injury due to the actions of other fans in attempting to retrieve footballs that land in the seating area. The trial court erred in finding that no duty existed and entering summary judgment in favor of Notre Dame. Reversed.

 For an extended version of the case and review questions to test your understanding of the material, please go to www.HumanKinetics.com/CaseStudiesInSportLaw.

Jaworski v. Kiernan

696 A.2d 332 (Conn. 1997)

The sole issue in this appeal is what duty of care the defendant, Harry Kiernan, owed the plaintiff, Cynthia A. Jaworski, while both were participating on opposing teams in an adult coed soccer game sponsored by the recreation department of the town of South Windsor.

The jury reasonably could have found the following facts. The South Windsor recreation department sponsors an outdoor adult coed soccer league. On May 16, 1993, during a game, the defendant made contact with the plaintiff while she was shielding the soccer ball from the opposition so that the goalie on her team could retrieve the ball. As a result of this incident, the plaintiff suffered an injury to her left anterior cruciate ligament, which caused a 15% permanent partial disability of her left knee.

The plaintiff brought this action against the defendant in two counts. In the first count, she alleged that the defendant failed to exercise due care and that his conduct was negligent and careless in that he "hit" and "tripped" her from behind and that he challenged a female player, both in violation of league rules. The plaintiff further alleged that the defendant's negligent conduct caused her injury. In the second count, the plaintiff alleged that the defendant's conduct was wanton and reckless, citing the same violations of league rules, and claiming that his conduct caused identical harm. The defendant moved to strike the plaintiff's negligence count, claiming that a participant in an athletic contest is, as a matter of law, not liable to a coparticipant for injuries sustained as a result of simple negligence during the playing of the game. The defendant's motion was denied. The defendant then filed a special defense to the plaintiff's action, alleging that the plaintiff's own conduct was negligent, and that the plaintiff's negligence exceeded his alleged negligence. The jury returned a verdict for the plaintiff on the first count of her complaint, the negligence count, and found no comparative negligence attributable to the plaintiff. The jury found for the defendant on the second count of the plaintiff's complaint wherein she had alleged

reckless conduct. The jury awarded the plaintiff damages in the amount of $20,910.33, the exact amount of her medical bills.

The defendant appealed from the judgment of the trial court to the Appellate Court, and we transferred the appeal to this court. Because we conclude that participants in a team athletic contest owe a duty to refrain only from reckless or intentional conduct toward other participants, we reverse in part the judgment and remand the case with direction to strike the first count of the plaintiff's complaint.

We first note that the determination of whether a duty exists between individuals is a question of law. Only if a duty is found to exist does the trier of fact go on to determine whether the defendant has violated that duty. When "the trial court draws conclusions of law, our review is plenary and we must decide whether its conclusions are legally and logically correct and find support in the facts that appear in the record."

Duty is a legal conclusion about relationships between individuals, made after the fact, and is imperative to a negligence cause of action. The nature of the duty, and the specific persons to whom it is owed, are determined by the circumstances surrounding the conduct of the individual. Although it has been said that no universal test for duty ever has been formulated; our threshold inquiry has always been whether the specific harm alleged by the plaintiff was foreseeable to the defendant. The ultimate test of the existence of the duty to use care is found in the foreseeability that harm may result if it is not exercised. By that is not meant that one charged with negligence must be found actually to have foreseen the probability of harm or that the particular injury which resulted was foreseeable, but the test is, would the ordinary person in the defendant's position, knowing what he knew or should have known, anticipate that harm of the general nature of that suffered was likely to result?

A simple conclusion that the harm to the plaintiff was foreseeable, however cannot by itself mandate a determination that a legal duty exists.

Many harms are quite literally "foreseeable," yet for pragmatic reasons, no recovery is allowed. A further inquiry must be made, for we recognize that duty is not sacrosanct in itself, but is only an expression of the sum total of those considerations of policy that lead the law to say that the plaintiff is entitled to protection. While it may seem that there should be a remedy for every wrong, this is an ideal limited perforce by the realities of this world. Every injury has ramifying consequences, like the ripplings of the waters, without end. The problem for the law is to limit the legal consequences of wrongs to a controllable degree. The final step in the duty inquiry, then, is to make a determination of the fundamental policy of the law, as to whether the defendant's responsibility should extend to such results.

Our first step in an analysis of whether a duty exists and the extent of the defendant's duty, therefore, is to determine the foreseeability of the plaintiff's injury (i.e., whether a reasonable person in the defendant's position, knowing what he knew or should have known, would have anticipated the harm that resulted from his actions). Soccer, while not as violent a sport as football, is nevertheless replete with occasions when the participants make contact with one another during the normal course of the game. When two soccer players vie for control of the ball, the lower limbs are especially vulnerable to injury. If a player seeks to challenge another player who has possession of the ball or seeks to prevent another player from gaining possession of the ball, the resulting contact could reasonably be foreseen to result in injury to either player. We conclude, therefore, that the plaintiff's injury was foreseeable.

Having concluded that the plaintiff's injury was a foreseeable consequence of the defendant's actions, we need to determine as a matter of policy the extent of the legal duty to be imposed on the defendant. In order to determine the extent of the defendant's responsibility, we consider (1) the normal expectations of participants in the sport in which the plaintiff and the defendant were engaged, (2) the public policy of encouraging continued vigorous participation in recreational sporting activities while weighing the safety of the participants, (3) the avoidance of increased litigation, and (4) the decisions of other jurisdictions.

In athletic competitions, the object obviously is to win. In games, particularly those played by teams and involving some degree of physical contact, it is reasonable to assume that the competitive spirit of the participants will result in some rules violations and injuries. That is why there are penalty boxes, foul shots, free kicks, and yellow cards. Indeed, the specific rules applicable to this game demonstrate that rules violations were expected in the normal course of the game. Some injuries may result from such violations, but such violations are nonetheless an accepted part of any competition. Simply put, when competitive sports are played, we expect that a participant's main objective is to be a winner, and we expect that the players will pursue that objective enthusiastically. We also anticipate that players in their enthusiasm will commit inadvertent rules violations from which injuries may result. The normal expectations of participants in contact team sports include the potential for injuries resulting from conduct that violates the rules of the sport. These expectations, in turn, inform the question of the extent of the duty owed by one participant to another. We conclude that the normal expectations of participants in contact team sports counsel the adoption of a reckless or intentional conduct duty of care standard for those participants.

A proper balance of the relevant public policy considerations surrounding sports injuries arising from team contact sports also supports limiting the defendant's responsibility for injuries to other participants to injuries resulting from reckless or intentional conduct. We too appreciate the tension between promoting vigorous athletic competition on the one hand and protecting those who participate on the other. As have most jurisdictions, we conclude that this balance is best achieved by allowing a participant in an athletic contest to maintain an action against a coparticipant only for reckless or intentional conduct and not for merely negligent conduct. We believe that participants in recreational sports will not alter their enthusiasm for competition or their participation in recreational activities for fear of liability for injuring someone because of their reckless or intentional conduct. We are convinced, however, that liability for simple negligence would have an opposite effect. We also are convinced that a recklessness standard will sufficiently protect participants in athletic contests by affording them a right of action against those who cause injuries not inherent in the particular game in which the participants are engaged. In other words, we believe that the reckless or intentional conduct standard of care will maintain civility and relative safety in team sports without dampening the competitive spirit of the participants.

A final public policy concern that influences our decision is our desire to stem the possible flood of litigation that might result from adopting simple negligence as the standard of care to be utilized in athletic contests. If simple negligence were adopted as the standard of care, every punter with whom contact is made, every midfielder high-sticked, every basketball player fouled, every batter struck by a pitch, and every hockey player tripped would have the ingredients for a lawsuit if injury resulted. When the number of athletic events taking place in Connecticut over the course of a year is considered, there exists the potential for a surfeit of lawsuits when it becomes known that simple negligence, based on an inadvertent vio-

lation of a contest rule, will suffice as a ground for recovery for an athletic injury. This should not be encouraged.

The majority of jurisdictions addressing this issue have chosen to adopt either a reckless or an intentional conduct standard of care when determining liability for injuries that occur during an athletic contest.

Applying the foregoing considerations to the facts before us, we conclude that, as a matter of policy, it is appropriate to adopt a standard of care imposing on the defendant, a participant in a team contact sport, a legal duty to refrain from reckless or intentional conduct. Proof of mere negligence is insufficient to create liability. The judgment is reversed in part and the case is remanded with direction to strike the first count of the plaintiff's complaint.

 For an extended version of the case and review questions to test your understanding of the material, please go to www.HumanKinetics.com/CaseStudiesInSportLaw.

Kleinknecht v. Gettysburg College

989 F.2d 1360 (3rd Cir. 1993)

Suzanne W. Kleinknecht and Richard P. Kleinknecht (collectively the Kleinknechts) appeal an order of the United States District Court for the Middle District of Pennsylvania granting summary judgment to appellee Gettysburg College (the College).

In September 1988, Drew Kleinknecht was a 20-year-old sophomore student at the College, which had recruited him for its Division III intercollegiate lacrosse team. Lacrosse is a contact sport. In terms of sports-related injuries at the College, it ranked at least fourth behind football, basketball, and wrestling, respectively. Lacrosse players can typically suffer a variety of injuries, including unconsciousness, wooziness, concussions, being knocked to the ground, and having the wind knocked out of them. Before Drew died, however, no athlete at the College had experienced cardiac arrest while playing lacrosse or any other sport.

In September 1988, the College employed two full-time athletic trainers, Joseph Donolli and Gareth Biser. Both men were certified by the National Athletic Trainers' Association, which requires, *inter alia*, current certification in both cardiopulmonary resuscitation (CPR) and standard first aid. In addition, 12 student trainers participated in the College's sports program. The trainers were stationed in the College's two training room facilities at Musselman Stadium and Plank Gymnasium.

Drew participated in a fall lacrosse practice on the afternoon of September 16, 1988. Coaches Janczyk and Anderson attended and supervised this practice. It was held on the softball fields outside Musselman Stadium. No trainers or student trainers were present. Neither coach had certification in CPR. Neither coach had a radio on the practice field. The nearest telephone was inside the training room at Musselman Stadium, roughly 200 to 250 yards away. The shortest route to this telephone required scaling an 8-foot high cyclone fence surrounding the stadium. According to Coach Janczyk, he and Coach Anderson had never discussed how they would handle an emergency during fall lacrosse practice.

The September 16, 1988 practice began at about 3:15 p.m. with jogging and stretching, some drills, and finally a "6-on-6" drill in which the team split into two groups at opposite ends of the field. Drew was a defenseman and was participating in one of the drills when he suffered a cardiac arrest. According to a teammate observing from the sidelines, Drew simply stepped away from the play and dropped to the ground. Another teammate on the sidelines stated that no person or object struck Drew prior to his collapse.

After Drew fell, his teammates and Coach Janczyk ran to his side. Coach Janczyk and some of the players noticed that Drew was lying so that his head appeared to be in an awkward position. No one knew precisely what had happened at that time, and at least some of those present suspected a spinal injury. Team captain Daniel Polizzotti testified that he heard a continuous "funny" "gurgling" noise coming from Drew, and knew from what he observed that something "major" was wrong. Other teammates testified that Drew's skin began quickly to change colors. One team member testified that by the time the coaches had arrived, "[Drew] was really blue."

According to the College, Coach Janczyk acted in accordance with the school's emergency plan by first assessing Drew's condition, then dispatching players to get a trainer and call for an ambulance. Coach Janczyk himself then began to run toward Musselman Stadium to summon help. The Kleinknechts dispute the College's version of the facts. They note that although Coach Janczyk claims to have told two players to run to Apple Hall, a nearby dormitory, for help, Coach Anderson did not recall Coach Janczyk's sending anyone for help. Even if Coach Janczyk did send the two players to Apple Hall, the Kleinknechts maintain, his action was inappropriate because Apple Hall was not the location of the nearest telephone. It is undisputed that two other team members ran for help, but the Kleinknechts contend that the team members did this on their own accord, without instruction from either coach.

The parties do not dispute that Polizzotti, the team captain, ran toward the stadium, where he knew a training room was located and a student trainer could be found. In doing so, Polizzotti scaled a chain link fence that surrounded the stadium and ran across the field, encountering student trainer Traci Moore outside the door to the training room. He told her that a lacrosse player was down and needed help. She ran toward the football stadium's main gate, managed to squeeze through a gap between one side of the locked gate and the brick pillar forming its support, and continued on to the practice field by foot until flagging a ride from a passing car. In the meantime, Polizzotti continued into the training room where he told the student trainers there what had happened. One of them phoned Plank Gymnasium and told Head Trainer Donolli about the emergency.

Contemporaneously with Polizzotti's dash to the stadium, Dave Kerney, another team member, ran toward the stadium for assistance. When he saw that Polizzotti was going to beat him there, Kerney concluded that it was pointless for both of them to arrive at the same destination and changed his course toward the College Union Building. He told the student at the front desk of the emergency on the practice field. The student called his supervisor on duty in the building, and she immediately telephoned for an ambulance.

Student trainer Moore was first to reach Drew. She saw Drew's breathing was labored, and the color of his complexion changed as she watched. Because Drew was breathing, she did not attempt CPR or any other first aid technique, but only monitored his condition, observing no visible bruises or lacerations.

By this time, Coach Janczyk had entered the stadium training room and learned that Donolli had been notified and an ambulance called. Coach Janczyk returned to the practice field at the same time Donolli arrived in a golf cart. Donolli saw that Drew was not breathing, and turned him on his back to begin CPR with the help of a student band member who was certified as an emergency medical technician and had by chance arrived on the scene. The two of them performed CPR until two ambulances arrived at approximately 4:15 p.m. Drew was defibrillated and drugs were administered to strengthen his heart. He was placed in an ambulance and taken to the hospital, but despite repeated resuscitation efforts, Drew could not be revived. He was pronounced dead at 4:58 p.m.

Prior to his collapse on September 16, 1988, Drew had no medical history of heart problems. The Kleinknechts themselves describe him as "a healthy, physically active and vigorous young man" with no unusual medical history until his death. In January 1988, a College physician had examined Drew to determine his fitness to participate in sports and found him to be in excellent health. The Kleinknecht's family physician had also examined Drew in August 1987 and found him healthy and able to participate in physical activity.

Medical evidence indicated Drew died of cardiac arrest after a fatal attack of cardiac arrhythmia. Postmortem examination could not detect the cause of Drew's fatal cardiac arrhythmia. An autopsy conducted the day after his death revealed no bruises or contusions on his body. This corroborated the statements by Drew's teammates that he was not in play when he suffered his cardiac arrest and dispelled the idea that contact with a ball or stick during the practice might have caused the arrhythmia. The National Institutes of Health examined Drew's heart as part of the autopsy but found no pathology. A later examination of the autopsy records by a different pathologist, and still further study by yet another physician after Drew's body was exhumed, also failed to reveal any heart abnormality that could have explained Drew's fatal heart attack.

The Kleinknechts present three general issues on appeal. They first argue that the district court erred in determining that the College had no legal duty to implement preventive measures assuring prompt assistance and treatment in the event one of its student athletes suffered cardiac arrest while engaged in school-supervised intercollegiate athletic activity. Second, the Kleinknechts maintain that the district court erred in determining that the actions of school employees following Drew's collapse were reasonable and that the College therefore did not breach any duty of care. Finally, the Kleinknechts urge that the district court erred in determining that both Traci Moore and the College were entitled to immunity under the Pennsylvania Good Samaritan Act.

A federal court exercising diversity jurisdiction must "apply the substantive law of the state whose laws govern the action." The parties agree that Pennsylvania law applies to the present dispute. "In cases where the state's highest court has not considered the precise question to be answered, the federal court is called upon to predict how the state court would resolve the issue should it be called upon to do so." Because the Supreme Court of Pennsylvania has not addressed the precise issues raised by the Kleinknechts, we must attempt to predict how that Court would rule in this case.

Whether a defendant owes a duty of care to a plaintiff is a question of law. In order to prevail on a cause of action in negligence under Pennsylvania law, a plaintiff must establish (1) a duty or obligation recognized by the law, requiring the actor to conform to a certain standard of conduct; (2) a failure to conform to the standard required; (3) a causal connection between the conduct and the resulting injury; and (4) actual loss or damage resulting to the interests of another.

The Kleinknechts assert three different theories on which they predicate the College's duty to establish preventive measures capable of providing treatment to student athletes in the event of a medical emergency such as Drew's cardiac arrest: (1) existence of a special relationship between the College and its student athletes, (2) foreseeability that a student athlete may suffer cardiac arrest while engaged in athletic activity, and (3) public policy.

The Kleinknechts argue that the College had a duty of care to Drew by virtue of his status as a member of an intercollegiate athletic team. The Supreme Court of Pennsylvania has stated that "[d]uty, in any given situation, is predicated on the relationship existing between the parties at the relevant time." The Kleinknechts argue that although the Supreme Court has not addressed this precise issue, it would conclude that a college or university owes a duty to its intercollegiate athletes to provide preventive measures in the event of a medical emergency.

Drew chose to attend Gettysburg College because he was persuaded it had a good lacrosse program, a sport in which he wanted to participate at the intercollegiate level. Head Trainer Donolli actively recruited Drew to play lacrosse at the College. At the time he was stricken, Drew was not engaged in his own private affairs as a student at Gettysburg College. Instead, he was participating in a scheduled athletic practice for an intercollegiate team sponsored by the College under the supervision of College employees. On these facts we believe that the Supreme Court of Pennsylvania would hold that a special relationship existed between the College and Drew that was sufficient to impose a duty of reasonable care on the College. Other states have similarly concluded that a duty exists based on such a relationship.

The Supreme Court of Pennsylvania has not specifically addressed the issue whether schools owe its athletes a duty based on that special relationship. Here, Drew was not acting in his capacity as a private student when he collapsed. Indeed, the Kleinknechts concede that if he had been, they would have no recourse against the College. There is a distinction between a student injured while participating as an intercollegiate athlete in a sport for which he was recruited and a student injured at a college while pursuing his private interests, scholastic or otherwise. This distinction serves to limit the class of students to whom a college owes the duty of care that arises here. Had Drew been participating in a fraternity football game, for example, the College might not have owed him the same duty or perhaps any duty at all. There is, however, no need for us to reach or decide the duty question either in that context or in the context of whether a college would owe a duty towards students participating in intramural sports. On the other hand, the fact that Drew's cardiac arrest occurred during an athletic event involving an intercollegiate team of which he was a member does impose a duty of due care on a college that actively sought his participation in that sport. We cannot help but think that the College recruited Drew for its own benefit, probably thinking that his skill at lacrosse would bring favorable attention and so aid the College in attracting other students.

In conclusion, we predict that the Supreme Court of Pennsylvania would hold that the College owed Drew a duty of care in his capacity as an intercollegiate athlete engaged in school-sponsored intercollegiate athletic activity for which he had been recruited.

This does not end our inquiry, however. The determination that the College owes a duty of care to its intercollegiate athletes could merely define the class of persons to whom the duty extends, without determining the nature of the duty or demands it makes on the College. Because it is foreseeable that student athletes may sustain severe and even life-threatening injuries while engaged in athletic activity, the Kleinknechts argue that the College's duty of care required it to be ready to respond swiftly and adequately to a medical emergency.

Foreseeability is a legal requirement before recovery can be had. The test of negligence is whether the wrongdoer could have anticipated and foreseen the likelihood of harm to the injured person, resulting from his act. The type of foreseeability that determines a duty of care, as opposed to proximate cause, is not dependent on the foreseeability of a specific event. Instead, in the context of duty, "[t]he concept of foreseeability means the likelihood of the occurrence of a general type of risk rather than the likelihood of the occurrence of the precise chain of events leading to the injury." Only when even the general likelihood of some broadly definable class of events, of which the particular event that caused the plaintiff's injury is a subclass, is unforeseeable can a court hold as a matter of law that the defendant did not have a duty to the plaintiff to guard against that broad general class of risks within which the particular harm the plaintiff suffered befell.

Even this determination that the harm suffered was foreseeable fails to end our analysis. If a duty is to be imposed, the foreseeable risk of harm must be unreasonable. The classic risk-utility analysis used to determine whether a risk is unreasonable balances "the risk, in light of the social value of the interest threatened, and the probability and extent of the harm, against the value of the interest which the actor is seeking to protect, and the expedience of the course pursued."

Although the district court correctly determined that the Kleinknechts had presented evidence establishing that the occurrence of severe and life-threatening injuries is not out of the ordinary during contact sports, it held that the College had no duty because the cardiac arrest suffered by Drew, a 20-year-old athlete with no history of any severe medical problems, was not reasonably foreseeable. Its definition of foreseeability is too narrow. Although it is true that a defendant is not required to guard against every possible risk, he must take reasonable steps to guard against hazards that are generally foreseeable. Though the specific risk that a person like Drew would suffer a cardiac arrest may be unforeseeable, the Kleinknechts produced ample evidence that a life-threatening injury occurring during participation in an athletic event like lacrosse was reasonably foreseeable. In addition to the testimony of numerous medical and athletic experts, Coach Janczyk, Head Trainer Donolli, and student trainer Moore all testified that they were aware of instances in which athletes had died during athletic competitions. The foreseeability of a life-threatening injury to Drew was not hidden from the College's view. Therefore, the College did owe Drew a duty to take reasonable precautions against the risk of death while Drew was taking part in the College's intercollegiate lacrosse program.

Having determined that it is foreseeable that a member of the College's interscholastic lacrosse team could suffer a serious injury during an athletic event, it becomes evident that the College's failure to protect against such a risk is not reasonable. The magnitude of the foreseeable harm—irreparable injury or death to one of its student athletes as a result of inadequate preventive emergency measures—is indisputable. With regard to the offsetting cost of protecting against such risk, the College prophesied that if this court accepts that the College owed the asserted duty, then it will be required "to have a CPR certified trainer on site at each and every athletic practice whether in-season or off-season, formal or informal, strenuous or light," and to provide similar cardiac protection to "intramural, club sports and gym class." This "slippery slope" prediction reflects an unwarranted extension of the holding in this case. First, the recognition of a duty here is limited to intercollegiate athletes. No other scenario is presented, so the question whether any of the other broad classes of events and students posited by the College merit similar protection is not subject to resolution. Second, the determination whether the College has breached this duty at all is a question of fact for the jury. This court recognizes only that under the facts of this case, the College owed a duty to Drew to have measures in place at the lacrosse team's practice on the afternoon of September 16, 1988, in order to provide prompt treatment in the event that he or any other member of the lacrosse team suffered a life-threatening injury.

In reversing the district court's grant of summary judgment to the College, we predict that the Supreme Court of Pennsylvania would hold that a college also has a duty to be reasonably prepared for handling medical emergencies that foreseeably arise during a student's participation in an intercollegiate contact sport for which a college recruited

him. It is clearly foreseeable that a person participating in such an activity will sustain serious injury requiring immediate medical attention. It may be that the emergency medical measures the College had in place were sufficient to fulfill this duty. It is also possible that the College could not foresee that its failure to provide emergency medical services other than those that it already had in place would substantially contribute to the death of an apparently healthy student. Nevertheless, "[W]hether in a particular case the plaintiff has demonstrated, by a preponderance of the evidence, that the defendant's negligent conduct was a substantial factor in bringing about the plaintiff's harm, is normally a question of fact reserved for the jury, and should only be removed from the jury's consideration where it is clear, as a matter of law, that reasonable minds could not differ on the issue." *Little v. York County*, 481 A.2d 1194, 1198.

Our holding is narrow. It predicts only that a court applying Pennsylvania law would conclude that the College had a duty to provide prompt and adequate emergency medical services to Drew, one of its intercollegiate athletes, while he was engaged in a school-sponsored athletic activity for which he had been recruited. Whether the College breached that duty is a question of fact. If the fact finder concludes that such a breach occurred, we think that the question whether that breach was the proximate or legal cause of Drew's death would likewise be a question of fact.

Finally, the Kleinknechts argue that the College owed a duty of care to Drew based on public policy considerations. Seizing upon the language from the Pennsylvania Supreme court, the district court held that the College had no duty to anticipate and guard against the possibility of a healthy, physically active, young athlete having a heart attack while engaged in intercollegiate athletic activity, candidly admit[ting] that [this] conclusion shades off into these broad areas of policy concern.

Again, we believe this determination fails to distinguish duty from legal cause. It also fails to appreciate the full import of the very language on which the district court says it relied. As already explained, two distinct theories establish that the College owed a duty of care to Drew as an intercollegiate athlete. A special relationship existed between the College and Drew in his capacity as a school athlete. His medical emergency was within a reasonably foreseeable class of unfortunate events that could arise from participation in an intercollegiate contact sport. If, as the Supreme Court of Pennsylvania has stated, the concept of duty "amounts to no more than 'the sum total of those considerations of policy which led the law to say that the particular plaintiff is entitled to protection,'" then it strengthens our belief that that Court would hold that the policies supporting these two theories are themselves sufficient to require the College to adopt preventive measures reasonably designed to avoid possible death from a life-threatening injury a recruited athlete suffers during an intercollegiate athletic activity.

Under the facts of this case, the College owed a duty to Drew to have reasonable measures in place at the practice on the afternoon of September 16, 1988, to provide prompt treatment in the event that he or any other member of the lacrosse team suffered a life-threatening injury. The determination whether the College in fact breached this duty is a question of fact for the jury.

Finally, we address the College's argument that Pennsylvania's Good Samaritan law provides immunity to both the College and its personnel who rendered emergency care to Drew. The parties do not dispute the district court's determination that neither Coach Janczyk nor Coach Anderson is entitled to immunity. The College, however, argues that it too is entitled to immunity because it is a "person" within the terms of the statute. In general, Pennsylvania statutory law defines the term "person" as including corporations, partnerships, and associations

unless the statutory context indicates otherwise. Section 8332, however, requires a person who seeks immunity to hold certification in an approved first aid, advanced life saving, or basic life support course. We think it is unlikely that the Pennsylvania General Assembly intended that corporations could achieve the requisite certification and receive immunity. As the Kleinknechts note, the statute encourages rescue and lending assistance at the scene of an emergency. These measures can only be taken by a natural person. Therefore, we reject the College's argument and predict that the Supreme Court of Pennsylvania will not hold that a corporation is entitled to immunity under the Pennsylvania Good Samaritan law.

The district court's holding that the College's duty of care to Drew as an intercollegiate athlete did not include, prior to his collapse, a duty to provide prompt emergency medical service while he was engaged in school-sponsored athletic activity will be reversed. The district court's holding that the College acted reasonably and therefore did not breach any duty owed to Drew following his collapse will likewise be reversed. We will remand this matter to the district court for further proceedings consistent with this opinion. We will reverse the district court's conclusion that the College is entitled to immunity under the Good Samaritan law.

 For an extended version of the case and review questions to test your understanding of the material, please go to www.HumanKinetics.com/CaseStudiesInSportLaw.

Knight v. Jewett

11 Cal.Rptr.2d 2 (Cal. 1992)

In this case, we face the question of the proper application of the assumption of risk doctrine.

On January 25, 1987, the day of the 1987 Super Bowl football game, plaintiff Kendra Knight and defendant Michael Jewett, together with a number of other social acquaintances, attended a Super Bowl party at the home of a mutual friend. During half time of the Super Bowl, several guests decided to play an informal game of touch football on an adjoining dirt lot, using a "peewee"

football. Each team had four or five players and included both women and men; plaintiff and defendant were on opposing teams. No rules were explicitly discussed before the game.

Five to 10 minutes into the game, defendant ran into plaintiff during a play. According to plaintiff, at that point she told defendant "not to play so rough or I was going to have to stop playing." Her declaration stated that "[defendant] seemed to acknowledge my statement and left me with the impression that he would play less rough prospectively." In his deposition, defendant recalled that plaintiff had asked him to "be careful," but did not remember plaintiff saying that she would stop playing. On the very next play, plaintiff sustained the injuries that gave rise to the present lawsuit. As defendant recalled the incident, his team was on defense on that play, and he jumped up in an attempt to intercept a pass. He touched the ball but did not catch it, and in coming down he collided with plaintiff, knocking her over. When he landed, he stepped backward onto plaintiff's right hand, injuring her hand and little finger.

Both plaintiff and Andrea Starr, another participant in the game who was on the same team as plaintiff, recalled the incident differently from defendant. According to their declarations, at the time plaintiff was injured, Starr already had caught the pass. Defendant was running toward Starr, when he ran into plaintiff from behind, knocked her down, and stepped on her hand. Starr also stated that, after knocking plaintiff down, defendant continued running until he tagged Starr, "hard enough to cause me to lose my balance, resulting in a twisting or spraining of my ankle."

The game ended with plaintiff's injury, and plaintiff sought treatment shortly thereafter. After three operations failed to restore the movement in her little finger or to relieve the ongoing pain of the injury, plaintiff's finger was amputated. Plaintiff then instituted the present proceeding, seeking damages from defendant on theories of negligence and assault and battery.

As every leading tort treatise has explained, the assumption of risk doctrine long has caused confusion both in definition and application, because the phrase "assumption of risk" traditionally has been used in a number of very different factual settings involving analytically distinct legal concepts. In some settings (e.g., most cases involving sports-related injuries), past assumption of risk decisions largely have been concerned with defining the contours of the legal duty that a given class of defendants (e.g., owners of baseball stadiums or ice hockey rinks) owed to an injured plaintiff. In other settings, the assumption of risk terminology historically was applied to situations in which it was clear that the

defendant had breached a legal duty of care to the plaintiff, and the inquiry focused on whether the plaintiff knowingly and voluntarily had chosen to encounter the specific risk of harm posed by the defendant's breach of duty.

Prior to the adoption of comparative fault principles of liability, there often was no need to distinguish between the different categories of assumption of risk cases, because if a case fell into either category, the plaintiff's recovery was totally barred. With the adoption of comparative fault, however, it became essential to differentiate between the distinct categories of cases that traditionally had been lumped together under the rubric of assumption of risk.

To simplify greatly, it has been observed that in one kind of situation, to wit, where a plaintiff unreasonably undertakes to encounter a specific known risk imposed by a defendant's negligence, plaintiff's conduct, although he may encounter that risk in a prudent manner, is in reality a form of contributory negligence. We think it clear that the adoption of a system of comparative negligence should entail the merger of the defense of assumption of risk into the general scheme of assessment of liability in proportion to fault in those particular cases in which the form of assumption of risk involved is no more than a variant of contributory negligence.

Although the difference between the primary assumption of risk–secondary assumption of risk nomenclature and the "reasonable implied assumption of risk"–"unreasonable implied assumption of risk" terminology embraced in many of the recent court of appeals decisions may appear at first blush to be only semantic, the significance extends beyond mere rhetoric. First, in "primary assumption of risk" cases, where the defendant owes no duty to protect the plaintiff from a particular risk of harm, a plaintiff who has suffered such harm is not entitled to recover from the defendant, whether the plaintiff's conduct in undertaking the activity was reasonable or unreasonable. Second, in "secondary assumption of risk" cases, involving instances in which the defendant has breached the duty of care owed to the plaintiff, the defendant is not entitled to be entirely relieved of liability for an injury proximately caused by such breach, simply because the plaintiff's conduct in encountering the risk of such an injury was reasonable rather than unreasonable. Third and finally, the question whether the defendant owed a legal duty to protect the plaintiff from a particular risk of harm does not turn on the reasonableness or unreasonableness of the plaintiff's conduct, but rather on the nature of the activity or sport in which the defendant is engaged and the relationship of the defendant and the plaintiff to that activity or sport. For these reasons, use of the "reasonable implied assumption of risk"/"unreasonable implied assumption of risk" terminology, as a means of differentiating between the cases in which a plaintiff is barred from bringing an action and those in which he or she is not barred, is more misleading than helpful.

The dissenting opinion suggests, however, that, even when a defendant has breached its duty of care to the plaintiff, a plaintiff who reasonably has chosen to encounter a known risk of harm imposed by such a breach may be totally precluded from recovering any damages, without doing violence to comparative fault principles, on the theory that the plaintiff, by proceeding in the face of a known risk, has "impliedly consented" to any harm. For a number of reasons, we conclude this contention does not withstand analysis.

First, the argument that a plaintiff who proceeds to encounter a known risk has "impliedly consented" to absolve a negligent defendant of liability for any ensuing harm logically would apply as much to a plaintiff who unreasonably has chosen to encounter a known risk, as to a plaintiff who reasonably has chosen to encounter such a risk.

Second, the implied consent rationale rests on a legal fiction that is untenable, at least as applied to conduct that represents a breach of the defendant's duty of care to the plaintiff. It may be accurate to suggest that an individual who voluntarily engages in a potentially dangerous activity or sport "consents to" or "agrees to assume" the risks inherent in the activity or sport itself, such as the risks posed to a snow skier by moguls on a ski slope or the risks posed to a water skier by wind-whipped waves on a lake. But it is thoroughly unrealistic to suggest that, by engaging in a potentially dangerous activity or sport, an individual consents to (or agrees to excuse) a breach of duty by others that increases the risks inevitably posed by the activity or sport itself, even where the participating individual is aware of the possibility that such misconduct may occur.

Third, the dissenting opinion's claim that the category of cases in which the assumption of risk doctrine operates to bar a plaintiff's cause of action properly should be gauged on the basis of an implied consent analysis, rather than on the duty analysis we have described above, is, in our view, untenable for another reason. Such an approach not only would be inconsistent with principles of fairness, but also would be inimical to the fair and efficient administration of justice. If the application of the assumption of risk doctrine in a sports setting turned on the particular plaintiff's subjective knowledge and awareness, summary judgment rarely would be available in such cases, for, as the present case reveals, it frequently will be easy to raise factual questions with regard to a particular plaintiff's subjective expectations as to the existence and magnitude of the risks the plaintiff voluntarily chose to encounter. By contrast, the question of the existence and scope of a defendant's duty of care is a legal question that depends on the nature of the sport or activity in question and on the parties' general relationship to the activity, and is an issue to be decided by the court, rather than the jury. Thus, the question of assumption of risk is much more amenable to resolution by summary judgment under a duty analysis than under the dissenting opinion's suggested implied consent approach.

In determining the propriety of the trial court's grant of summary judgment in favor of the defendant in this case, our inquiry does not turn on the reasonableness or unreasonableness of plaintiff's conduct in choosing to subject herself to the risks of touch football or in continuing to participate in the game after she became aware of defendant's allegedly rough play. Nor do we focus on whether there is a factual dispute with regard to whether plaintiff subjectively knew of, and voluntarily chose to encounter, the risk of defendant's conduct, or impliedly consented to relieve or excuse defendant from any duty of care to her. Instead, our resolution of this issue turns on whether, in light of the nature of the sporting activity in which defendant and plaintiff were engaged, defendant's conduct breached a legal duty of care to plaintiff.

As a general rule, persons have a duty to use due care to avoid injury to others, and may be held liable if their careless conduct injures another person. Thus, for example, a property owner ordinarily is required to use due care to eliminate dangerous conditions on his or her property. In the sports setting, however, conditions or conduct that otherwise might be viewed as dangerous often are an integral part of the sport itself. Thus, although moguls on a ski run pose a risk of harm to skiers that might not exist were these configurations removed, the challenge and risks posed by the moguls are part of the sport of skiing, and a ski resort has no duty to eliminate them. In this respect, the nature of a sport is highly relevant in defining the duty of care owed by the particular defendant.

Although defendants generally have no legal duty to eliminate (or protect a plaintiff against) risks inherent in the sport itself, it is well established that defendants generally do have a duty to use due care not to increase the risks to a participant over and above those inherent in the sport. Thus, although a ski resort has no duty to remove moguls from a ski run, it clearly does have a duty to use due care to maintain its towropes in a safe, working condition so as not to expose skiers to an increased risk of harm. The cases establish that the latter type of risk, posed by a ski resort's negligence, clearly is not a risk (inherent in the sport) that is assumed by a participant.

In some situations, however, the careless conduct of others is treated as an "inherent risk" of a sport, thus barring recovery by the plaintiff. For example, numerous cases recognize that in a game of baseball, a player generally cannot recover if he or she is hit and injured by a carelessly thrown ball, and that in a game of basketball, recovery is not permitted for an injury caused by a carelessly extended elbow. The divergent results of the foregoing cases lead naturally to the question how courts are to determine when careless conduct of another properly should be considered an "inherent risk" of the sport that (as a matter of law) is assumed by the injured participant.

Contrary to the implied consent approach to the doctrine of assumption of risk, discussed above, the duty approach provides an answer that does not depend on the particular plaintiff's subjective knowledge or appreciation of the potential risk. Even where the plaintiff, who falls while skiing over a mogul, is a total novice and lacks any knowledge of skiing whatsoever, the ski resort would not be liable for his or her injuries. And, on the other hand, even where the plaintiff actually is aware that a particular ski resort on occasion has been negligent in maintaining its towropes, that knowledge would not preclude the skier from recovering if he or she were injured as a result of the resort's repetition of such deficient conduct. In the latter context, although the plaintiff may have acted with knowledge of the potential negligence, he or she did not consent to such negligent conduct or agree to excuse the resort from liability in the event of such negligence. Rather than being dependent on the knowledge or consent of the particular plaintiff, resolution of the question of the defendant's liability in such cases turns on whether the defendant had a legal duty to avoid such conduct or to protect the plaintiff against a particular risk of harm. As already noted, the nature of a defendant's duty in the sports context depends heavily on the nature of the sport itself. Additionally, the scope of the legal duty owed by a defendant frequently will also depend on the defendant's role in, or relationship to, the sport.

These cases demonstrate that in the sports setting, as elsewhere, the nature of the applicable duty or standard of care frequently varies with the role of the defendant whose conduct is at issue in a given case. In the present case, defendant was a participant in the touch football game in which plaintiff was engaged at the time of her injury, and thus the question before us involves the circumstances under which a participant in such a sport may be held liable for an injury sustained by another participant.

The overwhelming majority of the cases, both within and outside California, that have addressed the issue of coparticipant liability in such a sport, have concluded that it is improper to hold a sports participant liable to a coparticipant for ordinary careless conduct committed during the sport (e.g., for an injury resulting from a carelessly thrown ball or bat during a baseball game) and that liability properly may be imposed on a participant only when he or she intentionally injures another player or engages in reckless conduct that is totally outside the range of the ordinary activity involved in the sport.

In reaching the conclusion that a coparticipant's duty of care should be limited in this fashion, the cases have explained that, in the heat of an active sporting event like baseball or football, a participant's normal energetic conduct often includes accidentally careless behavior. The courts have concluded that vigorous participation in such sporting events likely would be chilled if legal liability were to be imposed on a participant on the basis of his or her ordinary careless conduct. The cases have recognized that, in such a sport, even when a participant's conduct violates a rule of the game and may subject the violator to internal sanctions prescribed by the sport itself, imposition of legal liability for such conduct might well alter fundamentally the nature of the sport by deterring participants from vigorously engaging in activity that falls close to, but on the permissible side of, a prescribed rule.

In our view, the reasoning of the foregoing cases is sound. Accordingly, we conclude that a participant in an active sport breaches a legal duty of care to other participants (i.e., engages in conduct that properly may subject him or her to financial liability) only if the participant intentionally injures another player or engages in conduct that is so reckless as to be totally outside the range of the ordinary activity involved in the sport. As applied to the present case, the foregoing legal principle clearly supports the trial court's entry of summary judgment in favor of defendant. The declarations filed in support of and in opposition to the summary judgment motion establish that defendant was, at most, careless or

negligent in knocking over plaintiff, stepping on her hand, and injuring her finger. Although plaintiff maintains that defendant's rough play as described in her declaration and the declaration of Andrea Starr properly can be characterized as "reckless," the conduct alleged in those declarations is not even closely comparable to the kind of conduct—conduct so reckless as to be totally outside the range of the ordinary activity involved in the sport—that is a prerequisite to the imposition of legal liability on a participant in such a sport.

Therefore, we conclude that defendant's conduct in the course of the touch football game did not breach any legal duty of care owed to plaintiff. Accordingly, this case falls within the primary assumption of risk doctrine, and thus the trial court properly granted summary judgment in favor of defendant. Because plaintiff's action is barred under the primary assumption of risk doctrine, comparative fault principles do not come into play. The judgment of the court of appeals, upholding the summary judgment entered by the trial court, is affirmed.

 For an extended version of the case and review questions to test your understanding of the material, please go to www.HumanKinetics.com/CaseStudiesInSportLaw.

Lestina v. West Bend Mutual Insurance Company

501 N.W.2d 28 (Wis. 1993)

This is an appeal, from a judgment of the circuit court for Waukesha County, Patrick L. Snyder, Circuit Judge. The case comes to this court on certification by the Court of Appeals pursuant to § 809.61, Stats.1991-92. The sole question presented by the certification is what is the standard of care in Wisconsin for a [recreational] sports player who is alleged to have caused injury to another player during and as part of the [recreational team contact sports] competition. The circuit court determined that negligence was the governing legal standard.

Robert F. Lestina, the plaintiff, filed this personal injury tort action against Leopold Jerger,

the defendant, and Jerger's homeowner's insurer, West Bend Mutual Insurance Company, after the plaintiff was injured in a collision with the defendant. The collision occurred during a recreational soccer match organized by the Waukesha County Old Timers League, a recreational league for players over the age of 30.

The plaintiff was playing an offensive position for his team and the defendant was the goalkeeper for the opposing team on April 20, 1988, when the injury occurred. Shortly before the plaintiff was injured, he had scored the first goal of the game. After his goal the plaintiff regained possession of the ball and was about to attempt a second goal when the defendant apparently ran out of the goal area and collided with the plaintiff. The plaintiff asserted that the defendant "slide tackled" him in order to prevent him from scoring. Although slide tackles are allowed under some soccer rules, this league's rules prohibit such maneuvers to minimize risk of injury. The defendant claimed that the collision occurred as he and the plaintiff simultaneously attempted to kick the soccer ball.

The plaintiff seriously injured his left knee and leg in the collision and commenced this action, alleging that the defendant's conduct was both negligent and reckless. The defendant moved for summary judgment on the negligence issue, asserting that the plaintiff's allegations of negligence were insufficient as a matter of law to state a cause of action for injuries sustained during a recreational team contact sports competition.

After the jury returned a unanimous verdict finding the defendant 100% causally negligent, the defendant filed motions raising, among other issues, the question whether negligence was the appropriate legal standard. The circuit court denied the postverdict motions and entered judgment in favor of the plaintiff. The defendant appealed one issue to the court of appeals—whether negligence was the appropriate legal standard in this case. The court of appeals certified the cause to this court.

This case presents a single question of law: Is negligence the standard governing the conduct of participants in recreational team contact sports? Courts in other jurisdictions have applied three divergent legal theories to uphold actions for sports-related injuries: (1) intentional torts, (2) willful or reckless misconduct, and (3) negligent conduct.

Courts have historically been reluctant to allow participants in contact sports to recover money damages for injuries, absent a deliberate attempt to injure. The intentional tort in a recreational team contact sport is assault and battery. A battery is the intentional, unprivileged, harmful or offensive touching of a person by another. Both parties agree that a player in a recreational team contact sport should be liable for an intentional tort. Neither party urges us to hold that a player should be held liable only for intentional torts. The defendant asks the court to adopt the recklessness standard. The plaintiff urges that the negligence standard is appropriate.

Several courts have held that recklessness is the appropriate standard to apply in personal injury actions between participants in recreational contact team sports. From the various formulations courts have used to define reckless conduct, recklessness apparently falls somewhere on a continuum between an intentional act and an act of negligence. The Restatement (Second) of Torts (1965) describes recklessness "as acting without intent to inflict the particular harm but in a manner which is so unreasonably dangerous that the person knows or should know that it is highly probable that harm will result."

A third basis for actions for sports-related injuries is negligence. Negligence consists of failing to use that degree of care that would be exercised by a reasonable person under the circumstances. Few sports cases can be found that have allowed a complainant to recover on proof of negligence. We believe that the negligence standard, properly understood and applied, accomplishes the objectives sought by the courts adopting the recklessness standard, objectives with which we agree. Because it requires only that a person exercise ordinary care under the circumstances, the negligence standard is adaptable to a wide range of situations. An act or omission that is negligent in some circumstances might not be negligent in others. Thus the negligence standard, properly understood and applied, is suitable for cases involving recreational team contact sports.

The very fact that an injury is sustained during the course of a game in which the participants voluntarily engaged and in which the likelihood of bodily contact and injury could reasonably be foreseen materially affects the manner in which each player's conduct is to be evaluated under the negligence standard. To determine whether a player's conduct constitutes actionable negligence (or contributory negligence), the fact finder should consider such material factors as the sport involved; the rules and regulations governing the sport; the generally accepted customs and practices of the sport (including the types of contact and the level of violence generally accepted); the risks inherent in the game and those that are outside the realm of anticipation; the presence of protective equipment or uniforms; and the facts and circumstances of the particular case, including the ages and physical attributes of the participants, the participants' respective skills at the game, and the participants' knowledge of the rules and customs.

Depending as it does on all the surrounding circumstances, "the negligence standard can subsume all the factors and considerations presented by recreational team contact sports and is sufficiently flexible to permit the 'vigorous competition' that the defendant urges. We see no need for the court to adopt a recklessness standard for recreational team contact sports when the negligence standard, properly understood and applied, is sufficient." For the reasons set forth, we affirm the judgment of the circuit court. The judgment of the circuit court is affirmed.

Wilcox, Justice (dissenting).

I dissent because I conclude that the unique nature of contact sports calls for the application of a standard of care other than ordinary negligence. I disagree with the majority's basic premise that ordinary negligence is flexible enough to be applied under any set of circumstances. I believe application of the ordinary negligence standard in personal injury actions arising out of participation in contact sports will discourage vigorous and active participation in sporting events. I agree with the majority of jurisdictions that have considered this issue and concluded that personal injury cases arising out of athletic events must be predicated on reckless disregard of safety; an allegation of negligence is not sufficient to state a cause of action.

Participants in contact sports assume greater risks than do others involved in nonphysical recreational activities. Because rule infractions, deliberate or unintentional, are virtually inevitable in contact sports, I believe imposition of a different standard of conduct is justified where injury results from such contact. I would adopt the rationale of the majority rule and hold that a participant in a contact sport such as soccer is liable for injuries in a tort action only if his or her conduct is in reckless disregard for the safety of the other player, but is not liable for ordinary negligence. The allegation as to ordinary negligence did not state a cause of action and should have been dismissed.

 For an extended version of the case and review questions to test your understanding of the material, please go to www.HumanKinetics.com/CaseStudiesInSportLaw.

Lofy v. Joint School Dist. #2, City of Cumberland

166 N.W.2d 809 (Wis. 1969)

The action arises from a multiple vehicle auto accident and is for wrongful death and personal injuries. The trial court granted the motion for summary judgment of the defendant-respondent Joint School District #2, City of Cumberland, and judgment was entered dismissing the plaintiffs' complaint as to the school district, the municipalities in the district, and their insurers.

On March 13, 1965, Cumberland High School won the right to participate in the state high school basketball tournament to be held in Madison March 18-20. After a meeting with the high school students and their parents to determine how many students wanted to and would go to the tournament, Arthur D. Spoolman, principal of the school, arranged with the defendant, Wisconsin Northern Transportation Company, for

two 41-passenger buses and one 37-passenger bus to transport the students and faculty chaperons from Cumberland to Madison and return. The arrangements were made in writing by an instrument designated Commercial Charter Coach Order.

The written agreement provides that the students and chaperons were to be picked up at the school and were to leave Cumberland at 5:30 a.m., March 18. The destination was set forth as the Field House, Madison, and arrival time at 12:30 p.m., March 18. The route was stated best way and the return trip was to start at the Field House after last game March 20. The total charge for the three buses for the entire trip was stated in the agreement as $952. This sum was paid by check on March 23, drawn on the account of the

Cumberland High School Activity Fund. The school charged each passenger a proportionate share of the total cost.

During the trip to Madison on March 18, at a point on Interstate Highway 94 near Tomah, Wisconsin, the bus, driven by Gerald L. Winget, an employee of the transportation company, struck a car from the rear as a part of a multiple vehicle collision. The car was operated by Matthew G. Lofy, a faculty member of the Cumberland schools. His wife and children were passengers. They also intended to attend the tournament but were proceeding independently.

Mr. Lofy died as a result of the injuries he received; the passengers were injured. His wife, Phyllis Lofy, commenced this action as administratrix of the estate of Matthew G. Lofy and as general guardian of the children.

The complaint named the school district and the municipalities in which the district is located, the partners of the transportation company, Gerald L. Winget, the driver of the bus, their insurance carriers, and others as defendants. The school district, its insurer, and the municipalities of the district brought on for hearing the motion for summary judgment to dismiss the complaint as to those defendants.

The trial court was of the opinion that the transportation company was an independent contractor and that the school district could and did delegate its duties to the transportation company. Judgment was entered dismissing the complaint as prayed for. Plaintiffs appeal. The school district and its insurer have responded.

The issue for the court to decide is, "Is the school district liable for negligent operation of a bus contracted for with a licensed transportation company to transport students incidental to an extra-curricular school activity?"

To answer this question we determine whether the transportation company became an independent contractor and, if so, whether the duties of the district to third persons in the transportation of students to an extracurricular activity can be delegated.

In addition to the common law of *respondeat superior*, the Wisconsin statutes dealing with school transportation and municipal liability must be considered.

Transportation by school districts is, in the main, provided for and controlled by statutory enactment. Among other provisions, the use of bus transportation is restricted to not more than 50 miles beyond the border of the state. In addition, the school bus must be insured subject to the following limitations: "such policy shall provide bodily injury liability coverage with limits of not less than $10,000 for each person, and, subject to such limit for each person, total limits as follows: $100,000 for each accident for each such motor vehicle having a seating capacity of more than 36 but less than 50 passengers and property damage liability coverage with a limit of not less than $5,000." W.S.A. 40.53(4, 5) § 40.57.

We agree with the conclusion reached by the trial court that the legislature did intend that a school district can delegate to others its tort responsibility or liability by contract.

The school district is not obligated to provide transportation for extracurricular school events. The statute (§ 40.53(4) (a)) provides the school district may provide transportation for students for extracurricular activities. The word "may" used in its context in the statute here makes it discretionary as to whether the school provides such transportation.

In the event the school does decide to provide for the transportation, the statute (§ 40.53(5)(a)) gives it alternative methods including by contract with a common carrier, provided such common carrier has the liability insurance coverage required by §§ 194.41 or 194.42, Stats. The insurance required by these sections is equal to or in excess of that required for regular school buses.

There is nothing in this statutory scheme that prohibits a school from entering into a contract with a common carrier for transportation of students and others for extracurricular school activities; on the contrary we believe the legislature has given school districts specific authorization to do just that.

The affidavits in support of the motion for summary judgment make clear that Wisconsin Northern Transportation Company was a common carrier and did comply with the insurance requirements of §§ 194.41 and 194.42, Stats.

The appellants contend that the transportation company, by the terms of and in the performance of the contract, lost its character as a common carrier because the facilities used were not available to the public generally over a specified route. We do not believe it makes a material difference whether the transportation company was a common carrier or a contract carrier for this specific trip. The transportation company had the general or overall designation of common carrier. The fact that a very limited amount of its equipment for one designated trip was used to perform a contract that was consistent with the more limited legal concept of a contract or private carrier did not destroy its overall character as a common carrier. We are of the opinion the statutory designation of a common carrier was for the purpose of affording the school district a means of assuring the required liability insurance as indicated by § 40.57(9), Stats.

The contract entered into between the school and the transportation company was statutorily permissible and did afford the insurance protection required by statute.

We now consider whether the transportation company was an independent contractor.

Whether a person is an agent or an independent contractor has been decided many times. Several factors must be taken into consideration in determining the question. The most important single indicium is who has retained the right to control the details of the work.

The contract did not reserve any significant control of the details to the school. The school only designated the time and place of departure: 5:30 a.m. March 18 at the school; the approximate arrival time at the destination: 12:30 p.m. Field House at Madison; route: best route; and return departure time and place: Field House March 20 after the last game. This detail of control seems to be almost the absolute minimum. With less information it is questionable that there could have been a trip or a contract at all.

The specific buses, the driver, the route, the en route stops, the manner of driving, all significant factors as to possible liability, were within the complete control of the transportation company and its employees. The only duty assigned or performed by the faculty chaperons was to keep order among the students and make sure they got on the bus. The transportation company

was an independent contractor during the trip in question.

The general rule is that one who contracts for the services of an independent contractor is not liable to others for the acts of the independent contractor. There are exceptions to the rule, such as where services contracted for involve inherent danger, where the control of the safe place of a structure has not been relinquished or where the work contracted for was a nondelegable duty of the principal. The operation of a bus between Cumberland and Madison over modern highways cannot be considered inherently dangerous.

The appellants urgently contend that § 345.05, Stats., creates absolute liability on the part of the school district. We disagree. Section 345.05 and its predecessor, § 85.095, have been existent, in substance, for several years. The obvious purpose was to abrogate the doctrine of municipal immunity in the operation of motor vehicles under the terms of the statute and to create an exception to the overall doctrine of municipal immunity.

The appellants argue that the language of § 345.05, Stats., "For the purposes of this subsection, a motor vehicle shall be deemed owned and operated by the municipality if such vehicle is either being rented or leased," makes it impossible for the school district to absolve itself from liability for negligent acts of others.

In this instance the vehicle alleged to be negligently operated was neither leased nor rented but chartered by contract. The charter contract did not retain the control usually associated with a lease or rental agreement.

The underlying purpose of the statutes has been complied with. The trip was permissible. The liability insurance protection to users of the highway contemplated by the legislature has been afforded by the insurance protection acquired by the transportation company. The duty the school district owed to other users of the highway can be and was delegated to the transportation company as an independent contractor.

 For an extended version of the case and review questions to test your understanding of the material, please go to www.HumanKinetics.com/CaseStudiesInSportLaw.

Lowe v. California League of Professional Baseball

65 Cal.Rptr.2d 105 (Cal. App. 4 Dist. 1997)

John Lowe, plaintiff, was seriously injured when struck on the left side of his face by a foul ball while attending a professional baseball game. The Quakes, at their home games, feature a mascot who goes by the name of "Tremor." He is a caricature of a dinosaur, standing seven feet tall with a tail that protrudes out from the costume. Tremor was performing his antics in the stands just along the left field foul line. Tremor was behind plaintiff and had been touching him with his (Tremor's) tail. Plaintiff was thereby distracted and turned toward Tremor. In the next moment, just as plaintiff returned his attention to the playing field, he was struck by a foul ball before he could react to it. Very serious injuries resulted from the impact. As a result, the underlying action was commenced against the California League of Professional Baseball and Valley Baseball Club, Inc., which does business as the Quakes (defendants).

The case was resolved in the trial court by summary judgment entered in favor of defendants. Defendants were able to persuade the trial court, under the doctrine of primary assumption of the risk that defendants owed no duty to plaintiff, as a spectator, to protect him from foul balls. Such rationalization was faulty. Under *Knight*, defendants had a duty not to increase the inherent risks to which spectators at professional baseball games are regularly exposed and that they assume. As a result, a triable issue of fact remained, namely whether the Quakes' mascot cavorting in the stands and distracting plaintiff's attention, while the game was in progress, constituted a breach of that duty (i.e., constituted negligence in the form of increasing the inherent risk to plaintiff of being struck by a foul ball). Thus, the trial court improperly granted the motion for summary judgment and it must be reversed accordingly.

On said date and some time after the stated time and after the seventh inning, "Tremor" the Quake's mascot, came up into the stadium in the area where plaintiff and his group were seated. Tremor was accompanied by an usher as he performed antics and entertained the crowd. As John Lowe sat in his assigned seat, he was facing forward and looking toward the playing field when suddenly, and without warning or his consent, his right shoulder was touched by the tail of Tremor's costume. As he turned to his right to see who, or what, was touching him, baseball play had resumed and a batted ball, believed to be a foul ball, hit the plaintiff on the left side of his face breaking multiple facial bones.

The Left Terrace Section, where the plaintiff was seated with his group, is located northwesterly of the left field foul ball territory, and in the direct line of foul balls passing west of the third base line. Tremor's antics and interference, while the baseball game was in play, prevented the plaintiff from being able to protect himself from any batted ball and foreseeably increased the risks to John Lowe over and above those inherent in the sport. The notice contained no recitation of the grounds for the motion. However, as required by statute, defendants filed a separate statement of undisputed facts. Without the accompanying tabulation here of evidence for such statement of facts, they included:

> 1. On July 26, 1994, at approximately 7:05 p.m., plaintiff was in attendance at a baseball game between the Rancho Cucamonga Quakes and the San Bernardino Spirit at the Epicenter baseball facility and was seated in an area of the left terrace. 2. Plaintiff was struck by a foul ball by the Quakes mascot, Tremor [sic], who was entertaining in the area where plaintiff was seated. 3. The plaintiff had been to the Epicenter on at least two previous occasions. . . .

> Plaintiff Lowe had witnessed foul balls being hit into the stands on many occasions. 8. Plaintiff Lowe had personally witnessed at least one fan being struck by a foul ball. 9. Plaintiff Lowe did not request a protected seat. 10. The Epicenter did have protected seats. . . . 11. Many of the teams in the California League of Professional Baseball have mascots. 12. The mascots have become an intrical [sic] part of the game. . . . 14. The Epicenter stadium has approximately 2500 seats which are protected by screens.

Otherwise, the points and authorities observed, "[t]he California Supreme Court has stated (in the context of injuries to participants) that a defendant generally has no duty to eliminate, or protect a plaintiff from risks inherent to the sport itself, but has only a duty not to increase those risks. A mascot is not integral to the sport of baseball, as is required by *Knight*.

In pursuing his appeal, plaintiff, challenging to the propriety of the summary judgment, assigned as trial court error: (1) its improper application of the doctrine of the primary assumption of the risk; and (2) its reliance on a New York case, *Clapman v. City of New York* (1984) 63 N.Y.2d 669, 479 N.Y.S.2d 515, 468 N.E.2d 697. In responding to the appeal, defendants rely on a collection of cases that are readily distinguishable on their facts from those facts in this record and hence, because they are wholly inapposite, require no further discussion or analysis.

As prescribed by *Knight*, the burden to be surmounted by such filings was to show that any risk to spectators caused by the antics of the mascot did not operate to increase those inherent risks to which spectators at baseball games are unavoidably exposed. In other words, the key inquiry here is whether the risk that led to plaintiff's injury involved some feature or aspect of the game that is inevitable or unavoidable in the actual playing of the game. In the first instance, foul balls hit into the spectators' area clearly create a risk of injury. If such foul balls were to be eliminated, it would be impossible to play the game. Thus, foul balls represent an inherent risk to spectators attending baseball games. Under *Knight*, such risk is assumed. Can the same thing be said about the antics of the mascot? We think not. Actually, the declaration of Mark Monninger, the person who dressed up as Tremor, recounted that there were occasional games played when he was not there. In view of this testimony, as a matter of law, we hold that the antics of the mascot

are not an essential or integral part of the playing of a baseball game. In short, the game can be played in the absence of such antics. Moreover, whether such antics increased the inherent risk to plaintiff is an issue of fact to be resolved at trial.

Our view of the entire record leads to the conclusion that defendants offered nothing in the way of either relevant or competent evidence to resolve *prima facie* the dispositive issue of fact above recited; thus they failed to shift to plaintiff the burden contemplated by § 437c, subdivision (o)(2) of the Code of Civil Procedure. The same can be said of the *Clapman* case decided by the Court of Appeals of New York. In that case, a spectator at Yankee Stadium was struck by a foul ball. He contended that a vendor moving in front of him obscured his view. As to this contention, the court said that "respondents had no duty to insure that vendors moving about the stadium did not interfere with *Clapman*'s view." That is not this case. In *Clapman*, the plaintiff at all times was facing the field of play. Here, plaintiff, because of the distraction, had turned away. This presents a substantially different set of facts, recognized at once by anyone who has ever attended a professional baseball game. Based on the foregoing analysis, we hold that the trial court improperly granted the motion for summary judgment. The judgment is reversed with directions to the trial court to vacate its order of January 7, 1996, and to enter a new and different order denying defendants' motion for summary judgment.

 For an extended version of the case and review questions to test your understanding of the material, please go to www.HumanKinetics.com/CaseStudiesInSportLaw.

Maussner v. Atlantic City Country Club, Inc.

691 A.2d 826 (N.J. Super. A.D. 1997)

This case is one of first impression in New Jersey. The issue raised is whether golf course operators owe a duty of care to their patrons to protect them from lightning strikes. Plaintiffs Spencer Maussner and Colleen Maussner appeal from the entry of an order granting summary judgment to

defendants. In their appeal, plaintiffs contend that the trial court erred in summarily concluding that the owners and operators of a golf course owed no duty to golfers to protect them from lightning strikes. According to plaintiffs, a lightning strike on a golf course is a foreseeable risk that must be addressed by the owners of the course where various means of protection are feasible. Plaintiffs maintain that the dismissal of this case prior to the completion of crucial discovery denied them the opportunity to ascertain who bore the responsibility for failing to implement proper safety procedures at defendant's golf club.

We find, however, that where a golf course has taken steps to protect its patrons from lightning strikes, a duty of reasonable care arises to take these steps correctly under the circumstances. Finding that there is a triable issue as to whether defendant Atlantic City Country Club properly implemented its safety procedures, we reverse and remand to the trial court for proceedings not inconsistent with this opinion.

At approximately 7:30 a.m. on Sunday, March 28, 1993, plaintiff Spencer Van Maussner, a longstanding member of the Atlantic City Country Club (Club), arrived at the Club with his friends Michael McHugh, Robert Dusz, and Peter Costanzo. Although a snowstorm had been predicted for that morning, the sportsmen were not deterred from pursuing their scheduled golf match. The sky that morning was overcast with misty conditions, and it was drizzling rain by the time the group began to play. At approximately 8:00 a.m., the Club's starter directed the foursome to begin play at the tenth hole. As the group played their first two holes, the tenth and eleventh, the drizzle turned into a downpour, which subsided as they teed off at the twelfth hole. After hitting his approach shot to the twelfth green, McHugh noticed a lightning bolt, and the four players and their two caddies proceeded along the fairway intending to seek refuge at the clubhouse, which was approximately one-half mile away. There were no man-made shelters along this route. While walking, plaintiff put up his umbrella to avoid the rain.

On route to the clubhouse, the group crossed onto the seventh fairway. Walking on the seventh fairway, McHugh and Dusz were about 15 yards behind plaintiff and Costanzo. Suddenly there was a tremendous noise, and McHugh watched as a lightning bolt struck plaintiff, causing him substantial injuries. Both plaintiff and Costanzo fell to the ground. Dusz immediately went for help at the clubhouse, which was approximately 325 yards away, while McHugh remained behind

to assist his friends. One caddie was sent to the nearby police station to obtain additional assistance. After ascertaining that Costanzo was stable, McHugh administered CPR to plaintiff until the police and the medics arrived. According to McHugh, the Club caddie master and Club pro arrived at about the same time as the police. During this time, lightning continued to appear in the sky.

Plaintiff filed a complaint in the Superior Court, Law Division, Camden County, seeking damages for the injuries that he sustained in the above incident at the Atlantic City Country Club. The various defendants filed a timely answer to plaintiff's complaint, raising, *inter alia*, the defenses that they were under no duty to protect plaintiff from a lightning strike and that plaintiff's injuries were the result of an act of God.

Defendants moved for summary judgment asserting that plaintiff had not met his burden of establishing that defendants created or maintained a dangerous condition on the golf course. According to their moving papers, defendant:

> [U]sed reasonable care to make its premises safe for golfers. It monitored the weather channel and was in constant communication with the weather station. Signs were posted at the Country Club instructing members of its evacuation plan and how to proceed if inclement weather struck during play.

Defendant also argued that it was entitled to summary judgment because "[p]laintiff has not met its burden of establishing that a foreseeable risk was the proximate cause of his injuries." Accompanying its motion for summary judgment, defendant attached its answers to plaintiff's interrogatories. One such answer claimed that it had "no notice of [the lightning storm], however this defendant did have an effective evacuation plan which was put into effect immediately on notice of a lightning storm." This evacuation plan apparently consisted of the golf pro and the pro shop manager getting into golf carts, driving onto the course to locate golfers, and making sure that all the golfers vacated the course.

According to defendant, Club management generally monitored the weather by listening to the weather advisory channel and placing calls to the Naval Aviation Facilities Experimental Center (NAFEC). The Club consulted the National

Weather Service on the morning of the incident and, although inclement weather was predicted, there were no warnings that lightning was possible. The Club did not possess any equipment for detecting lightning, had not installed any audible warning devices, nor had they erected any shelters on the course. Club members were warned about the general risks of lightning by a notice from Don Siok, the Club golf pro, and a United States Golf Association (USGA) poster, which were both posted in the locker room.

The notice from Siok advises golfers that

> WEATHER CONDITIONS SOMETIMES NECESSITATE OUR GOLF COURSE EVACUATION PLAN TO BE IMPLEMENTED. WHEN AUTHORIZED PERSONNEL ADVISE YOU TO COME IN OFF THE COURSE, IT IS IMPERATIVE THAT YOU DO SO.

> OUR WEATHER MONITORING SYSTEM (NAFEC AND WEATHER ADVISORY CHANNEL) ADVISES US OF DANGEROUS ELEMENTS IN THE AREA AND GIVES US TIME TO CLEAR THE COURSE TO INSURE YOUR SAFE EVACUATION. THE U.S.G.A. RECOMMENDS YOU REACT IMMEDIATELY TO A DANGEROUS SITUATION AND TO SEEK SHELTER IF YOU FEEL DANGER FROM LIGHTING [sic] OR STORM IS IMMINENT.

In a responding certification, plaintiff claimed that these notices were not placed in the locker room until after he was struck by lightning. As described by the Club, their evacuation plan, which entailed Club employees retrieving golfers on the course at the first notice of thunder or lightning, had been in effect for approximately 40 years. Defendant also maintained that golfers were encouraged to retreat to nearby private homes in the event of a severe storm. Plaintiff and his friends, in response certifications, denied any knowledge that they would be welcome at these homes. Nonetheless, according to defendant, one caddie did make this suggestion while the golfers were walking back to the clubhouse. The golfers apparently rejected the idea. Plaintiff, however, disputes this contention.

As noted, there is no New Jersey case law that addresses the issue of whether a golf course owes its patrons a duty of care to protect them from lightning strikes. Cases from other jurisdictions are somewhat instructive on this issue. To summarize, courts have found that lightning is such a highly unpredictable occurrence of nature that it is not reasonable to require one to anticipate when and where it will strike. The risk to be guarded against is too remote to impose legal liability. In addition, courts have also emphasized that it was reasonable to infer that a reasonably prudent adult can recognize the approach of a severe thunderstorm and know that it is time to pack up the clubs and leave before the storm begins to wreak havoc. Further, courts discovered there is no industry standard to implement warning devices or shelters that are lightning proof.

In contrast, one court left open the possibility that, had there been an industry standard or customary conduct of protecting patrons from lightning strikes, the result might have been different. On the record reviewed in this case, there is some evidence that other golf courses in the immediate area of the Club utilized various methods to protect their patrons.

Golf course operators do owe a general duty to protect their patrons, but this duty does not necessarily extend to all potential harms. Although lightning is foreseeable in the abstract, its occurrence is so random and unpredictable that the risk it poses is quite remote even to persons who frequent the open expanses of golf courses. Even a remote risk, however, can be foreseeable and can give rise to a duty.

It is the responsibility of the courts to determine the scope of tort liability. Before recovery will be allowed under a negligence theory, a defendant must first owe a duty to a plaintiff. Although a foreseeable risk is the indispensable cornerstone of any formulation of a duty of care, not all foreseeable risks give rise to duties. Once the foreseeability of the injury has been established, considerations of fairness and policy will dictate whether the imposition of a duty is warranted.

Traditionally, premises liability has been governed by the common law distinctions between trespassers, licensees, and invitees. The property owner was deemed to owe a different duty of care to a person on his or her land depending on the category into which that person fit. Under this common law analysis, an owner or possessor of property owes a higher degree of care to the business invitee because that person has been invited on the premises for purposes of the owner that often are commercial or business related. To such an invitee, a landowner owed a duty of reasonable care to guard against any dangerous conditions on his or her property that the owner either knows about or should have discovered.

Traditionally, an act of God is the cause of an accident if it is a purely natural force that could not have been prevented by any amount of foresight and pains and care reasonably to be expected of [a defendant]. Under New Jersey law, a plaintiff can recover from a defendant even where the defendant's negligence coincides with an act of God. This view of liability is reflected in Model Jury Charge 5.14, which provides that:

> An act of God is an unusual, extraordinary and unexpected manifestation of the forces of nature, or a misfortune or accident arising from inevitable necessity which cannot be prevented by reasonable human foresight and care. If plaintiff's injuries were caused by such an event without any negligence on the part of the defendant, the defendant is not liable therefore.

> However, if the defendant has been guilty of negligence which was an efficient and cooperative cause of the mishap, so that the accident was caused by both the forces of nature and the defendant's negligence, the defendant is not excused from responsibility.

It is not clear, ultimately, how the act of God defense operates in the arena of recent tort jurisprudence. This line of cases stands for the proposition that where supposed precautionary measures actually and foreseeably increase the likelihood of a potentially lethal natural phenomenon and enhance the risk of injury, the negligent third party will not be excused from liability in any resulting accident simply because an act of God was involved. The present case is different, according to defendant, because defendant did nothing to increase the likelihood that lightning would strike the golf course. The act of God defense, in and of itself, does not exculpate defendant. Further analysis requires that we examine basic fairness under all of the circumstances in light of considerations of public policy.

As noted, *supra*, finding that one person owes a duty of reasonable care to another turns on whether the imposition of such a duty satisfies an abiding sense of basic fairness under all of the circumstances in light of considerations of public policy. This determination requires the balancing

of several factors: the nature of the attendant risk; the opportunity and ability to exercise care; and the public interest in the proposed solution.

A particular lightning strike is clearly unpredictable. There is no way that present technology can predict whether a bolt of lightning will strike a tree, a bush, a rock, or any of four golfers standing near them. Similarly, the path of a particular tornado or the eye of a hurricane may be difficult to predict. In the past these storms were truly acts of God; they came out of nowhere and unleashed tremendous destructive powers. Modern technology has rendered these storms more predictable. We now know, for example, when conditions are favorable for tornadoes, and we know by satellite imagery and computer modeling when a hurricane will strike land and the probability that it will hit at a particular place. These once unforeseeable forces of nature must now be considered, at least to a great extent, foreseeable.

As noted by plaintiff's expert and by Professor Flynn, there is now technology available that makes lightning's presence more predictable. This being the case, the presence of lightning is less an act of God and more a predictable destructive force. Thus, the nature of the attendant risk is that its presence is predictable, if not its individual manifestations. Similarly, the opportunity and ability to exercise care in the case of lightning is now greater than it has been in the past. A golf course can warn golfers of what to do in the presence of lightning, can warn golfers of the approach of lightning by using signals, and can create and maintain lightning-proof shelters. A golf course can now also detect the existence of lightning by using some of the new technology that is detailed in Berger's preliminary expert report and in Professor Flynn's article.

Lastly, the public interest in the proposed solution is clear. The great popularity of golf makes the reasonable protection of golfers an important public interest. There are now more people walking around on open plains carrying bags of steel shafts than there have ever been. We find that when a golf course has taken steps to protect golfers from lightning strikes, it owes the golfers a duty of reasonable care to implement its safety precautions properly. We do not go so far as to hold that golf course operators have an absolute duty to protect their patrons from lightning strikes. We refrain from finding this greater duty because it may still be cost-prohibitive to make all golf courses adopt particular safety procedures.

Our holding has the following consequences. All golf courses have a duty to post a sign that details what, if any, safety procedures are being utilized by the golf course to protect its patrons from lightning. If a particular golf course uses no safety precautions, its sign must inform golfers that they play at their own risk and that no safety procedures are being utilized to protect golfers from lightning strikes. If, however, a golf course chooses to utilize a particular safety feature, it owes a duty of reasonable care to its patrons to

utilize it correctly. This latter standard means, for example, that if a golf course builds shelters, it must build lightning-proof shelters; if a golf course has an evacuation plan, the evacuation plan must be reasonable and must be posted; if a golf course uses a siren or horn system, the golfers must be able to hear it and must know what the signals mean; and if the golf course uses a weather forecasting system, it must use one that is reasonable under the circumstances.

 For an extended version of the case and review questions to test your understanding of the material, please go to www.HumanKinetics.com/CaseStudiesInSportLaw.

Miller v. United States

597 F.2d 614 (7th Cir. 1979)

In this civil action arising under the Federal Tort Claims Act, the district court awarded Richard P. Miller $1 million for injuries he sustained in a diving accident at the Crab Orchard National Wildlife Refuge in southern Illinois. The United States appeals from the lower court's judgment on the issue of liability. We affirm the decision for the reasons noted below.

As a first step, we must briefly outline the relevant facts. The Crab Orchard National Wildlife Refuge is owned by the United States and administered by the Department of the Interior. Within the refuge is a 7,000-acre lake, approximately two-thirds of which is open to the public for water-related activities such as boating, fishing, swimming, and water skiing.

The accident in question occurred at a boat dock on the far west end of the lake. On the road that enters the dock, there is a sign that reads "Boat Launching." The area is not authorized for swimming or diving, but, at the time of the accident, there were no signs to that effect. The pier is not equipped with a swimmer's ladder or raft.

On May 23, 1972, 20-year-old Richard P. Miller arrived at the dock with a group of friends who had been searching for a place to go swimming.

A swimmer and diver for most of his life, Miller had never been to the dock area before the day of the accident. On arrival, he removed his tank top and sandals, and walked on the pier to a point that was approximately 10 feet from its end. The lake bottom at this point was not visible due to the murky water. Miller saw one man in the water toward the end of the pier who appeared to be treading water. In addition, he saw two or three people in the water along the left side of the pier about 20 feet from shore. After someone shouted that the water was fine, Miller dove into the lake from the left side of the pier. The water depth, however, was only about three feet, and he apparently struck his head on the lake bottom. Miller is now a quadriplegic.

The threshold legal issue on appeal concerns the applicability of the Illinois Recreational Use of Land and Water Areas Act, Ill.Rev.Stat. ch. 70, §§ 31-37. The Act was passed to encourage owners of land to make land and water areas available to the public for recreational purposes by limiting their liability toward persons entering thereon for such purposes. Accordingly, it provides that a landowner who permits his land to be used for recreational purposes has no duty of care to keep the premises safe for recreational use or to warn those who enter his land for recreational purposes of any dangerous condition thereon. However, the Act does not limit the landowner's liability for willful or malicious failure to guard or warn against a dangerous condition.

On appeal, the United States argues that a private individual who operates a recreational facility similar to Crab Orchard Wildlife Refuge would be entitled to the protection of the Recreational Use of Land and Water Areas Act. If this is a correct reading of the law, then, under the Federal Tort Claims Act, the United States would be entitled to the same protection, 28 U.S.C. § 2674.

The district court found, however, that the United States' liability is governed by the Recreational Area Licensing Act, Ill.Rev.Stat. ch. 1111/2, §§ 761-785, rather than the Recreational Use Act. Noting that the two statutes should be read *in pari materia*, the court concluded that the Licensing Act applies to areas such as the Crab Orchard facility that are maintained primarily for recreational purposes, while the Recreational Use Act applies only to lands that are used on a casual basis for recreational purposes.

In our view, a fair reading of the statutes supports this construction. As was noted earlier, the central purpose of the Recreational Use Act is to encourage owners of land to make land and water areas available to the public for recreational purposes. By contrast, the Licensing Act applies to areas of land that are specifically maintained for recreational use.

We agree with the district court, then, that the two statutes should be read *in pari materia*, and that the Recreational Use Act does not apply to areas such as the Crab Orchard facility that are primarily maintained for recreational use. Accordingly, the United States is not entitled to the protection of that act.

The central question thus becomes whether the United States breached a duty of care to the appellee. In our view there is credible evidence to support the district court's finding that the government was negligent in failing to post "no swimming" or "no diving" signs at the west end boat dock. On this point, the following facts are significant: (1) the boat dock was an improved area with restrooms, a wooden pier, and two paved parking areas; (2) the pier extended 50 feet into the lake; (3) the water was shallow but murky; (4) the appellant was aware of the water depths; (5) the appellant knew that individuals had previously used the boat dock area for swimming and wading; (6) the appellant's own safety plan recommended that warning signs giving notice that swimming is permitted only at designated beaches should be erected at all unsupervised locations where visitors are likely to swim. Under these circumstances, we cannot say the district court erred in concluding that the United States did not act with reasonable care when it failed to post any warnings or take any precautionary measures with respect to swimming and diving at the west end boat dock.

The district court also rejected the United States' claim that Miller was contributorily negligent as a matter of law. The court reasoned as follows:

> Plaintiff approached an improved area by way of a paved access road. There was a parking lot. There were wash room facilities. There was a path to the pier. The boat launch was separate and not visible from the pier. The pier extended out into the water 50 feet. The water near the shore was clear and plaintiff observed that the bottom was sandy and sloped. People were in the water about a third of the way out with the water at various points on their bodies. There was a man off the end of the pier in the water to his shoulders who appeared to be treading water. There were people at the end of the pier of whom plaintiff enquired about the water who responded to him that it was "fine." One of the plaintiff's friends had assured him that the spot was "perfect" for swimming. The evidence shows that her opinion was based on her own experience there when the water was at least 4 to 4-1/2 feet deep. Most significantly, there were no warnings of any kind.

Plaintiff's dive was not a deep one. The risk was a hidden one of which plaintiff had no comprehension or awareness.

On these facts, we are not persuaded that Miller was contributorily negligent as a matter of law. Accordingly, the judgment of the lower court is affirmed.

 For an extended version of the case and review questions to test your understanding of the material, please go to www.HumanKinetics.com/CaseStudiesInSportLaw.

Mogabgab v. Orleans Parish School Board

239 So.2d 456 (La. App. 4th Cir. 1970)

The plaintiffs, Joy Mogabgab and her husband, Dr. William J. Mogabgab, filed this suit against the defendants, Orleans Parish School Board, Robert E. O'Neil, head coach at Benjamin Franklin Senior High School, Sam A. Mondello, assistant coach, Estelle Barkemeyer, principal of the school, Dr. Carl J. Dolce, superintendent of Orleans Parish School Board, Jack Pizzano, supervisor of Health, Safety and Physical Education Division of Instruction of Orleans Parish School System, and Continental Casualty Company. Plaintiffs sued to recover a judgment in favor of Mrs. Joy Mogabgab in the amount of $55,000, and in favor of Dr. William J. Mogabgab in the amount of $56,634.75, together with a judgment against Continental Casualty Company for $1,693.50, a penalty of 12% on the total claim, and attorneys' fees and costs, which they assert are the damages incurred by the death of their son, Robert, and which they allege resulted from the negligence of the defendants in failing to perform their duty of providing all necessary and reasonable safeguards to prevent accidents, injuries, and sickness of the football players at Benjamin Franklin Senior High School, and, also, in failing to provide for prompt treatment when injuries or sickness occur.

The defendants answered and denied the allegations of negligence. The defendants plead the contributory negligence of the plaintiffs in permitting their son to play football when they knew, or should have known, he had periodic increases in blood pressure and abnormal heart sounds, and that they assumed the risk.

Following a trial on the merits, the lower court rendered judgment in favor of the defendants, dismissing the plaintiffs' suit, at their cost. From that judgment, the plaintiffs have perfected this appeal.

The record discloses that Robert Mogabgab was on the football squad of Benjamin Franklin Senior High School, and on August 16, 1966, he was engaged in training exercises, the second day of practice for that school year. The coaches, Robert E. O'Neil and Sam A. Mondello, were supervising the practice, which began at 3:45 p.m. at Audubon Park in New Orleans. At approximately 5:20 p.m., while participating in an exercise known as wind sprints, Robert displayed fatigue and fell down, after which he was assisted to the school bus by two of his teammates. He was nauseous and vomited prior to entering the bus and while en route to Benjamin Franklin Senior High School.

Robert Wissner, a teammate, testified that young Mogabgab appeared to collapse when climbing the steps of the bus and that he had to be carried onto the bus. Wayne Webb, a former student and football player at Benjamin Franklin, testified that Robert fell during the wind sprints and, within a minute or two, two boys carried him to the bus, with his feet on the ground, but that he was put into the bus, and the boys had difficulty getting him up the steps of the bus. Wayne Webb further testified that while seated on the front seat of the bus Robert seemed to lose himself. He estimated that the bus arrived at the school about 5:40 p.m., that Robert was helped into the school building, where he was placed on the cafeteria floor on a blanket, and the other players began undressing him. He described Robert's appearance as pale, tired, and exhausted. He did not observe Robert talking at any time. He further testified that Robert was later placed in the shower, was taken out about 5:50 p.m., placed on a blanket, with a blanket over him, and he was given an ammonia capsule by Coach Mondello. By this time, he was very clammy, pale, his breathing was heavy, and he was concerned about Robert's condition. Robert's arms were massaged and an unsuccessful attempt was made to give him salt water. Wayne Webb further stated that Coach O'Neil was in the office most of the time while Robert was receiving the afore described treatment, that a first aid book was brought into the cafeteria, and that both of the coaches discussed what was wrong and what should be done.

Dr. Howard W. Wissner and his wife, parents of Robert Wissner, arrived at the school at approximately 6:40 p.m., and observed Robert lying on the cafeteria floor. They described Robert as appearing grayish-blue, with his mouth hanging slightly ajar, his lips and the exposed hand and arm were bluish, and he was moaning. Dr. Wissner stated to Coach Mondello that Robert was critical and apparently in shock, and that a physician should be called; that when he offered to call a physician, Coach Mondello told him "no," and explained that Dr. Rinker, a member of the school board, would see that a doctor in the neighborhood would come quickly, if he were called, and that he would take care of it. Dr. Wissner stated that he observed two first aid journals where Coach Mondello was seated. Mrs. Wissner informed her husband that something must be done for Robert, after which Dr. Wissner reiterated his earlier statement, that if the coach did not call a physician, he would. At this point, Coach Mondello again stated that it was his responsibility, and, as Dr. Wissner was leaving the school to call a physician, Coach O'Neil called to him and stated that Robert's father was a physician and that his mother had indicated she would call Dr. Burch.

Mrs. Mogabgab was telephoned at approximately 6:45 p.m. She then called Dr. John H. Phillips, who arrived at the school at approximately 7:15 p.m. Dr. Phillips, a specialist in internal medicine and a subspecialist in cardiovascular diseases, was Robert's treating physician. He testified that he first saw Robert on April 16, 1962, and again on May 10, 1966, and on both occasions he found his health to be perfectly normal. Dr. Phillips explained that periodic rises in blood pressure and a heart murmur he detected were normal. He testified the next time he saw Robert was on August 16, 1966, at approximately 7:15 p.m., in response to a call from Mrs. Mogabgab about 7:00 p.m. He stated that when he saw Robert he was lying on the cafeteria floor on a blanket, on his abdomen, in an obviously sick condition; that he was unconscious, cyanotic, cool, clammy, actively sweating, with no pulse in any of his major vessels, no evidence of pressure, pupils were widely dilated, fixed, and not responsive to light, and, at that time, he diagnosed the condition as profound heat exhaustion with shock to an advanced degree, but not necessarily irreversible. Dr. Phillips testified that Robert's condition continued to worsen and, at 2:30 a.m. on August 17, 1966, he expired.

Dr. George Burch testified that he examined Robert around 8:00 p.m., at which time he found him seriously ill and in coma, and, in his opin-

ion, the prognosis was poor. He explained heat exhaustion and heat stroke and stated that when a person is unable to walk his condition is pretty severe and medical advice should be sought, so that medical treatment can be instituted before the patient's condition reaches an irreversible state. Dr. Burch pointed out that every effort should be made immediately to stop accumulation of heat and putting a blanket over a person with heat exhaustion or heat stroke is the wrong thing to do. He further explained that it is extremely important that such a patient be brought to a physician and hospital, since the quicker treatment is begun to reverse the condition caused by heat stress the better the prognosis; therefore, time is of the essence. Although Dr. Burch could not give a positive answer that Robert would not have died if proper medical treatment had been instituted when he first staggered and informed the coach of his illness, he did state that his death would have been much more unlikely.

Certainly it is plain that Robert E. O'Neil and Sam A. Mondello were negligent in denying the boy medical assistance and in plying an ill-chosen first aid. Moreover, the facts concerning the question of causality are at least reasonably clear. It is the legal significance of these facts that fashions the hub of the case.

The best synthesis of the medical evidence is that heat damage works its wreckage on the body in a continuum, causing progressive internal changes in the human system much as it causes progressive organic changes in a boiling egg. At some indefinite point in this continuum the process of heat damage becomes irreversible and past that point little can be done. All of this means that if appropriate medical assistance is available early, the chances of survival are good. If it is long delayed, there is little hope. Once symptoms appear each minute that passes without medical attention measurably reduces the chances of survival. All of the medical evidence, save that of Dr. Nadler (who played no part in treatment) both supports and reinforces these conclusions.

Here, the negligence of Coaches O'Neil and Mondello actively denied Robert access to treatment for some two hours after symptoms appeared. When he did see a physician, it was too late and he died. This much the plaintiffs proved.

It was not proved that he would have certainly lived if brought to a doctor sooner or for what precise period of time the condition remained reversible. We do not think, however, that the law demands such flawless precision. Casualty like most other facts in a civil action, may be proved by a preponderance of the relevant evidence. Stripped of unfortunate jargon concerning certainty, proof by a preponderance of evidence requires only that a litigant satisfy the court or jury by sufficient evidence that the existence of a fact is more probable or likely than its nonexistence.

Taken as a whole, the record supports the premise that it is more likely than not that Robert would have survived with reasonably prompt medical attention.

For the foregoing reasons, the judgment of the lower court is hereby affirmed, insofar as it dismissed the plaintiffs' suit against Mrs. Estelle Barkemeyer, Dr. Carl J. Dolce, and Mrs. Inez C. Pizzano, executrix of the succession of Jack Pizzano. The judgment is reversed insofar as it dismissed the plaintiffs' suit against the Orleans Parish School Board, Robert E. O'Neil, and Sam A. Mondello; and judgment is hereby rendered in favor of plaintiff, Mrs. Joy Mogabgab, in the sum of $20,000, in favor of plaintiff, Dr. William J. Mogabgab, in the amount of $21,634.75, and against the defendants, Orleans Parish School Board, Robert E. O'Neil, and Sam A. Mondello, jointly and *in solido*.

For an extended version of the case and review questions to test your understanding of the material, please go to www.HumanKinetics.com/CaseStudiesInSportLaw.

Nabozny v. Barnhill

334 N.E.2d 258 (Ill. App. 1975)

Plaintiff, Julian Claudio Nabozny, a minor, by Edward J. Nabozny, his father, commenced this action to recover damages for personal injuries allegedly caused by the negligence of defendant, David Barnhill. Trial was before a jury. At the close of plaintiff's case on motion of defendant, the trial court directed a verdict in favor of the defendant. Plaintiff appeals from the order granting the motion.

Plaintiff contends on appeal that the trial judge erred in granting defendant's motion for a directed verdict and that plaintiff's actions as a participant do not prohibit the establishment of a *prima facie* case of negligence. Defendant argues in support of the trial court's ruling that defendant was free from negligence as a matter of law (lacking a duty to plaintiff) and that defendant was contributorily negligent as a matter of law.

A soccer match began between two amateur teams at Duke Child's Field in Winnetka, Illinois. Plaintiff was playing the position of goalkeeper for the Hansa team. Defendant was playing the position of forward for the Winnetka team. Members of both teams were of high-school age. Approximately 20 minutes after play had begun, a Winnetka player kicked the ball over the midfield line. Two players, Jim Gallos (for Hansa) and the defendant (for Winnetka) chased the free ball. Gallos reached the ball first. Since he was closely pursued by the defendant, Gallos passed the ball to the plaintiff, the Hansa goalkeeper. Gallos then turned away and prepared to receive a pass from the plaintiff. The plaintiff, in the meantime, went down on his left knee, received the pass, and pulled the ball to his chest. The defendant did not turn away when Gallos did, but continued to run in the direction of the plaintiff and kicked the left side of plaintiff's head causing plaintiff severe injuries.

All of the occurrence witnesses agreed that the defendant had time to avoid contact with plaintiff and that the plaintiff remained at all times within the "penalty area," a rectangular area between the 18-yard line and the goal. Four witnesses testified that they saw plaintiff in a crouched position on his left knee inside the penalty zone. Plaintiff testified that he actually had possession of the ball when he was struck by defendant. One witness, Marie Shekem, stated that plaintiff had the ball when he was kicked. All other occurrence witnesses stated that they thought plaintiff was in possession of the ball.

Plaintiff called three expert witnesses. Julius Roth, coach of the Hansa team, testified that the game in question was being played under FIFA rules. The three experts agreed that those rules prohibited all players from making contact with the goalkeeper when he is in possession of the ball in the penalty area. Possession is defined in the Chicago area as referring to the goalkeeper having his hands on the ball. Under FIFA rules, any contact with a goalkeeper in possession in the penalty area is an infraction of the rules, even if such contact is unintentional. The goalkeeper is the only member of a team who is allowed to touch a ball in play so long as he remains in the penalty area. The only legal contact permitted in soccer is shoulder to shoulder contact between players going for a ball within playing distance. The three experts agreed that the contact in question in this case should not have occurred. Additionally, goalkeeper head injuries are extremely rare in soccer. As a result of being struck, plaintiff suffered permanent damage to his skull and brain.

The initial question presented by this appeal is whether, under the facts in evidence, such a relationship existed between the parties that the court will impose a legal duty on one for the benefit of the other. More simply, whether the interest of the plaintiff who has suffered invasion was entitled to legal protection at the hands of the defendant. There is a dearth of case law involving organized athletic competition wherein one of the participants is charged with negligence. There are no such Illinois cases. A number of other jurisdictions prohibit recovery generally for reasons of public policy. We can find no American cases dealing with the game of soccer.

This court believes that the law should not place unreasonable burdens on the free and vigorous participation in sports by our youth. However, we also believe that organized athletic competition does not exist in a vacuum. Rather, some of the restraints of civilization must accompany every athlete onto the playing field. One of the educational benefits of organized athletic competition to our youth is the development of discipline and self-control. Individual sports are advanced and competition enhanced by a comprehensive set of rules. Some rules secure the better playing of the game as a test of skill. Other rules are primarily designed to protect participants from serious injury.

For these reasons, this court believes that when athletes are engaged in an athletic competition; all teams involved are trained and coached by knowledgeable personnel; a recognized set of rules governs the conduct of the competition; and a safety rule is contained therein that is primarily designed to protect players from serious injury, a player is then charged with a legal duty to every other player on the field to refrain from conduct proscribed by a safety rule. A reckless disregard for the safety of other players cannot be excused. To engage in such conduct is to create an intolerable and unreasonable risk of serious injury to other participants. We have carefully drawn the rule announced herein in order to control a new field of personal injury litigation. Under the facts presented in the case at bar, we find such a duty clearly arose. Plaintiff was entitled to legal protection at the hands of the defendant. The defendant contends he is immune from tort action for any injury to another player that happens during the course of a game, to which theory we do not subscribe. It is our opinion that a player is liable for injury in a tort action if his conduct is such that it is either deliberate, willful, or with a reckless disregard for the safety of the other player so as to cause injury to that player, the same being a question of fact to be decided by a jury.

Defendant also asserts that plaintiff was contributorily negligent as a matter of law, and, therefore, the trial court's direction of a verdict in defendant's favor was correct. We do not agree. The evidence presented tended to show that plaintiff was in the exercise of ordinary care for his own safety. While playing his position, he remained in the penalty area and took possession of the ball in a proper manner. Plaintiff had no reason to know of the danger created by defendant. Without this knowledge, it cannot be said that plaintiff unreasonably exposed himself to such danger or failed to discover or appreciate the risk. The facts in evidence revealed that the play in question was of a kind commonly executed in this sport. Frank Longo, one of plaintiff's expert witnesses, testified that once the goalkeeper gets possession of the ball in the penalty area, "the instinct should be there (in an opposing player pursuing the ball) through training and knowledge of the rules to avoid contact (with the goalkeeper)." All of plaintiff's expert witnesses agreed that a player charging an opposition goaltender under circumstances similar to those that existed during the play in question should be able to avoid all contact. Furthermore, it is a violation of the rules for a player simply to kick at the ball when a goalkeeper has possession in the penalty area even if no contact is made with the goalkeeper. We conclude that the trial court erred in directing a verdict in favor of defendant. It is a fact question for the jury. This cause, therefore, is reversed and remanded to the Circuit Court of Cook County for a new trial consistent with the views expressed in this opinion.

Reversed and remanded.

 For an extended version of the case and review questions to test your understanding of the material, please go to www.HumanKinetics.com/CaseStudiesInSportLaw.

Rispone v. Louisiana State University and Agricultural and Mechanical College

637 So.2d 731 (La. App. 1 Cir. 1994)

This appeal challenges numerous aspects of the trial court's liability and quantum determinations. After a thorough review of the record, we find no error in the trial court's rulings, and we affirm.

Plaintiff, Joseph Samuel Rispone, filed this tort suit against Louisiana State University and its Board of Supervisors (LSU) after he sustained an injury at Alex Box Stadium on the LSU campus. The record reflects that on the evening of May 28, 1990, Mr. Rispone attended a baseball game at the stadium that would determine whether LSU would advance to the College World Series. The game had to be rescheduled twice due to rain. It rained the weekend preceding the game and the day of the game.

Mr. Rispone arrived at Alex Box Stadium, purchased a Coke and French fries at the concession stand, then headed toward the left field baseline to find his seat. The evidence established that the pathway to the left field bleachers had puddles of water and that mud and water were being tracked into the bleachers by patrons. Mr. Rispone and his companions entered a set of temporary bleachers on the left field baseline, climbing up in the middle of the bleachers. Later, they decided to sit elsewhere. As Mr. Rispone was going down the bleachers, he hit an "awkward" step and fell face forward. The evidence established that Mr. Rispone broke two ribs and ruptured his Achilles tendon as a result of the fall.

Following the presentation of the evidence, the trial court ruled that LSU failed to use reasonable care to provide a safe environment to its patrons. Specifically, the court found that the fall was caused by the existence of a nonuniform step in the temporary bleachers, which LSU was aware of, yet failed to provide a remedy or warning. The court assessed 90% fault to LSU, while allocating 10% fault to plaintiff for his "slight inattentiveness." Plaintiff was awarded $24,260.78 in lost wages and $80,000 in general damages. LSU appealed, challenging the liability, causation, and fault allocation rulings, along with the awards for lost wages and general damages. Mr. Rispone also appealed, contesting the trial court's allocation of 10% fault to him and the adequacy of the general damage award.

In challenging the trial court's liability ruling, LSU admits that one nonuniform step did indeed exist in the bleachers where Mr. Rispone fell. This nonuniform step resulted because the temporary bleachers did not fit together properly. The trial court found as a fact that the normal step existing between the bleacher seats was 12 inches. However, the distance between the steps where Mr. Rispone fell was approximately one inch. The evidence also established that LSU was aware that this nonuniform step existed, yet failed to remedy it and failed to warn of its existence. LSU insists that the existence of this nonuniform step did not render the bleachers unreasonably dangerous. In support of this argument, LSU relies on the fact that there were no reported accidents in over three years that the bleachers were in use. Also, LSU insists that even if the nonuniform step created a dangerous condition, it should have been obvious to all patrons, including plaintiff, and thus there was no duty to warn of the defect.

The trial court's finding that the nonuniform step created an unreasonable risk of harm to plaintiff is a factual finding that will not be reversed on appeal absent manifest error. After reviewing the record, we find that the court's conclusion was a reasonable one, which will not be disturbed by this court.

LSU disputes the trial court's factual finding that the existence of the nonuniform step caused plaintiff's fall, contending that the fall was caused by plaintiff's own inattentiveness. LSU also contests the trial court's allocation of only 10% fault to plaintiff for his inattentiveness, while Mr. Rispone charges the trial court should have found LSU solely at fault. However, these findings of fact are entitled to great weight and may not be disturbed in the absence of manifest error. After reviewing the record, we are unable to say that the trial court erred in its causation determination, or its allocation of the percentages of fault, and we therefore decline to disturb those rulings.

The trial court awarded Mr. Rispone $80,000 in general damages. Mr. Rispone suffered a severe rupture of the Achilles tendon. He spent months in casts, underwent extensive physical therapy, and has two permanent suture weights in the tendon to hold it in place. His treating physician opined that while Mr. Rispone has reached his maximum medical improvement, he will continue to have intermittent symptoms of swelling, tendinitis, and inflammation in the right leg.

The trial court also observed that Mr. Rispone's injured leg is smaller than the other, resulting from atrophy due to the injury.

Prior to the accident, Mr. Rispone was very active in athletics and community activities, including coaching. He also is an electrician whose company primarily does industrial contract jobs. Mr. Rispone was a field superintendent for his company and climbing for inspections was a regular part of his job. The medical evidence established that Mr. Rispone suffered a 12% disability to his lower extremity and a 5% disability to his body as a whole. He is restricted from climbing, lifting, or standing for prolonged periods. Further, he may not climb ladders at work, walk on scaffolding, or inspect above certain heights. All of these restrictions are permanent. As the trial court correctly observed, Mr. Rispone cannot assume full duties at work, and his coaching and other community activities are restricted due to the limitations.

An award may only be increased or decreased when it is beyond that which a reasonable trier of fact could assess for the effects of the particular injury to the particular plaintiff under the particular circumstances. The $80,000 general damage award is amply supported by the evidence in this case. After considering all of the evidence in this case, we cannot conclude that a rational trier of fact could not have fixed the award at the level set by the trial court, and we therefore decline to disturb it. Lastly, LSU challenges the award for lost wages. Because this award is supported by the evidence, we shall not decrease it.

Based on the foregoing, the judgment appealed from is affirmed. All costs of this appeal, in the amount of $419.73, are assessed to appellants, Louisiana State University and Agricultural and Mechanical College and Board of Supervisors of Louisiana State University and Agricultural and Mechanical College.

 For an extended version of the case and review questions to test your understanding of the material, please go to www.HumanKinetics.com/CaseStudiesInSportLaw.

Sallis v. City of Bossier City

680 So.2d 1333 (La. App. 2 Cir. 1996)

Plaintiff, Randy Sallis, injured his knee while participating in a softball tournament at a recreational complex owned and maintained by defendant, the City of Bossier City. The trial court found that plaintiff's injuries were caused by the City's negligence and that plaintiff and his wife were entitled to damages. The National Softball Association (NSA) sponsored the 1991 Rose Classic Softball Tournament played on May 18-19 at Tinsley Park, a recreational facility owned and operated by the City of Bossier City (the City). Plaintiff, Randy Sallis, played in the tournament on a team sponsored by Big Star Grocery Store of Many, Louisiana. Tinsley Park had four softball fields, two with grass infields (fields 3 and 4) and two with dirt infields (fields 2 and 5). Because of heavy rain on Saturday, Billy Walden, the supervisor at Tinsley Park, told Don Farrar, NSA regional director, that the grass fields could not be used on Sunday. The rain continued on Sunday and before play started, Walden "dragged" the two dirt fields with a tractor and scarifier.

Plaintiff's team played the fourth or fifth game on field 2 on Sunday. Plaintiff batted tenth in the lineup and on his first at bat hit a ground ball between first and second bases. The second baseman's attempt to throw plaintiff out was wide causing the first baseman to lean toward home plate to catch the ball. To avoid a collision, plaintiff slid headfirst into first base. During the slide, five feet from first base, plaintiff struck a steel shaft permanently fixed in the base path that ripped open his knee. Plaintiff was taken by ambulance to Willis-Knighton South Hospital.

On May 8, 1992, plaintiff and his wife, Gail Sallis, filed suit against the City and its insurer, American Guarantee & Liability Insurance Company. An amended petition named as additional defendants the NSA, its regional director, Don Farrar, and their insurer, Transamerica Insurance Company. Trial began on December 13, 1994, and at the close of evidence, the trial court dismissed all claims against NSA, Farrar, and Transamerica. Judgment in plaintiffs' favor was rendered on July 20, 1995. Randy Sallis was awarded general

and special damages and Gail Sallis was awarded damages for loss of consortium.

The City and its insurer have appealed, alleging that the trial court erred in imposing liability and alternatively, that the trial court erred in awarding excessive damages. The Sallises answered the appeal, seeking an increase in damages.

In the maintenance and operation of its public parks, playgrounds, and recreational areas, a city/parish owes a duty commensurate with ordinary and reasonable care under the circumstances. The city/parish is not the insurer of the safety of those using such facilities, nor is it required to eliminate every source or possibility of danger. Rather, it is held to the same degree of care as any other person or entity in possession and control of land. The owner or custodian of immovable property has a duty to keep the premises in a reasonably safe condition. He must discover any unreasonably dangerous condition on the premises and either correct that condition or warn potential victims of its existence.

Plaintiffs premised this action against the City on both negligence and strict liability. The elements that must be satisfied to impose liability on the City are essentially the same under either theory. Under either negligence or strict liability, it must be shown that: (1) the City owned or had custody of the thing that caused the damage, (2) the thing was defective in that it created an unreasonable risk of harm to others, (3) the City had actual or constructive knowledge or notice of the defect prior to the accident and failed to take corrective action within a reasonable time, and (4) causation. The City's ownership and custody were not disputed and the evidence clearly establishes that plaintiff's injuries were caused by his striking a steel shaft hidden in the base path. We must therefore determine whether plaintiffs showed that the steel shaft presented an unreasonable risk of harm and that the City had knowledge of the defect prior to the accident.

Billy Walden, maintenance supervisor with the City's Parks and Recreation Dept., stated that Bolco base anchors were installed in the softball fields at Tinsley Park. The base anchor is one method of securing base pads to the ground; other methods of attachment include straps, side stakes, and permanent installation. Because several of the base anchors had been bent by players sliding into base and by City employees when dragging and raking the fields, they were replaced with stakes of heavier gauge metal in 1990.

Because of a variety of baseball and softball leagues using different field dimensions, the City installed three permanent sets of base anchors on each field at distances of 60, 65, and 70 feet. The hollow steel shafts were set in concrete and covered with approximately 2 to 3 inches of dirt. Use of one set thus necessarily involved nonutilization of the other two sets.

Walden stated that when not in use, a thick mushroom-shaped rubber cap five inches in diameter was placed on the top of each unused base anchor. The caps served dual purposes; they kept mud and dirt out of the hollow shafts and prevented injury to players.

Although Tinsley Park was rented out to NSA for the softball tournament, maintenance of the fields remained the responsibility of the Parks and Recreation Dept. Because of the heavy rains on Saturday, the grass infields were being damaged. Walden informed Farrar, the tournament director, that no further games would be played on the two grass fields.

The tournament, however, was allowed to continue on the two dirt fields. Walden and his crew dragged these fields with a tractor and spiked attachment before any games began on Sunday. According to Walden, all that this accomplished was to "push the mud around." Walden stated that he did not check to see whether the protective rubber caps had been displaced and whether the anchor shafts were exposed during the previous day's games or as a result of his efforts to maintain the fields. He also testified that he did not inform any of the tournament officials or participants of the hidden and unused anchors in the base paths.

It is common and customary for softball to be played in the rain and mud. On this weekend, the fields were extremely muddy and base running was more difficult. Billy Walden and Don Farrar discussed implementing a "no slide" rule; however, the umpires, coaches, and players were

never notified of such a regulation. Charlie Mason and Larry Hattaway, who played on plaintiff's team, observed several players sliding in the game before theirs on Sunday. Mason and Hattaway observed that Randy struck a metal base anchor in the running path approximately five feet in front of first base. Both were unequivocal that the steel shaft did not have a protective rubber cap. Neither Walden nor Bob Carter, an employee of the Parks and Recreation Dept. who witnessed the accident, could remember whether the protective rubber cap was in place.

The City's installation of multiple sets of base anchors allowed for the easy adaptation of the park's fields for use by a number of baseball and softball leagues. Defendants, however, introduced no evidence of similar multiple base peg use in other recreational complexes or information concerning the safety of this type of installation. All of the witnesses, including the NSA regional director, testified that they were unaware that Tinsley Park was equipped with more than one set of base pegs.

The evidence clearly supports the trial court's finding that the steel shaft causing plaintiff's injury did not have its rubber covering and was hidden from view just below the dirt/mud. Given that softball is commonly played in the rain, that play in inclement weather softens the soil and tears up the field, that tournament play on a wet, muddy field causes excessive wear and tear to the field, we find that the unprotected and hidden steel shaft located five feet in front of first base constituted an unreasonable risk of harm.

Appellants' argument that the City was unaware of the hazard posed by the unprotected base peg is meritless. The base anchors were installed by City employees. There was a conscious decision by the City to install not one, but three pegs at different distances for each base on each field. In addition to the City's awareness of the presence of multiple base anchors, we find that the City knew or should have known that these base pegs, if unprotected, posed an unreasonable risk of harm and that it failed to implement a procedure to insure that each unused shaft was covered.

The officials, coaches, and players were not informed of the presence of the additional base anchors, nor were the base anchors at 60 and 70 feet checked to ascertain whether the weather, maintenance efforts, or tournament play had uncovered the unused stakes or dislodged their protective coverings.

As stated above, the trial court correctly found that the City was negligent and that this negligence caused plaintiff's injuries. In this case, the dangerous condition was an unprotected base anchor located five feet in front of first base. The testimony is uncontroverted that Farrar, NSA's representative, was unaware that there were base pegs in the base line of the Tinsley Park fields. Furthermore, Billy Walden, Tinsley Park supervisor, testified that he never told anyone from NSA that there were base anchors in the base paths.

There was no evidence that NSA or Farrar was aware of the dangerous condition (i.e., an unprotected base anchor in the base line); thus, they had no duty to plaintiff to prevent his injury. We also find no merit to defendants' assertion that NSA and Farrar were negligent for failing to terminate tournament play because of the inclement weather. Plaintiff's injuries were caused not by his playing softball on a muddy field, but by sliding into an unprotected stake located a few feet in front of the base. The trial court correctly granted co-defendants' motion for involuntary dismissal.

IT IS ORDERED, ADJUDGED, AND DECREED that plaintiff is awarded $9,000 for cost of retraining. IT IS FURTHER ORDERED that in all other respects the trial court's judgment is AFFIRMED. All costs are assessed to defendants/appellants, City of Bossier City, and American Guarantee & Liability Insurance Company. AS AMENDED, AFFIRMED.

 For an extended version of the case and review questions to test your understanding of the material, please go to www.HumanKinetics.com/CaseStudiesInSportLaw.

Schiffman v. Spring

609 N.Y.S.2d 482 (A.D. 4 Dept. 1994)

The New York Supreme Court should have granted the motion of defendants, John Spring and Fred Bright, for summary judgment dismissing the complaint.

Plaintiff, a member of the women's varsity soccer team at the State University of New York at Brockport, was injured on September 22, 1987, when her foot became stuck in mud on the playing field while she was participating in a soccer game held at the State University of New York at Geneseo (Geneseo).

Plaintiff alleged that Spring and Bright, the athletic director at Geneseo and the coach of the Geneseo women's varsity soccer team, respectively, were negligent in electing to hold the soccer game on a field that was wet, slippery, and muddy. Plaintiff testified at an examination before trial that, before play commenced, she was aware of the condition of the surface of the playing field. Additionally, plaintiff testified that she and other members of the team discussed that condition and complained about it to their coach. Nonetheless,

plaintiff voluntarily elected to participate in the game and played the first half without incident. She voluntarily returned to the field to play the second half. Plaintiff sustained her injury shortly after the second half commenced.

As a general rule, participants properly may be held to have consented, by their participation, to those injury-causing events that are known, apparent or reasonably foreseeable consequences of the participation. On the other hand, a defendant generally has a duty to exercise reasonable care to protect such participants from unassumed, concealed, or unreasonably increased risks. To establish plaintiff's assumption of risk, a defendant must show that plaintiff was aware of the defective or dangerous condition and the resultant risk, although it is not necessary to demonstrate that plaintiff foresaw the exact manner in which his injury occurred. Whether that conclusion can be made depends on the openness and obviousness of the risk; plaintiff's background, skill, and experience; plaintiff's own conduct under the circumstances; and the nature of defendant's conduct. Perhaps the most important factor, however, is whether the risk is inherent in the activity.

Defendants sustained their initial burden on their motion for summary judgment. They submitted evidentiary proof in admissible form to establish that plaintiff voluntarily participated in the soccer game, fully aware of the condition of the playing field and of the risk of injury. Defendants' proof established that plaintiff's injury was not the consequence of a failed duty of care on the part of the defendants but was a luckless accident arising from the vigorous voluntary participation in competitive interscholastic athletics. In opposition to the motion, plaintiff failed to raise a triable issue of fact whether defendants breached their duty to exercise reasonable care to protect plaintiff from unassumed, concealed, or unreasonably increased risks. Plaintiff failed to dispute defendants' proof that she voluntarily participated in the soccer game with knowledge and appreciation of the risks inherent in playing on a field that was wet, slippery, and muddy.

Order unanimously reversed on the law without costs, motion granted, and complaint dismissed.

 For an extended version of the case and review questions to test your understanding of the material, please go to www.HumanKinetics.com/CaseStudiesInSportLaw.

Vargo v. Svitchan

301 N.W.2d 1 (Mich. App. 1980)

Plaintiffs brought this action against defendants as a result of injuries sustained by Gregory Vargo. On the grounds of governmental immunity, the trial court granted accelerated judgment to defendants Svitchan, the athletic director, Mayoros, the high school principal, Hagadone, the school district superintendent, and the Riverview Community School District. Leave to appeal was initially denied by this court. Plaintiffs sought leave to appeal to the Supreme Court, which, in lieu of leave to appeal, remanded to this court to hear the case as on leave granted.

On June 25, 1973, Gregory Roy Vargo, a 15-year-old high school student, reported for the first of a scheduled series of weightlifting training sessions in preparation for high school football team try outs in the Fall. This session was conducted at the high school in the gymnasium. Allegedly urged on by the coach, Dr. Donald Lessner, to perform to the utmost, Gregory Vargo pushed himself to and beyond his limits, and, while lifting a 250- to 300-pound weight, he fell and received injuries resulting in paraplegia. It is alleged Gregory Vargo's two spotters failed to react quickly enough to seize the barbell before the fall.

Plaintiffs' complaint, twice amended, alleges that appellee Svitchan, the athletic director, appellee Ernest Mayoros, the principal, and appellee Hagadone, the school superintendent, negligently supervised Coach Lessner and allowed Lessner to abuse students and to threaten and pressure them into attempting athletic feats beyond their capabilities, resulting in Gregory Vargo's injury. The complaint further alleges that the gymnasium facilities were inadequate and defective because lack of sufficient ventilation caused Gregory Vargo to perspire excessively, contributing to his injuries.

M.C.L. § 691.1407; M.S.A. § 3.996(107), reads, "Except as in this act otherwise provided, all governmental agencies shall be immune from tort liability in all cases wherein the government agency is engaged in the exercise or discharge of a governmental function." The question as to whether the protection afforded a governmental unit by the above statute extends to its individual agents or employees is presently unsettled in Michigan. "It goes without saying that this area of the law is unsettled. Although we perceive a trend in Michigan to severely limit governmental immunity, as yet the problem of its applicability must be contended with." *McCann v. Michigan*, 247 N.W.2d 521.

"The extent to which a school principal is protected by immunity is dependent on whether the act complained of falls within the principal's discretionary or ministerial powers.

"A ministerial officer has a line of conduct marked out for him, and has nothing to do but to follow it; and he must be held liable for any failure to do so which results in the injury of another. A judicial officer, on the other hand, has certain powers confided to him to be exercised according to his judgment or discretion; and the law would be oppressive which should compel him in every case to decide correctly at his peril." *Wall v. Trumbull,* 16 Mich. 228, 234. "Discretionary acts are those of a legislative, executive or judicial nature. Ministerial acts are those where the public employee has little decision-making power during the course of performance, but rather his conduct is delineated." *Sherbutte v. Marine City,* 130 N.W. 2d 920.

In the case at bar, the plaintiffs, in their complaint, have set forth lengthy allegations concerning the purported negligence of Riverview Community High School principal, Ernest Mayoros. The plaintiffs have averred that Principal Mayoros was negligent by "inducing, suggesting, encouraging, intimidating and coercing plaintiff Gregory Roy Vargo to attend the weight lifting session and to attempt to lift and lower heavy weights without having inquired as to his experience or capabilities to lift such weights without properly instructing him and other members of the class as to techniques of safety that would avoid injury and without providing proper mechanical and/or human safeguards."

The plaintiffs have further alleged that Principal Mayoros was negligent "by failing to stop the illegally [sic] conducting of an organized summer program for varsity football players contrary to Michigan High School Athletic Association rules," and "by failing to promulgate adequate rules, regulations, procedures and safeguards, and by failing to properly instruct and train the coach, assistant coaches, and Athletic Director herein." The plaintiffs finally claim that Principal Mayoros was negligent because he failed to inspect the activities that were being conducted by Coach Lessner, because he permitted the use of an improperly-equipped room, and because he failed to take action on receiving a complaint and notice that Coach Lessner was "too rough" on his prospective football players.

According to the analysis set forth in *Cook (Cook v. Bennett,* 288 N.W.2d 609 [1979]), it appears that the principal in the instant case should not be covered by the cloak of governmental immunity. As in

Cook, Principal Mayoros had a duty to reasonably exercise supervisory powers so as to minimize injury to his students. The principal of the school maintains direct control over the use and condition of the facilities. Therefore, if the weightlifting room was, in fact, improperly equipped and designed for that use, the defendant principal would bear direct responsibility. Moreover, if the summer weightlifting program was, in fact, in violation of MHSAA rules and regulations, it would be the principal, Ernest Mayoros, who would be in charge of such a program. Finally, it must be noted that weightlifting is an activity that requires special training and supervision; overexertion and resultant injuries are foreseeable and frequent in the absence of proper supervision. If such a program was to be conducted in the high school, the principal had a duty to minimize injury to the participating students.

Although the liability (or lack thereof) of a school athletic director under the governmental immunity statute has not been previously addressed by this court, it seems that the above reasoning and outcome should apply with equal vigor to that person who is in direct control of the athletic program under which the plaintiff is injured. In the instant case, Athletic Director George Svitchan was directly in charge of the football program and Coach Lessner. As athletic director, the summer weightlifting program was not only within his knowledge but was also his direct responsibility. George Svitchan was the person in a position and authority to oversee the practices and stop any unsafe activities. Due to the specialized nature of the position, Mr. Svitchan, more so than the principal, should have promulgated reasonable safety precautions and minimized injury to the students. The athletic director must be presumed to know the nature of the class and the physical requirements and limitations of its participants. One cannot say that all reasonable men would agree that no negligence could be inferred under the circumstances. That question should be left to the jury.

We conclude that the plaintiffs' allegations are of active, personal negligence on the part of the athletic director. The alleged liability is not based on negligence committed as a public functionary. Since the plaintiff was injured in the course of an athletic activity, a trier of fact could find that defendant Svitchan abused a personal and direct duty to provide a safe weightlifting program. Defendant Svitchan is not entitled to the protection of the governmental immunity statute.

However, the same cannot be said for Superintendent T.E. Hagadone. We are unable to discern in the Complaint any allegations of "personal neglect" on the part of the superintendent. The essence of the plaintiffs' allegations is that Mr. Hagadone was negligent in his supervisory responsibilities. The possible negligence of the coach (and other school employees) cannot be imputed to him merely because he was in a supervisory position.

Plaintiffs also appeal from the trial court's decision that the defendant school district is immune from suit because it is not liable under the defective building exception to the governmental immunity statute, the pertinent part of which follows:

> Governmental agencies have the obligation to repair and maintain public buildings under their control when open for use by members of the public. Governmental agencies are liable for bodily injury and property damage resulting from a dangerous or defective condition of a public building.... M.C.L. § 691.1406; M.S.A. § 3.996(106).

The interpretation of this statutory exception has undergone recent revision by the Michigan Supreme Court. Early cases involving the public building exception consistently held that an exemption from governmental immunity is not made out under M.C.L. § 691.1406; M.S.A. § 3.996(106) unless the injury was sustained from a structural part of the building or a fixture attached thereto.

These cases make it clear that the exception to governmental immunity found in M.C.L. § 691.1406; M.S.A. § 3.996(106) is no longer to be governed by whether the instrumentality causing the injury was a fixture or structural part of the public building. Of concern now is whether the injury occurred in a "public place" and whether that public place was fit for its assigned and intended use.

In the instant case, the plaintiffs' allegations invoking the public building exception follow the vein of Bush (Bush v. Oscoda Area Schools, 250 N.W.2d 759 [1976]). The plaintiffs do not point to a particular fixture or part of the building as dangerous but aver that the defendant school district was negligent for the following reasons:

> providing a school building and room that was defective and inadequate for the activity required or directed to be performed; that there was inadequate ventilation, excessive heat and perspiration which caused or contributed to the injuries sustained, and/or by otherwise failing to use due care in the ownership, maintenance, operation, utilization of such school building and/or by otherwise failing to use due care.

The plaintiffs further allege that, at the time of the accident, the weightlifting room failed to have sufficient numbers of weightlifting safety machines or power racks to be used by the students and that the available floor mats or pads were not being used on the concrete floor to prevent possible slippage and lessen the likelihood of serious injury. Thus, the plaintiffs in the case at bar, like the plaintiff in Bush, have alleged the existence of a dangerous condition on the basis of "fitness for intended use" and the absence of safety devices.

However, as the defendant school district notes, in the present case, the complained-of room was being used as expected, as a gymnasium. Plaintiffs' argument that the gymnasium was dangerous because there was inadequate ventilation and consequent excessive perspiration (causing the barbells to slip) would possibly require a distorted interpretation of the statutory exception and the concept of "dangerous or defective." It is a common, and indeed unavoidable, experience that athletes perspire while in action. To allow the plaintiffs' claim in this regard would be to overextend the purpose and meaning of the statute. The plaintiffs' allegations fall more within the tenor of danger caused by the negligence (failure to exercise due care) of individual employees of the school district, rather than danger caused by the building itself. It appears from the facts that the lack of supervision, not a defect in the building, was the cause of the plaintiff's injuries.

In the instant case, the plaintiffs' allegations concerning a defective or dangerous condition stem not from the condition of the building itself but from the activities or operations conducted within the building. To hold otherwise would expand the public building exception far beyond its purpose and intent and do violence to the will of the Legislature.

The order of the trial court granting accelerated judgment to defendants Ernest Mayoros and George Svitchan is reversed, the grant of accelerated judgment to defendants Hagadone and Riverview Community School District is affirmed, and the matter is remanded for trial.

 For an extended version of the case and review questions to test your understanding of the material, please go to www.HumanKinetics.com/CaseStudiesInSportLaw.

Appendix

CASE FINDER

Name of case	Jurisdiction	Chapter	Page	Year	Level of sport	Key terms
AIAW v. NCAA	D.C. Cir.	1	2	1984	College	Women's sports
Averill, Jr. v. Luttrell	Tenn. App.	9	267	1958	Professional	Baseball
Banks v. NCAA	7th Cir.	1	6	1992	College	Agent rules, draft rules
Baugh v. Redmond	La. App. 2 Cir.	9	268	1990	Recreational	Softball
Bearman v. University of Notre Dame	Ind. App. 3 Dist.	9	271	1983	College	Football, spectator
Benjamin v. State	N.Y. Ct. Cl.	9	272	1982	College	Hockey, spectator
Blair v. Washington State University	Wash. Supreme Court	2	48	1987	College	Discrimination, women's sports
Boston Athletic Association v. Sullivan	1st Cir.	5	150	1989	Recreational	Athletic apparel, running
Brown v. Pro Football, Inc.	U.S. Supreme Court	1	12	1996	Professional	Developmental squad, salaries
Bunger v. Iowa High School Athletic Association	Iowa Supreme Court	7	200	1972	Public school	Alcohol
Burkey v. Marshall County Bd. of Education	D.C. W.Va.	4	128	1981	Public school	Equal Pay Act, female coaches, Title VII
Byrns v. Riddell, Inc.	Ariz. Supreme Court	6	174	1976	Public school	Football helmet
Chicago Professional Sports Ltd. Partnership v. NBA	7th Cir.	1	16	1996	Professional	Basketball, television rights
Cohen v. Brown University	1st Cir.	8	230	1996	College	Women's sports, Title IX
Concerned Parents v. City of West Palm Beach	S.D. Fla.	7	204	1994	Recreational	Americans with Disabilities Act
Cook v. Colgate University	2nd Cir.	7	207	1993	College	Women's sports, Title IX
Crawn v. Campo	N.J. Supreme Court	9	274	1994	Recreational	Softball
Dallas Cowboys Cheerleaders, Inc. v. Pussycat Cinema, Ltd.	2nd Cir.	5	155	1979	Professional	Football, trademark
Davis v. Monroe County Board of Education	U.S. Supreme Court	8	238	1999	Public school	Student-on-student sexual harassment

CASE FINDER *(continued)*

Name of case	Jurisdiction	Chapter	Page	Year	Level of sport	Key terms
DeFrantz v. USOC	D.C. Cir.	7	209	1980	Olympic	Amateur Sports Act
DeMauro v. Tusculum College, Inc.	Tenn. Supreme Court	9	277	1980	College	Golf
Denis J. O'Connell High School v. The Virginia High School League	4th Cir.	2	52	1978	Public school	Athletic association, private school
Dilger v. Moyles	Cal. App. 1 Dist.	9	280	1997	Recreational	Golf
Doe v. Taylor ISD	5th Cir.	2	56	1994	Public school	Civil rights, teacher-on-student sexual harassment
Dotzler v. Tuttle	Neb. Supreme Court	9	281	1990	Recreational	Basketball
Dudley Sports Co. v. Schmitt	Ind. App. 2 Dist.	6	176	1972	Public school	Baseball pitching machine
Eddy v. Syracuse University	N.Y.A.D.	9	282	1980	Recreational	Frisbee, gymnasium
Everett v. Bucky Warren, Inc.	Mass. Supreme Judicial Court	6	180	1978	Public school	Hockey helmet
Faragher v. City of Boca Raton	U.S. Supreme Court	7	214	1998	Recreational	Lifeguards, sexual harassment, Title VII
Favia v. Indiana University of Pennsylvania	W.D. Pa.	8	243	1993	College	Women's sports, Title IX
Federal Baseball Club v. National League of Professional Baseball Clubs	U.S. Supreme Court	1	20	1922	Professional	Baseball, Sherman Act
Filler v. Rayex Corp.	7th Cir.	6	183	1970	Public school	Baseball glasses
Flood v. Kuhn	U.S. Supreme Court	1	21	1972	Professional	Baseball, reserve system
Foster v. Bd. of Trustees of Butler County Community College	D. Kan.	9	284	1991	College	Basketball, recruiting, transportation
Franklin v. Gwinnett County Public Schools	U.S. Supreme Court	8	247	1992	Public school	Civil rights, teacher-on-student sexual harassment
Friedman v. Houston Sports Association	Tex. App. — Houston [1st Dist.]	9	287	1987	Professional	Baseball, foul ball, spectator
Gebser v. Lago Vista ISD	U.S. Supreme Court	8	250	1998	Public school	Civil rights, teacher-on-student sexual harassment
Gehling v. St. George's University School of Medicine, Ltd.	E.D. N.Y.	9	289	1989	College	Running

CASE FINDER *(continued)*

Name of case	Jurisdiction	Chapter	Page	Year	Level of sport	Key terms
Gillespie v. Southern Utah State College	Utah Supreme Court	9	291	1983	College	Basketball, trainer
Hall v. The University of Minnesota	D. Minn.	2	61	1982	College	Academics, basketball
Hanson v. Kynast	Ohio App. 5 Dist.	9	293	1987	College	Lacrosse
Hauter v. Zogarts	Calif. Supreme Court	6	184	1975	Recreational	Golf training device
Hayden v. Notre Dame	Ind. App.	9	295	1999	College	Football, spectator
Hegener v. Board of Education of City of Chicago	Ill. App. 1 Dist.	4	133	1991	Public school	Teacher-on-student sexual harassment
Hemphill v. Sayers	S.D. Ill.	6	188	1982	College	Football helmet
Hill v. NCAA	Calif. Supreme Court	2	66	1994	College	Drug testing
Jager v. Douglas County School District	11th Cir.	2	72	1989	Public school	Prayer
Jaworski v. Kiernan	Conn. Supreme Court	9	297	1997	Recreational	Soccer
Kelley v. Board of Trustees	7th Cir.	8	255	1994	College	Women's sports, Title IX
Kleinknecht v. Gettysburg College	3rd Cir.	9	299	1993	College	Cardiac arrest, lacrosse
Knight v. Jewett	Calif. Supreme Court	9	304	1992	Recreational	Football
Law v. NCAA	D. Kan.	1	24	1998	College	Restricted earnings coaches, salaries
Lestina v. West Bend Mutual Ins. Co.	Wis. Supreme Court	9	308	1993	Recreational	Soccer
Lofy v. Joint School District #2, City of Cumberland	Wis. Supreme Court	9	310	1969	Public school	Basketball, transportation
Los Angeles Memorial Coliseum v. NFL	9th Cir.	1	27	1984	Professional	Football, Sherman Act
Lowe v. California League of Professional Baseball	Cal. App. 4 Dist.	9	313	1997	Professional	Baseball, foul ball, mascot
Lyons Partnership v. Giannoulas	5th Cir.	5	157	1999	Professional	Mascot, trademark
Maussner v. Atlantic City Country Club, Inc.	N.J. Super. A.D.	9	314	1997	Recreational	Golf, lightning
Menora v. Illinois High School Association	7th Cir.	2	77	1982	Public school	Athletic apparel, religion
Miller v. United States	7th Cir.	9	318	1979	Recreational	Swimming
Mogabgab v. Orleans Parish School Board	La. App. 4th Cir.	9	320	1970	Public school	Football

CASE FINDER *(continued)*

Name of case	Jurisdiction	Chapter	Page	Year	Level of sport	Key terms
Monson v. State	Ore. App.	3	110	1995	College	Basketball, contract
Moore v. Notre Dame	N.D. Ind.	4	138	1998	College	Age discrimination
Nabozny v. Barnhill	Ill. App.	9	322	1975	Recreational	Soccer
NCAA v. Board of Regents of the University of Oklahoma	U.S. Supreme Court	1	34	1984	College	Sherman Act, television rights
NCAA v. Tarkanian	U.S. Supreme Court	2	80	1988	College	Civil rights
NFL v. McBee & Bruno's, Inc.	8th Cir.	5	160	1986	Professional	Copyright, football, television rights
Palmer v. Merluzzi	3rd Cir.	2	83	1989	Public school	Alcohol, drugs, due process
Pell v. Victor J. Andrew High School	Ill. App. 1 Dist.	6	191	1984	Public school	Gymnastics
Perdue v. City University of New York	E.D.N.Y.	4	141	1998	College	Gender discrimination, Title VII, Title IX
Pottgen v. The Missouri SHSAA	8th Cir.	7	220	1994	Public school	Eligibility, Rehabilitation Act
Rawlings Sporting Goods Co., Inc. v. Daniels	Tex. Civ. App. — Waco	6	194	1981	Public school	Football helmet
Rispone v. LSU	La. App. 1 Cir.	9	324	1994	College	Baseball, spectator
Roberts v. Colorado State Board of Agriculture	10th Cir.	8	259	1993	College	Women's sports, Title IX
Rodgers v. Georgia Tech Athletic Association	Ga. App.	3	114	1983	College	Contract, football
Sallis v. City of Bossier City	La. App. 2 Cir.	9	326	1996	Recreational	Softball
San Francisco Arts & Athletics, Inc. v. USOC	U.S. Supreme Court	5	164	1987	Olympic	Copyright, Lanham Act
Sandison v. Michigan HSAA, Inc.	6th Cir.	7	222	1995	Public school	ADA, eligibility, Rehabilitation Act
Schaill v. Tippecanoe County School Corp.	7th Cir.	2	86	1988	Public school	Drug testing
Schiffman v. Spring	N.Y.A.D. 4 Dept.	9	328	1994	College	Soccer
Smith v. Pro Football, Inc.	D.C. Cir.	1	41	1978	Professional	Football, Sherman Act
Spring Branch ISD v. Stamos	Tex. Supreme Court	2	92	1985	Public school	Eligibility, no-pass no-play rule
Stanley v. USC	9th Cir.	4	145	1999	College	Basketball, Equal Pay Act
Taylor v. Wake Forest University	N.C. App.	3	119	1972	College	College scholarship

CASE FINDER *(continued)*

Name of case	Jurisdiction	Chapter	Page	Year	Level of sport	Key terms
Tinker v. Des Moines Independent Community School District	U.S. Supreme Court	2	95	1969	Public school	Freedom of speech
University of Colorado v. Derdeyn	Col. Supreme Court	2	98	1993	College	Drug testing
University of Pittsburgh v. Champion Products, Inc.	W.D. Pa.	5	168	1983	College	Lanham Act, trademark
Vanderbilt University v. DiNardo	6th Cir.	3	121	1999	College	Breach of contract
Vargo v. Svitchan	Mich. App.	9	329	1980	Public school	Weightlifting
Vernonia School District 47J v. Acton	U.S. Supreme Court	2	103	1995	Public school	Drug testing

About the Authors

Andrew T. Pittman, PhD, is a professor in the department of health, human performance, and recreation (HHPR) at Baylor University, where he also serves as the director for the sport management program and as HHPR graduate program coordinator for admissions. Dr. Pittman has authored two other books as well as numerous chapters in books and articles in refereed journals. In addition, he is a frequent presenter at conferences ranging from the local to the international level on topics related to sport law.

Dr. Pittman is a member of many organizations, including the American Alliance for Health, Physical Education, Recreation and Dance; the National Sports Law Institute; the North American Society for Sports Management; the Sports Lawyers Association; and the Sport and Recreation Law Association.

John O. Spengler, JD, PhD, is currently an associate professor in the department of tourism, recreation, and sport management at the University of Florida. He is the chair-elect of the safety and risk management council and a research fellow of the American Alliance for Health, Physical Education, Recreation and Dance (AAHPERD). He was twice named Who's Who Among America's Teachers and was named the University of Florida College of Health and Human Performance teacher of the year.

Dr. Spengler has published more than 40 scholarly and practitioner-based journal articles and has written book chapters and two other texts in the areas of sport and recreation law and safety, including *Risk Management in Sport and Recreation.* He has also served as a safety consultant in recreation and sport and is an experienced sport participant and sport supervisor.

Sarah J. Young, PhD, is an associate professor in the department of recreation, park, and tourism studies at Indiana University. She has 11 years of experience in administering and programming campus intramural sport programs and teaches legal aspects courses to undergraduate and graduate students in sport and recreation. Young has published numerous articles and book chapters in sport and recreation publications and has given more than 50 presentations at professional conferences. She is a member of the Sport and Recreation Law Association, the National Intramural Recreational Sport Association, and the National Recreation and Park Association.

*You'll find
other outstanding
sport management resources at*

www.HumanKinetics.com

In the U.S. call

1-800-747-4457

Australia...08 8372 0999
Canada 1-800-465-7301
Europe...+44 (0) 113 255 5665
New Zealand..0800 222 062

HUMAN KINETICS
The Information Leader in Physical Activity & Health
P.O. Box 5076 • Champaign, IL 61825-5076 USA